SOCIOLOGY
AN INTRODUCTION

John E. Conklin
TUFTS UNIVERSITY

SOCIOLOGY
AN INTRODUCTION

Macmillan Publishing Co., Inc.
NEW YORK

Collier Macmillan Publishers
LONDON

Macmillan Publishing Company
866 Third Avenue, New York, New York 10022

Collier Macmillan Canada, Inc.

Library of Congress Cataloging in Publication Data

Conklin, John E.
    Sociology, an introduction.

    Includes bibliographies and index.
    1. Sociology.   I. Title.
HM51.C5995 1984   301   83-16182
ISBN 0-02-324190-X

Printing: 2 3 4 5 6 7 8   Year: 4 5 6 7 8 9 0 1 2

For photo credits see pages 532 and 533.

ISBN   0-02-324190-X

Preface

From time to time, many of us are overwhelmed by the complexity of the social world. At other times we look at society and wish we had the power to change it. Sociology is a tool that can help us understand how society works and how it can be altered. This book introduces you to sociology—its theoretical perspectives, its research methods, its findings, and its concerns.

Theoretical Orientation of the Book

Sociological theory organizes our perceptions of the world and calls our attention to certain social issues. The theoretical orientation of this book is eclectic, reflecting my belief that different theoretical positions each offer something unique and important for understanding the social world. Three major perspectives—functionalism, conflict theory, and interactionism—are introduced in Chapter 1 and used throughout the book. Debates among sociologists holding these perspectives are highlighted, and boxed selections, called "Sociology and Everyday Life," illustrate how these perspectives can be applied to the everyday world. For instance, in Chapter 3 we apply conflict theory's concept of cultural hegemony to the popular television show "Happy Days," and in Chapter 6 we show how interactionist theory can make sense of the way that hairdressers and their customers deal with each other.

Organization of the Book

The twenty chapters in this book are grouped into five main parts, each of which has a brief introduction. The table of contents paints a detailed picture of how the chapters and parts are organized. This book differs from some introductory sociology texts by including whole chapters on social interaction (Chapter 6) and the legal system (Chapter 15). In addition, the chapter on education (Chapter 12) focuses more on higher education than do many textbooks, an orientation that is designed to appeal to both students and instructors. The chapter on the economic system (Chapter 16) has a section on leisure, and includes a boxed selection on how modern technology has changed our leisure habits. Chapter 2, "Research Methods," is also significantly different from most textbook discussions of this subject; it takes the reader through three actual research projects to illustrate different methods and to show the logic of the research process.

Examples open many chapters of the book—see, for instance, the beginnings of Chapters 3, 7, and 19—and sociological concepts are illustrated throughout with photographs, cartoons, and other graphics. Unlike many books, which use statistical tables and charts as "filler," the only tables and charts that appear in this book are discussed in the body of the text, and the reader is directed to the statistical material at the appropriate time. The data in the tables and charts is as up to date as possible, in many cases drawn from the 1980 census or from even more recent sources.

One outstanding feature of this book is the fifty-five boxed selections called "Sociology and Everyday Life" and referred to as SELs in the body of the text. (See the list that follows the table of contents.) These lively, up-to-date passages are drawn from newspapers, magazines, and professional journals and books. Many are direct excerpts, and others are adapted from original sources. To illustrate ideas developed in the text, these selections present concrete examples from everyday life, both in our society and in others, including the Soviet Union, China, Japan, and Lapland. Also, in the body of the text the reader is "cued" as to when to read the selection and is shown how it illustrates a general sociological concept or theory.

I have limited the introduction of new terminology to what I think are the most important sociological concepts for introductory students. However, as in any other academic field, certain ideas are given specific meanings by sociologists. Throughout the text, these concepts are italicized and listed with definitions in the Important Terms section at the end of the book. In addition, the terms introduced in each chapter are listed at the end of the chapter, along with the page numbers on which they appear.

Each chapter of text ends with a comprehensive summary that students will find useful in studying for examinations. Following the Summary is a list of six to ten Suggested Readings.

This book was written to be easily understood by students with no background in sociology. However, because the book is clearly written does not mean that the ideas are examined in either a simplistic or a condescending way. My aim has been to instill a respect for the complexity of the social world and for the difficulty of systematically studying and understanding that world.

SUPPLEMENTARY MATERIALS

A student study guide that includes questions and exercises is available, both in booklet form and on computerized disk. In addition, an instructor's manual and a test-item file are available for help in preparing classes, examinations, and exercises. I would like to thank the following people: J. Robert Lilly, Northern Kentucky U. (Study Guide); Edgar L. Webster, Oklahoma State U. (Instructor's Manual); Richard Salem, Charles S. Green, and Hadley Klug of U. Wisconsin–Whitewater (Test Item File).

ACKNOWLEDGMENTS

Many people have contributed to the writing and production of this book. I would like to thank the following people for reviewing and commenting on the book manuscript in its earlier forms: Professor Craig Calhoun, University of North Carolina; Professor Ira J. Cohen, Rutgers University; Professor Joseph Faulkner, Pennsylvania State University; Professor Richard Gale, University of Oregon; Professor William Lane, State University of New York at Cortland; Professor Robert Lilly, Northern Kentucky University; Professor Richard Salem, University of Wisconsin—Whitewater; Professor Robert Szafran, University of Iowa; Dr. Kendrick Thompson, Northern Michigan University; Professor Ron Turner, Colorado State University; Professor Ronald Wohlstein, Eastern Illinois University. In particular, I would like to thank Joseph E. Faulkner for reviewing the manuscript at two stages. I did not take every suggestion offered by these reviewers, but many of their recommendations for changes did prove useful.

I also thank my colleagues at Tufts University, Professors Mary Jane Cramer, Susan Ostrander, and Barbara Tedlock, who offered excellent suggestions for improving various chapters; others, especially Professor Paul Joseph, pointed to additional sources of material and were generous in lending me books. I would also like to thank Margaret McCarthy, administrative assistant, and Maureen DeVito, secretary, for their efficient support in administering the Department of Sociology and Anthropology while I worked on this book.

There are many at Macmillan Publishing Company to whom I am deeply grateful. Senior Editor Kenneth J. Scott showed early faith in my ability to write this book, and Barbara Nonas and Louise Collazo provided able assistance in the first stages of the project. Senior Editor James D. Anker oversaw most of the writing of the book, and for his support and assistance I am deeply grateful. Kate Moran, Patricia Cabeza, and Susan Cooper also gave invaluable editorial assistance along the way; Judith Rodgers expertly copy-edited the manuscript; Cheryl Maunes supplied the photo research. Most importantly, Anne Pietropinto—with whom I spent hours on the telephone—offered professional advice, expert criticism, and sound suggestions for improving the book; I learned much from her.

I would also like to express my gratitude to my children, Chris and Annie, and to my wife, Sarah, for their support and tolerance during the long and arduous period that I was writing this book. This book is dedicated to them and to my daughter, Lydia.

BRIEF AUTHOR BIOGRAPHY

John E. Conklin is Professor of Sociology and Chair of the Department of Sociology and Anthropology at Tufts University in Medford, Massachusetts.

Professor Conklin was born in Oswego, New York, in 1943, and raised in Syracuse, New York. He is the father of three children—Chris, Anne, and Lydia, who was born to him and his wife Sarah as this book went to press.

After earning a bachelor's degree, with honors in economics, from Cornell University in 1965, Professor Conklin attended Harvard University, completing his doctorate there in 1969. He then worked for a year at Harvard Law School's Center for Criminal Justice. He started teaching at Tufts University in 1970, and now offers introductory sociology, crime and delinquency, deviant behavior and social control, and sociology of law.

Professor Conklin's first book, published in 1972, was *Robbery and the Criminal Justice System,* a study based on data gathered in Boston. In 1973, he edited a collection of papers on organized crime, *The Crime Establishment.* In 1975, Macmillan published his study of community reactions to crime, *The Impact of Crime.* An examination of white-collar crime was published in 1977, entitled *"Illegal but Not Criminal": Business Crime in America.* Most recently, Macmillan published Professor Conklin's *Criminology,* which is now being revised for a second edition.

Any readers' comments or suggestions on *Sociology: An Introduction* may be sent to Professor Conklin at Tufts University.

Contents

Sociology and Everyday Life Selections

part I
PERSPECTIVES AND METHODS

Everyone knows something about the social world, because each of us deals with other people. Without some knowledge of social behavior, we would find it difficult to lead our daily lives. However, the way that sociologists acquire their knowledge of this behavior is different from the casual way that most other people do.

Chapter 1, "Sociological Perspectives," investigates the ways in which sociologists look at the world. It describes how sociologists search for patterns of behavior, and for the social causes and social consequences of that behavior. This search is carried out systematically, in a way that relies on the scientific method, which we discuss in some detail in the first chapter and demonstrate in Chapter 2. In addition, in Chapter 1, we look at several careers that illustrate how sociology can be put to use. Then we examine three basic theoretical perspectives that guide different sociologists in their study of behavior—the functionalist, conflict, and interactionist perspectives.

Chapter 2, "The Research Process," looks at the way sociologists approach their study of the social world, and how they apply the scientific method to their study. This chapter takes the reader through the stages of a research project by describing three actual studies: of the causes of juvenile delinquency, of the sources of prison unrest, and of homosexual behavior in public places. These studies illustrate three important research strategies used by sociologists—surveys, experiments, and observation.

SOCIOLOGICAL PERSPECTIVES

Does welfare discourage people from working? Are women more likely than men to support legalized abortion? Does the death penalty deter people from murder?

You may have opinions on these issues. Sociologists have opinions, too; but in their professional capacity as sociologists they try to set aside their personal views and gather evidence about the social world in a systematic way. In fact, they may hold one opinion before they do a research project and change that opinion as a result of what they learn from the study.

The Sociological Approach

Sociology is the systematic study of relationships among people. If this definition seems broad, it is because sociology itself is so vast. Sociologists have addressed all of the questions mentioned above, as well as thousands of others. A quick glance through the table of contents of this book will give you a hint of the wide variety of topics dealt with by sociologists.

Sociologists begin their work by looking at the social world and choosing something they want to explain. Rather than speculate on ''plausible'' explanations, they search for informed explanations. They collect evidence that will help them understand a social phenomenon, whether it be the rising crime rate, the shrinking size of the American family, or the shift of the American population to the Sun Belt states. From their research, sociologists draw tentative conclusions that can be checked by other sociologists conducting their own studies. This systematic approach to the study of social behavior is the scientific method, which we examine later in this chapter and in more depth in Chapter 2.

This systematic approach is possible only because behavior is patterned and regular; if it were random, there could be no explanation for it. For example, in the United States people drive on the right side of the road; in other societies—such as Great Britain—people drive on the left. This behavior is socially patterned; societies have rules about which side of the road cars should drive on. This rule exists ''outside'' the individual drivers, but it influences their personal behavior.

WHAT DO SOCIOLOGISTS STUDY?

In conducting the systematic study of relationships among people, sociologists explore the social behavior of both individuals and the groups to which they belong. When sociologists study individual behavior, they are interested in the *social* aspects of that behavior. In other words, sociologists assume that people's behavior is influenced by the groups and organizations to which they belong, by broad aspects of the society in which they live, and by the specific social context or setting in which they find themselves at the moment.

For example, you may have sometime had the experience of feeling uncomfortable and behaving differently in one situation than in another. You may feel comfortable asking questions in a seminar or discussion group of ten students, but uneasy asking the same questions in a lecture hall filled with two hundred students. You might want to ask the same question in both settings, but your actual behavior would probably be quite different. In fact, your behavior might not be the same if you were one of ten students sitting in a circle around a small table rather than being one of ten students facing a professor in a large lecture hall. Both the size of the class and the seating pattern of the group are social characteristics that influence individual behavior and, as such, are open to study by sociologists.

The groups sociologists are concerned with range in size from small groups such as a married couple or a family and large organizations such as the IBM corporation to entire societies such as the United States. Groups are characterized by long-lasting relationships among the members. They also have distinct identities and a division of labor, meaning that different members perform specific tasks. For example, a club would have a particular group identity, and different jobs in the club would be assigned to a president, a secretary, and a treasurer. Most sociologists believe that the characteristics of groups differ from the traits of their individual members—in other words, that "the whole is more than the sum of its parts," and that the whole is worth studying as an entity in itself.

The Beatles were an example of such a group phenomenon. This rock group had a clear identity and a unique brand of music that excited millions of fans from 1963 until its breakup in 1971. After the group split up, the four Beatles continued to write and record individually, but most music critics and rock fans felt that these individual efforts lacked the "magic" of the original group. One way to explain the Beatles' success would be to say that the group consisted of four very talented individuals. Another explanation—one that would be favored by sociologists—would emphasize the interaction among the four members. This explanation would not assume that the Beatles' success—the result of their interaction—could easily have been predicted from knowing about the individual members.

The Beatles were a small group, but sociologists also study much larger groups and organizations. For example, they might look at General Motors, Chrysler, and Toyota and then identify the similarities and differences among these companies. How, for example, are workers recruited for jobs in these firms, and how are they rewarded for their efforts? Are women and minority groups discriminated against in hiring, pay, and promotion? How do the many positions and departments in the company fit together into a cohesive unit that manufactures and markets automobiles? How are decisions made in the organization? What part does advertising play in selling cars to the public? Answers to these questions for each of the companies would provide insight into the relative success or failure of each organization.

When sociologists examine whole societies, they look for the sources of broad trends, such as indus-

trialization and urbanization, and explore the effects of these changes on social behavior and social organization. For example, in many societies now undergoing industrialization and urbanization there tends to be a weakening of ties to kinfolk, a growth in the size of the workplace, and greater expectations for consumption of material goods. Sociologists also draw comparisons between societies, addressing questions of major concern, such as why have crime rates in the United States risen so rapidly in recent years, while crime in Japan has declined during the same period? Similarly, sociologists will study the same society at two different times, to answer questions such as why do 52 per cent of all American women hold jobs today, when in 1940 barely half that number were in the labor force?

THE SOCIOLOGICAL IMAGINATION

By studying the groups and organizations to which people belong and the social situations in which people find themselves, sociologists illuminate the link between personal life and the broader social world. The effort to relate individual behavior to larger social influences has been called using the *sociological imagination* (Mills, 1959). A student who is denied admission to a school on the basis of race might experience personal rejection, but a sociologist would see the rejection as one instance of a pervasive pattern of racial discrimination. Personal problems can sometimes be alleviated by soliciting help and support, but social issues require policies based on an understanding of the complex nature of the social world.

We are often unaware of the many ways in which our individual behavior is influenced by social factors. Few of us would consider marrying someone we did not love, and yet in many societies romantic love is not a condition for marriage. Men and women is such societies may marry to forge a political alliance between families or to enrich the woman's family through payment of a bride-price by the man's family. In the United States, on the other hand, men and women marry believing that they have made a personal choice based on a romantic emotion; but their "personal" motives for marriage actually reflect social values that they learned as children.

Sociologists are more interested in patterns of behavior, such as marriage for romantic love, than they are in the actions of specific individuals. An American couple who marry only for financial reasons would be of interest to a sociologist primarily

Sociologists make an effort to relate individual behavior to social influences. In the United States and many other Western cultures, marrying for romantic love is an example of how individual motives can reflect social values.

because their behavior is in contrast to the regular pattern of marriage for love. Television news reports and profiles in magazines such as *People* tell us about such curious deviations from general patterns of behavior, but sociologists are more interested in what such unusual cases tell us about overall patterns of social behavior. For example, a twenty-year-old man who married a seventy-year-old woman would make a good "human interest" story for the press, but only if a significant number of young men were to marry older women would sociologists study such behavior. They would look for the social causes of this behavior, phenomena that might include a shortage of young women who wanted to marry young men. Sociologists would also predict and discuss the social consequences of such behavior, including a drop in the number of children born in the society. In other words, sociologists would describe the patterns that the "unusual" behavior takes, and would study and report the causes and consequences of that behavior.

Sociologists often show how individual behavior is influenced by broad social forces, and tend to minimize the importance of "free will," the notion that individuals have unlimited freedom to choose their behavior. Some people resent sociologists for suggesting that behavior is predictable, for most of us would like to believe that we are in control of our destinies. To some degree, we choose how we will act in social situations, but our choices and behavior are limited and influenced by social factors, often in ways of which we are unaware. By studying sociology, we become more aware of these limitations, and this awareness can be liberating. For example, awareness of the differences in pay for men and women who do the same job makes it possible to develop laws to eradicate sex discrimination and to equalize pay. Learning about the ways that social forces limit individual behavior often directs attention to changing the social world.

WHAT DO SOCIOLOGISTS DO?

Why study sociology? To learn about how society works is one reason. At one time or another, most of us have felt that the world is too complex, even frighteningly so. Studying society helps to make it more understandable. This knowledge can be reassuring, although sometimes knowing more about society can be discouraging. The study of sociology thus contributes to a well-rounded education.

You may have a more practical purpose for studying sociology. The study of sociology is valuable in almost every career and position in society, and sociologists have recently begun to pay more attention to the application of sociology to everyday life (Salem and Green, 1982; Huber, 1982). In SEL 1.1 we see how Chris, a business executive, uses his undergraduate training in sociology in his work. A variety of careers are also open to people with more advanced training in sociology.

Most sociologists in the United States are professors at colleges and universities. Sociology professors, like professors in other fields, spend their time teaching, doing research, advising students about their curricula and their careers, writing articles and books, working on university committees, and serving the outside community. The job of one sociology professor, Shelley, is described in SEL 1.1.

Some sociologists do research on a full-time basis. A number of them have university appointments, but many work for private research firms, the government, or profit-making corporations. Full-time researchers often have less choice in what they will study than do university professors. They may work under the pressure of deadlines to complete research proposals and reports on their research. Marion is a full-time research sociologist whose career is described in SEL 1.1.

Other trained sociologists work as planners, using their skills to design transportation systems, plan urban development, or improve the efficiency of organizations. Sociologists with sophisticated research skills, including the ability to understand complex statistics and use computers, can often command higher salaries in industry than most universities can pay.

More and more often, the research of sociologists is being used by judges, lawmakers, and political officials in their decision making. The 1954 Supreme Court decision that made school desegregation illegal relied on social science evidence. Since then, the courts have used social research in their decisions on the death penalty, the size of the juries, and various other issues. National commissions studying urban riots, violence, marijuana use, and pornography have also made extensive use of social science research, sometimes even sponsoring new research efforts to tackle difficult questions. We are still a long way from the time when policy makers will systematically review all relevant social science research before making a decision, but in recent years this has become more of a reality.

SOCIOLOGY AND EVERYDAY LIFE 1.1
What Sociologists Do

Training in sociology is excellent preparation for many professional careers. College graduates who have studied sociology find work in a variety of settings. The three cases that follow suggest the wide range of careers open to sociologists.

PERSONNEL MANAGER

Most of his friends think of Chris as a business executive, not a sociologist. As personnel manager of a small, highly successful manufacturing firm, Chris landed his first job largely because of his background in industrial sociology and social psychology. (Chris went to work immediately after earning his B.A. in sociology.) He started with the company ten years ago as a personnel assistant; now he has considerable influence on his firm's strategies for hiring, training, supervising, and promoting. He considers himself a practitioner rather than a scholar, and says that he has not really kept up with sociological research over the past ten years. Yet he does read specialized publications on organizational behavior and industrial and business practices, and here his college training in sociology is very useful.

In the future Chris may be promoted to higher executive positions in his present firm or may join another organizaton, but for now he is working for one of the growing number of businesses whose top management understands that a background in sociology is useful for administrators and other executives.

UNIVERSITY PROFESSOR

As an undergraduate, Shelley decided to major in sociology, and her interest in teaching, research, and writing led her to pursue an academic career. Now she is one of six assistant professors of sociology at a major university, a busy member of a department with twenty-five faculty members who oversee the work of 400 undergraduate majors and seventy-five graduate students who are working toward master's and doctoral degrees. Shelley, in fact, recently earned her own Ph.D. in a similar department at another university, where she began teaching before she completed her dissertation.

In her current job, Shelley enjoys the company and mental stimulation of her faculty colleagues and finds her work with her students satisfying. She teaches five or six courses a year, including two advanced seminars. The material she covers in these graduate seminars is largely in the area of her own research, and she has been able to hire two graduate-student research assistants for a study financed by a federal grant.

Shelley's university salary combined with that of her husband — who teaches physics in the same university — is more than adequate. In the summers, instead of teaching, she works on a book for which, like any author, she has great hopes, although she realizes that scholarly books bring more prestige than income and that only a few basic textbooks in her field sell well in a highly competitive market. She also knows that she must publish articles and, ideally, a book before her tenure decision, due during her sixth year at the university, in order to maximize her professional options.

Despite all the pressures of the 1980s and the demands of her work, Shelley finds daily fulfillment in being a sociologist in a university setting.

RESEARCH INSTITUTE STAFF MEMBER

From its offices in a large city, the private research institute of which Marion is a staff member conducts sociological studies of specific problems of interest to government agencies, corporations, and political groups. Marion joined the institute with a brand new M.A. in sociology (with a concentration in research methods and statistics) and a job title of research assistant. Over the next several years she energetically added graduate work toward an M.S. degree to her on-the-job training. Today she is associate project director, responsible both for developing new projects and for supervising the actual research, much of which focuses on the city and its surrounding region. She has become very adept at constructing research proposals and at following them through revision to funding. She has demonstrated a talent for matching the appropriate research processes to clients' needs.

Marion's present salary is somewhat higher than the average for those in her graduating class and is likely to jump significantly as she achieves success in acquiring new contracts and advising clients. Her routine workday runs from nine until six, although when she is conducting interviews, supervising staff, or doing statistical analysis required for a report to a client, she may work evenings and weekends.

Her professional future offers several options. She can continue with her present employer, move to another research firm (some of which are nonprofit and associated with a university or the government), or establish her own agency. Whatever her next step, Marion's solid background in sociology and her professional research experience will serve her well.

Source: Based on American Sociological Association, *Careers in Sociology*. Washington, D.C.: American Sociological Association, 1977, pp. 6–8. Used by permission.

The Methods of Sociology

Why should a policy maker consider the work of a sociologist more seriously than the assertions of anyone else? The answer is that sociologists are regarded as experts with the professional skill to test their ideas. Anyone can have an idea or an opinion, but what distinguishes sociologists and other social scientists is that they test the validity of their ideas and opinions. For example, many people think that the threat of execution deters potential murderers, but there is almost no reliable social science evidence that this is so. Large segments of the American public are convinced that many welfare recipients are "cheats" who do not need the money they get from the government, but studies of welfare fraud consistently find that very few recipients collect money illegally. Sociologists are committed to testing the validity of ideas about the social world, even though they commonly find that widely held views are mistaken.

THE SCIENTIFIC METHOD

Sociological inquiry begins with curiosity, a desire to understand "what makes things tick." However, an inquiring mind is not enough. Sociological inquiry also entails the use of research methods that are designed to gather evidence and test ideas in a systematic or scientific fashion. The *scientific method*—which is used in both the social sciences and the natural sciences—is based on the assumption that there is an underlying order that can be understood by careful observation, exact measurement, accurate recording of findings, and thoughtful interpretation of results.

All science demands precision. As a result, scientists have developed a technical language to speak about and, particularly, to define basic concepts clearly. The precise definition of terms enables others in the same field to understand what the researcher has measured, and makes it possible for a second researcher to check the findings of the first by measuring the same concepts in the same way. In this book, we will introduce some terms that may be unfamiliar to you but that have meaning in sociology. Other terms that may be familiar will have a precise meaning that may differ from your previous understanding of these terms. For example, you may say to a friend that something has "status," meaning that it has high prestige or high standing. To a sociologist, however, the term "status" refers to a position in an organized set of social relationships. A sociologist would regard everyone in that set of relationships as having a status, not just those with the most prestige.

The research methods that we examine in more detail in Chapter 2 are designed so that the commonsense ideas or "hunches" that researchers have can be verified or disproved in the research they do. Sociologists must be detached enough from their research topics to allow their conclusions to contradict what they thought they might find in their studies. For example, not long ago one sociologist did a study on robbery, the crime in which an offender uses force to steal property from a victim. One question he wanted to address was whether robbers who carried weapons were more likely than unarmed robbers to injure their victims. At first, he thought that those who carried weapons might be the most likely to injure their victims. However, the evidence he collected from police records showed that robbers who carried pistols were *less* likely to hurt their victims than robbers who carried knives, and that robbers who carried knives were *less* likely to injure their victims than

In one sociological study it was found that criminals who carry firearms are actually less likely to hurt their victims than are those who carry knives or no weapons at all. The reason is that the victim is intimidated and is thus more likely to comply with the assailant's demands.

robbers who carried no weapon at all. Further examination of the evidence revealed that this was because unarmed robbers punched or pushed their victims to scare them into giving up their money, but robbers who carried weapons (especially firearms) intimidated their victims into handing over their money (Conklin, 1972). The initial idea was contradicted by the evidence, which provided a reasonable explanation for the results.

THE SEARCH FOR ORDER

All scientific research, including that done by sociologists, is based on the assumption that there is an underlying order or regularity that can be understood by applying the scientific method. Sociologists search for patterns and relationships among various aspects of the social world. One sociologist, looking for a relationship between juvenile delinquency and divorce, might ask the question: Are delinquents more likely than nondelinquents to come from broken homes? Another sociologist, wishing to see what relationship there was between religious beliefs and financial success, might ask: Are some religious beliefs more conducive to financial success than others, or does financial success influence the kinds of religious beliefs that people hold?

Sociologists are less interested in the specific findings of one study than in what that research can tell them about the social world in general. For example, the robbery study was of less interest for what it told about robbery in 1964 and 1968 in Boston than in what it might say about the crime of robbery as a form of behavior. Before the findings of one study can be generalized, however, similar research must be done in a variety of settings.

TENTATIVE CONCLUSIONS

Sociologists are tentative in drawing conclusions, because it is rare that a single research study offers evidence that can be generalized. A relationship that exists in one society or set of social circumstances may not exist in a different society or set of social circumstances. For example, a study of the United States might conclude that the elderly are held in low regard by the young, yet in many tribal societies the elderly are the most highly regarded group.

One way to present research results tentatively is to state conclusions as probabilities. For example, one study might find that the children of wealthy parents have a better chance, or probability, of earning high incomes as adults than do the children of poor parents. The fact that some children of poor parents become wealthy, and the fact that some children of wealthy parents become poor, do not invalidate the conclusion that there is a *relationship,* measured in terms of probability, between parents' income and the income their children earn as adults. Yet, even a conclusion as general as this may not apply in all societies to the same extent. For example, in Sweden, the government taxes the wealthy at a high rate in order to redistribute income from the rich to the poor. Thus, the relationship between the income of Swedish parents and that of their children will probably be weaker than in the United States, where less of an effort is made to redistribute income.

PREDICTING THE FUTURE

One test of the validity of research findings is whether they can predict the future. Carefully conducted research can increase our understanding of the social world and enable us to predict what will happen in the future. For example, sociologists were able to predict from the evidence of the large number of babies born in the United States immediately after World War II that, beginning in the early 1950s, there would be a need for more schools, and this proved to be so. In addition, and on a more general level, a declining rate of marriage at one time can be used to predict fewer births in the immediate future—which in turn will lead to a drop in the number of school-age children a few years later. Predictions like these can help us to prepare for the future, and to develop policies to minimize the negative consequences of social change.

Sociology and Common Sense

Commonsense or everyday assumptions about behavior are often the starting points for social research, but sociologists remain skeptical about such assumptions until they have evidence that they are correct. Early one winter morning in 1964, thirty-eight residents of Queens, New York, watched from their apartments as a man knifed to death a young woman named Kitty Genovese. Common sense might dictate that at least one of the bystanders would have tried to intervene to help the victim. Read the description of this event in SEL 1.2 and try to imagine how you would have behaved if you had witnessed this crime.

SOCIOLOGY AND EVERYDAY LIFE 1.2
Would You Have Helped?

As she arrived home in the early morning darkness, Kitty Genovese, a decent, pretty young woman of 28, was stalked through the streets close to her Kew Gardens apartment and stabbed again and again by a man who had followed her home and who took almost a half hour to kill her. During that bloody little eternity, according to an extraordinary account published in the New York *Times,* Kitty screamed and cried repeatedly for help. Her entreaties were unequivocal. "Oh, my God!" she cried out at one point. "He stabbed me! Please help me! Someone help me!" Minutes later, before the murderer came back and attacked her for the final time, she screamed, "I'm dying! I'm dying!"

The reasons the murderer's actions and his victim's calls are so well documented is that police were able to find 38 of Kitty's neighbors who admitted they witnessed the awful event. They heard the screams and most understood her cry for help. Peeking out their windows, many saw enough of the killer to provide a good description of his appearance and clothing. A few saw him strike Kitty, and more saw her staggering down the sidewalk after she had been stabbed twice and was looking for a place to hide. One especially sharp-eyed person was able to report that the murderer was sucking his finger as he left the scene; he had cut himself during the attack. Another witness has the awful distinction of being the only person Kitty Genovese recognized in the audience taking in her final moments. She looked at him and called to him by name. He did not reply.

No one really helped Kitty at all. Only one person shouted at the killer ("Let that girl alone!"), and the one phone call that was finally made to the police was placed after the murderer had got in his car and driven off. For the most part the witnesses, crouching in darkened windows like watchers of a Late Show, looked on until the play had passed beyond their view. Then they went back to bed.

Not all of these people, it must be said, understood they were watching a murder. Some thought they were looking on at a lovers' quarrel; others saw or heard so very little that they could not have reached any conclusion about the disturbance. Even if one of her neighbors had called the police promptly, it cannot be definitely stated that Kitty would have survived. But that is quite beside the point. The fact is that no one, even those who were sure something was terribly wrong, felt moved enough to act. There is, of course, no law against not being helpful.

On the scene a few days after the killer had been caught and had confessed, Police Lieutenant Bernard Jacobs discussed the investigation. "The word we kept hearing from the witnesses later was 'involved,'" Jacobs said. A dark-haired, thoughtful man, he was standing on the sidewalk next to two fist-sized, dark-gray blotches on the cement. These were Kitty's bloodstains and it was there that the killer first stabbed her. "People told us they just didn't want to get involved," Jacobs said to me. "They don't want to be questioned or have to go to court." He pointed to an apartment house directly across the quiet street. "They looked down at this thing," he went on, "from four different floors of that building." Jacobs indicated the long, two-story building immediately next to him. A row of stores took up the ground floor; there were apartments on the upper floor. "Kitty lived in one of them," Jacobs said. "People up there were sitting right on top of the crime." He moved his arm in a gesture that included all the buildings. "It's a nice neighborhood, isn't it?" he went on. "Doesn't look like a jungle. Good, solid people. We don't expect anybody to come out into the street and fight this kind of bum. All we want is a phone call. We don't even need to know who's making it.

"You know what this man told us after we caught him?" Jacobs asked. "He said he figured nobody would do anything to help. He heard the windows go up and saw the lights go on. He just retreated for a while and when things quieted down, he came back to finish the job."

Source: Loudon Wainwright, "The Dying Girl That No One Helped," *Life* 56 (April 10, 1964): 21. Loudon Wainwright/LIFE ©1964 Time Inc. Reprinted with permission.

Why did no one help Kitty Genovese? A series of social psychological experiments conducted in the aftermath of the event found that the context in which witnesses observe an emergency is the factor that determines whether help will be offered (Latané and Darley, 1970). From these and other experiments on bystander intervention in emergencies, we know something about the social circumstances in which observers are most likely to help a victim: a situation in which a solitary witness who personally knows the victim is asked by the victim to act in a specific way. In contrast to what common sense might dictate, there is actually *less* chance of help being offered if a group of witnesses is present than if there is only one witness. A single witness feels the entire responsibility for providing help, whereas a person in a crowd feels that he or she has no more responsibility than anyone else. If no one in a crowd offers help right away, each person may then feel that he or she has misinterpreted the situation and that no help is actually needed.

Commonsense attitudes often reflect distorted or fragmentary perceptions of the social world. People notice things that support their beliefs, and ignore information that is inconsistent with their convictions. One reason that sociologists distrust commonsense explanations that have not been verified is that it is often possible to come up with "plausible" or "logical" explanations for things that are not even true. Consider, for example, the following plausible explanation for Switzerland's high crime rate:

1. It is a wealthy nation, and so there are many opportunities for theft;
2. It is ethnically diverse, composed of three major language groups, and this diversity produces conflict among groups, leading to high crime rates;
3. Much of its population lives in cities, and urbanization is associated with high crime rates;
4. It has a large population of lower-class foreign workers, who might be discontented with their low standard of living and therefore turn to crime; and
5. Most of the population owns firearms, and firearms are associated with high rates of violent crime.

The only problem with this explanation is that Switzerland does not have a high crime rate, even though each of these statements is true. Indeed, Switzerland's crime rate is one of the lowest among industrialized nations, for a variety of reasons that include strong family ties, a close relationship between youths and their elders, strong community bonds, economic and social stability, and a tradition of citizen responsibility (Clinard, 1978).

COMMON SENSE AND SOCIAL POLICY

One problem with untested everyday assumptions is that they sometimes form the basis of social policies that fail to work or in some cases actually backfire. In 1973, the New York state legislature passed a law designed to curb the sale of narcotics by sentencing offenders to life imprisonment. Common sense told the lawmakers that this would deter drug sales, but research later showed that the law did not reduce drug trafficking (Joint Committee on New York Drug Law Evaluation, 1978). Similarly, an experiment intended to help poor families by providing them with income supplements actually undermined the stability of families who received the grants (Hannan and Tuma, 1978).

Much sociological research begins in the same way—with commonly accepted ideas that are examined and tested. This research often follows a set pattern—using the scientific method, sociologists collect and evaluate evidence, draw tentative conclusions, and predict the future. There are, however, some important differences among sociologists in the way they approach their study of the social world.

Theoretical Perspectives in Sociology

For centuries, people have speculated about the social world, but modern sociology, the systematic approach to examining social life, is barely a century old. By the middle of the 1800s, social thinkers were sharply divided in their views on how society should be analyzed. This disagreement continues today between functionalists and conflict theorists. A third perspective, the interactionist perspective, which developed in the twentieth century, is the other major approach that sociologists now use to study the social world.

A *theoretical perspective* is a general approach to the study of reality, a set of assumptions and interrelated concepts that provides a way of seeing the world. The adherents of each perspective ask distinct questions about society and expect to find different things when they study society.

FUNCTIONALISM

Biological organisms are composed of a variety of structures, or organs, that serve different functions (have different consequences) for the whole organism. These structures, such as the heart and the brain, are related in complex ways that enable the organism to maintain equilibrium, a balanced state of health. Some sociologists have been struck by the similarity between biological organisms and societies and social groups. Societies, they observe, also have a variety of structures, or institutions, that serve various interrelated functions necessary for maintaining a healthy, or balanced, society. This idea is the basis of *functionalism,* or structural-functionalism, as it is sometimes called, the perspective that sees each structure as serving a certain function for society. The *function* of an institution is not the conscious purpose for which the institution was designed, but rather the consequences or effects that the institution has on the rest of society.

Two social structures or institutions that you are familiar with are the family and the school. Both institutions serve the function of teaching the young to become members of society. In this way, the family and the school help to maintain the equilibrium of society by instilling societal values, such as loyalty and conformity to the law. These two institutions are, in fact, closely related. For example, most American communities have a Parent-Teacher Association (PTA) that links the family and the school.

The Beginnings of Functionalism: Comte and Spencer

The analogy between biological organisms and societies was first proposed in the nineteenth century by Auguste Comte (who coined the term "sociology" in 1838) and by Herbert Spencer. This analogy was revived by American sociologists in the 1930s.

Herbert Spencer helped to popularize sociology in the latter part of the nineteenth century. The writings of this English thinker, especially his *Principles of Sociology* (the first volume of which was published in 1876), stimulated interest in the new field in both Great Britain and the United States. Influenced by the work of the biologist Charles Darwin, Spencer claimed that societies evolved from simple to complex forms in much the same way that species evolved. Spencer's work became the basis of the philosophy of social Darwinism,

which stated that without government interference a society would either prosper or die off, and that the process of "survival of the fittest" (a term used first by Spencer, and not Darwin) would inevitably allow the best possible societies to survive. Though Spencer's work is rarely read today, he was important in his time because he increased public awareness of sociology and established the basis of the functionalist perspective.

The Problem of Social Order

Functionalists are concerned with the problem of social order, and ask the question: How does society manage to endure over time? They regard the shared beliefs and values of the members of society as the basis of social order, and examine the ways in which people come to acquire those beliefs and values and the rewards that people gain from conforming to the expectations of others. Functionalists also see social order as emerging from the complex interrelationships among people, groups, and institutions.

EMILE DURKHEIM. Perhaps the most influential analysis of social order was the massive body of scholarship produced by the French sociologist Emile Durkheim. Durkheim explored many social structures and phenomena, including religion, education, the law, and suicide. There was a prominent theme in all of his work—a concern with social order. Durkheim (1893, 1933) suggested that a major difference between traditional or tribal societies and modern industrial societies was the basis of social order. In traditional societies, order was based on shared beliefs and values; in other words, social cohesion was based on similarities. In contrast, in modern societies, the differences among people are what makes order possible—social solidarity is based more on the interdependence among people than on their similarity. This interdependence or division of labor produces a stable society. Durkheim was concerned with understanding the function that this division of labor served for society.

Durkheim's *Suicide* (1897, 1951), the first systematic effort by a sociologist to test and verify a theory with statistical evidence, showed that an individualistic form of behavior—taking one's life—was related to the way that society was organized. Durkheim found that suicide rates—the number of people who commit suicide divided by the total number of people in the group—varied

Functionalists point to shared beliefs and values as the basis of a smoothly functioning society. However, even the most harmonious societies can experience social disturbances from time to time.

considerably from group to group. Suicide was more common among divorced and widowed people than among married people, and married people with children were less likely to take their own lives than married people who had no children. In addition, the elderly were more likely than the young to commit suicide. From this and other evidence, Durkheim concluded that what affected a group's suicide rate was the social ties of its members: People with extensive ties to others were less likely to commit suicide than were people who were socially isolated. The single, the widowed, and the elderly were especially prone to suicide because they were relatively detached from other people.

MAX WEBER. Another sociologist who contributed to the development of functionalism was Max Weber, a German sociologist who was also concerned with the issue of social order. Weber examined the way societies were organized according to differences in social class, political power, and social prestige. His detailed examination of bureaucracies and organizations was one of the first systematic studies of the various bases of authority within different types of social systems. In his study of the origins of modern capitalism, Weber ex-

plored the influence of religious beliefs on economic development. In this work Weber, like Durkheim, showed how cross-cultural research can be used to advantage.

TALCOTT PARSONS. The functionalist perspective was further developed by the American sociologist Talcott Parsons, whose voluminous body of theoretical work was influenced by Durkheim and Weber. Parsons suggested that societies develop institutions or structures to serve certain functions that are essential to their survival. Economic institutions serve society by transforming raw materials into goods and services and distributing those goods and services to the members of society. Political institutions establish societal goals and develop policies to reach those goals. Other institutions, such as the legal system, serve to hold society together and integrate individuals and groups into a working unit. Religious institutions function to minimize the disruption of society and reinforce societal values. Each kind of institution has important consequences or functions for society, and all are related. For example, contract law defines social relations in a certain way, and also serves to protect the property of corporations, which are part of the economic system.

Functions and Dysfunctions

Sometimes social institutions have *dysfunctions*, or consequences that fail to serve the well-being of society. In other words, these institutions disrupt societal equilibrium or balance. For many years the family and other institutions in the United States were built on the traditional division of labor between men and women, and taught young girls to expect that the men they married would take care of them and their children. By denying women an independent source of income, this tradition caused women to become subordinate to men. Another consequence was to place on men the sole burden of financial support of the family. In the last two decades, however, the proportion of women working outside the home has increased dramatically. At the same time, there has been a large increase in the divorce rate. These two changes mean that the lesson little girls learned—that men will support them financially when they grow up—is no longer functional in today's world. Many parents continue to socialize their daughters in this way, but when these girls grow up they may experience personal conflict when they find that other people (including their husbands and working women) expect them to hold a job, and that judges may not award them alimony if they get divorced. The expectation that they will be supported by the men they marry may also be dysfunctional for single women because it may encourage them to be less committed to their jobs and careers.

Manifest and Latent Functions

Social institutions have some consequences that are obvious and intended, but often sociologists discover hidden and unintended results (Merton, 1968). A *manifest function*, or intended consequence, of American schools is to teach students the "three Rs"—reading, writing, and arithmetic. The ultimate effect of these skills is to produce educated voters and employable workers. However, the school also has *latent functions*, or consequences that are not intended or obvious. One latent function of American schools is to act as a "marriage market" where potential marital partners can meet. Because students usually attend schools in the communities where they live, and because people of similar social and economic background usually live in the same community, the public school system helps to ensure that adolescents interact chiefly with others from their own background. Because many marriages are made among people who meet during these years, there will be a tendency for husband and wife to have similar backgrounds. The school therefore serves the latent function of maintaining the class system. Some might see this as functional for maintaining the stability of society, but others would regard it as dysfunctional because it maintains inequality, which can lead to dissatisfaction and class conflict.

Critiques of Functionalism

Functionalism has been criticized, particularly by adherents of the conflict perspective, for tending consistently to support the existing social system, or status quo. This view suggests that functionalists are often conservative, that their perspective implicitly holds that institutions that contribute to social harmony are good for society. Although some of the work of functionalists has indeed been supportive of the status quo, the functionalist perspective does not seem to be inherently conservative. For instance the idea of dysfunction suggests that certain institutions may actually be harmful to society.

A more serious problem with functionalism concerns its method: Whether an institution is called functional or dysfunctional depends on the sociologist's values and preferences. From a conservative sociologist's point of view, high corporate profits might be functional for society in that they provide resources for reinvestment and economic growth, but a more radical sociologist might well see those high profits as dysfunctional, in that they are acquired by exploiting and underpaying workers. Even though both interpretations would be consistent with a functionalist perspective, the values of the sociologist—as to whether the consequences of high profits were beneficial or harmful to society—would determine whether the institution was considered functional or dysfunctional.

Another criticism of functionalism is that it overemphasizes societal harmony and thereby minimizes the importance of conflict and change. Functionalists sometimes write as if there were a complete consensus on values and beliefs, when in fact even the most harmonious societies include groups that differ in some of their values and beliefs. Some functionalists have tried to develop theories of conflict and change (Parsons, 1966, 1971, 1977), but their efforts are less satisfactory than those of conflict theorists.

Applications of Functionalism

Let us now look at the way that functionalists would analyze two aspects of society: the family and crime.

FUNCTIONALISM AND THE FAMILY. How would a sociologist taking the functionalist approach study the family? Such a study would explore the consequences of that institution for the rest of society and for the members of the family. According to functionalists, the family:

1. provides companionship and intimacy, including outlets for sexuality;
2. reproduces members of society; and
3. trains and educates the young.

As the primary agent of reproduction and socialization, the family enables a society to endure over time. Furthermore, early childhood training by the family lays the foundation for the educational system, by enabling the schools to assume that most children when they start school will have a background of certain skills and knowledge.

Functionalists examine the division of labor within the family. One such interpretation, which has been criticized as conservative and sexist, is that the complementary nature of sex roles in the traditional American family—with men earning the income and women raising the children and tending the home—is "functionally related to maintaining family solidarity in our class structure" (Parsons, 1954: 174–175). This perspective suggests that societal harmony depends on this traditional division of labor. However, this is not the only way a functionalist might examine the division of labor between the sexes. Another functionalist might interpret the large proportion of married women who work outside the home as functional for society in several ways (such as providing a larger pool of workers for the economic system, making possible higher standards of living for two-worker families, and increasing the independence and psychological rewards experienced by working women); but dysfunctional in other ways (such as reducing parental supervision of children whose parents both hold jobs). A detailed functionalist analysis of the family would find a variety of functions and dysfunctions.

FUNCTIONALISM AND CRIME. One kind of behavior that the public often decries as dysfunctional is crime. Yet some functionalists view crime as "nor-mal" because it exists in all societies (Durkheim, 1895, 1938: 64–75). In fact, some functionalists have even claimed that crime has positive consequences for society, because the punishment of those who violate social standards defines the boundaries of acceptable behavior and gives people guidelines about how they should act. Durkheim pointed out that crime is functional in uniting people in opposition to criminals who violate the law (Durkheim, 1893, 1933). However, the dysfunctions of crime in creating mistrust and suspicion probably outweigh any positive consequences (Conklin, 1975).

Another functionalist view of crime might emphasize "the crime industry"—the large number of agencies and workers who owe their jobs to the presence of crime in society. If there were no crime, there would be a much smaller police force, no criminal courts, and no prisons. One consequence of crime is to create work for some members of society. This can be regarded as a function of crime, but it could also be seen as a dysfunction because crime draws scarce resources away from more productive uses.

CONFLICT THEORY

The conflict perspective encompasses several approaches to the study of society, all of which stress conflict and competition among groups of people for scarce resources, such as wealth, power, and prestige (Collins, 1971, 1974; Oberschall, 1978; Flacks and Turkel, 1978). This perspective sees society as in a continuous state of flux and emphasizes the sources of change, rather than the bases of order, in all societies. *Conflict theory* looks at how some groups acquire power and maintain dominance over other groups, asking who gains and who loses from the way that society is organized. Conflict theory suggests that groups will act on the basis of self-interest and may even resort to force to achieve their goals.

The Marxist Perspective

The conflict perspective owes its development to the contribution of Karl Marx. Marx—a scholar who studied past and contemporary societies with the aim of directing the course of history—emphasized the importance of the economic system, which he claimed strongly influenced all the other social institutions, such as the family, the school, organized religion, and the legal system.

Marx was concerned with the conflict among groups that had different relationships to the "means of production"—that is, the resources, technology, factories, and labor used to produce goods and services. Marx observed that control over the means of production led some groups to oppress and exploit others. With the goal of eradicating social injustice, Marx developed a theory outlining the inevitable sequence of stages that all societies would pass through until the private ownership of the means of production disappeared in the final stage, which was communism.

Marx analyzed in great detail the origins of the capitalist system that prevailed in Western European and North American societies in the nineteenth century. We shall return to his analysis of capitalism in later chapters, but his central argument was that a capitalist class, or bourgeoisie, owned the productive resources and exploited the working class, or proletariat, which supplied the labor to produce goods and services. Marx predicted that when the oppressed working class became aware of its collective predicament, it would unite and, in a violent revolution, destroy the capitalist system, then take control of the means of production and establish a socialist economy. In functionalist terms, this revolution would constitute societal disequilibrium, an interpretation that would be criticized by Marxists as conservative and reinforcing of the status quo.

Marx contributed to contemporary sociology—and especially to modern conflict theories—in many ways. His use of historical evidence to understand contemporary societies is important; in recent years, a growing number of sociologists have done historical research (Wallerstein, 1974, 1979, 1980; Tilly, 1978, 1981; Skocpol, 1979). Marx also drew attention to the question of who gains from existing social arrangements, prompting him to search for the hidden consequences of these arrangements.

Marx's emphasis on class has influenced modern sociology, and today social class is one of the primary dimensions of social life studied by sociologists. The concept of class has been extended beyond Marx's original notion; today, sociologists regard class not just as position in the economic system of production—or awareness of that position—but have expanded the concept to include factors such as income, accumulated wealth, occupational prestige, education, and life style.

Modern Conflict Perspectives

Modern conflict theories, most of which are built on Marx's idea of class, also deal with conflict among different groups that are defined by race and ethnicity, religious beliefs, political allegiances, sex, age, and life style. For example, according to one conflict explanation, the Prohibition Amendment that made the sale and consumption of alcoholic beverages illegal in the United States from 1920 to 1933 was the result of a conflict between the middle-class, Protestant Americans who lived in small towns and rural areas and the working-class, Catholic immigrants who lived in large cities (Gusfield, 1963). The conflict that led to Prohibition did not take place between economic classes as much as between groups that sought prestige or high status in American society. These groups were defined more by life style, ethnicity, place of residence, and religion than by their relationship to the means of production.

The Prohibition Amendment that made the sale and consumption of alcoholic beverages illegal in the United States from 1920 to 1933 was the result of a conflict between middle-class, Protestant Americans who lived in small towns and rural areas and working-class, Catholic immigrants who lived in large cities.

For centuries, people have speculated about social behavior: why individuals act differently in a crowd, why life in the city differs from country living, why some people are wealthier than others. Sociologists go beyond mere speculation about behavior to study human action in a systematic way.

Sociologists ask members of the public about their attitudes and actions. Sometimes they perform experiments under controlled conditions. In other cases, sociologists carefully observe people engaged in daily activity. The kind of behavior that can be studied with these research methods is limitless: voting in elections, factory work, bank robbery, and interaction within families.

People are not born as social beings; they must learn how to behave. Every society has a distinct culture—a set of ideals and standards, a language, styles of dress, and food preferences. Customs that strike us as odd—such as eating alligator meat for dinner or wearing nothing but a large leaf for clothing—are accepted ways of life in other cultures.

Socialization is the process by which a culture is learned by the young and by immigrants, who eventually become members of the society. Parents play an important part in socialization; so do peer groups, schools, and the mass media (especially television). Sociologists look at the way that people learn new patterns of social behavior from the time they are born until they die.

People who are not socialized into the ways of a society's dominant culture, and people who behave according to standards that conflict with those of the most powerful group in the society, sometimes engage in deviance—the violation of accepted social standards or norms. When the norms that are violated are laws, deviance is crime.

Interaction among people is the primary building block of social structure—the regular and stable pattern of relationships among people. By studying interaction from several perspectives, sociologists have illuminated the way that groups, organizations, and societies develop and endure.

A family is one kind of social structure, and a large corporation such as IBM is another. Although most sociologists focus on social structures that are intermediate in size—such as families, schools, churches, and corporations—they may study groups as small as a "dyad" (two people) or as large as the world system of states.

One aspect of social structure is stratification, the ranking of people and groups according to social standards. Stratification may be based on income, accumulated wealth, occupational prestige, and power. Social classes based on these factors are associated with differences in quality of life and patterns of behavior.

Many societies are also stratified by race and ethnicity. In other words, the group that has the most income, wealth, prestige, and power often differs from other groups in terms of perceived physical features (race) or cultural background (ethnicity). The great diversity of racial and ethnic groups in the United States is a source of both cultural richness and social conflict.

Differences between men and women in income, wealth, prestige, and power mean that a society is stratified by gender—the social, cultural, and psychological aspects of maleness and femaleness. In the United States today, women earn less than men, even when they have the same amount of education. Inequality of this sort has led to efforts to change traditional patterns of behavior for men and women. Today a majority of women hold full-time jobs outside the home, and more men have taken on domestic tasks.

Changing gender roles have affected the family, one of the social arrangements, or institutions, that is found in all societies. Families come in various forms, from the nuclear family of a man, a woman, and their children, to families that include larger numbers of relatives, sometimes even multiple husbands and wives. The family has important consequences for society, especially the socialization of the young, but conflict also characterizes many families.

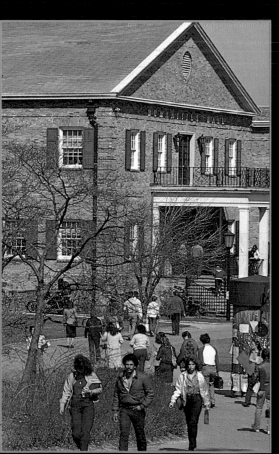

Another important institution is education. Schools provide students with the skills they need as workers and voters, and they instill the culture in new members of society. Americans have become more highly educated during the twentieth century, but some sociologists question whether the educational credentials required by employers are always necessary to perform the job.

Most societies have some form of religion—a set of beliefs, symbols, and rituals that focus on sacred matters. The United States contains a multitude of religions that worship the sacred in various ways. Recently, American religion has been characterized by more cooperation among churches, an explosion in the number of sects and cults, and a growth in the political activity of fundamentalists.

Sociologists study the political system, the institution that establishes and implements societal goals. Political participation ranges from voting to contributing to campaign funds, and from being a delegate to a nominating convention to holding office. Sociologists have described the American political system as a contest for power among competing interest groups, and as a system dominated by a small elite, often one that also controls the economic system.

Closely linked to the political system is the legal system. The law has social origins, and it affects social behavior in numerous ways. The legal system includes the police, the courts, and prisons and jails. These organizations have been investigated by sociologists, often with the aim of improving the way that the legal system operates.

There is tremendous variation in the economic systems of different societies. Some rely on the gathering of food that grows wild, and others depend on the trading of stocks or on high technology. Capitalist systems leave property in private hands, and socialist systems define productive resources such as factories as public property. Sociologists have explored the social consequences of factory work, unionization, inflation, and computerization.

One of the broad social processes that is changing the world's societies in dramatic ways is population growth, which is a product of lowered death rate and birth rates that remain high. Population growth has harmful consequences when it outstrips the growth in world's food supply and when it taxes the capacity of the natural environment. Industrialization has led to a high standard of living, but not without costs such as pollution of the water and the air.

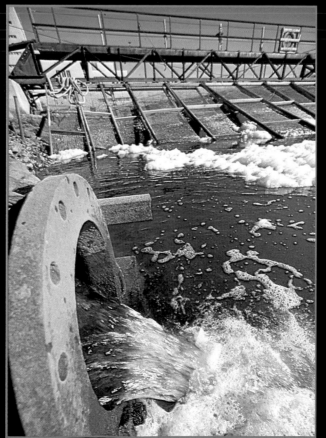

The increasing concentration of people in large communities has meant that the world's societies have become more urbanized. City life offers advantages such as cultural opportunities and a wide choice of friends, but it can also be associated with deteriorating housing, high crime rates, and lack of privacy. Sociologists have explored the patterns that cities form as they grow and the effects of urban life on residents.

Sometimes social behavior occurs relatively spontaneously, as in mass hysteria, fads, or crowds. Sociologists have developed various theories to explain such unstructured behavior and they have also looked at the way that people mobilize supporters, financial resources, and media attention to form social movements. In recent years, social movements such as civil rights, feminism, gay rights, and nuclear disarmament have changed American society.

Social change is the process by which societies are transformed. Some sociologists believe that progress occurs over the long run, others claim that societies rise and fall over time, and yet others take a pessimistic view of the future. The sociological study of the causes and consequences of social change, such as the impact of computers on our daily lives, can prepare us for the future and can even help us to change the kind of society in which we will live in the years to come.

One important modern conflict theorist is Ralf Dahrendorf. Dahrendorf (1959) sees conflict as intrinsic to any social organization in which there is an accepted difference in authority between groups. This conflict over authority encompasses Marx's notion of class conflict, but it also includes conflict between groups that are not defined by whether they own productive resources. For example, there may be conflict between secretaries and managers in a corporation, even though neither group owns the means of production. Dahrendorf's approach also can be used to analyze conflict in noneconomic organizations, such as between parents and children in a family or between teachers and students in a high school.

Another important conflict perspective is that of Lewis Coser. Coser's theory incorporates elements of both functionalism and conflict theory, as is evident from the title of his most important book, *The Functions of Social Conflict* (1956). Coser treats conflict as a pervasive quality of life in all societies, and he examines both the functions and dysfunctions of conflict for society. He shows how conflict between two groups can increase the internal cohesion of each group. For example, the members of a basketball team who are preparing for the "big game" may be drawn closer to each other, a feeling that would be absent if not for the sense of competition generated by the upcoming game. Conflict and competition also connect the opposing parties to each other, for conflict itself is a form of social interaction. Sometimes conflict increases social cohesion by leading groups to form coalitions against a common enemy. For instance, two juvenile gangs that had previously engaged in conflict might unite in the face of a common enemy. Conflict can also alert those in positions of power to the need for reform. The increase in the rate of crime in the United States during the 1960s was followed by increases in government expenditures for welfare. In the climate of the day, crime was interpreted by political decision makers as a sign of widespread discontent—especially among poor minorities living in large cities—and welfare benefits were increased to alleviate this discontent and maintain social harmony (Swank, 1981).

Critiques of Conflict Theory

Functionalists have sometimes criticized conflict theorists for paying too little attention to the question of what holds societies together, and too much attention to conflict and change. Other critics claim that, at least until recently, conflict theorists have made little use of modern research methods, such as statistical evidence and computer analysis. Conflict theorists sometimes respond that an analysis of the complexities of social life cannot be reduced to statistics and that doing so has caused some sociologists to become removed from their subjects and to lose compassion.

Applications of Conflict Theory

Let us now examine how conflict theorists analyze the family and crime.

CONFLICT THEORY AND THE FAMILY. The conflict perspective focuses on the way that the family is influenced by the economic system. In many simple economic systems, it was practical for women to perform chores associated with the home, because they were often pregnant or nursing. Men, being larger, often undertook acts that required physical strength, such as hunting game. In modern industrial societies, such as the United States, men and women are more likely to perform similar tasks: Many women hold jobs outside the home, and many men do household chores. However, conflict theorists note that women continue to be dominated by men. These theorists claim that inequality persists between the sexes not because of biological differences but because it serves the needs of a capitalist economy.

Conflict theorists regard the modern family as serving the economic interests of the society and the needs of the men who dominate it. Because women are paid less than men for comparable work, it is in the economic interest of the groups that dominate the economy to hire such low-paid workers. Sex discrimination in pay also reduces the financial independence of women and maintains male dominance, both in the economic system and in the family.

CONFLICT THEORY AND CRIME. Conflict analysis of crime begins with the premise that no behavior is inherently criminal. Instead, some types of behavior are socially defined as criminal, and these social definitions typically reflect the economic interests of groups that control the legal system. Conflict theorists point out that the criminal law reserves its harshest punishments for acts that are usually committed by members of economically disadvantaged groups. A man who steals $50 may spend more time in prison than an executive officer of a company whose fraudulent advertising costs consumers millions of dollars each year. The conflict perspective attributes this difference in punishment to the fact that the executive is a member of a class with more influence over the enactment and enforcement of law than is the poor person who steals $50.

The conflict perspective views the legal system in the context of society's economic system. The dominant class writes the law and influences the way the law is enforced, and in doing so gains and maintains economic advantage. Criminal sentences for robbery protect the property of owners; the lenient treatment of an executive makes profit-seeking behavior safe. The conflict perspective suggests that societies with different economic systems will regard different types of behavior as criminal and will create different forms of punishment. In the socialist system of the Soviet Union, the destruction of public property is treated more severely than in the United States, a capitalist society in which the law is written to protect private property.

INTERACTIONISM

Interactionism is a theoretical perspective that focuses on the ways that individuals direct and choreograph their interactions with each other. This perspective does not examine entire societies or even large institutions but instead concentrates on the behavior and perceptions of individuals within small groups. The interactionist perspective draws on Max Weber's call for an understanding of the meaning that behavior has to people as they interact with one another.

An important form of the interactionist perspective is *symbolic interactionism,* a theory that examines the way that participants in social interaction choose and agree on the meaning of *symbols,* things that stand for something else or have a meaning deeper than the surface aspect of the symbol. The meaning of symbols is assigned by the agreement of members of a group. Children learn to distinguish a police officer from a bus driver and from a football player by the uniforms they wear. Someone from a different society might see these uniforms as merely clothing. Those who have learned what the clothing symbolizes—specifying the job that the wearer performs—have another tool with which they can interact with one another.

Symbols sometimes make it possible for people to interact without communicating verbally. People respond to gestures, facial expressions, body language, and modes of dress. You can think of examples from your personal experience; you might approach someone at a party who seems friendly on the basis of nonverbal cues, and avoid another person who appears detached or hostile. Responses to symbols are learned and sometimes are not even conscious. When people have an intuition or a "bad feeling" about someone else, they are often reacting to nonverbal symbols.

Language is the most important set of symbols for social interaction. Words do not have intrinsic meanings, as you know if you have ever tried to understand someone speaking a foreign language. Words mean only what people say they mean. Communication through language is one kind of symbolic interaction.

The pioneers of symbolic interactionism in the United States were Charles Horton Cooley and George Herbert Mead. Both Cooley and Mead examined society as the product of the interactions of people who learned to interpret a variety of symbols. Both studied the process by which people develop images of themselves, or self-concepts, through their interaction with others; they both concluded that a person's self-concept was the product of the way in which that person was treated by other people, and how that person interpreted the treatment by others. A boy who is treated as a troublemaker by his parents, teachers, and friends is likely to develop a self-concept of a troublemaker, which may prompt him to cause trouble so that his behavior fits with his self-concept. A girl who is treated as a "fast learner" by her parents and teachers may think of herself as intelligent and good at schoolwork, enabling her to succeed in her academic pursuits.

Herbert Blumer is one contemporary symbolic interactionist. Blumer views society as a product of social interaction that people create in an ongoing, continuous way—meaning that people continually redefine the social situation through their interactions with one another. Blumer has applied the symbolic interactionist approach to the study of forms of collective behavior, such as crowds and social protest. He argues that social problems are most accurately seen as the products of collective definition that occurs through social interaction, rather than as the inevitable result of objective conditions such as poverty or crime (Blumer, 1971).

Symbolic interactionism is not the only form of interactionism. Another interactionist perspective is Erving Goffman's *dramaturgical approach,* which analyzes behavior in much the same way that one would analyze the presentation of a play to an audience. According to Goffman (1959), people present certain aspects of themselves to others, and the way that the self is presented depends on the social context. You have undoubtedly acted differently in an interview for admission to college or for a job than you have at parties with your friends.

Critiques of Interactionism

Interactionists have been criticized for paying too little attention to entire societies and large institutions. Their response is that societies and institutions are made up of individuals who interact with each other and do not exist apart from those members (Homans, 1964). They claim that an understanding of the process of social interaction illuminates the nature of these large social structures. However, interactionists have not, in fact, contributed as much to the study of societies and institutions and to an understanding of the process of social change as functionalists and conflict theorists have. Nonetheless, interactionism does complement functionalism and conflict theory in important ways, by examining the actual way in which people interact.

Applications of Interactionism

Let us now see how an interactionist would examine the family and crime.

INTERACTIONISM AND THE FAMILY. Interactionists would study the family in terms of how husbands and wives, and parents and children, relate to each other. They would examine the process by which the members of a family learn from their parents or friends how to behave toward other members of the family. They would also look at how the members of a family develop common understandings of each other's actions through both verbal and nonverbal communication and how this communication reflects differences among family members in wealth, power, and prestige.

Interactionists might note that parents begin more conversations, and speak and interrupt more often than their children do. They might observe that husbands do all of these things more often than their wives do. Because research shows that people who speak more, begin more conversations, and interrupt more often tend to have the most influence in making group decisions, an interactionist might conclude that, within the family, parents

According to interactionists, one indication of the differences in power within the family might be seating patterns at mealtime.

have more influence than children and husbands have more influence than wives.

An interactionist would also look for other indications of power differences within the family. One piece of evidence might be seating patterns at mealtime. The seating of the husband and father at the head of the table might symbolize his dominance over other members of the family. Another symbolic representation of the man's dominance might be that he, and not his wife, drives when the entire family is in the car.

INTERACTIONISM AND CRIME. An interactionist might begin a study of crime by looking at the way in which rules of behavior evolve through the interaction of group members. Crime is a collectively defined behavior that either produces actual harm (assault, rape, or murder) or symbolizes trouble to members of the group (loitering, vagrancy, or drug use). In the case of crime, the rules of behavior are the laws that define certain acts as punishable.

Interactionists also study the relationships between criminals and victims, and between police officers and suspects. A study of murder found that victims often contribute to their own deaths by being the first to use force or threaten the murderer in symbolic ways, such as through insults and obscene gestures (Luckenbill, 1977). Studies of police behavior find that officers rely on symbols—demeanor and verbal communication—to determine whether they should arrest suspects, warn them, or let them go (Piliavin and Briar, 1964).

Some types of unlawful behavior are learned through interaction. Pickpockets and burglars sometimes learn their trade through interaction with skilled thieves. A study of marijuana use found that social interaction was important for learning the proper smoking technique, how to recognize and interpret the effects of marijuana, and how to enjoy the drug's effects (Becker, 1973).

USING THE THREE PERSPECTIVES

Although many sociologists express a preference for one of the three theoretical perspectives, you do not have to choose among them. In the chapters that follow, we will take all three perspectives. Each has advantages and disadvantages, and many social phenomena are best understood by examining them from more than one perspective, as seen in our examples of the family and crime. The conflict perspective and functionalism would under-

emphasize the interaction among family members, and interactionism would not stress the relationship of the family to the economic system or the functions that the family serves for other social institutions. Yet all of these issues must be examined in order to understand completely the institution of the family. At some point in the future, someone might integrate these three perspectives into a single sociological perspective, but until then the best solution is to use each perspective as a different lens for examining social phenomena.

Summary

Sociology is the systematic study of relationships among people. Sociologists study patterns of behavior in order to discover the social causes and consequences of that behavior. They look at how people form groups, often identifying the characteristics of groups that cannot easily be predicted from knowledge about the individual group members. Sociologists show the relationship of personal life to broad social factors by making use of the sociological imagination.

Sociologists perform a variety of jobs. Many work in colleges and universities where they teach, do research, serve on committees, and contribute to the community. Others do full-time research work at a university, a private research firm, a government agency, or a private corporation. Sociologists also use their skills to plan for social change. Increasingly, the work of sociologists has been used by goverment policy makers to make informed decisions on matters of social importance.

Unlike other observers of the social world, sociologists test their ideas, and use the scientific method to gather the evidence with which to test those ideas. Sociological research is designed so that the idea with which a sociologist starts can either be proved or disproved in the study. Researchers assume that there are patterns to social life that can be studied and understood. The conclusions that sociologists draw from their research are usually tentative and qualified.

Sociologists sometimes begin their studies with commonsense ideas about what they will find, but then subject these everyday assumptions to systematic study. Commonsense notions may be proved correct, but sometimes they are disproved by research because they are only fragmentary or distorted descriptions of the social world.

A theoretical perspective is a framework that is used to study some aspect of the world. Three major sociological perspectives are functionalism, conflict theory, and interactionism. The study of many social phenomena benefits from the use of all three perspectives, rather than taking a single perspective.

Functionalism is based on a biological analogy to society. This perspective sees societies as composed of a variety of structures, or institutions, each of which has certain consequences for society. Functionalists are concerned with the problem of social order, and address the question of how people manage to form a cohesive society. Functionalists look at the consequences or functions of institutions for society; when these consequences disrupt social harmony, they are called dysfunctions. Some functions are manifest, or obvious and intended, and some functions are latent, or hidden and unintended. Functionalism has been criticized as conservative and supportive of the status quo, and for paying too little attention to conflict and change.

Conflict theory stresses conflict, competition, and the process of social change. Karl Marx, whose work laid the foundation of conflict theory, focused on class conflict, the clash between groups with different positions in the system of production. Other conflict theorists have examined conflict that is based on race and ethnicity, religion, politics, age, sex, and life style. Marx contributed to sociology his use of historical evidence, his emphasis on class and economic factors, and his attention to the process of change. Dahrendorf and Coser have developed conflict theories that differ in some ways from Marx's. Conflict theory has been criticized for paying too little attention to the problem of social order and for its infrequent use of statistical methods to test its ideas.

Interactionism examines how individuals direct their actions to each other. Symbolic interactionism examines the way that the participants in interaction attach meanings to symbols such as gestures, facial expressions, clothing, body positioning, and spoken language. Cooley and Mead looked at the way in which self-concepts were developed through symbolic interaction. Another interactionist perspective is Goffman's dramaturgical approach, which looks at the way that people present different aspects of themselves to the various audiences they confront. Interactionism has sometimes been criticized for paying too little attention to the broader social context within which people interact.

Important Terms

CONFLICT THEORY (15)
DRAMATURGICAL APPROACH (18)
DYSFUNCTION (14)
FUNCTION (12)
FUNCTIONALISM (12)
INTERACTIONISM (18)
LATENT FUNCTION (14)
MANIFEST FUNCTION (14)
SCIENTIFIC METHOD (8)
SOCIOLOGICAL IMAGINATION (4)
SOCIOLOGY (3)
SYMBOL (18)
SYMBOLIC INTERACTIONISM (18)
THEORETICAL PERSPECTIVE (11)

Suggested Readings

Pauline Bart and Linda Frankel. *The Student Sociologist's Handbook,* 3rd ed. Glenview, Ill.: Scott, Foresman, 1981. This useful tool for the beginning sociology student presents sociological perspectives, research and resource materials, and techniques for writing sociology papers.

Peter L. Berger. *Invitation to Sociology: A Humanistic Perspective.* Garden City, N.Y.: Doubleday, 1963. A well-written introduction to the sociological perspective on the world.

Randall Collins and Michael Makowsky. *The Discovery of Society,* 2nd ed. New York: Random House, 1978. A useful discussion of the history of sociological thought.

Bettina J. Huber. *Embarking upon a Career with an Undergraduate Sociology Major.* Washington, D.C.: American Sociological Association, 1982. A brief pamphlet that contains practical advice on how to find a job using sociological skills learned during the college years.

C. Wright Mills. *The Sociological Imagination.* New York: Oxford University Press, 1959. This perspective on sociology, by a renowned conflict theorist, emphasizes the relationship between individual experiences and broad social influences.

Everett K. Wilson and Hanan C. Selvin. *Why Study Sociology: A Note to Undergraduates.* Belmont, Calif.: Wadsworth, 1980. A short introduction to sociological perspectives and methods.

THE RESEARCH PROCESS

Why do sociologists use elaborate research methods to study a world that is familiar to everyone? One reason, as we mentioned in Chapter 1, is that commonsense, everyday assumptions are often inaccurate. At best, as we have seen, they are generally fragmentary and distorted reflections of social reality. Using various research techniques, sociologists apply the scientific method to the study of society. They insist on testing the accuracy of "what everyone knows" by collecting and analyzing *empirical data*—that is, the evidence that results from careful observation and exact measurement.

An understanding of the research methods described in this chapter will help you read sociological studies published in books and journals. The ability to comprehend such material may even be useful to you in your career (see the example of Chris in SEL 1.1). At the very least, a basic understanding of sociological methods will make you a better-informed consumer of the research that is presented in newspapers and on television. Sometimes this research is so poorly designed that the results are questionable. For example, public opinion polls conducted during the daytime are likely to omit the views of working men and women, and so it is dangerous to generalize the results.

In their research, sociologists use a variety of methods. Sometimes they analyze existing records that have been collected for some other purpose. The United States Bureau of the Census enumerates the nation's population every ten years and collects other data annually; sociologists have used Census Bureau reports to study issues such as changes in the divorce rate and differences in incomes among racial and ethnic groups. Although these records often leave out much information that a sociologist would like to have in carrying out a particular study, the advantage of using such sources is that the cost of collecting the evidence has already been borne by the agency that gathered the data.

Sociologists often gather data by selecting individuals or groups whom they question, test, or observe for the purposes of the study. One research method sociologists use is the *survey*, a study in which a representative group of people are asked to answer a prepared list of questions. Later in this chapter, we will discuss a survey of junior and senior high school students that tried to explain why some of them committed delinquent acts. Another method is the *experiment*, a more controlled type of research in which human subjects are treated in various ways to determine the effects of that treatment on their behavior and attitudes. We will analyze one experiment that explored the effects of imprisonment on social behavior and psychological well-being by assigning men to the roles of "prisoners" or "guards" in a mock prison. The third research strategy that we examine is *observation*, or watching social behavior in a systematic way. One observational study that we examine is a study of homosexual behavior in public restrooms. There are two reasons for considering this study; in addition to being a good illustration of one observational method—participant observation—it also aroused considerable controversy about the ethics of sociological research, a controversy that we examine in some detail.

Surveys

Conducting sociological research involves following, in a systematic way, a sequence of steps from the conceptualization of the problem to the presentation of the findings. We will examine the form that this process takes in the three major research strategies—surveys, experiments, and observation—using an actual study to illustrate each one.

DEFINING THE RESEARCH PROBLEM

How does a sociologist choose what to study? One way is to examine matters of personal interest. For example, I might study the crime of robbery because I believe that it is an important social problem that causes distress to victims and fear among the general public. Another sociologist might decide to compare two types of crime according to the way their perpetrators are punished—such as robbery, which usually is punished far more severely than white-collar crime, which costs society more than robbery in financial terms. Many sociologists acknowledge that they may be less than objective when selecting a topic for study, but they usually agree that data collection and analysis should be done as objectively as possible, free of the influence of personal preferences and beliefs.

Sometimes sociologists do research at the request of a group or organization seeking specific information or a solution to a practical problem. For instance, the government might hire a sociologist to evaluate the effects of an innovative educational program; a corporation might provide funds for a sociologist working for a market-research firm to determine if there is any consumer demand for a new product; or a political candidate might pay a sociologist to conduct a poll on voter preferences in an upcoming election. Thus, a major factor in the choice of a research topic is the funding that is available. Organizations often support research on controversial issues in the hope that the results will support their current goals. Other times, sociologists themselves take the initiative to conduct research on controversial issues; for example, they have studied the effects that busing for school desegregation has on the academic performance of students.

Often, a sociologist will choose a research topic that reflects the central assumptions and concepts of the theoretical perspective that he or she favors. In Chapter 1 we investigated three theoretical perspectives—functionalism, conflict theory, and interactionism—which serve as broad frameworks that orient sociologists to the world and influence their selection of research problems.

Theories are formal statements of the relationships among concepts. Theories make sociologists aware of problems that need to be studied and is-

A basic understanding of sociological methods will make you a better-informed consumer of the research that is presented in newspapers and on television.

sues that remain unresolved. Testing a theory is one of the purposes that sociologists have in conducting research. Theories also explain facts and organize the results of research. Research evidence may confirm or disprove a theory, and it may also make it necessary for a theory to be reformulated (Merton, 1968: 139–171).

REVIEW OF THE LITERATURE

After a sociologist chooses a particular research topic, the first step in the research process is usually to review thoroughly the published literature on that topic. This review of the literature serves a dual purpose: It indicates what research has already been done and what questions remain unanswered, and it helps the sociologist to refine the concepts that will be used in the research project. In addition, a systematic review of the literature can inform the researcher of the pitfalls that others have encountered in doing research on the same topic.

In the early 1960s, the sociologist Travis Hirschi (1969) decided to study the causes of juvenile delinquency. One of the first things he did was to review previous work on delinquency, and in doing so he came across three major theories of delinquency. One he called "strain theory." According to this theory, people become delinquent because they are unable to achieve goals such as financial success by conforming to the law. Hirschi saw several problems with this theory: It did not explain why delinquents actually conformed to the law most of the time; it did not explain why some delinquents later became law-abiding citizens; and it did not explain why members of the middle class often commit delinquent acts.

The second theory of delinquency Hirschi found was "cultural deviance theory," an interactionist approach that claimed that people learned to be delinquent by interacting with others who were already violating the law. Hirschi found this theory very abstract and difficult to test with research.

The third theory that Hirschi found was "control theory," an approach that assumes that people who are not attached to others are free to engage in delinquent behavior. The theory does not claim that everyone who lacks social ties or bonds will violate the law; it merely states that people who lack such attachments are free to violate the law. Because it leaves room for individuals to choose how to behave, control theory is less deterministic than the first two theories, which presume that everyone in the same social situation will behave similarly.

Hirschi's study of the causes of delinquency thus began with an investigation of earlier theoretical and empirical work. From his review of the literature, Hirschi concluded that control theory best fit the evidence that had been gathered by other researchers. He expanded some of the assumptions of control theory and used it as a guide as he went on to collect and analyze further data on delinquency.

STATING A HYPOTHESIS

A primary focus of Hirschi's control theory was the relationship between an adolescent boy's attachment to his parents and delinquency. Hirschi might have stated this relationship in formal terms as follows:

> The more closely attached an adolescent boy is to his parents, the less likely he will be to engage in delinquent behavior.

This formal statement is called a *hypothesis*, a tentative statement about the relationship between variables. A *variable* is a measurable characteristic or trait that differs from one subject (person or thing) to another, or over time for the same subject. There are two variables in Hirschi's hypothesis; one is attachment to parents, and the other is delinquent behavior. The subjects are the boys who filled out questionnaires for Hirschi. Attachment is a variable because it varies or changes from one boy to the next; one boy might be very attached to his parents, and another boy might be rather remote from his parents. Attachment to parents might also vary over time for the same boy; a boy might be more closely attached to his parents when he is thirteen than when he is seventeen. The other variable in the hypothesis is delinquent behavior, and this too differs from boy to boy, and over time for the same boy.

Variables can be classified according to whether they are "independent" or "dependent." In Hirschi's hypothesis, attachment to parents is the *independent variable* because it is not thought to be affected by changes in the other variable in the hypothesis. Delinquent behavior is a *dependent variable* because variations in delinquent behavior depend on variations in attachment to parents. Variables are only independent or dependent relative to each other. For example, in the above hypothesis delinquent behavior is thought to depend on variations in attachment to parents, but a different hypothesis might suggest that school performance depends on variations in delinquent behavior. Such a hypothesis would consider delinquent behavior the independent variable and school performance the dependent variable.

DESIGNING A RESEARCH PROJECT

A *research design* is an orderly plan for collecting, analyzing, and interpreting data, and often involves the testing of one or more hypotheses that may be part of a broader theory. Sociologists must make several decisions about their research projects before they actually begin to gather evidence.

The Dimension of Time in Research

One decision that the researcher must make is how to handle the dimension of time, and there are two main ways that this is done. A researcher who gathers evidence on subjects at just one point in time is conducting a *cross-sectional study*. Hirschi's research was cross-sectional, because he gathered information from a group of students at one time in 1965.

One difficulty with cross-sectional research is that it is often hard to determine which of two related variables is the cause and which is the effect. For example, if Hirschi had found that the boys who were less attached to their parents were the more likely to be delinquent, he might have explained that finding in a variety of ways. For instance, boys who are not close to their parents at one time may be likely to turn to delinquency at a later time. Another possible explanation is that boys first engage in delinquency, then detach themselves from their parents, or are rejected by their parents for their delinquent behavior.

It is difficult to determine cause and effect in cross-sectional research, because cause-and-effect explanations require the researcher to state which of two variables changes first and thus affects the other variable. Some of the problems of cross-sectional studies are avoided in *longitudinal studies*, which follow a group of people over time. For example, a longitudinal study might measure boys' attachment to their parents over a period of years and measure their delinquent activity over that same period. The sociologist conducting this type of study would be able to determine whether weakened attachment to parents preceded delinquent behavior, or whether delinquent activity preceded the weakening of bonds to parents.

OPERATIONALIZING THE VARIABLES

Taking abstract, general concepts and defining them in concrete, measurable terms is called developing an *operational definition*. Hirschi, for example, operationalized the variable "attachment to parents" by asking fourteen specific questions that dealt with various aspects of his subjects' relationships with their parents. Two of these questions and the possible answers to them are:

1. Do you share your thoughts and feelings with your father?
   a. usually
   b. sometimes
   c. never
2. How often have you talked over your future plans with your father?
   a. often
   b. occasionally
   c. never

For each of these questions, the boys had to select one of three answers. Such "forced-choice" questions enable researchers to compare the responses of many subjects.

Sometimes sociologists ask "open-ended" questions, which permit respondents to answer in their own words. This type of question leaves more room for individual expression, and can direct a researcher's attention to matters that he or she had not previously considered. However, it is difficult to analyze responses to open-ended questions because each subject answers the question in a different way. For instance, if Hirschi had allowed the boys to answer question 1 in their own words, instead of giving them three choices, he might have received responses like these: "yes," "no," "I'd rather not talk about it," "only when he's around," "my father doesn't live with me," and "I talk about sports with him but never discuss school." Hirschi would have had a difficult time testing his hypothesis with such a variety of answers; he would have had to group these responses into categories, and even then some of the answers would have been hard to classify.

One way that Hirschi operationalized the variable of attachment to parents was to combine each boy's answers to questions 1 and 2 into a dimension that he labeled "intimacy of communication with father." Scores on this scale ranged from 0 to 4. A boy received a score of 0 (little intimate communication) if he answered "never" to questions 1 and 2. He received a score of 4 (much intimate communication) if he answered "usually" and "often" to questions 1 and 2. Boys who gave other combinations of responses were scored 1, 2, or 3 on the scale.

How did Hirschi operationalize delinquent behavior, the other variable in the hypothesis? From his review of the literature and from his own training and research experience, Hirschi knew that delinquency is usually measured in one of two ways. One approach is to use police, court, and prison records to document incidents of delinquency. The other approach is to measure delinquency through self-reports, or anonymously-answered questionnaires that include a series of questions about delinquent acts that people might have committed in a specific period of time.

Hirschi used both of these measures of delinquency in his survey. He collected data from police records and from self-report questionnaires that were filled out by the students. He relied on the self-report measure of delinquency for most of his analysis of the data, although he did use the official data throughout his book. Hirschi defined delinquency as acts that could result in punishment by the agents of the larger society if these acts were detected (Hirschi, 1969: 47). He operationalized this rather abstract definition by asking the students the following questions:

1. Have you ever taken little things (worth less than $2) that did not belong to you?
2. Have you ever taken things of some value (between $2 and $50) that did not belong to you?
3. Have you ever taken things of large value (worth over $50) that did not belong to you?
4. Have you ever taken a car for a ride without the owner's permission?
5. Have you ever banged up something that did not belong to you on purpose?
6. Not counting fights you may have had with a brother or sister, have you ever beaten up on anyone or hurt anyone on purpose?

The subjects were asked to choose one of the following four answers for each of these six questions:

a. never
b. more than a year ago
c. during the last year
d. during the last year *and* more than a year ago.

From the responses to the six questions, Hirschi constructed a "delinquency scale"—the total number of the six acts that each boy admitted to having committed during the previous year. These delin-

quent acts might seem to be relatively trivial, but they fit Hirschi's definition of delinquency because each act is punishable by the juvenile justice system.

WRITING A QUESTIONNAIRE

In his study of delinquency, Hirschi used data from two secondary sources, school and police records, and one primary source, questionnaires completed by students. The questionnaire that Hirschi used is reprinted in his book and covers fifty-two pages. That may seem very long, but this was the length that Hirschi needed to gather all the information required to test his control theory of delinquency.

Researchers often "pretest" their questionnaires on people who are similar to those who will eventually participate in the actual survey. A pretest helps the researcher "get the bugs out" of the questionnaire; it identifies questions that do not elicit useful information and can be eliminated, or clarified to remove confusing or ambiguous wording. Writing a questionnaire is a more difficult job than it might seem. You might think that all you need is to know what you are interested in and then ask respondents questions about that topic. However, there are many ways to request information. For example, Hirschi might have asked his subjects the following question about their attachment to their parents: "How close are you to your father?" This straightforward question is one way to operationalize the variable of attachment to parents, but it is too broad to elicit specific details about the subjects' relationships with their fathers.

Another problem that researchers must watch for in writing questionnaires is "loading" a question, or wording a question so as to elicit a particular answer. It is often difficult to keep questions neutral; sometimes a question is loaded so subtly that it even escapes the notice of an experienced researcher until that question is pretested. The question "Have you committed any delinquent acts in the last year? " might seem to be neutral. However, the term "delinquent" might have a negative connotation for many respondents. Some who have engaged in petty theft or vandalism might not think that such acts are "real delinquency." Hirschi's method of asking about six specific acts was a more neutral way of gathering information on involvement in delinquency than a single question about delinquency itself.

Hirschi collected his data by having his subjects complete questionnaires in private. Sometimes

One method of conducting a survey is the self-administered questionnaire. In writing questionnaires, the researchers must be careful not to "load" the questions.

questionnaires, which are simply printed lists of questions, are used to conduct *interviews*—face-to-face encounters in which trained researchers ask respondents a series of questions and record their answers. Interviewers must be careful not to influence their subjects' responses by their inflection of certain words in the questions, by nonverbal signals such as body posture or yawning, or by appearing overly intrigued by a particular response. Interviewers should ask all respondents the same questions in the same way and try to keep from expressing their personal views in a way that influences the respondents. Sometimes the respondents try to give the interviewers answers that they think the interviewers want to hear. Interviewers should strenuously try to discourage all efforts by respondents to gain approval of the interviewer. An extreme example of how an interviewer can affect the views expressed by respondents might be a black interviewer who asks white respondents whether they approve of busing to integrate schools. White respondents might strongly oppose busing but still tell the black interviewer that they favor it in order to avoid offending the interviewer. In a survey on this subject, a researcher might have interviewers

question respondents of the own race in order to avoid distortion of the results.

CHOOSING A SAMPLE

Sociologists use a variety of methods to gather data with which to test their hypotheses. One method is the survey, or sample survey. By gathering information from a carefully selected *sample* of people chosen from a larger *population*, sociologists can draw accurate conclusions about the larger population from what they learn about the sample. Samples need not be very large, but it is important that they be representative of the population from which they are taken; in other words, the people who are studied must resemble as closely as possible the larger population to which the researcher wishes to generalize. The Gallup Poll periodically assesses American public opinion and voter preferences by questioning about 1,500 people; usually these polls accurately predict the results of national elections in which millions of people cast ballots. The Nielsen ratings of television shows are based on the viewing habits of about 6,000 carefully selected American households; these ratings are often used to justify cancelling poorly rated shows. Interviewing a representative sample of a population eliminates the need to gather information from everyone in the population.

In 1936, a magazine called *Literary Digest* tried to predict the winner of the presidential election by mailing ten million postcards to people chosen from telephone books and car registration lists. Based on the responses of the two million people who returned cards, *Literary Digest* announced that Alfred Landon would be the next President of the United States. Franklin D. Roosevelt won by a landslide. What went wrong?

There were two major problems with this study. First, the people to whom the postcards were mailed were probably not a representative sample of all voters; they only represented people who owned telephones and cars, which many people could not afford in 1936, during the Great Depression. As a result, there was no way to generalize about all American voters from those who were mailed cards. The second problem with this study was that only 20 per cent of those who were sent cards filled them out and returned them. Sociologists usually consider a *response rate* this low as incapable of providing information that accurately reflects the views of the original sample; in other words, there is a high probability that the 20 per cent who returned cards differed in some important ways from the 80 per cent who did not respond (Babbie, 1983). As a result, even if the ten million people who were sent cards were representative of all voters—and there is good reason to think they were not—the failure of most of those people to return completed cards is reason to distrust the results of the study.

Hirschi worked to avoid these problems in his survey. He chose his sample from the 17,500 students who entered the eleven junior and senior high schools in Western Contra Costa County in the San Francisco–Oakland area in the fall of 1964. Though this sample included 3,605 boys and 1,949 girls, his analysis in *Causes of Delinquency* focused only on the boys.

Was Hirschi's sample representative of all sixteen- to eighteen-year-olds in the country? The students he studied may have differed in some ways from those in other areas of the country, and they may have differed from students of that age today. Sociological research is usually limited in time and place; for this reason, researchers typically are tentative in presenting their conclusions. A more serious problem with Hirschi's sample is that he was unable to include school dropouts, who may well have been more delinquent than the students who filled out questionnaires. Hirschi's sample may not have been fully representative of all boys and girls in this age group, but it was carefully selected and probably is a close approximation of this population.

Another problem with surveys is dealing with the response rate. *Literary Digest*'s response rate of 20 per cent was below the commonly accepted standards of sociological research. Hirschi's response rate of 65 per cent was considerably higher, but we still need to ask if this 65 per cent of the sample differed in any major way from the 35 per cent who did not complete the survey. The major reason that the students in the original sample did not complete the study was that Hirschi was unable to obtain their parents' permission for them to participate. Because Hirschi's research dealt with the parent–child relationship as a possible cause of delinquency, this source of nonresponse may have distorted his results somewhat. Perhaps those parents who were most protective of their children and refused to allow them to take part in the study were also the parents who had the closest relationships with their children; this would be an important factor because Hirschi found that close parent–child relationships were associated with lower rates of delinquent activity. Another source of nonresponse was the absence of some students from school on the day the study was done. Those who were ill probably did not differ in any major way from those who were present; however, students who were truant may have differed from those who completed the study in some way that affected Hirschi's conclusions. Hirschi did find that those boys in the sample who completed questionnaires were less likely to be delinquent (based on police records) than those boys in the original sample who failed to complete questionnaires.

Hirschi was careful in choosing his sample, and he took pains to collect information from as many subjects in that sample as he could. He was aware of possible distortions that might have been introduced, either by the way the sample was selected or the way information was collected. He pointed out the shortcomings in his data and was cautious in generalizing from his findings. In addition, he discussed in great detail in *Causes of Delinquency* the way he chose the sample and gathered the information; this rigor gives others the opportunity to consider for themselves the basis of his conclusions.

GATHERING DATA

After a researcher has formulated a hypothesis, operationalized the variables, developed a questionnaire, and chosen a sample, the next step is to gather the data. Researchers sometimes encounter problems at this stage of the survey. They may find themselves unable to gain access to all members of their sample, thereby reducing the response rate and making their final sample unrepresentative of the population from which it was drawn. If they use interviews, they may find difficulty in communicating with their subjects. These and other problems often demand flexibility of the sociologist doing the research.

Before hypotheses can be tested, the raw information must be prepared for analysis. Sometimes answers to certain questions must be categorized, as Hirschi would have to have done if he had asked the open-ended question we mentioned earlier. A sociologist who asks respondents how much money they earned in the previous year would probably find it easiest to test hypotheses by first grouping all the answers into a few income categories, such as "under $10,000," "$10,000 to $25,000," and "over $25,000." Researchers often write codebooks, which contain standardized ways that different people can use to code or categorize responses to various questions.

After the data are coded, researchers can then do the statistical analysis needed to test their hypotheses. Today, most analyses of survey data are done by computer, greatly increasing the speed with which sociologists can complete their statistical work. Computer analysis also enables sociologists to explore a number of relationships among variables that they might have ignored if they had to analyze the data using pencil and paper.

ANALYZING THE DATA

After the data have been collected and prepared for analysis, the researcher can examine the results to see if they contradict or confirm the hypotheses. Sociologists examine their data in a variety of ways before drawing tentative conclusions. They develop explanations of their findings, citing the reasons why their hypotheses were confirmed or contradicted. Researchers often relate their results to the theories they designed their studies to test, and, if necessary, reformulate those theories to take the new evidence into account.

Reading a Statistical Table

Sociologists commonly use statistical tables to organize and summarize the findings of their research. Hirschi's book, *Causes of Delinquency* (1969), includes 100 tables. One of them, Table 2.1, provides evidence that tests the hypothesis: "The more closely attached an adolescent boy is to his parents, the less likely he will be to engage in delinquent behavior."

At first glance, this table may be somewhat confusing, but closer inspection reveals some interesting information that bears on Hirschi's hypothesis. The first step in reading any statistical table is to

TABLE 2.1
Self-Reported Delinquency by Intimacy
of Communication With Father (in Per Cent)

| | Intimacy of communication with father | | | | |
| | *Little* | | | | *Much* |
Self-reported delinquent acts	0	1	2	3	4
None	39	55	55	63	73
One	18	25	28	23	22
Two or more	43	20	17	15	5
Total percentage	100	100	100	101	100
Total number of boys	97	181	436	287	121

Source: Adapted from Travis Hirschi, *Causes of Delinquency.* Berkeley, Calif.: University of California Press, 1969, p. 91. Used by permission.

figure out what kind of information it contains and how that information is presented. The first thing to note about Table 2.1 is that it shows the relationship between self-reported delinquency and intimacy of communication with father; each variable is measured on a scale discussed earlier.

The title of the table informs us that the numbers are "in per cent," and an examination of the figures indicates that the percentages in each column add up to 100 per cent (except the fourth column, which totals 101 per cent because of rounding errors). One piece of information that is missing from the title but made clear in Hirschi's book is that the data in the table are for boys only.

Look next at the headings of the columns and rows. The column headings in Table 2.1 break down the variable of intimacy of communication into five categories (0, 1, 2, 3, and 4). The row headings break down the variable of self-reported delinquent acts into three categories: "none," "one," and "two or more." In other words, the three rows classify boys by whether they reported none of the six delinquent acts, one of them, or two or more of them.

The next step in interpreting Table 2.1 is to look at the numbers at the bottom of the table. These numbers summarize the information in each column. (Some tables also include numbers at the right side that summarize the information in each row.) "Total percentage" is the sum of the three figures in each column, and "total number of boys" is the number of boys in each of the five categories of the variable, intimacy of communication with father. For example, 97 boys scored 0 in intimacy of communication with father, and 39 per cent of those 97 boys reported that they had not committed any of the six delinquent acts.

One way to examine the data in Table 2.1 is to consider the figures across each row. For example, if we regard boys who report "two or more" delinquent acts as the most delinquent, we find that the percentages decline from 43 per cent to 5 per cent as we look across this row. Of the boys who had very little communication with their fathers (score of 0), 43 per cent reported two or more delinquent acts. Of those who had much intimate communication with their fathers (score of 4), only 5 per cent reported two or more delinquent acts. In other words, increases in intimate communication with father are associated with decreases in number of self-reported delinquent acts. This finding supports Hirschi's hypothesis.

A final step before leaving Table 2.1 is to consider what questions it leaves unanswered. For example,

you might wonder whether intimacy of communication with a boy's mother is also related to self-reported delinquency; it is, but not quite as strongly as intimacy of communication with his father. Another question that this table does not answer is whether the relationship between attachment to parents and actual arrests for delinquency is as strong as the relationship between attachment to parents and self-reported delinquency; Hirschi does not present this information.

Correlation and Causation

When the relationship between two variables is such that when one increases in value, the other either increases or decreases in value, we say that there is a *correlation* between the two variables. A correlation of $+1$ means that every increase in the value of one variable is accompanied by a proportionate increase in the value of the other variable. A correlation of -1 means that every increase in the value of one variable is accompanied by a proportionate decrease in the value of the other variable. If there is no relationship between the changes in the values of the two variables, the correlation is 0.

Hirschi might have used a correlation coefficient to describe the relationship between intimacy of communication with father and self-reported delinquent acts. This correlation coefficient would be negative, because increases in intimacy of communication with father are accompanied by decreases in self-reported delinquent acts.

The fact that two variables are correlated does not tell us anything about causation. The data presented in Table 2.1 are consistent with Hirschi's theory that lack of attachment to parents gives adolescents the freedom to commit delinquent acts. However, other interpretations of the cause-and-effect relationship between the two variables are possible. One alternative explanation of Table 2.1 is that boys who engage in delinquent acts then become less likely to communicate intimately with their fathers. In other words, the chain of causation might be the opposite of what Hirschi suggested in his theory. In fact, *both* of these cause-and-effect explanations may be correct; in other words, lack of intimate communication with a father might lead to delinquency, and delinquency might then reduce intimacy of communication. The correlation between delinquency and intimacy of communication can thus be the result of any of the following three cause-and-effect relationships; arrows show the direction of causation, and a two-headed arrow means that each variable has an effect on the other one:

1. Lack of intimate communication ⟶ delinquency

2. Delinquency ⟶ lack of intimate communication

3. Lack of intimate communication ⟷ delinquency

There is still another possible explanation of the relationship between intimate communication and delinquency: Some other variable might influence both intimacy of communication and delinquency so as to produce a correlation between them. For example, poor performance in school might suppress intimate communication between boys and their fathers, either because the boys are embarrassed about their poor grades or because their fathers reject them for their poor academic performance. Poor performance in school might also lead to delinquency, especially if the boys began skipping classes or "hanging out" with other delinquents. This three-way relationship can be shown as follows:

4.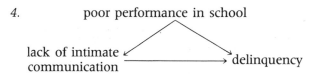

poor performance in school

lack of intimate communication ⟶ delinquency

If boys who perform poorly in school fail to communicate intimately with their fathers and also report more delinquent acts, the original correlation between intimate communication and delinquency might be spurious. In other words, the original relationship between intimate communication and delinquency was not "real" because it was actually a product of the effects of a third variable, school performance, on the two original variables.

Sociologists search for spurious relationships in order to uncover "real" or "true" cause-and-effect relationships. To find the best possible explanation of their research results, they use a variety of statistical methods. Researchers seek relationships between variables that have *statistical significance*. This term has a complex mathematical meaning, but the basic idea is that a relationship is statistically significant if it is unlikely to have been produced by chance. If the relationship between two variables is statistically significant, the researcher can say with a high degree of confidence that the relationship

that has emerged from the sample is also true of the population from which the sample was drawn.

Sociologists use statistics to examine relationships and to present and summarize their research results. A complaint that is sometimes heard about statistical evidence is that "you can prove anything with statistics" or that "figures lie, and liars figure." It is true that statistics have been used improperly, but the proper application of the scientific method, the correct use of statistics, and the careful interpretation of results can minimize such problems. Statistics are simply organized and classified facts, and methods for testing the meaning of those facts. Like any other research tool, statistics can be abused as well as used to illuminate and inform. An outright rejection of statistics usually reflects an ignorance of statistical techniques rather than an understanding of the pitfalls that need to be avoided in using statistics.

PRESENTING THE FINDINGS

Sociologists often present the results of their research in some public forum. Their presentations include papers read at professional meetings, articles published in scholarly journals, government research reports, books, or privately printed research monographs. Research that is published in journals and books is the most widely disseminated, enabling other sociologists to examine, consider, criticize, and even repeat the work done by their colleagues. This is the process by which sociologists have gained their understanding of social behavior.

Experiments

There are some issues that sociologists can investigate in situations where they can control the variables of interest to them (Bonacich and Light, 1978). This type of research design is the experiment. One experiment that has elicited much reaction from sociologists and psychologists in recent years is a study of a mock prison by Philip G. Zimbardo and his associates at Stanford University (Zimbardo, 1971, 1972; Zimbardo et al., 1973; Haney, Banks, and Zimbardo, 1973).

DEFINING THE RESEARCH PROBLEM

The study grew out of Zimbardo's interest in finding the sources of prison riots and corruption and

SOCIOLOGY AND EVERYDAY LIFE 2.1
Analyzing the Evidence: Some Basic Concepts

Sociologists summarize and present the results of their research with a variety of statistical measures. Because no single measure conveys all the information, sociologists tend to use more than one statistic to describe their research evidence.

To illustrate some of the basic statistical measures that sociologists use, let's consider an example. You happened to be in a class that had only nine students in it, and you decided to take a survey of the students' ages. The results of your survey were as follows: 16, 20, 20, 20, 22, 23, 25, 25, and 54.

One way to examine the ages of the students would be to do a *frequency distribution,* or simply list the number of times that each age appears in the group of your classmates:

Age	Frequency
16	1
20	3
22	1
23	1
25	2
54	1

Another way to look at these ages is by finding the *mode*—the number in the set that occurs most often. The mode for these nine ages is 20, because three of the nine students are 20 years old. The mode only tells us which of the numbers in a set is the most common; it tells us nothing about the rest of the measurements.

The *mean*, which is also referred to as the "average," is simply the sum of all the figures divided by the total number of figures in the set. In the case of the ages of your classmates, the mean is 25, which is the sum of all the ages (225) divided by the number of ages taken (9). The mean is commonly used to tell us something about the overall pattern of measurements. Its disadvantage is that an extreme measurement—such as the age of 54 for one of the students—inflates the mean. There is a difference between a class in which each student is 25 years old, and a class in which the students range in age from 16 to 54, even though the mean age of both of these groups is 25.

Another statistical measure is the *median,* which refers to the number that falls in the middle of a set of figures that are arranged in either ascending or descending order of magnitude. The median age of your classmates is 22, since half of the nine ages are greater than 22 and half are less than 22. The median does not tell us everything about the set of numbers, but it does tell us the midpoint. In this set of nine ages, the median is a better description of the students' ages than is the mean, because the mean is inflated by the age of 54 but the median treats the age of 54 merely as one measurement above the midpoint.

Another simple statistic that is sometimes used in conveying information about a set of numbers is the *range* of measurements. The range of the ages of your classmates would be 16 to 54. The range is often combined with other statistical measures to describe a set of data. For example, a good way to describe the ages of your classmates might be to say that they have a range of 16 to 54 with a median age of 22.

the reasons why prisons fail to rehabilitate inmates and keep them from relapsing into criminal behavior after they are released. Zimbardo's papers reporting on his experiment do not include a systematic review of the extensive literature on prisons, but they do demonstrate that he was aware of the issues raised in that literature when he designed his research.

Zimbardo did not test a formally stated hypothesis. Rather, he sought to gather evidence to evaluate what he called his "dispositional hypothesis"—the idea that "the state of the social institution of prison is due to the 'nature' of the people who administer it, or the 'nature' of the people who populate it, or both" (Haney, Banks, and Zimbardo, 1973: 70). This view is held by both defenders and critics of the prison system. Before beginning his experiment, Zimbardo thought that the "bad people" involved with prisons were probably much less responsible for prison riots, brutality, and corruption than was the social organization of the prison itself.

DESIGNING AN EXPERIMENT

The main problem Zimbardo faced in designing his research was that any prison already in existence would already have the social organization of a prison, and would be composed of administrators, guards, and prisoners who could be considered responsible for bad prison conditions. Zimbardo's problem was how to design a study that would separate the effect of the "bad people" on prison conditions from the effect of the prison organization itself. Zimbardo's solution was to create a mock prison with many of the characteristics of a real prison, except that "healthy and normal people" would be assigned as "guards" or "prisoners." This enabled Zimbardo to eliminate the possibility that the "guards" and "prisoners" he studied were "bad people" disposed to violence and corruption, leaving him free to study the effects of the prison organization on behavior.

Zimbardo randomly assigned experimental subjects to be either "guards" or "prisoners." This means that each subject had an equal chance of being a guard or a prisoner; assignment to one group or the other was decided on the basis of a coin flip. Each group was an *experimental group*, be-cause both guards and prisoners were exposed to an independent variable—the prison situation—in order to see its effects on their behavior and attitudes.

In some experiments, one group of subjects is a *control group* that is not exposed to the independent variable in order to provide a base line to which any changes in the behavior or attitudes of the experimental group can be compared. For example, one experiment with actual prisoners sought to evaluate the effects of group counseling, a form of therapy that tried to change the prisoners so they would not commit any more crimes after they were released from prison. The sociologists who conducted this experiment found that about half of the inmates who had received group counseling while in prison returned to prison within three years of their release. Did group counseling work for the half of the prisoners who stayed out of prison, or did it fail for those who returned? There is no way to know how effective the group counseling was without knowing how many of the prisoners would have returned to prison if they had not received any group counseling. For this reason, the experimenters also studied a control group of prisoners who did not receive group counseling.

The motivation for Zimbardo's research was his interest in the sources of prison riots and corruption and the reasons that prisons fail to rehabilitate their inmates.

They found that about half of this group also returned to prison within three years of their release. Comparing this control group to the group that had received group counseling enabled the researchers to say that group counseling was ineffective in preventing released prisoners from returning to prison (Kassebaum, Ward, and Wilner, 1971).

Researchers must be aware that the mere fact of participating in an experiment sometimes alters the behavior of experimental subjects in subtle and unexpected ways. One important experiment on worker productivity was conducted not in a laboratory, but in a factory. The experimenters found that productivity improved when lighting was made brighter and when workers were given more coffee breaks. However, productivity also increased when the lighting was dimmed and when the number of coffee breaks was reduced. The researchers concluded that the attention paid to the workers by the experimenters affected productivity, apart from any effect of the actual working conditions. The effect that participation in an experiment has on a dependent variable is now often called the *Hawthorne effect,* after the name of the factory where the study was done (Roethlisberger and Dickson, 1939, 1964).

OPERATIONALIZING THE VARIABLES

Before setting up his mock prison, Zimbardo identified a number of variables that seemed relevant to understanding the organization of prison life. He then designed the setting in which these variables were operationalized. Prisoners were kept in small cells with steel bars and with no furniture; these cells were constructed in the basement of the psychology building at Stanford University. Prisoners were kept in this prison twenty-four hours a day. They had little privacy and some of their basic civil rights were taken away, though they were not to be subjected to physical abuse. Guards worked eight-hour shifts of three guards each. They were told to maintain order in the prison, but were given no specific instructions on how to do this.

The social organization of the prison was Zimbardo's independent variable; he was interested in its effects on the behavior and attitudes of the prisoners and the guards. Zimbardo hypothesized that being thought of and treated as a guard or a prisoner would produce "significantly different, reactions on behavioral measures of interaction, emotional measures of mood state and pathology, attitudes toward self, as well as other indices of coping and adaptation to this novel situation"

(Haney, Banks, and Zimbardo, 1973: 72). Zimbardo measured these dependent variables in several ways. There were two types of dependent variables: "transactions between and within each group of subjects, recorded on video and audio tape as well as directly observed; and individual reactions on questionnaires, mood inventories, personality tests, daily guard shift reports, and post experimental interviews" (Haney, Banks, and Zimbardo, 1973: 73). Zimbardo thus had information from different sources with which to measure the dependent variables of behavioral and psychological responses to the prison experience.

CHOOSING A SAMPLE

To rule out the suggestion that any harmful effects of the prison that he found were due to sadistic and power-hungry guards or trouble-making and rebellious prisoners, Zimbardo selected experimental subjects who were normal and healthy. He ran a newspaper ad offering to pay $15 per day for up to two weeks of participation in a study of prison life. Seventy-five men responded to the ad. Questionnaires and interviews were used to screen them so that only the most stable, the most mature, and the least involved in antisocial behavior such as crime would be chosen. The experimental subjects who passed these screenings were randomly assigned to the two groups, ten prisoners and eleven guards. The subjects were male college students; most of them were middle class and white.

GATHERING THE DATA

Zimbardo used a variety of methods to gather his data. To measure the changes that occurred over the course of the study, Zimbardo and his research associates had the prisoners and guards fill out questionnaires before, during, and after the experiment. They videotaped about twelve hours of the behavior of the prisoners and guards, and they audiotaped about thirty hours of conversations between and among the prisoners and guards. The experimenters also asked the guards to make daily reports on their own observations, and they had the prisoners keep informal diaries.

ANALYZING THE DATA

To analyze the tapes, Zimbardo and his associates devised a way to categorize the data into distinct types of incidents. These categories included asking questions, giving commands, and making threats. Two people who were not part of the experiment judged the taped material as falling into the various categories and scored the behavior, for example, by determining whether a prisoner or a guard asked a question or made a threat.

Statistical tests were used to determine whether changes in the psychological variables that occurred during the experiment were greater than might have been expected by chance; in other words, these tests were used to determine whether the prison experiment produced statistically significant changes in the subjects.

The analysis of the data led Zimbardo and his associates to conclude that the general outlook of *both* prisoners and guards became more negative as the experiment progressed. For members of both groups, feelings about themselves became more negative. Encounters between prisoners and guards were usually "negative, hostile, affrontive and dehumanizing" (Haney, Banks, and Zimbardo, 1973: 80). The guards were active in interactions with the prisoners; they were more likely to ask questions, give commands, and make threats. The prisoners were more passive; they asked few questions, gave few commands, and rarely made threats.

The mock prison setting apparently re-created the social conditions of an actual prison. Five of the ten prisoners had to be released before the end of the experiment because of "extreme emotional depression, crying, rage and acute anxiety" (Haney, Banks, and Zimbardo, 1973: 81). The experiment was terminated after only six days, rather than the two weeks for which it was initially scheduled, because of the extreme reaction of some of the subjects. The prisoners were happy to have the experiment end, even though they could simply have walked out of the prison and forfeited their pay at any time. Two prisoners later commented:

". . . The way we were made to degrade ourselves really brought us down and that's why we all sat docile towards the end of the experiment."

". . . I began to feel I was losing my identity, that the person I call ————, the person who volunteered to get me into this prison (because it was a prison to me, it *still* is a prison to me, I don't regard it as an experiment or a simulation . . .) was distant from me, was remote until finally I wasn't *that* person, I was 416. I was really my number and 416 was really going to have to decide what to do" (cited in Haney, Banks, and Zimbardo, 1973: 88).

The guards, however, were unhappy when the experiment ended because they had come to enjoy their power. One guard later said, ". . . Acting authoritatively can be fun. Power can be a pleasure"; another remarked ". . . we were always there to show them just who was boss" (cited in Haney, Banks, and Zimbardo, 1973: 88). Some of the guards even worked extra hours without pay.

DEBRIEFING THE SUBJECTS

Because subjects are treated in unusual ways, sometimes even in ways that can harm them, researchers often hold debriefing sessions after an experiment in which they tell the subjects what went on, and how they may have been deceived about the real purpose of the study. Following his experiment, Zimbardo held three sessions with the experimental subjects—one for prisoners, one for guards, and another for all of the subjects together. The subjects discussed their feelings about the experiment and analyzed the moral issues raised by their experiences. These subjects were contacted again during the following year. The experimenters concluded that "the negative effects of participation had been temporary, while the personal gain to the subjects endured" (Haney, Banks, and Zimbardo, 1973: 88). The gain was what the subjects had learned about themselves and the nature of authoritarian settings such as prisons.

Some critics of this experiment feel that it is unethical to conduct such studies with human subjects if even temporary distress is produced. Critics also suggest that the subjects of experiments such as Zimbardo's may actually suffer long-term consequences; for instance, the men who served as guards might have lost regard for themselves after learning that they could behave so brutally, and the prisoners' self-esteem might have suffered from the treatment they received during the experiment. Studies that have harmful effects of this sort can also undermine the credibility of social scientists who wish to conduct studies in the future.

PRESENTING THE FINDINGS

Zimbardo and his associates have presented the results of their experiment in several places. They have published their most technical reports in scholarly journals such as the *International Journal of Criminology and Penology* (Haney, Banks, and Zimbardo, 1973). They have written articles for mass-circulation magazines such as *Society* (Zimbardo, 1972) and *The New York Times Magazine*

(Zimbardo et al., 1973). Zimbardo (1971) has also used this study as the basis for Congressional testimony on prisons. The results of this experiment are well known to sociologists and psychologists, agents of the criminal justice system, lawmakers, and the general public. The study calls for a shift in responsibility for prison riots, brutality, and corruption away from the personal failings of administrators, guards, and inmates, and onto the shoulders of the social organization of the prison itself.

Observation

Sociologists use a variety of observational methods to study social behavior (Emerson, 1981). By watching small groups of people interact in laboratories, they note how a group identity develops and how leaders emerge from a collection of people. They make field observations of how people act during a riot or after a flood. Sometimes they use "unobtrusive measures," such as studying patterns of human traffic by observing where paths are worn across a college campus or where tiles are most frequently replaced in a museum (Webb et al., 1981). In one form of systematic observation, sociologists are active participants in the groups they are studying.

PARTICIPANT OBSERVATION

Suppose you wanted to learn about the lives of men who hang out on the streetcorners of an urban slum. You could write a questionnaire and approach these men on the street, but you might find that they had no interest in answering your questions. They might even react to you in a hostile manner. If they did fill out questionnaires, they might tell you after they completed them that your questions did not have much to do with their daily lives. Unless you had some prior notion of how they lived, you would not be able to write questions that were relevant to their experiences.

How then would you study the lives of these men? This was a problem faced by Elliot Liebow, a white anthropologist who wanted to study the streetcorner behavior of black men in Washington, D.C. He decided that the best approach would be to use a method that had been developed by anthropologists and sociologists, the method of *participant observation*. This research strategy requires the scholar to become personally involved in a group in some capacity in order to observe the group's behavior. SEL 2.2 contains an excerpt from Liebow's book, *Tally's Corner*, in which he tells how he defined his role in the lives of the streetcorner men.

SOCIOLOGY AND EVERYDAY LIFE 2.2
Observing Life on a Streetcorner

Elliot Liebow, a white anthropologist, spent a year and a half in 1962 and 1963 observing streetcorner life among black men in Washington, D.C. This selection gives us an idea of what the method of participant observation is like from the perspective of the social scientist.

On several different counts I was an outsider* but I also was a participant in a full sense of the word. The people I was observing knew that I was observing them, yet they allowed me to participate in their activities and take part in

*From the outset, I had decided that I would never shoot crap, pool, or play cards for money, or bet money in any way (numbers excepted, since playing numbers is safely impersonal), and would meticulously avoid the slightest suspicion of a personal involvement with any woman. These self-imposed restrictions to some extent did underline my marginality. My explanation that I couldn't afford to chance a fight or bad feelings because of my job was usually accepted and I was generally excused from participating in these activities rather than excluded from them.

their lives to a degree that continues to surprise me. Some "exploited" me, not as an outsider but rather as one who, as a rule, had more resources than they did. When one of them came up with the resources—money or a car, for example—he too was "exploited" in the same way. I usually tried to limit money or other favors to what I thought each would have gotten from another friend had he the same resources as I. I tried to meet requests as best I could without becoming conspicuous. I was not always on the giving end and learned somewhat too slowly to accept food or let myself be treated to drinks even though I knew this would work a hardship on the giver.

When in the field, I participated as fully and as whole-mindedly as I could, limited only by my own sense of personal and professional propriety and by what I assumed to be the boundaries of acceptable behavior as seen by those I was with.

Occasionally, when I wanted to record a physical description of say, a neighborhood, an apartment, or a social event, I tried to be an observer only. In practice, I found it impossible to keep all traces of participation out of a straight observer role.

One Saturday night, with my observer role clearly in mind, I went to a dance at the Capitol Arena where more than a thousand people were jammed together. I was the only white male, this was my first time at such an event, the music was so foreign to me that I picked out the wrong beat, and I was unable to identify several of the band instruments. I was, willy-nilly, an observer. But here are a few lines excerpted from the field observation:

It was very hot, it was very noisy, it was very smelly, and it was all very exciting. It was impossible to remain simply an observer in a place like this, even for someone as phlegmatic as I. It was only a few minutes after Jackie Wilson started singing that I discovered that the noise wasn't nearly loud enough, the heat wasn't nearly hot enough, and the odor from more than a thousand closely packed people was not really strong enough at all. Like everyone else, I wanted more of everything.

Almost from the beginning, I adopted the dress and something of the speech of the people with whom I was in most frequent contact, as best I could without looking silly or feeling uncomfortable. I came close in dress (in warm weather, tee or sport shirt and khakis or other slacks) with almost no effort at all. My vocabulary and diction changed, but not radically. Cursing and using ungrammatical constructions at times—though they came easily—did not make any of my adaptations confusable with the speech of the street. Thus, while remaining conspicuous in speech and perhaps dress, I had dulled some of the characteristics of my background. I probably made myself more accessible to others, and certainly more acceptable to myself. This last point was forcefully brought home to me one evening when, on my way to a professional meeting, I stopped off at the Carry-out in a suit and tie. My loss of ease made me clearly aware that the change in dress, speech, and general carriage was as important for its effect on me as it was for its effect on others.

In retrospect, it seems as if the degree to which one becomes a participant is as much a matter of perceiving oneself as a participant as it is of being accepted as a participant by others.

Source: From *Tally's Corner: A Study of Negro Streetcorner Men* by Elliot Liebow. Copyright ©1967 by Little, Brown and Company (Inc.). Excerpted by permission, pp. 253–256.

Sociologists and anthropologists who engage in participant observation to study social behavior have to focus on particular aspects of the behavior they are studying. Liebow investigated the street-corner men's perceptions of work and their relationships with one another, and with their lovers and their wives. One advantage that participant observation has over more formal research methods such as surveys and experiments is that it is more flexible in allowing researchers to notice things they were unaware of when they began their work.

The sociologist who conducts observational research must decide how active he or she will be in the group that is being observed. This raises a problem for researchers: Too much participation can make it hard to conduct detached and professional observation, but too much distance from the group can make it difficult to gain information about the subjects of the study. In SEL 2.2 Liebow discusses how he resolved this issue.

Participant observation is especially useful for uncovering information and generating hypotheses that can later be investigated more formally in surveys and experiments. Because observation is usually done on one group at a time, the question is sometimes raised as to how representative this group is of all other groups. Some researchers solve this problem by taking a survey.

One obstacle that participant observers confront is gaining access to the groups they wish to study. Slight changes in clothing or speech patterns can be useful in establishing rapport with the subjects of the study. Most sociologists agree that participant observers should tell their subjects that they are sociologists studying them, rather than deceive the subjects about the true reason for their presence in the group.

Observers also need to develop ways to record information without disrupting the normal behavior of the group. One problem with participant observation is that subjects may react to the presence of an outsider and change their behavior in certain ways, thus giving the sociologist a distorted view of the group's activities. Observers must also be careful not to give too much weight to the behavior or words of active or talkative members of the group. They must try to get a balanced picture of the group as a whole and avoid treating the most appealing or aggressive members as representative of the group.

Observing "Tearoom Trade"

Ever since its publication in 1970, Laud Humphreys' observational study of homosexual behavior in public restrooms has received much attention. Humphreys studied behavior that had never been explored systematically: how men who are strangers to each other interact during sexual encounters in public places, known as "tearooms" in the slang of the homosexual world. Humphreys felt that he could not fully understand this behavior simply by having men fill out questionnaires, for many would have denied that they participated in such behavior, and others would not have told Humphreys all that he wished to know.

Humphreys was a participant in the behavior that he studied, but he did not engage in homosexual sex. Instead he played the role of a "watchqueen," a third party to the interaction who acted as a lookout to make sure that no outsiders intruded on the men who were having sex. Sociologists disagree as to whether Humphreys acted deceptively in this phase of his study. Defenders argue that he did indeed act the part of the watchqueen and therefore deceived no one; but according to critics, although he acted as a watchqueen, he deceived his subjects because his real motive for being in the restroom was to collect information as a sociologist, and he did not inform his subjects of this.

Humphreys' observations did yield some information that was previously unknown outside the homosexual world. He found that the men usually did not speak to each other, but made agreements to have sex on the basis of glances, body positioning, and other nonverbal signals. One function of this elaborate process was to prevent men who were looking for sexual partners from approaching anyone who was not interested. This protected those engaged in the "trade" from the anger of unsuspecting outsiders to their world.

By placing himself within their world, Humphreys was able to see, from the participants' perspective, the risks of the "tearoom trade." He saw that the police were a threat to these men, and he personally experienced the terror caused by teenage "toughs" who harassed the men with taunts

Humphreys studied behavior that had never been explored systematically before: how men who are strangers to each other interact during sexual encounters in public places.

and violence. From his observations, Humphreys concluded that the tearoom trade posed no serious danger to straight society, but that some police officers and teenagers did present risks to the men.

As excerpts in SEL 2.3 reveal, the ethical standards of Humphreys' research aroused considerable controversy. Probably even more controversial than his observations in the tearoom was the second phase of his study, in which he took a survey of the men he had observed engaging in homosexual acts. Humphreys recorded the license plate numbers of the men's cars, something that was easy to do because the restroom was in a park to which most of the men would drive. He traced their license numbers and added the men to a sample interviewed in survey on social health. Disguising himself somewhat, Humphreys questioned the men in their homes more than a year after he had been the watchqueen in the tearoom. Humphreys claims that there was no indication that any of these men recognized him from the tearoom when he interviewed them in their homes.

In this phase of the study, Humphreys used both survey methods and participant observation. He asked the men questions from the social health survey, but he also closely observed their homes, families, and life styles while he interviewed them. This part of his study has aroused some heated opposition, for Humphreys had a written record of men who had violated the law, and had it fallen into the wrong hands, that record might have been used for blackmail or extortion. The fact that Humphreys carefully protected the list does not negate the risk that he took, and he later had second thoughts about this aspect of his research. Humphreys did deceive the men about the reason for visiting their homes. The men were part of the social health survey, but they were not selected randomly for questioning, as other members of the sample had been. In addition, Humphreys' observations of the men's homes, families, and life styles went beyond the survey that he told them he was conducting.

Humphreys was able to gather certain types of information about the men only because he used deception. He found that about half of the men were married, and some had children. These facts prompted him to conclude that many men who engage in impersonal sex in tearooms do not identify themselves as homosexuals, even though they engage in homosexual behavior. This conclusion suggests that a person's behavior (homosexual acts, for example) may not always determine the way that person defines himself (as a homosexual, for example).

The men whom Humphreys interviewed were more politically conservative than their neighbors. Many of the "trade" had what appeared to the outside world to be good marriages. Their incomes were higher than their neighbors', and they worked more hours each week. The homes, cars, and clothing owned by these men were unusually neat. Humphreys suggests that these men tried to create an impression to the rest of the world of leading very respectable lives in order to hide "the discreditable nature of their secret behavior" (Humphreys, 1975: 135).

This study of the tearoom trade used participant observation and survey research to uncover information that was new to sociology. However, Humphreys took substantial risks in collecting his data. Social scientists and journalists have expressed strong feelings about the ethics of this study. Read the opinions in SEL 2.3 and see how you feel about the ethical issues raised by Humphreys' research.

SOCIOLOGY AND EVERYDAY LIFE 2.3
The Ethics of Research

In 1970 Laud Humphreys published Tearoom Trade: Impersonal Sex in Public Places, *a report of his research on homosexual behavior in public restrooms. The book, which aroused a storm of controversy, included a seven-page postscript on the question of ethics in his research. An enlarged edition was published in 1975 that included fifty-eight pages of discussion (among a number of social scientists and a journalist)* of the ethics of Humphreys' research. Here we look at some of the issues raised in that discussion.

LAUD HUMPHREYS (1970)

So long as we suspect that a method we use has at least *some* potential for harming others, we are in the extremely awkward position of having to weigh the scientific and social benefits of that procedure against its possible costs in human discomfort (Erikson, 1967: 368).

In the article from which I have quoted, Erikson develops an argument against the use of disguises in gaining entrance to social situations to which the researcher would otherwise be denied admission. My research in tearooms required such a disguise. Does it, then, constitute a violation of professional ethics?

Antecedent to Erikson's focus on *methods,* there is a larger question: Are there, perhaps, some areas of human behavior that are not fit for social scientific study at all? Should sex, religion, suicide, or other socially sensitive concerns be omitted from the catalogue of possible fields of sociological research? At first glance, few would answer yes to this question. Nevertheless, several have suggested to me that I should have avoided this research subject altogether. Their contention has been that in an area of such sensitivity it would be best to "let sleeping dogs lie."

I doubt that there are any "sleeping dogs" in the realm of human interaction, and certainly none so dormant as to merit avoidance by those whose commitment should be to the enhancement of man's self-knowledge. Even if there are, sexual behavior in public places is not among them. The police, the press, and many other agents of social control *make* that behavior their concern . . .

NICHOLAS VON HOFFMAN (1970)

We're so preoccupied with defending our privacy against insurance investigators, dope sleuths, counterespionage men, divorce detectives and credit checkers, that we overlook the social scientists behind the hunting blinds who're also peeping into what we thought were our most private and secret lives. But they are there, studying us, taking notes, getting to know us, as indifferent as everybody else to the feeling that to be a complete human being involves having an aspect of ourselves that's unknown. . . .

Humphreys said that he did everything possible to make sure the names of the men whose secrets he knew would never get out: "I kept only one copy of the master list of names and that was in a safe deposit box. I did all the transcribing of taped interviews myself and changed all identifying marks and signs. In one instance, I allowed myself to be arrested rather than let the police know what I was doing and the kind of information I had."

Even so, it remains true that he collected information that could be used for blackmail, extortion, and the worst kind of mischief without the knowledge of the people involved.

IRVING LOUIS HOROWITZ AND LEE RAINWATER (1970)

Von Hoffman says he is talking about the invasion of privacy, but his celebration of the "aspect of ourselves that's unknown" shows a deeper worry about making rational and open what he conceives to be properly closed and dark in human reality. Von Hoffman concentrates his outrage on the methods Humphreys used to learn what he did, but we believe that at bottom he is not much different from other critics of behavioral science who make exactly the same points that von Hoffman makes with respect to research, even when it involves people who freely give their opinions, attitudes and autobiographical data to interviewers. This, too, is regarded as a threat because eventually it will remove some of the mystery from human life.

But von Hoffman recognizes that his most appealing charge has to do with privacy, and so he makes much of the fact that Humphreys collected information that could be used for "blackmail, extortion, and the worst kind of mischief without the knowledge of the people involved."

Here his double standard is most glaringly apparent. Journalists routinely, day in, day out, collect information that could be used for "blackmail, extortion, and the worst kind of mischief without the knowledge of the people involved." But von Hoffman knows that the purpose of their work is none of those things, and so long as their information is collected from public sources, I assume he wouldn't attack them. Yet he nowhere compares the things sociologists do with the things his fellow journalists do. Instead, he couples Humphreys' "snooping around," "spying on people" with similarly "well-motivated" invaders of privacy as J. Edgar Hoover and John Mitchell.

To say the least, the comparison is invidious; the two kinds of enterprises are fundamentally different. No police group seeks to acquire information about people with any other goal than that of, in some way, prosecuting them. Policemen collect data, openly or under cover, in order to put someone in jail. Whatever it is, the sociological enterprise is not that. Sociologists are not interested in directly affecting the lives of the particular people they study. They are interested in those individuals only as representatives of some larger aggregate—in Humphreys' case, all participants in the tearoom action. Therefore, in almost all sociological research, the necessity to preserve the anonymity of the respondent is not an onerous one, because no purpose at all would be served by identifying the respondents.

In this respect, journalists are in fact much closer to policemen than sociologists are. Journalists often feel that their function is to point the finger at particular malefactors. Indeed their effort to acquire information about individuals is somewhat like that of the police, in the sense that both seek to affect importantly the lives of the particular individuals who are the object of their attention. Perhaps this kind of misconception of what the sociologist is about, and the total absence of any comment on the role of the journalist, leads von Hoffman to persistently misinterpret Humphreys' research as "invading some people's privacy." Yet everything Humphreys knew about the deviant behavior of the people he studied was acquired in a public context (indeed, on public land).

DONALD P. WARWICK (1973)

In sum, there are three ethical objections to the research tactics reported in *Tearoom Trade*. First, the researcher took advantage of a relatively powerless group of men to pursue his study. Had Humphreys passed as a voyeuristic gardener or chauffeur for a prominent family he would have been subject to legal and other kinds of retaliation. The men in the tearooms could not fight back. A critic might argue that Humphreys' subsequent acceptance by homophile organizations, including his election to a position on the National Committee for Sexual Civil Liberties, testifies to the fact that he did not exploit the people he studied. However, the men he studied are probably not represented in these organizations because of the covert nature of their activities. Even if they were, one could still object to the manipulation and deception of research subjects for whatever end. Second, through his research tactics Humphreys reinforces an image already prevalent in some circles that social scientists are sly tricksters who are not to be trusted. The more widespread this image becomes, the more difficult it will be for any social scientist to carry out studies involving active participants.

The third and strongest objection is that the use of deception, misrepresentation, and manipulation in social research encourages the same tendencies in other parts of society. A democratic nation is ultimately built upon respect for constitutional processes and restraint in the use of means. If one group arrogates to itself the right to use non-constitutional means for advancing its ends others will do likewise. The same lesson applies to the social sciences. If we claim that our causes justify the use of deception and manipulation, those advocating contrary causes will apply the same logic to their choice of means.

MYRON GLAZER (1972)

Yet it is crucial to emphasize that Humphreys' respondents knew full well that he had no legal means by which to keep the potentially explosive data from falling into the hands of police or other authorities. Humphreys' informants were totally dependent on his shrewdness. Social scientists, I would stress, are vulnerable to subpoena and, unlike physicians, lawyers, and clergy, cannot promise their respondents any legal immunity. . . .

Did his work illegitimately infringe on the rights of those observed? Here, as I see it, the answer is far more complex and must be divided into the two major phases of the approach Humphreys followed. His first encounter with the men occurred in a *public* bathroom. He had as much right to be there as any of the participants. Indeed, as the lookout, he took the same risks as those he observed. Arrest, harassment, and physical violence could have been his lot.

The situation was markedly different, however, in the second stage of the research design. Here Humphreys visited the men in their own homes. He watched them prepare barbecues, have their evening drinks, and converse with their families. Humphreys was an invited outsider. He took no personal risk by being there, but his presence did pose a potential threat to the men and their families. Humphreys' account is the only one available, and we do not know whether any of the respondents were frightened by the researcher's home visit. There has been no follow-up inquiry to alert us to any anxiety that they may have suffered as a result of the coverage that the research has received in the mass media. . . .

While admiring Humphreys, I know that I could not pursue such research myself and would attempt to dissuade others from such a path. The dangers to respondents, to the researcher, and to the precious sense of respect for the privacy of others seem too great for the returns. Had Humphreys faltered, had his data been secured by police officials or unscrupulous blackmailers, Humphreys would have been branded a rogue and a fool. He can now legitimately reject these epithets. Others, particularly those whom we hope to help by our efforts, should not be put in such jeopardy except with their explicit consent.

LAUD HUMPHREYS (1975)

I am forced to agree with my critics regarding that part of my study in which I traced license numbers and interviewed respondents in their homes. At the time, although troubled and cautious about my research strategies, I justified them [in certain ways]. It seemed that I was interviewing subjects in the least disturbing and least dangerous manner possible. I now think my reasoning was faulty and that my respondents were placed in greater danger than seemed plausible at the time. . . .

Since then, although I remain convinced that it is ethical to observe interaction in public places and to interview willing and informed respondents, I direct my students to inform research subjects before interviewing them. Were I to repeat the tearoom study, I would spend another year or so in cultivating and expanding the category of willing respondents. . . .

Years have passed since I studied the tearoom encounters and those who enact a hidden portion of their lives in them. There is no reason to believe that any research subjects have suffered because of my efforts, or that the resultant demystification of impersonal sex has harmed society.

Source: Laud Humphreys, *Tearoom Trade: Impersonal Sex in Public Places,* enlarged edition. Hawthorne, N.Y.: Aldine Publishing Company, 1975, pp. 167–232 (abridged). Used by permission.

Ethics in Social Research

Guidelines for ethical research with human subjects have been developed by the federal government, universities, and the American Sociological Association. There is general agreement that subjects should voluntarily agree to participate in a study and should be told how the research might affect them. To require informed consent may make some research difficult or even impossible, but it protects subjects from being harmed by researchers. Ethical standards also require that research results remain confidential so as to protect subjects from harm or embarrassment. The subjects' right to privacy must be protected, even though this requirement may conflict with sociologists' conviction that their profession requires them to learn as much as they can about social behavior. Subjects should be told at the conclusion of the research exactly what happened during the study. When the results of the project are published, the authors should acknowledge any personal beliefs, values, or affiliations that may have affected the study. They should also include information about the sources of any funds they used to carry out the research.

The ethical standards of the researchers who have carried out a particular study can be evaluated by considering the following questions:

1. Did the study harm any subjects, or was there a substantial risk of such harm?
2. Did the study have any actual or potential benefit for the subjects or for society as a whole?
3. Was the privacy of the subjects violated?
4. Did the researcher deceive the subjects to collect the data?
5. Was a less risky method of data collection available?

All researchers must carefully weigh the answers to these questions. Ethical research protects the public, and it also serves to maintain and enhance the reputation of sociological research. The violation of ethical standards can harm research subjects and may make it more difficult for sociologists to carry out studies of social behavior in the future.

Summary

Sociologists test everyday assumptions and commonsense ideas by means of the research process, an application of the scientific method to the study of social behavior. They use a variety of strategies to conduct their research; three of the most common are surveys, experiments, and observation.

Each of these research designs involves a series of stages. The first step is for the sociologist to define a research problem; personal preferences and theoretical perspectives often act as guides in choosing a research topic. This stage often involves a systematic review of the existing literature on a particular topic to generate ideas and help the researcher decide how to study the topic. The researcher then states a hypothesis, a tentative relationship between variables.

In designing a research project, the sociologist must determine whether to conduct a cross-sectional study and collect the data at one point in time or to do a longitudinal study and gather evidence over time. Longitudinal studies are often more expensive and time-consuming, but they help researchers examine cause-and-effect relationships in ways that are not possible with cross-sectional data.

An important part of any study is to operationalize the variables, that is, to define the concepts in precise and measurable terms. Often, sociologists operationalize variables by writing a series of questions to be asked in a survey, by designing an experiment, or by choosing certain types of behavior to observe.

The next step of the research process is to select a sample to study. Survey research uses samples that are representative of a larger population so that the researcher can generalize from the results of questioning a sample of respondents to the population from which that sample was selected. Experiments also use samples, groups of experimental subjects who are treated in different ways by the experimenter. Observational methods do not use a sample as that term is commonly understood, but sociological observers usually pick groups to study that can tell them something of general significance about social behavior.

In the process of gathering data, researchers sometimes find it necessary to adapt their methods to overcome certain obstacles. The data-gathering phase sometimes raises ethical issues about the deception of the research subjects, the violation of the right to privacy, or potential harm to the subjects. In some studies, especially experiments, researchers debrief their subjects after the study in order to avoid deception and prevent long-term harm.

After gathering the data, the researcher analyzes the results. Many surveys and experiments are analyzed statistically by computers. Participant observers systematically examine their field notes in order to draw general conclusions from what they have observed.

Finally, the researcher presents the findings of the study. If the results are published in a book or an article, other sociologists can examine, consider, and criticize the research, and can even conduct similar studies to check on the accuracy of the researcher's conclusions.

This research process is applied in a variety of research designs. In this chapter we have examined in detail examples of three of the designs most often used by sociologists: surveys, experiments, and observation. In addition to following the steps of the research process, sociologists must also conduct their studies according to certain ethical standards, striving to avoid harm, deception, and violation of the right to privacy. This not only protects the public, but it also makes it possible for sociologists to continue to do research in the future.

Important Terms

CONTROL GROUP (34)	LONGITUDINAL STUDY (26)
CORRELATION (31)	
CROSS-SECTIONAL STUDY (26)	OBSERVATION (23)
DEPENDENT VARIABLE (25)	OPERATIONAL DEFINITION (26)
EMPIRICAL DATA (23)	PARTICIPANT OBSERVATION (37)
EXPERIMENT (23)	POPULATION (28)
EXPERIMENTAL GROUP (34)	RESEARCH DESIGN (26)
HAWTHORNE EFFECT (35)	RESPONSE RATE (29)
HYPOTHESIS (25)	SAMPLE (28)
INDEPENDENT VARIABLE (25)	STATISTICAL SIGNIFICANCE (32)
INTERVIEW (28)	SURVEY (23)
	THEORY (24)
	VARIABLE (25)

Suggested Readings

Earl R. Babbie. *The Practice of Social Research,* 3rd ed. Belmont, Calif.: Wadsworth, 1983. A readable text that discusses the major research methods used by sociologists in a clear and understandable fashion.

Stephen Cole. *The Sociological Method: An Introduction to the Science of Sociology,* 3rd ed. Chicago: Rand McNally, 1980. A brief introduction to qualitative and quantitative methods of testing ideas about social behavior.

Norman K. Denzin. *The Research Act: A Theoretical Introduction to Sociological Methods.* Hawthorne, N.Y.: Aldine, 1978. This book examines research methods in sociology, particularly nonstatistical methods such as participant observation, and emphasizes the use of research to test theory.

Myron Glazer. *The Research Adventure.* New York: Random House, 1972. A look at some of the obstacles faced by sociological researchers.

Phillip E. Hammond, ed. *Sociologists at Work.* New York: Basic Books, 1964. A collection of essays by sociologists about research projects on which they have worked.

Jeffrey Katzer, Kenneth H. Cook, and Wayne W. Crouch. *Evaluating Information: A Guide for Users of Social Science Research,* 2nd ed. Reading, Mass.: Addison-Wesley, 1982. An introduction to the use and evaluation of research results.

part II
BECOMING A MEMBER OF SOCIETY

Newborn babies and immigrants are not members of a society until they learn to act and think like other people in the society. In this section we look at the process by which people become full participants in society.

In Chapter 3, "Culture," we examine the shared meanings that form the culture of a society. We look at the values, or ideals, of a culture; the norms, or standards that guide behavior; and the language that people use to communicate. We also examine material culture, which includes technology and the meanings that people give to physical objects. We see what happens when people come into contact with a culture very different from their own, and we stress the variety that exists in complex cultures such as that of the United States.

Chapter 4, "Socialization," looks at the process by which culture, which is at first "outside" an individual, is internalized. This process is called socialization or enculturation. To behave as social beings, people must learn their culture's way of life. They learn the values and norms of the culture from parents, teachers, peers, and, in industrial society, from the mass media. Because socialization extends over a person's entire lifetime, we explore how, over the course of their lives, people learn intellectual abilities, emotional responses, and social skills.

Chapter 5, "Deviance and Crime," looks at behavior that violates norms, and explores four major sociological theories of deviance. According to strain theory, deviance is the product of frustration that develops when people cannot achieve societal goals through socially accepted means. Control theory sees deviance as the result of the lack of close ties to other people. Cultural transmission theory regards deviance as behavior learned during socialization. The labeling perspective stresses the social definition of rule-breaking behavior and looks at interaction between rule-breakers and those who make and enforce the rules.

CULTURE

In 1972, the Pioneer 10 spacecraft was launched on a flight headed toward the stars, beyond the most distant planets of our solar system. On this craft was a plaque (see next page) that was designed to communicate information—about where the craft came from and who built it—to any resident of outer space who might discover it.

This plaque was designed in part by Carl Sagan, who saw it as a way to convey certain kinds of information to other advanced civilizations. Sagan admits that the meaning of the plaque might be obscure to the average earthling. See if you can figure out what it means. The only thing that would be clear to most people are the figures of the man and the woman, which Sagan suggests may actually be the most difficult part of the message for another civilization to comprehend. The rest of the plaque "is written in the only language we share with the recipients: Science" (Sagan, 1973: 18). This language conveys a picture of a hydrogen atom, a key to a star figure that locates the Earth with respect to fourteen radio-wave-emitting pulsars, a diagram of the solar system, a sketch of the spacecraft, and information in binary numbers that indicates how large the two people are (Rothstein, 1981).

This plaque brought much public response. Its interest for sociology is that it tells us a lot about the people who designed it and the people who reacted to it. The plaque itself is an artifact, or physical object, that is part of American culture. The information this artifact contains tells us something about the values and knowledge of those who launched the craft.

The message on the plaque assumes many things about the creatures who might intercept it. It assumes that they will see the plaque as carrying a message that is distinct from the rest of the craft. It assumes that the use of line drawings to represent three-dimensional objects will make sense to these extraterrestrials. The plaque also assumes that an "advanced civilization" will have a science that sees the physical world in much the same way as American scientists do (Rothstein, 1981). Another assumption is that these extraterrestrials will be enough like humans physically to interpret the two figures as living beings. The British humor magazine *Punch* imagines how one extraterrestrial might respond to the plaque:

"Speaking as a fourteen-legged and extremely thin spider," said a voice from the back of Andromeda 9, "I have studied this post-card from the Earthlings and I take it as a snub. The caricature of our species is both crude and inept, suggesting, amongst other things, that we've got a right leg longer than all the rest. Furthermore, the geometric being which is standing at the back has clearly turned its back on us and one of the other two is pointing five antennae in a frankly sordid gesture. There seems little reason to doubt, amongst us intelligent spiders, that this thing is intended as a declaration of war. The illustrated talent for the creature on the right to be capable of firing arrows from the shoulder is a particularly sinister turn and one that bodes badly for a long and bitter struggle with the Earthlings." (cited in Sagan, 1973: 31).

Silly as it is, the *Punch* article shows us some of the hidden assumptions in the plaque. Clearly, a different civilization might interpret the picture in ways that we cannot even imagine. The plaque contains a variety of symbols, or signs that are intended to convey a meaning deeper than the surface meaning of the symbol. A *culture* is a system of symbols that a group of people share to help them make sense of the world. Only someone who shares the culture of the scientists who designed the plaque would interpret the hidden meanings of the various symbols in the way that is intended. A different being, such as a fourteen-legged spider,

Pioneer 10 Plaque.

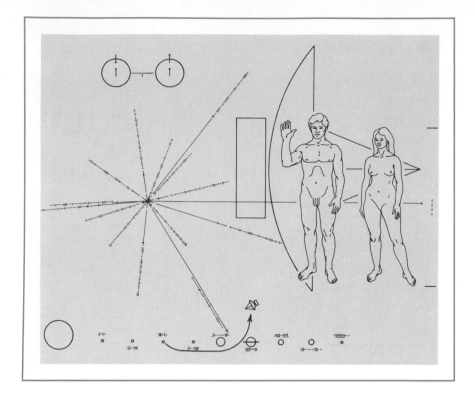

might miss the intended meaning of the plaque altogether.

The response of earthlings to this plaque also tells us something of the diversity of culture on this planet. In fact, different groups in American society saw the plaque in quite different ways. One person criticized its depiction of a naked man and woman as sending pornographic filth into space. A Catholic magazine protested that everything was depicted except God and suggested that the plaque should have included a pair of praying hands. The man's raised hand was intended as a sign of greeting to the universe; the designers claimed that on Earth this is a widely accepted sign of friendly feelings, although one person pointed out that a civilization with knowledge of the Earth's history in the 1940s might assume that the Nazis had conquered the world. Another reaction to the plaque was *Playboy's* complaint about government censorship of the woman's genitals. Some feminists also felt that the omission of the woman's sex organs was inappropriate, and also criticized the woman's apparent passivity, and the fact that she did not offer a greeting to the universe.

People interpreted the meaning of the plaque's message in accordance with their own perspectives on the world. When we consider that all of these viewpoints share at least certain aspects of American culture and yet each is a unique interpretation, we can reasonably question whether a being from an extraterrestrial civilization would be able to make any sense of the information in the plaque.

What Is Culture?

What can we learn about American values and beliefs from the Pioneer 10 plaque? The plaque's message presumes that differences between men and women are worth representing to extraterrestrials. Two figures could have been drawn to represent other differences between people, such as race or age. The choice to represent sex differences, without including any information about how humans reproduce, suggests that there are important *social* differences between men and women in American society. The plaque also indicates that science is highly valued in American society, at least by the designers of the plaque. Science is less important in other societies; some of them might have preferred to send an example of their artwork into space. The plaque, then, says something about the culture of the United States, even though that information is not explicit.

What exactly is culture? This term has a variety of meanings to anthropologists and sociologists. One type of definition stresses the content of culture, such as knowledge, technology, laws, and the arts (Tylor, 1871, 1958). This position treats culture as a collection of "things." Another way to define culture is as a shared set of meanings that are used to interpret and make sense of the world (Geertz, 1973; Hall, 1981). Social scientists who hold this view search for the underlying meanings that are expressed in the content of culture. For example, an anthropologist or sociologist who took this approach would ask what meaning a tool or a sculpture had for the members of a group. This approach treats culture as a screen between people and the external world that directs their attention to certain matters and structures the world for them (Hall, 1981).

How is a culture different from a society? Sometimes the difference is not clear, and often the two terms are used interchangeably. However, there is an important difference. A "society" is a group of people who interact mostly with each other and live in a defined territory; societies are relatively independent of each other (see Chapter 7). Cultures are sets of meanings that people share. Some cultures, such as the Jewish culture, go beyond the boundaries of a society, and transcend national borders. Sometimes a culture outlives the society that gave birth to it. Elements of the culture of ancient Rome, such as the Latin language and classical sculpture, still exist today, even though Roman society died off centuries ago. In fact, the human figures in the Pioneer 10 plaque were drawn according to models of classical sculpture.

A culture is a "design for living" that is shared by a group and learned from others in the group (Kluckhohn, 1949). Culture is a characteristic of groups; we cannot speak of the culture of a single individual, although an individual can be thought of as a bearer of culture. Newborn babies and immigrants become members of a society before they learn the culture of its people. Babies and immigrants interact with others members of the society from the time they enter it, but they require years to learn the culture. "Socialization" or "enculturation" is the process by which the culture that is at first "outside" the person becomes internalized, through learning from parents, teachers, peers, religious leaders, and other sources. Culture is passed from generation to generation through this process of socialization, which we examine in the next chapter.

Culture provides us with a great advantage: We do not have to figure out how to accomplish a task or how to interpret the world, for we can rely on the traditions of our ancestors. Each new generation does not have to reinvent the wheel, rediscover fire, or redesign the computer. New generations sometimes discard aspects of the culture that no longer seem relevant or important, and they modify other aspects of the culture to fit their own needs. Today, people are more likely to pick up the telephone than write a letter, a more common practice a century ago. The phone is better adapted to a modern society in which speed is valued and people move a lot.

MATERIAL CULTURE

What functions does culture serve for society? One answer to this question is that culture makes it possible for people to meet certain needs in order to survive. Culture enables people to adapt to the environment in which they live. Lower animals rely on instincts—complex and specific types of behavior that are inherited and not easily altered—to help them adapt to the environment. These instincts, which do not have to be learned from other animals, appear in animals soon after birth.

Human behavior is not determined by instincts. People do have some inborn reflexes, or automatic reactions to external stimulation. These reflexes include responses to keep from falling and to protect against loud noises; both of these responses are evident in infants who have not had the chance to learn them. People also have biological needs, or drives, such as hunger and sex. In recent years, the discipline of *sociobiology* has tried to explain social behavior in biological terms (E. Wilson, 1975, 1978). People are indeed biological organisms with inborn drives that must be satisfied, but the tremendous variety of ways that people satisfy these needs suggests that biology establishes only broad limits to human behavior rather than determining that behavior, as the sociobiologists suggest. In fact, biological needs have probably had less impact on behavior with the spread of communication among the peoples of the world, enabling them to borrow ways of meeting their needs from other cultures.

People need to eat in order to survive, but every culture has its own customs about what can be eaten and how food is to be prepared. Hindus in India will not eat the meat of cattle, even though cattle are plentiful in this underfed society. Most cultures condemn cannibalism, but the Jalé of New Guinea eat human flesh, as did the ancient Aztecs; however, cannibalism is usually for symbolic reasons, not for protein. People who gather vegetables and hunt game would be shocked to learn that Americans sometimes eat "lemon cream pies" that contain neither lemons nor cream but are made entirely from synthetic chemicals.

Another basic human need that is met in different ways in different cultures is protection from the weather. The way that people dress is a part of their culture. In a few cultures, people wear practically nothing at all, though even in hot climates societies have customs that require the body to be covered in some way. People who live in cold climates need clothing in order to survive, but their dress varies greatly from culture to culture. Eskimos wear parkas made from the skins of animals they have killed, whereas Americans are more likely to buy coats made of synthetic materials.

Clothing is part of *material culture*, the tangible and physical aspects of culture. *Artifacts* are objects that are part of material culture because they have been given meaning by people; one example is the plaque that was sent into space. A disk-like stone that lies on the ground but is not used by anyone is not an artifact. If that stone is used as part of a vehicle that provides transportation, it is an artifact, because it then serves a human need and holds meaning for people. People create artifacts to help them accomplish their tasks and meet their needs. For example, the Zulus of nineteenth-century Africa developed a short spear called an *assegai* that was very effective in hand-to-hand combat; with this weapon, the Zulus were able to conquer other tribes and expand the territory they controlled. One artifact may also be given different meanings in different cultures. For instance, the wheel was invented by the Incas of South America, who used it only in children's toys and not for transportation because of the mountainous terrain in which they lived.

Material culture includes *technology*, the practices, tools, materials, skills, and methods of organization that people use to manipulate the environment for their own purposes. Technology is cumulative; that is, it builds on past developments in a progressive way. Technology sometimes creates unexpected problems, in addition to conferring benefits on a society. Modern industry has raised the standard of living of millions, but it also threatens human health and the natural environment by causing pollution. The computer has greatly increased the efficiency of modern industrial societies, but according to some people, the video games that have become popular with the young may cause them to become less involved in athletic activities or be less willing to do homework. Yet, technology sometimes offers solutions to the problems it creates: It can supply the techniques needed to control industrial pollution, and can make schoolwork more exciting for students who learn to work with computers.

EXPRESSIVE CULTURE

Culture includes more than artifacts and technology. It also includes ideas, beliefs, values, and customs—all of which comprise the *expressive* part of culture, which serves to express people's emotional needs and helps them to interpret the world. In recent years both anthropologists and sociologists have become more interested in what they can learn about how people interpret the physical and social world and how they make sense of their own place in that world (Geertz, 1973; Giddens, 1976, 1979; Hall, 1981).

Imagine a visitor from outer space watching two short films of boys who are contracting their right eyelids. To the alien, these films might seem indistinguishable. However, if you closely examined each film, you might discover two quite different meanings in the eyelid contractions. One film might show a boy suffering from an involuntary twitch; the meaning of his behavior is that he has a physiological problem that is beyond his control. In contrast, you might notice that the eyelid contraction in the second film seems deliberate and directed at someone else. You can "tell" that this eyelid contraction is a wink, a conspiratorial signal to others. This boy intends to convey a message by his behavior, but this message can only be interpreted properly by someone familiar with the culture of the boy who is winking (Geertz, 1973: 6–7).

A culture is a set of meanings attached to particular kinds of behavior, such as eyelid contractions. The designers of the plaque that is now speeding through space assumed that a raised hand would clearly signal friendship to extraterrestrials because many cultures on Earth give it this meaning. However, there is no reason to think that creatures from another planet will share this meaning of the raised hand. In fact, they may use the same signal to indicate hostility or a desire for sexual relations. Even on Earth, the raised hand has not always conveyed friendliness; as used by the Nazis, it symbolized hostility and evil intentions to many people.

According to the interpretive view of culture, the system of codes and meanings that form a culture enables the people who share the culture to interact smoothly with one another. This view of culture contrasts with the position that emphasizes the artifacts and technology of a culture. The interpretive approach sees culture as a context within which behavior makes sense to people. The members of a society who share a culture understand the significance of objects, gestures, clothing, grooming, and other aspects of culture; however, to understand the culture, social scientists must interpret the meaning of what those people take for granted. Social scientists understand culture by watching the activities of people and interpreting the meaning that behavior holds for them. Sociologists and anthropologists have a complete picture of a culture only when they can participate in it as full-fledged members (Geertz, 1973; Giddens, 1976, 1979).

The interpretive approach to culture seeks to understand the meaning that people give to aspects of material culture such as clothing. Clothing serves to protect people from inclement weather, but, of course, clothes do much more than protect people from the elements. Some types of apparel, such as necklaces and headdresses, have magical implications; wearers believe that they acquire some type of mysterious power when they wear such things. Clothing can also be a way to indicate wealth and social position. In 1899, the American economist, Thorsten Veblen, wrote that mode of dress was "evidence of ability to pay"; in addition to signifying social worth, clothes were worn to convey the impression that the wearer was wealthy enough not to have to work for a living. Veblen illustrates this point as follows:

Much of the charm that invests the patent-leather shoe, the stainless linen, the lustrous cylindrical hat, and the walking-stick, which so greatly enhance the native dignity of a gentleman, comes of their pointedly suggesting that the wearer cannot when so at-

tired bear a hand in any employment that is directly and immediately of any human use. . . . The woman's shoe adds the so-called French heel to the evidence of enforced leisure afforded by its polish; because this high heel obviously makes any, even the simplest and most necessary manual work extremely difficult. The like is true even in a higher degree of the skirt and the rest of the drapery which characterises woman's dress. The substantial reason for our tenacious attachment to the skirt is just this: it is expensive and it hampers the wearer at every turn and incapacitates her for all useful exertion (Veblen, 1899, 1918: 170–171).

Clothing, then, has several functions, or consequences, for society. It protects people from the elements. It offers comfort and makes some kinds of work easier or safer. As Veblen shows, clothing can also symbolize to others that the wearer has a certain identity or social standing. Clothing also serves to seduce; some clothes are intended to attract erotic attention. One observer even suggests that a society's birth rate is higher when men's clothing and women's clothing are more distinct from each other, and that fewer children are born during times of "unisex" clothing (Lurie, 1981: 213–214).

The conflict perspective regards drastic changes in fashion that take place over short periods of time in advanced capitalist systems such as the United States as reflections of the power of advertising and business to entice consumers to discard their old clothes and buy new ones. For example, many women in the mid-1960s who at first would never have worn miniskirts did adopt this style after a while; today, many of these women cannot imagine how they wore skirts that short and claim they never would again. In SEL 3.1, Alison Lurie looks at some of the cultural meanings of the punk or New Wave style that developed in Great Britain in the late 1970s and spread to the United States soon thereafter.

SOCIOLOGY AND EVERYDAY LIFE 3.1
The Punk Look

Social protest and social disaffection both tend to adopt some characteristic costume. The Beatniks, Teddy Boys, and Zoot Suiters of the postwar period, the Mods, the Rockers of the 1950s, the Skinheads and the Hippies of the 1960s, all expressed themselves eloquently in the language of clothes. Today alienation from mainstream values is just as fluently set forth by what were known first as Punk and later as New Wave styles.

The original Punk Look appeared in London in the late 1970s among marginally employed or unemployed working-class teenagers. It featured hair cropped to a fuzz and dyed startling, unnatural colors: often very pale yellow, sometimes red, green, orange or lavender. Faces were powdered pasty white, with sooty eyes and heavy lipstick. In clothing, red, black and white were the favorite colors. Punks wore black leather jackets and jeans decorated with metal studs and superfluous zippers; T-shirts printed with vulgar words and violent and/or pornographic pictures—often images of rape and murder. Artificially torn and soiled clothing, held together with outsize safety pins, exposed areas of pale, unhealthy flesh, which were often bruised and scratched. One favorite accessory was the dog or bicycle chain, which might be pulled tight round the neck or used to fasten one leg to the other. Punk chicks might also wear this costume, or they might vary it with hot pants, side-slit skirts, tight angora sweaters and spike-heeled sandals . . .

In the language of clothes, the Punk style was a demand for attention, together with a cry of rage against those who should have paid attention to these kids in the past but had not done so: parents who were too immature or too exhausted; callous or helpless teachers and social workers; a welfare state that seemed uninterested in their welfare and had no jobs for most of them. The motorcycle-gang outfits, the chains and razor blades, the real and artificial bloodstains and scars, the exposure of flesh, were intended to offend and to frighten. It was necessary to go to these extremes to get any reaction because the street costumes of the late sixties and early seventies were already fairly outrageous, and because the ordinary man and woman had become so familiarized with violence and sex through the media.

At the same time, other aspects of the Punk Look appealed not only for attention, but for the love and care that we give to very small children, especially to injured ones. After all, where else had we seen that fluffy Easter-chick hair, those pale scratched faces and scraped knees, those torn shirts and jeans, those ill-fitting, often half-undone jackets and leggings? As for that Punk trademark, the outsize safety pin stuck through a cheek or earlobe, it could not help but remind every mother of the awful moment when she ran one just like it into her darling instead of into his nappie. The chain that linked one leg to the other not only suggested violence, bondage and sexual perversion—it also gave its wearer the short, halting, appealing gait of a toddler.

It was this double message, as of a viciously angry miserable baby, that made the Punk Look so deeply disturbing. Most new styles cause only surprise, scornful amusement or admiration; the Punk Look made people in Britain feel rage, guilt, compassion and fear simultaneously; it was fashion moving toward political protest, possibly toward political action. The recent American equivalent, known as New Wave, is a watered-down version of its original, more theatrical than serious in intent. It is not associated with the working class, and it de-emphasizes the damaged-baby indicators— quite logically, since American children are more apt to be spoiled than neglected. New Wave fashions, too, are usually worn at night, to parties and bars and discos and concerts; they seldom appear in public in the daytime. As might be expected, therefore, the New Wave Look has aroused relatively little public outrage; its principal message seems to be that some American teenagers are bored and restless (so what else is new?) and looking for cheap, relatively safe thrills.

Source: Excerpted from *The Language of Clothes*, by Alison Lurie, pp.161–164. Copyright © 1981 by Alison Lurie. Reprinted by permission of Random House, Inc.

Elements of Culture

Since 1945, millions of American children have read or heard the story of Tootle, a young engine that wants to grow up to be a big locomotive. To do this, Tootle goes to engine school, where he learns to stop at red flags and stay on the tracks. One day Tootle leaves the tracks to race a horse; later he wanders into the meadows to enjoy the flowers and play with the butterflies. When his errant behavior is discovered, the townspeople of Lower Trainswitch decide to take action. The next time Tootle leaves the tracks for the fields, he meets red flags everywhere. The only visible green flag is on the tracks, so, to the applause of his neighbors, he returns to the rails. He vows never again to leave the tracks. Later he grows up to be a "Two-Miles-a-Minute Flyer" who advises young engines: "Work Hard. . . . Always remember to Stop for a Red Flag Waving. But most of all, Stay on the Rails No Matter What" (Crampton, 1945: n.p.).

Children who hear or read this story probably could not articulate its exact meaning, but they

Clothing is part of material culture. Here the "punk look" demonstrates eloquently a form of alienation from mainstream Western cultural values.

undoubtedly understand its message at some level. The story tells children that they will be successful if they follow the rules. They learn that experienced adults will help guide them to achieve rewards such as applause and adult status. Adults are portrayed as tolerant and appreciative of good behavior. In the real world, the signals toward the path to success are rarely as clear as the flags confronted by Tootle. The rewards of adult status in the real world are usually not as positive as the story suggests, nor are adults always as helpful or tolerant as the townspeople of Lower Trainswitch (Riesman, 1950: 107–111).

VALUES

All cultures have stories, myths, folklore, and fairy tales like the story of Tootle that convey the values of the culture. *Values* are abstract and shared ideas about what is desirable, good, or correct—they represent the ideals of the culture. The value of

success conveyed in Tootle's story is an ideal; rarely is the real world so rewarding.

Values are emotion-laden. In other words, the reason that the members of a culture share a value such as conformity or politeness is because they *feel* that such behavior is right. This feeling is learned from fairy tales and folklore, and from parents, teachers, peers, and religious leaders. Values are the very general shared preferences of a culture rather than the preferences of its individual members, although people internalize the values of the culture and are guided in their behavior by those values, just as Tootle was.

A culture's values are organized in a value hierarchy, a set of priorities among values. The hierarchy is not always apparent; often it can be seen most clearly when there is a conflict between values. Consider an extreme example: In 1980 a New Jersey couple tried to trade their fourteen-month-old son for a 1977 Corvette. The car dealer's first reaction was to agree to the swap, but after a bit of reflection he decided it would be wrong and he called the police. He asked himself, "How could this boy cope with life knowing he was traded for a car?" (Goldman, 1980: B1). This bizarre incident shows a conflict between two important values of American culture: family ties and material success. Critics of American culture often point to its strong emphasis on materialism, but the unanimous, negative response to this attempt to trade a baby for a car suggests that Americans probably value the parent–child relationship even more than the trappings of success.

Because values are very general, many types of behavior fit with the values of a culture. Often, different values seem to be possible guides to behavior; actual behavior sometimes conflicts with one value but is compatible with a different value. One value of American culture is that everyone should have equal opportunity to be hired for a job. However, a majority of Americans would deny an avowed homosexual a job as a school teacher. This action is incompatible with the value of equal employment opportunity, but it does conform to a different value—protection of the young from those who might seduce them into a deviant life style. This value of protecting the young from homosexuals is based on emotion rather than evidence, for rarely are children seduced into homosexuality in this way; indeed, the risk of seduction by a heterosexual teacher may be greater.

NORMS

Values express general goals and establish broad guidelines for behavior. *Norms* are more specific rules about appropriate behavior. Norms state expectations about how a particular person should behave, think, or feel in a specific situation. In this way, norms organize social behavior and make the actions of others predictable, at least within certain limits.

Norms are specific to the person and the situation. For example, when you go to the beach, you are expected to wear a bathing suit or casual clothing. At most beaches in the United States, you would be stared at, criticized, or even arrested if you appeared in the nude. In contrast, on some European beaches you would be stared at or criticized for wearing a bathing suit, because the norm is to swim in the nude. Wearing a tuxedo or a formal gown on either the American or the European beach would violate the norm about appropriate beachwear. One person who might be expected to

dress differently on the beach is a police officer. An officer who patrolled the beach in a bathing suit or in the nude would probably violate social expectations about how police officers should dress while on duty.

Clothing that is appropriate for the beach is inappropriate in other situations. If you showed up for a job interview in a bathing suit, you probably would not be hired, unless you were applying for the job of lifeguard. Formal dress that is inappropriate for the beach is often required at banquets and ceremonies. The norm of how to dress is related to the particular person and the specific social context.

Most norms, including how to dress, are somewhat flexible, rather than rigid, requirements for a specific kind of behavior. At some beaches you can swim in the nude, wear a bathing suit, or dress casually. Even wearing a formal gown or a tuxedo would probably not elicit much more reaction than a puzzled glance. At some parties, acceptable apparel ranges from formal to relatively casual. However, not all norms are so flexible. In some nudist camps, visitors must disrobe, leave cameras at the gate, avoid staring, and refrain from touching others (Weinberg, 1965; Lowney, Winslow, and Winslow, 1981: 46–64). Some formal affairs require black tie, and some expensive restaurants will not seat couples if the man is not wearing a jacket and tie or if the woman is wearing denim.

A rigid type of norm is a law, a formal rule defined by a political authority that has the power to punish violators. The more closely a law conforms to the informal norms of a culture, the easier it is to enforce. When norms support behavior that is illegal, conflict may develop between law enforcers and the rest of the population. The widespread use of marijuana has produced conflict between users and the police in recent years, just as the Prohibition Amendment created conflict among federal agents, bootleggers, and drinkers in the 1920s and 1930s.

SANCTIONS

If you take off your bathing suit at a beach where nudity is prohibited you might be stared at, criticized, or arrested. These reactions to your violation of the norm (or the law) are called *sanctions*. Sanctions reveal the meaning that a culture gives to behavior. In the mid-1970s the fad of "streaking" naked through a public place was often punished with arrest, but because this violation of the norm against nudity was viewed as a harmless prank, the actual punishments were usually mild. On the other hand, indecent exposure has a very different meaning; it is seen as a threatening act with sexual overtones and is typically punished more severely than is streaking.

Sanctions can be positive as well as negative. A soldier who acts "above and beyond the call of duty" to rescue another soldier in a battle might be sanctioned positively (or rewarded) for heroism by receiving a commendation or a medal. A soldier who deserts under fire might be negatively sanctioned by being courtmartialed. Both heroes and cowards violate norms, because they do not behave as expected in the particular situations in which they find themselves. Both are often sanctioned for their violations of norms.

Sanctions serve to reinforce the norms of a culture by rewarding people for behavior in accordance with cultural values and by punishing people for disvalued behavior. Military medals and promotions are used to encourage heroism and conformity; courtmartials and denials of leave are used to discourage cowardice and deviance. Sanctions control the future behavior of those who are rewarded or punished, and they help to ensure that people channel their behavior in approved directions.

Behavior is influenced by the threat of punishment and the promise of rewards. However, daily behavior is probably less influenced by these sanctions than by the values and norms that individuals have learned from the culture and internalized as parts of their personalities and consciences. Socialized individuals conform most of the time because they believe that they should, not because they fear negative sanctions (See Chapter 4). Tootle learned to stay on the tracks because of the social rewards the townspeople gave him for following the green flag; by the time he grew into a big locomotive, he probably stayed on the tracks because it seemed the only way to do things, not because he continued to fear disapproval for wandering off to enjoy the flowers.

Language

Eskimo language includes more than twenty different words for various types of snow. The Slave Indians of northern Canada have thirteen different words for ice. Snow and ice are an important part of the daily lives of these people, and their languages reflect the great attention they pay to the weather. Most Americans speak simply of snow and ice, although skiers sometimes use different terms to distinguish among types of snow on skiing surfaces.

A *language* is a set of words and rules of grammar for the use of those words. Words are symbols that stand for ideas and objects that are important in a culture. A word is merely a combination of sounds and letters that have no meaning apart from that which is assigned to it by the language. In English, the letters c-a-r stand for an automobile, but in French an automobile is symbolized by the word *voiture*, in German it is called *Wagen*, and in Spanish it is referred to as *coche*. Some languages do not even have a word for automobile.

Many languages borrow from other languages. A primitive tribe that is exposed to automobiles may add to their language the word for car that is used by the people who have introduced the car to their culture, or the tribe may make up a new word for car. The French had no word in their language for bulldozer when they first used this piece of equipment. A government commission whose aim is to preserve the French language created a new word for bulldozer: *bouteur*. Rather than use the new word, however, the French people adopted the English term "bulldozer."

Language not only helps people interpret the world, but it is also an important part of the cultural identity of a people. The national commission that attempts to create new French words rather than adopt foreign ones grew out of the traditional importance of the French language to the identity of the French people. The editor of a dictionary of English terms that have been adopted into French has said, "France is not one of the big powers. We must accept the successive imperialisms of the world, but it can be hard for us. Here we have a nostalgia for the past time, the impression of having lost our power first, then our riches and now our language" (Rey-Debove, cited in Eder, 1981: 19).

A language enables a people to store knowledge and transmit their culture to succeeding generations. In this way, language helps to define and perpetuate a culture. The French worry about the importation of English words because they fear that it will undermine the cultural unity of the French people. However, the group cohesiveness that a language creates and reinforces can have a negative consequence—conflict between groups that speak different languages. The bitter division between French-speaking Canadians and English-speaking Canadians is largely a product of language differences. Many Native Americans have had problems when they attend government schools where they are forced to speak English rather than their native language. For example, the Navaho language is verb-oriented and does not use adjectives in the way that English does. This creates problems for Navaho children who are required to learn English, which places more emphasis on adjectives and less on verbs (Kluckhohn and Leighton, 1946). Imposing a language on another group is one form of cultural domination.

LANGUAGE AND SOCIAL REALITY

To an extent, language shapes our perceptions of reality. People whose language includes twenty terms for snow or thirteen words for ice perceive aspects of the natural environment differently from the way English-speakers see the world. Languages also differ in the ways they describe and interpret time. English has many words that represent divisions of time (minutes, hours, and days) and has grammatical rules that tell when an action occurs (verb tenses). In contrast, the language of the Hopi Indians of the American Southwest has no words to symbolize divisions of time, nor does it employ verb tenses that make it clear to an English-speaker when an action has occurred. The idea that language influences the way that people see the world—whether it be the natural world, the dimension of time, or social relationships—is called the *Sapir–Whorf hypothesis,* after the two linguists who developed the idea. One succinct statement of this idea is: "Every language has an effect upon what the people who use it see, what they feel, how they think, what they can talk about" (Kluckhohn and Leighton, 1946: 197).

The hypothesis that language influences perceptions of the world has been a major reason that the feminist movement has tried to eliminate "sexist" terms from English. Feminists have argued that the use of words that distinguish between males and females emphasizes, and even serves to perpetuate, social inequality between the sexes. The English language has traditionally used male nouns, pro-

Because the structure of their language varies a great deal from English, American Indians often have difficulty when they must speak English in government schools.

nouns, and adjectives to refer to people who might be either male or female. In the statement, "Each student should now put down his pen," the adjective "his" is masculine, even though the class may well include both males and females. More recent English usage would make it more likely that this statement would now read, "Each student should now put down his or her pen" (note that the masculine adjective still usually comes first) or "All students should now put down their pens." Even though these changes might seem awkward or unnecessary to some people, they do make it clear that there are females in the class. Occupational terms have also been altered to be "sexually neutral." The statement, "The fireman put out the fire" might now read, "The fire fighter put out the fire." Sexist terminology has been eliminated from the most recent edition of *Roget's Thesaurus*, a book of synonyms and antonyms that has been published for over 130 years, which now refers to "mankind" as "humankind" and "countryman" as "country dweller." The editor of this thesaurus says that such changes make "much more explicit the existence of women. Before, they were just assumed" (Lloyd, cited in Glass, 1982: 25).

Whereas the Sapir–Whorf hypothesis would suggest that sexist language influences perceptions of relationships between males and females, another interpretation would suggest that sexist language is a product of the inequality between the sexes that is present in the social world. In other words, social conditions influence language, rather than language influencing perceptions of social reality. This hypothesis would imply that changes in sexist language could not alone affect relationships between men and women, for these relationships would have to change before language could change (Adams and Ware, 1979). Still another view is that language and social reality affect each other in reciprocal fashion. According to this view, sexist language does influence perceptions of relationships between the sexes, and inequality between men and women does affect language. This approach would suggest that if either the relationship between the sexes or sexist language were altered, the other might change.

Changes in material culture sometimes affect language. The development of modern telecommunications has introduced new terms to the English language; for example, one phone system has features called "meet-me conference," "directed call pickup," and "camp-on." Computer technology has also introduced many new words to the languages of modern industrial societies. Terms such as "input," "output," "software," and "microchips" have been added to English in recent years, and the French language has borrowed some of these terms directly from English rather than invent new words.

Contact between Cultures

One afternoon during an extended visit to Japan, the American anthropologist Edward T. Hall returned to his hotel room to find that someone else's belongings were spread about his room and his things were missing. After checking to make sure he was in the right room, Hall asked the desk clerk what had happened and was told that he had been moved. He went to his new room and found his personal belongings laid out just as they had been in the other room. A short time later this happened to him again in a different Japanese hotel; later he was actually moved from one hotel to another. An American might well think that he or she was being treated rudely and inconsiderately, but Hall's investigations showed that exactly the opposite was true. He uncovered two aspects of Japanese culture, a formal and ceremonial side that is often all that foreign visitors see, and a warm and friendly side that is reserved for those who are accepted as "members of the family." Hall discovered that, by being moved about, he was actually being treated in a friendly and intimate fashion, because that is how the Japanese treat their relatives or close friends. What at first struck Hall as insulting behavior was in fact the best possible treatment he could have received (Hall, 1981: 57–69).

CULTURE SHOCK

Visitors to other countries often experience *culture shock,* a sense of anxiety, confusion, and disorientation that occurs when one comes into contact with a different culture. Even an anthropologist who is trained to expect that other people will behave in ways very different from those to which the anthropologist is accustomed can experience culture shock. In SEL 3.2, the anthropologist Napoleon A. Chagnon reveals his startled and negative reactions when he first encountered the Yąnomamö tribe of South America. Not only was Chagnon personally disgusted by the tribe's physical appearance, but, after spending some time with them, he also was irritated by their constant demands of him: "Give me a knife, I am poor!"; "If you don't take me with you on your next trip to Widokaiya-teri I'll chop a hole in your canoe!"; "Don't point your camera at me or I'll hit you!"; and "Share your food with me!" (Chagnon, 1968, 1977: 8). The constant beg-

ging and threatening were shocking to Chagnon, who came from a culture that emphasized privacy and personal possessions. Eventually he adjusted to life among the Yąnomamö, but his initial reactions show the problems that can develop when members of different cultures come into contact with one another.

SOCIOLOGY AND EVERYDAY LIFE 3.2
Culture Shock

The Yąnomamö are a warlike tribe that lives in southern Venezuela and northern Brazil. This is an account of one anthropologist's first encounter with them, and the culture shock that he experienced.

We arrived at the village, Bisaasi-teri, about 2:00 PM and docked the boat along the muddy bank at the terminus of the path used by the Indians to fetch their drinking water. It was hot and muggy, and my clothing was soaked with perspiration. It clung uncomfortably to my body, as it did thereafter for the remainder of the work. The small, biting gnats were out in astronomical numbers, for it was the beginning of the dry season. My face and hands were swollen from the venom of their numerous stings. In just a few moments I was to meet my first Yąnomamö, my first primitive man. What would it be like? I had visions of entering the village and seeing 125 social facts running about calling each other kinship terms and sharing food, each waiting and anxious to have me collect his genealogy. I would wear them out in turn. Would they like me? This was important to me; I wanted them to be so fond of me that they would adopt me into their kinship system and way of life, because I had heard that successful anthropologists always get adopted by their people. I had learned during my seven years of anthropological training at the University of Michigan that kinship was equivalent to society in primitive tribes and that it was a moral way of life, "moral" being something "good" and "desirable." I was determined to work my way into their moral system of kinship and become a member of their society.

My heart began to pound as we approached the village and heard the buzz of activity within the circular compound. Mr. Barker [an American guide] commented that he was anxious to see if any changes had taken place while he was

away and wondered how many of them had died during his absence. I felt into my back pocket to make sure that my notebook was still there and felt personally more secure when I touched it. Otherwise, I would not have known what to do with my hands.

The entrance to the village was covered with brush and dry palm leaves. We pushed them aside to expose the low opening to the village. The excitement of meeting my first Indians was almost unbearable as I duck-waddled through the low passage into the village clearing.

I looked up and gasped when I saw a dozen burly, naked, filthy, hideous men staring at us down the shafts of their drawn arrows! Immense wads of green tobacco were stuck between their lower teeth and lips making them look even more hideous, and strands of dark-green slime dripped or hung from their noses. We arrived at the village while the men were blowing a hallucinogenic drug up their noses. One of the side effects of the drug is a runny nose. The mucus is always saturated with the green powder and the Indians usually let it run freely from their nostrils. My next discovery was that there were a dozen or so vicious, underfed dogs snapping at my legs, circling me as if I were going to be their next meal. I just stood there holding my notebook, helpless and pathetic. Then the stench of the decaying vegetation and filth struck me and I almost got sick. I was horrified. What sort of welcome was this for the person who came here to live with you and learn your way of life, to become friends with you? They put their weapons down when they recognized Barker and returned to their chanting, keeping a nervous eye on the village entrances.

Source: From *Yąnomamö: The Fierce People* by Napoleon A. Chagnon, pp. 4–5. Copyright © 1977, 1968 by Holt, Rinehart and Winston. Reprinted by permission of Holt, Rinehart and Winston, CBS College Publishing.

A phenomenon that is similar to culture shock is what the American social critic Alvin Toffler (1970) has called "future shock"—the confusion and disorientation that result from the rapid and accelerating rate of change in contemporary industrial societies. People who learn one culture when they are young often find that by the time they are adults the culture of their society has changed so dramatically that the lessons they learned as children are outdated. The elderly, and even the middle-aged, often hold values and norms that no longer fit with the latest ways of doing things.

ETHNOCENTRISM

Because they were anthropologists, Hall and Chagnon tried to understand the people they encountered. When someone makes a negative judgment of the values, norms, and behavior of a culture, elevating the standards of his or her own culture, we say that person is behaving ethnocentrically. *Ethnocentrism* is the judgment of a culture as inferior, undeveloped, barbaric, backward, or immoral in comparison to the culture of the person making the judgment. People who have not been exposed to a diversity of cultures often regard the strange and exotic as inferior or backward. Even people who have experienced other cultures sometimes make these ethnocentric judgments, as Chagnon did of the Yąnomamö.

Ethnocentrism can lead to conflict between people from different cultures. When whites came to North America, they assumed that they could make treaties with Native Americans and acquire their land. However, Indian cultures did not include a conception of land as something to be privately owned and transferred between people, and so these treaties had no meaning in the context of these cultures. Whites ethnocentrically assumed that everyone would share their ideas about the purchase and trading of land. This misunderstanding led to prolonged conflict in which hundreds of thousands of Native Americans died at the hands of whites, and smaller numbers of whites died at the hands of Indians (Brown, 1970).

Another dysfunction of ethnocentrism is that it can discourage borrowing from a different culture. People in one society might be able to meet some of their goals or adapt better to the environment if they felt that the exotic ways of a different culture were worth emulating. The !Kung San of Central Africa gather vegetation that satisfies their nutritional needs, but other societies, even when faced with starvation, have been slow to cultivate these nutritional crops. The rigidity of ethnocentric attitudes can cause a culture to stagnate or die rather than adapt to the world by borrowing from others.

The ethnocentrism of a culture is often reflected in an "origin myth," a tale about the beginnings of "the people." According to the Yąnomamö's origin myth, blood spilled from the heavens onto the part of the earth where they live, causing them to become fierce and warlike (Chagnon, 1968, 1977: 1). Like many other origin myths, the origin myth of the Navaho describes the people of that tribe as the center of the world (Kluckhohn and Leighton, 1946: 123). By implication, the existence of others is not acknowledged, or they are seen as less worthy than the people who share the same culture.

Although most of the effects of ethnocentrism are negative, it can also have certain benefits. Ethnocentrism helps to maintain the stability of a culture because the members of a society identify with the traditions of the culture and transmit them to new members, whether they are children or immigrants. Ethnocentrism promotes loyalty and conformity to the standards of the culture, and it can also encourage cooperation among people who share a culture.

Changes in the modern world have eroded ethnocentrism, although it is still widespread and harmful to relations among different peoples. The mass media, especially radio and television, have spread information about the diversity of cultures to people who were previously isolated from such knowledge. The spread of mass education and literacy has also counteracted ethnocentrism to some extent. Exposure to other cultures not only breaks down ethnocentrism, but it also helps one learn about one's own culture, because underlying assumptions about the world are challenged by alternative ways of seeing and doing things. This is one reason why the study of foreign languages and cultures is commonly thought to be essential to a well-rounded education.

CULTURAL RELATIVISM

Social scientists who study other cultures know that there is great variety to human behavior. They know that there is no one "human nature" that is reflected in culture, even though ethnocentric people often assume that their culture best represents human nature. *Cultural relativism* is the view that no culture is better than another, and that cultural diversity should be tolerated, understood, and appreciated, rather than ethnocentrically condemned. Cultures should be judged in their own terms, rather than in terms of the values and norms of the person who is observing that culture from outside. Cultural relativism stresses the need for detachment and objectivity in the analysis of other cultures. This is well-stated by Edward T. Hall (1981: 7):

A massive cultural literacy movement that is not imposed, but which springs from within is called for. We can all benefit from a deeper knowledge of what an incredible organism we really are. We can grow, swell with pride, and breathe better for having so many remarkable talents. To do so, however, we must stop ranking both people and talents and accept the fact that there are many roads to truth and no culture has a corner on the path or is better equipped than others to search for it. Furthermore, no man can tell another how to conduct that search.

One standard that is often used to judge other cultures is technological progress. Technologically advanced cultures are often seen as superior to technologically backward cultures. In fact, people who live in both types of culture often place the same value on technological progress. Cultures can indeed be ranked according to how technologically advanced they are, for technology is one aspect of culture that is cumulative and progressive. However, this does not necessarily imply that it is better to be technologically advanced. Technological progress improves the standard of living, lowers the death rate, and has other benefits, but it also causes industrial pollution and dissatisfaction with factory jobs.

Countercultures

Native American cultures include religious beliefs that show deep reverence for certain holy practices, places, and people. The religious ceremonies of these tribes also include "burlesques by clowns who parodied serious rituals, introduced obscenity into sacred places (by drinking urine, eating feces, and simulating sexual intercourse), and showed open disrespect to the gods themselves" (Wallace, 1966: 136). We also find examples of these "rituals of rebellion" in the dominant culture of the United States; on Halloween children and adolescents behave in ways that are discouraged or punished at other times, such as eating sweets, staying out late, harassing adults, demanding treats, and engaging in acts of minor vandalism.

These practices all violate widely accepted values and norms. Their presence in society suggests that the culture is not completely uniform, and that it is better to examine the variety of values and norms a culture contains than to analyze it as a unified and consistent set of values and norms. Indian clowns and American trick-or-treaters share the values and norms of the dominant culture, even though they violate those cultural expectations at certain prescribed times and places.

In some cases, the variety that exists within a single culture can take the form of a *counterculture*, "a set of norms and values of a group that sharply contradict the dominant norms and values of the society of which that group is a part" (Yinger, 1977: 833). Countercultures emerge when a group feels that it cannot achieve its desires within the existing cultural context. As a result, this group develops a new interpretation or behavior to deal with the world.

The dominant culture of most societies can usually be identified, as we shall see later in this chapter, when we investigate the dominant culture of the United States. In addition, most cultures also include countercultures that contradict dominant values and norms in certain ways. Countercultures consist of many kinds of social phenomena, such as religious sects, delinquent gangs, life styles associated with different generations, political protests and revolutions, social movements such as feminism and gay rights, and new forms of the arts (Yinger, 1977, 1982).

Countercultures sometimes reverse the values and norms of the dominant culture, and other times they emphasize a minor theme of the dominant culture and give it predominance. For instance, punk rock, which emerged in the late 1970s, often lacks the melody and instrumentation of classical music or the easy-listening music that you might hear in a supermarket or at the dentist's. In fact, punk rock reverses many of the conventions of traditional rock and roll. It has been the basis of a small but highly publicized counterculture that has tried to create an entirely new kind of music by altering the techniques of early forms. Other countercultures emphasize a minor theme in the dominant culture rather than reverse its values and norms. Two values prominent in American culture are "saving for a rainy day" and deferring gratification until the future, but there is a minor theme of going on a spending spree when a person suddenly has a lot of money. This "subterranean" theme of tolerance for extravagance is a major

Drawing by Mankoff; © 1980 The New Yorker Magazine, Inc.

value for some delinquent youths, who elevate it to a dominant position in their counterculture, so that gang members who steal a large sum of money are expected to "blow it" immediately (Matza and Sykes, 1961; Cohen, 1955; Yinger, 1977, 1982).

THE FUNCTIONALIST INTERPRETATION OF COUNTERCULTURES

A functionalist would see such countercultural practices as Indian clowning or Halloween trick-or-treating as contributing to the health of the whole society. Religious rituals of rebellion permit the participants to do the "wrong thing," and in the process help to maintain social order and traditional religious practices by allowing people to express impulses that are frustrated by the established religion (Wallace, 1966: 135). This suggests that no dominant institution such as religion can satisfy everyone's needs all the time, and that countercultural religious practices or even countercultural religions such as sects and cults can act as "safety valves" through which people can "blow off steam," instead of attacking and destroying the existing religious institution.

The theft and violence of delinquent gangs might seem to have little benefit for society at large, but a functionalist could interpret even this destructive behavior as having certain positive consequences. Much gang delinquency is a product of the social conditions in which lower-class and working-class adolescent males live. This group has a very high rate of unemployment and a relatively high rate of dropping out of school. Gang delinquency by this segment of the population may be functional for society because it diverts their attention from the political and economic system that has caused their low level of education and their high rate of unemployment. Instead of becoming political revolutionaries seeking to overthrow the existing social order, the boys turn to theft and violence against others, usually others from the working class and lower class. Their behavior is harmful to individuals and to society in certain ways, but it is less disruptive than militant political action would be. In this way, the counterculture of delinquents can be seen as functional for the social system.

THE CONFLICT INTERPRETATION OF COUNTERCULTURES

A conflict theorist would see countercultures as reflecting the contradictions of society and as expressing the "strongly ambivalent feelings" that are inevitable in a culture that is not completely integrated (Yinger, 1977: 844). Countercultures keep various values and norms alive without requiring participants in the counterculture to be fully committed to those values and norms or forcing them to withdraw their allegiance from the dominant culture.

A Marxist would begin by looking at the relationship between culture and the economic system. A counterculture would, in this view, be treated as a reflection of the conflict between the classes that play various roles in the productive process. Marx emphasized the ways in which a society's culture was influenced by its economic system, but he paid scant attention to the ways that culture can affect the economic system. For example, he did not thoroughly explore the ways by which the dominant capitalist culture could inhibit the growth of working-class consciousness and thus reduce the chance that workers would forcibly take control of the means of production.

The influence of culture on the economic system was explored by the Italian Marxist Antonio Gramsci in the 1920s and 1930s (Boggs, 1976; Miliband, 1977). Gramsci developed the concept of *cultural hegemony* (or ideological hegemony), the principle that the dominant group in any repressive system will impose its values, norms, attitudes, beliefs, and morality on all other groups in the society in order to maintain and enhance its advantageous position. Gramsci argued that the dominant class would do this by establishing control over such institutions as the school, the political system, the economic system, and the media. He was most concerned with cultural hegemony by the capitalist class in capitalist systems, and pointed to the control that capitalists exercised over culture and tradition to explain the lack of revolutionary action by the working class in such systems. He suggested

that the working class and the intellectuals who supported them needed to create an alternative set of meanings and ideas that could be used to wrest control from the capitalists and establish the cultural hegemony of the working class. One contemporary observer suggests that the best example of cultural hegemony today may be found in the Soviet Union, where the Communist party has established an "ideologically prescribed social order" and regulated daily life, the expression of feelings, and the production and distribution of goods and services (Bell, 1978: xxiii).

Cultural hegemony can be established in a variety of ways. The professionalization of sports in the United States conveys the idea that money is a natural part of athletic competition; in other societies, sports are usually played by amateurs. One critic suggests that the professionalization of American sports may lead people to think of life in general as pervaded by commercial values, with success in competition being measured by salary (Miliband, 1977: 52).

In advanced industrial societies, whether capitalist or socialist, control of the mass media, such as radio and television, is a main route to establishing cultural hegemony. In societies in which television is owned by the government, political leaders can present the population with a single point of view. When television networks are privately owned, as they are in the United States, the media are less likely to reflect a single point of view, but the media in such societies have been criticized for presenting material that perpetuates the dominance of big business (Ben-Horin, 1977; Gitlin, 1979; Kellner, 1979). Sometimes this works in subtle ways. In SEL 3.3 we can see how the popular television show, *Happy Days*, upholds the values of American culture by the way in which the hero Fonzie chooses to resolve his "dilemma."

SOCIOLOGY AND EVERYDAY LIFE 3.3
Fonzie and the American Way of Life

Television situation comedies center on a conflict or problem that is resolved neatly within a preconceived time period. This conflict/resolution model suggests that all problems can be solved within the existing society. For example, a 1976 episode of *Happy Days* saw the teen hero Fonzie out with an attractive older woman. He learns she is married, and a set of jokes punctuate his moral dilemma. Finally, he sits down with the woman, tells her he hears she's married, and when she says, "Yes, but it's an open marriage," he responds: "No dice. I've got my rules I live by. My values. And they don't include taking what's not mine. You're married. You're someone else's." He gets up, shakes her away, and is immediately surrounded by a flock of attractive (unmarried) girls—a typical comical resolution of an everyday moral conflict that reinforces conventional morality. In a 1977 episode of *Happy Days*, dealing with the high school graduation of the series' main characters, Fonzie moralizes, "It's not cool to drop out of school." In a 1978 episode, when his friend Richie is seriously injured in a motorcycle wreck, the Fonz "reveals his compassion in an emotional prayer for his friend" (*TV Guide* description), praying with eyes to heaven, "Hey Sir. He's my best friend. . . . Listen, you help him out and I'll owe you one." Here ideologies of religion and exchange reinforce each other; television attempts to be not the "opiate of the people" but their active instructor and educator.

Interestingly, the working-class character Fonzie, here used as the spokesman for middle-class morality, represents a domestica-

tion of the James Dean/Marlon Brando 1950s rebel. Whereas Dean in movies like *Rebel without a Cause* was a hopeless misfit who often exploded with rage against the stifling conformity and insensitivity of those around him, Fonzie quits his gang (the Falcons) and comes to live in the garage apartment of the middle-class Cunninghams. Fonzie's defense of the dominant morality creates a melting-pot effect, where all good people seem to share similar values and aspirations. Hence, *Happy Days* provides a replay of *Ozzie and Harriet* and earlier TV family morality plays, with Richie Cunningham starring as David Nelson, the all-American good boy, and Fonzie as the irrepressible Ricky Nelson, whose "hipness" made him an effective salesman for the middle-class way of life.

Source: Douglas Kellner, "TV, Ideology, and Emancipatory Popular Culture," *Socialist Review* 9 (May–June 1979): 19–20. Used by permission.

Contemporary Marxist sociologists acknowledge that American television does present the contradictions that exist within American culture rather than presenting a unified cultural perspective (Kellner, 1979). Programs have dealt with the problems of a poor black family (*Good Times*), a white working-class bigot (*All in the Family*), middle-class adolescents in the 1960s (*Happy Days*), and a single middle-class working woman (*The Mary Tyler Moore Show*). Even such apparently controversial material as *Roots* was commercially successful. Television thus reflects the cultural variety of American society; it does not overtly try to convert viewers to the dominant culture (except maybe through commercials), but support of the dominant culture by all groups is often conveyed by the ways that characters choose to solve their problems (see SEL 3.3). A short series called *Loose Change* dealt with the lives in the 1970s of three women who attended the University of California at Berkeley in the 1960s, a period of student unrest focused on the Vietnam War. One critic of this series felt that it "reduced the explosive politics of the 1960s to melodrama, emphasizing the pain and punishment inflicted for not conforming and the rewards for adjusting to the existing order. It presented the 1960s as a disorderly, chaotic period to be eschewed for the order and stability of the present" (Kellner, 1979: 20). The message conveyed by this series—that conformity to dominant standards

brings happiness—is much the same as the message of *Tootle*; both serve to maintain the dominant culture.

Explaining Cultural Similarity, Variety, and Change

Eskimo males traditionally offered their wives to guests who spent the night with them; American men are more likely to offer their visitors a cocktail. The Yanomamö eat monkeys, rodents, alligators, and caterpillars; the French prefer snails, veal, potatoes, beans, wine, and pastries. Gypsies wear many layers of clothing; the Tasaday wear a leaf or two. The amount of cultural diversity in the world is staggering, and yet all cultures contain certain common characteristics.

The general traits shared by all cultures are called *cultural universals*. Every culture has customs of hospitality, methods of food preparation, and styles of body adornment, although the forms that these take vary from culture to culture. Other cultural universals include language, art, mythology, religion, family, education, government, property, housing, dancing, sports, and incest taboos (Wissler, 1923; Murdock, 1965).

Often the form that cultural universals take within a particular culture changes over time. In the United States, bathing suits covered much more

Often the form that cultural universals take within a particular culture changes over time. In the United States, standards of dress for women have changed greatly since the turn of the century.

of the body in the nineteenth century than they do today. In the 1970s, a designer tried to introduce the topless bathing suit for women, but this style was not widely adopted. Standards of modesty had changed over the years, but not to the point that many American women were willing to reveal their breasts in public. Today, as in the past, the culture of the United States includes standards of dress, but those standards have changed over time: Men no longer wear detachable collars on their shirts, and women no longer wear multiple petticoats.

In their analysis of cultures, sociologists and anthropologists try to answer three questions:

1. Why do all cultures share certain cultural universals?
2. Why is there so much cultural diversity?
3. Why do cultures change over time?

They have offered a variety of answers to these questions.

BIOLOGY AND CULTURE

Sociobiologists claim that all people have certain biological needs, such as hunger and sex, and that people develop cultural practices to meet these needs. Sociobiologists point to cultural universals as evidence that a common biological makeup has led to similarities among the cultures of the world (E. Wilson, 1975, 1978; Gregory, Silvers, and Sutch, 1978). Cultural universals such as the incest taboo are claimed to have a genetic basis, and the institution of the family is thought to exist in all cultures because it meets biological needs for intimacy and sex. However, the family is organized differently in various cultures, and the sociobiological perspective does not explain this cultural diversity. There are great differences among the cultures of the world but little variation in human biology (Harris, 1979).

Sociobiologists explain cultural change with the claim that genetic traits evolve over time to meet people's needs. Genetic change alters behavior so that people can adapt better to the world in which they live. The difficulty with this explanation is that cultural change often occurs very quickly, long before genes can change. Since the late 1940s, when it was introduced, television has changed the leisure habits of Americans, but there is no reason to think that this cultural change corresponds at all to changes in the genetic makeup of Americans. Groups sometimes respond to a crisis by developing new practices. A plane carrying a Uruguayan rugby team crashed in the Andes in 1972. The survivors kept alive by eating human flesh, even though their culture condemned cannibalism (Read, 1974). These passengers did not change genetically, but they did develop a new form of behavior in order to survive.

CULTURE AND THE ECOSYSTEM

Another way to explain cultural similarity, diversity, and change is in terms of the *ecosystem*—the complex and self-sustaining system of all living and nonliving things in a particular area. The ecological approach focuses on the total environment in which people live, including the geography, climate, and productivity of the land.

The harsh climate in which Eskimos live and the shortage of food in that environment led them to develop the practices of voluntary suicide by the elderly and murder of female infants. A culture that developed in a different environment might have a surplus of food to feed the nonproductive elderly and the young.

Another cultural practice that is rooted in the ecosystem is the Hindus' refusal to slaughter cows. India is a nation where hunger is widespread, and the millions of cows in the country could be a good source of food. However, the density of India's population and the poor quality of its land mean that people must keep their cows to bear the oxen that plow their small and unproductive farms and to provide the manure with which to fertilize the land. Without cows, many Indians would starve to death, and so the Hindu practice of treating cows as sacred makes sense in the context of the environment in which the Indian people live (Harris, 1974, 1977).

The ecological explanation correctly claims that environment sets broad limits on the kind of culture that a people can develop. Those who live in the tropics do not wear parkas or play ice hockey, and residents of arctic regions do not wear bikinis or become long-distance swimmers. The limits that the ecosystem imposes on cultural development are probably most important for cultures that lack an advanced technology, because they have less capacity to control the environment for their own purposes. An advanced technology broadens the range of possible cultural practices. Eskimos could become expert long-distance swimmers if they had the technology and resources to build indoor swimming pools, and many Americans do swim indoors during the coldest days of winter.

The ecological argument does not explain cultural diversity very well, as people who live in similar environments often have very different cultures. In the American Southwest, there are great cultural differences among "Anglos" (white Americans), Mexican-Americans, and Native Americans. Similarly, in the large cities of the Northeast, there are great cultural differences among the different racial and ethnic groups that live in the same environment. All these groups have experienced cultural change as they have borrowed the practices of other groups. This cultural change is a product of learning from others, not the result of changes in the environment in which people live.

INTERNAL SOURCES OF CULTURAL CHANGE

We have seen that cultures often contain a variety of values and norms. Countercultures emphasize values and norms that are different from those of the dominant culture, and sometimes, when a counterculture grows strong and takes hold, cultural change is the result. The student antiwar movement of the 1960s affected American culture in several ways. It spread opposition to the Vietnam War to adults who shared the dominant culture in other ways. It would be overstating the impact of the antiwar movement to say that it made Americans more politically liberal, but even in the 1980s the arguments of the antiwar movement were raised when the Reagan administration considered American intervention in El Salvador. Another effect of the student antiwar movement on American culture was a change in grooming styles, as long hair, beards, and mustaches became more popular than they had been in the 1950s.

According to conflict theorists, the contradictions within a culture and the shifts in the relative power of different groups are the sources of cultural change. Differences in emphasis on values and norms can also explain why one culture differs from another. Both the Japanese culture and the American culture value individual success and loyalty, but Japanese culture places more emphasis on loyalty, and American culture stresses personal accomplishments to a greater degree.

CULTURAL BORROWING

One possible explanation of cultural universals is that the practices of one culture may spread to another culture through diffusion and borrowing. Often cultural borrowing occurred so long ago that the members of a society consider their culture to be entirely of their own invention.

The introduction of an element from one culture into another culture can upset the organization of a society. The Yir Yoront of Australia traditionally used stone axes and developed patterns of authority and religious rituals that were based on this simple tool. Leaders controlled the stone axe and shared it only with those thought worthy of using it. When steel axes were introduced by outsiders, social relationships among the Yir Yoront changed dramatically. The stone axe was no longer a source of authority and prestige, and its religious significance declined (Sharp, 1952). The culture of the Yir Yoront was a cohesive whole that was disrupted when new technology was introduced from the outside.

The rituals of rebellion of several American Indian tribes have changed greatly as a result of the influence of the dominant culture of the United States. One dramatic change was produced by the moon landing in 1969. The Zuñi saw this as a violation of the sacred "source of all light and life" and developed new rituals to deal with this threat. They created new burlesque skits in which "clowns dressed as satellites, rockets, and astronauts ran madly around the village, threw one another into the air, and fell off roofs" (Tedlock, 1979: 72). The purpose of these skits was to shock others into laughter or disapproval and to help relieve the tension that the moon landing had produced. The discovery of the Pioneer 10 plaque could produce a similar disruptive effect on the culture of some extraterrestrial civilization.

Cultural borrowing can explain why different cultures have some common characteristics and why cultures such as the Yir Yoront and the Zuñi undergo drastic changes in short periods of time. It is possible that by adapting borrowed culture to meet the needs of their people, the cultures of the world became so diverse. The Zuñi did not borrow the technology of space exploration, but they did incorporate the moon landing into their traditional forms of clowning and religious ritual. The same aspect of a culture can be given very different meanings by people who already hold different values and norms.

The American Value System

In 1970, two books that presented different views of the value system of the United States were published. One was the third edition of *American Society*, a popular text by Robin M. Williams, Jr. The other was the first edition of Philip Slater's *The Pursuit of Loneliness: American Culture at the Breaking Point*, which he revised in 1976. Williams emphasizes the existence of a dominant system of American values, and Slater stresses the conflict between an "old culture" and a "new culture" that emerged in the 1960s.

THE DOMINANT AMERICAN VALUE SYSTEM

In his book Williams outlines the dominant values of American culture, although he also discusses a variety of countercultural themes within that culture. He suggests that dominant values can be recognized by how extensively they are held in the population, how long they have endured, the intensity with which they are held, and the prestige of those who hold them (Williams, 1970: 448).

According to Williams, Americans value individualism and self-reliance. When they succeed, they take credit as individuals; when they fail, they usually blame themselves or "bad luck" rather than the society of which they are a part. Americans value personal accomplishment and success, especially at their jobs. Work is valued both as an end in itself and as a means to monetary rewards and social recognition. Americans also value efficiency and practicality, and often disparage abstract and unworkable ideas. This emphasis on pragmatism is closely related to the value placed on science and rationality as ways to control nature to meet people's needs. Americans have faith that the future will be better than the present, and they often believe that science and technology will be the means to that brighter future.

The dominant American value system includes an emphasis on individual freedom from government interference, a value that has persisted since immigrants settled in the United States after escaping the political and religious oppression of their homelands. This value was enthusiastically embraced by Ronald Reagan in the 1980 presidential campaign. The value of freedom from government control often goes hand in hand with a strong emphasis on patriotism and national loyalty. Another important value is equality for all people; however, the implementation of this goal—as when legal measures are taken to ensure equality—sometimes conflicts with the value of freedom from government interference.

Williams outlines several other values, but these are some of the ones that are central to his portrait of the dominant American value system. The relationship among these values and the way they are manifested in actual behavior are complex and difficult to understand. Individualism is sometimes incompatible with patriotism and dedication to the nation. Equality often conflicts with freedom from government interference. These values are all part of an identifiable dominant culture, even though there are contradictions within that culture. Shifts sometimes occur in the emphasis given to different values. It was this process of cultural change in American society that Slater sought to understand in *The Pursuit of Loneliness.*

AMERICAN CULTURE AT THE BREAKING POINT

Slater's 1970 critique of American culture tried to make sense of the turmoil of the 1960s, including student protests over the Vietnam War, urban riots in black ghettos, the hippie movement, widespread drug use, and crime in the streets. Although he and Williams were analyzing American culture at the same time, Slater focused more on conflict over values and less on the dominance of one set of values.

Slater suggests that there were two cultures in American society in the 1960s, an "old culture" that emphasized scarcity and the need to compete in order to gain personal satisfaction, and a "new culture" that challenged this old culture by claiming that scarcity and the need to compete were artificial concepts. Slater describes the values of these two cultures as follows:

There are an almost infinite number of polarities by means of which one can differentiate between the two cultures. The old culture, when forced to choose, tends to give preference to property rights over personal rights, technological requirements over human needs, competition over cooperation, violence over sexuality, concentration over distribution, the producer over the consumer, means over ends, secrecy over openness, social forms over personal expression, striving over gratification, Oedipal love over communal love, and so on. The new counterculture tends to reverse all of these priorities (Slater, 1970: 100).

Slater claimed that the various countercultures that comprised the new culture could better satisfy Americans' needs for a sense of community, engagement with important social issues, and dependence and cooperation. He stopped short of predicting that the new culture would become the dominant culture of the future, but he did state that any successful society needs countercultures in order to generate new cultural patterns that can respond to a changing world.

THE AMERICAN VALUE SYSTEM TODAY

Whose view of the American value system best describes American society in the 1980s? The answer depends in part on whether you emphasize the values that Americans share with each other or the differences that exist among Americans. Certainly the themes that Williams emphasized more than a decade ago are still important dimensions of American culture. A description of today's American value system might have a somewhat different emphasis than Williams' picture, but it would be possible to describe today's value system using the themes that Williams outlined.

Conflict in American culture has attenuated, or at least become less violent, since the 1960s, and it seems clear that Slater's new culture has not become the dominant American value system. In fact, today there is considerable conflict between the old culture and the liberal center that Slater thought would fade away. The efforts of the Moral Majority to impose their values and norms by banning books from libraries, stamping out obscenity in every imaginable form, and forcing changes in school curricula to eliminate values they consider anti-family, anti-God, and anti-American have been opposed by liberal groups that seek to protect freedom of speech and cultural diversity. The new culture is not dominant on college campuses today. Instead, most students value hard work, individual success, and material comfort, all themes that Williams emphasized in his analysis of American culture in 1970.

Summary

Culture is a shared set of meanings or a "design for living" that includes knowledge, artifacts, technology, the arts, religion, values, and norms. Societies consist of people who interact with each other; sometimes the culture of a society outlasts the society itself. Culture is transmitted from generation to generation through socialization, so that new generations do not have to create technology anew or develop meanings of the world.

One aspect of culture is material culture, which includes artifacts and technology. Material culture is given meaning through expressive culture, the interpretations that people who share a culture place on artifacts and technology. For instance, clothing has a variety of meanings other than to protect people from the weather; it can be used to attract erotic attention, demonstrate social standing, or gain magical power.

Fairy tales and myths reveal the values of a culture. These values are abstract and emotion-laden ideals about what is desirable, good, or correct. Some values are given more importance than others in the value hierarchy of a culture. Values are only general guides to behavior, and many types of behavior are compatible with at least one value of a culture.

Norms are more specific rules or expectations about what kind of behavior is appropriate for a particular person in a certain social situation. Many norms are somewhat flexible, although laws have less flexibility than informal norms. A sanction is a reaction to the violation of a norm; it may range from a stare of disapproval to capital punishment. Sanctions help to maintain conformity to norms by rewarding behavior that fits with cultural values and by punishing behavior that clashes with those values.

Language is a set of symbols (words) and rules of grammar for arranging those symbols in a way that makes sense to people. Language enables people to interpret the meaning of the world; it also maintains a people's identity. Language enables people to transmit their culture to the next generation or to immigrants who become part of their society. Language influences the way that people perceive reality; for example, sexist language can affect perceptions of the social relationships between men and women. However, language is also a product of social reality, so that sexist language may reflect inequality between the sexes rather than cause it.

Culture shock sometimes occurs when someone from one culture comes into contact with a different culture. Anthropologists often reflect on their initial reactions to an exotic culture by trying to interpret the meaning of that culture, but other people may react to a different culture ethnocentrically and make negative judgments. Ethnocentrism can produce conflict between people from different cultures; it can also discourage borrowing from different cultures that might help a people adapt to their environment or fulfill their needs. Ethnocentrism can strengthen the stability of a culture or promote loyalty to the culture, but most of its effects are harmful to relations among people. Cultural relativism is a position that counteracts ethnocentrism by arguing that every culture should be interpreted in its own terms, rather than in terms of the culture of an outside observer.

Countercultures are sets of norms and values that sharply contradict the dominant culture.

Countercultures can be functional in allowing people to "blow off steam" rather than destroy the dominant culture. The presence of countercultures suggests that there are contradictions within the society, such as class differences. Conflict theorists emphasize the concept of cultural hegemony, the idea that dominant groups impose their own norms and values on all groups in the society in order to maintain their advantageous position. Often this domination is made possible by control of the mass media.

Three important issues in the analysis of culture are the explanation of cultural universals, cultural diversity, and cultural change. Sociobiologists seek to explain these in terms of biological inheritance. They consider cultural universals as evidence that all people have common biological needs, but they are unable to explain cultural diversity or cultural change in terms of human biology. The ecological approach tries to explain cultural universals, diversity, and change in terms of the environment in which people live. Some very broad cultural differences may be attributable to the ecosystem, but environment cannot explain very well why groups that live in similar environments often have drastically different cultures or why culture often changes much faster than environment. Another explanation of the sources of culture is in terms of contradictions that exist within a culture. Changing emphasis on certain values and norms can explain cultural change, and it can also account in part for cultural diversity. Another source of cultural universals is borrowing from other cultures; differences in the ways that borrowed aspects of a culture are adapted to the needs of a people may explain cultural diversity.

The values of American culture have been analyzed in a variety of ways. In 1970, two influential explanations were published. Robin Williams, Jr., explored the dominant value system of the United States in terms of the themes of individualism, accomplishment and success, efficiency and practicality, progress, freedom from government interference, and equality. In contrast to this view of the dominant value system, Philip Slater emphasized a conflict between an "old culture" and a "new culture" and suggested that the new culture could better fulfill needs that the old culture could not meet. Williams' description is probably a more accurate picture of American culture today than is Slater's.

Important Terms

ARTIFACT **(52)**	EXPRESSIVE CULTURE **(52)**
COUNTERCULTURE **(62)**	LANGUAGE **(57)**
CULTURAL HEGEMONY **(64)**	MATERIAL CULTURE **(52)**
CULTURAL RELATIVISM **(61)**	NORM **(56)**
CULTURAL UNIVERSAL **(65)**	SANCTION **(56)**
CULTURE **(49)**	SAPIR—WHORF HYPOTHESIS **(58)**
CULTURE SHOCK **(59)**	SOCIOBIOLOGY **(51)**
ECOSYSTEM **(66)**	TECHNOLOGY **(52)**
ETHNOCENTRISM **(61)**	VALUE **(55)**

Suggested Readings

W. Arens and Susan P. Montague, eds. *The American Dimension: Cultural Myths and Social Realities.* Port Washington, N.Y.: Alfred Publishing Co., 1976. A fascinating collection of essays on American culture that focuses on the content of the mass media and observations of social interaction.

Ruth Benedict. *Patterns of Culture,* with a new introduction by Margaret Mead. Boston: Houghton Mifflin, 1934, 1959. A classic study of different cultures from a comparative perspective.

Edward T. Hall. *Beyond Culture.* Garden City, N.Y.: Doubleday, 1981. A well-written introduction to the study of expressive culture that presents some intriguing examples.

Alison Lurie. *The Language of Clothes.* New York: Random House, 1981. A lavishly illustrated and entertaining account of the meaning conveyed by clothing.

Philip Slater. *The Pursuit of Loneliness: American Culture at the Breaking Point,* rev. ed. Boston: Beacon Press, 1976. A new edition of the author's 1970 critique of the culture of the United States and the conflicts intrinsic to it. This version includes a new chapter on economic issues, and eliminates passages on campus conflict, conflict between the generations, the "counterculture," and political conflict.

Robin M. Williams, Jr. *American Society: A Sociological Interpretation,* 3rd ed. New York: Alfred A. Knopf, 1970. A detailed account of the themes that define the dominant culture of the United States.

J. Milton Yinger. *Countercultures: The Promise and the Peril of a World Turned Upside Down.* New York: Free Press, 1982. A comprehensive examination of social groups and movements that hold values and norms contradicting the dominant culture.

SOCIALIZATION

Genie had . . . personal habits that were not socially acceptable. She blew her nose onto anything or nothing, often making a mess of her clothing. At times, when excited or agitated, she would urinate in inappropriate places—leaving her companion to deal with the results. But it was her lack of socialization that was most difficult to deal with, especially in public. Genie had a special fondness for certain things— anything made of plastic, certain foods, certain articles of clothing or accessories. If anyone she encountered in the street or in a store or other public place had something she liked, she was uncontrollably drawn to him or her, and without obeying any rules of psychological distance or social mores, she would go right up to the person and put her hands on the desired item. It was bad enough when she went up to someone else's shopping cart to reach in to take something out; but when the object of attention was an article of clothing, and Genie would simply attach herself to the person wearing that clothing and refuse to let go, the situations were extremely trying (Curtiss, 1977: 20).

Genie's odd behavior is a result of her unusual upbringing. From about the age of two until she was thirteen and a half, she was kept in a locked room by her father, who communicated with her only by growling or barking like a dog. During the day, she was strapped to a child's potty seat, and at night she was tied into a straitjacket contraption and placed in a cagelike enclosure. There was little noise in her house, and she developed no ability to make vocal sounds. When Genie did make noises, her father beat her. As a result, she developed no language skills; even after she was given special training in language, she was unable to learn to speak like a normal child.

As sad and unusual as Genie's case is, she is by no means the only child who was raised in isolation. The sociologist Kingsley Davis (1949) documented two similar cases during the 1940s. One was of a girl named Anna, who, when she was found at the age of six, could not walk or talk; she was indifferent, expressionless, unpredictable, and did not seem fully human. Anna was an illegitimate child who had been hidden in an upstairs room by her grandfather since she had been a baby. She was sheltered and fed just enough to keep her alive, and she had little contact with other people. Anna was put in a special school, but by the time she died about five years later her behavior was only that of a normal two- or three-year-old. She did try to converse in short phrases, learned to keep herself and her clothes clean, and helped other children. Anna's mental capacity may well have been limited, and so it is difficult to know how far she might have progressed, but in spite of her probable limitations she developed a number of skills that she had not had before being taken from isolation.

Another similar case is that of Isabelle, the illegitimate child of a deaf-mute mother. Isabelle was kept in a darkened room and communicated with her mother only by gestures, and, when she was found at the age of six and a half, she could not speak. However, with special treatment, within two years after being discovered she reached a relatively normal stage of development, and was able to attend school with other children her age. Isabelle's contact with her mother and the special training she was given in language—a tool necessary to understanding the meaning given to the world by people who share a culture—probably account for the fact that she progressed faster and farther than Anna. Differences in their inherited mental capacities might also have played a part.

Socialization and Social Isolation

Genie, Anna, and Isabelle were all inadequately socialized, because they grew up isolated from people who would teach them the values and norms of the culture. *Socialization* is the process by which people learn the culture of a society and become full participants in that society. Socialization makes social behavior possible, and it establishes the basis of social order. Socialization is usually the result of interaction with parents, teachers, and friends; in industrial societies, the mass media—especially television—also act as agents of socialization.

The socialization process takes place over the entire lifetime of an individual, but social scientists have paid much less attention to socialization in adulthood than to childhood socialization. At various points in their lives people learn to perform certain "roles," or to behave in ways that are considered "right" for the positions they hold in society (see Chapter 7). Socialization also includes the acquisition of *cognitive skills*—intellectual abilities such as reasoning, thinking, remembering, and using language. Another aspect of socialization is *affective development*, the learning of emotions and feelings. You might think that feelings such as love are a basic part of human nature, but the indifference that Anna showed toward others indicates that isolation from human contact can prevent a person from developing such "natural" feelings.

Defective socialization is a result of the absence of contact with other people. One experiment that demonstrated this was Harry Harlow's work (1962) with rhesus monkeys. We must be careful when generalizing about humans from research with monkeys, but the experimental setting that Harlow used enabled him to manipulate certain conditions in the laboratory that could not have been controlled in a study of human infants. Harlow raised monkeys in isolation from other monkeys. He found that monkeys actually preferred a wire "mother" covered with cloth to a wire "mother" that was not covered with cloth but that fed them continually. Monkeys preferred the warmth of bodily contact with a cloth surrogate mother to the regular feeding provided by the surrogate mother that was not covered with cloth. These results suggest that there may be an inherited need for social contact among monkeys. Many observers believe that humans also have an inborn need for contact and affiliation with other people.

Harlow discovered that the rhesus monkeys who were raised in isolation did not exhibit "typical" monkey behavior when in the presence of other monkeys. They did not get along peaceably with others. They were not sexually attracted to other monkeys and did not know how to mate, even though it is often thought that this behavior comes

naturally. The inability of the monkeys raised in isolation to get along with other monkeys suggests that their behavior is, to a large extent, learned from other monkeys through interaction, rather than determined by instinct.

Harlow's research showed that the damage that isolation did to the social development of monkeys could not be easily remedied by reestablishing social contact. Some of the damage to Genie, Anna, and Isabelle was reversed, though to varying degrees for each of them. Of the three, Isabelle made the most progress; she had had the most extensive contact with another person and had learned how to communicate with others.

Interaction with others is crucial to the socialization of a child. Those who do not have contact with caring people are limited in their emotional, physical, and social development. Children learn by modeling their behavior after the people with whom they interact, and clearly their opportunity to copy the behavior of others is reduced with lack of contact. Children can also learn behavior that violates cultural norms and values. For example, many parents who abuse their children were abused by their parents when they were young. However, most of the social contacts that children have with others teach them to behave in culturally approved ways. Even parents who are criminals rarely teach their children to commit crime; they want their children to grow up to be law-abiding citizens.

THE NATURE–NURTURE DEBATE

For years, scholars have debated the source of human behavior. Some have argued that "nature," or inherited traits, determines or strongly influences behavior (E. Wilson, 1975, 1978). Others have claimed that "nurture," or the attention given to the young by others, has more impact on behavior than heredity. This debate has never been resolved, and it probably never will be.

A sensible approach is to pay attention to both inherited traits and learned behavior in seeking a full explanation of human behavior. People are biological organisms capable of learning many types of behavior. However, because of limitations imposed by inheritance, they cannot learn some kinds of behavior; for example, people cannot learn to fly without mechanical assistance because they simply lack the biological apparatus to fly. Of course, people do have the innate capacity to develop a technology that enables them to fly and to

Interaction with others is crucial to the socialization of a child. Children may be severely limited in their emotional, social, and sometimes physical development unless they develop strong social ties with one another and with caring adults.

create a training course to teach pilots how to operate aircraft. Although all people probably have the potential to develop a culture with this technology, most of the cultures of the world have never used their potential to create the technology necessary to fly.

Biology establishes broad limits to behavior, and within those limits many types of behavior are possible. As the cases of Genie, Anna, and Isabelle suggest, although the capacity to learn from others seems to be innate, social interaction is necessary before this capacity can be used to develop behavior that fits with cultural norms and values.

Biological inheritance sets the limits within which people develop, but these limits tend to be broad, and many people do not fully use the potential with which they were born. Probably many people are born with the capacity to become professional athletes, but few actually develop those skills. Some who are born with that potential become lawyers or physicians because they were taught by their parents and teachers to pursue academic work rather than sports. Others, who receive less encouragement to study hard, may spend more time playing sports when young and thereby de-

velop their skills to become athletes. The social environment influences the way that people actually use their biological potential. Of course, even a favorable social environment will not make a professional athlete out of someone who lacks the physical coordination or muscle to succeed in sports.

THE ROLE OF PEOPLE IN THEIR OWN SOCIALIZATION

Sometimes, analyses of socialization overemphasize the extent to which culture and society control innate biological drives (Freud, 1930, 1962; Wrong, 1961). Biological drives such as hunger and sex are channeled through socialization, but people can resist socialization and act in self-serving ways that do not meet the expectations of others. In other words, people often take an active role in their own socialization and consciously choose to behave in particular ways, rather than simply being passive recipients of lessons taught them by others.

As people get older, they have more input into their socialization. Adolescents have more to say about how they will behave and what values they will adopt than infants do. Adults often choose to undergo socialization experiences such as psychotherapy and job training because of their own needs and desires. Socialization is a learning process, but it also involves interaction between those who are learning the ways of the culture and the agents of socialization, such as parents, teachers, and friends.

Agents of Socialization

The people, groups, and organizations that transmit culture are referred to as *agents of socialization*. These agents transmit culture by teaching people values and norms and otherwise influencing their behavior to make them full members of society. In preliterate societies, socialization is carried out primarily by the family and, to a lesser extent, by the *peer group*, people who are of the same age and roughly equal in authority. The agents of socialization that are most important in industrial societies like the United States are the family, the school, the peer group, and the mass media. Other important agents of socialization in such technologically advanced societies are work organizations, the military, the community, voluntary associations (such as the Boy Scouts), and organized religion. The effect of these different agents is often reinforcing, in that they tend to socialize people in the same values and norms, though sometimes they conflict, by teaching incompatible values and norms. For instance, schools tend to stress individualism, whereas the military and work organizations emphasize loyalty to the group over personal success.

THE FAMILY

In most societies, children are socialized in their first few years of life by the family into which they are born. Socialization is the result of intimate interaction with parents, brothers and sisters, and other relatives. Some of this socialization takes place through the direct teaching of lessons, such as "Hang up your clothes" or "Say thank you," but socialization also takes place as children imitate the actions of the adults around them. The organization of the family and the relationship of children to their families vary from society to society, but in industrial societies most of the socialization in early childhood is done by a child's biological parents. Exceptions to this pattern include children who are institutionalized, adopted, or illegitimate. Some

societies have tried to replace the natural parents with assigned caretakers—one example is the Israeli *kibbutz*—or even with the peer group (See SEL 4.1).

In many societies, children are socialized by their families according to a method that is passed from one generation to the next with little thought; children are raised in much the same way that their parents were raised. In fact, one of the things that is learned in the socialization process is how to raise children, and children apply this lesson when they become adults and raise offspring of their own. In some societies, including the United States, parents carefully examine and evaluate child-rearing practices. They are conscious of how they might affect their children, and they strive to socialize their sons and daughters to produce the kind of children they want.

The socialization of children is influenced by the parents' motives for having children; by the relative importance that they attach to their own fulfillment and to the needs of their children; and by the size and the structure of the family. In small families, each child receives considerable parental attention. There is opportunity in a small family for parents to communicate their expectations more effectively than would be possible in a large family. Children from smaller families perform better in school, score higher on intelligence tests, and are less likely to be delinquent, although some of these differences may be due to the fact that middle-class families tend to be smaller, on the average, than working-class families; in other words, economic advantage rather than family size may be responsible for these differences (Douglas, 1964; Clausen, 1966; Hirschi, 1969). There is also evidence than children who are born first in a family are more successful later in life than children born later in the same family. First-born children receive more attention as infants, and because they have more opportunity to talk with their parents when young, they can thus learn their parents' expectations about school performance and everyday behavior (Douglas, 1964; Clausen, 1966).

In the United States in recent years more mothers have taken jobs outside the home. As a consequence, increased numbers of children have spent their early years in day-care centers and nursery schools. There is disagreement about how this has affected their socialization. Some claim that no person or group can replace the biological parents in raising the young. Some critics do concede that a perfectly designed day-care center *might* almost equal the parents as an agent of socialization, but they claim that few if any centers approach this ideal (Fraiberg, 1978). Some evidence indicates that day-care centers can replace parents for a good part of the day and may even socialize children more effectively in cultural goals than can their parents (Bronfenbrenner, 1970). Supporters of day-care centers also point out that a mother who wants to work but cannot find child care may communicate her frustration and do a less effective job of bringing up her children.

Socalization in the United States and the Soviet Union

Not everyone wholeheartedly approves of the American way of child-rearing. One critic charges that, in American families, children spend relatively little time with their parents, are segregated from other adults, and develop poor images of themselves because of parental neglect (Bronfenbrenner, 1970). In the Soviet Union, the style of rearing children is quite different, as we see in SEL 4.1. Russian children spend a lot of time in close contact with adult supervisors and peers in day-care centers. These peer groups adopt the norms and values of adults and reinforce those expectations in play activities. As a result of adult supervision and peer-group pressure, the collectivist values of sharing and cooperation are transmitted to Russian children at an early age. The American system of socialization is, however, more compatible with the culture's emphasis on individualism.

SOCIOLOGY AND EVERYDAY LIFE 4.1
Maternal Care in the Soviet Union and the United States

From his research and observations, Urie Bronfenbrenner has found three major differences in maternal care in the Soviet Union and the United States.

PHYSICAL CONTACT

Russian babies receive substantially more physical handling than their American counterparts. To begin with, breast feeding is highly recommended and virtually universal. And even when not being fed, Russian babies are still held much of the time. The nature of this contact is both highly affectionate and restricting. On the one hand, in comparison with American babies, the Russian child receives considerably more hugging, kissing, and cuddling. On the other hand, the infant is held more tightly and given little opportunity for freedom of movement or initiative. . . .

SOLICITOUSNESS

The mobility and initiative of the Soviet child are further limited by a concerted effort to protect him from discomfort, illness, and injury. There is much concern about keeping him warm. Drafts are regarded as especially dangerous. Once the child begins to crawl or walk, there is worry lest he hurt himself or wander into dangerous territory. For example, children in the park are expected to keep in the immediate vicinity of the accompanying adult, and

when our youngsters—aged nine and four—would run about the paths, even within our view, kindly citizens of all ages would bring them back by the hand, often with a reproachful word about our lack of proper concern for our children's welfare.

DIFFUSION OF MATERNAL RESPONSIBILITY

The foregoing example highlights another distinctive feature of Russian upbringing, the readiness of other persons besides the child's own mother to step into a maternal role. This is true not only for relatives, but even for complete strangers. For example, it is not uncommon, when sitting in a crowded public conveyance, to have a child placed on your lap by a parent or guardian. Strangers strike up acquaintances with young children as a matter of course, and are immediately identified by the accompanying adult or by the child himself as "dyadya" (uncle) or "tyotya" (auntie).

Nor is the nurturant role limited to adults. Older children of both sexes show a lively interest in the very young and are competent and comfortable in dealing with them to a degree almost shocking to a Western observer. I recall an incident which occurred on a Moscow street. Our youngest son—then four—was walking briskly a pace or two ahead of us when from the opposite direction there came a company of teenage boys. The first one no sooner spied Stevie than he opened his arms wide and, calling "*Ai malysh!*" (Hey, little one!), scooped him up, hugged him, kissed him resoundingly, and passed him on to the rest of the company, who did likewise, and then began a merry children's dance, as they caressed him with words and gestures. Similar behavior on the part of any American adolescent male would surely prompt his parents to consult a psychiatrist.

Given this diffusion of nurturant behavior toward children, it is hardly surprising that So-viet youngsters exhibit less anxiety than their American age-mates when their mother leaves them in the care of another person or in a nursery. Such delegation of the care of the child is, of course, standard practice in the U.S.S.R., a nation of working mothers in which 48 per cent of all age-eligible women are in the labor force.

Source: From *Two Worlds of Childhood: U.S. and U.S.S.R.*, by Urie Bronfenbrenner, pp. 7–9. Copyright © 1970 by Russell Sage Foundation. Reprinted by permission of the publisher.

THE SCHOOL

In preliterate cultures, basic knowledge and skills are often passed on from one generation to the next by word of mouth. Most industrial societies have found it necessary to have a system of formal education transmit the complex array of knowledge and skills that are required for everyday life to proceed smoothly in that social system. Because a literate population is needed in order for complex societies to operate efficiently, children are often required to begin school at the age of five or six; many have spent a few years in day-care centers and nursery schools by the time they enter elementary school.

The intended consequence (or manifest function) of the school is to impart to students certain technical knowledge and skills, including the "three Rs" (reading, writing, and arithmetic). Children need these skills to understand the world, through the lens of the culture, and to play roles such as employee, informed voter, and taxpayer. These skills give children the necessary equipment to solve problems and continue their education and training.

In addition to instilling certain skills and knowledge, schools also socialize children by demanding adherence to the values of the culture. Children are taught to get along with other students, and teachers' evaluations often include the child's social adjustment as well as academic performance. Teachers try to motivate children to want to learn and to succeed by the standards of the culture. Research indicates that children who are most industrious in their early years are most likely to enjoy good mental health in adulthood, possibly because these children learn to derive satisfaction from conforming to others' expectations (Sobel, 1981).

Another value that is taught in school is patriotism. Children learn this value by reciting the pledge of allegiance and by studying American history from a particular perspective. In American schools, the value of individualism is also stressed by teachers, who ask children to do their school work alone and then grade their efforts as individuals. In collectivist societies, school systems emphasize cooperation and sharing. This cooperation might be defined as cheating in an American school, but it would be rewarded in a school in the People's Republic of China. On the other hand, individual efforts that are rewarded in an American school might actually be treated as antisocial activities in a Chinese school.

The school is, for many children, the first setting in which they have an extended opportunity to interact with people with whom they are not intimately involved. The bonds between students and teachers are not emotional and personal in the way that the bonds between children and their parents are. One result of this experience is that children learn to be loyal to an institution outside the family and to respect authority that is not derived from a personal relationship.

Socialization in school affects children's attitudes toward themselves. By conforming to their teachers' expectations, students are rewarded with high grades and praise, and thereby develop a sense of competence that makes schoolwork enjoyable and satisfying. Other students, who fail to meet their teachers' demands, lose self-esteem; they come to think of themselves as incompetent, and their future behavior may reflect their image of themselves as unable to perform as others expect. Socialization in school can thus affect a child's self-image and behavior, in addition to teaching specific skills and values. The effort to develop the child's character is

Schools socialize children in the values of the culture, as well as teaching them certain skills and knowledge.

stated more openly in the Soviet Union, where government manuals include clear objectives about character development for students of different ages, but American schools do have significant, if unintended, effects on the character of students (Bronfenbrenner, 1970: 23–69).

THE PEER GROUP

In a peer group—a collection of people of about the same age who have the same relationship to authority—individuals interact and cooperate with one another, and they often have an influence on one another that socializes them in certain ways.

Children relate to others in their peer groups as equals, which is different from their experiences in the family and in the school, where adults have authority over them and supervise their behavior. The earliest peer-group experience usually occurs around age three or four in a play group or in nursery school. Peer groups are also important to adolescents, and they sometimes play an important part in the socialization of adults, such as in the military, at work, or in the community.

Peer groups act as agents of socialization by offering the reward of social approval in return for conformity to group standards. Many peer groups are joined by choice, which increases the motivation to behave in ways that will please other members of the group. Peer groups are important in providing children with an identity apart from their relationships with parents and teachers. These groups provide models of behavior that children have not yet been exposed to, and thus open up new possibilities for socialization. Until adolescence, the most influential peer groups are usually composed of others of the same sex (McCandless, 1969: 808–809).

To some extent, peer groups adopt the norms and values of adults and teachers, and so help to reinforce the standards of the culture. However, peer groups in the United States sometimes develop norms and values that contradict those of parents or teachers, or at least emphasize themes different from those stressed in the dominant culture. Peer groups sometimes socialize children in ways to "beat the system"—for example, by sharing ways to cope with the demands of parents or how to find shortcuts to fulfill their teachers' expectations.

During adolescence, which lasts from about age twelve until about age twenty-one, peer groups are especially important. Adolescents sometimes develop a counterculture that stresses different values and norms than those of the dominant culture, but even these adolescents continue to share many aspects of the dominant culture. Parents and teachers stress the importance of academic achievement, but adolescents often emphasize popularity, which traditionally is measured by athletic skill for boys and by attractiveness for girls (Coleman, 1961). Of course, popularity is important to adults and teachers, too, so the adolescent peer group may best be seen as emphasizing one theme of the dominant culture rather than contradicting that culture altogether.

Although peer groups may not consciously act to socialize their members, they have a powerful influence on behavior. Because their acceptance by peers is so important to adolescents, the expectations of others of the same age become very important. Peer groups help adolescents make the difficult transition from childhood to adulthood.

In the United States, peer groups exist for people of all ages, but the adolescent peer group has been given the most attention by social scientists and by the popular press. Single people—including those who have never married, and those who are separated, divorced, or widowed—have recently developed their own peer groups. These singles' groups, which are a result of a rising divorce rate and a delay in marriage until later years, provide social support in a mostly-married culture and provide the opportunity to form new relationships with others in similar situations.

THE MASS MEDIA

The *mass media* are the instruments of large-scale communication—including television, radio, movies, magazines, and newspapers—which transmit information and symbolic material to a large, unorganized, and dispersed group of people (Janowitz, 1968). This transmission process does not involve any face-to-face interaction between people and it is one-way; the audience does not communicate to the media.

The mass media use advanced technology to communicate with large masses of people. Technology is neutral, but its uses in the mass media have profound effects on the ways that people are socialized. The mass media can reinforce the values and norms of the culture, or they can expose people to new values and norms. The mass media can provide balanced information and viewpoints, or they can transmit distorted and one-sided information.

In the United States and other industrial societies, the most important mass medium is television. Television can and has been used to socialize children and adults. The program *Sesame Street* has had demonstrated effects in developing its viewers' cognitive skills. The series *Roots* rekindled interest in the exploration of people's ancestry, enhanced a sense of ethnic identity, and educated viewers about the history of blacks in the United States. Programs on the Public Broadcasting System and, to a lesser extent, on the national networks provide opportunities for viewing plays, ballets, operas, and other educational programs to which people would otherwise not have had access.

In spite of its benefits, television has been criticized more often than praised for its impact on behavior and values. Children often neglect their schoolwork, friends, and parents in favor of watching television. Television can actually clash with the goals of school. One study of six-year-olds found that those who watched the most television used "fewer adjectives, fewer adverbs, and [spoke] in shorter, simpler sentences"; heavy viewers also had more trouble reading (Singer, cited in Preston, 1981: B1, B4).

Children between the ages of two and eleven watch an average of nearly twenty-eight hours of television each week. The average high school student has watched about 15,000 hours of television and has seen around 18,000 fictionalized murders. There is evidence that children are socialized into these viewing habits by modeling their own behavior after the behavior of their parents. More than 95 per cent of all American households contain at least one television set, so exposure to television is nearly universal throughout society. One result may be an increasing homogeneity of American culture and behavior, because television is an agent of socialization for all members of society.

In addition to replacing other activities in the lives of children, adolescents, and adults, television also has what many regard as negative effects. Television viewing is correlated with aggressive behavior and delinquency (Muson, 1978). It is difficult to design research that shows conclusively that television viewing *causes* aggressive behavior, because children who are already predisposed to behave aggressively may choose to watch more television, but some experiments do show that watching aggressive behavior actually produces similar behavior (Bandura, Ross, and Ross, 1961; Liebert and Baron, 1972; Cater and Strickland, 1975). In recent years, some longitudinal research has indicated that television viewing precedes aggressive behavior and can be treated as a cause of that behavior. A summary of about 2,500 studies and reports published since 1970 concludes that there was overwhelming scientific evidence that watching excessive television violence produces aggressive and violent behavior in children and adolescents. This report—by the National Institute of Mental Health—calls television "a formidable educator whose effects are both pervasive and cumulative" (cited in Reinhold, 1982: C27).

Television can also desensitize viewers to real-life violence (National Commission on the Causes and Prevention of Violence, 1970; Goldsen, 1977). When people see a lot of crime on television, they may learn to accept it as more commonplace than it really is (Duffy, 1982; *The Boston Globe,* January 10, 1983, p. 3). This can dull their emotional responses to actual crime and lead them to adopt a passive, voyeuristic perspective on the world. Children who watch a lot of television have been found to be more fearful of the world than children who watch less television (Flast, 1977). In addition, children who watch a lot of television may also be more likely to demand constant stimulation and entertainment; one result may be that playing with friends or sitting in class may seem less exciting than watching television.

The mass media present children, adolescents, and adults with models on which they sometimes base their own behavior, even though those models are probably relatively less important in the socialization process than parents, teachers, and peers. In the United States, the models in the mass media are commonly athletes, comedians, and people who use violence. The active and skilled people who do appear are usually young or middle-aged white males; blacks, females, and the elderly are less often portrayed as competent. This way of presenting blacks, women, and the elderly—that is, stereotypical images—reinforces prejudices and social inequality. Popular songs on the radio also reinforce a traditional division of labor between men and women; listeners may come to accept the subordinate status of women as inevitable and natural, rather than subject to change through social action. These songs reinforce the belief that romantic love is a good basis for enduring relationships between the sexes, by tending to downplay or neglect the importance of cooperation and mutual respect to a good relationship.

Television, radio, movies, magazines, and newspapers in the United States all convey repeated messages that the consumption of material goods is a worthy activity. Television commercials and, to a lesser extent, the content of the actual programs

The mass media in the United States repeatedly convey the message that the consumption of material goods is a worthy activity.

present models of behavior that imply, sometimes not so subtly, that people who have and spend more money are better and enjoy life more than nonconsumers. The encouragement of consumption by the mass media might even lead people to seek high-paying jobs that they do not find especially satisfying in order to have the resources to maintain a life style filled with expensive material possessions. The materialism conveyed by the mass media can also lead to property crime by people who feel they lack the opportunity to earn as much money as they would like through legitimate pursuits; this crime might take the form of petty theft by the poor or embezzlement by executives whose desires are not satisfied by the income they earn on the job. Some commercials also encourage unhealthy dietary practices, such as eating sugar-laden foods rather than more nutritious fare. In television commercials, alcohol use is often associated with an exciting life style such as sailing in the South Seas or racing a sports car through the mountains. This portrayal may prompt nondrinkers to drink, and it may lead some people to drink to excess and thereby increase alcoholism in the society.

The mass media reflect the culture and the society of which they are a part, but the material presented in the mass media also influences behavior. In fact, businesses invest millions of dollars in producing and presenting commercials in the mass media on the assumption that those commercials *do* influence behavior. The types of behavior that the mass media encourage are not necessarily the kinds of behavior that people might encourage if they were able to develop a social policy about what would be presented in the mass media; commercial considerations, rather than careful examination of social goals, determine what is presented in the mass media in many industrial societies.

Socialization and the Life Cycle

The agents of socialization have an ongoing effect throughout the *life cycle*, the orderly sequence of events between birth and death. The stages of the life cycle correspond roughly to chronological age, but those stages are defined in distinctive ways by different cultures and in different historical periods (Elder, 1975). In the United States and other industrial societies, the life cycle is most commonly divided into the stages of childhood, adolescence, and adulthood; adulthood is sometimes subdivided

into early, middle, and late phases. In each of these stages people confront different problems and behave in different ways.

Childhood did not emerge in Western societies until the sixteenth century. Up until then, those we now define as children were treated much like adults. By the age of eight, people in the Middle Ages dressed like adults and worked beside them in the field and in the home (Ariès, 1962; Postman, 1982). Not all cultures define a stage of childhood, but in the contemporary United States this stage is defined as the time between birth and about the age of twelve.

Adolescence is a socially defined stage in the life cycle in industrial societies, but this stage has only existed since the Industrial Revolution and has been called "adolescence" for less than a century. This stage is a transition from childhood to adulthood, roughly from the age of twelve to the age of twenty-one. There is no stage of adolescence in most tribal, preliterate societies, where formal ceremonies known as "rites of passage" mark an abrupt transition from childhood to adulthood. However, in industrial societies adolescence is a time when people continue their education, which is needed in an economic system based on a complex technology, and do not work at a full-time job, because the labor of teenagers is superfluous in an advanced economic system.

The beginning of adulthood varies from culture to culture; it may begin in the early teens or not until the early twenties or later. Adulthood includes what we often call old age, a stage that begins at very different ages in various societies. In the United States, the elderly are often defined as those past the age of sixty-five, which until recently was the typical age for retirement from most jobs. Now that the retirement age has been shifted to seventy, the social definition of old age may be revised upward. In many cultures old age begins much sooner, largely because people do not live as long. Among the Ik of Africa, for example, old age begins in the late twenties, largely as a consequence of the physical decline that occurs due to a shortage of food (Turnbull, 1972). In all cultures, old people confront similar problems, such as learning how to deal with poor health and death and how to interact with younger generations.

Because people confront different problems in each stage of the life cycle, they continue to be socialized throughout their lives. They learn the culture's ways of dealing with such tasks as becoming independent of their parents, choosing a spouse, raising children, and dealing with the prospect of death. Psychologists have traditionally emphasized socialization in early childhood, but social scientists of all sorts have started to pay more attention to socialization in the later stages of the life cycle. The rapidly developing field of gerontology brings together several academic fields in the study of the problems of the aged, including the socialization that occurs when they deal with the death of a spouse, the loss of a job, and declining health.

TWO APPROACHES TO SOCIALIZATION

Social scientists use two major theoretical perspectives to examine socialization throughout the life cycle—a developmental approach and an interactionist approach—that we shall now describe. Then, in the rest of the chapter we look at the three major stages in the life cycle—childhood, adolescence, and adulthood—first from the developmental perspective and then from the interactionist perspective.

The Developmental Approach

The developmental approach to the study of socialization usually focuses on a child's or an adolescent's progression through a sequence of stages that have both physical and mental characteristics. This approach stresses the process by which "normal" children learn skills and ways of coping with the environment and society. Children and adolescents are thought to be molded by their culture and society, but they are also individuals who cannot move to the next stage in the developmental sequence until they have completed the stage they are in. We will examine four major developmental theories: Sigmund Freud's theory of personality; Jean Piaget's theory of cognitive development; Piaget's and Lawrence Kohlberg's theories of moral development; and Erik Erikson's theory of identity. Of these theories, only Erikson's extends beyond adolescence. However, as we look at adult socialization, we will discuss some recent efforts to identify stages in the development of men and women (Sheehy, 1976; Levinson, 1978).

A CRITIQUE OF THE DEVELOPMENTAL APPROACH. "Dialectical psychology" is a recent approach that sees socialization as a product of both the biological makeup of people and the social, cultural, and historical context in which they live (Riegel, 1976, 1979). Dialectical psychologists criticize develop-

mental theorists for limiting their work to a specific social, cultural, and historical setting—such as Freud's Vienna in the early twentieth century—and then generalizing to all other cultures, times, and places. Dialectical psychology explores individuals' interactions with one another, and thus has something in common with the interactionist approach, but it also deals with historical factors that are usually neglected by interactionists. The dialectical perspective treats crises in an individual's life as important opportunities for personal growth, rather than as difficulties to be resolved, which is how developmental theorists usually deal with crises.

The Interactionist Approach

Interactionists assume that people change over the life cycle, but they usually reject the idea held by developmental theorists that changes occur in some unvarying and inevitable sequence of stages. Interactionists see the stages of the life cycle as socially defined; that is, in the culture, which arises out of the interaction of members of society, there are ideas about the various stages of the life cycle.

Interactionists are particularly interested in the emergence of the *self*—that sense of identity of oneself as something separate from the rest of society, while still living in it. For interactionists, socialization is a continuous process in which the self is defined through communication with others. Because communication is so important in the socialization process, the acquisition of a language is essential to the formation of a social self.

Children play an active part in their own socialization by developing meanings and creating strategies for interacting with others (Denzin, 1977). For instance, children between the ages of two and three often test the boundaries of behavior acceptable to their parents, their parents respond by setting rules, and the children adjust their behavior; some children will do as they are told, others will continue to rebel openly, and still others will maintain a well-behaved front while breaking the rules in secret. Adolescents and adults play an even more active part in their own socialization, with adolescents accepting or rejecting the values and norms of adults, and adults often entering voluntarily into socialization experiences such as psychotherapy or job retraining.

Through interaction with others, people learn new roles. Children learn how to behave in nursery school or elementary school from their parents, their teachers, and their peers. Adolescents often try on new roles associated with adulthood, such as working at a job or forming a romantic attachment. Socialization in adulthood occurs when people adopt new roles such as spouse, parent, employee, and retired person. Interactionists focus on the way that these and other roles are learned from others.

Socialization in Childhood

In the twelve or so years that are called childhood, people develop an identity, or sense of self. They acquire cognitive skills, such as reasoning and remembering, and affective traits, such as the ability to love and trust others. During this stage, children learn to want to please others, to obey and to question authority, and to act in what they and others define as a moral way.

DEVELOPMENTAL THEORIES OF CHILDHOOD SOCIALIZATION

Developmental theorists have delineated a series of stages through which all children pass on their way to becoming functioning members of society. Different theorists have emphasized various aspects of behavior and personality; here we look at theories of the development of personality, cognitive skills, morality, and identity.

The Development of Personality: Sigmund Freud

Sigmund Freud (1930, 1962) saw socialization as a continuous conflict between the individual's instinctual drives and culture, which channels and curbs those drives. He assumed that children learned the norms and values of the culture primarily from their parents and that the individual personality was essentially formed by the age of five or six. Freud saw adulthood as a time in which earlier unresolved conflicts were reenacted, rather than a new stage in the progressive development of the individual. According to Freud, one way to facilitate change in adulthood is psychoanalysis, a process through which the conflicts of the early years are brought to the surface and resolved by working with a psychiatrist.

Freud used three intellectual concepts, or "constructs," to describe the structure of what we might call a "social personality": the id, the ego, and the superego. The "id" consists of the urges and drives that people are born with. For example, newborn babies want to satisfy their hunger, and they act aggressively and without consideration for others. The "ego" is the rational or conscious aspect of the personality that seeks to satisfy the impulses of the id in a socially acceptable way. The ego mediates between the drives of the id and the demands of the culture. The "superego" is the conscience; it represents parental authority expressed in the individual as a continuing acceptance of cultural norms and values. For Freud, socialization is a process through which innate instincts are repressed by the culture as the child internalizes norms and values.

One basic human drive is the desire for sexual gratification. During different stages of development, sexual pleasure is associated with various parts of the body. At first the child associates pleasure with the mouth and the act of sucking. Later, gratification is linked to self-control and the satisfaction of parental expectations about toilet-training. After this stage, the child begins to associate pleasure with his or her sexual organs. This is followed by a stage in which sexuality is repressed, and then a stage in which the young adolescent begins to associate pleasure with sexual intercourse. Freud saw these stages as a natural and inevitable progression in the normal sexual development of children, although his critics have pointed out that this model might only be an accurate description of the sexual development of his own patients.

The Development of Cognitive Skills: Jean Piaget

Jean Piaget examined the development of the mental faculties of perception, thought, reasoning, memory, and speech that an individual needs to understand the social world and to carry out social interaction. His work contrasts with Freud's in that Freud examined the development of the affective (feeling) part of the personality and Piaget looked at the development of cognitive (intellectual) abilities. Like Freud, Piaget examined the development of personality in children; but unlike Freud, who based his theories on the childhood memories of his adult patients, Piaget directly observed children.

Piaget claimed that all children pass through the same stages of cognitive development and that they cannot pass to a later stage before integrating the experiences of the earlier stages. Cognition develops cumulatively, because intellectual abilities depend on biological development and because certain skills, such as writing, cannot be learned

By directly observing children, Piaget studied the development of the mental faculties that the individual needs to understand the social world.

from others until more basic skills, such as spoken language, have been mastered. Children pass through the stages at different speeds that are determined in part by the social context. The exact content of what children learn in each stage varies from culture to culture.

Piaget's theory of cognitive development describes four stages (Piaget and Inhelder, 1969; Elkind, 1968). During the first stage, infants acquire the language that is necessary to define objects, store memories, and think about the physical world. In the second stage, which lasts roughly from two until seven, children learn to communicate with others and understand the ideas to which words refer. During the third stage of cognitive development, which lasts from about seven to twelve, children learn to understand cause-and-effect relationships and deal with abstract concepts such as weight and number. The cognitive development of some people stops at this point, but many continue into a fourth stage, during which they learn to think rationally and abstractly, apply general principles to actual cases, and contemplate their futures.

The Development of Morality: Piaget and Kohlberg

Both Piaget and Lawrence Kohlberg have found that children develop a sense of right and wrong in an orderly way. Piaget and Kohlberg treat moral development as a kind of cognitive development, for they are more interested in the intellectual components of morality than in the actual behavior of children in different stages of moral development.

JEAN PIAGET. Piaget claims that children first see the rules by which they abide as external to them (Piaget, 1932, 1948; Maccoby, 1968: 231–235). Only later do they accept the obligation to conform to those rules in spite of the fact that they did not create them. Children learn to obey the spirit, rather than just the letter, of the rules. They develop the ability to take a specific rule and apply it to a new situation. Only in the later stages of moral development do children fully internalize rules and come to believe that they should abide by those rules for the good of society. At this point they support the rules by consent, rather than because they feel forced to by an external authority.

LAWRENCE KOHLBERG. Based on his decades of work on the development of a sense of morality in children, Lawrence Kohlberg (1981) has outlined a sequence of stages that he claims is to some extent independent of cultural differences. All children pass through these stages in the same order, and they cannot skip over one stage to a later one. The exact age at which children pass through each stage is unclear and varies from culture to culture and among groups within a single society. In fact, some people never reach the later stages of moral development.

In the first stage of moral development, children react only to the direct threat of punishment by their parents. Later they develop a sense of reciprocity, the idea that they will be rewarded if they behave according to others' expectations, and eventually they act out of a desire to please others. By observing others' reactions to them, they develop notions of right and wrong. Only later do they realize the possibility of conflict among their ideas of right and wrong. Finally, children develop an internalized sense of good and bad—principles of justice and morality that guide their actual behavior, even when those principles conflict with their self-interest. Some people do not reach this stage, but those who do have passed through all of the preceding stages in order.

The Development of Identity: Erik Erikson

One of the few developmental theories that covers the entire life cycle is that of Erik Erikson (1950; Elkind, 1970). Erikson identifies eight stages of development, each of which is defined by an "identity crisis" or set of problems that arise because of changes in physiology, psychology, and social context. Specific problems must be resolved at each stage, although some problems can recur in later stages, when the individual must deal with them again. In many cases, solutions to these crises are available in the culture; that is, individuals do not have to work out solutions to their developmental problems entirely on their own. When the problems of a particular stage are resolved and a stable identity has been created, the individual can pass to the next stage.

In the first year of life, the central conflict is between trust and mistrust. Consistent love and support from parents creates in the child a sense of comfort, security, and trust. When parents are erratic, uncaring, or neglectful, their children are socialized to become mistrustful and insecure.

Between the ages of one and three, the central conflict is between autonomy and doubt (or shame). The child develops skills to deal with the social world. The reactions of others to these early efforts at independence are important. If the child is protected from the consequences of failure but allowed to try out new skills, a sense of autonomy and competence will emerge. If the child is not allowed to act independently, doubt about his or her abilities may develop. The failure to satisfy others' expectations can impede the development of a stable identity.

At about age four or five, the central conflict is between initiative and guilt. At this age, children begin to take the initiative in dealing with the world. When their actions are reinforced by approval and support from others, they develop a stable sense of themselves. Children will develop a sense of guilt and low self-esteem if others respond negatively to their efforts to take the initiative at this stage.

From about age four to age twelve, there is a conflict between industry and inferiority. The reactions of teachers and peers, as well as parents, will determine whether the child develops a sense of mastery or a sense of inferiority in dealing with the world. At this stage children are judged for the first time by people with whom they do not have an intimate relationship; their teachers judge their academic and social skills, and their peers accept or reject them.

INTERACTIONISM AND THE EMERGENCE OF THE SELF

Interactionists emphasize the way in which the self, that coherent image of who one is, develops from behavior that is oriented toward other people. This process actually extends beyond childhood, because the self continues to develop throughout the life cycle (Gecas, 1982). However, it is in the early years that most people form a stable sense of who they are; later in the life cycle this self may be altered, but any alterations are usually modifications of a basic pattern that is established in childhood.

Charles Horton Cooley

Charles Horton Cooley (1903) was an interactionist who was interested in how people form a sense of themselves. He felt that interaction with other people is essential to this development of the self. In their early years, people see themselves as others see them. They watch how others react to them, and eventually they are able to imagine how others will respond to them even before they actually do respond. People are sensitive at an early age to the ways that others evaluate them, and they learn that these judgments can cause them to feel good or bad. These perceptions of how others see them may not even be accurate, but the perceptions still influence their sense of self. If others treat you as bright, you will come to think of yourself as intelligent; if others act as if you are stupid, your sense of self will include a low estimate of your own intelligence.

The self is often called a *social* self because it develops out of interaction with other people. Because the responses of others are so important in the formation of a self, Cooley called this sense of personal identity a *looking-glass self*: The self is the image that reflects off the "mirror" of other people. This looking-glass self includes both identity ("who I am") and self-esteem ("how good I am").

Cooley recognized that the self continues to develop throughout life, but he paid particular attention to the role of communication during childhood. Parents provide an important "mirror" for children in the first years of life, and children often develop a self that reflects how their parents respond to them. Play groups are also important in the development of the self, because children learn how their friends see them by playing with them in the park or in a day-care center or nursery school. Cooley developed the idea of a "primary group" to describe groups such as families and play groups in which people interact with each other face to face; he felt that primary groups were critical to the development of the social self.

George Herbert Mead

George Herbert Mead (1934) was a philosopher and social psychologist who emphasized the way that the self is created from social experiences. Mead saw the self as a process composed of the interaction between two aspects of the person. The aspect he called the "I" acts in a spontaneous and individualistic way, and another aspect of the person called the "me" reflects on that behavior and how other people respond to that behavior. For Mead, the self emerges from a "conversation of gestures" within the individual's mind between the spontaneous "I" and the "me," which represents the learned conventions of the culture.

Like Cooley, Mead felt that the self was influenced by observations of other people's attitudes toward oneself and by communication with others. An important quality of the self, in Mead's view,

was its objectiveness; people can reflect on themselves as separate and unique things in the world. He claimed that there are multiple selves within a single person and that different selves become important when interacting with others in various social situations.

Mead explored the way that children develop a sense of self from others. He claimed that children first learn to imitate the behavior of others who are important to them, especially their parents; Mead referred to these important people as *significant others*. Children then begin to develop a consciousness of self and a sense that others respond to them. They act out and practice the behavior of these significant others; by pretending to be them, they adopt their perspectives. By switching from one role to another, children learn to understand the roles and perspectives of others. They also learn to arouse others to behave in certain ways that complement their own needs and desires, and this leads to joint activity in which they interact with others (Denzin, 1977).

By the age of eight or nine, children begin to play games in which they learn to take the broader perspective of the group, rather than the more limited perspective of the significant others with whom they interact. Mead calls this broader perspective the *generalized other*, because it extends beyond the significant others in the daily life of the child. In games such as hide-and-seek and baseball, children show they can take the perspective of an organized group, see the relationship among various roles in the game, and follow rules to achieve the goals of the game. The social self develops as children extend their awareness of the world from their own inner state to the expectations of significant others, then to the broader expectations of the generalized other of the group and finally to the perspective of the whole society.

Socialization in Adolescence

In the United States and other industrial societies, children enter the socially defined stage of adolescence at about age twelve. This is often a stressful phase, because adolescents are usually still financially dependent on their parents, and yet they want and attempt to abandon their childish ways. They may be expected to act as grownups, but they are denied the opportunity to engage in adult behavior such as marriage and full-time work.

Teenagers continue to have strong bonds to their parents during adolescence, but their peer groups often emphasize values and norms different from those of their parents' dominant culture. Adolescents often place more value on popularity with their peers than on scholastic success, and they sometimes adopt an antiauthority stance and reject their parents and their life style. Still, adolescents do share many of the values and norms of their parents. Probably the slang, dress, and music of adolescents are better seen as part of an effort to define themselves as distinct from adults, rather than as a real effort to create an entirely new culture.

Developmental theorists and interactionists have examined socialization in adolescence, but they have given less attention to this than they have to childhood socialization. Let us now look at the developmental and interactionist theories of adolescence.

THE DEVELOPMENTAL PERSPECTIVE

The developmental theories that we have already examined include stages that occur, at least in part, in adolescence. Freud's theory of sexual development sees adolescence as a stage in which libidinal pleasure becomes associated with sexual intercourse, even though norms in many industrial societies encourage adolescents to refrain from intercourse until marriage. Piaget's theory of cognitive development sees adolescence as a time when teenagers learn to think rationally and abstractly and to reflect on their own thoughts and ideals. Piaget and Kohlberg treat moral development during adolescence as an emerging willingness to abide by rules for the mutual benefit of everyone.

Erikson asserts that identity formation is by no means complete in childhood; he believes that people confront a fifth crisis in adolescence—the conflict between identity and role confusion. He sees the task at this stage as the integration of the various issues of the first four stages into a coherent identity. At this stage, people undergo physical changes and new social experiences. These changes cause anxiety and confusion, but the successful integration of these changes leads to the formation of a stable identity.

THE INTERACTIONIST PERSPECTIVE

Interactionists look at changes in patterns of social interaction during adolescence. In early childhood most interaction is with parents and teachers, but in adolescence social relationships are broadened and the peer group becomes more important. Spending time with peers is a way to weaken bonds to parents and anticipates the independence that will come with adulthood. Adolescents become sensitive to the judgments of their peers, and acceptance or rejection by peers is a daily concern for teenagers.

Adolescents play an active role in their own socialization. They reflect on their behavior and choose among different values. They begin to grow independent of their parents, and this can create stress if their parents want them to remain children longer than they wish to (Campbell, 1969). SEL 4.2 shows that in recent years there have been some changes in the boundary between childhood and adolescence, and also between adolescence and adulthood. The literature read by children and by adolescents is increasingly filled with issues that previously were examined only by adults or older adolescents, and television exposes children and adolescents to information they did not have access to in the past (Winn, 1981; Postman, 1982).

SOCIOLOGY AND EVERYDAY LIFE 4.2
Changing Definitions of Childhood and Adolescence

In recent years there has been growing concern in the United States that children are becoming adolescents at an ever-younger age, with pre-teens now being exposed to issues that until recently they did not deal with until adolescence. Some of this concern is also directed at the increased awareness that teenagers now have of issues that were previously of concern only to adults. This selection shows that these changes are reflected in the books that children and adolescents now read.

Once upon a time, children read books about fairies and animals, about other children engaged in the innocent pleasures of childhood. Today, children read about different subjects:

A beautiful girl of 14 lives in a small town where her father is a barber and her mother a humble laundress. The girl dreams of romance and fame but is obliged to spend her days in drudgery, cleaning houses and baby-sitting. At last she decides to run away from home and seek her fortune in the big city.

(So far the story resembles the familiar tales of the past. But it continues.)

On her first day in the big city, she meets a handsome man who befriends her when she is lost. She falls in love with him. Alas, he turns out to be a pimp. He compels her to become one of his prostitutes. At first she is appalled. She cannot believe that she has to do "it" with all sorts of strange men. Soon, out of love for her protector she becomes one of his most successful hookers, which arouses the jealousy of her colleagues. One of the other girls puts LSD into our heroine's soft drink and she has a bad trip. Finally, after many adventures, she finds her way into a rehabilitation center for runaway children. There she gets "therapy" and prepares to return to her small-town home—sadder but wiser.

Books such as this one, "Steffie Can't Come Out To Play," written by Fran Arrick and published in 1978 by Bradbury Press, are widely distributed and read by 10-, 11-, 12-year-olds. This new genre deals with subjects heretofore considered unsuitable for children. George A. Woods, children's book editor of The New York Times, describes with amazement recent submissions for review: "It's not just sex that defines the change. I've got books coming in on children with harelips, epilepsy and insanity as well as the usual alcoholic parents, drug-addicted children, child beaters, divorce, acne and death."

It is generally acknowledged that Ursula Nordstrom, publisher of Harper Junior Books from 1941 to 1973, was the primary force behind many innovations of the last 25 years. The first departure came in the 1960's, when she published an excellent book called "Stevie," by John Steptoe, which strayed from the "nice" middle-class, white patterns that had long monopolized children's books by telling, in nonstandard speech patterns, of the life of a black ghetto child.

But the first real "breakthrough," as these books came to be called in the trade, was a small volume for young children by John Donovan published by Harper & Row in 1969, called "I'll Get There: It Better Be Worth the Trip," a story about a boy, his friend and his dog. The uproar occasioned by this book centered on a brief scene in which two 13-year-old boys who are having a sleep-over at one of their houses are suddenly drawn to each other and find, to their surprise, that they are kissing. A homosexual episode in a children's book, though so subtly presented that many readers overlooked it, represents far more than increased openness. Donovan's book, and Steptoe's before it, were signs that a decision had been made by important cultural forces to end a period of vestigial Victorianism. In the years to come, books were to serve a new function: In addition to entertaining or teaching about the past, they would also prepare young children for future complexities in an increasingly troubled society.

Source: Marie Winn, "What Became of Childhood Innocence?" The New York Times Magazine, January 25, 1981, p. 17. ©1981 by The New York Times Company. Reprinted by permission.

Adolescents often engage in *anticipatory socialization*, the effort to learn the roles associated with the adult status that they will soon attain. They may model their behavior on heroes from the mass media, peers who act in a grown-up manner, or adults such as their parents and teachers. By anticipating how they will be expected to behave, adolescents practice playing adult roles. Anticipatory socialization is one way that adolescents play an active part in the development of their own identities.

Socialization in Adulthood

Adulthood in the United States usually begins at about age twenty-one. People have usually acquired a stable identity by the end of adolescence, and socialization during adulthood builds on that identity, reshapes the individual, and poses new problems of adjustment (Brim, 1966, 1968; Mortimer and Simmons, 1978). Socialization in childhood and adolescence inculcates the culture's norms and values; in adulthood, socialization focuses more on the performance of new roles, such as parenthood, and the acquisition of new skills. When adults undergo experiences such as brainwashing, military training, or rehabilitation in prison, we speak of *resocialization*, or intensive efforts by agents of socialization to get people to unlearn old ways of doing things and adopt new identities, values, norms, and behavior.

The only developmental theory that explicitly deals with adult socialization is Erikson's, but research by Levinson and by Sheehy on the crises experienced by adult men and women does illuminate the process of socialization after adolescence.

Interactionists have not studied adult socialization in much detail either, but we can examine the roles that adults commonly play and learn as a result of their interaction with others. We subdivide the long period of adulthood into early, middle, and late phases.

EARLY ADULTHOOD

The phase of early adulthood begins when people finish high school or college and extends roughly to the age of forty. This stage is defined rather vaguely at both ends because once people have passed

When adults undergo experiences such as brainwashing, military training, or rehabilitation in prison, we speak of resocialization. Here a veteran discusses his war experiences with a counselor in a government-sponsored "vet center."

through adolescence they exercise considerable choice over when they assume various adult roles.

The Developmental Perspective

According to Erikson, the basic conflict over identity that must be resolved in the early years of adulthood is between intimacy and isolation. During this stage, men and women learn to form close attachments to people of the opposite sex. Some people have difficulty forming these ties because they fear that they will be submerged by a relationship. This conflict between intimacy and isolation must be resolved in order for a person to develop a stable identity in young adulthood.

Another developmental perspective is taken by Daniel Levinson (1978), who conducted a study of adult socialization among forty middle- and upper-middle-class men. He found that in the early years of adulthood these men established homes apart from their families and began to separate emotionally and financially from their parents. They chose occupations and began to establish relationships with women. They started to develop an adult way of life while still keeping open their options to change. In their thirties, these men set goals for their lives, formed ties to older people who could sponsor or guide them in the adult world, developed careers, and married and had children. Levinson's study focused on certain crises or transition points that seemed important in the developmental process, enabling the men to take stock of the past and plan for the future.

Gail Sheehy (1976), following the lead of Levinson and other researchers, has developed an approach to adult socialization that looks at changes in both men and women and at the way those changes affect couples. After taking 115 life stories, Sheehy concluded that "the tempo of development is not synchronized in the two sexes" and that this creates "predictable crises for couples" (Sheehy, 1976: 15):

During the twenties, when a man gains confidence by leaps and bounds, a married woman is usually losing the superior assurance she once had as an adolescent. When a man passes 30 and wants to settle down, a woman is often becoming restless. And just at the point around 40, when a man feels himself to be standing on a precipice, his strength, power, dreams, and illusions slipping away beneath him, his wife is likely to be brimming with ambition to climb her own mountain (Sheehy, 1976: 15).

Additional research is needed before we can know how generally the patterns of development discerned by Sheehy and by Levinson apply to adult men and women.

Interactionism and New Roles

To some extent, we are socialized to the performance of adult roles when we are children and adolescents: We observe our parents interact with each other, watch how our parents treat us and our brothers and sisters, and listen to our parents discuss their jobs. However, we continue to learn how to perform roles such as spouse, parent, and worker after we become adults. We learn what our husbands and wives expect of us, we react to the needs and the demands of our children, and we learn from our bosses and fellow employees how to do our jobs. The active part that adults play in this socialization process makes it difficult to specify a single model of adult socialization, but we can examine how people learn to perform certain adult roles.

MARRIAGE. Socialization into the marital role actually begins when young children see how their parents interact; this knowledge is one influence on the way that children will deal with their own spouse. Parents sometimes actively influence their offspring's choice of a spouse, but even when they do not, they have an indirect influence over the choice of a spouse through the values they have taught their children. Children and teenagers also prepare for the marital role by acquiring the motivation to marry from their parents, peers, popular songs, movies, magazines, and television shows. In American society, children and adolescents learn that marriage should be based on love rather than on financial need or some other practical reason. Dating and courtship during adolescence provide an opportunity to "practice" relating to the opposite sex. In addition, increasing numbers of young people have entered "trial marriages" to see how capable and willing they are to live with another person before actually getting married (Hill and Aldous, 1969).

Most people enter marriage with the expectation that it will be permanent, even though statistics show that the chance that a marriage will end in divorce is quite high. Because they define marriage as permanent, husbands and wives adjust to each other in many ways. Adjustment can entail such mundane matters as how clean the bathroom will be kept or whether the bedroom window will be open at night; it also involves such major adjustments as spending evenings alone while the other person pursues a career. Socialization in the marital role requires husbands and wives to agree on how to handle the family finances, allocate housework, visit the in-laws, and decide where to live (Brim, 1968; Hill and Aldous, 1969).

PARENTHOOD. Voluntary childlessness has increased somewhat in recent years in the United States, but most married people eventually do have children. Adjustment to the presence of children in the home is an important socialization experience for most young adults. Social scientists have typically looked at the way that parents socialize their children, but it is also true that children socialize their parents. (Consider the bumper sticker, "Insanity is hereditary; you catch it from your children.") Children are not passive recipients of their parents' teachings. They have their own needs and desires, and they express them to their parents, who in turn adapt to their children. Parents of young children often change the ways they use their leisure time, watching *Sesame Street* or *Electric Company* instead of the news, and learning to enjoy trips to the zoo or the circus instead of dining out or attending a play. Parents learn to spend less quiet time alone with each other, and they adjust to a family situation rather than the intimacy of being a couple. Parents of young children may also learn to live with less sleep, and they may divide the housework and financial responsibilities in different ways.

The cost of raising children creates financial strain for some parents, who must learn to sacrifice to meet the needs of their children. If both parents work, they may assign some of the care and socialization of their children to day-care centers, nursery schools, and baby-sitters. To do this, many young parents must alter the conception of the nature of parenthood that they learned when young.

WORK. During early adulthood, most men and women undergo socialization to an occupation (Brim, 1968; Moore, 1969). This may begin with training in a professional or graduate school program, such as law, medicine, dentistry, or business. Many companies train their workers in new skills and knowledge, loyalty to the employer, and inter-

personal relations with other workers. When workers are promoted or change jobs, often they must be socialized to their new position. During childhood and adolescence, there is relatively little preparation for the daily routine of a job; as a result, some young adults are surprised at how much they must learn in order to succeed in the world of work.

MIDDLE ADULTHOOD

In the years from about forty to sixty-five, most adults do not undergo major transformations of their identities, but their socialization continues in a variety of subtle ways. Many people move during this time and have to adjust to a new community. Moving sometimes involves a step up the social ladder, and this may require them to change their behavior to fit the expectations of their neighbors. During this period men and women are sometimes promoted in their jobs, and they may be socialized in new work skills such as management and decision making.

The Developmental Perspective

During middle age, the major conflict over identity is between generativity and stagnation. Erikson uses the term "generativity" to refer to the decision to grow, continue to be creative and productive, and teach a new generation. This often involves an increased sense of responsibility for future generations and a desire to ensure the survival of the species by training a replacement for oneself. Stagnation is the lack of self-fulfillment that comes from the failure to grow and change. Resolution of the conflict between generativity and stagnation enables the middle-aged person to establish a stable identity.

In middle age, people review and appraise their lives, examining what they have gained and what they have missed. This stock-taking often leads middle-aged people to withdraw from the world and focus more on themselves (Neugarten, 1966, 1973; Levinson, 1978). During this period, they try to create realistic goals for the future, and many sense their own mortality for the first time and begin to think about the number of years they have left rather than the number of years they have already lived. This can lead to despair, but it can also lead to a sense of renewal and an effort to leave a legacy for future generations.

Interactionism and New Roles

During the middle years of adulthood, people often abandon old roles and adopt new ones. One of the most important changes of this period occurs when the children leave home. Other important changes include preparation for impending retirement, dealing with the death of parents and friends, and coping with declining physical health.

THE "EMPTY NEST SYNDROME." A major adjustment that adults in their middle years must make is to the situation in which they find themselves suddenly alone, as their children have either gone off to college or are living by themselves. The absence of the children to whom they have devoted years of their lives leaves many men and women with a sense of purposelessness, which is often called the *empty nest syndrome*. This problem has traditionally been seen as a problem faced by women, because until recently most women were full-time mothers. Today, with many women working outside the home, the loss of purpose that accompanies the empty nest may be less severe. Little attention has been paid to how fathers are affected when their children leave home. One effect in families in which the father is the only full-time breadwinner may be a reduced commitment to work because there are fewer people depending on his income. As traditional family roles for men and women change, fathers may increasingly experience a greater sense of loss than in the past, and women's sense of loss may be lessened by their increased involvement in the labor force.

LATE ADULTHOOD

The stage of the life cycle after sixty-five is called late adulthood or old age. In the United States, where the culture stresses youthfulness, beauty, health, and physical activity, the elderly are disvalued because they are less likely to have these traits. Because Americans are not socialized to old age during childhood, adolescence, or early or middle adulthood, they often experience anxiety and confusion as they enter this stage.

The Developmental Perspective

The primary conflict over identity in old age is between integrity and despair. According to Erikson, people who enter old age with a sense of the integrity, or wholeness, of their lives and a satisfaction with their past accomplishments are able to continue to pursue personal interests, express themselves, make peace with others, and confront death. Those who despair over lost opportunities and bad decisions that they have made have difficulty forming a coherent identity in this stage; they have difficulty sustaining close personal relationships and have more problems in facing their own death.

Interactionism and New Roles

In late adulthood, people usually give up roles that have been important to them as a source of identity throughout their lives. Probably the two most important changes are loss of a spouse through death and retirement from a job. Declining physical health can evoke a feeling that one is deteriorating and reduce self-esteem. Impending death also becomes a major source of concern for the elderly.

WIDOWHOOD. Women in the United States live an average of nine years longer than men. As a result, there are many more widows than widowers, and many elderly women (and a smaller number of men) live for years after their spouse dies. The death of a spouse often leads elderly people to establish new friendships with other members of the same sex, an abrupt change after decades of intimate communication with someone of the opposite sex.

RETIREMENT. Most employers in the United States now require their workers to retire at the age of seventy, even if the individual can still work satisfactorily (Atchley, 1982). A functionalist might point to the way that this benefits society; jobs are made available to younger workers, and those workers who can no longer do their jobs effectively are not stigmatized. However, retirement reduces the income of the elderly, and this often lowers their standard of living if they do not have savings. The loss of a job also strips them of an important source of identity and forces them to turn to other sources of self-expression and satisfaction to fill their increased leisure time. Late adulthood seems to be easiest for those who develop new outlets for their talents and skills, continue productive work, and maintain close relationships with others.

Concern with Death

The elderly are more *concerned* with the issue of death than younger people are, but they *fear* death less than the young do (Marshall, 1980: 78). Many people assume that the fear of death is an inevitable part of old age; one person who holds this belief is Elisabeth Kübler-Ross, a physician who has worked for years with terminal patients. Her research indicates that these patients go through several stages. Because fear of death is inevitable, according to Kübler-Ross (1969), their first reaction is to deny the fact of their impending death. Then they express anger at the prospect of leaving the world. After this, these terminal patients try to ''strike a bargain,'' usually by praying to God that they will be content to die if only they can reach one final goal. Next they become depressed, experiencing a grief that is preparatory to departure from the world, and finally they accept their impending death. Knowledge that many dying people pass through these stages may help the elderly better prepare themselves for death and help them understand the emotions they feel. One critic of Kübler-Ross's research suggests that these reactions are by no means inevitable (Marshall, 1980: 68−69). Many of Kübler-Ross's patients were not elderly, and the denial of death might well be normal, because so few people die young. Kübler-Ross also withheld information from some terminal patients about the fatal nature of their diseases, so their denial of death may be an understandable response to incomplete information about their health.

The elderly experience many other emotions as well as fear of death. Some fear the pain of dying or the physical deterioration of their body. Others are concerned with the end to experience, the unknown nature of life after death, or the consequences of their death for their dependents (Diggory and Rothman, 1961). Some do not fear death at all, but are indifferent toward it or see it as a blessing. Many elderly people plan for their deaths by purchasing insurance, writing wills, making financial plans, and helping to plan their funerals. Such planning suggests that not all elderly people deny death out of fear; many can plan for their own death in a rational way.

SOCIOLOGY AND EVERYDAY LIFE 4.3
Learning to Cope with Dying

Since 1974, hospice care has developed rapidly in the United States as a way to help terminal patients and their families accept death. Hospices do this by providing medical and emotional support for dying patients and their families, either in residential facilities for the dying or at home. One way that the patients and their families are sometimes socialized to impending death is to have them witness an actual death so that they can see that they will not be abandoned when they are dying.

The goal of hospice programs is to manage terminal disease in ''a way that patients live until they die, that their families live with them as they are dying—and go on living afterward,'' says Dr. Sylvia Lack, a medical director of a hospice program in New Haven, Connecticut (p. F1).

The son of a sixty-four-year-old man who died in the care of New Haven's hospice program describes the experience as follows:

''He was bitter,'' Bob Gery recalls of his father. ''I think almost anybody would be bitter if you're told a year or so after you've retired that you have less than six months to live.

''He was bitter. He argued with my mother. He argued with me, with my wife. Things that in normal health would be considered just small things.

''At first I kept saying, 'Dad, how could you treat Mom like this?' realizing I was talking from my perspective, a healthy person.

''In the last couple of months, when we had the understanding and he had the appreciation of the things told to him by the people at hospice and by us, there really wasn't any need to do any more arguing.

"The people at hospice were straightforward and told him he was going to die and that how he chose to die over the next several months depended on him and on what they could do for him if he let them.

"He could die with dignity or could die in any other manner he chose. If he wanted to go back to the hospital or some extended care facility, they could do that, too. He chose to die at home.

"I think hospice let myself and my wife and my mom cope with the grief that we had. And it gave my dad a feeling of being able to care for himself. To dictate the circumstances of living out his last several months. Hospice gave us hope in a time of no hope. It allowed us to put ourselves together, all of us" (p. F1).

This hospice program provides home visits during the day and at night, seven days a week. For example, one fifty-four-year-old widow who moved to New Haven from Buffalo, N.Y., was dying from cancer of the mouth. She had great difficulty speaking and eating and was very much alone. One hospice volunteer helped her find a store where she could buy a present for a grandchild, and a minister brought her some material to proofread. This woman comments: "People like Shirley and Mr. Abbott come to see me every other day. . . . I feel like I'm making friends. A bunch of people are tuned in on me. Not a day goes by that someone from hospice doesn't call me or come by." Then she adds: "I feel ugly. I'm in pain now. I look forward to peace. I'm not afraid to die" (p. F1).

Source: Based on George Esper, "Hospice Helps Patients to Live until They Die, Families to Cope," *The Bridgeport Post*, January 15, 1978, p. F1. Used by permission.

Death in American society is not the forbidden subject that it was a short time ago. The work of Kübler-Ross has alerted the public to ways to cope with death. Many colleges and universities have introduced courses on the topic. Hospices have been established to help terminal patients and their families prepare for death (See SEL 4.3). Still, death in the United States is usually a matter of concern mainly to the dying, their families, and the medical personnel and funeral directors with whom they deal. Because most of the elderly die in hospitals or nursing homes, their deaths are usually hidden from the rest of the community. Death is still not an issue of broad community concern, nor are people socialized during the earlier stages of the life cycle to accept their impending death (Rosow, 1974; Marshall, 1980).

Summary

Children who spend the first few years of life in relative isolation do not behave in ways that we consider fully human, for they have not been socialized in the values, norms, intellectual skills, emotions, and behavior that are part of the culture.

The most important agents of socialization in industrial societies are parents, teachers, peers, and the mass media. Socialization in the first few years of life occurs mainly as a result of the interaction of children with their parents, although the way that children are reared varies from society to society and from group to group within the same society. The school is another important agent of socialization in industrial societies, because a certain amount of formal education is needed to do most jobs. Schools also instill the culture's values and norms; in the United States, these include patriotism, discipline, and hard work. In addition, children's self-images are influenced by the way that their teachers and their peers respond to them. Peer groups are especially important in the socialization of adolescents, but they also play an important part in the socialization of children and adults. A fourth agent of socialization is the mass media, which include television, radio, movies, magazines, and newspapers. For example, by merchandising products in an appealing way, television teaches viewers to value the consumption of material goods. The media deflect attention from schoolwork, athletics, and social relationships, and retard the development of reading and writing skills. In addition, television viewing is closely associated with aggressive and delinquent behavior.

Developmental theorists treat the socialization process as a relatively invariant sequence of stages; individuals do not skip stages, and they only pass from one stage to the next when they have completed the work of the first. Freud emphasized the way that culture curbs individual drives; he looked at the development of personality through the internalization of cultural norms and values. Piaget's theory of cognitive development looks at the learning of intellectual skills such as memory and the ability to reason. Both Piaget and Kohlberg have explored the way that children develop an abstract sense of right and wrong, after initially viewing rules as externally imposed standards that must be obeyed in order to avoid punishment. One of the few developmental theories that covers the entire life cycle is Erik Erikson's theory of identity formation, which includes eight stages of development, each of which contains a different set of conflicts that must be resolved to form a stable identity.

The interactionist perspective on socialization explores the relationship between the agents of socialization and the individuals who are being socialized, treating those who are being socialized as active participants in their own socialization. Cooley and Mead have investigated the way that the self is formed through interaction; people notice others' reactions to them and the judgments implied by those reactions, and they develop ideas about themselves that reflect others' reactions to them.

Most developmental theories focus on the way that children are socialized by their parents, but interactionists emphasize the give-and-take between children and their parents, teachers, and peers. In adolescence, peer groups become even more important in the socialization process.

Socialization continues into adulthood, with adults taking an even more active role in their own socialization than do adolescents. Developmental theorists such as Erikson focus on the issue of establishing intimate relationships in early adulthood, and they also look at the way that young adults break away from their families and begin careers. Interactionists look at the new roles adopted by young adults—marriage, parenthood, and work—and the way that they learn new types of behavior from others. In the middle years of adulthood, people are often socialized into new communities and new jobs.

During this time, people become aware of their own mortality, a realization that leads many to try to grow and continue to be creative so that they have a legacy to leave future generations. An important change in roles in this stage is the "empty nest syndrome," the situation that arises when children have grown up and left home. In late adulthood people continue to integrate their experiences into a coherent identity; a sense of dissatisfaction with the past can cause despair, but a successful integration of the past can produce contentment. In this stage people often give up roles that have been important to them in their adult years, and they look for new sources of satisfaction. Many women and somewhat fewer men experience the death of a spouse, and they often form friendships with members of the same sex after a lifelong intimacy with someone of the opposite sex. People also retire, and the loss of work strips away an important source of identity and income. The elderly are concerned with their impending death, but this does not necessarily lead them to fear death; often they plan for their own death in a rational way. Death has become more widely discussed in American society in recent years, and the elderly and their families have increasingly been socialized to impending death.

Important Terms

AFFECTIVE DEVELOP-
MENT (74)
AGENTS OF SOCIALIZA-
TION (76)
ANTICIPATORY SOCIALIZ-
ATION (89)
COGNITIVE SKILLS (74)
"EMPTY NEST SYN-
DROME" (93)
GENERALIZED OTHER
(87)

LIFE CYCLE (82)
LOOKING-GLASS SELF
(87)
MASS MEDIA (80)
PEER GROUP (76)
RESOCIALIZATION (90)
SELF (83)
SIGNIFICANT OTHER (87)
SOCIALIZATION (74)

Suggested Readings

Urie Bronfenbrenner. *Two Worlds of Childhood: U.S. and U.S.S.R.* New York: Russell Sage Foundation, 1970. A comparative study of childhood socialization and the source of SEL 4.1.

Sigmund Freud. *Civilization and Its Discontents*, trans. by James Strachey. New York: Norton, 1930, 1962. Freud's classic statement of how culture curbs basic drives through the socialization process.

David A. Goslin, ed. *Handbook of Socialization Theory and Research*. Chicago: Rand McNally, 1969. The essays in Part III present a comprehensive review of socialization research on different stages in the life cycle.

Marvin R. Koller and Oscar W. Ritchie. *Sociology of Childhood*, 2nd ed. Englewood Cliffs, N.J.: Prentice-Hall, 1978. This textbook presents a solid, thorough discussion of socialization in the early years.

Daniel J. Levinson, with Charlotte N. Darrow et al. *The Seasons of a Man's Life*. New York: Ballantine, 1978. An intensive examination of the socialization experiences of forty middle-class and upper-middle-class men during their adult years.

Victor W. Marshall. *Last Chapters: A Sociology of Aging and Dying*. Monterey, Calif.: Brooks/Cole, 1980. A thorough sociological analysis of the last stage in the life cycle.

Peter I. Rose, ed. *Socialization and the Life Cycle*. New York: St. Martin's Press, 1979. A collection of essays that consider the socialization process at different ages.

DEVIANCE AND CRIME

If you were to kill a classmate or a relative, you would probably be arrested and tried for murder. You would have committed an act that violates a norm which exists in virtually every society: "Thou shalt not kill." Your act would be *deviance* because it violates a norm that is part of the culture, and it would also be a *crime* because that norm is a law.

If you killed one of the enemy while in the military and fighting a war, you might be praised or given a medal. This kind of behavior is normative for soldiers; it conforms to the expectations of the role. If you intentionally killed another soldier in your own platoon, however, you would probably be tried for murder.

You would not have committed a crime if you were a police officer and you shot and killed a man who was trying to escape from the scene of a serious crime that he had just committed. Police officers are allowed to use lethal force to stop a fleeing felon. Even though this killing is not legally a murder, it might well be seen as an act of deviance by the criminal's friends or neighbors, who feel that the use of lethal force was an excessive response.

An example of the use of lethal force that is rewarded rather than punished is the work of a public executioner. This employee of the state is paid to put people to death; indeed, this type of killing has the support of the law. Even though it is a legitimate occupation, public executioners are apt to conceal the nature of their work from friends and relatives, who are likely to see such work as unsavory or deviating from general expectations about how one should earn income.

These examples show that even the act of killing another person is subject to a wide variety of social definitions; the act itself does not have an intrinsic meaning apart from the role of the killer and the social context of the killing. Taking the life of another person can be both deviant and criminal, as

in the case of murder. It can also be noncriminal but still deviant, as in a police killing or a public execution. In wartime, a soldier's taking the life of the enemy is seen as neither deviant nor criminal by most members of society.

Every culture has norms that establish expectations about what types of behavior are appropriate for particular people in certain social situations. When a person violates a norm, members of society respond by recognizing the act as deviant. One kind of deviance is crime, which may be punished by the state because a legal norm has been violated. All crimes are deviant, but some deviant behavior, such as alcoholism or attempted suicide, is not criminal because the norms have not been made into law by a recognized political authority.

The Social Definition of Deviance

No act is inherently deviant; it must first be defined by other people as deviant from a norm. Deviance is a "property *conferred upon* behavior" rather than an intrinsic quality of behavior (Erikson, 1966: 6). In some instances, such as witchcraft, it is not even necessary for a person to engage in actual nonconforming behavior to be classified as a deviant.

Various cultures interpret the consumption of alcoholic beverages in very different ways. In the Jewish culture, drunkenness is treated as deviant behavior. However when the members of the Camba tribe of Bolivia gather together from the fields in which they work, they are expected to get drunk to the point of passing out, then to continue drinking when they revive (Heath, 1962).

Taking the property of others is also responded to in a variety of ways. In some tribal societies, people are expected to make use of the property of others if they need to. In the United States, such behavior

Socialization is the primary means of producing conformity to society's norms, but law enforcement is also an important mechanism of social control.

would be considered theft, and the person who took the property of another would be arrested and punished if found guilty. In Colombia, on the other hand, thieves are not punished as criminals if they steal to meet a pressing need for food or clothing, lack the legal means to satisfy those needs, refrain from violence, and take no more than they need (Radzinowicz and King, 1977: 116).

Within a culture, the social definition of deviance also changes with time. In the early 1900s, many middle-class American women used laudanum, an opiate, to relieve menstrual cramps and other pains. Many of these women were addicted to the drug, but they were not classified as deviant, much less criminal. A few decades later, when the law made narcotics use and possession punishable, the social definition of opiate users changed; it was still not illegal to *be* an addict, but it was illegal to possess or use opiates such as laudanum and heroin.

The social definition of alcohol use also changed in American culture in the earlier part of this century, when temperance groups that had been fighting to outlaw the sale and consumption of alcoholic beverages finally succeeded in having the Prohibition Amendment enacted (Gusfield, 1963). From 1920 to 1933, the sale and consumption of alcohol were illegal, although many groups did not

see alcohol use as deviant from their own standards. The temperance forces regarded alcohol as a symbol of changes in American society that they resisted; they also sought to prohibit cigarette smoking, which they succeeded in doing in a few states for short periods of time, and they even opposed such "lewd" forms of entertainment as jazz and the fox trot.

MORAL ENTREPRENEURS

Some behavior is socially defined as deviant through the actions of *moral entrepreneurs*, people who oppose certain behavior and support laws to prohibit that behavior (Becker, 1973). Harry J. Anslinger is one such person. Anslinger worked first for the Prohibition Bureau and then devoted his life to lobbying for laws to prohibit the sale and use of such drugs as heroin and marijuana; he succeeded both in the United States and with the United Nations. The temperance forces that supported Prohibition were also moral entrepreneurs; they distributed leaflets and posters to convince people of the evils of alcohol, claiming that it led to degeneracy and the breakup of the family. A recent moral entrepreneur is Anita Bryant, who has lobbied against efforts to grant homosexuals equal rights; her efforts were curtailed when she revealed that her own behavior sometimes violated social norms.

Not all moral entrepreneurs seek to prohibit behavior. E. M. Jellinek (1960) spent years trying to convince the United States government, the medical establishment, law enforcement agencies, and the United Nations that alcoholism should be treated as a disease rather than as a crime or a sin. To a large extent he was successful in altering the social definition of alcoholism.

THE MEDICALIZATION OF DEVIANCE

Jellinek's efforts were part of a trend in the social redefinition of deviance in the twentieth century—the increasing interpretation of rule breaking in medical terms (Conrad and Schneider, 1980). The social definitions of behavior such as alcoholism, drug addiction, and homosexuality have been "medicalized." Heroin addiction is still regarded as a law enforcement problem in the United States, but the opening of methadone clinics in the 1960s represents a willingness by law enforcers to deal with addiction through medical treatment. Since 1920, Great Britain has dealt with addiction as a medical problem; addicts register with the government and are given prescriptions for addictive drugs by their physicians (Judson, 1974; Trebach, 1982). Until the late 1970s, homosexuality was defined as a medical or psychiatric problem in the United States, but gay rights groups have succeeded in getting the American Psychiatric Association to "demedicalize" homosexuality.

In spite of the trend toward medicalizing deviance, law enforcement continues to play a major role in dealing with rule-breakers in American society. For example, in the 1940s various communities organized and established committees to write new laws to deal with sex offenders, usually after a series of sex crimes had been committed in the community. Psychiatrists were called in to help design these laws, and so the social definition of sex crimes was in part medical, even though the end result was the passage of new laws to punish sex offenders through the criminal justice system (Sutherland, 1950).

THE FUNCTIONS AND DYSFUNCTIONS OF DEVIANCE

What consequences does deviance have for society? You would probably first think of the dysfunctions, or negative effects, of behavior that breaks the rules. Assault, rape, and murder hurt people physically. Vandalism and theft destroy or cause the loss of property. Suicide and alcoholism harm those close to the persons who commit the deviant acts, as well as the deviants themselves.

Aside from the effects of deviance on its victims, the violation of norms can also disturb social peace. Functionalists often regard deviation from society's norms as harmful to the social order; in extreme cases, deviance can cause citizens to withdraw support from the government and the social system. Conflict theorists are more likely to see deviance as the product of social inequality, and they often point out that "deviance" is an emotion-charged word used by groups with power to protect their advantaged position in society.

Deviance has positive consequences for society as well as dysfunctions. Behavior that violates norms alerts people to their shared interests; when confronted with a rule-breaker, people reflect on the shared norm that has been broken. The French sociologist Emile Durkheim suggested that deviance may actually bring a group closer together by accentuating their shared norms, but deviance such as serious crime can also cause mistrust within a community (Durkheim, 1893, 1933; Conklin, 1975).

The violation of norms establishes the boundaries of behavior for a group (Erikson, 1966). Norms are often vague guides to behavior, and behavior that tests the limits of tolerable behavior makes the group's expectations clearer by forcing the group to define and defend its boundaries of accepted behavior.

The responses of a group to rule-breaking behavior can also be functional in deterring people from certain acts. A negative sanction applied to one rule-breaker can dissuade other potential violators from deviating from the same rule (see Chapter 15). If some people gain advantages over others by breaking rules, the rest of society may become angry, even to the extent of taking direct action against suspected deviants. Sanctions applied to rule-breakers by institutions such as the courts may be functional in preventing such vigilante action.

Deviance is also functional in that it allows people to "blow off steam," which prevents frustration from building up and possibly causing political and social upheaval. Deviant behavior also serves to warn those in positions of authority about social discontent and defects in the social structure that can be remedied through new social policies. In this way, rule-breaking behavior can be a source of social change. For example, the high crime rate of young black males who live in large cities has made government officials more aware of and concerned about the high unemployment rate of this group and the need to create more jobs for them.

SOCIAL CONTROL

In spite of the functions that deviance serves for society, most societies try to inhibit the violation of norms and laws. Groups with power use the law to impose their own values and norms on the rest of the society. The conflict perspective treats the law—the set of norms formalized by a political authority—as the product of competition among groups to define the standards of the society. Functionalists regard the law as a reflection of the norms shared by the members of society; law enforcement is treated as an effort to maintain the consensus that gave rise to the law.

Both functionalists and conflict theorists are aware that the law is only one way to control be-havior. Other mechanisms of *social control*, the process that brings about conformity to society's norms, include the family, the school, peer groups, and organized religion. Socialization is the primary means of social control. This *informal* mechanism of social control is especially important in the first few years of life, but as we saw in Chapter 4, socialization continues throughout the life cycle. Through socialization the members of society learn values and norms that guide their behavior. They also learn the motivation to conform to society's norms. According to one hypothesis, deviance is the result of the defective socialization of people who break the rules.

Deviance is more common in some communities than in others, suggesting that the structure of a community may be related to the frequency of rule-breaking behavior. In communities where people remain relatively anonymous, there is less informal pressure to conform from relatives, friends, and neighbors than in communities where everyone is known to each other. Crime and other

"How do I feel about being mugged? Well, naturally I didn't enjoy it and I certainly don't condone violence or threats of violence as a means toward social change. However, I can empathize with my assailant and realize that in his terms this is a valid response to the deteriorating socio-economic situation in which we find ourselves."

Drawing by Lorenz; © The New Yorker Magazine, Inc.

forms of deviance are more common in large cities than in small towns, in part because the informal control of behavior is weaker in large communities where people are less likely to know their neighbors. Within large cities, some communities have more deviance than others. One reason is that potential rule-breakers are more likely to be deterred by knowing they will provoke negative responses from residents of certain communities (Conklin, 1975). One architect has even suggested that it is possible to design public housing that creates a "defensible space," an area in and near a building that will be relatively crime-free because residents feel a sense of territoriality and will challenge intruders who might commit crime in that area (Newman, 1972).

Socialization and community structure are often effective informal social controls, but formal controls such as the criminal justice system are often thought to be most important in the control of rule-breaking. Residents of communities with little crime often attribute their low rate to the effectiveness of informal controls such as socialization and community action. People who live in areas with a lot of crime commonly attribute that high rate to the ineffectiveness of formal controls such as the police and the courts (Boggs, 1971).

In recent years, there has been considerable debate over whether the police can reduce crime. The low rate at which the police arrest suspects may not pose enough risk to offenders to stop them from violating the law; the police in the United States arrest a suspect in only one-fifth of all serious crimes that are reported, and many of those suspects are either not convicted, or, if they are convicted, do not go to prison. A well-designed study done in Kansas City, Missouri, found that the number of police patrol cars in an area was not related to how much crime that area had (Kelling et al., 1974). Some American cities have four times as many police officers per capita as other cities, but there is no apparent relationship between the size of the police force and a city's crime rate (President's Commission on Law Enforcement and Administration of Justice, 1967: 96, 106). Supporters of the police suggest that the police could reduce crime if they had more personnel and resources, if the courts convicted more suspects, and if offenders were sentenced to longer prison terms. However, there is little evidence that such changes could be made without abridging constitutional rights or that crime rates would drop even if these changes were made. Formal mechanisms of controlling deviance are probably less effective than the informal means of socialization and community control, even though Americans and their political leaders have repeatedly turned to the criminal justice system to reduce crime rates.

Sociological Theories of Deviance

Many explanations of deviant behavior have been proposed. An early theory was Cesare Lombroso's (Ferrero, 1911) idea that criminals are biological reversions to a more primitive stage of humanity; a more recent explanation focuses on the role of abnormal chromosomal patterns (Witkin et al., 1976). There are, in addition to these biological theories, several psychological ones, which claim deviance to result from feeblemindedness and criminal personality traits. Here we focus on four major sociological explanations of deviance and crime.

The first theory we examine is strain theory, which traces the source of deviance such as suicide, crime, and mental illness to *anomie*, the sense of normlessness and frustration that is a product of the way that society is organized. The second theory we examine also looks at the important role that social ties play in determining whether a person will violate norms. A third approach to the study of deviance is cultural transmission theory, which proposes that deviance is learned in much the same way that conforming behavior is learned—from others, through the socialization process.

These three theories consider deviance as a form of behavior to be explained, even though each theory uses different ideas to explain rule-breaking. The fourth theory is the labeling perspective, an approach derived from interactionism and conflict theory. The labeling perspective distinguishes between rule-breaking, which is simply behavior that violates a norm, and deviance, which is rule-breaking that has been labeled and treated in negative ways by a group. The labeling perspective also looks at the role of group dominance; certain groups that have more power control the enactment and enforcement of norms and laws and impose their definition of deviance on others.

STRAIN THEORY

Strain theory suggests that the organization or disorganization of society causes anomie, which leaves people confused about what norms should regulate their behavior. Strain develops when these norms are unclear or in conflict with other norms, or when they fail to provide opportunities for people to meet their needs. This leads to frustration, a sense of rootlessness, and uncertainty, which often produce behavior that violates social norms.

Durkheim's Study of Suicide

The idea of anomie was first used to explain deviant behavior by Emile Durkheim (1897, 1951) in his study of suicide. Durkheim used official statistics to examine the social sources of suicide. He concluded that suicide occurs when people are insufficiently integrated into social groups (egoistic suicide), and when they are excessively integrated into social groups (altruistic suicide). Suicide can also be caused by the insufficient regulation of people by social norms (anomic suicide) and by the excessive regulation of people by social norms (fatalistic suicide).

Egoistic suicide is common among people who are isolated from strong group supports. Durkheim used this concept to explain why Jews had lower suicide rates than Catholics, and why Catholics had lower suicide rates than Protestants. He suggested that among Protestants there is less integration into the religious group than for the other two groups, and that Jews are the most strongly integrated into a religious group. Egoistic suicide was also more common among unmarried people than among married people of the same age, and more common among married people without children than among those with children.

The opposite condition of excessive integration into a group accounts for those rare cases of altruistic suicide when people sacrifice their lives for the good of others. This explanation fits the Eskimo practice of suicide among the elderly and the infirm who cannot contribute to their own survival; the Hindu practice of *suttee*, in which widows throw themselves on the funeral pyres of their deceased husbands; and the Japanese practice of *junshi*, in which a leader's followers kill themselves to follow him into the hereafter.

Fatalistic suicide is a rare type that occurs when a person is excessively regulated by social norms. Durkheim dealt with this only in a footnote and saw it as an explanation of suicide among slaves. Anomic suicide, on the other hand, arises from inadequate regulation by social norms. Durkheim saw anomie as the cause of suicide that resulted from rapid economic and social change that left people unsure about how to behave.

One interpretation of Durkheim's theory of suicide suggests that it might be more simply reformulated as follows: "The *more* integrated (regulated) a society, group or social condition is, the *lower* its suicide rate. . . . The *higher* the level of egoism (anomie) prevailing in a society, group, or social condition, the *higher* the suicide rate" (Johnson, 1965: 886).

Merton's Theory of Anomie

An important effort to link anomie to deviant behavior was made in 1938 by Robert K. Merton (1968). Merton distinguishes between culturally defined goals such as material success and the norms that regulate the means to achieve those goals. In American society, material success is, for many, a symbol of personal worth, and the culture includes norms about how this societal goal is to be reached. These norms derive from the values of the culture, not from their efficiency in achieving societal goals. A bank robbery may be a quick way to get a few thousand dollars, but it is prohibited by the law. On the other hand, working at a job may be a less efficient way to get rich, but it is a socially approved way.

Equilibrium exists when people who use the accepted means achieve socially approved goals and experience satisfaction. When the goals and the means are not in harmony, anomie or normlessness results. Merton is a functionalist, and he sees this disequilibrium or anomie as dysfunctional to society. Anomie can cause deviant behavior when people are denied access to accepted means to reach approved goals, which they have been socialized to believe they actually can attain. For instance, in the United States women and minority-group members have more difficulty than men and white Anglo-Saxon Protestants (WASPs) in gaining access to the jobs that lead to financial success; according to Merton's theory, we would expect anomie to be more common among women and minorities.

Merton developed a model, shown in Table 5.1, of five ways that people who find themselves in different social circumstances adapt to societal goals and the approved means to reach those goals. The first mode of adaptation is "conformity," the condition in which people accept both the societal goals and the approved means to reach them. Functionalists see the congruence between goals and means as functional for society, but a conflict theorist might argue that the goals that some groups aspire to are the product of socialization by a dominant class, and not in their own best interest.

TABLE 5.1
Merton's Five Modes of Adaptation

Modes of adaptation	Societal goals	Approved means
I. Conformity	Accept	Accept
II. Innovation	Accept	Reject
III. Ritualism	Reject	Accept
IV. Retreatism	Reject	Reject
V. Rebellion	Reject, and substitute new goals	Reject, and substitute new means

Source: From Robert K. Merton, *Social Theory and Social Structure,* 1968 enlarged edition. New York: Free Press, 1968, p. 194. Used by permission.

"Innovation" is the mode of adaptation whereby people seek to achieve approved goals by means that are not approved by the society. This is especially common when the goal is strongly desired, as material well-being is in the United States. Innovation describes a variety of types of rule-breaking. It includes both embezzlement of funds by well-paid corporate executives and theft by poor people to feed their families. Innovation was the basis for the rise of organized crime in the United States. The domination of organized crime today by Italian-Americans has been attributed to the fact that when Italians arrived in the United States, they found commerce and business controlled by WASPs and big-city political machines controlled by Irish-Americans. As a result, some Italian immigrants turned to organized crime during the Prohibition Era as a way to achieve material well-being through disapproved means (Bell, 1962).

The third mode of adaptation in Merton's analysis is "ritualism," the condition in which a person continues to behave in an expected fashion after abandoning any hope of achieving societal goals. A worker who takes a job when young, hoping to climb the corporate ladder, but finds years later that he or she has not advanced very far, may continue to work at the job but give up any idea of success.

"Retreatism" involves a rejection of both societal goals and institutionalized means to reach those goals. Drug addicts and skid-row alcoholics no longer seek material success, nor do they engage in the approved means of legitimate work. Some forms of retreatism are defined as crime because they seem to be a challenge or affront to those who strongly believe in societal goals.

The fifth mode of adaptation is "rebellion." Rebels reject societal goals and substitute new ones in their place; they also replace accepted means with new ones. Behind the rebel's attempt to change the goals and the means is the desire to create a new social order. To this end, rebels may even commit political crimes, but their acts are motivated by an altruistic wish to improve the lot of others, not a desire to improve their personal well-being (Schafer, 1974).

Anomie and Gang Delinquency

One explanation of juvenile delinquency relies on Merton's approach and also draws from cultural transmission theory (which we look at later): Cloward and Ohlin's (1960) theory of differential opportunity. They suggest that Merton did not go far enough by only looking at some people's lack of access to legitimate opportunities; they argue that not everyone has equal access to *illegitimate* opportunities either. In other words, when access to the approved means to reach societal goals is blocked, some people will turn to innovation, but not everyone has the opportunity to innovate successfully.

Cloward and Ohlin regard delinquency as a product of the opportunities available for adolescents to reach socially approved goals through legitimate and illegitimate means. They describe three types of delinquent gangs: criminal gangs that seek material gain through theft, conflict gangs that seek peer approval through fighting, and retreatist gangs that use drugs. Criminal gangs innovate in their quest for societal goals; they do this through illegal acts of theft. Conflict gangs develop in neighborhoods where adolescents lack both legitimate *and* illegitimate means to attain material success; the absence of both job opportunities and lucrative criminal careers leads them to form gangs, in which they can gain prestige among their peers by being tough. Cloward and Ohlin suggest that "double failures"—those who cannot use either legitimate or illegitimate means to achieve success and who lack the skill to be good fighters—turn to retreatist gangs that use drugs.

Another interpretation of gang delinquency that is based on Merton's theory of anomie is Albert Cohen's (1955) theory. Cohen concluded that working-class boys develop norms and values that are the opposite of those of the dominant culture because they feel that the educational system and the job market thwart their chances of attaining success. The norms and values they create are the reverse of the middle-class norms and values by which they are negatively judged. Middle-class culture favors the control of aggression, so these youths reward each other for violent behavior. Middle-class values revere property, so they engage in vandalism to destroy property. The middle-class defers pleasure until the future, so gangs seek immediate gratification.

Assessing Strain Theory

Strain theory is most easily applied to instrumental acts that violate norms—that is, behavior in which the deviant seeks to attain some goal by violating a rule. Robbery and white-collar crime can be interpreted as innovations to achieve societally approved goals. However, strain theory does not contribute much to our understanding of certain types of expressive deviance, such as impulsive murder, rape, and homosexuality, which give vent to emotions such as rage or sexual desire.

Strain theories assume that rule-breakers are frustrated by their efforts to achieve societal goals, and this assumption has some problems. Some research indicates that deviants are not in fact more frustrated than nondeviants, nor do deviants necessarily have different goals and norms (Short and Strodtbeck, 1965; Hirschi, 1969). Strain theories also assume that it is possible to describe a set of societal goals, but as we saw in Chapter 3 most cultures in industrial societies contain a diversity of cultural and countercultural themes. Still, strain theory does describe an important factor that underlies some rule-breaking—the quest for societal goals in a social system in which the approved means are limited or distributed differentially among groups.

CONTROL THEORY

Control theory extends Durkheim's idea that social ties among people are important determinants of behavior. This theory claims that people who lack intimate attachments to parents, teachers, and peers and who also lack the aspirations and moral beliefs that link them to a law-abiding life are free to violate norms. Freedom from social attachments and cultural norms means that the opinions of other people matter little, leaving the individual free to break the law or violate a norm with little fear of social disapproval. This theory assumes that from time to time everyone has the impulse to deviate, and that the attachments to others and to conventional behavior inhibit many people from deviating more often than they do. One control theorist says that the theory is not designed to tell us why people deviate. Instead, he says, "The question is, 'Why don't we do it?' There is much evidence that we would if we dared" (Hirschi, 1969: 34).

In our examination of research methods in Chapter 2, we saw that Travis Hirschi discovered that adolescent delinquents are much less closely tied to their parents than boys of the same age who do not engage in delinquency. Other research indicates that heroin addicts also have weaker ties to their parents than those who do not use heroin (Chein et al., 1964). What is important in inhibiting deviance is the "psychological presence" of parents in the mind of an individual who has an opportunity to break a rule; the actual physical presence of the parents is less important. Those who are more intimately involved with their parents are more concerned with their good opinion, and this close bond restrains deviant behavior of which the parents would disapprove.

Delinquency is least common in families in which there is good communication between parents and children. Divorce has often been cited as a cause of delinquency, but there seems to be a weaker relationship between delinquency and divorce than between delinquency and the *quality* of the relationship between children and their parents. The relatively weak relationship between divorce and delinquency is probably explained by the fact than many single parents communicate well with their children and thus inhibit deviant behavior, whereas some parents in intact families do not

Control theory holds that social ties among people are important determinants of behavior: Freedom from intimate attachments to parents, teachers, and peers leaves the individual freer to violate norms.

communicate well with their children and leave them free of the controls that would inhibit rule-breaking.

The school is another institution that is important in controlling delinquency. Students who are successful academically are less apt to engage in delinquency because they are more attached to the school and its teachers than are students who do not do well. Adolescents are more apt to be delinquent if they are not concerned with their teachers' opinions of them. Academic incompetence leads students to dislike school and reject the authority of teachers and administrators; this reduces controls that would otherwise inhibit delinquent behavior. Delinquents who do not have close relationships with their teachers are also more likely to have weak relationships with their parents (Hirschi, 1969).

There is mixed evidence about the importance of peers to delinquents. Hirschi found that, compared to nondelinquents of the same age, delinquents are less likely to have close relationships with their peers. Delinquents also tend to view those with whom they spend time in a negative light, and they are less apt than nondelinquents to say they have close friends (Hirschi, 1969). Other studies indicate that delinquents band together for mutual support and see their gangs as a source of prestige and camaraderie (Cohen, 1955; Cloward and Ohlin, 1960; Empey and Lubeck, 1971). Another view of

juvenile gangs is that they are loosely structured groups in which members are only minimally committed to each other (Yablonsky, 1966). Juvenile gangs probably provide many delinquents with their closest social relationships, even though in absolute terms those bonds are not very strong.

Control theory proposes that individuals who have conventional goals such as education and work are inhibited from engaging in delinquent behavior or other forms of deviance because such rule-breaking would jeopardize their pursuit of socially approved goals. Those who do not aspire to conventional goals are free to deviate from social norms. They may even gain social rewards from violating norms, because their deviance is a demonstration to themselves and others that they do not regard conventional goals as worth pursuing. Delinquents who see a bleak future for themselves often feel that their high school years and the years immediately afterward will be the happiest period of their lives. This frees them from conventional pursuits like education and work, leaving them in a situation in which they can deviate with little fear of losing something of value to them.

Neutralizing Social Norms

The socialization process teaches everyone to abide by social norms to some extent, and yet most of us deviate from norms at times. How is this possible?

Before people can violate norms, they must have some justification for committing the deviant act. Even people who become hardened criminals or committed deviants must at some point justify their initial violation of a norm they have learned through socialization.

There are in the culture a set of justifications that have been called *techniques of neutralization* (Sykes and Matza, 1957). These techniques, which are learned through socialization, are a central part of control theory because they provide a mechanism by which people can break their bonds to the conventional world that would inhibit them from violating rules. These techniques of neutralization are often learned through the process of cultural transmission, which we examine shortly.

One technique of neutralization is the "denial of responsibility," the claim that a deviant act was an accident or was due to forces beyond the individual's control, such as negligent parents or wayward friends. This technique enables people to deny that they are personally responsible for their behavior, thus making it easier for them to break rules they know that most people accept. Delinquents use this technique to explain why they break windows with their friends, and President Nixon used this technique when he blamed his staff members for the Watergate burglary.

Another technique is the "denial of injury," the claim that no one is hurt by certain acts that "technically" violate norms. Robbers sometimes justify theft by claiming that their victims can recover their losses from their insurance company, even though the company and its clients lose in the end. Auto thieves justify their crimes with the claim that they only "borrowed the car temporarily" and did not intend to deprive the owner of the car permanently. Shoplifting in large department stores is sometimes rationalized with the claim that the company can afford the loss.

"Denial of the victim" is a technique that is used to justify a deviant act as rightful retaliation against

---

SOCIOLOGY AND EVERYDAY LIFE 5.1
Justifying a Life of Crime

Criminals often give elaborate justifications for their repeated violations of the law. When asked whom he blamed for the events of his life—which included heroin addiction, theft, work for organized crime, imprisonment, and drug therapy—one man offered the following justification:

Society created the situation where you have to have dope fiends. Dope fiends exist, not because they are pathological inferior humans, but because people make millions off the poppy, the pharmaceuticals—and booze, for that matter. . . .
   Everybody in control of this system contributes to criminality, drug addiction, and the bone-raped, insular poverty of our ghettos. Somehow, some way, in our modern industrial society we have created numerous situations and conditions where people are unhappy, alienated, disgusted. Especially poor folks and disenfranchised minorities. The pressures of making it on the square get too difficult. Life gets too harsh too early, and you turn to drugs, or wine, or just robbing and killing (Rettig, Torres, and Garrett, p. 175).

A professional fence—a receiver in stolen goods who buys things cheaply from thieves and resells them to a public that is looking for a bargain—gives another kind of justification for a career of crime:

The way I look at it, I'm a businessman. Sure I buy hot stuff, but I never stole nothin' in my life. Some driver brings me a couple of cartons, though, I ain't gonna turn him away. If I don't buy it, somebody else will. So what's the difference? I might as well make money with him instead of somebody else (Klockars, p. 139).

This justification is factually wrong on a number of counts: This fence did steal when younger, he was legally committing theft as a fence, and it is not clear that thieves would know another fence to buy the merchandise they had stolen. This fence also rationalized his crimes by pointing out that the companies from which the property had been stolen were very profitable and were insured against losses. Overall, he saw his criminal activities as no reason to condemn him:

Sure I've done some bad things in my life. Who hasn't? Everybody's got a skeleton in his closet somewhere. But you gotta take into account all the good things I done too. You take all the things I done in my life and put 'em together, no doubt about it, I gotta come out on the good side (Klockars, p. 151).

Sources: Based on Carl B. Klockars, *The Professional Fence.* New York: Free Press, 1974; and Richard P. Rettig, Manual J. Torres, and Gerald R. Garrett, *Manny: A Criminal-Addict's Story.* Boston: Houghton Mifflin, 1977.

someone who deserves to be victimized, such as the government, a prostitute, a homosexual, an unscrupulous shopkeeper, or a large corporation. This technique is often used to justify deviant acts against groups that the larger society defines as deviant.

The "condemnation of the condemners" is a technique used by a deviant to blame those who make and enforce the rules for being no better than those who are accused of violating the rules. This "you do, too" attitude rationalizes breaking the rules by pointing to police brutality and corruption or to deviance by people in positions of power and influence. Some people convicted of tax evasion a few years ago pointed out that they were no worse than President Nixon, who had underpaid his own taxes by more than $400,000.

Another technique that is used to justify the violation of norms is the "appeal to higher loyalties," the assertion that the demands of a group to which one belongs—such as a juvenile gang or a corporation—require behavior that violates the norms or laws of some larger group. Using "national security" to justify burglarizing the offices of a political opponent or "going along with the guys" as a reason for breaking windows are examples of appealing to loyalties higher than the law.

Techniques of neutralization are part of the general culture. They are closely related to widely accepted values, such as lack of hypocrisy and loyalty to others. These techniques enable people to justify rule-breaking without feeling morally unworthy. Though there is limited research on whether rule-breakers actually use techniques of neutralization before violating norms, some research supports the idea that these techniques are an essential part of the process by which people free themselves from controls that would otherwise inhibit deviance (Cressey, 1953, 1971; Hirschi, 1969; Davis, 1974).

Assessing Control Theory

Control theory distinguishes between rule-breakers and conformists in the areas of attachment to other people and the pursuit of conventional courses of action. The assumption that everyone has impulses to violate norms is probably accurate, but we lack good information about the frequency with which different people have impulses to break rules. Some people probably have these impulses more often than others, and this, as well as the lack of social bonds, may account for differences in the rates of deviance among people.

The sequence of events leading to deviance has not yet been specified by control theory (Wiatrowski, Griswold, and Roberts, 1981). It is not clear that the techniques of neutralization are always used before a norm is violated; they may sometimes be used after a deviant act is committed, to rationalize it. Weak ties to other people may lead to deviance, but the violation of a norm can also weaken ties to other people. Poor relationships with parents can free adolescents to engage in delinquency, but a child's being labeled delinquent in juvenile court can also prompt parents to rejection. Control theory identifies important factors involved in rule-breaking behavior, but it has yet to show exactly how these variables are related to deviance.

CULTURAL TRANSMISSION THEORY

Cultural transmission theory explains deviant behavior in terms of socialization to norms, motives, and skills that differ from those of the dominant culture. Walter Miller (1958) has proposed that lower-class delinquents violate the law because they conform to norms and values that are part of a lower-class culture in which they have been socialized. This set of norms and values includes the themes of trouble, toughness, smartness, excitement, fate, and autonomy. Miller identifies the content of the values and norms that he claims are related to delinquency, but he does not develop a theory of how those values and norms are learned.

The most influential effort to examine the way that rule-breakers learn the motives and the skills to violate norms is *differential association theory*, a form of cultural transmission theory developed by Edwin H. Sutherland (1978). Differential association theory seeks to explain why individuals become criminal and why crime rates vary from group to group in society. This theory is very general; as a result, it has stimulated more theoretical work than empirical research.

Differential association theory states that all criminal behavior is learned; it denies the effect of biological inheritance on such behavior. This theory claims that crime is not invented anew by individuals but is learned through face-to-face interaction with other people. Criminals learn from others both the motives to violate the law and the specific techniques of crime. The mass media are considered unimportant in this learning process. This omission may be due to the fact that Sutherland developed his theory before television became widespread.

Differential association theory assumes that people orient their behavior to the law. Through socialization everyone learns "definitions favorable to violation of the law" and "definitions unfavorable to violation of the law." Some people learn to see an unattended bicycle as an opportunity for theft (a definition favorable to violation of the law), but others perceive the same situation as a chance to warn the owner about a potential theft (a definition unfavorable to violation of the law).

The "principle of differential association," the crux of Sutherland's theory, states that people become criminal when they have *more* definitions that support violation of the law than definitions that oppose violation of the law. Everyone learns both types of definitions; it is the ratio of the two that determines behavior. In addition to the number of each type of definition, Sutherland considers the length of time during which people are exposed to each kind of definition, how early in childhood these perceptions of the law develop, and the source of the definition. For example, prolonged exposure at an early age to definitions favorable to violation of the law that are transmitted by parents is more important in causing criminal behavior than fleeting exposure in adulthood to definitions favorable to violation of the law that are transmitted by a neighbor or co-worker.

Differential association theory has been modified and extended in other cultural transmission theories (Akers, 1977). One such theory focuses on the way that people choose models for their behavior, suggesting that the modeling process does not necessarily require direct interaction with others. This theory, which has been called "differential identification theory," proposes that "a person pursues criminal behavior to the extent that he identifies himself with real or imaginary persons from whose perspective his criminal behavior seems acceptable" (Glaser, 1956: 440).

Assessing Cultural Transmission Theory

One of the shortcomings of cultural transmission theory is that it explains *how* criminal behavior develops but not *why* it does. In other words, this theory focuses on the process of learning but does not describe the social structure that provides the opportunities for this process to occur. This is in contrast to both strain theory and control theory, which focus on the organization of social relationships that are conducive to criminal behavior.

Cultural transmission theory, especially differential association theory, has been criticized for being so general that it is difficult or even impossible to test. There is much evidence that is consistent with differential association theory, even though this evidence does not usually test hypotheses that have been derived from a formal statement of the theory. Juvenile delinquents often learn criminal motives and skills from their peers in gangs, and they are cut off from definitions unfavorable to violation of the law because of their weak ties to parents and teachers. Professional thieves also learn how to commit crime from other thieves. For instance, pickpockets learn specific skills from other thieves; part of their socialization to this trade involves learning a complex "argot," a specialized language that they use to describe the world (Maurer, 1964). Call girls—expensive prostitutes who contact clients from their apartments by phone—undergo an apprenticeship during which they learn from pimps and from other call girls how to deal with clients (minimize interaction), how to regard their clients (as exploitative but exploitable), and how to work (with a minimum of effort and without drugs) (Bryan, 1965, 1966). White-collar criminals learn values, norms, motives, and skills from others in the business world and to some extent are cut off from outside pressures to abide by the law. This situation is conducive to learning behavior such as bribing foreign officials and collusion with other executives to fix prices (Conklin, 1977: 83–85).

Not all evidence is consistent with differential association theory. Research on offenders in rural communities, check forgers, and rent-control violators does not support the theory (Clinard, 1944, 1952, 1969; Lemert, 1953). Still, the bulk of research is at least compatible with this cultural transmission theory, even though it does not prove the theory in a definitive way.

THE LABELING PERSPECTIVE

The three theories of deviance and crime that we have examined so far all try to explain rule-breaking behavior. Strain theory, control theory, and cultural transmission theory search for the causes of deviant behavior, either in the culture and the social structure or in the background of the deviants themselves. In recent years, sociologists have developed a different way of looking at rule-breaking behavior that is known as the *labeling perspective*.

This approach focuses on the interaction between rule-breakers and those who label or stigmatize them as deviants. This perspective treats deviance as *problematic*: in other words, sociologists should study the process by which behavior comes to be called deviant rather than assume that deviance has a reality of its own apart from what people make of rule-breaking behavior. This perspective pays little attention to the background of rule-breakers, and focuses instead on their interaction with the people who label them deviant. This perspective treats deviance "not as a static entity but rather as a continuously shaped and reshaped *outcome* of dynamic processes of social interaction" (Schur, 1971: 8). The labeling perspective carefully examines the ways that the label of deviant affects the self-concepts of rule-breakers, closes social opportunities (such as jobs) to them, gives rise to organized groups of deviants such as the gay rights movement, and pushes rule-breakers into deviant careers.

Like control theory, the labeling perspective assumes that from time to time many people have impulses to break rules, even though they usually do not act on those impulses. Some people intend to break rules; they may avoid the constraints of socialization to conventional norms if they are already free of attachments to others who support those norms. Other people use the techniques of neutralization to justify their violations of norms. However, not everyone who violates a norm intends to do so; some break rules accidentally or because they are ignorant of the rules. Whether the rule-breaking is intended or not, people sometimes respond to the individual who violates a norm as a deviant, beginning a labeling process that often forces the rule-breaker into a socially constructed category of deviant or outsider (Becker, 1973).

Labeling is done by people who sift details of behavior from an individual's broad repertoire of actions, and then use those details to create a "master status," a definition of the individual in terms of a single label (Kitsuse, 1964; Erikson, 1966). A professional football player who sells insurance in the off-season will be labeled a homosexual if he is discovered engaging in sex with another man; the many other characteristics of this person are played down and his identity becomes that of homosexual. This process of sifting through the details of a rule-breaker's life and then recasting that person's identity in terms of deviance includes stereotyping, retrospective interpretation, negotiation, and role engulfment (Schur, 1971, 1979). Organizations also play an important part in processing rule-breakers and treating them as deviants.

Stereotyping

Rule-breakers are often seen in terms of the stereotypes shared by many members of society. *Stereotypes* are caricatures or simplified pictures that sometimes contain an element of truth but exaggerate the differences between those they depict and the rest of the society. Stereotypes allow some people to see themselves as "normal" and therefore different from the outsiders who are labeled deviant. Stereotypes are a part of the culture and are learned from parents, teachers, peers, and the mass media. In SEL 5.2 we can see how the mentally ill are stereotyped; these stereotypes determine how the mentally ill are treated by others and even how they see themselves. These stereotypes may also inhibit some people from seeking needed psychiatric care because of a fear of being labeled mentally ill.

SOCIOLOGY AND EVERYDAY LIFE 5.2
Stereotypes of the Mentally Ill

Deviant behavior develops in a social context that includes the stereotyping of those who do not conform to norms. This selection examines the stereotypes that are commonly used to describe people who have been labeled mentally ill.

In newspapers it is a common practice to mention that a rapist or a murderer was once a mental patient. Here are several examples: Under the headline "Question Girl in Child Slaying," the story begins, "A 15-year-old girl *with a history of mental illness* is being ques-

tioned in connection with a kidnap-slaying of a 3-year-old boy." A similar story under the headline "Man Killed, Two Policemen Hurt in Hospital Fray," begins "A *former mental patient* grabbed a policeman's revolver and began shooting at 15 persons in the receiving room of City Hospital No. 2 Thursday."

Often acts of violence will be connected with mental illness on the basis of little or no evidence. For instance, under the headline "Milwaukee Man Goes Beserk, Shoots Officer," the story describes the events and then quotes a police captain who said, "He may be a mental case." In another story, under the headline, "Texas Dad Kills Self, Four Children, Daughter Says," the last sentence of the story is "One report said Kinsey (the killer) was once a mental patient." In most large newspapers there apparently is at least one such story in every issue.

Even if the coverage of these acts of violence was highly accurate, it would still give the reader a misleading impression because negative information is seldom offset by positive reports. An item like the following is almost inconceivable:

Mrs. Ralph Jones, an ex-mental patient, was elected president of the Fairview Home and Garden Society at their meeting last Thursday.

Because of highly biased reporting, the reader is free to make the unwarranted inference that murder and rape and other acts of violence occur more frequently among former mental patients than among the population at large. Actually it has been demonstrated that the incidence of crimes of violence (or of any crime) is much lower among former mental patients than in the general population. Yet, because of newspaper practice, this is not the picture presented to the public. Newspapers have established an ineluctable relationship between mental illness and violence. Perhaps as importantly, this connection also signifies the incurability of mental disorder; that is, it connects *former* mental patients with violent and unpredictable acts. . . .

Reaffirmation of the stereotype of insanity occurs not only in the mass media but indirectly in ordinary conversation: in jokes, anecdotes, and even in conventional phrases. Such phrases as "are you crazy?" or "it would be a madhouse," or "it's driving me out of my mind," or "we were chatting like crazy," or "he was running like mad," and literally hundreds of others occur frequently in informal conversations. In this usage, insanity itself is seldom the topic of conversation, and the discussants do not mean to refer to the topic of insanity, and are usually unaware that they are doing so.

I have overheard mental patients, when talking among themselves, using these phrases unthinkingly. Even those mental health workers, such as psychiatrists, psychologists, and social workers, who are most interested in changing the concept of mental disorder often use these terms—sometimes jokingly but usually unthinkingly—in their informal discussions. These terms are so much a part of ordinary language that only the person who considers every word carefully can eliminate them from his speech. Through verbal usage, the stereotype of insanity is an inflexible part of the social structure.

Source: Thomas J. Scheff, *Being Mentally Ill: A Sociological Theory.* Hawthorne, N.Y.: Aldine Publishing Company, 1966, pp. 71–76. Used by permission.

Stereotypes in our society may lead some members to label this group of adolescents a gang of "juvenile delinquents."

The stereotype of deviant is sometimes used to close off opportunities to people, forcing them instead to behave in some way that is consistent with the stereotype. During the 1972 presidential campaign, when it was revealed that he had undergone shock treatment for psychiatric problems in the past, Senator Thomas Eagleton withdrew as Democratic candidate for Vice-President. The stereotype of mental illness thus closed off the opportunity for him to serve in high office.

Retrospective Interpretation

Closely related to the stereotyping of rule-breakers is *retrospective interpretation* (Schur, 1979: 231–240). This is a process by which people respond to an act of rule-breaking by reassessing the individual as a whole person, searching for other behavior or characteristics that seem compatible with the rule-breaking. The process of reevaluating someone who had previously appeared "normal" in light of a violation of a norm is dramatically illustrated in SEL 5.3. The process can also extend into the future as well as reflect on the past; a current act of deviance might be used as the basis for assessing all of the rule-breaker's future actions, so that otherwise "normal" behavior in the future will be seen in light of the individual's earlier rule-breaking behavior.

Retrospective interpretation sometimes takes place in "status-degradation ceremonies," rituals such as criminal trials in which a rule-breaker is publicly redefined as a deviant (Garfinkel, 1956). Sometimes a rule-breaker will have his or her identity changed by a "specialist in biographical reconstruction" such as a psychiatrist (Schur, 1971, 1979; Rosenhan, 1973). These specialists choose selectively from past behavior to develop a new identity for the individual as a deviant. This process of redefining rule-breakers is functional for these specialists, because those who interpret the meaning of past behavior through the filter of knowledge about current rule-breaking often gain prestige and income from their work with those who violate norms (Szasz, 1970).

SOCIOLOGY AND EVERYDAY LIFE 5.3
"Can I Tell You a Secret?": A Case of Retrospective Interpretation

This exchange occurred a few years ago between two men who had been friends for many years.

"Can I tell you a secret?"
"Of course," I said.
"Well, I think you ought to know that I'm going to be a woman."
I don't honestly remember what I answered. Nothing, I think, for a second or two and then, "Good God" or some such thing. After all, as more than one person who thought he knew James Morris was to remark in the next few years, "You read about this sort of thing in the newspapers sometimes, but it simply doesn't happen to your friends!" Yet as I gazed at James, with innocent astonishment, it was suddenly very clear that it was indeed happening to him.
"It won't make any difference to you, will it?" he asked anxiously; and as I shook my head, still dumbstruck, his eyes filled with tears. All at once the vaguely disturbing oddities of appearance and behavior that had been accumulating for some time around the familiar and formerly manly figure of James Morris *fell into a new and coherent shape.* There was the wonderfully youthful bloom and smoothness of his skin—previously so puzzling in a man well past 40—and the strangely high-pitched voice on the telephone; there was the growing sense of elfin shyness, as of one who belonged to some other, secret world, and, most conclusively, as James briefly and deliberately opened the jacket buttoned high over his chest, there was the reason he had developed of late a curious habit of hugging himself in round-shouldered intimacy: two budding breasts that showed beneath his shirt. A moment before he had still been James Morris to me, in spite of these hints of femininity. Now he seemed Hermaphroditus incarnate, and I wondered why on earth I hadn't guessed his secret all along.

Source: David Holden, "James and Jan," *The New York Times Magazine*, March 17, 1974, p. 19 (emphasis added here). For Morris's account of the actual sex-change operation and its effects on her attitudes and behavior, see Jan Morris, *Conundrum.* New York: Harcourt Brace Jovanovich, 1974.

Negotiation

In interaction between rule-breakers and those who label them deviants, the rule-breakers sometimes have the power to negotiate with the labelers about an appropriate label (Schur, 1971, 1979). A voluntary patient of a psychiatrist can discuss the psychiatrist's interpretation of his or her behavior, rejecting certain interpretations and accepting others. Rule-breakers sometimes reject or disavow a label altogether, feeling that the label misinterprets their actions or claiming that they have changed since the label was attached. Alcoholics Anonymous, Overeaters Anonymous, and Gamblers Anonymous are three groups that have had some success in "destigmatizing" deviants by redefining their identities.

Role Engulfment

Another aspect of the labeling process is *role engulfment*, the tendency of the labeled rule-breaker to be engulfed or swallowed up in a deviant role (Schur, 1971, 1979). Deviants first engage in "primary deviation," which is also called rule-breaking. At this stage, the individual violates a norm, but this violation is either unnoticed by others or treated as eccentric but not deviant. Only when other people respond to rule-breakers with rejection or negative sanctions such as ridicule or criminal punishment will the rule-breakers be socially defined as deviants. Primary deviation, or repeated breaking of rules, may continue for some time, but "secondary deviation" does not emerge until the behavior has been socially defined as deviant. When this happens, the rule-breaker accepts his or her identity as a deviant and organizes his or her life around this master status (Lemert, 1951).

Labeling a deviant as such often involves imputing to the rule-breaker a motive for violating socially recognized conventions. When rule-breaking is socially defined as intentional deviance, the rule-breaker may be perceived as a challenger to accepted norms. This response not only causes the deviant to adopt a new self-concept, but it often leads the deviant to associate with others who are also labeled deviant. This can set in motion the development of a deviant career, a series of stages through which the individual becomes increasingly committed to rule-breaking.

One example of role engulfment is found in Edwin Lemert's (1951) innovative study of deviance. Lemert used his concepts of primary and sec-ondary deviation to explore stuttering, a deviant form of speaking. Stuttering does not seem to have biochemical origins, but is instead a response to stress. Some societies do not even have stuttering, but it is relatively common in the United States, especially among boys around the age of six or seven. Stutterers engage in primary deviation when they have difficulty speaking, but this behavior can be repeated frequently without the speaker developing the self-concept of a stutterer. Only when parents and peers react to the child with amusement, ridicule, or unease does the speaker begin to develop the identity of stutterer. To avoid embarrassment, the child speaks less and withdraws from interaction whenever possible. Parents often respond by being overly protective, shielding the child from situations in which speech is necessary, and reducing their expectations of the child. This creates more stress and even more withdrawal from social contacts. Rejection by peers and teachers can cause the child to be quiet in class; stutterers tend to have average intelligence levels but low academic performance. The social response to stuttering thus changes the child's identity. As the child adjusts to rejection, he or she loses opportunities for social life and academic success. Eventually this can even lead the stutterer to take a low-paying job that does not require verbal skills or interaction with people. Stutterers tend to delay marriage, and they become isolated from others. In his analysis of stuttering, Lemert provides a clear example of how labeling can alter self-concepts and social behavior as primary deviation becomes secondary deviation (Lemert, 1951: 143–174).

Organizational Labeling

Labeling theorists draw attention to the power of organizations in applying labels to deviants (Schur, 1971, 1979). One sociologist even suggests that the total deviance in a society remains relatively constant over time because the capacity of the social control apparatus of a society remains roughly the same over time (Erikson, 1966). This would suggest that if the number of police officers remained the same over some period, they would make about the same number of arrests, even if one type of crime actually became less common. This idea is the reason why some prison reformers have responded negatively to proposals to build new prisons. These critics fear that more cells will simply mean more people sent to prison, rather than a reduction of prison overcrowding, the ostensible basis of most proposals to build new prisons.

The organizational processing of deviants has become an important issue in the United States during the twentieth century; some have even characterized this society as a "therapeutic state" in which the government and its agencies have increasingly taken over the treatment of deviants such as juvenile delinquents, drug addicts, alcoholics, and the mentally ill (Kittrie, 1971). The increasing use of organizations and professionals to deal with deviants creates a "buffer zone" between the public and the deviants, allowing most people to feel that deviants will be taken care of by specialists, at the same time that these deviants are isolated from the rest of society in prisons, mental institutions, and other custodial care settings. Workers in these organizations often hold stereotyped views of deviants, treat them in ways that reinforce their deviant behavior, and socialize them in a variety of ways.

One deviant-processing organization is the juvenile court. This organization first emerged in the United States in 1899 as a result of efforts by "child savers" to prevent children from being labeled criminal and sent to prisons with adults (Platt, 1977). Many sociologists today believe that the juvenile court has a labeling effect that causes those who appear before a judge to reconceptualize themselves as delinquents rather than see themselves as basically "normal" people who happen to have deviated from a norm. One study found that boys who appear in juvenile court do not think that this status-degradation ceremony will change the way that they are seen by their parents, teachers, or friends. These boys did feel that their court appearance might cause the police to pay more attention to them or might give them difficulty in finding jobs in the future (Foster, Dinitz, and Reckless, 1972).

Another organization that socializes deviants is the mental hospital (Perrucci, 1974). As a part of one study, several people with no history of mental disorder gained admission to mental hospitals by claiming that they heard voices that told them that life was empty (Rosenhan, 1973). Once they had gained admission, these pseudopatients no longer exhibited any symptoms. No one on the hospital staff recognized these people as pseudopatients; instead, they were most often labeled schizophrenic. Each patient had a case history written by an examining therapist. Many of these case histories interpreted the patient's past in terms that fit a textbook description of a schizophrenic's child-

hood. The hospital staff interpreted as signs of mental illness even such apparently normal behavior as waiting outside a cafeteria half an hour before lunch was to be served; this was perceived as a sign of the "oral-acquisitive nature of the syndrome." The pseudopatients were also given large numbers of pills to keep them under control and to help them sleep. This experiment suggests that once a person has been labeled deviant, others will treat that person in ways that are consistent with the label without necessarily reassessing the accuracy of the label.

Assessing the Labeling Perspective

The labeling perspective has made an important contribution to the sociology of deviance. It focuses on the way that norms are developed and applied to rule-breakers. It also examines the effects of a label on the rule-breaker, including changes in self-concept, behavior, and interaction with other deviants.

One criticism of the labeling perspective is that although it is very useful in describing the process by which primary deviation becomes secondary deviation, it adds little to our understanding of how and why that initial violation of the rule occurred. This criticism reflects the position that rules and violations of rules are real and distinct behaviors, and that it is necessary to ask why some people violate certain norms sometimes. Labeling theorists focus on the way that the rules are socially constructed and on the meaning given to behavior that breaks those rules, rather than on background characteristics or social arrangements that are conducive to rule-breaking behavior.

The labeling perspective does not explain very well why some rule-breaking behavior leads to changed self-concepts or to deviant careers without being labeled by others as deviance (Gove, 1980). Rule-breakers can engage in "self-labeling" of themselves as deviant, without actually being subjected to a status-degradation ceremony in which others label them. The labeling perspective does take into account the possibility that the label that others try to attach to a rule-breaker may be disavowed or accepted only in part; this perspective does not require the rule-breaker to accept the label that others try to impose.

One criticism that both functionalists and conflict theorists have leveled against labeling theory is that in its focus on the interaction between rule-breakers and those who label them, this perspective pays too little attention to aspects of the larger social structure, such as inequalities in wealth and power (Taylor, Walton, and Young, 1973; Harris and Hill, 1982). In recent years, labeling theorists have begun to incorporate some of the insights of conflict theory into their perspective by focusing on the role of inequality in making and enforcing rules.

Criminal Behavior

Over the last two centuries, several types of rule-breaking behavior that were once treated as private matters have been redefined as matters of public concern that require the intervention of the criminal justice system. Acts of rule-breaking that were once sanctioned informally have increasingly become the subject of formal social control by the state and its agencies. Drug use that was permitted in the nineteenth century has been redefined as a crime, and for a time the sale and consumption of alcoholic beverages was punishable as a crime.

Crime is rule-breaking behavior that is punishable by the state because it is regarded as an act against the state rather than as a private wrong against the victim. Ideally, crimes are defined by laws that are specific, uniformly applied, dispassionately enforced, and compatible with the informal norms of the culture (Sutherland and Cressey, 1978: 5–8).

THE COSTS OF CRIME

Behavior is usually defined as crime because the public, the lawmakers, or some influential group determines that the behavior is costly or harmful in some way. The costs of crime can be measured in financial terms, in terms of the physical harm to the victims, and in social terms, such as the cost of staying off the streets at night or mistrusting neighbors.

The Financial Costs of Crime

There are many ways to measure the financial costs of crime. Offenses such as arson and vandalism involve direct losses of property through destruction. Theft involves the transfer of property from a rightful owner to the thief, although to the victim it is a loss. Other financial costs are the wages lost by

a disabled victim and the hospital fees for injured victims.

Some calculations of the overall cost of crime include the money spent on illegal goods and services such as narcotics, gambling, and prostitution. Money spent on these things is diverted from legitimate expenditures, but this money can also be regarded as expenditures on leisure pursuits, although illegal ones. Another cost of crime is the money spent on the enforcement of the law—including the salaries of police officers, judges, and correctional officers—and the funds that go to maintain courthouses and prisons.

The Joint Economic Committee of Congress estimated that the total cost of crime in the United States in 1976 was $125 billion (*The New York Times*, January 2, 1977, sec. 3, p. 15). The largest component of this is white-collar crime, which cost about $44 billion. *White-collar crime* is a punishable violation of the law by otherwise respectable people of high social standing who engage in criminal acts in the course of their legitimate work (Sutherland, 1949, 1961). Bribery, kickbacks, stock fraud, embezzlement, computer crime, price fixing, and other white-collar crimes cost the public more each year than the conventional crimes of robbery, burglary, larceny, and auto theft (Conklin, 1977).

The Joint Economic Committee estimated that expenditures on the criminal justice system in 1976 were about $22.7 billion. In the same year, about $21.4 billion was spent on illegal narcotics, about $10 billion on prostitution, and about $5.9 billion on illegal gambling. All conventional crimes against property cost victims about $4 billion, a large amount in absolute terms but less than one-tenth of the loss from white-collar crime. Offenses such as illegal immigration, arson, and illegal liquor sales accounted for much of the remaining cost of crime. Crimes such as murder, aggravated assault, and rape also produced financial losses for victims and their families.

Physical Harm from Crime

In addition to the financial costs of crime, many offenses cause physical harm. People are murdered and raped, suffer injuries in assaults, and are poisoned by contaminated food and a polluted atmosphere. Although white-collar crime is often thought to be nonviolent, in many cases there is harm to the victims, even though this harm is usually a result of negligence rather than intent. Air pollution sometimes is due to the violation of crim-

White-collar crimes, such as bribery and kickbacks, cost the public more each year then the conventional crimes of robbery, burglary, larceny, and auto theft.

inal laws, and many respiratory diseases are caused by such pollution. Deaths result from the sale of contaminated food and intravenous drugs, and from the sale of dangerous products to unsuspecting consumers.

The most easily measured type of physical harm from crime is the number of people murdered each year. There were 22,516 people murdered in the United States in 1981, a high number of murders as compared to other industrial societies, even when differences in population are taken into account (Webster, 1982). Between 1970 and 1974, more Americans were murdered in the United States than were killed in the Vietnam War.

Another violent crime that is less easily measured than murder is forcible rape, a sexual attack

on a woman by the use or the threat of force. In 1981, 81,536 rapes were reported to the police in the United States, but probably two to four times that number were actually committed. A total of 643,720 cases of aggravated assault were reported to the police in 1981; this crime is an unlawful attack, often with a weapon, that is intended to cause bodily injury to the victim. In 1981, there were 574,134 reported cases of robbery, the theft of property by force or threat of force against the victim. Probably 75,000 to 100,000 of these robbery victims were injured seriously enough to warrant medical attention (Conklin, 1972; Hindelang, Gottfredson, and Garofalo, 1978). Other kinds of crime that produce physical harm include child abuse and police brutality, although there are few reliable statistics on how common these offenses are.

Some crimes do not seem to harm victims, even though they violate widely shared norms. These are often called *victimless crimes* because there is usually no victim who is willing to report the crime to the police. Victimless crimes include gambling, homosexuality, and drug use. Defining an act as a crime when there is no self-perceived victim makes it difficult for the police to enforce the law. Such laws often lead rule-breakers to develop an elaborate network to hide their deviance from outsiders (Schur, 1965; Schur and Bedau, 1974).

The Social Costs of Crime

The quality of life in a community rests on a sense of personal security, and that sense of security is influenced by the way that residents perceive the threat of crime (National Advisory Commission on Civil Disorders, 1968: 266). The social costs of crime include fear and anxiety, suspicion of strangers and neighbors, the widespread ownership of firearms, the skepticism of voters about the honesty of their political leaders, and the wariness of investors in the stock market that results from white-collar crime.

A capitalist economy depends in part on private investment, which can be eroded if white-collar crime causes mistrust of the business community and thus less investment. A presidential crime commission has stated that white-collar offenses are "the most threatening of all [crime]—not just because they are so expensive, but because of their corrosive effect on the moral standards by which American business is conducted" (President's Commission on Law Enforcement and Administration of Justice, 1967: 5). Illegal campaign contributions and bribes to political officials can make it difficult to mobilize public support for political leaders. Political corruption and white-collar crime can also set an example of disobedience that is emulated by the general public.

Conventional crimes such as rape, assault, and robbery have a variety of social costs in addition to the financial loss and the physical harm they produce (Conklin, 1975). A fear that is pervasive among Americans is the fear of an unprovoked attack in public by a stranger. This is a fear of murder, rape, and robbery, even though these crimes are relatively rare in comparison to such offenses as burglary, auto theft, and larceny. This fear of crime is fundamentally a fear of strangers, even though the chance of being murdered by a stranger is about one-tenth the chance of dying in a car accident and about one-third the chance of dying in an accidental fall (President's Commission on Law Enforcement and Administration of Justice, 1967: 52; Silberman, 1978: 6).

Fear of crime has a number of consequences. It can destroy the atmosphere necessary for learning to take place in school. It creates a generalized fear of dark streets, reducing human traffic on the streets and making them even more dangerous for those who do venture outside at night. Crime also reduces trust in other people. Imagine the effect of the following incident on the lives of one couple:

It was in Briarcliffe, N.Y., where a young couple went to dinner one evening at a local restaurant, and returned to find their car apparently stolen. After reporting it to the local police, they returned to their home and the next morning were surprised to see the car in the driveway, with an envelope on the windshield.

"There was an emergency and we had to borrow the car," the note read. "Please excuse the inconvenience, but perhaps these two theater tickets will make up for it." The couple, surprised but pleased, told the police that their car had been returned, and the next Saturday used the theater tickets.

When they returned that night, they found that their house had been completely looted (Andelman, 1972: 49).

Fear of crime can even lead people to react negatively to others who mean well, such as ex-convicts who sincerely want to end a career in crime. These ex-convicts often have difficulty disavowing the label that others attach to them, and they have trouble finding jobs and housing because others do not trust them. In many cases they return to crime because they are denied access to legitimate ways to earn money.

Sometimes the fear of crime reduces people's involvement in their community, as they come to see their neighborhood as a place filled with threatening people. Crime can even cause mistrust of long-time neighbors or lead people to move to what they think will be a safer community.

MEASURING CRIME

Determining the exact amount of crime that occurs in any society is no easy task. To measure crime, sociologists have used three different techniques: official statistics, victimization surveys, and self-report studies. Each of these methods has its shortcomings, but each has provided valuable information about crime.

Official Crime Statistics

Sociologists sometimes use official records to measure crime, while remaining aware that these records are imperfect indicators of crime. Since 1930, the Federal Bureau of Investigation has collected crime reports from local police departments. The FBI assumes that a more accurate measure of crime can be derived from crime reports produced by the police than from other agencies of the criminal justice system. Because some crimes do not lead to an arrest, some arrested suspects are not convicted, and some convicted offenders are not sent to prison, the most complete information about crime comes from police records of crime incidents.

The FBI tabulates reports that are supplied on a voluntary basis by local and state police agencies. Today these reports cover most of the country. One problem with these statistics is that they reflect only those crimes the police hear about and decide to record. The public fails to report crimes to the police for a variety of reasons, including the inconvenience of calling the police and testifying in court, the triviality of their losses, the feeling that the police cannot do anything after the crime has been committed, and the desire to protect an offender who is known to the victim (President's Commission on Law Enforcement and Administration of Justice, 1967; Hindelang, 1976). Sometimes the police do not record a crime that is reported; they may not think that a crime actually occurred, or they may wish to keep their city's official crime rate low.

Every year since 1930 the FBI has published an annual report on the amount of crime recorded by local police departments; this report also includes information on arrested suspects, police personnel, and assaults on officers. This annual report now provides details on eight "serious" crimes that, when added together, form a crime index. These eight crimes have been selected by the FBI because they are regarded as serious by the general public, because they occur relatively often, and because they commonly come to the attention of the police. The FBI calculates a crime rate for each of the eight crimes by dividing the total number of reported crimes by the total estimated population, and expressing the result as number of crimes for every 100,000 people. The crime rate in 1981 for each of the eight index crimes is shown in Table 5.2.

The FBI's method of calculating crime rates has some serious flaws; for example, it does not make much sense to calculate a rate of forcible rape by

TABLE 5.2
Crime Rates in the United States, 1981

Index crime	Rate per 100,000 people
Murder	9.8
Forcible rape	35.6
Robbery	250.6
Aggravated assault	280.9
Burglary	1,632.1
Larceny—theft	3,122.3
Motor vehicle theft	468.7
Arson	*
Total	5,799.9

*Arson was added to the crime index in 1979, and the FBI does not yet have complete statistics available on this offense.

Source: William H. Webster, *Uniform Crime Reports: Crime in the United States, 1981.* Washington, D.C.: U.S. Government Printing Office, 1982, p. 39.

dividing number of reported rapes by the *total* population of the country, because only women can be victims of this crime.

Victimization Surveys

The first large-scale survey to measure criminal victimization by questioning a cross section of the population was conducted in the United States in 1965. Since 1972, the United States Bureau of the Census and the Department of Justice have carried out similar surveys to measure the extent of victimization in the country.

Victimization surveys have discovered a large "dark figure," which is the amount of crime that actually occurs but does not make its way into official police records, either because it is never reported to the police or because the police fail to record it. The dark figure is especially high for forcible rape, because the negative social response to being a rape victim inhibits many women from reporting this crime. The criminal justice system and the general public often treat rape victims as deviants rather than as victims of other people's rule-breaking (Weis and Borges, 1973).

Victimization surveys do not provide a "true" measure of crime any more than official statistics do. There are a variety of problems in gathering information from people about their experiences as crime victims. Some minor crimes are forgotten. Crimes that occurred in the distant past are sometimes reported as having occurred within the previous year so that the subject will have something to talk about with the interviewer (Levine, 1976, 1978; Singer, 1978). In spite of these and other methodological problems, victimization surveys have provided a more complete record of crime than have official statistics.

Self-report Studies

A third measure of crime relies on questionnaires that are filled out anonymously by people who report the crimes that they have committed during a given period of time. These studies have also discovered a large amount of hidden crime. Self-report studies demonstrate that most people commit at least a few trivial offenses, and that a small number of people commit many crimes, including several serious ones.

Self-report studies provide a useful measure of crime, but they have some methodological problems that make it impossible for the results to be used as a "true" measure of crime. People who fill out self-report questionnaires sometimes exaggerate their criminal activity, and sometimes they conceal it for fear of being discovered, even though they have been guaranteed that their responses are confidential. In general, however, self-report studies seem to be quite accurate in measuring criminal involvement. So far, the real drawback to these studies is that most have been done with juvenile subjects and have focused on relatively minor offenses; as a result, they tell us little about crime by adults and little about the most serious violations of the law.

CRIME IN THE UNITED STATES

Crime rates in the United States differ by region, by size of a community, and by sex, age, race, and class. Sociologists analyze the ways that crime rates vary in a society because this information supplies the data that theories of crime must explain.

FBI crime statistics show variations from region to region. The South has regularly had higher murder rates than the rest of the country, but recently the rate in the South has become more like that of the rest of the nation. The western states now have higher rates of burglary and larceny than other regions. Some sociologists have sought to explain the higher murder rate in the South, but few have paid much attention to regional differences in rates of property crime.

Another regularity is that crime rates generally increase with the size of a community. The robbery rate in rural areas was only 22.1 per 100,000 people in 1981; the rate in towns with populations between 10,000 and 25,000 was 92.5; the rate in cities with populations between 50,000 and 100,000 was 228; and the rate for cities with populations over 250,000 was 843.8 (Webster, 1982). Other serious crimes do not show quite as dramatic an increase with size of the community, but all of the offenses in the FBI crime index (see Table 5.2) are more common in large communities. Victimization surveys do not always support this conclusion; burglary, personal assault, and personal theft do not vary much with the size of the community in some surveys, but this may be because these surveys ask victims where they live rather than where the crime occurred (Law Enforcement Assistance Administration, 1976).

Within metropolitan areas, crime rates are usually highest near the center of the city; rates decline with distance from the center (Shaw and McKay, 1969). Delinquency is most common in areas with low income, dilapidated housing, transiency, high unemployment rates, high rates of broken families, and occupancy by minority groups; these areas are usually in the center of the city (Chilton, 1964; Turner, 1969).

A major source of variation in crime rates in all societies is sex. Some part of the difference in crime rates between males and females might be attributed to biological differences (such as hormones that predispose men to aggressive behavior), but most of the difference is due to the different roles that men and women play in society. The crime rates of males and females are probably more alike in the United States than they are in any other society, suggesting that sex roles are as interchangeable in the United States as they are anywhere. Nevertheless, American males commit much more crime than American females, except for crimes such as prostitution. Table 5.3 shows that in 1981 more males than females were arrested for each of the eight index crimes. Only for the crime of larceny, which includes shoplifting (a crime often committed by women), are a substantial number of the arrested suspects females, and even for that crime more than twice as many men as women are arrested.

Age is another trait that is strongly associated with law-violating behavior. Young people commit

TABLE 5.3
Suspects Arrested for Index Crimes, by Sex, Age, and Race, 1981

Index crime	Sex		Age		Race		
	% male	% female	% under 18	% over 18	% white	% black	% other*
Murder	87.3	12.7	9.1	90.9	49.6	49.0	1.4
Forcible rape	99.1	0.9**	14.8	85.2	50.2	48.2	1.6
Robbery	92.8	7.2	28.6	71.4	38.9	60.0	1.1
Aggravated assault	87.4	12.6	14.0	86.0	61.3	37.3	1.4
Burglary	93.7	6.3	42.6	57.4	68.5	30.3	1.2
Larceny	70.9	29.1	34.8	65.2	66.3	31.8	1.9
Auto theft	91.1	8.9	40.5	59.5	68.1	30.2	1.7
Arson	88.5	11.5	42.4	57.6	78.4	20.5	1.1
Total	80.9	19.1	33.5	66.5	64.3	34.1	1.6

*American Indian, Alaskan Native, Asian, or Pacific Islander.
**A woman may be arrested for forcible rape if she acts as an accomplice to a man who commits the actual rape.

Source: Adapted from William H. Webster, *Uniform Crime Reports: Crime in the United States, 1981.* Washington, D.C.: U.S. Government Printing Office, 1982, pp. 177–179.

disproportionate amounts of crime. Table 5.3 shows that in 1981 about one-third of all arrested suspects were under the age of eighteen, and most of them were between twelve and eighteen years old. Suspects arrested for property crimes are generally younger than those arrested for violent crimes. Overall, fewer than one-eighth of all arrested suspects are thirty-five years old or more.

There are also significant variations in crime rates in the United States by racial and ethnic group. The rates for Jews, Japanese-Americans, and Chinese-Americans are lower than the rates for the rest of the population, but the crime rates for blacks and Hispanics are higher than those of other groups (Voss, 1963; Wolfgang, Figlio, and Sellin, 1972; Webster, 1982).

The FBI annual report provides information on the race of suspects arrested for the eight index crimes. These figures are shown in Table 5.3. Blacks are arrested much more often than whites for all of the index crimes, although the discrepancy is greatest for violent crimes. Overall, about one-third of all suspects arrested in 1981 were black, but blacks constituted only about 12 per cent of the population. It is important to keep in mind that the victims of most of these crimes are also black, even though there is widespread fear among whites of crime by blacks (Furstenberg, 1971). It does not appear that FBI arrest figures distort the relative contribution of blacks and whites to crime,

because there is little research to show that the police are more likely to arrest a black offender than a white offender (Conklin, 1981).

What the FBI crime statistics do omit is the amount of property lost due to white-collar crime, and most of that crime is committed by white offenders. The types of crime that form the crime index are disproportionately committed by blacks, but that index omits the most costly offenses, with the exception of some cases of arson for profit. The difference between blacks and whites in index crimes and white-collar crimes reflects differences in access to both legitimate and illegitimate opportunities for the two groups.

There has been considerable debate in recent years about the relationship between class and crime (Tittle, Villemez, and Smith, 1978; Hindelang, Hirschi, and Weis, 1979; Braithwaite, 1981). Self-report studies suggest that index crimes are committed more by the lower classes than by those higher in social standing. Criminals from the lower classes are also more likely to be arrested than criminals with higher income, more education, and more occupational prestige. Thus, there is a real difference between the classes in the commission of index crimes, but not as great a difference as is suggested by arrest statistics. Of course, white-collar crime, the most costly of all crimes, is by definition committed by people of relatively high social position.

Summary

Behavior is not inherently deviant; it is only the social response to rule-breaking that makes an act deviant. The same behavior can be treated as deviant in one society but not in another, or at one time but not another time in the same society. Moral entrepreneurs seek to change social norms by striving to have certain behavior treated as deviant or reinterpreted by society. In this century, several violations of norms have been redefined in medical terms.

Deviance has dysfunctions for society, such as disturbing the social order and harming both victims and rule-breakers, but it also has several functions. It alerts people to their shared values and establishes the boundaries of acceptable behavior in a group. Deviant acts can also be a signal of discontent and lead to new social policies, and they often enable people to "blow off steam."

Societies try to curb rule-breaking by exercising social control. Formal social control is the application of sanctions by official agencies of the state such as the police. Informal social controls, such as socialization and community opinion, are probably more effective than formal controls in inducing people to conform to a culture's norms.

Four sociological explanations of deviance are strain (or anomie) theory, control theory, cultural transmission theory, and labeling theory. Strain theory proposes that deviance arises from a discrepancy between societal goals and the approved means to reach those goals. Those who seek the goals but lack legitimate means to reach them become frustrated and turn to deviance. Access to illegitimate means as well as legitimate means accounts for the different forms that deviance takes among people in different social circumstances. This theory offers a plausible account of some kinds of goal-seeking deviance (such as theft), but it does not explain deviance that is the product of emotional needs (such as impulsive murders).

Control theory proposes that people break rules when they lack intimate attachments to parents, teachers, or peers and lack commitment to conventional forms of behavior such as education and work. This theory assumes that we all have the motivation to violate norms, but only those of us who are free of close attachments will actually do so. This theory suggests that people who are attached to others and to conventional norms need to justify their deviance before violating norms; this is made possible by techniques of neutralization. Control theory is consistent with many research findings, but so far the exact sequence of events leading to deviance has not been specified.

The most influential cultural transmission theory is differential association theory. This theory proposes that rule-breaking is the product of a socialization process in which definitions of the law that are conducive to violating the law are learned in interaction with other people. This theory is so general that it is difficult to test, but it is compatible with much research.

The labeling perspective regards deviance as socially defined rule-breaking. This approach focuses on interaction between rule-breakers and those who make and enforce rules. Deviants are created in part by a stereotyping process in which a few details of a person's behavior are accentuated and used to characterize the whole person. Sometimes one act of deviance causes other people to reevaluate the past behavior of the rule-breaker through retrospective interpretation. In some circumstances a rule-breaker is able to negotiate with those who are doing the labeling over the actual label that is applied. Often the labeling process leads to role engulfment, with rule-breakers redefining themselves in terms of the label that others have given them. This turns primary deviation, or the simple violation of norms, into secondary deviation— changes in self-concept, behavior, and friendships that result from being labeled deviant. Organizations such as juvenile courts and mental hospitals commonly play an important part in this labeling process. The labeling perspective has incorporated some of the insights of conflict theory, but it has not explained the sources of primary deviation.

Crime is deviance that violates the law and is punishable by the state. Often it is financially costly, physically harmful, and socially disruptive. Sociologists usually measure crime in three ways. Official crime statistics, which measure the extent and distribution of crimes that are reported to and recorded by the police, give an incomplete picture of all the crime that actually occurs. Victimization surveys that are based on interviews with a cross section of the population have revealed a large "dark figure" of unreported crime, as have self-report studies that ask people how many crimes they themselves have committed.

In the United States, the South has historically had the highest murder rates; in recent years, the West has had the highest rates of property crimes. The crime rates for the eight index offenses increase with the size of a community. People with certain social characteristics are especially likely to be arrested; for example, arrested suspects are particularly likely to be male, young, black, and from the lower classes. These variations in crime rates are facts that sociological theories try to explain.

Important Terms

ANOMIE (103)

CONTROL THEORY (106)

CRIME (99)

CULTURAL TRANSMISSION THEORY (109)

DEVIANCE (99)

DIFFERENTIAL ASSOCIATION THEORY (109)

LABELING PERSPECTIVE (110)

MORAL ENTREPRENEUR (100)

RETROSPECTIVE INTERPRETATION (113)

ROLE ENGULFMENT (114)

SOCIAL CONTROL (102)

STEREOTYPE (111)

STRAIN THEORY (103)

TECHNIQUE OF NEUTRALIZATION (108)

VICTIMLESS CRIME (118)

WHITE-COLLAR CRIME (116)

Suggested Readings

Howard S. Becker. *Outsiders: Studies in the Sociology of Deviance.* New York: Free Press, 1973. An influential statement of the labeling perspective, with an examination of moral entrepreneurs and an analysis of marijuana use and jazz musicians.

John E. Conklin. *Criminology.* New York: Macmillan, 1981. An expanded treatment of the discussion of crime in this chapter.

Peter Conrad and Joseph W. Schneider. *Deviance and Medicalization: From Badness to Sickness.* St. Louis: Mosby, 1980. A comprehensive examination of the way that various forms of deviance have been redefined in medical terms.

Walter R. Gove, ed. *The Labelling of Deviance: Evaluating a Perspective*, 2nd ed. Beverly Hills, Calif.: Sage Publications, 1980. A collection of essays that assess the accuracy and usefulness of the insights of the labeling perspective.

Travis Hirschi. *Causes of Delinquency.* Berkeley, Calif.: University of California Press, 1969. A lucid statement of control theory and a test of the theory with survey data.

Jeremiah Lowney, Robert W. Winslow, and Virginia Winslow. *Deviant Reality: Alternative World Views*, 2nd ed. Boston, Mass.: Allyn and Bacon, 1981. First-hand accounts of various kinds of deviant behavior, with theoretical analysis of those accounts.

Edwin M. Schur. *Interpreting Deviance: A Sociological Introduction.* New York: Harper & Row, 1979. A well-written text that examines and illustrates the major ideas of the labeling perspective.

part III
THE ORGANIZATION OF SOCIAL LIFE

*Human behavior follows regular patterns; it has a structure
that can be studied by sociologists. In the next five chapters we
look at the way that social life is organized, and pay special
attention to the issue of social inequality.*

*Chapter 6 focuses on the interaction of people in their daily
lives. Three theories are presented that explain behavior that is
so familiar to you that you might not even think to analyze it
in a systematic way. The systematic study of this "trivial" behavior is, however, essential to understanding how society is
organized.*

*The network of relationships among people — what sociologists
call "social structure"—is explored in Chapter 7. Social structure includes patterned interaction between groups as small
as two people, as in a college interview or in a marriage, and it
also includes patterned interaction in large groups such as corporations and governments. We have all had many experiences
with different social structures, but we often forget how important these structures are in our daily existence.*

*Chapter 8 examines an important aspect of the social struc-
ture—social stratification, the ranking of people, or categories of
people, in a hierarchy by income, wealth, prestige, or power.
Class—a central concept in many sociological studies—is one
major dimension along which societies are stratified.*

*Another basis for stratification is race or ethnicity. Most societies
contain multiple groups that differ in physical characteristics or
cultural traditions, and it is common to find that one group
dominates the others. In Chapter 9 we explore the various ways
that dominant groups treat those who are subordinate to them,
and the responses of those minority groups to such treatment.*

*The final chapter in this section, Chapter 10, investigates an-
other basis of social inequality—gender. Men and women have
unequal access to opportunities to acquire valued resources such
as income and occupational prestige, and in this chapter we
explore how sex affects social interaction and the stratification
of society.*

SOCIAL INTERACTION

Why is *social interaction*—the response of individuals to one another—so important? There are several reasons. When individuals interact they develop shared meanings about the world that form the basis of culture, as we saw in Chapter 3. Social interaction is also the mechanism by which the values and norms of an existing culture are transmitted from generation to generation. We saw in Chapter 4 that the basis of the socialization process is the interaction between unsocialized children and the parents, teachers, and peers who convey culture to them. In Chapter 5 we looked at cultural transmission theory, which proposes that deviance is also a result of socialization, but based on interaction with people who are sources of norms and values that are conducive to rule-breaking behavior.

In addition, interaction is important because it is the basis of social order. By orienting their behavior to one another and by considering other people's reactions to them, people develop an understanding of behavior; they can repeat behavior and share expectations about what that behavior means. This makes future behavior somewhat predictable and leads to the emergence of social structure—groups, organizations, and societies that endure in a recognizable form (see Chapter 7).

In this chapter we investigate three major theoretical perspectives on social interaction, some of which were examined briefly in Chapter 1. One perspective is symbolic interactionism, an approach that looks at the way that meanings develop from interpersonal behavior. We explore the meanings attached to language and to nonverbal expressions, gestures, and postures. The second perspective, ethnomethodology, employs some unusual strategies to discover the unspoken rules that make easy interaction possible. The third perspective is the dramaturgical approach, which uses the analogy of a theatrical play to analyze interaction. It focuses on the details of how we create impressions of ourselves for those with whom we interact, our "audiences." An understanding of these three perspectives might enable you to see social interaction in a new light, for all of us act on the basis of many assumptions that we usually take for granted.

Types of Interaction

Before we look at the three theories of social interaction, we must examine some of the many ways in which people interact. One form of interaction is the trading of goods, services, social approval, and other desired things; gift-giving at Christmas is one such exchange, and so are making love and buying groceries. People sometimes compete for the same limited goal; only one team can win a league championship and only one corporate vice-president will become president. At other times, people cooperate to reach a shared goal; for instance, a husband and a wife might both work overtime to pay for a new house or a car. Conflict is a kind of interaction in which one party tries to dominate the other; war is conflict between societies, and assault is conflict between individuals. The dimension of domination and subordination is important in many forms of interaction, especially conflict.

EXCHANGE AND RECIPROCITY

Many human needs cannot be met unless people interact with one another. People must cooperate to meet their basic requirements of food, water, shelter, and clothing. They depend on each other for a sense of security and attachment to others, and their sense of self-esteem is a product of others' responses to them. People also have a need for self-actualization—the fulfillment of personal potential—and meeting this need often requires the help and approval of other people (Maslow, 1968). One kind of interaction that is important in meeting these needs is *exchange*, a process in which people give and receive rewards in a mutually satisfying way.

Exchange theory assumes that people are motivated by self-interest and interact with one another to satisfy their personal needs (Homans, 1974; Emerson, 1976). People calculate and weigh the possible gains and losses they might derive from an interaction. They enter into relationships only if they expect that the rewards from doing so will balance or exceed the costs, such as the time and energy they must put into the interaction.

Values and norms influence the kinds of exchange that are acceptable in a society. Prostitution, the exchange of money for sex, is widely disapproved in many cultures. Exchange in the marketplace, where money is paid for a product, is encouraged. It is acceptable for students to exchange notes from lectures they miss, but it is not acceptable for them to exchange answers during an examination.

George C. Homans (1974) has proposed that the social order develops from interactions that are repeated because the participants wish to gain the same rewards over and over again. He assumes that people are rational, in that they carefully consider the benefits and costs of past, present, and future interactions. They repeat behavior that they have found rewarding in the past and expect to prove rewarding again. If they get enough of a particular reward, they are less likely to repeat the behavior because the reward will be less valuable to them. A millionaire might refuse paid work, because he or she would not need the money, but the same person might do the work if the reward were the gratitude of a friend or public notoriety.

Norm of Reciprocity

People often bring to their interactions with others the expectation that people are obliged to help and not to harm those who have helped them (Gouldner, 1960). This norm, called the *norm of reciprocity*, requires that each person give and receive things that are perceived in roughly equal terms. When people gain rewards from an exchange, they will be motivated by self-interest to interact again in the same way to gain additional benefits. Rewarding exchanges in which each party

gains thus are repeated and a pattern or regularity of behavior develops. When the norm of reciprocity is violated, an exchange is less likely to be repeated because the individual who has spent time and energy in the interaction but has not been rewarded will no longer be motivated to enter the exchange.

The norm of reciprocity implies that people expect exchanges to be fair and just. In the eighteenth century B.C., the Code of Hammurabi stated that justice required "an eye for an eye, a tooth for a tooth." Some people have interpreted this as a demand for harsh justice, but in fact it states the norm that punishment by the state should correspond to the harm that the offender has inflicted. "An eye for an eye" would literally mean that a person who poked out the eye of another person would have his or her own eye poked out in return. A fine would be too lenient, and execution would be too severe. The idea that justice is served when a penalty fits a crime is based on the norm of reciprocity.

Economic transactions are exchanges that involve specific, often quantifiable obligations. One party agrees to pay a specific amount of money for a particular good or service. Sociologists are more interested in *social* exchanges that create a more diffuse, less specific obligation between people (Blau, 1964; Cook and Emerson, 1978; Caplow, 1982a). "Love" can be seen as an emotion, but it is also a part of a social exchange. "Falling in love" often involves behavior by one person to elicit a response from the person who is the object of the love. The love-object's response may then stimulate more behavior to express the feeling of love, and this may in turn elicit additional responses. People may be "in love" with someone from whom they receive no response, but this emotion will usually disappear if there is no response at all. People expect the expression of their love to elicit an emotionally rewarding reaction from the one who is loved. Ongoing relationships involve similar exchanges. People often do things for each other without receiving any response, but they usually expect at least a "thank you" or a small favor in return.

Exchange and the norm of reciprocity link people in relationships that form the basis of the social order. Exchange establishes bonds of friendship and creates relationships of domination and subordination. These relationships, as well as the rewards derived from the interaction, become important to people and can even lead them to sustain interaction after it no longer provides concrete rewards (Blau, 1964). Some relationships are based on impersonal and material exchanges, such as paying a hairdresser or buying a movie ticket. Other exchanges are based on personal obligations and emotional commitments, such as marriage and friendship. Preliterate, nonindustrial societies are usually held together by personal and emotional exchanges; gifts often play an important role in maintaining cohesion in these societies (Mauss, 1925, 1954). Industrial societies are bound to a greater extent by impersonal obligations and material exchanges; money becomes an important medium of exchange in these societies.

COOPERATION

Cooperation, a form of interaction in which people strive for a common goal, requires people to share a definition of the situation and to depend on each other. It can be a spontaneous response to a situation that requires people to act together, or it can be based on long-established customs. Cooperation can be demanded by a higher authority, or it can be formally agreed upon by equal partners (Nisbet and Perrin, 1977). Cooperation is often an efficient way to accomplish tasks, because it allows for greater effort than individuals could exert on their own, and because it provides intrinsic rewards such as gratitude from other parties to the interaction. In some instances, however, cooperation stifles individual initiative and creativity by forcing people to adjust to the needs of the group or by allowing some people to minimize their contributions to a group effort.

COMPETITION

The parties to *competition* seek the same limited goal and agree to abide by certain rules in their efforts to reach that goal. Because competitors strive for scarce rewards such as money, power, prestige, or attention, one person's gain is another's loss. In

Competition is one form of social interaction. In competition the participants seek the same limited goal and agree to abide by certain rules in their efforts to reach that goal.

competition, the important thing is the achievement of the goal, rather than the domination of the competitor; as a result, competition is relatively impersonal and the competitors are expected to be gracious winners and good losers. In SEL 6.1 we see that one resource that people compete for, usually unconsciously, is attention in their conversations with others.

SOCIOLOGY AND EVERYDAY LIFE 6.1
Competing for Attention

One form of competition that you probably have not thought much about is the competition for attention that occurs when you talk with other people. Charles Derber has analyzed this "pursuit of attention" in great detail. He believes that Americans seek attention in their interactions with others because their culture emphasizes individualism and encourages "self-interest and self-absorption."

Derber examines a variety of clever but often unconscious strategies that we use to direct attention to ourselves in conversation. He shows that this "conversational narcissism" occurs both in formal settings such as work organizations and in informal settings such as dining. He suggests that a careful analysis of conversation can reveal much about the social order. For instance, he finds that men are more likely than women to be self-oriented and to use attention-getting devices in conversation; women are more apt to give attention to other participants in the conversation.

One way to direct attention to oneself is to introduce a topic of conversation. There are unwritten rules about how others should respond when a person introduces a new topic of conversation; for example, it is considered discourteous to change the subject too abruptly or to show no interest at all.

Derber points out the subtle techniques by which people divert attention from others to themselves. One strategy is a "shift-response," a conversational reaction to another person's statement that draws attention away from that person. Derber (p. 24) gives the following example:

John: I'm feeling really starved.
Mary: Oh, I just ate.

This shifts the topic from John's feelings to Mary's feelings. John may then respond to Mary's statement by asking her what she had to eat, and the conversation has been refocused on her. Mary will have successfully competed with John for the scarce resource of attention. She might also have responded to John's statement with what Derber calls a "support-response," a reaction that encourages John to continue the conversation with himself as the focus of attention:

John: I'm feeling really starved.
Mary: When was the last time you ate?

This slight difference is nuance makes a significant difference in who holds attention in the interaction, even though John and Mary may not be aware of this process.

Diverting attention to oneself can be done in an active way by introducing one's feelings into a conversation as if they are an elaboration on a point that the other speaker has just made. Derber (p. 26) gives the following example to show that what seems to be a response to another person is actually an active effort to shift attention away from that person:

Mary: My summer place has been such a blessing this year.
John: I know, I sure would like a place like that, the way I've been feeling, but I've got to earn the bread first, you know?
Mary: Yeah.
John: I figure that if I work enough this year and next, I'll be able to check that place out in Vermont again and maybe. . . .

Sometimes attention is shifted more passively if one does not respond enthusiastically to the other person's conversation. Instead of asking questions to get that person to elaborate on a point, an individual may respond with brief comments that convey little interest in the topic of discussion, as Mary does in the above conversation with "Yeah." Showing minimal interest in a conversation may shut off the other person and leave the field open for the passive conversationalist to take that initiative and introduce a new topic, although Mary did not do this with John.

Source: Based on Charles Derber, *The Pursuit of Attention: Power and Individualism in Everyday Life*. Cambridge, Mass.: Schenkman Publishing Company, 1979.

Not all competitors begin a competition on an equal footing. When this is so, competition may cause resentment among those who feel they cannot compete on an equal basis with those who have an advantage. It has been suggested that giving minority groups equal opportunity to compete for income or prestige with groups that have long had greater access to those rewards is much like taking a ball and chain off a convict's leg and telling him he is now free to compete equally in a foot race with an Olympic champion. One consequence of competition between those who do not begin on an equal footing is that the winners can develop an inflated self-esteem and feel contempt for the losers, and the losers can suffer a loss of self-esteem and feel bitterness toward the winners. These effects can disrupt the social order and lead to open conflict.

Competition can be inefficient in allocating some rewards. For example, the total amount of money that research firms spend in writing research proposals for a single government contract can surpass the amount of the contract on which the firms are bidding. Of course, for the winner in the competition, the resources have been spent wisely. In terms of the efficient use of society's resources, it might not make sense to have several research firms collectively spend $500,000 writing proposals for a $100,000 project.

CONFLICT

Conflict is a struggle over scarce resources in which one party seeks to eliminate, defeat, destroy, or neutralize the opposition in order to achieve a desired goal. Conflict is a form of interaction that binds antagonists in a relationship (Coser, 1956). In a conflict, each party is aware of the other; this is unlike competition, in which people can strive for the same goal without even being aware of or interacting with each other. Conflict often occurs within certain limits; even war is generally conducted by certain rules. However, the parties to a conflict often have a basic disagreement over the social order, and thus there is less consensus on the rules of interaction than is the case for exchange, cooperation, or competition.

Conflict between groups often increases the internal cohesion of each group (Coser, 1956). Conflict enables a group to define its boundaries in a struggle against another group, even though this process separates the groups from each other. During wartime, citizens often pull together as they experience a heightened sense of patriotism and common purpose, in spite of the division and hostility the war creates between nations. Some observers have suggested that the Argentine invasion of the Falkland Islands in 1982 was intended by the ruling military junta to bolster support by drawing Argentines together in opposition to a common enemy. The capture of American hostages by Iranian militants in 1979 had a similar effect in uniting Americans in opposition to a common enemy.

Conflict can be productive when it is realistic, that is, when it is a means to a specific end. Realistic conflict arises when one of the participants in an interaction calculates that there are possible gains from the conflict. One example of realistic conflict is labor–management conflict that leads to a strike over wages and benefits. In contrast, nonrealistic conflict is an interaction that is based not on rival goals, but rather on the need for tension-release and the expression of emotions such as anger. A riot at a soccer match or a rock concert and the lynching of a black person by a white mob during a period of economic insecurity are examples of nonrealistic conflict (Coser, 1956).

DOMINATION AND SUBORDINATION

Interaction often involves a relationship of domination and subordination. The German sociologist Georg Simmel (1950) has suggested that the party that holds authority in an interaction rarely dominates the subordinate party completely, but instead expects to elicit a response that will make the interaction with the subordinate party rewarding to the dominant party. Simmel treated dominant–subordinate relationships as a form of interaction, as a give-and-take process, rather than as the absolute imposition of the will of one party on another. Sometimes the dimension of authority is not obvious in an interaction, even though it strongly influences the way that people respond to each other. For example, in SEL 6.2 we see that women are sometimes afraid to express their preferences to their hairdressers because they believe that their hairdressers "know best." In this way, hairdressers exert a subtle domination over their female customers.

SOCIOLOGY AND EVERYDAY LIFE 6.2
Interaction in the Beauty Salon

In the strange and enchanted world of the beauty salon, the hairdresser may be many things to many women. To the rich and the social, he may be a father confessor, a son, an escort, a dear friend. To the beauties whose faces appear in fashion magazines or on television screens, he is more of a technical adviser. To ordinary women who lead ordinary lives, he is a friendly sorcerer who, with a wave of the scissors, makes them feel a little prettier, a little younger, a little more self-assured.

Then there are a small number of women who profess to have problems with hairdressers in the city's top salons, although for reasons perhaps best known to themselves, they continue to patronize them.

Seen through their eyes, the salon is a source of instant intimidation—"All those wavy walls and mirrors and Art Deco furniture." Other customers inspire envy—"Everywhere you look there's a tall, thin blonde with cheekbones." The hairdressers themselves seem arrogant and remote—"I don't dare tell him how I want my hair done, he gets so huffy."

"And these are not incompetent women," says Marlene Fedin. "I've seen executives who would never be intimidated in a business situation almost reduced to supplicants in a beauty salon. And these women are paying $50 and up."

Miss Fedin is a sales executive for a fabric company and the winner in a recent power struggle with a hairdresser who, she suspects, "wanted to make me into a punk rocker."

A similar battle was won by Anne Thompson. She is a press agent for films, not a stuffy job. Still, she did not fancy a pink streak in her hair and told her hairdresser so.

"I stood up to him, but I felt bad," she admitted with a sigh. "To me, it's a haircut, but to him, it's an art form. He wanted to try something new and, I guess, I felt boring. If you like your hairdresser, you want his approval."

Why is it that otherwise competent women experience twinges of insecurity when they don those little salon smocks? The masters themselves, stylists such as Monsieur Marc or Kenneth or Xavier, chalk it up to "bad feelings" about themselves or "bad experiences" in lesser hands.

"Sometimes we have to be the victims for what has happened to them in the past," Xavier Zietounian said with a shrug. "We have to understand and make them more relaxed about hair, to have a sense of humor about hair."

But other experts, those who teach women to get what they want through assertive training techniques, consider the problem deeper and far more complex. In many cases, women lack the basic skills required to communicate their needs to the hairdresser, they say. In other cases, they fail to use the skills because of vague and admittedly irrational fears that the hairdresser will retaliate by ruining their hair.

Perla Knie finds that women in her assertiveness training workshops view hairdressers as they do doctors or lawyers—as authority figures.

"Of course, some hairdressers play into this by using negative reinforcement," Miss Knie pointed out. "They will be curt or unresponsive to any request a woman makes so she won't dare bring it up again."

Why doesn't the woman leave? Miss Knie laughed and conceded that she once put up with a haughty hairdresser because he kept telling her, "If it wasn't for me, you'd still look like Brooklyn." She said that, like many women, she chose to believe that her hairdresser possessed "some secret, magical knowledge that would make me look right" and that "the known misery is better that the unknown."

Other women say they hesitate to switch hairdressers or even salons for fear of being labeled "a promiscuous customer." A lawyer, who once left Eric for Pamela and then returned to Eric, recalls being terrified that her "infidelity" would be discovered. "I invented this elaborate story about being abroad," she admitted.

Not surprisingly, hairdressers deny that they are such temperamental or dictatorial creatures, although they do not deny that a handful of customers might have this misconception. The truth, they say, is that no hairdresser of any reputation can afford to ignore a client's preferences and that the worst client may be the one who expresses no preference at all.

Every once in a while a new client will appear in Kenneth's chair and say: "You're the artist. Do whatever you want." Experience has taught Kenneth Battelle to be wary of such women.

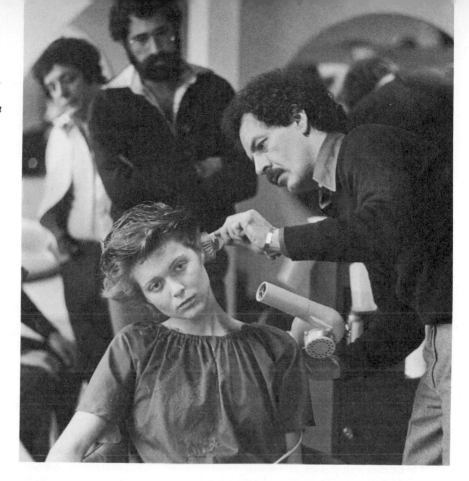

We see how hairdressers can—with the wave of scissors or a hairdryer—make women feel a little prettier or a little more self-assured. Or they can be a source of subtle intimidation.

"Listen, I don't think I should cut your hair today," he tells her gently. "Go home and think about it or look through these magazines and tell me what you think is pretty hair."

Noting that "hair is a woman's security blanket," Mr. Marc agreed. "I put myself in the client's place," he said, "and always I listen.

When the hair is too short, she is very unhappy. And you? Why, you are the worst hairdresser in the world."

Source: Georgia Dullea, "Standing Up to the Hairdresser Can Take a Kind of Courage," *The New York Times*, January 12, 1981, p. B4. Reprinted by permission.

Dominance can be used to control scarce and valued resources, and it can also be used to provide intrinsic rewards, such as flattery or gratitude from subordinates. Subordinates can also derive rewards, such as protection, from an exchange with those who dominate them. Sometimes people submit to authority to avoid the responsibilities that freedom imposes; Erich Fromm (1941) called this response the "escape from freedom" and suggested that it is conducive to the rise of totalitarian governments such as that of Nazi Germany.

Laboratory research with unorganized gatherings of students shows that even if everyone is equal when they first begin to interact, over time patterns of interaction will emerge in which some students assume the role of leader and others willingly become followers who subordinate themselves to the leaders (Hare, 1976). Domination and subordination seem to be an intrinsic part of social interaction.

In a famous experiment, Stanley Milgram (1973) found that people will obey those they perceive as exercising legitimate or proper authority, even if those people ask them to hurt others. In this study, the experimenter told participants to administer electrical shocks to volunteers who failed to perform correctly on a word-association test. The experimenter told the subjects that their cooperation was necessary to meet the goals of science and that no one would be hurt in the study. When a subject administered the shocks to the other participant in the experiment (who was actually an associate of the experimenter and was not really receiving any shocks at all), this other participant screamed, complained of a heart problem, and eventually remained silent when the strongest shocks were "administered." Many of the subjects continued to administer electrical shocks even after it seemed that the other person had become unconscious. This study suggests that under certain conditions some people will submit to authority, even to the point of hurting others, if they feel that the authority has a legitimate basis. In this experiment, that basis of authority was the prestige of science and scientific researchers.

Symbolic Interactionism

In Chapter 4 we looked at George Herbert Mead's theory of the self. Mead and other symbolic interactionists (e.g., Stryker, 1980) emphasize the socialization process, especially the way that people learn to adopt the perspectives and roles of others. Herbert Blumer is one symbolic interactionist who focuses instead on the way that people develop "joint action" or social behavior through interaction with each other. He sees social structure—the groups, organizations, and societies that we examine in the next chapter—as people "who are engaging in action" with each other (Blumer, 1969b: 6).

Blumer proposes three premises of symbolic interactionism, a term he coined in 1937 that has been applied to several different approaches. First, people "act toward things on the basis of the meanings that the things have for them" (Blumer, 1969b: 2). Words, gestures, and objects have symbolic meaning; that is, they stand for or represent something for those people who agree to their meaning (Charon, 1979). Several different meanings can be attached to the same object. For example, a cross has one meaning to a Christian, and a different one to a member of a tribal society who worships a number of gods. The meaning given to an object is often taken for granted and may seem so obvious to those who share a culture that it does not even warrant consideration.

Blumer's second premise is that the meaning of an object arises out of social interaction among people, rather than being intrinsic to the object. According to Blumer, people interpret and consider the actions of others with regard to an object and adjust their behavior accordingly. For example, the meaning of a tree depends on how others treat that object; lumberjacks will think of trees differently than will the members of a suburban garden club. Blumer's theoretical position would suggest that the plaque that we looked at in Chapter 3 would not have the same meaning for its extraterrestrial discoverers as for its terrestrial creators unless both groups were able to respond to each other's reactions to the plaque.

The third premise of Blumer's version of symbolic interactionism is that the meanings of objects are modified through an interpretative process that individuals use in their dealings with the objects they encounter. Meaning is not simply aroused within the person and applied to the object; rather, people create meaning by interpreting the world, not just by reacting to it. People must notice and consider those things that have meaning for them; noticing and considering are part of a social process because people respond to other people's reactions to objects. In this process of interpretation, the individual "selects, checks, suspends, regroups, and transforms the meanings [of the object] in the light of the situation in which he is placed and the direction of his action" (Blumer, 1969b: 5).

Joint action or social behavior emerges when people take into account what each other is doing and fit their behavior accordingly. To establish joint action, people can rely to some extent on meanings they have developed in past interactions. Even though new interactions are influenced somewhat by past interactions between the participants, each new interaction also requires the participants to establish a shared understanding about the meaning of their behavior. Words, gestures, and objects must have the same meaning for the participants in an interaction to communicate effectively and engage in joint action. A robber's order to "stick 'em up" indicates that the victim is supposed to submit to the thief's demands, that the robber intends to steal the victim's property, and that the interaction is a holdup. If the victim understands these meanings of the simple command, the robbery will proceed smoothly. If the victim does not understand what is going on, the thief may use physical force or try to find a different victim. Similarly, if one person in a verbal disagreement makes an insulting slur or pulls a knife, this may change the meaning of the interaction and prompt the target of those symbolic actions to use lethal force against the person who spoke the slur or pulled the knife (Luckenbill, 1977).

Shared meanings often develop through verbal communication, but much of the meaning of interpersonal behavior is communicated through such nonverbal "language" as facial expressions, physical gestures, and physical distance between people.

FACIAL EXPRESSIONS

One source of information in most interactions is the facial expressions that the participants make. By watching another person's expressions, you can learn that he or she is bored with the conversation, angry at you, disgusted with something that has just happened, or surprised to see you. Because you understand the meaning of these expressions, you know how to respond to that person in a way that makes for smooth interaction.

You might think that facial expressions were a product of socialization to the ways of a particular culture, but there is some evidence that facial expressions have similar meanings in a wide variety of cultures. The possiblity that the meaning of facial expressions is innate rather than learned is suggested by the fact that people who are blind from birth express their emotions with facial expressions very much like those of sighted people, even though the blind have not had the chance to learn those expressions by observing others. Another source of support for the possibility that some facial expressions are culturally universal is research by Paul Ekman (Ekman, 1980; Goleman, 1981), who found that members of the Fore tribe of New Guinea, a group that had not seen Caucasian faces before Ekman and his co-workers, were able to match a series of simple stories with photographs of Caucasians expressing different emotions. Ekman asked a different group of New Guineans to make expressions they thought were appropriate for the people in these stories. When he showed videotapes of their facial expressions to a group of college students in the United States, he found that they were also able to match facial expressions with stories. The photographs on page 136 show New Guineans and Americans expressing sadness, happiness, and disgust. This research is not conclusive evidence that facial expressions are the same in all cultures, but it does show a striking similarity of expressions and associated meanings in two very

different cultures that have had little contact with each other.

Through facial expressions, people sometimes inadvertently give information to others about their real feelings that is not consistent with the feelings they wish to communicate. This "leakage" may embarrass the person, who may try to control the emission of these unintended signals. The other person in the interaction may disregard this inconsistent information, look away so that the first person can preserve the intended impression, or interpret the information as a sign of insincerity, deceit, or hypocrisy. Inconsistency between verbal communication, nonverbal symbols such as facial expressions, and actual behavior often creates problems for continued interaction because it makes it difficult for the participants to share the same meaning of the interaction.

PHYSICAL GESTURES

Although facial expressions have similar meanings in different cultures, physical gestures—the movement of parts of the body—seem to have meanings that are unique to a specific culture, and in fact often to particular situations within that culture. The upraised middle finger that is an obscene gesture in the United States does not convey the same meaning in most of the world's cultures. The upraised hand in the plaque sent into space is a sign of greeting in many but not all cultures, and it is very possible that it would not convey a friendly greeting to extraterrestrials. A physical collision between pedestrians on the street requires a verbal apology in some cultures but not in others, and even in cultures in which an apology is generally expected it would not be expected if the person were fleeing from a burning building or running from a car that had gone out of control (Ashcraft and Scheflen, 1976).

Often physical gestures communicate information in subtle ways of which people are unaware. Physical posture can communicate laziness, boredom, rebelliousness, or sexual availability. Crossed legs and arms can communicate an unwillingness to talk openly with another person. Sometimes people receive this information without thinking much about it, but those who are aware of the symbolic meaning of gestures and postures can use it to their advantage. For instance, in some cultures direct eye contact during conversation indicates attentiveness and interest, even though in other cultures such eye contact is considered rude

Facial expressions seem to be innate traits of humans. Similar expressions convey the same meaning in different cultures, as we can see in these three sets of photographs comparing New Guinean and American ways of expressing sadness, happiness, and disgust.

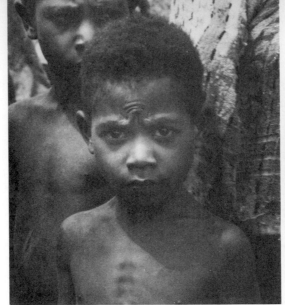

Sadness

Happiness

Disgust

(Ashcraft and Scheflen, 1976). As a result, a person who wishes to show interest in another person might consciously seek to establish direct eye contact with that person (Mazur et al, 1980).

PERSONAL SPACE

Another important symbolic aspect of social interaction is the meaning that is given to the physical space between the people who are interacting. *Personal space* is the unoccupied area that people feel must be maintained around themselves in order to be safe and comfortable. This need for an unoccupied space around oneself has been attributed to a territorial need of all animals, including humans, for a "safe space" that cannot be entered by those who are potentially threatening (Ardrey, 1966; Hall, 1966).

In some cultures, people stand or sit very close to one another when they interact, and in other cultures people stand or speak at a greater distance. In any culture, discomfort will result when another person "invades" the culturally defined personal space by standing or sitting "too close" (Hall, 1959, 1966). In the United States, speaking distance is usually about three feet, unless the speakers are intimate with each other. Smaller distances are typical of many cultures. Consequently, Americans are often seen by people from other cultures as unfriendly because they seem to stand too far away or be aloof.

"Comfortable" speaking distance depends in part on the relationship between the participants in an interaction. People who are of similar social background, age, education, and wealth are likely to stand or sit closer together than people of dissimilar backgrounds (Burgoon and Jones, 1976). Personal space is also related to the nature of the interaction and its location. On the basis of his observations and interviews with a group of middle-class adults living in the northeastern United States, Edward T. Hall (1966: 113–129) has distinguished four zones of personal space. Intimates usually place themselves less than eighteen inches apart when interacting. This "intimate distance" has symbolic meanings of protection, sexual interest, comfort, and affection, and it enables people to have sensory responses to each other's bodies. In public situations in which people are forced to be this close to nonintimates, they develop "distancing" strategies; for example, subway riders avoid eye contact, and elevator passengers keep their hands at their sides and carefully watch the number of the floor on the overhead panel. "Personal

distance" is between eighteen inches and four feet, and it is commonly used among friends and acquaintances to signify their personal relationships and to discuss personal matters. "Social distance" ranges from four to twelve feet and is used in formal and impersonal relationships such as job interviews or consultations among co-workers. "Public distance" is more than twelve feet and is used in situations such as a speech or a lecture when an individual with higher social standing wishes to maintain distance from the audience. The amount of personal space between people who are interacting tells us something about their relationship, and it also influences the way in which they interact. When one person feels that the space that is appropriate to the interaction is "invaded," he or she may back away, change posture, become hostile, build obstacles, or leave the scene.

People sometimes try to structure personal space by adopting or designing certain seating patterns or furniture arrangements. It is considered acceptable for people to sit side by side with strangers in a movie theater if the theater is crowded, but if you enter a theater and take a seat beside the only other person in attendance your behavior would be interpreted quite differently. A group of three men or three women in a dating bar may effectively thwart efforts at conversation by members of the opposite sex by facing each other around a small table. This arrangement communicates their desire for intimate conversation with one another and an unwillingness to have their space invaded by strangers (Scheflen and Ashcraft, 1976).

Furniture arrangements can affect interaction. The positioning of office desks and chairs influences interaction among workers and can encourage or discourage certain patterns of friendship in the office (Gullahorn, 1952; Wells, 1965). A desk may be positioned so that it comes between the worker and his or her clients; the desk than acts as a barrier and creates personal space between the participants in the interaction. In contrast, living room furniture is usually placed so that there are no barriers between people and so they can interact on an equal basis while sitting close to one another.

People sometimes use "markers" to designate a certain territory as belonging to them in their absence (Sommer, 1969; Goffman, 1971). These markers, which symbolize possession and an intent to return, vary in their effectiveness in conveying these meanings to others. Leaving valuable and personal items such as a coat on a chair in the library is more likely to reserve your spot than leaving a newspaper or magazine, an item that is more likely to be removed by someone who wants to sit in "your" seat. A city dweller might place an empty garbage can or sawhorse in a parking space that he or she has spent hours shoveling out. Disagreement about whether it is possible to reserve a personal parking place on a public road has led to some disputes about the meaning of such markers. Markers have meaning only when people acknowledge them as symbols of the right of an individual to reserve a place for personal use.

Ethnomethodology

Ethnomethodology is a term that was coined by Harold Garfinkel (1967) to describe an approach to the study of social interaction that seeks to understand and describe people's efforts to make sense of the world (Handel, 1982). Ethnomethodologists try to discover the underlying rules and formal structures of routine daily life. This approach focuses on the "taken-for-granted" aspect of behavior and looks at the ways that people create shared definitions of the world through the process of interaction.

Ethnomethodologists see people as capable of exercising judgment when they confront a situation, and they think that people develop "a meaningful course of situationally appropriate action" (Abrahamson, 1981: 59). People do bring rules of behavior to their interactions with one another, but the meaning of a specific interaction must usually be "negotiated" within a set of general rules. When people interact, there is considerable room for defining the nature of the situation, even if the participants have some agreement as to the rules of interaction. Negotiating meaning is especially difficult for people from different cultures, but even people with the same cultural background must establish the meaning of their interaction. Social order exists because people can make sense of the situations they confront by agreeing to common meanings. Social reality is an "ongoing accomplishment of the concerted activities of everyday life" (Garfinkel, 1967: vii).

Ethnomethodologists strive to describe the "formal properties of common sense activities" by discovering the general rules that people use to make their interaction meaningful (Garfinkel, 1967: viii). One way they have done this is through a careful analysis of everyday conversation. They have found that much conversation is conducted through shorthand phrases, incomplete sentences, and tacit assumptions that make the meaning of a conversation intelligible to the participants but unclear to outside observers. It is necessary to know something about the speakers' backgrounds, the context of the conversation, the meaning of the sequence of utterances, and the importance of omissions in order to know the full meaning of a conversation. Consider the example below, which is provided by Garfinkel (1967: 25–26). First read the conversation in the left-hand column to see what was actually spoken by the two participants, and then read the conversation again and look at the meaning that was conveyed by the spoken words (the right-hand column).

Husband: Dana succeeded in putting a penny in a parking meter today without being picked up.	This afternoon as I was bringing Dana, our four-year-old son, home from the nursery school, he succeeded in reaching high enough to put a penny in a parking meter when we parked in a meter zone, whereas before he has always had to be picked up to reach that high.
Wife: Did you take him to the record store?	Since he put a penny in a meter that means you stopped while he was with you. I know that you stopped at the record store either on the way to get him or on the way back. Was it on the way back, so that he was with you or did you stop there on the way to get him and somewhere else on the way back?
Husband: No, to the shoe repair shop.	No, I stopped at the record store on the way to get him and stopped at the shoe repair shop on the way home when he was with me.
Wife: What for?	I know of one reason why you might have stopped at the shoe repair shop. Why did you in fact?

Husband: I got some new shoe laces for my shoes.

As you will remember I broke a shoe lace on one of my brown oxfords the other day so I stopped to get some new laces.

Wife: Your loafers need new heels badly.

Something else you could have gotten that I was thinking of. You could have taken in your black loafers which need heels badly. You'd better get them taken care of pretty soon.

Another technique that ethnomethodologists have used to examine the implicit rules of social behavior is to disrupt accepted patterns of interaction and note the responses of the participants. By acting in this unusual way, a researcher can learn the tacit or unspoken rules of interaction from people's reactions to the disturbance of routine behavior. Garfinkel asked some of his students to behave in their own homes as if they were boarders rather than members of the family. They addressed their parents in formal terms (Mr. and Mrs.) and requested permission to have a snack rather than helping themselves. Some students could not keep up this pretense for long because it made them and their parents uncomfortable. Their parents were "stupefied" and reacted with "astonishment, bewilderment, shock, anxiety, embarrassment, and anger, and with charges . . . that the student was mean, inconsiderate, selfish, nasty, or impolite" (Garfinkel, 1967: 47). In their efforts to restore the normal routine of family interaction, family members demanded to know what was going on, and some suggested that the student was ill, overworked, or had been fired from a job. The strong reactions of the parents indicate that the simple and commonly accepted rules of normal family behavior are important to smooth interaction. This experiment helped to reveal some of the rules that guide this type of interaction.

Disruption of normal routines reveals the accepted rules of daily behavior. Casual conversation often depends on the acceptance of shorthand phrases and simple answers to routine questions. This was demonstrated by some of Garfinkel's students when they probed for detailed responses to routine questions, and thereby changed a superficial conversation into an upsetting situation. For example, one person said to another member of the

same car pool, "I had a flat tire." The experimenter replied, "What do you mean, you had a flat tire?" The first speaker was stunned, but then answered angrily, "What do you mean, 'What do you mean?' A flat tire is a flat tire. That is what I meant. Nothing special. What a crazy question!" (Garfinkel, 1967: 42). Another example is that casual comments such as "How are you?" are expected to be given superficial answers such as "Fine," rather than detailed accounts of one's physical and mental health, the number of uncompleted homework assignments, and the quality of one's sex life. Through such disruptions of expectations, the rules of everyday conversation are revealed.

Instead of assuming—as do most sociologists and most other people—that social order exists "out there" (that is, has a reality of its own), ethnomethodologists suggest that social order exists only because people have the *"capacity to convince each other* that society is out there" (Turner, 1982: 415). Ethnomethodologists search for the techniques and strategies by which people construct and sustain a vision of an orderly and patterned social world. According to ethnomethodologists, the substance of this perceived social order can only be inferred, but the *methods* that people use to create an impression of social order can be observed directly.

The Dramaturgical Approach

Erving Goffman has said, "All the world is not, of course, a stage, but the crucial ways in which it isn't are not easy to specify" (1959: 72). This statement is the basis of the dramaturgical approach to the study of social interaction—one that likens behavior to a theatrical performance in which people play different roles and act out scenes for the "audiences" with whom they interact.

People take into account the expectations of others and present only those aspects of themselves that fit with those expectations. In this sense, the self is situational; it has a variety of facets that are shown in different contexts. Different audiences reinforce or challenge the part of the self that an individual presents, and the individual responds by trying to play the role that the situation and the audience demand.

IMPRESSION MANAGEMENT

People try to control the reactions of those with whom they interact by presenting themselves in certain ways. The way that people present themselves to others defines the interaction and elicits a certain response. For example, most people try to create a "good first impression" by their dress and demeanor. *Impression management* is the process of trying to convey particular kinds of information to others to get them to respond in a desired way. Both verbal and nonverbal communication are used to create and to maintain impressions. Sometimes people are aware of using these techniques, but often they do not fully recognize how they create impressions.

The cooperation of the audience with whom a person is interacting is essential to a successful presentation of the self. Usually an audience will cooperate in an individual's effort to create a particular impression. Sometimes individuals make mistakes in this presentation by revealing information that is inconsistent with the impression they wish to create or by revealing emotions that do not fit with their behavior. They may do this by a slip of the tongue, a trembling voice, excessive sweating, a telling facial expression, or inappropriate dress. When the presentation of the self is disrupted in these ways, often an audience will nevertheless continue to support the impression that the individual wishes to create. Audiences can offer support by behaving courteously and helping people to restore the desired impression, or they can ignore errors made in the presentation of the self. In other situations audiences may seek information about the true intentions of the individual or even disrupt the presentation with a direct challenge. An individual's social self requires the cooperation of others, because this self is defined through social interaction.

ALIGNING ACTIONS

An *aligning action* is an effort to maintain or reestablish an impression that a person wishes to con-vey to an audience (Stokes and Hewitt, 1976). When people err in presentation, they usually try to correct with an aligning action. One type is a "disclaimer," an explanation for behavior that is about to occur and that will seem out of character with the intended impression (Scott and Lyman, 1968; Hewitt and Stokes, 1975). Another type is an "account," an explanation for inappropriate behavior that has already occurred. Accounts include both excuses, the admission that wrong has been done but that the individual was not responsible for the inappropriate behavior, and justifications, the acceptance of responsibility for the wrongdoing along with a denial that the behavior was improper under the circumstances. Justifications can be used repeatedly, but excuses cannot be repeated effectively because they imply lack of intent to do wrong and repeated behavior suggests that intent is present. The techniques of neutralization that we examined in Chapter 5 are disclaimers, because they precede behavior that violates rules, though these techniques are often used to justify deviant behavior that has already occurred (Sykes and Matza, 1957).

PERSONAL PROPS

Part of the staging of impression management involves the "actors" in an interaction using certain personal props to convey or reinforce a particular impression. Uniforms are one type of personal prop; the police, the military, and nurses all wear clothing that conveys information to an audience about what kind of behavior can be expected from them. Speech patterns and technical terms also convey information about the speaker's social standing or area of expertise. A beard, a pipe, or a "beeper" might be used to create a particular impression. In SEL 6.3 we can see how an applicant to a prep school might behave to create the impression desired by those who run the school.

SOCIOLOGY AND EVERYDAY LIFE   6.3
Getting into Prep School: The Interview

You will see from the following selection that the creation of a proper image—in this case, the "preppy" image—depends on dress, demeanor, reading tastes, hobbies, and friends and relatives.

This humorous piece makes it clear that the creation of the "right" impression is a complex undertaking filled with many details, including the correct personal props.

The most significant element of the Prep school entrance application is the interview. You're smart and you've done well on the SSAT's but so have other applicants, and the administration needs to get a look at you to see if you're right for student life pictures in future catalogs.

It helps if a campus building is named after a family member—an endowment fund is better—but even without these assets you can shine in the interview by adhering to a few cardinal rules.

DOs

1. Dress conservatively. Boys must wear a blue blazer, gray flannels, Weejuns, a white shirt and a red-and-blue rep tie (unless you're applying to a Bohemian Prep school, in which case sport white corduroys, a flannel shirt, and an incongruous tie). Girls have no choice but to wear a plaid kilt, button-down shirt, plain stockings, and loafers.

2. Your parents should be jovial and well-dressed. Rehearse Daddy on his hearty laugh and firm handshake. Make sure Mummy clasps her hands in her lap.

3. Tell about your epiphany (SSAT word) of the human need for salvation while reading *The Catcher in the Rye*, your favorite book.

4. Check ahead to uncover which is the school's perennially bad team and stress your prowess in that sport ("Except for my trophy in track, I don't feel I've reached my potential.")

5. Name-drop all siblings, cousins, and close friends who went or go to the school and "looooove it." This suggests that you'll fit right in and not become a loner who reads Sylvia Plath.

6. Feign interest in the school's curriculum, emphasizing the courses not offered in your day school. ("I saw in the catalog that you have classes in modern theology and . . .").

7. Ask about extracurricular programs and react with enthusiastic fervor to every activity.

8. After campus tour, remark on the beauty of the grounds, the modernity of the facilities, the handsomeness of the buildings.

DON'Ts

1. Wear Lacoste shirts, khakis and sneakers—implies an untrustworthy casualness. Absolutely no polyester or pens in pockets. (Sure, they want to groom you, but not *that* much.) Girls should stay away from short skirts, low-cut blouses, and platform shoes. Any suggestion of sartorial eccentricity should be reserved for impressing fellow students *after* you've been accepted.

2. Allow parents to talk about the trouble they've had with you at home and in school. They should not speak until spoken to (or they may overshadow you).

3. Discuss the *Communist Manifesto* and how it raises some unsettling questions about capitalism.

4. Groan when the interviewer outlines the school's compulsory athletic program or let him know you were impeached by your Little League team.

5. Admit to being second cousin to the student who tear-gassed last year's commencement ceremony.

6. Go into your interest in music or art—this makes you sound like the type who won't respect the school's "classic" curriculum. *Never* mention TV.

7. Inquire about the number of overnight or weekend leaves.

8. Query the whereabouts of cigarette machines, liquor stores, and sister or brother schools. Don't ask if the school fence extends through the woods at the back of the campus.

Source: Lisa Birnbach, ed., *The Official Preppy Handbook*. New York: Workman Publishing, 1980, pp. 54–55. Reprinted with permission of the publisher.

SETTING THE SCENE

The presentation of self often requires that the setting in which people interact reinforce the intended impression and make certain behavior possible.

People often decorate their homes to create a particular impression for visitors; those who sell furniture often say they are selling a "life style" rather than simply furniture. The term "coffee-table book" is used to refer to large, illustrated books

People often decorate their homes to convey a certain image. What impression do you think the owners have tried to create here?

that are laid out on tables for display purposes rather than to be read carefully. Restaurants often convey a certain atmosphere or "image" in their decor; butcher-block tables and hanging plants are common "scenery" in restaurants that appeal to young professionals and college students.

Scenery often includes a "front-stage" area and a "back-stage" area. The front-stage area is where the actual performance or presentation takes place. Often the presentation requires "teamwork," the cooperation of several people in creating a certain impression for an audience. The back-stage area is a place that is concealed from the audience; there the team that is trying to create an impression in the front-stage area can relax, share secrets, make preparations, practice their performance, and speak critically of the audience. In this back-stage area the members of the team often intentionally contradict the impressions they create in the front-stage area. Back-stage areas include the bathrooms of singles' bars and off-camera areas of television studios.

Goffman (1959) observed that the behavior of waiters and waitresses in a hotel restaurant was quite different in the dining room (front-stage) and in the kitchen (back-stage). In the dining room, employees were polite and deferential to guests; in the kitchen they often spoke vulgarly and criticized the guests. Occasionally back-stage behavior becomes known to the audience, destroying impressions that the team has worked hard to create. A kitchen door that is mistakenly left open in a restaurant can reveal aspects of the employees' behavior that are usually concealed from the diners. Sometimes back-stage behavior is concealed from the audience by collusion among the team members; an argument between a waiter and a *maitre d'* will be glossed over when they interact before the guests in the dining room.

Another example of front-stage and back-stage behavior involves professors and students. In the classroom, professors seek to create an impression that they are knowledgeable instructors who thoroughly understand their fields, and students try to create the impression that they are hard-working and attentive. As a result, professors may be reluctant to admit that they cannot answer a question or do not understand some aspect of their field, even though they may admit this to other professors in back-stage areas such as their offices or faculty lounges. Professors sometimes rely on teamwork with their teaching assistants and with other professors to maintain the impression that they know their fields thoroughly. Students sometimes use disclaimers and excuses to explain their absence from class or their poor performance on an examination. In private, they may tell other students that they were bored with the lectures or the reading material, or that they had better things to do with their time. These reactions are shared in back-stage areas such as dormitories, libraries, or student lounges, where students often exchange very different opinions of their professors from those they try to convey in the classroom (just as professors commonly exchange opinions of their students among themselves). On those rare occasions that a student or a professor "invades" the back-stage area of the other, information might be revealed that clashes with the front-stage presentation of the self in the classroom.

DRAMATURGICAL ANALYSIS: TWO EXAMPLES

Goffman's concepts of impression management, aligning actions, personal props, and setting the scene can be applied to a multitude of daily interactions. Here we examine two kinds of social interaction that have been analyzed by sociologists: a gynecological examination and a singles' dance.

Pelvic Examination in a Doctor's Office

Henslin and Biggs (1971) have used the dramaturgical approach to examine the interaction between gynecologists and their patients who are undergoing pelvic examinations. Because of the way they are socialized, many American women feel that their sense of modesty and even their self-concept are threatened when they undergo such examinations. Some even avoid checkups because of these feelings. Consequently, physicians have developed a "play" with a number of "scenes" that desexualize and depersonalize this examination and make the interaction between doctor and patient easier for both.

While the woman waits outside the doctor's office, she still retains her identity as a complete person; she has not yet been redefined as a patient who is about to undergo a pelvic examination. The nurse then calls the woman's name, directs her to the examination room, and weighs her. Often the woman sees this weighing process as an aspect of competent medical care that signals the beginning of her treatment as a patient.

The nurse next takes the patient into the doctor's office, where he greets her, asks her some questions, and decides if a pelvic examination is necessary. If the doctor determines that the examination is required, he calls the nurse, who then assumes the role of "pelvic preparer." When the nurse enters the room, the doctor leaves. The patient then undresses in the doctor's absence to eliminate any sexual connotations from her disrobing. She then lies on her back on an examining table with her knees bent and her feet in metal stirrups at the corners of the table, and wears a sheet draped over her pelvic area. This depersonalizes the examination and conceals the pelvic area from the patient while revealing it to the doctor.

The doctor then reenters the room and conducts the examination in the presence of the nurse, who provides emotional support for the patient and legal protection for the physician. The patient is treated as "a pelvis to be examined" rather than as a complete person. The doctor usually does not engage in personal conversation with the patient, nor does he typically make eye contact with her. The draped sheet reinforces the impersonal nature of the interaction at this stage.

When the examination is done, the physician leaves the examining room. The patient often expresses relief that it is over, and she gets dressed. The doctor then reenters the office and interviews the woman again, giving her information about the results of the examination and treating her as a whole person once again. The woman then leaves the office and returns to the normal routine of her life.

This interaction between doctor and patient makes a situation that many women find quite threatening much more comfortable. The woman is first treated as a complete person, then as a patient, and finally as "a pelvis to be examined." This change in her identity "medicalizes" the interaction and keeps the examination on an impersonal level. After the examination, she returns to the patient role and finally is treated as a complete person again before leaving the office.

Managing Impressions at a Singles' Dance

Dances and parties for single people are opportunities to meet and form relationships with people of the opposite sex. Those who attend such functions recognize this, but the purpose also implies—negatively—that they have to depend on such gatherings to establish relationships with others. As a consequence, these single people strive to create a good first impression and to present themselves in ways that indicate that they are not "desperate losers" (Schwartz and Lever, 1976; Berk, 1977).

Singles' dances and parties are often held in attractive settings such as well-known clubs and hotels. Some of these affairs are limited to "young professionals," although this kind of advertising is designed primarily to enhance the prestige of those who attend and to create a favorable public impression of single people. The settings in which these dances and parties are held often have dim lighting (to conceal physical defects) and loud music (to ensure casual rather than intimate conversations).

Men and women who attend singles' dances often present themselves as busy people who do not need the companionship of members of the opposite sex, although their very presence at the dance contradicts this impression. Singles sometimes show this by arriving late or by leaving early, by circulating among the other people there to avoid any commitment to one person, and by remaining aloof and "above the battle." Some try to distinguish themselves from the crowd by saying that this is the first singles' dance they have attended or that a friend forced them to attend. Those who are ignored by others often criticize them as "cliquey."

Singles' gatherings place a premium on physical appearance. Because people do not know each other, physical attraction is a major basis for social interaction. Because first impressions count in this setting, even those who complain that these events are "meat markets" try to look as attractive as possible and carefully examine others before they engage in conversation with them.

These strategies are intended to create favorable impressions and to "save face" (prevent embarrassment) when the goal of meeting others is not met. Face-saving strategies are also used to terminate conversations when one person finds another to be unattractive or incompatible or when one encounters an unwanted sexual advance. Singles often have difficulty ending a conversation while preserving the other person's feelings. They may excuse themselves to go to the bathroom or say they have to return to a friend who has been left alone. They may also say they want to "look around" or speak to someone they have not seen in a while. When these excuses cannot be made credibly or are not accepted by the other person as a reason to end an interaction, the individual who wishes to be free of the interaction can spend hours in an unwanted conversation and feel at the end of the dance that it was a waste of time.

Summary

Interaction has various forms. One form is exchange, a give-and-take process in which participants each seek rewards. If the norm of reciprocity is violated in an exchange, the participants may not continue to interact with each other. Another type of interaction is cooperation, the striving together for a common goal. Competition is a form of interaction in which people strive for the same goal, but with some of them winning and others losing. Conflict is interaction in which one party tries to eliminate or defeat the other. In many interactions, especially conflict, domination–subordination is an important dimension that influences the way that people deal with each other.

One important perspective on interaction is Herbert Blumer's version of symbolic interactionism. Blumer's theory explores the way that people act toward things on the basis of the symbolic meanings of those things. These meanings are developed from interaction among people and from an individual's interpretation and consideration of the meaning of things. Joint action exists when people take each other into account and adjust their behavior accordingly.

Much important interaction is nonverbal. This kind of interaction depends on the symbolic meanings of facial expressions, physical gestures, and personal space. Facial expressions have certain similarities across cultures, as we saw in one study that compared the meaning of the facial expressions of Americans and New Guineans. The meaning of physical gestures varies more from one culture to the next. Personal space is the amount of territory that a person needs around him or her to feel comfortable; norms of personal space vary across cultures and with the social background and interpersonal relationship of the participants in an interaction.

A second perspective on interaction is ethnomethodology, the study of the "taken-for-granted" techniques by which people make sense of the world. This perspective regards people as active participants in the development of meaningful kinds of behavior. Ethnomethodologists look for the rules that make interaction possible by carefully analyzing the hidden meanings of casual conversations and by disrupting expected behavior to discover the formal structures of interaction.

Dramaturgy is the third perspective on interaction that we examined. This approach likens human interaction to a play in which people follow scripts and act out scenes for an audience. The self is situational; people present only certain aspects of themselves to others in particular contexts. In doing so, they try to create impressions that elicit desired behavior from others. When this impression management is disrupted, people use aligning actions such as disclaimers, accounts, excuses, and justifications to bring the interaction back into line with the impression they are trying to create. Sometimes people use personal props and scenery to convey or reinforce a particular impression. We saw how personal props, scenery, aligning actions, and impression management were used in a doctor's office during a pelvic examination and at a singles' dance.

Important Terms

ALIGNING ACTION (140)
COMPETITION (129)
CONFLICT (131)
COOPERATION (129)
ETHNOMETHODOLOGY (138)
EXCHANGE (128)

IMPRESSION MANAGE-MENT (140)
NORM OF RECIPROCITY (128)
PERSONAL SPACE (137)
SOCIAL INTERACTION (127)

Suggested Readings

Herbert Blumer. *Symbolic Interactionism: Perspective and Method*. Englewood Cliffs, N.J.: Prentice-Hall, 1969. One of the best presentations of the symbolic interactionist perspective; the first chapter is an especially useful summary of this position.

Erving Goffman. *The Presentation of Self in Everyday Life*. Garden City, N.Y.: Doubleday, 1959. Goffman's first presentation of the dramaturgical method for analyzing interaction.

Edward T. Hall. *The Hidden Dimension*. Garden City, N.Y.: Doubleday, 1966. An examination of territoriality and the norms of personal space in the United States and other cultures.

Warren Handel. *Ethnomethodology: How People Make Sense*. Englewood Cliffs, N.J.: Prentice-Hall, 1982. A brief introduction to this perspective presented in relatively simple language. Contains several applications of this approach to the study of interaction.

George C. Homans. *Social Behavior: Its Elementary Forms*, rev. ed. New York: Harcourt Brace Jovanovich, 1974. A statement of exchange theory and its uses in analyzing social interaction.

Howard Robboy and Candace Clark, eds. *Social Interaction: Readings in Sociology*, 2nd ed. New York: St. Martin's Press, 1983. A comprehensive collection of essays that look at many aspects of society from a symbolic interactionist perspective.

SOCIAL STRUCTURE

Your high school is probably much the same today as it was when you attended it. Administrators still hire and fire teachers; teachers still assign, collect, and grade homework; and both teachers and administrators continue to enforce disciplinary rules. Students are still concerned with athletics and popularity, as well as with their academic work. Students band together in groups, and some of them feel excluded from the groups they would like to join.

What is different about your former high school is that the specific people who are administrators, teachers, and students have changed somewhat since you graduated. If you returned to the school a few decades from now you might not know anyone, and yet if you closely watched the behavior of those in the school it would probably remind you of your high school days.

Social structure is interaction among people that recurs in regular and stable patterns over time. Social structure—the form or shape of social relationships—is distinct from the actual people who interact with one another. Thus, the social structure of your high school endures, even though students graduate, teachers leave their jobs, and administrators change.

The social structures that sociologists study are as small as two people engaged in interaction, as in a marriage, a confession in the Catholic Church, or a job interview. On the other hand, social structures can be as large as the international community of nations, although few sociologists study structures larger than a single society.

The family is one kind of social structure that exists in all societies. Just by seeing a man, a woman, and a child on the street or in a restaurant, you would not know that they were a family. You would need to know the meaning that they and other people give to their relationship and how they interact with each other in order to determine if they were a family.

Social structures are stable, even though they change and develop over time. A husband and wife with one child constitute a family. If they later have four more children and move in with the wife's parents, they are still a family, even though the form of the structure has changed.

Social structure has an *emergent* nature; that is, it has unique qualities that cannot easily be predicted from knowledge of its individual components. As we saw in Chapter 1, there is no way to determine exactly how individual musicians will interact when they form a group or exactly how individual players will interact as a team, even if we have detailed knowledge about the musicians or the players before they form a unit. In other words, a social structure has a reality that is distinct from its component parts. It endures over time, even with turnover in the individuals who occupy positions within the structure, as we saw in the example of the high school or as the cartoon shows.

Individuals who occupy positions in a social structure are affected by that structure in a variety of ways. Social structures place constraints on behavior and channel it in certain directions. First-year students at a college or university learn the rules of the school and the expectations of their peers. New employees learn the "company way" in their early years on the job. The "company way" is a characteristic of the organization that has emerged over time out of the interaction of workers who hold various positions in the firm. It may alter the new workers' hours of sleep, leisure time, mode of dress, manners, and commitment to people outside the company.

The social structure does affect the behavior and attitudes of people who occupy positions in it, but individuals can also change the social structure through their own actions. A social structure does not fully control and dominate people, even though it does influence them in many ways. The rise of labor unions changed the relationship be-

"*Merry Christmas, folks. And I want to say I couldn't be president of this great company without the support of each and every one of you, or people very much like you.*"

Drawing by Wm. Hamilton; © 1980 The New Yorker Magazine, Inc.

tween workers and management within American corporations from one of domination–subordination to one that more closely resembles an exchange between equals. Some married couples have modified the structure of the American family by communal living or by having the wife work at a full-time job outside the home and having the husband take care of the children and the house.

Components of Social Structure

Social structures consist of positions within the structure and behavior that is associated with those positions. Sociologists call these positions *statuses*, and the behavior that is associated with them *roles*.

STATUS

The term status, as used in sociology, should not be confused with the popular usage of the same word to mean prestige. A person who occupies a high status or position in a social structure may indeed have prestige (the respect of others), but the term status refers to the position itself, not the prestige or respect associated with the position. The president of General Motors occupies a status with high prestige attached to it; a janitor in the same company also occupies a status, but one with much less prestige.

Furthermore, statuses in a structure are independent of the characteristics of any specific individual who might occupy the status at a particular time. The status of president, for example, has meaning only in relation to the rest of the social structure and the other statuses within it. In fact, another way to look at social structure is as a set of relationships among a number of statuses.

Master Status

A single person often occupies several different statuses. The president of General Motors may also be a spouse, a parent, a member of a school board, and a trustee of a bank. A *master status* is the most important status in a person's life, the one that determines his or her social identity. As we saw in Chapter 5, where we looked at the master status "deviant," how other people react is an important factor in determining one's master status. However, each person also plays an active part in defining his or her own master status. The president of General Motors will probably acquire the master status of "corporate president" in the eyes of other people, but might also choose to make the status of "parent" or "spouse" a master status.

Their young age is a master status for children, and in many societies a person's sex is also a master status. For many Americans, occupation is a master status, as is evident from the fact that the first question people often ask when meeting someone is "What do you do?" The answer helps to place the person in the structure of society.

In recent years, some people have tried to cast off unwanted master statuses so that others will treat them as whole persons rather than in terms of a single master status. Feminists have sought to destroy the idea that an individual's sex is enough information to place a person in the social structure, and the gay liberation movement has tried to convince people that an individual's sexual prefer-ence is an inadequate basis for understanding the whole individual.

Ascribed and Achieved Statuses

Each of us has certain statuses known as *ascribed statuses*, or social positions assigned to us by others at birth or at some later stage in the life cycle. Personal choice or effort has nothing to do with ascribed statuses, which can be based on biological inheritance (sex or race), the traits of one's parents (class or ethnicity), or one's stage in the life cycle (adolescence or old age). Ascribed statuses depend on the symbolic meanings attached to certain traits in a culture. People with some Negro ancestry are classified as "black" in the United States, but Brazilians with some Negro ancestry are classified along a continuum by the shade of their skin color rather than lumped into the single status "black." The status of race is thus linked to the cultural meaning given to skin color, rather than to specific biological characteristics (see Chapter 9).

An *achieved status* is one that a person acquires by choice, effort, or merit. Unlike an ascribed status, it is based on individual behavior. As a result, people

By looking at the people in this photograph, we can get some idea of each one's as-cribed status in the social structure.

have some control over the statuses they achieve. A social structure that emphasizes achieved status over ascribed status can use talent more effectively and has some built-in flexibility. However, the people who occupy statuses in this social structure might experience anxiety in trying to achieve certain positions, and they might have difficulty explaining to others and to themselves why they fail to achieve certain statuses. Some statuses are relatively easy to achieve, such as the status of parent, but other statuses, such as physician or company president, are more difficult to achieve.

Achieved and ascribed statuses are closely intertwined, for relatively few positions are fully accessible by personal achievement. Consequently, most achieved statuses are filled by people with certain characteristics. Three traits that are especially important in achieving certain statuses are a person's sex and age, and the social class of his or her parents. Males who are born into a wealthy family and who have reached a certain age are more likely than young women from poor families to achieve the status of corporate president. The status of professional football player is an achieved status, but the achievement of this occupational position is limited to those who are male, an ascribed status. Until 1947, the ascribed status of race prevented blacks from achieving the status of major league baseball player.

ROLE

Each status is associated with one or more roles, the behavior that is expected of a person in a particular status. Individuals *occupy a status* and are expected to *play the role* attached to the status. Those who occupy the status of professor are ex-

pected to teach and advise students; at many colleges and universities they are also expected to do research, write, publish articles and books, and serve on committees. These activities constitute the variety of roles that are associated with the status of professor.

The expectations of a role are embodied in the norms of the culture. We learn many roles through socialization by our families, teachers, peer groups, and the mass media (see Chapter 4). These agents of socialization transmit cultural expectations about the behavior that is appropriate for people who occupy various statuses. When people have not learned roles through socialization, they must discover through interaction with others what behavior is expected of them in a particular situation. For example, people may be uncertain what behavior is appropriate for them on their first visit to a psychiatrist; only by interacting with the psychiatrist will they learn where they should sit, whether they can ask the psychiatrist personal questions, and how the psychiatrist will react to missed appointments. Through interaction these people begin to play the role of patient.

Some roles are flexible, in that there are various ways in which an individual who occupies a status can meet the demands of the role. For instance, professors can play the role of teaching students in different ways. They can lecture, lead a class discussion, show a film, or bring in a guest lecturer. However, the role does limit the professor's behavior, because the expectations of the role of teaching will not be met by discussing a topic that is irrelevant to the course or by missing half of the classes. In SEL 7.1 we see how the roles associated with the status of heir-apparent to the throne of England limited Prince Charles in his choice of a wife.

SOCIOLOGY AND EVERYDAY LIFE 7.1
Being King of England

The English royal family is a social structure that is part of the larger structure of government. Within the royal family, Prince Charles occupies the status of prince, which is also a status within the government, for he is the immediate heir to the throne. When he becomes king, Prince Charles will move from one status (heir-apparent) to another status (king). As king, he will perform such roles as giving the winning party in elections official permis-

sion to form a government. As king, he will also occupy the status of titular head of the Church of England; the roles associated with this position are largely ceremonial.

One expectation associated with the status of prince and heir-apparent to the throne is to select a "proper" wife. For years, Prince Charles's relationships with women received much attention from the press and the public. His selection of Lady Diana Spencer to be his wife met several different requirements for this role. It was necessary that he marry, because he had to father future heirs to the throne. His wife could not be either Catholic or divorced. She had to reinforce the monarchy as "a public symbol of family morality and family life" (p. 25). In playing the role of selecting a wife, Prince Charles fulfilled another expectation that was both personal and a reflection of his culture: He married someone with whom he was "in love." In the past, future kings and queens had entered arranged marriages in which their spouses were selected by their families so as to build a political alliance with another country. Prince Charles also had to marry a woman who was willing to merge her identity with his; he said that his future wife "not only marries a man. She marries into a way of life—a job" (p. 25). With all these limitations, it took Prince Charles several years and quite a few courtships before he found a wife, but Lady Diana Spencer fulfilled all expectations.

Lady Diana Spencer—now Diana, Princess of Wales—was related to royalty before her marriage to Prince Charles, and she was also accustomed to wealth. By joining the royal family, she acquired a new status that is associated with a variety of roles. Her life as the future king's wife has been described as follows:

She will never have to wash her own dishes, worry about her mortgage, change her children's diapers or fret about their education. She'll have a choice of seven places to call home.

Her children's job prospects look pretty good, too. But the price she must pay for all this is unenviable. She must make polite conversation to interminable mayors at interminable dinner parties, and take a passionate interest in Girl Scouts and women's institutes. She must cut ribbons, plant trees, lay foundation stones, declare things open, declare things closed. She must maintain a polite smile at all times, and be very careful what she says. She must never—but never—appear anything other than radiant and gracious (p. 25).

Source: Based on Tony Holden, "The Prince Says He's Finally Found Love," *The Boston Globe*, March 2, 1981, pp. 25, 27.

Role Performance

A role is the expected behavior associated with a status, and *role performance* is the actual behavior of a person who occupies the status. Role performance differs from the role itself; the actual behavior occurs within broad limits set by the role, but it is also affected by the self that a person has developed through socialization and by the situation in which the person finds himself or herself. For instance, the presidency of the United States is a status in the social structure of government. One role associated with that status is to make decisions about the deployment of the armed forces. Each president performs this role somewhat differently because each has different beliefs about when and where troops should be used, because the specific crises that arise are different, and because public support for military intervention changes over time. Different presidents thus act differently as commander-in-chief of the armed forces, but the expectations of the presidential role require all presidents to make decisions about how troops will be deployed.

Role Set

When several different roles are attached to a single status, we speak of a *role set* (Merton, 1968). A person who occupies several different statuses will also have several role sets, each of which is tied to a particular status. For example, a woman may occupy the statuses of mother, wife, and employee. Each of these statuses is tied to a role set. The status of employee may be associated with the role of supervising a group of secretaries as well as meeting the demands of her boss. The status of mother is associated with the roles of providing affection to the children and feeding them. The status of wife is tied to the roles of being a social companion and a sex partner. Thus a working mother occupies several different statuses, each of which is associated with a role set.

Role Conflict

Role conflict is said to occur when two or more roles that a person is expected to play are incompatible; if the demands of one role are met, it becomes difficult to play another role. A working mother might experience role conflict by having to pay attention to her children, act as a companion to her husband, and perform her job satisfactorily. A professor who is advisor to a student might experience role conflict in trying to grade that same student objectively. Black police officers are expected by other blacks to be loyal to the black community, and they are expected by their supervisors to be loyal to the police department. These expectations can be in

A working mother may experience role conflict in providing attention for her children and performing her job satisfactorily.

conflict if the officer is required to control a riot in a black community or arrest a black suspect (Alex, 1969).

Role conflict can be dealt with in a variety of ways. One way is to deny that there is a conflict. Another way is to respond to the demands of one role unemotionally or to give that role lower priority than another one. Thus a working mother might make clear to her children and her husband that working at home in the evening is necessary to her career. Role conflict is sometimes minimized by performing roles in different locations. Making it clear that work will be "left at the office" and that family members are not to call the person at work might reduce conflict between work roles and family roles. If role conflict persists, a person might withdraw from one role. Thus, continuing conflict between the role of wife and the role of worker might prompt a woman to get a divorce or to quit her job.

Role Strain

Role strain occurs when a person experiences the expectations of a single role as incompatible, making it difficult to perform the role. For example, physicians are expected to provide an objective diagnosis of a medical problem but also be personable and supportive of their patients. Military chaplains teach religious ideals of love and forgiveness but also encourage soldiers to kill the enemy (Burchard, 1963; Zahn, 1969).

Unclear and changing expectations about appropriate role behavior are common sources of role strain. For instance, changing expectations for husbands and wives are probably associated with role strain that underlies recent increases in divorce rates and in the number of men seeking psychiatric care for sexual problems.

Role strain is also associated with the assumption of new roles and with the giving up of old roles.

People may not be adequately prepared for a new role, be unwilling to give up an old role, or have difficulty making the transition from the old role to the new one. For example, adolescents often experience role strain because they are expected to stop acting like children and start acting more like adults, even though they are still expected to obey their parents and are not expected to adopt adult roles such as full-time employee or parent.

Another source of role strain is incompatibility among the expectations held by different people with whom an individual interacts. For instance, a husband's expectations about his wife's behavior as an employee ("Leave your work at the office") can conflict with the employer's expectations about her behavior ("Finish this report by tomorrow morning"). When the woman tries to meet the expectations of both her husband and her employer, she might experience role strain.

Groups

A *group* is a set of relationships among people who interact on a face-to-face basis over time. A group has a defined membership, a set of interrelated statuses and roles, common values and norms, and an identity. For a group to exist, people must interact repeatedly and communicate with one another. Over time, patterns of interaction develop and a social structure of linked statuses and roles emerges. Expectations develop among the members of the group as to the proper behavior for people occupying different positions. Groups have an identity, or sense that they are different from those who are not members of the group, and an *esprit de corps*, or feeling of being a unit with a distinct identity. Groups have their own values and norms, although these are often similar to those of the larger culture of which the group is a part. One common group norm is the norm of reciprocity (see Chapter 6).

The nature of groups is emergent; that is, they become more than the sum of their parts. Some sociologists claim that groups can be analyzed solely in terms of the behavior of their members and that groups have no separate reality of their own (Homans, 1964). However, most sociologists believe that groups have a character of their own that influences members in certain ways. The fact that fraternities and sororities, colleges and universities, and neighborhoods and communities have identifiable "images" does suggest that groups have different characteristics. One way that groups

influence their members is by pressuring them to conform to the norms of the group. Experiments have demonstrated that some members of a group will conform to group norms rather than stand up for what they personally believe, whereas other members are able to maintain their stance in opposition to group pressure (Asch, 1955).

Groups are not merely random collections of people. An "aggregate" is simply a collection of individuals who are in one place at one time. A crowd at a rock concert or the patients in a doctor's waiting room are not groups, because they do not interact over time, do not relate to each other in a structure of statuses and roles, do not share common values and norms, and do not have a distinct identity as a group. In some cases, aggregates do develop into groups, because physical closeness is conducive to the formation of a group.

A "category" is a collection of people who share some personal or social characteristic. People can be classified as "elderly" if they are over the age of seventy. Other categories are defined by sex, race or ethnicity, income, and educational attainment. Categories are simply statistical groupings or classifications of people with similar traits; they do not have the characteristics of groups, although people with similar characteristics are probably more likely to form groups than people with different characteristics.

PRIMARY GROUPS AND SECONDARY GROUPS

A *primary group* is a relatively small group whose members interact on a regular and intimate basis (Cooley, 1909, 1963). Primary groups have a strong sense of identity, a "we-feeling" that distinguishes them from the "they" who make up the rest of the world. Primary groups are relatively permanent and endure over time. Individual members are not easily replaced. Members of primary groups are treated as whole persons rather than as a means to some end. Relationships within primary groups are based on expressive or emotional needs, rather than on instrumental values such as the ability to perform specific tasks well. Individual deficiencies do not become a basis for throwing a person out of a primary group. However, the emotions felt by the members of primary groups are not always positive, because intimate interaction can lead to intense conflict.

Primary groups are especially important in the early stages of the life cycle. The prototype of a primary group is the family; the play groups of young children are another example. Primary groups link individuals to the larger society, and they are important in the socialization process. Families, play groups, and other primary groups satisfy the human need for intimacy, offer social support, and help resocialize people who wish to change. Self-help groups such as Alcoholics Anonymous and Overeaters Anonymous are primary groups in which social interaction is designed to support people in reaching a goal. Encounter groups and consciousness-raising groups are also primary groups that serve the expressive needs of their members.

Secondary groups are usually larger and more complex than primary groups, and less personal and intimate. Members of secondary groups generally work toward specific goals and are usually less emotionally involved than in primary groups. The specialization of tasks is greater in most secondary groups, and individuals are treated according to what they can contribute to the group. Compared to a primary group, interaction in secondary groups is relatively limited, superficial, and temporary. Secondary groups include labor unions, professional associations, and committees.

Secondary groups are instrumental; they seek to accomplish specific tasks, even though participation in the group can also serve expressive needs for the members. For example, the manifest function, or stated goal, of the various groups involved in the civil rights movement of the 1950s and 1960s was to achieve equality for blacks, but a latent function of that movement was to meet the participants' expressive needs, including the development of a sense of personal identity and effectiveness. Secondary groups that achieve their stated goals sometimes develop new goals in order to continue their existence. The March of Dimes, for example, spent twenty years raising money to help polio victims, but it changed its goals rather than disband when a vaccine was developed for this disease (Sills, 1958).

The concepts of primary group and secondary group are *ideal types*—composites of a set of general characteristics showing the essence of a social phenomenon—rather than descriptions of actual groups. Few groups fit an ideal type; many groups, for example, have some of the characteristics of both primary groups and secondary groups. Historically, as societies have grown larger and more complex, secondary groups have grown more important and primary groups have declined in importance. In tribal societies, the family and the peer group are important primary groups. In industrial

societies such as the United States these primary groups continue to be important, but secondary groups such as industrial organizations and schools have become more important than they are in less complex societies.

Primary groups sometimes develop within larger secondary groups. A work group is a kind of primary group that sometimes develops within a large industrial organization. Primary groups also develop in the armed forces. The primary groups that developed among soldiers during World War II and during the Korean War were characterized by intimate interaction, sharing of personal property, and mutual efforts to protect one another in combat (Little, 1970). American soldiers in Vietnam did not develop these primary groups to the same extent; because they knew in advance when their tour of duty would end, they defined their roles individually, rather than in group-oriented terms (Moskos, 1975).

REFERENCE GROUPS

A *reference group* is a group or a category that people use to evaluate themselves and their behavior (Merton, 1968). It provides guidelines that people use in developing a self-concept, in learning attitudes and beliefs, and in defining appropriate role performance. Often, reference groups are actually categories with which people identify, rather than specific groups of individuals. For example, a recent college graduate might use "adults" as a reference group. Also, college students sometimes compare their grades with those of other students at their own or similar schools, even though these reference groups are categories and not groups in the strict sense of the term (Bassis, 1977).

The main difference between a reference group and primary and secondary groups is that an individual may use as a reference group a group to which he or she does not actually belong. Some reference groups are membership groups, but groups that people wish to join or wish to avoid joining are also reference groups. Anticipatory socialization into a reference group occurs when people alter their behavior and attitudes to fit the expectations of the group that they plan to join in the future. Law students use practicing attorneys as a reference group even before they complete law school; in fact, undergraduates who hope to attend law school sometimes use practicing attorneys as a reference group. In neither case are the students actually members of the reference group. Practicing attorneys are members of the reference group of all attorneys, and they usually demonstrate this by joining a bar association. These attorneys are influenced by the expectations of other lawyers; these expectations are formalized in the bar's Code of Professional Responsibility.

Some reference groups are positive reference groups that people want to emulate; others are negative reference groups from which people want to distinguish themselves. Some law students, for example, might use public-interest lawyers such as Ralph Nader as a positive reference group; they might use public defenders who work with suspects charged with petty crimes as a negative reference group. These orientations can influence law students' behavior and attitudes—including their selection of courses, their political beliefs, and the job interviews they seek.

Socialization over the course of the life cycle involves changes in reference groups (see Chapter 4). Twelve-year olds begin to compare themselves with adolescents and distinguish themselves from children. College students also experience changes in reference groups. A famous study of students at Bennington College found that most students tended to become more liberal politically as they progressed through school, which was due to the shift in the students' reference group from their parents to their peers and their professors. Those who remained as conservative as they were when they started college continued to use their parents as a positive reference group. Students who became more liberal while at Bennington were still more politically liberal as adults than were other people of similar social and economic standing (Newcomb, 1963, 1967).

ASPECTS OF GROUP STRUCTURE

As they interact, people often develop a group structure that gives their relationship meaning, predictability, and stability (Bales, 1951). The structure of a group can be described by its boundaries, size, pattern of interaction, roles, and decision-making process (Hare, 1976; McGrath, 1978).

Boundaries

Groups are distinguishable from the social environment. They are cohesive units with their own boundaries. Some boundaries are natural, such as those based on territorial location, but other boundaries are more arbitrary, such as the exclusion of any person with Negro ancestry from a "whites-only" social club. The boundaries of a group can be defined by recurring patterns of interaction, by formal membership requirements, by culturally meaningful symbols such as uniforms and badges, and by conflict with other groups.

Size

The number of members in a group is an important structural characteristic that influences the behavior of a group's members in a variety of ways (Simmel, 1950; Blau, 1977). Large groups are always secondary groups and have the characteristics of secondary groups. Small groups can be either primary groups or secondary groups, but even those that are secondary groups often have some traits of primary groups, such as face-to-face interaction.

A "dyad," or group of two people, is fragile, because the group ceases to exist if one person leaves. In a dyad, the behavior of one member cannot easily be concealed from the other, so the members relate to each other intimately, with the norm of reciprocity often guiding their exchanges. The addition of new members to a dyad changes it in various ways.

In a "triad," or group of three people, coalitions are possible (Caplow, 1969). Two members can join forces against the third. Unlike a dyad, if one member of a triad leaves, the group continues to exist; the two remaining members might continue as a dyad or replace the third member. In a triad, interaction can continue when one person is absent or does not participate. When two members of a triad interact, the third person is an audience who can influence the way the other two interact with each other and with the third person. Conflicts between two members can be resolved by a third person, or the third person might exacerbate the conflict by manipulating the other members of the group.

Groups of five have certain advantages over smaller or larger groups (Berelson and Steiner, 1967; Hare, 1976). Because five is an uneven number, there is less likelihood of an even split of "votes" when there is disagreement. A group of five is more likely than a smaller group to offer each member a chance to find another person who shares the same opinion on an issue. Groups of five are also less likely than larger groups to split into factions that disrupt the group. Conversation is relatively easy in groups of five, but in larger groups the speaker is more apt to speak formally to the group as a whole rather than to converse with others as equals. Larger groups also require more coordination among members, causing formal leaders to emerge.

We can see the effect of group size on behavior by looking at classes of different sizes. In small seminars or discussion sections, there is often considerable interaction between the instructor and the students, and a lot of interaction among the students themselves. In larger seminars, communication is more likely to be between the professor and the students, with less among the students themselves. In small lecture classes, the professor might adopt a more formal style of presentation and only occasionally take questions from students. In larger lecture classes, students may be intimidated by the size of the class and tend to ask fewer questions; these classes often take the form of lectures presented by the professor to the students.

Pattern of Interaction

The pattern of interaction in a group can be graphically depicted in a diagram that shows patterns of influence, communication, and friendship in the group. A close-knit group (see Figure 7.1,A) includes a large number of strong ties among the members; a loose-knit group (see Figure 7.1,B) includes a small number of weak ties among members. Strong ties produce cohesive and well-integrated groups, but they also create sharper boundaries between the group and the social environment. Even weak ties *between* groups are important for the cohesion of the whole society; without these weak ties between groups, a society would lack integration and become splintered into its component groups (Granovetter, 1973).

Group Roles

Laboratory research with college students shows that several different roles emerge as an aggregate develops into a group over time (Bales, 1951; Bales and Slater, 1955; Parsons and Bales, 1955; Mills, 1967; Bales, 1970; Hare, 1976). A few roles are common—especially the role of talker, and the role of resolver of group differences and creator of harmonious relations. Another role involves offering new ideas to the group, and "clowns" often emerge to alleviate tension within the group through joking.

FIGURE 7.1

In both A and B, a two-headed arrow represents a mutual choice of friendship, and a one-headed arrow represents a one-way choice of friendship. Solid arrows show strong ties, and broken arrows show weak ties.

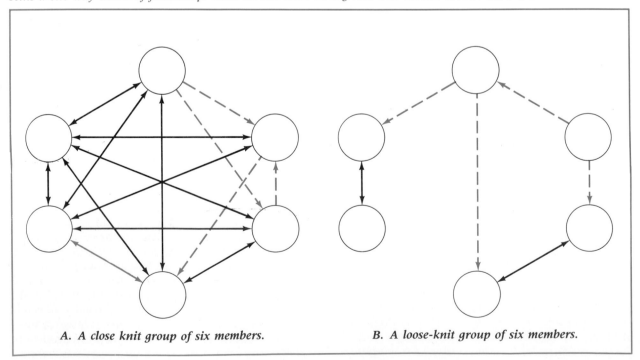

A. *A close knit group of six members.*   B. *A loose-knit group of six members.*

In most groups one important role is the leader. Leaders sometimes emerge through the interaction of the members, but in other groups they are formally appointed or elected. Leaders help the group set goals, coordinate relations among members, insure smooth communication and interaction, and assist in the making of decisions (Hare, 1976).

Groups require leaders to perform two kinds of tasks. "Instrumental leaders" make decisions and direct the group toward its goals. "Expressive leaders," on the other hand, are oriented toward the emotional aspects of the group, such as maintaining morale, insuring harmony, and providing support to the members (Bales, 1951, 1953; Slater, 1955; Sherif, 1956; Hare, 1976). At first, many groups select one person to play both instrumental and expressive roles, but as time passes these roles are usually divided between two people. Performing instrumental tasks commonly makes it difficult for a person to continue as an expressive leader, and a second person then takes over that role. The instrumental leader and the expressive leader usually continue to interact on a regular basis.

Group leaders use different styles to perform their roles. Democratic leaders try to sound out group opinion and win members' support before taking action. Authoritarian leaders are more assertive in directing a group and give orders to members. Laissez-faire leaders make relatively few efforts to guide the group, letting it take its own course with little direction.

Group Decision Making

Groups follow similar sequences in making decisions (Bales and Strodtbeck, 1951). First they consider a problem and gather information that is relevant to solving it. Then they evaluate the information that has been collected and consider alternative solutions. In making a decision, the group is sometimes torn by internal dissension. This leads to efforts to restore harmony; joking and mutually supportive activities help return the group to a cohesive state. This sequence is particularly common among groups that are oriented toward accomplishing specific goals (Talland, 1955).

Formal Organizations

In an industrial society such as the United States or Japan, people spend much time outside primary groups. They are educated in schools, work for large companies, and belong to churches or temples. Sociologists refer to these large, complex secondary groups as *formal organizations* (Blau and Scott, 1962).

Formal organizations are deliberately created to achieve certain goals. Colleges and universities are designed to educate students, conduct research, and provide knowledge to the larger society (see Chapter 12). Large corporations are designed to make profits by providing the public with goods and services (see Chapter 16).

Formal organizations are characterized by a *division of labor*, which orders work into a set of interrelated, specialized tasks. In order to operate smoothly, these organizations require well-defined lines of authority, clear channels of communication, and coordination among various statuses and roles. In contrast to primary groups, interaction within formal organizations is often emotionally uninvolving, because individuals are treated in terms of the tasks they perform for the organization rather than as complete persons. Obligations and rights are attached to statuses in the organization, rather than to the people who occupy those statuses at a particular time. Individual members of the organization are replaceable, but the organization continues to endure even with a turnover of personnel.

Organizations develop a variety of strategies for dealing with the external environment. To reduce disruption by the external world, they expand, alter the organizational structure, eliminate competitors, specialize in a particular task, or diversify their goals. Technological change sometimes requires an organization to develop new goals or adapt in other ways. For years, Parker Brothers was a leading manufacturer of children's board games. With the introduction of computer technology, the company developed a line of video games, although it was relatively late in entering this lucrative market. Profit-making organizations often adapt to their external environment by seeking new markets. Coca-Cola has expanded its market to the People's Republic of China. Nestlé's has tried to increase its sales of baby formula by persuading nursing mothers in developing countries to give up breast-feeding; this effort to expand its market caused considerable controversy because the formula was both more expensive and less safe than breast-feeding.

VOLUNTARY ASSOCIATIONS

A *voluntary association* is an organization whose members freely participate, such as a church or a campaign committee. These organizations are not rigidly organized, often lack a formal authority structure, and have many aspects of secondary groups.

People join voluntary associations in their spare time and are free to quit at any time. Members are not paid for their participation, as are the employees of formal organizations such as a corporation. Many people join voluntary associations to fill their leisure time in a pleasurable way or simply to interact with others who have similar interests. Some voluntary associations have specific goals, such as the improvement of local schools (the Parent–Teacher Association), lobbying for political change (a local political organization), or the expression of religious beliefs (a local church).

In the United States, the people who are most likely to join voluntary associations are middle-aged, married, and have relatively high levels of income and education (Hodges, 1964; Babchuk and Booth, 1969; Curtis, 1971). Voluntary associations have been criticized for the superficiality of their members' involvement, but they do meet expressive needs and are a testing ground for pro-

grams and policies that might later be adopted by a larger organization or by the government.

TOTAL INSTITUTIONS

People sometimes belong to organizations against their will. For example, they may be sentenced to prison, committed to a mental hospital, or drafted into the military. These organizations rely on coercion to motivate their members, often have nearly full control over all important aspects of an individual's daily life, and frequently isolate the individual from contact with the outside world. Erving Goffman (1961) has called organizations of this sort *total institutions*, although the term "institution" has another meaning in sociology that we discuss later in this chapter.

Total institutions such as prisons, the military, mental hospitals, and prisoner-of-war camps strive consciously to resocialize their members by creating for them a new sense of self and a new outlook on the world. The goal of these efforts at resocialization (see Chapter 4) is to create uniformity out of

Many people work for voluntary associations in their spare time and are free to quit at any time. Here a volunteer member of a blood donor organization leads a donor to a chair.

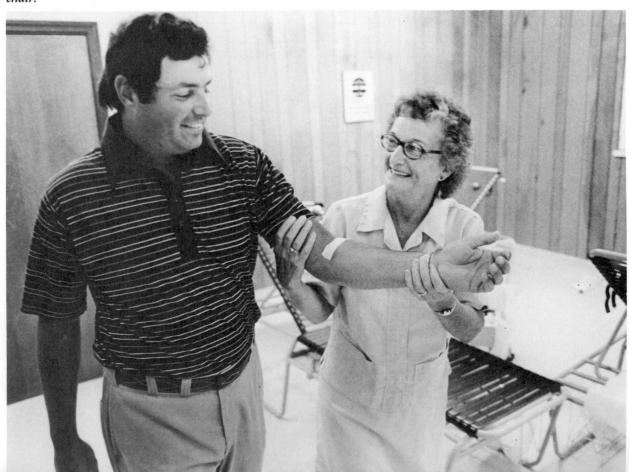

diversity—to take a group of people with different social identities and instill in them norms and values that become the basis of a new and common identity. Resocialization in total institutions often begins by isolating members from the outside world and from social support for their old identities. This is done by physical isolation, by consuming large amounts of the recruits' time, and by attacking those people who support the old social identity. It is also accomplished by stripping people of their old identities by altering their physical appearance. For example, recruits in the armed forces have their hair cut short and are made to wear uniforms.

After the old identity is destroyed or suppressed, the agents of socialization in charge of a total institution start to give new members the basis of a new identity. Rituals create group unity and encourage learning from the peer group. Members are given opportunities to play the role into which they are being resocialized. Sometimes old members are assigned the task of introducing new members into the organization. When partially resocialized individuals teach even newer recruits about the ways of life in the organization, these partially resocialized members often deepen their commitment to the roles in the organization by publicly affirming the organization's norms and values (Goffman, 1961, Van Maanen, 1976).

Not all total institutions are alike. Some are better able than others to isolate their members from the outside world. Also, membership in some is more voluntary than in others; for instance, some mental hospital patients will be voluntary admissions and others will be committed by a court, but all prison inmates are involuntarily locked up. The administrators of total institutions have different degrees of power to expel members; a patient in a mental hospital can be discharged relatively easily, but an unruly prison inmate cannot simply be released. The experience of being in a total institution affects members in different ways; some are able to neutralize the efforts to resocialize them, but others are influenced in major ways by these organizations (McEwen, 1980).

BUREAUCRACY

A *bureaucracy* is a formal organization that emphasizes the rational and efficient pursuit of goals through a highly structured network of statuses and roles. The German sociologist Max Weber (1925, 1947) viewed bureaucracies as technically efficient but dehumanizing organizations that are like machines, with the individual members of the organization acting like parts of a machine. Weber outlined the characteristics of the ideal type of bureaucracy; these characteristics are the abstract elements that define a bureaucracy, not actual traits of each and every bureaucratic organization in the real world.

Characteristics of Bureaucracies

One characteristic of a bureaucracy is a clear division of labor. Tasks are specialized, and each position or status (or "office") in the bureaucracy is attached to a specific job. Specialization enables individuals who occupy different statuses to develop expertise and become skilled and efficient at performing their jobs. Jobs are organized into units (or bureaus) that have specific functions to perform for the bureaucracy as a whole.

Bureaucracies have a hierarchy of positions or statuses in which authority and lines of communication are formally spelled out. *Authority* is the acknowledged right of those who occupy certain positions to exercise their will over others. The ranking of statuses by authority within a bureaucracy often takes the form of a pyramid, with a few people at the top exercising great authority and a large number of workers in lower positions controlled by those with more authority. Through this hierarchy, the various statuses are integrated into an efficient organization.

Formal rules and procedures govern the behavior of the members of a bureaucracy. These rules and procedures are written down, making behavior within the bureaucracy predictable and creating a stable organization that endures over time, even if there are changes in the personnel who occupy the various positions. For example, the Roman Catholic Church has endured for centuries, even though there are frequent changes in the Pope, the clergy, and the membership. The exact expectations of each status in a bureaucracy are spelled out in rules and procedures, which assign tasks to those who fill each position. This concreteness creates discipline, standardizes behavior, reduces the need for continuous supervision, and avoids the need to issue new orders continuously. Rules enable members of the organization to meet goals without having to develop a strong emotional commitment to the tasks they perform.

Bureaucracies are impersonal in their treatment of clients and customers. The application of rules and procedures to specific cases dealt with by the members of the bureaucracy requires formality and impartiality. This makes a bureaucracy efficient and predictable, even though at times it may seem insensitive to its clients.

Most bureaucracies use material rewards in the form of salaries, wages, commissions, and bonuses to motivate workers to achieve organizational goals. These workers are regarded as rational individuals who have instrumental needs and will respond to material incentives. This view is the basis of the "scientific management" school of industrial relations, an approach that emphasizes the specialization of tasks and the use of material rewards to motivate workers. The "human relations" approach, on the other hand, was developed from research on workers' behavior; it stresses the need to take into account the interpersonal dynamics of the work group, rather than the individual nature of work. This approach points to the need for such noneconomic rewards as social approval and job satisfaction to motivate workers. Recently, many organizations have sought to encourage workers' compliance with the firm's goals through the use of both material and nonmaterial rewards.

In bureaucracies, workers are hired and promoted on the basis of their qualifications and credentials, rather than on the basis of their personality traits or their personal relationships with members of the organization. Experience is also taken into account, because experience at a job minimizes the amount of training that a new worker must be given before being able to perform efficiently. Nevertheless, most employees are trained in some specific skills and learn to be loyal to the corporation. They are reviewed and evaluated regularly, and records are kept of their performance. Employee morale and technical efficiency are sustained by rewarding and promoting workers on the basis of merit and seniority. This is made possible by the different rewards—income, prestige, authority, and peer esteem—that are associated with each position in the bureaucracy's hierarchy. SEL 7.2 shows how one large American corporation, Citicorp, hires and evaluates its employees. In SEL 16.1, on page 377, we see how a different set of rewards is used to motivate workers in Japanese corporations.

SOCIOLOGY AND EVERYDAY LIFE 7.2
Hiring and Firing at Citicorp

This selection shows how the hiring and promotion practices of one large American corporation, Citicorp, fit some of the criteria of Weber's ideal type of bureaucracy.

In 1980, Citicorp recruiters interviewed about fifteen thousand college and business-school graduates around the world and hired more than a thousand of them. (The interviewers were not all full-time recruiters; every year, each of the company's business groups has at least one high-potential young executive drop his regular duties and spend that year exclusively in recruiting for his particular phase of the business). Among the institution's alluring aspects for talented officer candidates are its almost unequalled opportunities for assignment overseas—over half of all Citicorp employees work abroad at any given time—and its reputation for granting rapid promotions. One of every four officer-level employees is promoted every year, and the average age of the Policy Committee, consisting of twenty-nine of the company's top officers, hovers around fifty. Chief among the deterrents to applicants is Citi-

corp's well-deserved reputation for firing a significant percentage of new officer-candidate employees within their first few years of service.

Once hired, such an employee is trained in a particular aspect of the business—lending and account management, say, or systems and data processing, or money markets. The length of the training period varies according to the job and the employee's aptitude. In the corporate banking group—right up to the vice-presidential level—there is an evaluation procedure twice a year, in which both the employee and his or her supervisor fill out a sort of report card on the employee's progress in acquiring skills. Employee and supervisor do their reporting separately, and then meet to compare results, in what must often be a rather chilling session. To top that off, at least once a year each rising executive—in this case, without his participation—receives from his supervisor a performance appraisal, calculated to let him know as categorically as possible whether or not he is valued by Citicorp, and, if so, how much.

At the higher levels, appraisals are more baroque and more secret. Until a few years ago, top management maintained a color-coded list of the two or three hundred people considered the best prospects for top-management jobs. Those on the list whose names where underlined in gold were the ones most favored of all, like Abou ben Adhem in the angel's book of gold. People on the list, and especially those marked in gold, were not supposed to know it, but they usually managed to find out. . . . The color-coded list was superseded a while back by a new list of potential replacements for the holder of each of Citicorp's hundred or so top jobs; those on this list were roundly referred to as "corporate property." Again, people who were "corporate property" were not supposed to know but often did; none of them seem to have asked when or how the corporation had acquired title to them, or for what consideration. Citicorp officers say that the term "corporate property" has been officially dropped but is still used informally from time to time. . .

Source: John Brooks, "Profiles—The Money Machine," *The New Yorker*, January 5, 1981, p. 53. © 1981. Reprinted by permission.

The Problems of Bureaucracies

The ideal type of bureaucracy stresses the functions or positive aspects of such a formal organization, although Weber recognized that both the ideal type as well as real bureaucracies also had a number of negative functions (Weber, 1925, 1947; Udy, 1959; Hall, 1963).

One problem with bureaucracies is that formalized rules and procedures can elicit a similar response to all situations, even when new or unexpected circumstances demand different responses. The rules and procedures that were designed to deal with typical cases can cause confusion and inefficiency when they are relied on in an inappropriate situation. Rules encourage unimaginative responses, because finding creative solutions might be too time-consuming or be seen as a threat to promotions that are based on conformity to written rules and procedures. Bureaucrats often respond with ritualism (see Chapter 5), following formal rules and procedures to the letter, rather than following the intent of those rules and procedures (Merton, 1968). In SEL 7.3 we see how one worker in a large organization does his job in a ritualistic fashion. There is, however, some evidence that bureaucratization is consistently but not strongly related to "greater intellectual flexibility, higher valuation of self-direction, greater openness to new experience, and more personally responsible moral standards" (Kohn, 1971: 472). This might be because bureaucracies, compared to other organizations, recruit a more highly educated group of workers; but it seems more likely to be the result of the greater job protections, higher incomes, and more complex job requirements that are a part of bureaucratic organizations.

SOCIOLOGY AND EVERYDAY LIFE 7.3
Ritualism in the Office

This passage from Revolutionary Road, *a novel by Richard Yates, portrays ritualism in a bureaucracy.*

[Frank had begun to dwell on the] comic aspects of the job: the absurd discrepancy between his own ideals and those of Knox Business Machines; the gulf between the amount of energy he was supposed to give the company and the amount he actually gave. "I mean the great advantage of a place like Knox is that you can sort of turn off your mind every morning at nine and leave it off all day, and nobody knows the difference.". . .

Frank dropped his foot from the drawer and got settled at his desk. He had to think, and the best way to think was to go through the motions of working. This morning's batch of papers was waiting in his IN basket, on top of last Friday's, and so his first action was to turn the whole stack upside down on his desk and start from the bottom. As he did each day (or rather on the days when he bothered with the IN basket, for there were many days when he left it alone) he tried first to see how many papers he could get rid of without actually reading their contents. Some could be thrown away, others could be almost as rapidly disposed of by scrawling "What about this?" in their margins, with his initials, and sending them to Bandy, or by writing "Know anything on this?" and sending them to someone like Ed Small, next door; but the danger here was that the same papers might come back in a few days marked "Do" from Bandy and "No" from Small. A safer course was to mark a thing "File" for Mrs. Jorgensen and the girls, after the briefest possible glance had established that it wasn't of urgent importance; if it was, he might mark it "File & Follow 1 wk.", or he might put it aside and go on to the next one. The gradual accumulation of papers put aside in this way was what he turned to as soon as he was finished with, or tired of, the IN basket. Arranging them in an approximate order of importance, he would interleave them, in the same order, with those of the six- or eight-inch stack that always lay near the center of the desk, held down by a glazed ceramic paperweight that Jennifer had made for him in kindergarten. This was his current work file. Many of the papers in it bore the insignia of Bandy's "Do" or Ed Small's "No,"

and some had been through the "File and Follow" cycle as many as three or four times; some, bearing notes like "Frank—might look into this," were the gifts of men who used him as he used Small. Occasionally he would remove a piece of current work and place it in the equally high secondary pile that lay on the far right-hand corner of the desk, under a leaden scale model of the Knox "500" Electronic Computer. This was the pile of things he couldn't bring himself to face just now, and the worst of them, sometimes whole bulging folders filled with scrawled-over typewritten sheets and loose, sliding paper clips, would eventually go into the stuffed bottom right-hand drawer of the desk. The papers in there were of the kind that Ordway called Real Goodies, and that drawer, opposite to the one that served as a foot rest, had come to occupy a small nagging place in Frank's conscience: he was as shy of opening it as if it held live snakes.

Source: Richard Yates, *Revolutionary Road.* Boston: Little, Brown, 1961. pp. 77, 85–86. Reprinted by permission of International Creative Management.

Because bureaucrats sometimes apply rules almost automatically, clients may feel that they are being dealt with insensitively and as "cases" rather than as individuals with particular needs. For instance, college students sometimes complain that they are treated as a "number in a computer" rather than as a unique individual. This treatment is especially disturbing because adolescence is a time when personal identity is a major source of concern. Even though some people criticize "bureaucracy" for being unfeeling and insensitive, most people feel that they have been treated quite well by the actual bureaucrats with whom they have interacted (Katz et al., 1975).

The need to coordinate the many statuses and roles in a bureaucracy sometimes results in complicated sets of rules and procedures that occupy more of the workers' time than does the actual fulfillment of the organization's goals. Such "red tape" can cause behavior that is not consistent with the rationality and efficiency that characterize the ideal type of bureaucracy. The following passage describes the problems the novelist Ford Madox Ford had with the French civil service when he tried to trace a missing postal order:

. . . Mr. Ford decided to go directly to the *Direction de la Seine des P. T. T.* on the Boulevard Montparnasse.

At two o'clock he was ushered into the Director's office by a smiling charwoman. After a half hour the Director returned from lunch and scrutinized the documents with great care. Following further consultation with an official in a blue uniform, the Director announced that Ford should betake himself to the "Chief Sub-office for the Recovery of Money Orders" on the other side of Paris. There he was directed to Room V on the sixth floor. While he conversed with an attractive young woman for an hour about face powders and the like, her chief examined the papers and asked questions about Ford's war record and family, finally instructing him to return to the Boulevard Montparnasse, this time to Room XVI on the third floor. From there he was sent back to Room XI in the Chief Sub-office; thence to Room IV, Boulevard Montparnasse; next to Room III, Chief Sub-office; and finally to the "open sesame"—Room XIII, on Montparnasse. Although assured there that he would receive his money by the first delivery the following day, it actually arrived seven weeks later, only after a generous tip had been showered upon the postman (Sharp, 1931, cited in Blau and Meyer, 1971: 101).

Another problem that can develop in bureaucracies involves communication. Often, the flow of information is downward, from higher positions to lower ones, rather than upward to those with greater authority. Communication between posi-

"I'm sorry, dear, but you knew I was a bureaucrat when you married me."

Drawing by Weber; © 1980, The New Yorker Magazine, Inc.

tions is often imperfect, as information is withheld or distorted and decisions are based on incomplete or inaccurate information. The way that Japanese corporations have tried to counteract this problem is described in SEL 16.1, on page 377.

Another difficulty faced by bureaucracies is described by "Parkinson's law," which states that work expands to fill the time available for its completion (Parkinson, 1957). This means that if a bureaucrat is assigned a task that can be finished in less time than is actually available for its completion, the task will still take as long as the time that has been allotted. This idea also applies to the tendency of bureaucracies to increase the size of their staff. In order to increase their power and prestige within the organization, bureaucrats often try to increase the number of people under their supervision. Thus a bureaucrat may hire an additional secretary or administrative assistant, even if the work could be accomplished without more personnel. The newly hired workers find tasks to keep themselves busy and thereby justify their continued employment. In this way inefficiency and duplication of effort are encouraged. Parkinson's law fits the impressions held by some people who have

worked in bureaucracies, although one study found no evidence to support this "law" (Reimann, 1979).

Another problem with some bureaucracies is that the members' personal goals—such as accumulating power or finding a shortcut to finish a job—often come before organizational goals. The *iron law of oligarchy* is the tendency of an organization to become increasingly dominated by a small group of people (Michels, 1915, 1962). After examining the labor movement and political parties in Germany just before World War I, Robert Michels concluded that organizations become more bureaucratized over time because their leaders grow more concerned with maintaining their power and prestige than with attaining the explicit goals of the organization. The iron law of oligarchy describes a common but not inevitable process in organizations. For example, a study of a typographers' union found that no oligarchy developed, not because the members were apathetic about the union, but because there was little division between the members and their leaders, and because elections allowed for the regular replacement of leaders (Lipset, Trow, and Coleman, 1962).

FORMAL AND INFORMAL STRUCTURE

A bureaucracy is a formal organization that is deliberately designed to accomplish certain goals. However, in most bureaucracies there is also an *informal structure* in addition to the formal structure (Blau and Meyer, 1971). The informal structure consists of the patterns of interaction, friendships, personal behavior, "common knowledge," and informal authority, which differ from the practices specified in the rules and procedures of the organization. Spontaneous or unofficial behavior in a bureaucracy can contribute to inefficiency, but often it helps accomplish organizational goals and it may even lead to changes in the formal structure of the organization.

The behavior of work groups in industrial plants is significantly influenced by informal expectations. Work groups violate formal rules and procedures in several different ways. For example, in industrial plants where workers are expected to do their jobs independently of each other, they may actually help one another. This sometimes increases the group's overall output, thereby helping to meet the organization's goal of productivity even though the formal rule of independent work is violated. This kind of behavior can also increase worker morale and job satisfaction (Roethlisberger and Dickson, 1939, 1964). On other occasions, however, and perhaps as often, work groups restrict output by pressuring members to limit production. Workers may fear that if they produce at a high level, they will be required to produce at that level regularly; they may also fear that high productivity will lead to layoffs because supervisors will feel that the same output can be achieved with fewer workers. Sanctions used by work groups to restrict output include criticizing workers as "rate-busters" and excluding them from the social activities of the group (Roethlisberger and Dickson, 1939, 1964; Roy, 1952).

One example of informal practices that were incompatible with the formal rules and procedures of a bureaucracy comes from a study of United States postal workers (Harper and Emmert, 1963). Postal workers often "cut corners" to do their assigned tasks more easily than they could have by following the formal rules and procedures. One rule required them to deliver mail in the order specified in a route book, but often they changed their routes so they could finish more quickly. Some workers violated rules by using their own cars to deliver mail and by holding low-priority mail until a day

that they had little to deliver. These informal practices speeded mail delivery and enhanced job satisfaction. Eventually some of these informal practices were incorporated into the formal rules and procedures of the Post Office.

The "real" structure of an organization includes both formal and informal practices. People who occupy higher positions must often deal with those at the lower levels to accomplish the goals of the organization (Blankenship, 1977; Day and Day, 1977). For example, prisons are formal organizations, but they also contain important informal structures among the inmates (Sykes, 1958; Irwin, 1970). These informal structures are so important in the daily routine of prisons that administrators and correctional officers must deal with this inmate social organization in order to meet the prison's goals of custody and treatment. The process of negotiation between those in different positions of authority can lead to changes in the formal organization, such as the inmate grievance boards that have developed in prisons in recent years.

Institutions

For a society to survive and prosper, certain basic needs must be met. Members of the society who die must be replaced, and the new members must be socialized in the values and norms of the culture. Goods and services must be produced and distributed. Conflicts must be resolved, and behavior that causes harm must be held in check. The society must also be protected from external enemies. If these needs are not met, the society and its way of life may be destroyed (Aberle et al., 1950; Parsons, 1951).

To ensure their continued existence, societies develop *institutions*, or stable clusters of values, norms, statuses, and roles that enjoy wide support. Institutions thus contain elements of culture (values and norms) and social structure (statuses and roles). These institutions develop and become ingrained parts of society in order to meet basic needs; the process by which they are created is called *institutionalization*.

One institution that exists in all societies is the family (see Chapter 11). This institution serves to replace the members of society and to socialize them into its culture. It meets the human need for association with others and fulfills the sex drive. A family of a husband, wife, and children is a primary group, but the institution of the family is the pattern of values, norms, statuses, and roles that is common to a society. In the United States, the institution of the family includes laws about marriage and divorce, a norm of marrying within a religious organization, a value of bearing children, and a limited role for grandparents in the socialization of children. The institution of the family in other societies includes quite different values, norms, statuses, and roles, even though it still meets the basic needs that are met by the American family.

Education is another institution (see Chapter 12). It may include the formal organization of the school, or it may involve informal instruction of the young by the elders of a tribe. The institution of education imparts knowledge and skills and inculcates the values and norms of the culture. This institution fits closely with the institution of the family. The family is expected to prepare children for education in school, and the school is expected to teach values that are compatible with those of the parents. The institutions of a society are closely integrated with each other; a change in one often sets off a reaction in another. For example, the introduction of sex education in schools has drawn loud protests from some parents.

Another important institution is religion (see Chapter 13). This institution serves to meet people's needs for answers to questions such as the meaning of life. Religion unifies believers, even though it sometimes divides the members of a society that contains different religions. This institution includes formal organizations such as churches, as well as a variety of values, norms, statuses, and roles. For example, in the United States the law requires that religion be free of government interference, and the culture includes an informal norm that everyone should believe in some religion, although none in particular is specified.

By setting broad goals and making policies to reach those goals, the political institution maintains the unity of a people (see Chapter 14). Children are taught by their parents and teachers to be "responsible citizens" who vote and support the government. Socialization thus links the political institution with the family and education. One part of the political institution is the legal institution, a system that tries to insure predictability and justice through the application of formal rules and procedures (see Chapter 15). The legal institution has important effects on all the other institutions in the society; for example, the United States Supreme Court regularly decides cases that deal with the

family, education, religion, the political system, and the economic system.

The economic institution has been studied by sociologists as well as by economists (see Chapter 16). This institution is concerned with the production, distribution, and consumption of goods and services by the people of a society. Like the other institutions, the economic institution is closely linked to the rest of society's institutions. In addition to its other functions, the family is an important economic unit of production and consumption, and public schools are supported through taxation, an economic process.

Because the institutions of a society fit together into an integrated whole, it is difficult to change one without changing another. Functionalists stress the interconnectedness of institutions; they usually see the traditional, conservative nature of institutions as functional for the social order. Conflict theorists point out that institutions often favor those groups that gain from the established way of doing things and oppress those groups that are not well served by a society's institutional structure. Modern conflict theorists stress the interrelationship of all institutions and the difficulty of changing one without changing others, but many of these conflict theorists place greatest emphasis on the need to transform the economic system before the rest of society will change.

Societies

A *society* is a self-perpetuating social structure or set of institutions that is relatively self-sufficient, endures beyond the lifetimes of its members, and occupies a specific territory. Societies can be tribal groups of a few dozen people, or they can be large nation-states with populations of hundreds of millions. Both kinds of societies can exist, at least theoretically, without assistance from those outside the society, even though they may actually engage in exchanges with outsiders. The United States engages in international trade, but it could subsist on its own because it includes all of the institutions necessary to meet basic social needs. Families and work organizations are not societies because they must rely on other institutions to meet their basic needs.

Societies have distinctive cultures. Their members share values, norms, and usually a language. Societies perpetuate themselves through reproduction and, to a lesser extent, through immigration;

Traditional societies are small and simple—modern societies, large and complex.

both methods of replacing the members of a society require the socialization of new members. A society is a social structure, but it is closely associated with a culture, even if that culture includes considerable diversity.

Sociologists have developed a variety of ways to describe societies. One classification is based on the society's primary means of economic subsistence; this approach focuses on the economic institution and is examined in Chapter 16. Sociologists have also classified societies by the relative importance they give to primary and secondary groups and by the complexity of their division of labor (Tönnies, 1887, 1957; Durkheim, 1893, 1933; Redfield, 1941). There are some differences among these various classification schemes, but they overlap in many ways. These classifications essentially analyze societies on a continuum from traditional to modern.

TRADITIONAL AND MODERN SOCIETIES

Traditional societies are societies in which social relationships are relatively simple. They are like large primary groups, because they have few specialized roles and people interact as whole persons. The members of traditional societies share values and norms, including a strong sense of loyalty to the society; these shared values and norms are the basis of the social order. Socialization is often done by word of mouth rather than by formal education, because many traditional societies are preliterate. Relationships and behavior are based on statuses ascribed at birth; sex and age are often given great importance in the assignment of roles. There is little emphasis on individualism, and conformity to norms is encouraged through group pressure and the application of legal sanctions. The family is the most important institution in traditional societies.

At the other end of the continuum are *modern societies.* They are usually larger than traditional societies, and the number of statuses and roles is considerably greater. Interpersonal relations are less emotional and more often are based on legal contracts, rather than on personal bonds and long-standing customs, as they are in traditional societies. Modern societies are held together by the interdependence of statuses in a complex division of labor, rather than by similarities among the members of the society. The greater specialization of tasks means that interaction less often involves the whole person and is more likely to be based on the specific task that an individual performs. Many modern societies consist of diverse groups that have different norms and values; this makes conflict more common than it is in more homogeneous traditional societies, and it provides a source of social change in modern societies. One major change is urbanization, the process by which large numbers of people move from rural areas to cities. Individualism is more pronounced in modern societies, but it is often accompanied by anonymity and a sense of detachment from primary groups. In contrast to traditional societies, the family is less important in modern societies, and the economic and political institutions are relatively more important. Science and technological advances are important in modern societies, and they require a highly educated work force and much job specialization. Formal organizations are important in modern societies; in fact, the characteristics of the ideal type of bureaucracy are similar to the traits of modern societies.

Summary

Social structure is a pattern of interaction that has stability and regularity over time. Social structures derive their meaning from a shared culture. They are emergent in nature; that is, as a whole they differ from the characteristics of their component parts, and they have a division of labor or specialization of tasks.

A status is a position in a social structure. Statuses that are very important in defining the social identity of an individual are called master statuses. Some statuses are ascribed, or assigned to individuals by other people, and other statuses are achieved, or acquired by individual efforts. A role is the behavior expected of a person occupying a status; it reflects the self that has been developed through socialization and the situation in which the role is played. A role set is the cluster of roles that are associated with one status. Role conflict occurs when a person is expected to perform two or more roles that are incompatible, and role strain occurs when there is incompatibility among the expectations of a single role.

A group is a set of relationships among people who interact face to face over time. A group has a defined membership, a set of interrelated statuses and roles, shared values and norms, and an identity. Primary groups are small groups whose members interact on a regular and intimate basis, and secondary groups are larger groups in which relationships are less intimate and people are treated as means to certain ends rather than as complete persons. As societies have grown larger and more complex, secondary groups have become more important and primary groups less important. Reference groups are groups or categories against which people evaluate themselves and their behavior; they may be general categories of people, membership groups, groups that people aspire to, or groups that people wish to avoid.

Groups acquire cohesion by establishing boundaries that distinguish them from other people and groups. Size is an important characteristic of groups that influences the interaction of the members. The pattern of interaction in a group can be diagrammed to show networks of influence, communication, friendship, and authority. Through interaction, different roles develop within groups, including the role of leader. Groups often require two types of leaders—an expressive leader who fills the emotional needs of the members and an instrumental leader who helps the group achieve its goals.

A formal organization is a large, complex secondary group that is deliberately created to achieve a specific goal. It has a division of labor and clear differences in authority among the statuses. One type of formal organization is a voluntary association, an organization that people choose to participate in freely, often in their spare time. Many total institutions, or formal organizations that exercise coercive control over their members, are involuntary associations.

A bureaucracy is a formal organization that stresses rationality and efficiency in a highly structured network of statuses and roles. A bureaucracy has a clear division of labor, a hierarchy of authority, formal rules and procedures, and different rewards attached to various statuses. Bureaucracies have been criticized for their routine and uncreative responses to problems, their "red tape," and their overstaffing. Understanding the behavior of individuals in bureaucracies and other formal organizations requires attention to both the informal structure as well as the formal structure of the organization.

Institutions are stable clusters of values, norms, statuses, and roles that meet basic social needs and enjoy wide support in a society. The institutions are usually integrated, so that a change in one institution sets off changes in others. The major institutions we examine in later chapters are the family, education, religion, and the political, legal, and economic systems.

A society is a self-perpetuating social structure or set of institutions that is relatively self-sufficient, endures beyond the lifetimes of its members, and occupies a specific territory. Societies perpetuate themselves through reproduction and immigration, and transmit their culture to new members of the society through socialization. Sociologists have devised classifications of societies based on the means of economic subsistence, the relative importance of primary and secondary groups, and the complexity of the division of labor. One classification describes societies as traditional or modern, with most societies falling somewhere between these extremes.

Important Terms

ACHIEVED STATUS (149)	PRIMARY GROUP (153)
ASCRIBED STATUS (149)	REFERENCE GROUP (154)
AUTHORITY (159)	ROLE (148)
BUREAUCRACY (159)	ROLE CONFLICT (151)
DIVISION OF LABOR (157)	ROLE PERFORMANCE (151)
FORMAL ORGANIZATION (157)	ROLE SET (151)
GROUP (153)	ROLE STRAIN (152)
IDEAL TYPE (154)	SECONDARY GROUP (154)
INFORMAL STRUCTURE (164)	SOCIAL STRUCTURE (147)
INSTITUTION (164)	SOCIETY (165)
INSTITUTIONALIZATION (164)	STATUS (148)
IRON LAW OF OLIGARCHY (163)	TOTAL INSTITUTION (158)
MASTER STATUS (148)	TRADITIONAL SOCIETY (167)
MODERN SOCIETY (167)	VOLUNTARY ASSOCIATION (157)

Suggested Readings

Peter M. Blau and Marshall W. Meyer. *Bureaucracy in Modern Society*, 2nd ed. New York: Random House, 1971. A good introduction to bureaucratic organizations.

Rosabeth Moss Kanter and Barry Stein, eds. *Life in Organizations: Workplaces as People Experience Them.* New

York: Basic Books, 1979. A collection of first-hand accounts of work in formal organizations.

Robert K. Merton. *Social Theory and Social Structure*, 1968 enlarged ed. New York: Free Press, 1968. An important work containing essays on roles and bureaucracies.

Robert Nisbet and Robert G. Perrin. *The Social Bond*, 2nd ed. New York: Alfred A. Knopf, 1977. A useful analysis of social structure and social integration.

Michael S. Olmsted and A. Paul Hare. *The Small Group*, 2nd ed. New York: Randon House, 1978. A brief introduction to the nature of behavior in small groups.

Charles Perrow. *Complex Organizations: A Critical Essay*, 2nd ed. Glenview, Ill.: Scott, Foresman, 1979. A good introduction to the sociology of formal organizations.

Jerome H. Skolnick and Elliott Currie, eds. *Crisis in American Institutions*, 5th ed. Boston: Little, Brown, 1982. A collection of essays that examine American society and its institutions from the conflict perspective.

SOCIAL STRATIFICATION

Members of all societies share unequally in social rewards, or things that are valued. In primitive societies, people who are the tallest or strongest are likely to be the most skilled at hunting or fighting and are thus more able to get the "lion's share" of food and other valued items. In industrial societies, some people earn more money or hold more power than others. Some kinds of inequality are based on individual traits; certain people possess great strength, skill, or intelligence, and consequently have an advantage in fulfilling their needs and desires. However, much inequality is social in origin and based on factors that include race, sex, and family wealth.

Social stratification, which is one aspect of social structure, is the ranking of individuals and categories of people in terms of valued things, such as income or social honor. Status, or position in the hierarchy, influences life in many ways and is thus of central concern to sociologists. For example, position in the system of stratification is closely related to life expectancy, physical and mental health, educational opportunity, marriage and family life, leisure activity, treatment by the criminal justice system, and political behavior.

Rankings in a social hierarchy reflect cultural values. In other words, status is determined by the possession of what a society considers valuable. For example, people may be ranked on the basis of income, with some groups earning more than others—males more than females, or whites more than blacks. In some societies, the elderly are given more respect than the young, whereas in other societies the middle-aged are accorded more honor than either the elderly or the young. In nearly every society, status is influenced by the family into which a person is born; the opportunity for a child to change position when he or she becomes an adult varies from society to society, ac-

cording to the type of stratification system that a society has.

Types of Stratification Systems

Stratification systems differ according to the ease with which people at one level can move upward or downward into a different stratum. This movement is called "social mobility," a concept that we will explore later in the chapter. In "open systems," movement from one level to the next is relatively easy, but in "closed systems" such movement is difficult.

CLOSED SYSTEMS

Closed systems of stratification are based on ascribed statuses. These statuses are assigned to people because of innate traits (such as sex or skin color) or because of the social characteristics of their parents (such as religion, ethnicity, or slave status). Here we look at three types of stratification systems based on ascribed status—slave systems, estate systems, and caste systems.

A "slave system" is a closed stratification system in which some people are defined as property and in which, from the time of birth, there is almost no movement from the status of slave to the status of free person. Although slave systems are uncommon in the world today, about one million people are still enslaved, mostly in North Africa, the Middle East, and southern Asia (Nossiter, 1981).

A stratification system that contains several distinct hierarchies, each serving a different social purpose, is called an "estate system." In feudal times, these hierarchies were the nobility, the clergy, and the peasants or serfs. Family heritage determined the estate to which a person belonged; thus nobility—and the land and privileges that

This photograph was taken in Pretoria, South Africa, where a caste system based on race is rigidly enforced.

went with it—was inherited rather than achieved. Estate systems were common in the Middle Ages and still exist in some Latin American countries today, where powerful landowners dominate tenant farmers and where the military and the clergy also play important roles.

In "caste systems," found most notably in India and in South Africa, status is ascribed at birth on the basis of a family's position in the system. Status in a caste system is rigidly dictated, often being reinforced by religion or the law. There is little or no marriage outside the *caste* into which a person is born. People cannot change castes, although sometimes whole castes or subcastes rise or fall in the stratification system. The relationship between whites and blacks in the United States, particularly in the South before World War II, has sometimes been described as a caste system.

OPEN SYSTEMS

In contrast to the three types of closed stratification systems, "class systems" are relatively open. Statuses are largely but not exclusively achieved through talent, skill, education, and hard work. In other words, to a great extent performance rather than individual characteristics or family traits determines position in an open system.

A *class* is a category of people who have a similar social standing or rank based on economic resources, political power, social honor, or life style (Lenski, 1966; Coleman and Rainwater, 1978). Movement from one class to another is not prohibited by law or religion, but it is often impeded by social arrangements, as we shall see when we examine social mobility later in this chapter. Because so many elements enter into the definition of class, the boundaries between classes are not always clear, unlike the distinct divisions between strata in slave, estate, and caste systems. Most people marry others from the same or similar class backgrounds, but marriage between members of different classes is relatively common. A young woman lawyer working in a large law firm and earning $45,000 a year is most likely to marry a man who is also well-educated, working in one of the professions, and earning a good income; however, she might marry a millionaire or an auto mechanic.

The Sources of Stratification

Why is social inequality present in all societies? This question is the basis of a long-standing debate among sociologists. The conflict position holds that stratification is a result of exploitation by groups that seek to maintain and enhance their advantage over other groups. Functionalists, on the other hand, claim that stratification is necessary for societies to accomplish tasks that are essential to their survival. This debate raises the question of how inevitable is social inequality and how important is it in determining the extent to which inequality can be reduced or eliminated.

THE CONFLICT POSITION

Conflict theorists argue that the pursuit of individual and group interests leads to conflict over scarce resources. When a group manages to get control of these valued things—money or power, for instance—it will work hard to keep the "have-nots" from taking these things away from it. Inequality exists in all but the most primitive social and economic systems, but some societies permit or even encourage exploitation and domination more than others do.

Karl Marx (1848, 1967) defined classes by their position in the economic system, with clear boundaries existing between classes that were related in different ways to the "means of production"—the factories, machinery, and raw materials that are used to produce goods for consumption. In capitalist systems the bourgeoisie owns the means of production, but it is only able to make a profit by hiring workers. These workers, members of what Marx called the proletariat, are paid a wage or a salary that is less than the value of the goods they produce. The bourgeoisie, or capitalist class, makes a profit from this surplus value, the difference between the market value of the goods and the wages that workers are paid. Thus, according to Marx, capitalism is a system based on the exploitation of one class by another.

According to conflict theorists, each class in a capitalist system has its own interests to pursue, but workers are often unaware of how they are exploited by capitalists. This lack of awareness of their own best interests is called "false consciousness," which is maintained by cultural hegemony—the use of the mass media, public education, organized religion, and other institutions to teach all members of the society the values of the bourgeoisie. One consequence of false consciousness is that workers often try to reform society rather than take the reins of political and economic power to alter society in a radical way that would serve their own interests. Marx predicted that the numbers of exploited workers would increase over time and that they would eventually become aware of their own oppression. Their new-found class consciousness, or shared sense of common interests, would prompt them to take control of the means of production in a violent overthrow of the ruling class. They would first create a socialist state in which the proletariat was the dominant class, and then a classless communist society would develop. In fact, socialist revolutions have not occurred in advanced capitalist systems, as Marx predicted, but rather in societies such as the Soviet Union, China, and Cuba. Still, Marx's work was important in drawing attention to class and class conflict as forces that generate social change.

THE FUNCTIONALIST POSITION

The functionalist perspective regards stratification as both necessary and useful in accomplishing tasks that are essential to the survival of a society (Davis and Moore, 1945). This position is succinctly summarized as follows: "Social inequality is thus an unconsciously evolved device by which societies insure that the most important positions are conscientiously filled by the most qualified persons" (Davis, 1949: 367). An important job that few people have the skill and intelligence to perform will be rewarded more highly than a job that many people can do. Functionalists see the difference in rewards as reflecting the importance of a position to society and the relative scarcity of people who can fill that position (Lenski, 1966: 15). Indeed, there is evidence that income and respect are determined by the importance that people attach to a job and the training that is needed to do the job (Cullen and Novick, 1979).

A functionalist would argue, for example, that to motivate people to become physicians, they must be offered high salaries and social respect to induce them to undergo years of education and then enter a profession that requires long hours of work and produces much stress. These rewards also motivate doctors to continue in the profession after they have entered it. It is far from obvious, however, that the large differences in rewards among various jobs are really needed to motivate people to do certain work. Is it not possible, for example, that many people would become doctors for more altruistic reasons than money and social respect? In addition, the expense of a medical school education and the limited number of places available in medical schools prevent many qualified people from becoming doctors. Because the medical needs of many Americans are not being met, we might say that the stratification system in this case is dysfunctional for society.

The functionalist perspective has been criticized for suggesting that there is a close relationship between rewards such as income and prestige and the social importance of a job. Professional athletes and entertainers earn some of the highest salaries in the United States. Their skills are in short supply and people are willing to pay to be entertained, but the importance of these jobs for the survival of society is certainly questionable, especially when compared to nurses, social workers, or police officers, who are paid much less.

SOCIOLOGY AND EVERYDAY LIFE 8.1
What Is a Job Worth?

Functionalists and conflict theorists disagree on the issue of whether rewards for different jobs reflect their value to society. In recent years, there have been a few efforts to increase the pay of workers in certain occupations because the rewards of their jobs do not reflect the social worth of the work they do. Unlike charges of discrimination against a worker because of race or sex, this claim is that whole occupations are underpaid. So far the courts have rejected these claims of discrimination against entire job categories, stating that the law only recognizes discrimination against individuals.

There are indeed large discrepancies in salaries among occupations. In some cities sanitation workers (or garbage collectors) who have not even completed high school are paid starting salaries higher than teachers who have an M.A. degree. Professional athletes in the same city might make more than ten times as much as either the sanitation workers or the teachers. Indeed, professional athletes sometimes earn much more than doctors or the President of the United States. Do these differences reflect the social value of these jobs? If not, how would you go about determining the worth of a job?

One agency in the United States Department of Labor, plus the AFL-CIO, and others have endorsed the idea of trying to determine the value of different jobs. Studies have been conducted to compare the worth of jobs to each other. One approach is to grade a job by assigning points to the effort, skill, and responsibility required of a worker. A few efforts to evaluate the worth of jobs in systematic ways have been tried—including a German system to measure the worth of secretarial jobs by counting the number of finger movements per second. No system has yet been devised that pleases everyone, but it is possible that in the future such systematic efforts to measure the worth of jobs may be used to make rewards better reflect the importance of different kinds of work for society.

Source: Based on Vivienne Killingsworth, "Labor: What's a Job Worth?" *Atlantic Monthly* 247 (February 1981): 10–22. Used by permission.

In addition, social inequality, rather than motivating people to enter certain occupations, as functionalists suggest, often leads to inefficient use of the talents of the members of a society. Many blacks and women, for example, are probably discouraged from entering certain occupations or from seeking promotions to positions for which they are qualified because American society is stratified by race and by sex.

The biggest criticism of the functionalist position, however, is that it can be used to justify social inequality. Some critics find that it is a small jump from saying that stratification is functional and has useful consequences for society to saying that inequality *should* exist (Tumin, 1953).

A SYNTHESIS

One effort to provide a synthesis of the conflict and the functionalist perspectives is Gerhard Lenski's (1966) work on stratification in societies with different economic means of subsistence. Lenski focuses on the development of inequality as societies evolve from simple hunting and gathering bands to the most complex industrial societies. He sees conflict over scarce resources—such as wealth and power—as inevitably leading to inequality, because some people are more capable or intelligent than others. The stratification system that results from this conflict is functional for society in some ways and provides a rough match between skills and rewards. However, conflict over scarce resources produces more inequality than is needed to motivate people to fill the positions that are important for society's survival. Often, then, stratification is not functional but instead leads to exploitation and the inefficient use of scarce resources.

Although Lenski argues that stratification and inequality are inevitable in any but the most primitive societies, he does say that inequality can be reduced in most societies without impairing the ability of a society to survive or to accomplish certain tasks. He acknowledges that there is general agreement in most societies about the relative significance of different jobs and the degree to which they should be rewarded, but he also points out that power and influence are commonly used to maintain and enhance the advantages held by certain groups. Stratification initially develops to meet societal needs, but it is maintained and exaggerated by people who pursue narrow interests for themselves, their families, and their social groups.

Dimensions of Stratification

Max Weber (1918, 1949) suggests that Marx's definition of class in terms of the ownership or nonownership of the means of production overemphasizes economic factors. Weber instead treats stratification as the result of differences in the amount of money or wealth that people possess (property), the degree of social honor or respect that people are accorded (prestige), and the extent to which people can impose their will on others (power). Although he acknowledges that economic factors are very important in stratification systems—income, for example, often being a basis of prestige and power—Weber is also aware that prestige and power differ in important ways from property.

PROPERTY

Property is the set of rights and obligations attached to the ownership of money, goods, and services. Property has two aspects: income and wealth. *Income* is a type of property derived from personal labor or from the use of capital; it is the money, goods, and services that a person gains over a given period of time. Income commonly takes the form of a wage or a salary paid to an employee, but it can also be the interest on a savings account or the dividend on stock. *Wealth*, on the other hand, is income that has been accumulated or invested. It can be the result of investment by a person who earns income, but it can also be inherited. Wealth usually

Ownership of a mansion such as this is probably the result of accumulated wealth.

takes the form of savings, stocks and bonds, real estate, business assets, or personal possessions such as works of art or antiques. If you earned $1,500 at a summer job, that would be income; but if you used $500 of that income to buy a painting and put another $500 into a savings account, you would have accumulated $1,000 in wealth. The painting would not produce any additional income for you, although it might grow in value over time. You would, however, derive some additional income from your savings in the form of interest.

Class standing is related to both income and wealth, although annual income is used more often as a measure of position in the stratification system than is accumulated wealth (Henretta and Campbell, 1978). Most people live on their wages and salaries, but those at the top of the stratification system often rely on both wealth and income to support themselves. The rich might live in a large home inherited from their family, but they still need to pay the heating and electric bills and other expenses. The house might be inherited wealth, but other expenses are paid with income derived either from a job or from interest and dividends on accumulated wealth.

PRESTIGE

Prestige is the respect, deference, and social honor that are voluntarily given to a person by others. Because each person's prestige is related to the prestige given to everyone else in a stratification system, prestige is limited. If you gain prestige, others lose prestige relative to you; not everyone can have high prestige.

Prestige is based on many criteria, including family background, area of residence, style of dress, accent, and membership in clubs. People who recognize each other as roughly equivalent in prestige—such as the graduates of a particular college or the members of an exclusive country club—are called a *status group* (Weber, 1918, 1949). Status groups sometimes develop ways to indicate membership in the group that are independent of property and power. The exclusive boarding schools, or "prep" schools, that became popular in the United States at the end of the nineteenth century were designed to strengthen the identity of one status group—the old established families. However, these schools actually helped to integrate these "old families" with the *nouveaux riches*, newly rich families whose ancestors had been in the country for shorter periods of time. What began as a way of reinforcing one status group—the old aristocracy—ended up merging that group with "new money" to form a single, cohesive upper class that was able to maintain control of finances and power (Levine, 1980). Today, a prep school education continues to be an indicator of the status group to which a person belongs.

Prestige and membership in a status group are often judged by symbolic cues such as mode of dress, type of car, area of residence, and accent. These "status symbols" can help members of the same status group identify one another, and thus influence patterns of interaction. However, these cues are an imperfect guide to where a person fits in the stratification system, because people can adopt styles of dress and manipulate status symbols—for example, by affecting an accent or by wearing "preppy" clothes—to suggest that they belong to a different status group than they actually do.

Today in the United States and other industrial societies, prestige is based largely on the kind of work a person does, although there is some evidence that people see income rather than occupation itself as the best measure of where a person ranks in the stratification system (Coleman and Rainwater, 1978). Nonmanual work—such as teaching, social work, or scientific research—is generally rated higher in prestige than manual labor—such as working in a factory or doing road repairs—because nonmanual work usually requires more mental exertion, initiative, and autonomy. Occupational prestige commonly reflects the amount of education needed to do a job; thus professions such as medicine and the law, which require postgraduate training, are ranked higher than jobs such as store clerk and garbage collector, which require little formal education. The prestige ranking of an occupation is also related to how selective recruitment is for the job, how socially important the job is seen as being, and how much income and power are associated with the job (Cullen and Novick, 1979; Hope, 1982a).

Occupational Rankings

One way to determine the prestige of an occupation is to ask people how they evaluate various jobs. This has been done, with a cross section of a population asked to rate various occupations, for example, as excellent, good, average, below average, or poor. An overall prestige ranking is then constructed by taking the average prestige score of each occupation and listing the occupations from the one with the highest score to the one with the

TABLE 8.1

Selected Occupations from the Standard International Occupational Prestige Scale

Occupation	Prestige score	Occupation	Prestige score	Occupation	Prestige score
Chief of state	90	Draftsman	55	Carpenter	37
Ambassador	87	Journalist	55	Model	36
Supreme Court justice	82	Librarian	54	Fireman	35
Governor*	82	Professional nurse	54	Undertaker	34
Astronaut	80	Secretary	53	Plumber	34
Judge	78	Actor	52	Mason	34
Physician	78	Computer		Mail carrier	33
University professor	78	programmer	51	Baker	33
Physicist	76	Union official	50	Miner	32
Mayor, large city*	75	Flight attendant*	50	Building painter	31
High armed forces		Radio or TV		Butcher	31
officer	73	announcer	50	Cook	31
Secondary school		Weatherman	49	Cashier	31
principal	72	Real-estate agent	49	Masseur	30
Architect	72	Professional		Weaver	30
Lawyer*	71	athlete	48	Lives off social	
Dentist	70	Bank teller	48	security	30
Civil engineer	70	TV cameraman	47	Barber	30
Head of large firm	70	Traveling salesman	47	Taxi driver	28
Biologist	69	Farmer	47	Fisherman	28
Chemist	69	Dancer	45	Sewing machine	
Professional		Steel mill worker	45	operator	26
accountant	68	Keypunch operator	45	Textile mill worker	26
Sociologist	67	Insurance agent	44	Gas station	
Banker	67	Automobile dealer	44	attendant	25
Business executive	67	Electrician	44	Bartender	23
Psychologist	66	Office clerk	43	Waiter	23
Airline pilot	66	Garage mechanic	43	Faith healer	22
Middle-rank civil		Printer	42	Janitor	21
servant	66	Radio or TV		Meter reader	21
Pharmacist	64	repairman	42	Longshoreman	21
High school teacher	64	Tailor	40	Logger	19
Mining engineer	63	Policeman	40	Migrant worker	18
Author	62	Cabinet maker	40	Servant	17
Veterinarian	61	Locksmith	40	Lives on public	
Economist	60	Prison guard	39	assistance	16
Clergyman	60	Welder	39	Beggar	15
Postmaster	58	Railroad conductor	39	Newspaper seller	14
Medical technician	58	Soldier	39	Hotel bell boy	14
Optician	57	Tobacco factory		Garbage collector	13
Artist	57	worker	39	Shoe shiner	12
Social worker	56	Telephone operator	38	Moonshiner	6
Stock broker	56	Jazz musician	38	Narcotic peddler	6

*Term adapted from original source.

Source: Adapted from Donald J. Treiman, *Occupational Prestige in Comparative Perspective.* New York: Academic Press, 1977, pp. 235–260. Used by permission.

lowest score (Treiman, 1977: 31–41). Table 8.1 shows a ranking of occupational prestige based on surveys conducted in different nations.

There has been little change in the relative ranking of occupations in the United States since 1925, with the exception of slight increases in the prestige of certain scientific occupations and blue-collar jobs and slight drops in the prestige of some white-collar and political jobs (Hodge, Siegel, and Rossi, 1966; Curtis and Jackson, 1977). Moreover, people from a variety of social backgrounds rank occupations in much the same way. In fact, occupational rankings are remarkably alike in all contemporary societies, whether they are industrialized or are just beginning to develop (Inkeles and Rossi, 1956; Hodge, Treiman, and Rossi, 1966; Hauser and Featherman, 1977; Treiman, 1977). These studies of occupational prestige have been criticized for omitting a variety of jobs from the survey, questioning unrepresentative samples, and failing to ask respondents how much prestige jobs *should* have rather than what prestige jobs *do* have (Kemper, 1976; Coxon and Jones, 1978).

POWER

A third dimension of stratification—in addition to property and prestige—is *power,* the ability to impose one's will on another, even if that person does not wish to comply. Power is sometimes based on the use or threat of physical force; for example, the police have power based on law when they yell at a fleeing criminal, "Stop or I'll shoot." Power can also be derived from expertise in a particular field; a computer programmer would hold power in a company if he or she were the only employee who knew how to produce paychecks. Power can also come from holding political office, from working at a job in a bureaucracy, from having personal traits that inspire others, and from tradition and custom. The chief of a tribe has power that is based on tradition. The power of the President of the United States is derived from that office; unlike the chief, the president gains power by popular election rather than by tribal custom and family heritage. If the president has personal traits—such as an eloquent style of speaking or a brilliant mind—he will have additional power; Weber calls power based on such individual characteristics "charismatic power." We look at the various forms of power in more detail in Chapter 14, "The Political System."

STATUS CONSISTENCY AND MASTER STATUS

The multidimensional approach to class makes it possible to have inconsistencies in one individual's status in the stratification system (Stryker and Macke, 1978). *Status consistency* means that a person's rankings in terms of property, prestige, and power are all about equal. Status inconsistency is present when a person who ranks high on one or more of the three dimensions ranks lower on another dimension. For example, the job of professional baseball player does not have high occupational prestige, even though this job provides some of the highest annual incomes in the United States today. Likewise, some high-prestige occupations produce incomes that are lower than jobs with less prestige—judges earn less money than some actors, gangsters, or professional athletes, for example.

Status inconsistency also occurs when people are assigned a social position based on traits over which they have no control, such as their ethnic group, sex, or age. Thus, a young woman who is a skilled surgeon may find that she is treated according to stereotypes about how women and how young adults are expected to behave, rather than given the respect and deference usually accorded a surgeon. Social movements such as the black civil rights movement and the feminist movement have sought to make ascribed traits such as race and sex irrelevant to the assignment of social status.

People usually prefer to define themselves by the highest rank that they hold. For example, a gangster will define himself by his ranking on the property dimension rather than his ranking on the dimension of prestige. However, a member of the upper class who distinguishes "old money" from "new money" will probably be concerned with the source of the gangster's money and therefore rank him much lower.

Classes in the United States

Herbert J. Gans (1973: xi) describes America as "an unequal society that would like to think of itself as egalitarian." Americans are aware of differences in social standing, although they see the class structure as a continuum without sharp divisions between the classes. Marx's demarcation between the bourgeoisie and the proletariat does not fit most Americans' perceptions of class. Weber's three dimensions of stratification—property, prestige, and power—better capture the sense that most Americans have of class: a social standing or rank that is determined by income, occupation, education, and style of life (Coleman and Rainwater, 1978).

Sociologists have measured class in a variety of ways: by asking people to describe stratification in their community (the "reputational method"); by asking them to place themselves in one of a number of classes (the "subjective method"); and by using statistical measures such as income, educational level, and occupational prestige to rank people (the "objective method"). More recently, an explicitly Marxist study of the American class structure has defined class in terms of control over investments, participation in decision making, authority to determine other people's work, and autonomy to control one's own work (Wright et al., 1982). Each method of measuring class gives a somewhat different description of the stratification system, and each has its advantages and its shortcomings.

Sociologists generally consider the United States to have anywhere from three classes (upper, middle, and lower) to six (the division of the upper, middle, and lower classes into two sections each). One useful description is a five-class system: upper class, upper-middle class, lower-middle class, working class, and lower class (Rossides, 1976; Rothman, 1978).

TABLE 8.2
Family Income, United States, 1981

Family income	Percentage of all families
Under $5,000	5.8
$5,000 to $9,999	11.5
$10,000 to $14,999	13.6
$15,000 to $19,999	12.6
$20,000 to $24,999	12.6
$25,000 to $34,999	20.2
$35,000 to $49,999	14.9
$50,000 and over	8.9
Median income	$22,388

Note: Income is a readily available measure of class, but the cut-off points for assigning people to different classes are arbitrary. For example, whether one calls "middle class" those with incomes between $15,000 and $34,999 (45.4 per cent of all families) or whether one limits the middle class to those with incomes between $20,000 and $34,999 (32.8 per cent of all households) is an arbitrary decision.

Source: U.S. Bureau of the Census, *Statistical Abstract of the United States, 1982–83.* Washington, D.C.: U.S. Government Printing Office, 1982, p. 432.

FIGURE 8.1
Percentage of Total Income Earned by Each Fifth of Families, United States, 1981

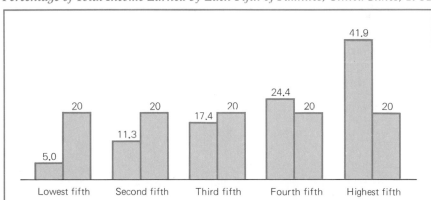

Source: U.S. Bureau of the Census, *Money Income and Poverty Status of Families and Persons in the United States: 1981.* Washington, D.C.: U.S. Government Printing Office, July 1982, p. 11.

The bar to the left of each pair shows the actual percentage of all income earned by each fifth of the families, and the bar to the right shows the percent of the total income that each fifth would have earned if income were equally distributed among all families—that is, each fifth would have earned 20 per cent of the total income.

SOCIOLOGY AND EVERYDAY LIFE 8.2
The American Social Ladder: The Top and the Bottom

One way to see the tremendous variation in the American class structure is to look closely at those who are at the very top of the stratification system and those who are at the very bottom.

Forbes magazine publishes a list of the 400 wealthiest Americans, based on estimates of income and the worth of stock, land, and other holdings. In 1982, a person needed about $100 million to make this exclusive "club."

Who exactly are the people who belong to this group? Oil fortunes account for eighty-nine of the places on this list, and sixty-three others made their money in real estate. The mass media—publications and broadcasting—were the source of forty other fortunes. These three sources thus accounted for nearly half of the top 400, but a few people accumulated their wealth in more unusual ways. Bob Hope, whose estimated worth is $280 million, did it with jokes (and wise investments). Two made the list through their criminal activities: Robert Vesco, who looted millions from Investors Overseas Services, and the late Meyer Lansky, reputed to be the "moneyman" for organized crime.

About three of every four people on the *Forbes* list made their money themselves rather than inheriting it from their parents, although their parents often provided them with a good start in life, particularly through education. One who made the list with only a limited education is J. R. Simplot, who

did it with spuds. He got mad at his father, quit eighth grade, sorted potatoes and raised hogs till he had his own potato field. His big break was meeting Ray Kroc (the founder of McDonald's and a fellow member of the 400) and owning the patent on frozen french fries. His estimated worth: $500 million (Kleinfield, p. 35).

At the other extreme of the social ladder is a growing number of railroad hobos, men—and an increasing number of women—who spend hours in freight yards trying to catch a ride on a train. Some have a specific destination in mind, but many are simply traveling around. Many of these hobos are out of work because of the high unemployment rate, and most lack a car or the bus fare to look for jobs. According to one, hitchhiking is more difficult today than it was in the 1960s.

Some hobos seem to like the lives they lead. One even claims that he would ride the rails if he had a thousand dollars in his pocket, saying, "It's enjoyable. I've met 10,000 friends around this country riding freights. I know where to get free meals, free clothes, free haircuts, free showers. Not that I use showers that much. I had one a couple days ago" (Peterson, p. 4).

The hobo's way of life has a tradition, a language, and a set of norms; it is a kind of counterculture. Only first names are used. Another norm that is learned from other hobos is that it is relatively safe to ride in an empty boxcar, but that arrest is often the consequence of being caught in a car containing merchandise. Hobos travel with few personal possessions, but they are often seen with a gallon jug of water for their long train rides.

The life of the hobo is dangerous. Some have been killed while trying to jump aboard a moving train, and others have died under the wheels when they fell off a car while drunk. Hobos tell of being knifed and beaten, and they have often been the victims of theft. Many have criminal records; one representative of a railroad company describes them as "a kind of lumpen-proletarian criminal class" (Peterson, p. 4).

Sources: Based on N. R. Kleinfield, "Forbes's Hunt for Richest 400," *The New York Times,* September 11, 1982, pp. 35, 41; and Iver Peterson, "More Take Up Life of the Railroad Hobo," *The New York Times,* January 15, 1983, pp. 1, 4.

THE UPPER CLASS

Although this class consists of no more than two or three per cent of all families in the United States, it controls a disproportionately large amount of property, prestige, and power. People in this class derive a high percentage of their incomes from interest, dividends, and investments rather than from regular salaries and wages. In 1972, the last year for which information is available, the one per cent of

"The Clarksons and the Baldwins are old money, the Schaefers and McNallys are new money, the Judds, the Lamberts, the Walters are no money . . ."

Drawing by Tobey; © 1981 The New Yorker Magazine, Inc.

families who controlled the most wealth held 20.7 per cent of all the wealth in the society (U.S. Bureau of the Census, 1982: 449).

The members of the upper class emphasize family heritage, traditional life styles, "tasteful" spending, education at the "right" schools, membership in exclusive clubs, and marriage with other members of the upper class. The members of the upper class often distinguish between an upper-upper class ("old money" and family heritage) and a lower-upper class ("new money" and no family background in the upper class). This distinction may not be apparent to those lower in the stratification system, but it is important to those at the top, as the cartoon illustrates.

THE UPPER-MIDDLE CLASS

About one-tenth of the families in the United States are in the upper-middle class. Members of this class

have high incomes and hold prestigious occupations such as physician and lawyer, but they live on earned income rather than on accumulated wealth. The parents of the members of the upper-middle class are often professionals or business executives and thus members of the upper-middle class themselves. Members of this class are career oriented, and have weak or minimal ties with relatives other than spouses and children so as to facilitate the geographic moves necessary to career advancement. The occupations of the upper-middle class often require a college degree or even an advanced degree, and they allow for considerable autonomy on the job.

THE LOWER-MIDDLE CLASS

People with white-collar, nonmanual jobs—such as teachers, nurses, lower-level business managers, and the owners of small businesses—are part of the lower-middle class that includes about a third of the population. People in this class have often had some college education. They are less career oriented than the upper-middle class, for they see few opportunities to move to better occupational positions. For example, schoolteachers receive annual salary increases, but they remain teachers performing the same duties year after year.

THE WORKING CLASS

The working class, which is nearly half the population, includes clerical and sales personnel and skilled and unskilled manual workers. These people earn regular incomes for working at relatively uninteresting jobs that have little prestige. They have limited opportunities to advance within their fields, and they see their jobs as a source of income rather than as a source of personal fulfillment.

THE LOWER CLASS

The lower class, which forms perhaps 20 per cent of the population, includes a variety of types of people who live on low earned incomes or on welfare assistance. This class includes some of the elderly, recent immigrants, criminals, transients, people with no job skills, people who have fallen into poverty from the lower-middle class or the working class, and families who have been on welfare for years. Jobs held by members of this class are low in prestige and often only temporary. Education is limited, and many people in the lower class have not completed high school.

Social Mobility

Most Americans believe in the possibility of *social mobility*, the movement of people from one position to another in the stratification system. They may not believe that everyone has an equal opportunity to end up at the top of the stratification system, but they do think that everyone can improve his or her social standing. People at the top are more likely than those at the bottom to believe in equal opportunity; after all, the system has worked well for them (Rytina, Form, and Pease, 1970). This faith in mobility weakens identification with a particular social class, because class position is seen as temporary and the stratification system as a whole is perceived as fluid rather than rigid. There are two types of social mobility: horizontal mobility and vertical mobility.

Horizontal mobility is movement from one position in a stratification system to another position at the same level. An example would be a worker in a Southern textile mill who moves to Detroit and takes a job on an automobile assembly line. Horizontal mobility does not increase or decrease a person's standing in terms of property, prestige, or power.

Vertical mobility, on the other hand, is movement upward or downward in a stratification system. Upward vertical mobility is movement from one position to another with greater income, wealth, respect, or power; a promotion from department manager to corporate vice-president would be one example. Downward vertical mobility is movement to a position of lower status, such as a foreman who is required to go back to working as a manual laborer under someone else's supervision.

As we noted earlier, class systems are much more open to social mobility than are slave, estate, or caste systems—even though there is some mobility in these relatively closed systems. In fact, barriers to social mobility are also present in open systems. For example, parents try to pass on their advantages to their children, making it more difficult for "have-nots" to gain those advantages. Discrimination against racial and ethnic groups and discrimination against women are other obstacles to mobility. In addition, people high in the stratification system discriminate against people from the lower class and the working class. This sometimes takes the form of limiting the upward mobility of people with "bad manners" or those who do not dress or speak "properly."

There tends to be more social mobility in modern societies than in traditional societies (see Chapter 7). One reason is that industrialization is associated with a complex division of labor that offers more high-status positions and greater rewards such as income and prestige. This kind of occupational structure provides more opportunities—and increased motivation—for upward mobility. In addition, birth rates decline with industrialization, a decline that is especially great for those at the top of the stratification system. Because these people do not have enough children to fill all the high-status positions, the way is opened for people lower in the system to move up.

Social mobility is also increased by migration because immigrants often take low-status jobs, in effect pushing other groups into higher positions. Urbanization, which increases with industrialization, can also enhance mobility, because the anonymity of the city makes it possible for people to be judged by their achievements rather than by family background, ethnicity, or other ascribed traits. People raised in cities and people who live in cities experience more upward mobility than people raised or living elsewhere (Blau and Duncan, 1967).

CAREER MOBILITY

A change in social position over the course of a person's lifetime is called *career mobility*. Many people are employed in occupations that have a career line; they enter an occupation at a low level where they gain experience and training, and later they are promoted to higher levels of the same occupation. Upward career mobility also occurs when people leave one occupation for another that has higher income, prestige, or power. Mobility is influenced by many factors, including one's sex, race, mental ability, ambition, education, the status of one's parents, and whether one's parents were divorced or married during one's childhood (Blau and Duncan, 1967).

INTERGENERATIONAL MOBILITY

In a completely open class system, the position a person attains in the stratification system would not be affected by the position his or her parents had attained. No stratification system is this open, and there is always some correlation between parents' status and the status of their offspring when they become adults. *Intergenerational mobility* is movement in a stratification system from the level occupied by a person's parents.

Upward intergenerational mobility is related to several factors. It is greatest for those who learn initiative and obedience in childhood. It is also more common among those who have few brothers and sisters and among those who are raised in stable families. Mobility is enhanced by parents who place a strong emphasis on education as a way to get ahead. Parents can also increase their children's chances of moving up in the stratification system by paying for their college education or by providing them with an inheritance to begin a career. The first job that a person takes and the amount of education that he or she has completed also influence mobility, although level of educational attainment is closely related to the status of one's parents. Mobility is less likely for people who have many children and for people who get divorced or separated (Blau and Duncan, 1967;

Duncan, Featherman, and Duncan, 1972; Jencks et al., 1979).

MOBILITY IN THE UNITED STATES VERSUS MOBILITY IN OTHER NATIONS

The amount of mobility that exists in the United States depends on how mobility is defined and measured, the most common way being to compare the income or the occupational prestige of people with that of their parents. Surveys have discovered that there is more upward mobility than downward mobility in the United States: About half of men are upwardly mobile, about one-third do not change class position, and the rest are downwardly mobile (Blau and Duncan, 1967; Hauser and Featherman, 1977). Most movement in the class system occurs in short increments rather than in big jumps. A large amount of mobility has been from farm jobs to blue-collar positions in cities, and from the working class into an expanded number of white-collar jobs. In other words, changes in the economy—and the occupations that are part of the economic system—account for much social mobility. In spite of these changes in the occupational structure of American society, there has been little increase or decrease in the total amount of social mobility in recent years (Blau and Duncan, 1967; Lipset, 1972; Hauser and Featherman, 1977; McRoberts and Selbee, 1981). One exception is young and well-educated blacks, who have experienced an increase in upward mobility in recent years (see Chapter 9).

The democratic ideology of American society more strongly supports social mobility than do the ideologies of most other industrial societies, but cross-national surveys do not show that there is much more upward mobility in the United States than elsewhere. Surveys that have compared mobility in the United States with that in countries such as Great Britain, Japan, France, and Sweden have, for the most part, found that in the United States there is a greater chance for a person from a lower-class or working-class background to attain a position high in the stratification system. However, in the United States there is also a greater chance that a person born to parents high in the stratification system will inherit their advantaged position. Although these surveys sometimes draw different conclusions about whether the total amount of mobility in the United States is greater or less than the total amount in other countries, the conclusion they seem to point to is that there is slightly more upward mobility in the United States, but not as much more as the differences in the ideologies of the different societies might suggest (Lipset and Bendix, 1959; Fox and Miller, 1965; Treiman and Terrell, 1965; Blau and Duncan, 1967; Duberman, 1976; Tyree, Semyonov, and Hodge, 1979; McRoberts and Selbee, 1981). The similarity of upward mobility in all industrial societies has been attributed to a similar occupational structure in these societies and to the ambition of people of all nationalities to gain the rewards associated with a higher position in the stratification system (Bendix and Lipset, 1959). The differences in mobility that do exist among industrial societies seem attributable to variations in occupational structure; for example, Great Britain seems to have somewhat more mobility than France or Sweden because it has a larger proportion of its workers in bureaucratic occupations (Hope, 1982b).

The Promise of Equal Opportunity

American culture includes a belief that ability, hard work, and ambition will be rewarded (Kluegel and Smith, 1981). This belief, which grew out of a past that was free of a hereditary privileged class, is incorporated in the Declaration of Independence, which declares that everyone is equal—a value learned through socialization in school. Is the "rags-to-riches" ideal a myth or a reality? There are arguments for both sides of the question, and even studies of social mobility do not give a definitive answer. Before we try to answer the question for ourselves, we need to look at what sociologists mean by the term "poverty."

POVERTY

Poverty is a condition in which people have too little money to afford the basic necessities of life. One way to define poverty is to establish a minimum income that is needed to buy the goods and services that will enable a family to survive. In 1981, this minimum income level was $9,287 for a nonfarm family of four (U.S. Bureau of the Census, 1982: 440). This figure was set by the Department of Agriculture, which establishes certain minimum nutritional standards for people living in different kinds of communities. Because incomes have not increased as fast as prices in recent years, the amount of money needed to maintain a standard of living above the poverty level has risen. However, the government has revised upward the dollar in-

come needed to stay out of poverty each year in order to take into account the effects of inflation.

Recently there has been considerable discussion about how to define poverty. Until a few years ago, most people agreed that the poverty line should be defined by a specific dollar income, but some critics have suggested that this measure exaggerates the extent of poverty (Browning, 1976; Browning and Johnson, 1979; Pear, 1982b; Herbers, 1982c). Family income does not include "in-kind benefits" such as school lunch programs, food stamps, subsidized housing, and health care (Medicaid and Medicare); and these noncash benefits have been an important part of federal efforts to reduce poverty. In 1980, more than one-sixth of all American households received at least one of these types of in-kind assistance. However, many of these benefits did not reach those living in poverty, as about two-fifths of all poor families did not receive any of these benefits (Rich, 1982). Cutbacks by the Reagan administration have limited the extent to which some of these programs can reduce poverty by supplementing cash income.

Who Are the Poor?

It is not easy to distinguish between what people need to survive and what they learn to want by being socialized in a particular culture. People may be able to survive while living in a dilapidated slum tenement, eating unnourishing food, and wearing worn clothing, but their lives would be unpleasant because of the negative reactions of others and because of the psychological pain they would suffer when they compared their standard of living with that of the rest of the population. In addition, a family defined as poverty stricken by American standards might have a life style that would be acceptable in another part of the world.

Whatever definition of poverty we use, it is clear that not everyone in American society is equally likely to be poor. In 1981, 14 per cent of all people in the United States lived below the poverty level. However, there were significant differences in the poverty rates of various racial and ethnic groups; for instance, only 11.1 per cent of whites lived in poverty, compared to 34.2 per cent of blacks and 26.5 per cent of Hispanics. Children under age sixteen lived below the poverty level more often than any other age group; and 15.3 per cent of those over age sixty-five lived in poverty, only slightly more than the 14 per cent figure for the population as a whole. Southerners also had a higher-than-

In 1981, 14 per cent of all people in the United States lived below the poverty level—a fact that limits their "life chances."

average chance of living in poverty; 17.4 per cent of people who lived in the South fell below the poverty level, the highest percentage for any region (U.S. Bureau of the Census, 1982: 440, 442).

Different types of families have different likelihoods of living in poverty. In 1981, 11.2 per cent of all families in the United States fell below the poverty level. However, only 6.8 per cent of families that included a married couple lived in poverty. Male-headed families with no wife present lived in poverty 10.3 per cent of the time, but female-headed families with no husband present fell below the poverty level in 34.6 per cent of the cases (U.S. Bureau of the Census, *Money Income and Poverty Status*, July 1982: 21). This extraordinarily high rate of poverty among families headed by women has been called "the feminization of poverty" (Pearce, 1978; National Advisory Council on Economic Opportunity, 1980: 17; see Chapter 10).

The percentage of families with incomes below the poverty line declined during the 1960s as a result of the War on Poverty, a series of programs sponsored by the now-defunct Office of Economic Opportunity, and because of a set of laws that increased benefits for the poor. In 1960, 22.2 per cent of all American families were living in poverty, but by 1970 that figure had declined to 12.6 per cent. The proportion of the population living in poverty did not decrease significantly during the 1970s, and in 1981 it stood at 14 per cent (under a slightly revised definition of poverty).

Why Does Poverty Exist?

Poverty exists, and seems to persist, for several reasons. Job discrimination against racial and ethnic minorities and against women is a cause of some poverty. Company policies that require workers to retire at age seventy leave some Americans below the poverty line, even with social security payments, Medicare, and other benefits. Technological advances can create poverty by making certain job skills outmoded and reducing the need for unskilled labor; the introduction of computer technology has and will continue to make some jobs outmoded (such as cash register clerk at a grocery store) and reduce the need for other skilled workers (as, for example, by replacing two typists with one typist and a word processor) (Serrin, 1982b). Still another source of poverty is change in the technology of agriculture—such as the modern machinery and marketing strategies of "agribusiness"—that has made many small farms unproductive, creating poverty in rural communities or in those cities to which displaced farmers move.

In some ways, poverty is functional for society as a whole, even though it is dysfunctional for the poor (Gans, 1973: 102–126). Poverty provides society with a group that is willing to do "dirty work" such as dishwashing and cleaning out bedpans in a hospital; this source of inexpensive labor enables tasks to be done that most people would resist doing. Indeed, some Southern states have seasonally reduced welfare benefits to encourage the poor to take jobs in the fields. The poor sometimes work as domestics or gardeners for the wealthy, who are thus freed for other work or for leisure pursuits. In addition, the poor provide society with a group that will pay for shoddy merchandise, stale food, second-hand clothing, and dilapidated housing.

Precisely because poverty has some useful consequences for society as a whole, it has proved difficult to eradicate, although many nations have succeeded in reducing the proportion of people living in poverty. We can see from SEL 8.3 that public attitudes are one source of opposition to efforts to reduce poverty in the United States. Later in this chapter we examine some of these measures to reduce poverty.

SOCIOLOGY AND EVERYDAY LIFE 8.3
"Blaming the Victim": Who Should Get Welfare?

"Welfare" is a loaded word—it sometimes evokes images of fraud and cheating or laziness and unwillingness to work. These attitudes toward poverty were demonstrated in a poll which found that Americans supported reductions in "public welfare" but wanted to retain "aid to the needy"; the two are essentially the same, but "public welfare" has a negative connotation that "aid to the needy" does not.

In fact, the level of income provided by welfare benefits does not permit a style of life that many people would choose, especially in the United States, where, from childhood on, everyone is bombarded with messages in the mass media to spend and to consume. Most welfare recipients cannot work, either because they are too young or too old, ill or disabled, or in school. In 1981, for example, of those people fifteen years old and over whose incomes fell below the poverty level and who did not work at all during the year, the main reasons that they did not work were as follows:

keeping house	33.3%
ill or disabled	23.2%
going to school	16.5%
retired	15.1%
unable to find work	9.3%
all other reasons	2.6%

Overall, 21.9 per cent of people age fifteen and over who did not work in 1981 fell below the poverty level. In addition, 7.3 per cent of Americans of this age who did work in 1981 still had incomes below the poverty level; and, somewhat surprisingly, 2.9 per cent of people who worked full time throughout the whole year nevertheless fell below the poverty level. In spite of these facts, some states have tried to substitute "workfare" for welfare, requiring welfare recipients who are able-bodied to work for their benefits or be trained for employment if they lack marketable skills.

Many welfare recipients are poor for a short time, even though there are some people who were raised on welfare and later bring up their own children on welfare. Also, cases of welfare fraud are relatively rare, probably accounting for less than 1 per cent of all claims for benefits. Still, many Americans above the poverty line—and indeed some below it—"blame the victims," the poor, for their own plight.

Sources: Based on John Herbers, "Conflict Is Found in Views on Needy," *The New York Times*, February 14, 1982, p. 31; and William Ryan, *Blaming the Victim*, rev. ed. New York: Vintage Books, 1976. Statistics are from U.S. Bureau of the Census, *Money Income and Poverty Status of Families and Persons in the United States: 1981*. Washington, D.C.: U.S. Government Printing Office, July 1982.

LIFE CHANCES AND PATTERNS OF BEHAVIOR

Sociologists have found that class standing and poverty, however they are measured, are closely related to the quality and the kind of lives that people live (Rossides, 1976; Rothman, 1978).

Life Chances

The opportunities that people have to survive until old age, eat nutritious food, enjoy good physical and mental health, live in adequate housing, and get a good education are called "life chances." These are directly related to income level and other indicators of social class.

LONGEVITY. The average number of years that a newborn infant can expect to live is related to such correlates of class as housing conditions, sanitation, medical care, diet, and education. Because people of the lower classes fare less well in these terms than those of higher standing, the poor have a shorter life expectancy (Fuchs, 1974; Gortmaker, 1979). Children of the rich are not as likely to die before they reach the age of one, and high-income mothers are less likely to die in childbirth. Diseases such as tuberculosis, pneumonia, and influenza do not strike the upper classes as often as they do the poor. The poor are also more likely to die from accidents, occupational diseases, lead poisoning, wartime service, murder, and suicide (Kitagawa and Hauser, 1968; Zeitlin, Lutterman, and Russell, 1973).

PHYSICAL HEALTH. People with higher incomes are less likely than the poor to have heart disease, diabetes, anemia, and arthritis. The rich seek medical care more often for the problems they do have, visiting physicians and hospitals before their health has deteriorated and thereby preventing serious complications. This is because the rich have more money to pay for medical services, are more likely to have medical insurance, and have greater access to medical facilities than do people who live in poverty-stricken communities (U.S. Bureau of the Census, 1980: 87, 109).

NUTRITION. People below the poverty level consume fewer calories, less protein, less calcium, less iron, and fewer vitamins than people with higher incomes (U.S. Bureau of the Census, 1982: 128). This can be attributed in part to the lack of money, even though the poor spend a higher percentage of their limited incomes on food than do people with higher incomes. The rich pay less for food of higher quality than do the poor, who often shop in grocery stores located in slum communities (Caplovitz, 1963). In addition, higher-income people are more likely to know better what constitutes a healthy and balanced diet. For the children of the poor, lack of good nutrition can impair brain function and development, thus lowering academic performance and closing off opportunities for an advanced education and a good job.

MENTAL HEALTH. Class position is closely associated with mental health. People of higher social position are happier and have fewer psychological problems than people of lower status (Hollingshead and Redlich, 1958; Cameron, 1974; Campbell, Converse, and Rodgers, 1976; Weeks, 1977; Rushing and Ortega, 1979; Kessler and Cleary, 1980). In mental hospitals, the poor are more likely than wealthier patients to be held for long periods of time and to receive custodial care rather than effective treatment (Hollingshead and Redlich, 1958; Meyers and Bean, 1968). Many poor people who are mentally ill receive no treatment at all; they are more likely to suffer from depression and from psychosomatic problems than are the upper classes, but the upper classes tend to suffer more from anxiety (Srole et al., 1977).

HOUSING. The poor spend a greater proportion of their incomes on housing than do people with higher incomes, but the poor still live in houses that are often in disrepair, have dangerous wiring, are infested with rats and cockroaches, and have inadequate heating and ventilation. These aspects of housing contribute to their inferior physical and mental health and lower their life expectancy.

EDUCATION. In the United States, children usually attend schools in their own neighborhood. These schools are typically financed with taxes from property owners in the community. Consequently, schools in upper-class areas are better financed. Children from upper-class backgrounds also score higher on intelligence tests and do better in their schoolwork than children from poor families.

The percentage of children enrolled in colleges and universities drops with declining family income, and so the poor suffer educationally because they are less able to afford to attend college (U.S. Bureau of the Census, 1982: 160). Education is important in locating a person's first job and in gaining promotions over the course of a career.

TABLE 8.3
Median Income by Level of Education Completed, Year-round Full-time Workers, Males and Females 25 Years Old and Over, 1981

Level of education completed	Median income	
	Males	*Females*
Less than 8 years	$12,866	$8,419
8 years	$16,084	$9,723
1 to 3 years of high school	$16,938	$10,043
4 years of high school	$20,598	$12,332
1 to 3 years of college	$22,565	$14,343
4 years of college	$26,394	$16,322
5 years or more of college	$30,434	$20,148
Median income, total	$21,689	$31,259

Source: U.S. Bureau of the Census, *Money Income and Poverty Status of Families and Persons in the United States: 1981.* Washington, D.C.: U.S. Government Printing Office, July 1982, pp. 13–14.

Because the poor are less likely to have high educational attainment, they hold low-prestige jobs and earn salaries that are often near or below the poverty line. We can see clearly from Table 8.3 that workers' incomes are closely linked with their levels of education. In Chapter 10, we look at the reasons for the large differences in income between men and women with the same amounts of education.

Patterns of Behavior

Position in the stratification system is closely associated with patterns of behavior such as consumption, leisure activites, political behavior, criminal behavior and treatment by the criminal justice system, family life, and child-rearing practices. These patterns of behavior form a "life style," the daily activities of people with a similar status. Life style is related to class because income, wealth, prestige, and power influence how people eat, what they wear, where they live, with whom they associate, and how they see the future.

CONSUMPTION PATTERNS. The ways in which income is spent vary with class standing. Members of the upper-upper class are concerned with "tasteful" displays of wealth rather than with ostentation; they frown on the *nouveaux riches,* or lower-upper class, for their inability to spend their newly earned money in ways that reflect tradition and restraint. The lower-upper class and the upwardly mobile members of the middle class often engage in "conspicuous consumption," the expenditure of money in ways calculated to attract the attention of other people and symbolize financial success outwardly. For instance, a former sideman of Elvis Presley remarked on the decoration of Graceland, Presley's home: "That house is filled with everything you'd walk into a furniture store and *not* buy" (cited in Marsh, 1981). In contrast, most members of the working class are not concerned with ostentation; rather, they spend their income so as to demonstrate that they are respectable; for example, they often spend money on home improvements.

LEISURE ACTIVITIES. People of different classes engage in different leisure pursuits. This is a result of the amount of income they have to spend on leisure activities, but it is also due to class differences in upbringing and education. People with higher incomes, more education, and professional occupations often spend their free time enjoying the performing arts, including classical music concerts, plays, the opera, and the ballet. Wealthy people also engage in athletic activities more often than members of the lower classes, who are more likely to be spectators at sporting events (Hodges, 1964). The proportion of Americans who say that watching television is their favorite evening activity

Here two couples enjoy an evening of bowling. What class do you think they belong to?

is greatest at lower levels of income and education (U.S. Bureau of the Census, 1980: 537, 540).

POLITICAL BEHAVIOR. People of higher social standing are more likely to register to vote, to vote in an election, and to be active in political organizations. Working-class and lower-class people tend to be liberal on economic issues; they support labor unions, government regulation of business, and social benefits such as unemployment compensation and social security. Middle-class and upper-class people are more conservative on economic issues, tending to favor big business and support inequality of income and wealth. However, the middle and upper classes are more liberal on non-economic issues such as tolerance toward minority groups, and the lower and working classes are more conservative on these issues. In the United States the working class and the lower class have traditionally been Democrats, and the middle class and the upper class have traditionally been Republicans, but these affiliations have weakened in recent years.

CRIME AND THE CRIMINAL JUSTICE SYSTEM. Members of the lower and working classes commit more crimes of personal violence, such as murder, rape, and assault, than do members of the middle and upper classes. Certain types of property crimes such as robbery, burglary, and auto theft are also more common among the lower classes. Some petty forms of theft are about equally common at all levels of the class system (Conklin, 1981: 139–141).

The most expensive crimes in terms of lost property are white-collar crimes such as embezzlement, income tax evasion, price-fixing, and false advertising. Crimes such as these, which are committed by middle- and upper-class people, account for about ten times as much financial loss as the conventional crimes of robbery, burglary, larceny, and auto theft, which are more often committed by people of lower status (Conklin, 1977: 1–8).

If a lower-class person and a middle-class person commit the same crime, the chances are greater that the lower-class person will be arrested, prosecuted, convicted, and sent to prison. The poor are less likely to be released on bail before trial, because such release requires money. The poor are also less able to afford private attorneys to handle their cases, and the defense provided by court-appointed lawyers is often inadequate. In addition, the poor are more likely to return to crime after their release from prison, because they often lack the job skills and the education that make hiring them an attractive prospect to employers.

FAMILY LIFE. The working and lower classes tend to emphasize family life more than the higher classes do; people in higher positions derive relatively more satisfaction from their jobs, from leisure pursuits outside the home, and from participating in voluntary associations (Cohen and Hodges, 1963). Lower-class and working-class people are more likely to interact socially with relatives than are the middle and upper classes, who tend more to associate with their friends and acquaintances. In addition, working-class and lower-class families often follow traditional sex roles: Women wait on their husbands, prepare meals, care for the children, and clean the house; men earn the income and discipline the children.

CHILD-REARING PRACTICES. Classes differ in the ways in which they socialize children. For instance, parents of each class try to train their children for the same work roles that they occupy (Kohn, 1963, 1969, 1976). Because middle- and upper-class parents often hold jobs in which they determine the pace of their own work and make their own decisions, they socialize their children to take the initiative and to be responsible. These parents reason with their children rather than demand obedience; punish them by withholding love and approval; and, when they behave as desired, reward them with affection and other symbolic rewards.

In contrast to the middle class, lower-class and working-class parents are more likely to demand obedience and compliance from their children and to punish them physically for disobedience. Socialization of this sort prepares working-class children for what their parents assume will be their future jobs, in which they will have to cooperate with other workers and obey a higher authority. From this, it is clear that child-rearing practices help to perpetuate the existing class system.

REDUCING POVERTY AND CLASS DIFFERENCES

Because the matter of class and standard of living is so essential to survival, the question of whether poverty can be reduced or eliminated altogether is important. There has been much debate over whether the goal of social policy should be to provide everyone with equal opportunity—that is, to treat everyone equally—or to strive for equal results such as the same income for everyone (Lewis et al., 1982). If the goal is not absolute equality, then the problem becomes agreeing on exactly how much inequality is tolerable. Methods to diminish social inequality include public education, embourgeoisement, taxation policy, and direct assistance to the poor.

Public Education

An industrial society requires a system of public education to provide people with the skills and the knowledge needed to hold jobs in an advanced economy. Public education helps to reduce differences among the classes by giving people the opportunity to acquire the knowledge and the skills—and the credentials—that will allow them to improve their position in the stratification system. Societies with systems of public education probably tend to have less social inequality than societies in which only people at the top of the stratification system can afford an education. However, the educational system can also serve to perpetuate stratification. In the United States, for example, financial support of public education comes from local property taxes and thus reinforces existing class differences at the community level. In Great Britain, ''public schools'' (which Americans would call private schools) help to maintain an elite status group by reinforcing an upper-class life style.

Embourgeoisement

In recent years, sociologists have proposed that class differences are being eroded by *embourgeoisement*, the process by which manual and blue-collar workers develop a life style much like that of the middle class or bourgeoisie. This change has been attributed to rising levels of income and education among the working class that provide them with the resources to develop patterns of behavior much like those traditionally characteristic of the middle class. At the same time, bureaucratization and the expansion of service jobs have increased the number of nonmanual and white-collar jobs that have some of the characteristics of working-class jobs, such as repetitiveness (Wright et al., 1982).

There is, however, little empirical evidence that embourgeoisement has transformed the working class. In Great Britain, neither higher incomes nor different kinds of jobs have led workers to become more like the middle class in their political attitudes and behavior (Goldthorpe et al., 1969). A study of different classes in Providence, Rhode Island, found that blue-collar workers and white-collar workers saw the same form of consumption—home ownership—in very different terms. The blue-collar workers saw home ownership as a way to become free of landlords, whereas the white-collar workers emphasized the financial advantages and the prestige associated with owning a home (Mackenzie, 1973). Today most blue-collar workers still identify themselves as working class, in spite of incomes and educations that are sometimes like those of the middle class. In addition, the high unemployment rates of recent years have caused some downward mobility among the working class, rather than a movement into middle- and upper-class positions.

Taxation Policy

One strategy for reducing inequality is to try to make people equal in terms of personal characteristics that influence income—such as education—in the hope that this will in turn create more equality in income or occupational prestige. However, this strategy is likely to be less effective in reducing inequality than the direct redistribution of income, because family background—which cannot be directly changed by government policy—has a major influence on the jobs that people get and the incomes that they earn (Jencks et al., 1972, 1979). In other words, policies that try to create equal *results*—through taxation or direct payments to the poor, for example—are more likely to reduce inequality than are efforts to equalize *opportunities*, such as educating everyone in the same way.

All industrial societies influence the distribution of income and wealth through their policies of taxation. Many societies use a progressive income tax to try to make incomes more equal. A "progressive tax" requires that people with higher incomes pay higher percentages of their incomes in taxes than are paid by people with lower incomes, thereby redistributing income to those lower in the stratification system. Although higher incomes are taxed at a higher rate in the United States, the federal tax system does provide many deductions or loopholes that are used more readily by the wealthy than by the poor. Thus some high-income people pay about the same percentage of their incomes in taxes as people with lower incomes do. For example, people who rent apartments or houses cannot deduct rental costs from their incomes before paying federal taxes, but homeowners and apartment building owners can deduct from their incomes all interest paid to the bank on mortgage loans and all

property taxes paid to the town or city. This provision favors homeowners and landlords over people who rent, and by doing so gives an advantage to those with greater wealth and income. The actual percentage of total income paid in federal taxes by the average millionaire is about the same as the percentage paid by someone earning between $5,000 and $7,000, but of course the same percentage applied to the income of a millionaire produces many more tax dollars (Rossides, 1976).

One way to equalize incomes is to reduce the number of loopholes that allow the wealthy to avoid or minimize paying taxes. However, some deductions do serve useful purposes, such as encouraging people to make donations to charity or providing people with a financial incentive to buy a home (which stimulates the construction industry). Another way to reduce inequality is to tax inheritances heavily, although this policy might create a disincentive for some people to work, especially older workers who plan to leave their accumulated wealth to their children.

Direct Assistance to the Poor

A more direct way to minimize social inequality is by direct cash or in-kind benefits paid to those who pass a "means test," that is, those who fall below a certain income level or who have been unemployed for a specified period of time. One proposal to alleviate poverty that has been debated but not enacted is a guaranteed minimum income that would make direct cash payments to people below a certain "floor" in order to bring their incomes up to a minimum level. Welfare programs in the United States have been aimed more at reducing poverty than have the programs in European welfare states, many of which provide services such as health care to all of the population (Piven and Cloward, 1982).

During the 1960s and 1970s, the United States government implemented several programs to raise the standard of living of the poor: Aid to Families with Dependent Children, medical assistance (Medicare and Medicaid), food stamps, housing subsidies, school lunch programs, aid to the elderly and the disabled, and emergency fuel assistance. CETA, the Comprehensive Employment and Training Act, established training programs for the unemployed and provided them with jobs in the public sector. In the late 1970s about half of the total income of the poorest 20 per cent of the population came from benefits of this sort.

The effort to reduce poverty was halted and reversed in part in the early 1980s. The Reagan administration has been ideologically opposed to supporting the poor with federal tax dollars, and so the policies of "Reaganomics" have sought to reduce federal spending on social programs that help the poor. Even CETA, a program aimed at training the unemployed for productive work, was "zero-budgeted," a euphemism for being eliminated. A recent examination of the reasons for this "attack on the welfare state" concludes that by reducing support for the poor and by increasing the unemployment rate, the Reagan administration hopes to increase profits for business, the source of its political support. Profits would be increased by reducing workers' wages and salaries—something that tends to happen when the poor and the unemployed feel they must take any job, even at low pay. This exerts a downward pressure on wages and salaries because people who are searching for work, especially when they have limited access to government benefits, will underbid the wages and salaries earned by those who are currently working. One result will be to undercut the bargaining power of workers and labor unions, because they fear being replaced by the readily available and inexpensive laborers (Piven and Cloward, 1982).

The Reagan administration designed its strategy of budget and tax cuts to produce gains for higher-income families and losses for poorer families. The "supply-side" economic theory that underlies this policy of increasing social inequality assumes that the economy can only be stimulated by creating incentives for work, saving, and investment. The cause of poverty, in this view, lies with the poor themselves, rather than with the social structure as a whole. This explanation of poverty is, of course, functional for those at the top of the stratification system, for whom the social structure has worked to advantage.

Summary

There is social inequality in every society; the ranking and classification of people by their control over scarce resources such as income, wealth, prestige, and power is called social stratification. Open systems of stratification, in which movement from one stratum to another is relatively easy, differ from slave, estate, and caste systems, which are more closed to social mobility.

Conflict theorists claim that differences in the control of valued resources are the result of the pursuit of individual and group interests. Marx saw the crucial difference among classes in capitalist societies as one of control of the means of production; the bourgeoisie controlled these resources, and the proletariat sold its labor to these capitalists. In contrast, functionalists see social inequality as a way to motivate people to do tasks that are necessary to the survival of society. They argue that the greatest rewards go to the skilled people who perform the jobs that are most valuable to society. One synthesis of these two perspectives suggests that stratification is the product of a need for unequal rewards to get certain tasks done well, but that conflict between groups leads to more inequality than is required to get these essential tasks done.

Weber went beyond Marx's economic analysis of classes and proposed three distinct dimensions of stratification: property (including both income and wealth), prestige, and power. Power, which has a variety of sources, is explored in detail in Chapter 14. Prestige in the United States is based largely on the respect accorded to different occupations, although it also reflects level of education, area of residence, family heritage, and other differences among people. Occupational rankings are remarkably similar in all contemporary societies, and they have not changed much in the United States in this century. When an individual is ranked at about the same level on all dimensions of stratification, this is called status consistency.

Many methods have been used to describe the class system of the United States; these methods usually yield between three and six classes. We briefly described five classes: the upper class, the upper-middle class, the lower-middle class, the working class, and the lower class.

Movement from one position in a stratification system to another is called social mobility. Mobility can be horizontal, or it can be upward or downward. Career mobility occurs within an individual's lifetime. Sociologists have paid more attention, however, to intergenerational mobility, the movement from the status occupied by one's parents to a different status during one's own lifetime. Intergenerational mobility is influenced by factors such as childhood socialization, educational attainment, and number of children in one's family. The ideology of the United States stresses equal opportunity for upward mobility, but cross-national surveys do not find significantly more upward mobility in the United States than elsewhere. More Americans do move into the top positions from positions lower in the stratification system, but Americans are also more likely than people in other societies to inherit a top position from their parents.

The American ideology of an open system with equal opportunity is contradicted by the reality of considerable inequality and poverty. Poverty has been defined in different ways, the usual way being in terms of a socially defined minimum income for a family of a particular size in a certain type of community. The poor are especially likely to be women and children in homes without fathers, members of minority groups, the uneducated, and the unskilled. Poverty persists because it is functional for society in certain ways, while being dysfunctional for the poor. Compared to those of higher status, the poor do not live as long, do not have as good physical and mental health, do not eat as well, live in unsatisfactory housing, and receive inadequate educations. Class differences are also closely associated with consumption patterns, leisure activities, criminal behavior and treatment by the criminal justice system, family life, and child-rearing practices.

A variety of measures might reduce poverty. Public education is an effort to give everyone an equal opportunity to acquire the skills and the knowledge necessary to find a good job. However, family background affects educational attainment, and education by itself is not an effective way to reduce social inequality. Embourgeoisement is a process by which improvement in the education and the income of the working class causes it to acquire a middle-class life style. This process has not yet produced a dramatic reduction in social inequality. Taxation policy, especially the progressive income tax, has been used to reduce income differences by redistributing scarce resources to the poor. Loopholes for the wealthy have made this an ineffective policy, even though income inequality has been reduced somewhat by this measure. The most promising way to reduce inequality and poverty is direct aid to the poor. Efforts of this sort by the United States government during the 1960s and 1970s did reduce by about half the proportion of all families living below the poverty level, but the

early 1980s saw a reversal of this trend as a result of the economic policies of the Reagan administration.

Important Terms

CAREER MOBILITY (183)
CASTE (172)
CLASS (172)
EMBOURGEOISEMENT (190)
HORIZONTAL MOBILITY (182)
INCOME (175)
INTERGENERATIONAL MOBILITY (183)
POVERTY (184)
POWER (178)

PRESTIGE (176)
PROPERTY (175)
SOCIAL MOBILITY (182)
SOCIAL STRATIFICATION (171)
STATUS GROUP (176)
STATUS CONSISTENCY (178)
VERTICAL MOBILITY (182)
WEALTH (175)

Suggested Readings

Ken Auletta. *The Underclass.* New York: Random House, 1982. A detailed look at America's "underclass"—long-term recipients of welfare, street criminals, hustlers, and transients—and some recent efforts to improve their social position.

Peter M. Blau and Otis Dudley Duncan. *The American Occupational Structure.* New York: Wiley, 1967. One of the most important studies of stratification and mobility in the United States.

Richard Coleman and Lee Rainwater. *Social Standing in America.* New York: Basic Books, 1978. A report on recent surveys of perceptions of class standing in the United States.

Christopher Jencks et al. *Who Gets Ahead? The Determinants of Economic Success in America.* New York: Basic Books, 1979. An important piece of research on social mobility.

Frances Fox Piven and Richard A. Cloward. *The New Class War: Reagan's Attack on the Welfare State and Its Consequences.* New York: Pantheon, 1982. A historical treatment of the background to recent cuts in federal benefits for the poor, how this policy serves those in higher positions, and a prediction for the future.

Daniel W. Rossides. *The American Class System.* Lanham, Md.: University Press of America, 1976. A comprehensive textbook on stratification and mobility in the United States.

Robert A. Rothman. *Inequality and Stratification in the United States.* Englewood Cliffs, N.J.: Prentice-Hall, 1978. A brief and clearly written introduction to social stratification.

W. Lloyd Warner and Paul S. Lunt. *The Social Life of a Modern Community.* New Haven, Conn.: Yale University Press, 1941. A classic study of stratification in a small Massachusetts town.

RACIAL AND ETHNIC GROUPS

Many societies contain groups and categories of people with different skin colors, languages, and religious practices. These physical and cultural traits form the basis of social distinctions that are used to rank or stratify people. Position in this stratification system is based on ascribed traits that people either are born with (skin color or facial features), acquire from their parents (religion), or learn through socialization in childhood (ethnic traditions). Often, individuals are assigned a status in the stratification system on the basis of a group or a category to which they belong.

The ranking of racial and ethnic groups and the social interaction among the members of those groups are important parts of a society's social structure. Intergroup relations sometimes produce conflict among individuals and groups, having consequences that range from full acceptance of a group to its extermination. The diversity of racial and ethnic groups in a society can be a source of tension and violence, but it can also enrich a culture and provide a source of new ideas that lead to social change.

Race, Ethnicity, and Minority Groups

Physical and cultural differences among groups are often associated with differences in property, power, and prestige. We describe these differences—and the social meanings attached to them—with the concepts of race, ethnicity, and minority group.

RACE

Race is commonly thought of as an inherited set of physical traits that distinguish large categories of people from one another. These traits are present at birth and cannot be changed, even though they evolve over thousands of years, as people adapt to the environment. In the United States, race is usually defined by skin color, although facial features, hair texture, height, and other physical characteristics are also used to distinguish racial groupings.

Biologists and anthropologists have not been able to agree on the number of clear and distinct races that exist in the world. One division among races is Caucasoid, Negroid, and Mongoloid. However, within each of these groupings there is considerable variation in physical features, and there is much overlap in traits from one grouping to another. Because of the difficulty of defining races in biological terms, most contemporary scholars have abandoned such efforts.

Although race seems to be a concept without any precise biological meaning, it does have an important social meaning. Race is a socially ascribed characteristic, for people believe that physical differences among people are associated with certain kinds of behavior. These beliefs, though inaccurate, nevertheless are important in determining the interaction among the members of a society or among the members of different societies. In SEL 9.1 we see how arbitrary the classification of racial groupings can be, and the important ways that such classification influences life chances and social interaction in South Africa.

In the United States, the category "black" includes all people with some recognizable Negroid ancestry, even though people assigned to that racial grouping sometimes have more Caucasoid ancestors than Negroid ones. About three-fourths of all people classified as blacks in the United States have at least one white ancestor, and one-fifth or more of all "whites" have at least a single Negroid ancestor (Hunt and Walker, 1974). People of mixed ancestry are assigned to one racial grouping or another, with assignment to a racial grouping being based on social definition rather than on bio-

SOCIOLOGY AND EVERYDAY LIFE 9.1
Racial Classification in South Africa

Apartheid, the racist policy used by the domi-
nant white group in South Africa, classifies all
citizens by race. This selection describes how
arbitrary that process of categorization is, and
also how it maintains rigid barriers between
people assigned to different racial groupings.

When my son's birth was registered in Johan-
nesburg the government sent me a document
reading: "Please note that Pogrund, Gideon
Ezra, identity number 730106 5123 00 7, has
been classified as a white person for the purposes of the Population Registration Act, 1950."

The document measures only 4½ inches by
5½ inches. In one way, it's a priceless piece of
paper. It sets my son at the top of the pile in
this race-ridden society. It makes him heir to
the best things that South Africa can offer,
overwhelmingly reserved for those classified as
whites.

In another way, it's a shameful thing to have,
evoking memories of the Nazis' Nuremberg
laws and serving as a reminder of the privileged status of whites.

Every single person in South Africa is racially
pigeonholed. It is a fundamental aspect of
apartheid. Without it, the system could not
work.

Every other of the vast range of racial laws
flows from population registration.

Once your classification is known, it determines where you can live, where you can work,
and even in some instances what work you can
do. It determines what kindergarten, school or
university you can attend, which movie houses
or restaurants you can go to, which trains and
buses you can use, which hospitals will accept
you, and in which cemetery you are buried.

The chief purpose of race classification is to
maintain white "purity"—despite the known
evidence that, in the case of Afrikaners, whose
forbears came from Holland in 1652, there was
until recent times a regular infusion of "colored" blood.

The government's racial division goes far
beyond mere white and black. On the black
side, there is further division into some 10
tribal ethnic groupings. Black intermarriage is,
however, allowed.

Mixed-race "colored," as well as Indians, are
divided into seven subgroups, including "other
colored" and "other Asian."

But even now, 31 years after it began, people
are officially moving from one classification to
another. They can appeal to government tribu-
nals and bring evidence to argue for a change.

Last year, 152 persons were reclassified. By
government edict, and by a stroke of the official
pen, 133 "Cape coloreds," as they are termed,
became white overnight, one white became colored, and four Indians became colored. Three
Malays—a colored subgroup—were "transformed" into Indians, six coloreds were made
Indians, three whites became Chinese, one
white a Malay, and one Indian a Malay.

To maintain the system, racially mixed marriages are forbidden. So is sex across color
lines, and several hundred people are prosecuted each year under the Immorality Act for
sleeping with someone of the "wrong" color. It
is well known that the criminal prosecutions are
a small fraction of the actual contraventions.

A South African man who goes to another
country to marry across the color line faces the
problem that his marriage remains illegal in
South Africa—and if he returns home with his
wife and sleeps with her he can be charged for
immorality.

Faced by prosecution, "mixed" couples regularly go to live, and to marry, in neighboring
countries.

Before any marriage can be performed in
South Africa, the man and woman must produce their race classification. So must the parties to any property transaction, to prove that
they are allowed to live in a particular area.

When the Population Registration law was
first introduced—in 1950, shortly after the present Afrikaner Nationalist government came to
power—there was a period of a few years in
which classification was applied throughout the
country.

After centuries in which whites and blacks
lived alongside each other, there were difficulties
in defining "borderline" cases.

There was one stage, in which vindictive
neighbors tipped off the authorities that someone of the "wrong" color was living next door.
And there were, inevitably, cases in which families were split by racial laws.

Employing crude tests, government-appointed
race classification officials would push a pencil
through a person's hair to check its texture, and
they would examine a person's fingernails.

The tests had to be changed over the years: Not only were the earlier methods often ineffective, but they could not overcome the practical difficulties of trying to fit people neatly into assigned slots.

Until 1962, acceptability by the community was the chief test applied. But then the definition of a "white" person was made tighter, with appearance and acceptance being considered together. Further, the new definition was later made retroactive to 1950, giving the authorities the right to reclassify people.

In 1967, the tests were tightened again. "Descent" became the determining factor in proving a person's race. But, in the absence of proof that both parents had been classified "white," a person had to undergo a number of tests in connection with "appearance" and "general acceptance," the earlier standards.

His habits, education, speech and deportment in general were to be considered. He had to be generally accepted as white where he usually lived, worked and mixed socially.

In 1967, however, a judge ruled invalid an old law allowing for the division of "coloreds" into seven subgroups—so a law was promptly passed to reinstate the subgroups.

The existence of the antiracial mixing Mixed Marriages Act and the Immorality Act has caused a certain amount of embarrassment to whites in South Africa in recent years, and there have been repeated calls that they should be scrapped.

However, it is unlikely that these laws will be scrapped. To do so would be to breach the entire system of population registration, on which apartheid in its present form depends.

Source: Benjamin Pogrund, "S. Africa Relaxing Racial Classification," *The Boston Globe,* August 13, 1981, p. 3. Reprinted courtesy of *The Boston Globe.*

logical inheritance. There is much variation among the people categorized as members of a particular racial grouping; "blacks" vary in skin color from very dark to quite light, and the same is true of "whites." Skin color is a symbol of membership in a socially defined racial grouping; it is a physical trait that is given a social meaning by the culture. This definition of race is learned through socialization, just like other aspects of the culture; people have to learn to see themselves and others as members of distinct racial groupings.

ETHNICITY

An *ethnic group* is a "people" that is defined by a common cultural or national identity that sets it off from other groups. Sometimes, ethnicity is linked to a socially defined racial grouping, as it is among black Americans; but often it is based on cultural traditions that are not associated with physical traits, such as the distinction between the Irish-American ethnic group and the Italian-American ethnic group.

Ethnic groups are socially defined by language, religion, ancestry, life style, cultural traditions, nationality, and sometimes by physical features. Ethnicity, or a sense of "peoplehood," is passed from one generation to the next through socialization.

Because children learn what ethnic group they belong to at a very early age, we say that ethnicity is an ascribed rather than an achieved characteristic. The common national origin, language, religion, and holiday traditions of an ethnic group create boundaries between it and other social groups and individuals, giving members of the ethnic group a sense of belonging and identity and sometimes serving their own political and economic interests as well.

Children learn the dominant culture of a society from the perspective of their own ethnic group, just as they learn the values and norms of their group through socialization. They might learn to make distinctions within their ethnic group that outsiders do not make; for example, Italian-Americans often distinguish between those whose ancestry can be traced to southern Italy and Sicily and those whose ancestry can be traced to northern Italy, even though other Americans usually lump them all together as Italian-Americans.

Members of an ethnic group develop patterns of interaction with each other. Sometimes this takes the form of marrying only other members of the same group. Membership in an ethnic group is often a source of personal and social identity that is not easily abandoned. Marginal individuals are people of mixed ancestry and people who switch

Ethnic groups are socially defined by language, religion, ancestry, life style, cultural traditions, nationality, and sometimes by physical features. This photo illustrates an ethnic group of Chinese-Americans.

ethnic identities, such as Italian-Americans who marry Irish-Americans and are absorbed into that ethnic group. Marginality is commonly associated with stress, because marginal people often lack a clear sense of identity in a culture that emphasizes ethnic group membership.

MINORITY GROUP

When sociologists speak of minority groups, they do not necessarily mean a group that is a numerical minority of a population, even though this is true of many minority groups. Black South Africans, for instance, are a minority group in the sociological sense, even though they make up 70 per cent of all South Africans. The 20 per cent of the South African population that is white is a dominant group. On the other hand, in the United States WASPs (White Anglo-Saxon Protestants) constitute only 35 per cent of the population, but they are not considered a minority group. What, then, do sociologists mean by a minority group?

A *minority group* is a category of people that has common traits and is subordinate in the stratification system of a society. Minority groups have less power than dominant groups, those groups that are able to impose their will on minority groups and define the dominant culture of a society. The existence of minority groups is often functional for dominant groups, because minority groups can provide a source of inexpensive labor, do undesirable "dirty work" such as street-sweeping or fighting wars, and purchase lower-quality food and merchandise that is not wanted by members of the dominant group (Gans, 1973).

Minority groups can be either racial or ethnic groups; that is, they can have either physical or cultural traits that make them socially distinct from others and provide a source of shared identity. These traits enable the dominant group to single out members of the minority group for unequal treatment that works to their disadvantage. Minority groups are often unable to control their own fate because they are the objects of prejudice and discrimination. Membership in a minority group is sometimes a source of pride, but membership is not voluntary or achieved. Instead, it is an ascribed status that prevents people from fully participating in the daily life and institutions of the society (Wirth, 1945: 347).

Minority groups are common in the societies of the world; one study found that more than 90 per cent of all nation-states have at least one minority group (Conner, 1972). A group sometimes acquires minority-group status when it migrates to a society in which another racial or ethnic group is dominant. A minority group can also develop when a nation-state expands to incorporate a different people; the expansion of the United States in the nineteenth century to include people of Mexican ancestry is one example. Minority-group status sometimes develops when a territory is colonized by members of a different racial or ethnic group; for example, the native populations of North America and Australia were relegated to minority-group status by the whites who colonized these continents.

Prejudice and Discrimination

Relationships between dominant groups and minority groups are often marked by hostility and unequal treatment. Hostility takes the form of prejudice, ethnocentrism, and unwillingness to interact with the members of other groups. Differential treatment is called discrimination, the actual behavior that excludes individuals from full participation in a society because they belong to a particular racial or ethnic group.

PREJUDICE

Prejudice is a belief that individuals can be evaluated by their membership in a group or a category. It is a prejudgment, a like or a dislike that is formed before one has all the information needed to judge an individual as a whole person. Prejudice is a generalization, an effort to select, accentuate, and interpret information in order to form a general picture of a whole group or category of people. Prejudice is the product of lack of contact with, and lack of understanding of a different group, but prejudice also resists modification through experience. New information about a group or an individual that would seem to contradict the prejudice is often ignored or reinterpreted to maintain the prejudice (Allport, 1958).

Prejudice is learned through socialization by parents, teachers, peers, and the mass media. Usually prejudice is negative (dislike of a group), but people also prejudge others favorably because of their membership in a particular group. Prejudice can take the form of negative beliefs about women, the elderly, or other categories of people, but usually it refers to negative attitudes toward racial and ethnic groups. One useful definition of ethnic prejudice is Gordon Allport's (1958: 10): "an antipathy based upon a faulty and inflexible generalization. It may be felt or expressed. It may be directed toward a group as a whole, or toward an individual because he is a member of that group."

Racism is prejudice in the form of a coherent set of beliefs (or ideology) that physical differences among groups determine differences in behavior among those groups. (The terms "sexism" and "ageism" have been coined to refer to prejudice based on differences in sex and age.) Racism often develops to justify the unequal treatment of a group; it serves the dominant group by helping to justify its advantages over a minority group. A racist system of beliefs developed among whites to rationalize their enslavement of blacks in the United States before the Civil War; this racist set of beliefs was supported by religion, the law, and dominant cultural values. The dominant culture often includes values and norms that encourage the members of a minority group to accept their own inferior social position. Racism often becomes a self-fulfilling prophecy; the unequal treatment of a group that is based on a belief in that group's inferiority often forces that group into an inferior position in the stratification system, which is used in turn to support the racist belief in the group's inferiority.

Ethnocentrism and Social Distance

Prejudice and racism are often closely related to ethnocentrism, the tendency to see one's own group or people ("we") as the center of the universe and superior to other groups and peoples ("they"), who are peripheral and less worthy (see Chapter 3). Ethnocentrism defines the boundaries of a group, and it is commonly associated with prejudice toward those who are not members. Ethnic or national pride is sometimes increased by disparaging others. When group members interact primarily with members of the same group, there tends to be suspicion and hostility toward strangers. The belief in the superiority of one's own group can generate and reinforce negative judgments about other groups.

Each person can be thought of as belonging to various groups of different sizes and degrees of intimacy. You belong to a family, a set of friends, a community of neighbors, a student body, a nation of citizens, and the world community. One way to measure your acceptance of the members of another racial or ethnic group is to ask at what point you would exclude others from the groups to which you belong. You might be willing to let others enter your country both as visitors and potential citizens, be willing to attend classes with them, but feel that they should not live in your neighborhood, join your group of friends, or marry one of your relatives. The indicator of how much intimacy you would be willing to allow the members of a different group is called *social distance* (Allport, 1958; Bogardus, 1959). The social distance between you and the members of another group would be great if you would not even admit them to your country; it would be little if you were willing to marry a member of that group. Social distance is often used as a measure of prejudice. Social distance can also give a rough idea of how people will behave when they interact with members of another group, but, as we will see later in this section, prejudice does not always tell us how people will actually behave when faced with a member of a different racial or ethnic group.

Stereotypes

We all need mental pictures to simplify the complex social world we deal with on a daily basis; it is not possible to react to every person and situation without some preconceptions. People sometimes simplify social reality by relying on stereotypes, generalized and exaggerated pictures that they use to describe entire categories of people (see Chapter 5). Often, these generalizations are wrong in predicting how an individual member of the stereotyped group will behave, but many people nevertheless use these stereotypes as guides to behavior.

Stereotypes take the form of a caricature or a myth, such as that blacks have "natural rhythm," that Jews are "clannish," or that WASPs are "uptight." Stereotypes sometimes contain a "kernel of truth," because the social conditions in which a group has lived can lead to identifiable traits that stereotypes then distort and exaggerate. The conditions of slavery might have made the music brought from Africa by blacks an especially important part of their culture. The need to main-

tain an image suitable to a position high in the stratification system might lead some WASPs to avoid any show of eccentricity. The hostility directed against Jews throughout history might have made family ties especially important to them. One sociologist has commented on the stereotype of Jews as being good at business as follows:

Are Jews better businessmen than others? This is impossible to prove. Yet there is enough evidence present to suggest that they indeed might have an edge in this area. For one thing, Jews have been in business for centuries. Forbidden to own land by the Roman Catholic Church and denied entry into the craft guilds during medieval times, Jews were forced to turn to moneylending to survive.

The Jewish religion and, in particular, the Talmud, with its emphasis on abstract thinking, also has played a role. From childhood on, the stress was on sharpening the mind, and when economic opportunities arose the Jew was able to apply his intellectual acumen to that sphere as well. After all, interest, futures, options, stocks, and, most importantly, money itself, were also abstractions. Yet another factor was that lacking a homeland for centuries, never certain when persecution might strike, Jews came to see money as the only means of survival, something with which to buy protection or acquire certain rights (Helmreich, 1981: A27).

Stereotypes might be somewhat accurate in describing the differences among groups, but they usually take small differences among groups, exaggerate those differences, generalize to entire groups of people, cast the generalization in negative terms, and influence the way that all members of the group are treated. Stereotypes are rigid ideas that are not easily modified by new information or direct contact with members of the stereotyped group.

Reducing Prejudice through Contact

For years, social scientists and community leaders felt that prejudice could be reduced by bringing the members of different racial and ethnic groups into direct contact. This idea was based on the assumption that prejudice reflected insufficient knowledge of other groups and that interaction could provide this information, and so dispel prejudice. Some studies did show that contact could reduce prejudice, but other studies found that contact either had no effect on prejudice or even increased it. Sometimes the members of the dominant group did not generalize favorable impressions they gained about specific members of the minority group to all members of that group, and sometimes members of the dominant group simply said that those with whom they had interacted were exceptions to their negatively stereotyped views.

Personal contact among members of different racial and ethnic groups is most likely to reduce prejudice if the individuals are of equal status, if their interaction has the support of a legitimate authority such as the government, if they are emotionally involved in the interaction, if they gain social rewards such as prestige or power from the experience, and if the members of the different groups are interdependent in striving for a common goal. Contact is unlikely to reduce prejudice if the members of the different groups are of unequal status. Competition rather than cooperation can actually increase prejudice. Tension during the social interaction and fear that one group will lose prestige or power can also increase prejudice (Amir, 1969; Ford, 1973). Thus, under the proper social conditions, contact can change beliefs about other groups, but contact alone does not guarantee that beliefs will change when members of different racial and ethnic groups meet.

DISCRIMINATION

You might assume that people who discriminate against others are acting on the basis of prejudice, but often this is not so. Prejudiced people do not necessarily treat the objects of their prejudice unequally, and people who do discriminate are not necessarily prejudiced against the targets of their discrimination. Prejudice is a belief that is not necessarily associated with the behavior of discrimination.

Discrimination is the treatment of people in a systematically negative way because they are members of a socially disvalued group or category. Discrimination is arbitrary: It is based on group traits rather than on individual characteristics. Discrimination denies opportunities to members of a group *because* they are members of the group. For example, job discrimination denies work to people who belong to a particular racial or ethnic group but provides employment for those who are no more (and perhaps less) qualified simply because they are members of a different group. Black Americans have encountered job discrimination by whites, and in some states Italian-Americans have in the past faced job discrimination by Irish-Americans. This sort of discrimination is based on group traits that are not relevant to the situation. Thus, a law firm's unwillingness to hire a law school graduate

because she is a woman is sex discrimination if she is as well qualified as the man who got the job; the failure to hire a man as a Playboy bunny is not sex discrimination because sex is relevant to performance of the job.

One type of discrimination is *segregation,* the forced spatial separation of a group. *Desegregation* is the elimination of this spatial barrier between groups, but it is not the same thing as *integration,* the actual social interaction of the members of different groups. Thus, an elementary school is technically desegregated if blacks and whites attend it. However, if black and white students are assigned to separate classrooms or separated by seating assignments within a classroom, this desegregated school is not integrated. Integration occurs when the students begin to play together, talk, and accept one another into their peer groups (Davidson, Hofmann, and Brown, 1978).

Discrimination is self-perpetuating. The refusal to hire the members of a minority group can be justified by saying that although they have the necessary educational credentials, they have attended inferior schools. However, job discrimination serves to keep the income of minority-group members low, preventing them from moving to higher-income communities with better schools that their children can attend. As a result, their children attend schools in poorer communities, where they receive an inferior education that can then be used to justify continued discrimination in the hiring process.

Until recently, many social scientists thought that prejudice led to discrimination; for example, in *An American Dilemma,* his classic study of American race relations, Gunnar Myrdal (1944, 1962) saw discrimination against blacks as rooted in white prejudices. More recently, sociologists have recognized that reference groups (see Chapter 7) often mediate between prejudice and discrimination (Feagin and Feagin, 1978; Smith, 1981). The expectations of friends, relatives, and peers influence a person to discriminate against others, whether or not that person is prejudiced against the group. If a person is rewarded with social approval for treating another group unequally, that person may discriminate even if he or she does not personally believe in the inferiority of the group that is being treated unequally.

Two different studies illustrate how prejudice and discrimination sometimes do not go together. In a study done in the 1930s, Richard LaPiere (1934) traveled around the United States with a Chinese couple; the three were refused service in only one of the 251 hotels and restaurants at which they stopped. Six months later, LaPiere wrote to these establishments and asked whether they would serve Chinese people. Ninety-two per cent of the hotels and restaurants said that they would refuse service. These refusals reflect a prejudice against the Chinese, even though the managers did not discriminate when they met the Chinese couple.

A second study found that about three-fourths of the police officers in Boston, Chicago, and Washington, D.C., spontaneously expressed prejudice against blacks to observers who were riding in their patrol cars. However, the observers found no consistent pattern of physical brutality by the police directed against blacks as opposed to whites (Reiss, 1971). The police were prejudiced, but did not discriminate on the basis of their prejudices. These two studies show that role expectations (see Chapter 7) often stop people from discriminating, even when they are prejudiced against a minority group.

Institutional Racism

We have defined racism as a set of prejudicial beliefs that physical differences among groups determine differences in behavior among groups. This "individual racism" has been contrasted with *institutional racism*, the social practices and policies that lead to the unequal treatment of a racial group (Carmichael and Hamilton, 1967; Feagin and Feagin, 1978; Feagin and Eckberg, 1980). Institutional racism is actually a pattern of discriminatory practices rather than a set of racist beliefs, although racist beliefs may support discriminatory practices.

The basis of much institutional racism is competition and conflict over scarce resources such as jobs, prestige, and political power. Discriminatory practices can be used to gain access to these rewards and to justify those rewards that have already been accumulated. Conflict theorists have pointed out that racist beliefs and discriminatory practices can serve the capitalist class by dividing workers by race and ethnicity, and by preventing the development of worker solidarity to create a socialist society or even to reform a capitalist one. Racism can also be a source of profits, as we can see in the exploitation of racial antagonisms in the world of boxing depicted in SEL 9.2. Individual and institutional racism are dysfunctional for society in that they cause social disorder and drain energy from more productive purposes, even though prejudice and discrimination can be functional for dominant groups in certain ways.

"Pride vs. Glory"—Larry Holmes (right) and Gerry Cooney (left) in their 1982 match for the heavyweight championship of the world.

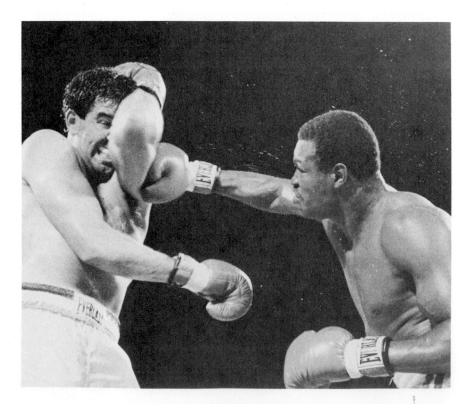

SOCIOLOGY AND EVERYDAY LIFE 9.2
Racism for Profit: The Case of Boxing

Conflict theorists claim that racism has been used to increase profits for the business class in American society. One group that has made huge profits is boxing promoters, who have exploited racist feelings in matches between fighters of different racial and ethnic groups.

The 1982 match between Larry Holmes and Gerry Cooney was described in advance by Don King, the black promoter of the bout, as "Pride vs. Glory." King said:

"It means that you have the champion, Larry Holmes, who rose as a poor black man to the top—only to play second fiddle to Muhammad Ali and now, again, to the contender—fighting for the pride of recognition; against Gerry Cooney, a fine white Irish-Catholic lad who could have been a salesman for GM or Exxon but who went into the Sweet Science for the glory of being heavyweight champion" (p. 39).

When asked if he was selling the fight as a battle between the races, King replied, "Absolutely not. I don't have to. The fight is built on racism . . . it's a natural element. The best thing to do is let it go" (p. 39).

Racism in boxing has a long history. In 1895, the editor of a New York City newspaper wrote of a black fighter, "We are safe at present from having a black world champion. How long can we escape? Wake up pugilists of the white race or you'll permit yourself to be parried by the black race" (p. 55).

Thirteen years later, author Jack London publicly asked a white man who had been heavyweight champion to come out of retirement to fight the reigning champion, a black man. London wrote, "Come back from your alfalfa fields and wipe the golden smile off the black champion" (p. 55). The ex-champion took London's advice, but was knocked out in a 1910 bout.

The call for a "Great White Hope" to defeat a black champion did not reemerge until the 1960s. Sonny Liston was a less popular champion than the preceding black heavyweight champions, and Muhammad Ali fed white antagonisms by claiming the status of conscientious objector to military service and by his boastful manner. Before his 1970 match with Ali, Jerry Quarry said, "This is the good white guy against the bad black guy. It means a lot to the country on just that. It's time a white man was on top in this game" (p. 55). Quarry lost the match. Another unsuccessful white challenger, Chuck Wepner, showed up for his 1975 match with Ali with his followers wearing buttons that said WIN, which they explained meant "Whip the Insolent Nigger." Ali's assistant yelled throughout the fight, "Kill the white man, kill the white man" (p. 55). A 1981 match between Ken Norton and Gerry Cooney was publicized as "The Caucasian Assassin vs. the Great White Hope."

Promoters are aware that bouts between boxers of different races, ethnic groups, and nationalities have an extra appeal for fans. Some of these promoters deny that this appeal is based on racial prejudice. One has said, "I get so irritated that people always try to read bigotry into race and religion. There's nothing wrong with whites cheering for whites and blacks cheering for blacks. It's a matter of pride. They try to make people ashamed of what they are" (p. 55). Still, many fans do insist on seeing boxing matches as fights between representatives of different racial or ethnic groups, rather than as matches between individuals. Promoters have profitably exploited this aspect of boxing for decades.

Source: Based on Steve Marantz, "Boxing's Formula: Black + White = Green," *The Boston Globe,* February 28, 1982, pp. 39, 55. Used courtesy of *The Boston Globe.*

Intergroup Relations: Dominant-Group Policies

One way to examine the relationships between dominant and minority groups is to look first at the policies of dominant groups toward minority groups, and then investigate the responses of minority groups to their treatment by dominant groups. An influential and popular textbook on racial and ethnic minorities by Simpson and Yinger (1972) provides us with a useful classification of six kinds of dominant-group policies toward minorities: assimilation, pluralism, legal protection of minorities, population transfer, continued subjugation, and extermination.

Cultural integration can be encouraged through a system of public education and by the mass media. "Sesame Street" was one of the earliest children's programs to present members of various racial groups on an equal basis.

ASSIMILATION

Assimilation is the absorption of a minority group into the larger society. When a group becomes assimilated, its boundaries are weakened and eventually disappear, and its members are treated by the dominant group as individuals rather than as members of a distinct group. Assimilation is sometimes forced on a minority group by a dominant group that requires the minority group to abandon its language, traditions, and religion for those of the dominant group. Assimilation can also be voluntary, occurring slowly over many years as a racial or ethnic group is absorbed into the society at its own pace. Voluntary assimilation is easiest if there are social, cultural, and physical similarities between the minority group and the dominant group.

Assimilation often takes the form of *acculturation*, a process by which a group adopts the dominant culture. This cultural integration can be encouraged through a system of public education that provides all groups with a common cultural background and a common language. In industrial societies, the mass media also play an important part in acculturating a diversity of racial and ethnic groups. Acculturation in the United States has been called "Anglo-conformity," because racial and ethnic minorities have usually been expected to adopt the culture of Americans who trace their ancestry to England (Cole and Cole, 1954; Gordon, 1964).

Amalgamation occurs when a group is assimilated by intermarriage with other groups. This kind of assimilation is what is meant by the phrase, "the melting pot," which was first used in 1908 to describe an American society in which all racial and ethnic groups would contribute to a common blend. This implies that all groups will contribute significantly, if not equally, to this common blend. Intermarriage among American racial and ethnic groups has been limited, however, and several distinct groups continue to exist today. Ethnic identity gives people a sense of belonging, a social identity, and continuity with the past; as a result, members of these groups do not always desire absorption into a common blend.

One observer has described the United States as a "triple melting pot," featuring marriage within the major religious groups—Protestants, Catholics, and Jews (Kennedy, 1944, 1952). Since the time that this idea was proposed, however, intermarriage between members of different religious groups has become more common. Today, race is the most important barrier to an amalgamated society (Glazer and Moynihan, 1970). There is now considerable marriage among people from different white ethnic groups, but relatively little intermarriage among whites, blacks, Asian Americans, Hispanics, and Native Americans (Indians). One area of the United States where a variety of racial and ethnic groups have amalgamated is Hawaii.

There has been some *structural assimilation* in the United States. This is the process by which people of different racial and ethnic groups participate in both the primary and secondary groups of the larger society, including private clubs, community organizations, businesses, and government (Gordon, 1964). In a structurally assimilated society, people of all racial and ethnic backgrounds would have equal access to all positions in the social structure. Today, WASPs make up a substantial part of the American elite, but various other racial and ethnic groups are also represented in top positions in business, labor, political parties, government, and the mass media (Alba and Moore, 1982).

PLURALISM

When a dominant group allows minority groups to retain their cultural identity and the minority groups do not seek assimilation, a variety of distinct groups may coexist side by side in the same society. This situation is called *pluralism*. In a pluralistic society, each group accommodates itself to the other groups and tolerates cultural diversity. Each group retains aspects of its own culture, such as a language, a mode of dress, and religious holidays. Group differences are not a source of negative

discrimination in a pluralistic society, and no group suffers from a minority status. No one group seeks to dominate other groups, and it is difficult to identify a hierarchy among the groups. In most pluralistic societies, intimate interaction and marriage usually continue to take place within each group, enabling the groups to retain their own identity and to avoid assimilation into a homogeneous society.

Switzerland is a pluralistic society in which people who speak German, French, Italian, and the ancient language of Romansh coexist peacefully. Another pluralistic society is China, where fifty-five ethnic minorities—sixty million people, but only 6 per cent of China's huge population—are encouraged to retain their distinct identity while adhering to a "vision of harmony in which the Han Chinese [the dominant group] are elder brothers" (Wren, 1982b: A2). This official policy of pluralism represents a change from a policy of assimilation only a few years ago.

LEGAL PROTECTION OF MINORITIES

Dominant groups can also adopt policies that legally protect minority groups from unequal treatment. The Thirteenth, Fourteenth, and Fifteenth Amendments to the United States Constitution were aimed at the legal protection of blacks who had just been freed from slavery. Between 1957 and 1965, federal civil rights laws were passed in response to the civil rights movement; these laws provided federal enforcement of blacks' right to register to vote. Federal legislation also defines acts of police brutality or mob violence against minority-group members as a violation of their civil rights that is subject to federal prosecution; similar acts against members of the dominant group are not subject to federal action.

Affirmative action taken by the United States government in recent years has tried to correct abuses caused by past discrimination against minority groups by encouraging structural assimilation. These policies, which are sometimes called "reverse discrimination" by their opponents, ask private industry, universities, and other employers to establish hiring goals. Proponents of affirmative action avoid using the term "quota" in favor of "hiring goals." These goals are not strictly enforced, nor are employers expected to abandon the usual job qualifications to hire members of minority groups. Affirmative action does require employers to seek out qualified minority-group candidates aggressively and to favor them over other candidates if they are as well qualified for a job.

Affirmative action has been seen as a way to correct past injustices against minority groups by giving them preferential treatment in the present. Because much hiring has traditionally been done through an "old-boy network"—a set of informal social relationships that has usually excluded minority groups—affirmative action is necessary for minority-group candidates to be considered for jobs in the first place. One criticism of these policies is that members of dominant groups may be excluded from consideration for certain jobs simply because of their racial or ethnic background, even though it was their ancestors rather than they themselves who discriminated against minorities in the past.

The Supreme Court has upheld affirmative action policies, with some qualifications, if they are intended to correct obvious patterns of discrimination that have occurred since passage of the 1964 federal civil rights law. The constitutionality of affirmative action is still somewhat unclear because of the narrow way in which the Court has decided some of its cases; it has not decided for or against affirmative action as a general policy. Affirmative action has some support among whites; most agree that special programs must be devised to help minorities, although three-fourths also feel that minority-group members must succeed on the basis of merit (Harris, 1978).

POPULATION TRANSFER

Policies that create spatial separation among racial and ethnic minorities are called *population transfer*, which can be done by peaceful means or by forcing a group out of a country. Groups can be relocated within a country, or they can be pressured or required to migrate. "Expulsion" is a policy that forces a minority group to leave the country in which it lives. Jews were expelled from Nazi Germany during the 1930s, and they have been expelled from the Soviet Union in recent years. In 1972 Idi Amin forced about 27,000 people of Indian ancestry to leave Uganda, even though many had never lived in India and considered Uganda to be their homeland. "Exclusion" is a policy that attempts to maintain a society's homogeneity by keeping members of a racial or ethnic group from entering the country in the first place. Orientals were barred from entering the United States from 1924, when a federal law was passed, until the late 1960s, when those restrictions were lifted.

Another kind of population transfer is the "subdivision" or "partition" of a country, with certain groups living in particular areas. One example was the division of India and Pakistan, with Hindus dominating India and Moslems dominating West Pakistan and East Pakistan (now Bangladesh). Another example of the internal subdivision of a nation is the creation in South Africa, since 1976, of ten independent, tribal "homelands" for blacks; 53 per cent of all black South Africans lived in these economically backward states in 1980. The United States used a policy of internal subdivision when it created reservations for Native Americans.

CONTINUED SUBJUGATION

Often the domination of a minority group continues over a long period of time because it provides advantages to the dominant group. Whites have dominated blacks in South Africa for many years, and since the end of World War II this subjugation has increasingly been given the support of the law. The federal government of the United States has tried to use the law to lessen the subjugation of minority groups, but these groups continue to be discriminated against by the dominant group.

One approach to the study of minority-group oppression likens it to colonization (Blauner, 1969, 1972; Hechter, 1975; Geschwender, 1978). This "internal colonialism model" suggests that the first stage in the subjugation of a minority group is often its forced entry into a society dominated by another group, which systematically destroys the culture of the minority group. The dominant group controls the minority group through elective office, government bureaucracy, and law enforcement. Members of the minority group are only allowed to work at low-status, poorly paid jobs. Internal colonialism is typically accompanied by a racist ideology that justifies discrimination. This model has been used to describe black–white relations in the United States, but it also applies to ethnic group relations in other societies.

EXTERMINATION

Extermination, or *genocide*—the deliberate and systematic elimination of a racial or ethnic group— usually involves killing members of a group, but it can also be done through forced sterilization. The murder of six million Jews by the Nazis is the most prominent example of extermination; other examples include the destruction of the Tasmanians by the British in Australia and the elimination of the Hottentots by white settlers in South Africa. Another instance of genocide was the destruction of 1.5 million Armenians by the Turks in 1915. White Americans systematically killed large numbers of Native Americans during the nineteenth century; about two-thirds of all Indians died during this time from disease, starvation (due largely to destruction of the buffalo), and warfare (Brown, 1970). One common element in these cases of genocide was the use of a racist ideology to portray the group being exterminated as inferior or subhuman.

Intergroup Relations: Minority-Group Responses

A minority group can respond in any of a number of ways to its treatment by a dominant group (Simpson and Yinger, 1972). Members of a minority group sometimes migrate from a society in which they suffer prejudice and discrimination, but this is rare. Also uncommon are efforts by individuals to "pass" as members of the dominant group. More often, minority groups accept their subordinate status; sometimes, this produces self-hatred. Another common reaction by minority groups is collective action to improve their lot.

WITHDRAWAL

An extreme but relatively uncommon response to subordination is for a minority group to leave a society. They may migrate as a group, as the Jews did from Nazi Germany and from the Soviet Union, in recent years. The Marcus Garvey Movement among black Americans during the 1920s urged blacks to return to Africa, though few did.

Sometimes a minority group moves from one part of a country to another where the group hopes to find more hospitable conditions. Blacks moved in large numbers from the South to the North during the twentieth century, beginning during World War I when many jobs became available in the large cities of the North.

Occasionally a racial or ethnic group will try to subdivide a country by secession. Black Muslims have argued that they should be given land in a few states to form their own nation, although this proposal has never been supported by a majority of black Americans. Another effort to secede is the current movement among French-speaking Canadians to establish their own country (Jacobs, 1980).

PASSING

Sometimes individual members of minority groups try to "pass" as members of the dominant group. They might change their life style to conform to that of the dominant group. Upwardly mobile members of an ethnic group sometimes change their behavior—abandoning a traditional mode of dress or converting to a different religion—in order to fit the expectations of the dominant group; this often occurs through the process of anticipatory socialization (see Chapter 4). Passing can also involve changing one's name so that it sounds "less foreign" and more like the names of the dominant group. In some cases, passing even takes the form of altering one's physical appearance to look more like the dominant group. Often this is not possible; for example, most black Americans cannot pass for white, but some do have skin that is light enough to do so. However, passing takes its toll, because those who pass must suffer the pain of rejecting their own group and cope with the fear of being discovered by members of the dominant group.

ACCEPTANCE

Members of a minority group sometimes silently accept prejudice and discrimination by the dominant group with little external show of anger or resentment. This was typical of black Americans a few decades ago, and it was the usual response of the untouchables, or outcastes, in India before Gandhi's efforts to change that society.

Passive acceptance of a subordinate status sometimes leads minority-group members to act in ways that confirm the stereotypes and prejudices of the dominant group. This can lessen the stress that would accompany the sanctions one would face in deviating from the dominant group's expectations, and it can even be rewarded by the social approval of the dominant group. Completely passive acceptance of subordinate status is uncommon; often, minority-group members joke among themselves about the dominant group, and they sometimes use the dominant group's stereotypes of them to manipulate the dominant group.

Acceptance of minority-group status is most common among the socially isolated. Direct contact with members of the dominant group or with upwardly mobile members of the minority group can evoke hopes for a better life and an unwillingness to accept prejudice and discrimination. Often the mass media provide models of a better life and lead a minority group to reject its subordinate position.

SELF-HATRED

Self-hatred and low self-esteem are a common reaction to prejudice and discrimination; this is especially likely when a subordinate status is accepted passively. We saw in Chapter 4 that people's self-concepts reflect the way that others treat them, so if they encounter prejudice and discrimination, they might feel unworthy and develop low self-esteem. This can produce "self-hatred," an internalization of the dominant group's prejudice. This takes the form of joking about one's own group, denigrating oneself in the presence of dominant-group members, and denying membership in the minority group by trying to pass.

Recent studies have found that the self-esteem of black Americans has risen in recent years and today is about as high as that of whites (Rosenberg and Simmons, 1971; Banks et al., 1977; Simmons et al., 1978; Porter and Washington, 1979). Many blacks have developed adaptive mechanisms to cope with prejudice and discrimination, regarding those who are prejudiced against them as ignorant and attributing discrimination to efforts by whites to keep their own jobs. Increased black militancy during the late 1960s and the 1970s shifted the blame for personal failure from the self to the social system as a whole, and this improved self-esteem (Porter and Washington, 1979). Sometimes members of minority groups assert that they do not fit the negative stereotype of their group held by the dominant group, even though residual self-hatred may prompt them to suggest that *other* members of their group fit that stereotype. Such efforts to dissociate oneself from the rest of one's group can maintain individual self-esteem but create stress associated with a marginal status.

COLLECTIVE ACTION

The members of a minority group often band together in collective action to change the way that they are treated by the dominant group. This can result in peaceful protests and demonstations designed to reform the social structure through legal change, or it can take the form of violent disturbances aimed at a more basic alteration of the society. The civil rights movement that sought to improve the position of blacks in American society involved both peaceful and violent forms of protest. This movement encountered white hostility and mob violence, but it did succeed in extending the voting rights of blacks, desegregating schools, and providing access to public facilities such as buses and hotels. Participation in this movement also increased black pride and strengthened a belief in the efficacy of collective action.

Although the civil rights movement significantly improved the status of black Americans, it did not lead to their structural assimilation into American society. In the mid-1960s, blacks turned to alternative strategies for social change. During this period there was much debate among black leaders about "black power." The black power movement was an effort to counteract institutional racism by establishing community control, creating a sense of identity among all blacks, defining common goals, and organizing to reach those goals (Carmichael and Hamilton, 1967). Black power was a militant stance which held that political and economic power were needed for blacks to bargain with the dominant group from a position of strength.

The collective action that received the greatest national attention during the 1960s was the urban riot. During this century, blacks have shifted from a group living mostly in the rural South to a group living primarily in large cities, many of them in the industrial North. Living conditions in urban ghettos, especially a high unemployment rate and inadequate housing, have led to widespread discontent. The riots of the 1960s were confined to black ghettos, but many of the specific targets of the rioters were symbols of white domination, such as shops owned by white merchants. The rioters' disruptive behavior can be interpreted as part of an exchange interaction (see Chapter 6) in which blacks would guarantee civil peace and social stability in return for concessions from political leaders (Piven and Cloward, 1977; Isaac and Kelly, 1981). As the Reverend Martin Luther King, Jr., said, "A riot is the language of the unheard" (cited in Killian, 1968: 109).

The riots of the 1960s often began with a confrontation between a black person and a white police officer. These confrontations commonly occurred in a "disturbed social atmosphere" (National Advisory Commission on Civil Disorders, 1968: 6) in which there had been a series of incidents that had heightened tensions in the weeks or months before the outbreak of violence. After this initial confrontation, a crowd would gather, rock-throwing would begin, and eventually looting and arson occurred.

After the series of disturbances following Reverend King's assassination in 1968, riots became less common, although they have occurred from time to time. A 1980 riot in Miami, which followed the acquittal of four white police officers accused of beating a black businessman to death, left eighteen people dead and destroyed $80 million of property. Some of the grievances of the blacks who rioted in Miami in 1980—and again in 1982—were similar to those of blacks who rioted in the 1960s: too few black police officers, too few black-owned stores, too few blacks holding elective office, and high rates of unemployment and poverty that had increased over the previous decade. One difference was considerable resentment by blacks in Miami about the success of Hispanic (primarily Cuban) business entrepreneurs in securing government loans (Thomas, 1981). This intergroup rivalry was exacerbated in the months immediately preceding the riot when over 100,000 Cuban exiles entered Florida while many black Haitians were denied political asylum in the United States.

Collective action such as riots and demonstrations can be functional for a society in that political leaders are made aware of social conditions that need to be changed. Such protests can signal the possibility of an even greater threat to the social order by disadvantaged groups. In addition to stimulating changes in social policies by the dominant group, collective action can give members of a minority group a sense of identity and raise their self-esteem when they succeed in changing their position in society.

Racial and Ethnic Groups in the United States

There are a diversity of racial and ethnic groups in the United States. Only one American in five cannot be classified as belonging to a single racial or ethnic group; some of these people are of mixed ancestry and others refuse to categorize themselves. Another 35 per cent are WASPs (White Anglo-Saxon Protestants), the group that is usually treated as the society's dominant group. The other 45 per cent of Americans can be classified into one of several minority groups.

BLACK AMERICANS

Blacks differ from other racial and ethnic groups in the United States in that they are the only group that was forcibly brought to this country as slaves. They also differ from the dominant group more visibly than some of the other minority groups, making their assimilation more difficult. Today, blacks constitute 11.8 per cent of the population.

Blacks have been the target of prejudice and discrimination since their entry into the country. This unequal treatment is inconsistent with American cultural values such as equality, liberty, and freedom (see Chapter 3). This incompatibility between general ideals and specific practices has been called "an American dilemma" (Myrdal, 1944, 1962). Throughout American history, whites have justified the discrepancy between their values and their behavior by claims that blacks are innately inferior to whites, by arguments that the Constitution did not include blacks when it stated that everyone was created equal, and by assertions that American cultural values do not apply to relations between the races. Nevertheless, the strain between cultural values and actual behavior persists, and blacks and other minority groups can appeal to general cultural values in their efforts to be treated equally.

The Family

The structure of the average black family is somewhat different from that of the typical white family. Fewer black families are composed of a married husband and wife, and so more black families are headed by a woman with no husband present in the household. This difference between blacks and whites is due to higher rates of divorce, desertion, and illegitimacy among blacks. Another difference between the typical white and black family is the average number of children per family, with blacks having somewhat more children than whites.

A controversial report issued in 1965 titled *The Negro Family: The Case for National Action*, but popularly referred to as the Moynihan Report, argued that a "defective" family structure was the source of "pathology" in the black community—its high crime rate, low educational level, high rate of school dropouts, high unemployment rate, and widespread alienation. This report presented data which showed that in comparison to whites, blacks had high rates of broken marriages, illegitimacy, and dependency on welfare. This report was intended to give the Johnson administration a basis for developing a federal policy to strengthen the black family, but when parts of it were leaked to the press it elicited harsh criticisms, often from people who had not even read the complete report. Critics charged Moynihan with selective use of the data and oversimplified conclusions. They correctly claimed that Moynihan had paid insufficient attention to the variety of family structures in the black community, among both the poor and the middle class. These critics also said that Moynihan had failed to compare black families with white families from the same social class; had he done so, he would have found that the divorce rate among poor whites was also high. Critics assailed Moynihan for failing to see that in a white-dominated society the type of family structure that he described as typical of the black community might be functional in helping blacks adapt to prejudice and discrimination. Perhaps most telling was the charge that Moynihan had paid too little attention to the effects of current institutional racism on the black family and had instead located the sources of the troubled black family in slavery and the Reconstruction Era after the Civil War. Critics charged that this interpretation might be used to justify inaction in the present, even though the report was intended to be the basis of federal efforts to help black families. Another major shortcoming of the report was that the great majority of black families in the United States were composed of a husband and wife living together with their legitimate children; to accentuate differences between black and white families, Moynihan had painted a picture of the black family that was actually characteristic of perhaps one-fourth of all black families (Rainwater and Yancey, 1967).

Housing

One important area of racial discrimination is housing. Blacks are more likely than whites to live in overcrowded, dilapidated housing that lacks adequate plumbing, heating, and ventilation. Some of this is because blacks have lower incomes, on the average, than whites do; but, even when they have the money, blacks often face obstacles to finding good housing. "Restrictive covenants" that limited the right of property-owners to sell to blacks were not ruled unconstitutional by the Supreme Court until 1948, and by then patterns of housing segregation were well established. Housing segregation was a deliberate federal policy until 1950, with federal mortgages being given only to homes in "stable" (racially homogeneous) communities. Only since 1962 has the federal govern-

ment encouraged housing integration, and this policy has had a limited impact in reversing past patterns of segregation. Federal efforts at urban renewal have often meant the removal of blacks from one segregated community to another (see Chapter 18).

Today banks "red line" low-income areas of cities and refuse to lend money to home-buyers in those areas; this form of income discrimination works to the disadvantage of blacks, because they typically have lower incomes than whites (Squires, DeWolfe, and DeWolfe, 1979). Suburbs that adopt zoning restrictions and refuse to permit the construction of low-income housing also exclude many blacks from the community. The Supreme Court ruled in 1977 that zoning was constitutional as long as it was not intended to discriminate by race, but income discrimination has the effect of doing just that. Even blacks who can afford to buy homes in predominantly white suburbs have a difficult time being shown homes on the market in those communities, because real-estate agents "steer" them to homes in inexpensive black communities or occasionally show them a home in an expensive white suburb (Pearce, 1979).

Education

Institutional racism in the housing market, one of the last areas to be touched by federal legislation, reinforces other kinds of discrimination. Because most children attend schools near their homes, discrimination in housing produces segregated schools. Today, segregated schools are a result of *de facto* (in fact) segregation rather than *de jure* (by law) segregation. In 1954, the Supreme Court ruled segregated schools inherently unequal and therefore unconstitutional in the landmark decision of *Brown* v. *Board of Education of Topeka, Kansas*. This case eliminated legal support for school segregation, but it did not eliminate the institutional racism that perpetuates a segregated educational system.

The desegregation of schools has been a slow process that has met resistance from whites. This process has been especially slow outside the South, where it has existed without legal support, making it difficult to attack through the courts. One strategy that has been used to desegregate schools in residentially segregated communities is busing children from their own neighborhood to schools in communities inhabited by members of other racial groups. This policy can be either voluntary or forced. It is not one that has broad public support.

One strategy that has been used to desegregate schools in a residentially segregated community is busing school children from their own community to schools in communities inhabited by members of other racial groups.

A 1978 poll found that 85 per cent of whites and 43 per cent of blacks opposed busing for the purpose of desegregation. Many whites and most blacks did favor school desegregation, but they disapproved of busing as the way to do it (Harris, 1978).

Blacks and whites differ in educational attainment. Table 9.1 shows the years of education completed by blacks and by whites who are twenty-five years old or more. This table shows that more whites than blacks have finished high school and

that more whites have received some college education. These figures reflect past inequalities in education, because they are for people who have for the most part finished their schooling. Statistics on younger blacks and whites indicate that they are more equal in educational attainment today than in the past. Today, blacks are almost as likely as whites to be enrolled in colleges and universities, although more of the blacks are enrolled in two-year or vocational schools.

TABLE 9.1 *Educational Attainment of Persons 25 Years Old and Over, 1981*

Years of school completed	White	Black	Hispanic
Less than 12th grade	28.4%	47.2%	55.5%
12th grade	38.5%	31.6%	26.3%
1 to 3 years of college	15.3%	13.1%	10.5%
4 years or more or college	17.8%	8.2%	7.7%
Median number of years completed	12.6	12.1	10.7

Source: U.S. Bureau of the Census, *Statistical Abstract of the United States, 1982–83.* Washington, D.C.: U.S. Government Printing Office, 1982, p. 143.

Politics

In recent years, black Americans have made significant gains in the political system. Although they officially gained the right to vote more than a century ago, discriminatory practices—especially in the South, where most of them lived—prevented them from exercising the right to vote. For example, in some communities blacks were required to recite the Constitution in order to register; whites did not have to pass the same test. Civil rights laws in 1964 and 1965 increased federal pressure on the states to register blacks, and this has produced a significant gain in voter registration among blacks. Although blacks and whites are about equally likely to be registered today, blacks actually vote less often at election time. This is mainly because people with lower levels of education and income are less apt to vote than those with more education and income, rather than because blacks are prevented from voting by discriminatory practices.

Blacks have also made important gains in holding elective political office. In 1981, they held more than three times as many elective positions as they had in 1970. Most of the positions held by blacks are in local government, and they are still underrepresented in elective offices at the highest levels of state and federal government.

Employment

Blacks also fare less well than whites in the area of employment. In recent years, their unemployment rate has been about twice that of whites. This does not even consider the fact that many blacks have given up the search for a job and dropped out of the labor force, nor does it indicate that many blacks are paid less than whites for the same work.

Unemployment rates are even higher for young blacks. In March 1983, the unemployment rate for blacks between the ages of sixteen and nineteen was 45 per cent, a figure about twice as high as for whites in the same age bracket (*The New York Times*, April 19, 1983, p. A14). This unemployment rate for black teenagers is very high, but it obscures the fact that in recent years most blacks in this age bracket have been enrolled in high school or college. In 1980, more than seven-tenths of all sixteen-to-nineteen-year-old blacks said that their primary activity was school or college; only 7.8 per cent of all blacks in this age bracket were actually searching for a job and unable to find one (Keller, 1981).

Blacks have a higher unemployment rate than whites for several reasons. They are, on the aver-age, less well educated than whites, and low level of education is an impediment to finding a job. The black population in the United States is, on the average, younger than the white population, and young people lack the experience and the skills needed for many jobs. In some cities industry has moved to the outlying suburbs, making many jobs inaccessible to blacks, who more often live in the center of a city. Black unemployment rates are also high because of racial discrimination by some labor unions and employers. In addition, the fact that the United States has not experienced a full employment economy in recent years has worked against blacks. Because of job discrimination, blacks are often ''the last hired, and the first fired,'' and the lack of full employment creates the conditions for these discriminatory hiring practices to drive up the black unemployment rate (DiPrete, 1981).

Income

Another area of continuing inequality between blacks and whites is income. Blacks have considerably lower incomes than whites, even when blacks and whites with the same amount of education are compared. Blacks are more likely than whites to hold jobs that do not pay well, and sometimes they are even paid less than whites who hold the same kind of job.

In 1981, the median income of black families was $13,266, considerably lower than the median income of $23,517 for white families (U.S. Bureau of the Census, 1982: 432). Black families thus had a median income that was only 56 per cent of the median for white families, a figure that is about the same as it was in 1950.

The income gap between the races is narrower if we compare only those families in which both husband and wife are present in the home and holding jobs. In these kinds of families, blacks now have a median income that is about 85 per cent of the median for similar white families, and this gap has been narrowing in recent years. This suggests that single-parent households account for much of the overall discrepancy in family incomes between the racial groups, and single-parent households are more common among blacks than among whites. Because these households are usually headed by women, and because women generally earn less than men (see Chapter 10), black families overall have a lower median income than white families.

There is some evidence that the number of middle-class blacks has risen significantly in recent years, but blacks are still more likely than whites to be poor. In 1981, for example, 34.2 per cent of all blacks and only 11.1 per cent of all whites were living below the poverty level (U.S. Bureau of the Census, 1982: 440).

Race or Class?

We have seen that there is much inequality between blacks and whites, as well as considerable inequality between the black middle class and the black lower class. In recent years, a heated debate has developed over the source of black poverty. Some attribute it to continued discrimination (Willie, 1979; Clark, 1980), whereas others argue that it is perpetuated by the economic conditions of a modern industrial society (W. Wilson, 1978).

This debate has centered around William Julius Wilson's book, *The Declining Significance of Race* (1978), a scholarly analysis of the relative importance of race and class in determining the position of blacks in the stratification system. Wilson, a black sociologist at the University of Chicago, claims that there is no economic incentive for businesses to discriminate against blacks in a modern economy. He shows that the black middle class has grown substantially larger since the 1960s, and he argues that the evidence indicates that well-educated blacks now have about as good a chance as whites with the same education to have a rewarding career. Wilson claims that the structure of the economic system and federal efforts such as affirmative action have provided job opportunities for educated blacks. He is speaking not so much about the declining significance of race in general, as the title of his book suggests, but rather about the declining significance of racism in the job market (Payne, 1979: 133). Racial antagonisms continue to exist in American society, but they center on scarce resources such as political power, funds for public schools, housing, and municipal services, rather than on jobs.

Wilson shows that economic change has left behind a large and growing black underclass in poverty-stricken ghettos. These poor people receive inadequate educations, live in substandard housing, and do not have access to good jobs, many of which have moved to suburban locations. Although Wilson believes that the origin of black poverty lies in the institutional racism of the past, he says that today it is perpetuated by economic conditions rather than by racial discrimination. Economic change has created a sharp schism between the black middle class and poor blacks, with

the threat that the black underclass might become permanent. According to Wilson, to eradicate poverty among blacks will require economic policies rather than policies directed at racism itself.

Wilson's thesis has been widely attacked by civil rights leaders and by scholars. His critics charge that blacks still face racial barriers at all levels of the stratification system; even middle-class blacks are aware of their race as "a consuming experience" (Willie, 1979: 157), feeling that they still have to prove themselves to whites. Another critic argues that many blacks in professional positions work at jobs that are race-related, such as "community relations"; he suggests that many of these blacks have little job security and do not compete with their white peers for promotions to important line positions (Clark, 1980).

Black civil rights leaders and scholars have also attacked Wilson for having a false optimism that threatens to undermine the commitment of whites to policies to eradicate racism. They fear that whites may oppose civil rights legislation such as affirmative action if they feel that racial discrimination is no longer a problem (Clark, 1980). This kind of criticism is based more on the policy implications of Wilson's work than on his interpretation of the data. Others have questioned Wilson's interpretation of the data by showing that the size of the black middle class is still quite small and that the gap between the races in income has not narrowed much in recent years (Hill, 1979).

Wilson and his critics agree that racism continues to plague American society. The critics claim that the eradication of racism itself would improve the condition of all blacks, including the poor. Wilson disagrees, saying that "even if all racial discrimination were eliminated today, the situation of poor blacks will not be substantially improved unless something is done to remove the structural barriers to decent jobs created by changes in our system of production" (W. Wilson, 1979: 170). This is more than an academic debate; it is one that will influence government policy toward poor blacks in the years to come.

HISPANIC AMERICANS

Hispanic Americans are the second largest American minority group, but they are difficult to define precisely. They have been defined as people who trace their ancestry to a country in which Spanish is the primary language, as people who have Spanish surnames, or as people who speak Spanish as their native language. The three largest groups of

Hispanics in the United States are Mexican-Americans, Puerto Ricans, and Cuban-Americans; there are smaller numbers of Hispanics from other Latin American nations. Together, the 14.6 million Hispanic Americans counted in the 1980 census made up 6.4 per cent of the population, but as many as another three to five million Hispanics—many of them illegal aliens from Mexico—might not have been counted. Hispanic Americans are today one of the fastest growing ethnic groups in America, due to immigration and a high birth rate. Although they have a common language and religion (Catholicism), there are physical, cultural, and social differences among the various Hispanic groups.

About 60 per cent of the Hispanics in the United States are Mexican-Americans, or "Chicanos." Most Chicanos live in the West and the Southwest, especially in California and Texas. Until recently, Chicanos lived primarily in rural areas, but today about half of them live in the central cities of metropolitan areas where they are segregated in *barrios*. In 1980, the median family income of Mexican-Americans was $15,200, lower than for whites but higher than for blacks. The proportion of Chicanos living in poverty is higher than for whites but lower than for blacks, and the unemployment rate of Mexican-Americans also falls between those of blacks and whites. This ethnic group has been discriminated against in the educational system because of its lack of fluency in English, but several states now require schools to provide instruction in Spanish. Although they have a high dropout rate, Mexican-Americans have made gains in education in recent years, even though smaller proportions of them attend college than is true of either whites or blacks.

Puerto Ricans can travel freely and inexpensively between the United States, of which they have been citizens since 1917, and their homeland, a commonwealth under American jurisdiction. Because of intermarriage among Spanish-speaking whites, blacks, and Indians in Puerto Rico, many members of this ethnic group have dark skin. As a result, they sometimes are discriminated against because of their skin color as well as their lack of fluency in English. Puerto Ricans began to move to the United States in large numbers in the 1940s and 1950s, and today most of them live in the New York City area. There are now about 1.8 million Puerto Ricans in the United States, but many of them move back and forth to Puerto Rico. The ease with which they can return might reduce their motivation to assimilate into American society. In 1980, the median income of this group was only

$9,900, less than half of that of all American families. Moreover, the gap between the income of Puerto Rican families and the income of other American families has widened significantly since 1959. Today, about 40 per cent of Puerto Ricans live below the poverty level.

Cuban-Americans are a third large Hispanic group, numbering about one million in the 1980 census. Until 1980, Cuban-Americans were primarily a well-educated group that was concentrated in business and the professions. Most of them had been members of the middle class in Cuba, which many had left in 1959 when Fidel Castro came to power. In 1980 the median family income of this group was $17,500, the highest of any Hispanic group and about 90 per cent of the median for all families in the country. This figure was calculated before the influx in 1980 of 125,000 Cuban exiles, a group that was younger, less well educated, and poorer than Cuban-Americans already in the country. Some of these new immigrants had been released from prisons and mental hospitals in Cuba. These Cuban-Americans will probably be slower to assimilate than the group that preceded them. Today, most Cuban-Americans live in Florida and in the New York City area.

ASIAN AMERICANS

The 3.5 million Asian Americans and Pacific Islanders in the United States—most of whom are Chinese, Japanese, and Filipino in ancestry—account for about 1.6 per cent of the population of the United States. The 1980 census found that Asian Americans, who are concentrated in California and Hawaii, had a median family income higher than that of all American families, and that a larger proportion of them than of all Americans had completed high school.

Chinese-Americans began to immigrate to the West Coast in the 1840s, with the peak years of immigration coming in the 1870s. There they worked on the railroads and in the mines, later turning to farm labor. In 1882, their immigration was ended by federal law, in response to white hostility and mob violence. At this time many Chinese-Americans moved into Chinatowns, urban ghettos where they developed a tightly knit community that controlled deviant behavior and provided help for the poor. As a result of discrimination, many of them began small businesses, primarily laundries and restaurants. Today, many Chinese-Americans still live in these Chinatowns—the largest of which are in Los Angeles, San Francisco, New York City, and Boston—but the social structure of these communities has broken down somewhat, and crime, delinquency, drug addiction, and gang fighting have become more common. Large numbers of Chinese-Americans have improved their position in the stratification system, so that as a group they are better educated and earn more than white Americans. However, some immigrants with few skills and little education have arrived in the United States from mainland China in recent years. The 800,000 Chinese-Americans in the country in 1980 make them the largest Asian-American group (Lyman, 1974; Lindsey, 1982).

Japanese-Americans first came to the United States in the 1880s, the peak years of their immigration being the early 1900s. At first, they worked on the railroads and in logging camps. Later, they moved into agriculture, a change that dispersed them and probably hastened their assimilation. In 1924, federal law ended the immigration of all Orientals, a restriction that was not lifted until 1965. In 1942, the United States government placed more than 100,000 Japanese-Americans in internment camps, an act that was the culmination of a long history of racism toward this group, according to a federal report issued in 1983 (see SEL 9.3). Today, the culture of the 700,000 Japanese-Americans emphasizes education and work, and they are heavily represented in the professions, engineering, and management. On some indicators of status—such as occupational achievement, educational attainment, and life expectancy—Japanese-Americans fare better than white Americans (Montero, 1981; Woodrum, 1981).

SOCIOLOGY AND EVERYDAY LIFE 9.3
Concentration Camps in the United States

Ten weeks after the Japanese attack on Pearl Harbor, President Franklin D. Roosevelt signed Executive Order 9066, which gave the military the power to exclude from specified areas anyone thought to be a risk to commit sabotage, espionage, or fifth-column activity. This order, which a commission more than forty years later called a result of "race prejudice, war hysteria and a failure of political leadership" (p. A12), set the stage for the removal of more than 100,000 Japanese-Americans from their homes on the West Coast into "relocation centers" that have also been called concentration camps.

Families could bring only what they could carry to these centers; many had to abandon property and promising careers. The average family lost about $10,000 in property through confiscation by the government. In the relocation centers, the Japanese-Americans lived in "tar-papered barrack rooms of no more than 20 by 24 feet. Each room housed a family, regardless of family size" (p. A12). There was little privacy, and eating and bathing were done in large groups. The experience of life in these camps disrupted traditional patterns of authority in the Japanese-American family; as a result, the power of husbands over their wives and of parents over their children was reduced. In addition, the experience stigmatized these people as potentially disloyal and unworthy of trust.

There were rumors after the attack on Pearl Harbor that Japanese-Americans living in Hawaii had acted as spies for the Japanese, but these rumors were soon found to be false by the American government. Nevertheless, political officials and military officers allowed the American people to continue to believe these rumors, which were used as a basis for the internment of Japanese-Americans as security risks. This was done "despite the fact that not a single documented act of espionage, sabotage or fifth-column activity was committed by an American citizen of Japanese ancestry or by a resident Japanese alien on the West Coast" (p. A12). This "grave injustice," as it was called by the Congressional Commission on Wartime Relocation and Internment of Civilians in 1983, was based on racism. All Japanese-Americans were treated as potentially disloyal simply because of their ethnicity. Moreover, Italian-Americans and German-Americans, who also traced their ancestry to nations with which the United States was at war, were not forced into relocation centers far from their homes.

Sources: Based on Harry L. Kitano, *Japanese-Americans: The Evolution of a Subculture*, 2nd ed. Englewood Cliffs, N.J.: Prentice-Hall, 1976; Judith Miller, "Wartime Internment of Japanese Was 'Grave Injustice,' Panel Says," *The New York Times*, February 25, 1983, pp. 1, A12; and "Excerpts from Summary of Report on Internment in U.S. in World War II," *The New York Times*, February 25, 1983, p. A12.

Between 1970 and 1980, the size of the Asian-American population increased faster than that of any other ethnic group. The lifting of restrictions on immigration in 1965 has led to an influx of people from the Philippines. Today there are about 775,000 Filipino-Americans in the country, most of whom live on the West Coast. Another important trend in recent years has been the arrival of large numbers of poor, uneducated, and unskilled people from Southeast Asia. With the fall of the South Vietnamese government in 1975, a large number of Vietnamese "boat people" entered the United States, so that by 1980 there were 262,000 Vietnamese in the country. Another important factor in the recent increase in the Asian-American population is that both Taiwan and the People's Republic of China have been assigned quotas of 20,000 immigrants per year by the federal government.

NATIVE AMERICANS

Native Americans, or Indians, have been treated by whites as if they were a single people, but in fact they belong to many different tribes with distinct cultures. About two-thirds of the population of American Indians died during the nineteenth century in battles with whites, from diseases to which they had no immunity, and from starvation because of the slaughter of the buffalo. Since then, the Indian population has increased to about 1.4 million, well under 1 per cent of the population of the country.

Most Indians live in urban areas, but a significant number live on reservations, many of them in the Southwest. These reservations are administered by the Bureau of Indian Affairs, an agency of the United States Department of the Interior. Since 1871, Indians have been treated as wards of the state; this policy has been criticized as "paternalistic racism" because it reflects an assumption that Indians are not competent to manage their own affairs without government assistance. Efforts to "terminate" this wardship status have also created a variety of social problems for Native Americans. Indians were granted full citizenship rights in 1924, but they are still treated as second-class citizens today.

Indians are the poorest ethnic group in the United States, with a median income that is about one-third that of whites. The average Indian has about eight years of education, and about one-fourth of them are illiterate. Government-run reservation schools do not prepare Native Americans well for life in modern society, much less for college studies. Many Indians live in dilapidated housing on reservations or in urban slums, and their homes often lack plumbing, electricity, and heat. Native Americans also have very high unemployment rates, as much as 40 or 50 per cent on some reservations. Life expectancy among Indians is about ten years less than for the rest of the population, and this group has very high rates of suicide and alcoholism.

In recent years, Indians have won legal suits against state governments to compensate them for lands taken from them in the nineteenth century. Because many Native American cultures did not include a concept of private property that could be transferred from one person to another, the treaties made between Indians and whites in the last century had a very different meaning for each group. Another sign of increased activism by Indians, aside from their actions in the courts, has been the development since the 1960s of organizations such as the American Indian Movement (AIM) that seek to create pride in Indian culture and to effect political change to improve the living conditions of Native Americans (Josephy, 1982; Matthiessen, 1983).

WHITE ETHNICS

Americans with ancestral roots in Italy, Ireland, Greece, and Eastern European countries—collectively referred to as white ethnics—make up about 28 per cent of the population of the country. When they entered the United States in the nineteenth and early twentieth centuries, these groups were less accepted than were the earlier immigrants from England, Germany, and the Scandinavian countries. These "new immigrants" came to the United States at a time when there was less need for manual labor than there had been in the past. Except for the Irish, few spoke English, and many were Catholic, relatively poor, and unaccustomed to urban life. A great many settled in ethnic communities, where they maintained the traditions of the "old country" and resisted acculturation.

Today there is considerable heterogeneity among white ethnics, and this variety is a source of differences among them in political participation, alcohol use, and sexual behavior (Greeley, 1974). For several generations, ethnic heritages have remained distinct, and their effect on behavior is independent of the effects of class and religion.

White ethnics have average incomes, are middle class, and often live in or at least maintain ties to ethnic communities. They have become well as-

Italian-Americans celebrating the San Gennaro festival in New York City.

similated into the larger society (Greeley, 1976). Each successive generation of a given white ethnic group has tended to marry outside the group to an increasing extent, hastening the process of amalgamation (Goering, 1971; Alba, 1976). At the same time that these groups have become assimilated, they have also begun to develop an increased interest in their cultural heritage. These white ethnics have sometimes been described as traditional and conservative, but evidence suggests that, relative to WASPs, they are more supportive of a guaranteed annual income, more opposed to pollution, more favorably disposed to government aid to the poor, and more in favor of racial integration (Greeley, 1974).

JEWISH AMERICANS

Jewish Americans are members of an ethnic group based on common religious beliefs and a shared cultural heritage. About 4 per cent of Americans are Jewish, although identification with this group ranges from negligible to the all-encompassing life style of the Hasidic Jews. Although some Jews entered the United States as early as the seventeenth century, they arrived in large numbers in the mid-1800s, in reaction to persecution in Europe. Having lived in the cities of Europe for generations, they adjusted quickly to life in American cities. Today about half of all Jewish Americans live in the New York City area; the total number of Jews in this region is greater than the Jewish population of any other city in the world.

Jews have encountered prejudice and discrimination (or anti-Semitism) in the United States. They have been excluded from jobs, clubs, and neighborhoods; and in the 1930s some colleges and universities restricted the number of Jewish students they would accept. The Jewish religion maintains the boundaries of this group by strongly encouraging marriage within the group, but Jews have had a high rate of intermarriage with non-Jews (Heilman, 1982). This intermarriage, coupled with the relatively small size of the average Jewish family, might in time lead to the amalgamation of Jewish Americans. Structural assimilation of Jewish Americans has occurred over the years. Compared to other Americans, Jews are twice as likely to have a college degree, more likely to work in the professions and in business, and have higher family incomes.

THE FUTURE OF RACE AND ETHNICITY

Racial and ethnic groups will continue to play an important part in American society in the future. The lifting of federal restrictions on immigration in 1965 has enabled new people to continue to enter the country from abroad. The willingness to take in large groups of foreigners in times of crisis—the Vietnamese in 1975 and the Cubans in 1980—also indicates that many people of different racial and ethnic groups will be admitted to the United States from time to time. Even if no new immigrants were to enter the country, race and ethnicity would still be an important part of the identity of many Americans.

One of the costs of racial and ethnic diversity is group conflict. Prejudice and discrimination still plague American society, even though they have diminished in recent years. Pride in one's own group is often associated with hostility toward other groups, and this sometimes takes the form of discrimination or even mob violence. The federal government's commitment to eliminating discrimination waxes and wanes. Many of its policies have become institutionalized, slowly reducing the unequal treatment of racial and ethnic minorities and improving their living conditions. The continuation of these efforts in the future will not eradicate the cultural diversity of American society, but it can minimize the disadvantages of being a member of a minority group.

Summary

Almost every society has at least one racial or ethnic group that is distinct from the dominant group. Biologists and anthropologists have been unable to agree on a single definition of race, but the social definition of race influences interaction. Ethnicity is a characteristic of a people with a shared culture or national identity; and ethnic groups differ in language, religion, ancestry, life style, nationality, and race. A minority group is a category of people that has recognizable traits and is subordinate in a stratification system. Many minority groups are racial and ethnic groups; they are not necessarily a numerical minority of a population, although they often are.

Prejudice is a belief that is formed about a person or a group before all available information has been considered. Social distance is the degree of intimacy in social interaction that a person will allow the members of another group. Social distance is related to ethnocentrism, the tendency to exclude outsiders as different from the members of the group. Ethnocentrism is reinforced by stereotypes—generalized and exaggerated pictures that purport to describe entire categories of people and that simplify reality and influence social interaction. Under certain conditions, prejudice can be reduced through social contact between the members of different groups.

Discrimination is the treatment of people in a systematically negative way because of their membership in a socially disvalued group. Discrimination is often self-perpetuating, in that treatment as inferior can reinforce a minority group's lower position in the stratification system. Discrimination can be linked to prejudice, but it is also closely related to the impact of reference groups on behavior. Prejudiced people do not always discriminate, and people who discriminate do not always harbor personal prejudices.

Racism is a set of beliefs which hold that physical differences among groups determine differences in behavior. Institutional racism is discrimination that is built into the institutional arrangements and social policies of the society.

When a minority group is absorbed into the larger society, it is said to be assimilated. This can result from the acculturation or cultural integration of the group, and it can be coerced by the dominant group or can be voluntarily chosen by the minority group. The United States has been described as having an Anglo-conformity model of acculturation, one in which ethnic groups adopt the culture of Americans who trace their ancestry to England. Assimilation can also be a result of amalgamation, the absorption into society of a group through intermarriage with other groups. A structurally assimilated group is one that participates fully in the primary and secondary groups of the larger society.

Pluralism is a situation in which several different racial and ethnic groups live side by side in a society without trying to dominate each other. Another kind of dominant-group policy is to protect minority groups through legal measures; one such policy is affirmative action, the effort to give disadvantaged groups certain advantages to make up for discrimination in the past. Sometimes dominant groups adopt a policy of population transfer; this can take the form of expulsion or exclusion of a group from a country, or the partition of a country. Dominant groups can also continue to oppress a minority group, a process that has sometimes been described as internal colonialism. The deliberate extermination of a minority group is called genocide.

Minority groups respond in various ways to their subordinate status. They may actually leave a society rather than tolerate unequal treatment. Individuals sometimes try to pass as members of the dominant group. Often, the members of a minority group accept their subordinate status in order to avoid conflict with the dominant group, but this can produce self-hatred and low self-esteem. At other times, the members of a minority group band together in collective protest to change their political and social situation.

Black Americans have been discriminated against for centuries, even though American culture stresses the equal treatment of all people; this produces "an American dilemma." Blacks and whites differ today—as they have for centuries—in family structure, housing conditions, education, political rights and behavior, employment rates, and income. In recent years there has been a heated debate about whether the disproportionate number of blacks living in poverty owe their plight to racial discrimination or to the structural conditions of the American economy.

Most Hispanics in the United States are Mexican-Americans, who live mostly in the Southwest and have a somewhat higher social standing than blacks; Puerto Ricans, who travel freely to and from their homeland and usually live in the New York City area; and Cuban-Americans, who live in Florida and in the New York City area and until recently came mostly from the Cuban middle class. Asian Americans are composed mostly of Chinese-Americans, who today enjoy a higher standard of living than the average white American; Filipino-Americans; and Japanese-Americans, who have become structurally assimilated into American society. Native Americans, or Indians, are the poorest minority group in the country; most of them live in cities and on reservations. White ethnics trace their origins to Italy, Ireland, Greece, and Eastern European nations. They suffered prejudice when they arrived in the country, but today they are quite well assimilated and have standards of living as high as WASPs. Jewish Americans compose about 4 per cent of the American population. They have also suffered prejudice and discrimination, but today their standard of living is higher than that of any other ethnic group in the country.

Important Terms

ACCULTURATION (204)	MINORITY GROUP (198)
AFFIRMATIVE ACTION (205)	PLURALISM (205)
AMALGAMATION (204)	POPULATION TRANSFER (206)
ASSIMILATION (204)	PREJUDICE (199)
DESEGREGATION (201)	RACE (195)
DISCRIMINATION (201)	RACISM (199)
ETHNIC GROUP (197)	SEGREGATION (201)
GENOCIDE (206)	SOCIAL DISTANCE (200)
INSTITUTIONAL RACISM (202)	STRUCTURAL ASSIMILATION (205)
INTEGRATION (201)	

Suggested Readings

Joe R. Feagin. *Race and Ethnic Relations*. Englewood Cliffs, N.J.: Prentice-Hall, 1978. A good introduction to the study of racial and ethnic groups in the United States.

James A. Geschwender. *Racial Stratification in America*. Dubuque, Iowa: William C. Brown, 1978. A good discussion of different models of racial and ethnic group relations, and a detailed discussion of blacks in American society.

Andrew M. Greeley. *Ethnicity in the United States: A Preliminary Reconnaissance*. New York: Wiley, 1974. A technical and important contribution to the sociology of white ethnics in the United States.

Jane Jacobs. *The Question of Separatism: Quebec and the Struggle for Sovereignty*. New York: Random House, 1980. An examination of the conflict between English-speaking and French-speaking Canadians that has threatened to partition the country.

Vincent J. Parrillo. *Strangers to These Shores: Race and Ethnic Relations in the United States*. Boston: Houghton Mifflin, 1980. A thorough treatment of the great variety of racial and ethnic groups in American society.

George E. Simpson and J. Milton Yinger. *Racial and Cultural Minorities: An Analysis of Prejudice and Discrimination*, 4th ed. New York: Harper & Row, 1972. A comprehensive and widely used textbook on racial and ethnic groups and the relations among them.

William Julius Wilson. *The Declining Significance of Race: Blacks and Changing American Institutions*. Chicago: University of Chicago Press, 1978. A controversial book that argues that economic conditions rather than racial discrimination is now perpetuating black poverty.

GENDER ROLES

In every society, men and women differ in the economic tasks they perform, in their roles within the family, in their modes of dress, and in a multitude of other matters. Differences between the sexes are the basis of one type of social stratification: In all societies, males have greater access to valued rewards such as property, prestige, and power. Males and females everywhere differ physically in the same way, and yet there is significant variation from one society to the next as to what is considered appropriate behavior for men and women and for boys and girls. In most societies, men carry out economic tasks and women raise the children, but in some societies women provide for the family and men nurture the young. In most societies, men are more sexually aggressive, but in some the female is more aggressive than the male. The great cross-cultural variation in the roles played by men and women is evidence that the "appropriate behavior" for each sex is a matter of social definition rather than one of innate predispositions.

Sex and Gender

Sex is a biological characteristic. One of twenty-three pairs of human chromosomes determines an individual's sex; males have an XY chromosome pair, and females have an XX pair. The first of the pair is an X chromosome from the mother's egg cell; the second in the pair—the chromosome that determines the baby's sex—is from the father's sperm. Males and females differ in their genital organs and in their balance of hormones—chemical secretions in the body. Sex is a trait that is fixed for life, with the rare exception of people who undergo hormone treatments and surgery to change their sex; even these people retain their original chromosomes. The biological trait of sex is, from a sociological point of view, an ascribed status, for

the sex of a person is used as a basis for assigning people to a variety of roles. Moreover, the assignment to these roles causes and perpetuates inequality between the sexes.

In contrast to sex, which is determined at conception, *gender*—the social, cultural, and psychological aspects of maleness and femaleness—is socially defined through interaction (Kessler and McKenna, 1978). With the rare exception of hermaphrodites, we can think of the sexes as either male or female, though genders are best described on a continuum from the most "masculine" to the most "feminine." Biological males exhibit behavior from the very masculine to the very feminine, and the same is true of biological females. A transvestite—a person who enjoys dressing in the clothes of the opposite sex—belongs to one sex while exhibiting behavior that is characteristic of the opposite sex; a transvestite is either a male behaving in a feminine way, or a female behaving in a masculine way.

Gender roles are the kinds of behavior that are typically expected of the members of a particular sex. For example, men are expected to dress in certain ways in the United States, and women in other ways. Cultural pressures exist to make gender-role behavior conform to that which is typical of a particular sex in the culture. One of these pressures is "homophobia," the fear of being seen by others as a homosexual. Men who dress in a feminine way, or express themselves in typically feminine ways, may be labeled "homosexual" by others; the negative connotation of this label encourages men—both heterosexuals and even many homosexuals—to behave in ways that are characteristically masculine.

We saw in Chapter 4 that an individual's sense of self develops through interaction with others. One important aspect of this self is *gender identity*, the socially learned part of the self that results from a person's recognition that he or she is a man or a woman, or a boy or a girl. Gender identity is a set of social and psychological traits associated with cultural conceptions of masculinity and femininity. In some cases, gender identity differs from sex. One study of people who were assigned the wrong sex at birth, usually because they had sexual characteristics of both males and females, found that their behavior was more closely related to their gender identity—a product of socialization—than to their biological sex, which was determined by their chromosomes (Money and Ehrhardt, 1972; Money and Tucker, 1975; Money, 1977; Money, 1980). If behavior were determined by the chromosome pair present at conception, then those who were biologically male but had a female gender identity should have behaved in typically masculine ways, and those who were biologically female but assigned to the male gender should have behaved in a feminine manner.

VARIATIONS IN GENDER ROLES

All societies have a set of gender roles that distinguish masculine behavior from feminine behavior, although this distinction is clearer in some societies than in others. According to one study, there are similarities in most societies in the upbringing of males and females. In 82 per cent of the societies examined, girls were taught by their parents to be nurturing, to help and comfort others. Boys were taught to be achievement oriented in 87 per cent of the societies and self-reliant in 85 per cent of the societies. In the rest of the societies there was either no distinguishable difference in gender-role socialization in terms of nurturing, achievement orientation, and self-reliance, or the socialization process actually taught boys and girls to behave in ways opposite to the usual pattern (Barry, Bacon, and Child, 1957). The fact that many societies did not follow the most common pattern of socialization of boys and girls indicates that gender-role behavior does not necessarily correspond to differences in sex. In other words, gender differences vary from culture to culture, even though sex differences are much the same everywhere.

Margaret Mead's (1935, 1963) study of three tribal societies in New Guinea provides dramatic evidence that gender is not inextricably linked to sex. Mead found that in all three cultures there

Would you say this little girl is having problems with gender identity—or is she simply having fun?

were expectations that males and females would behave in somewhat different ways, but she also discovered that in two of the tribes—the Arapesh and the Mundugumor—there were no significant differences in the temperament or personality of males and females. The culture of the Arapesh—a gentle people who lived in the mountains—contained norms that both sexes would be emotional, noncompetitive, nurturing, and passive; these traits are associated with the feminine gender role in most societies. As with the Arapesh, both males and females of the fierce and cannibalistic Mundugumor tribe were expected to have similar personality traits, except those traits were the traits typically defined as masculine in most societies: aggressiveness, suspiciousness, and hostility. The third tribe, the Tchambuli, did make a distinction between the temperaments of men and women, but it was the opposite of what characterized most of the world's societies: Tchambuli women were taught to be domineering and independent, and they fished and hunted game for the tribe; and Tchambuli men were expressive and emotional, spending much of their time gossiping or grooming themselves. Mead (1935, 1963: 310) concluded from her comparison of these three societies that "the personalities of the two sexes are socially produced."

In addition to anthropological evidence that gender roles vary from one society to another, we also find major differences in these roles at different times in the same society. For example, "the preindustrial era saw a greater degree of sharing of work and emotional roles by men and women than the industrial era which followed" (Bell, 1981: 307). In Colonial America, for example, the home was often a center of economic production; this was true of both farms and craft shops in the cities. There was more equality of men and women in this preindustrial society; women worked to provide for the family, and men played a greater part in raising the children. With industrialization, women often stayed home to take care of the children and men went to work in factories. Gender roles became more distinct with industrialization than they had been before (Rothman, 1978; Lerner, 1979; Bell, 1981).

Even in modern industrial societies we find significant differences in gender roles. For example, in socialist societies there tends to be more equality between men and women than in capitalist societies, as we can see from SEL 10.1. In fact, even within a single society we often find important differences in gender roles for various classes and ethnic groups. Working-class people in the United States, for example, typically make sharper distinctions between expected behavior for males and females than do people in the middle class (Komarovsky, 1967; Rubin, 1976). The working-class man is expected to be the breadwinner and the disciplinarian of the children; his desires and needs are treated as more important than those of the other members of the family. The working-class woman, on the other hand, defers to the man; she favors the notion of the man as breadwinner, although economic reality often forces her to join the labor force. In contrast to the working class, members of the middle class are more likely to share household, child-care, and work tasks; they also communicate more intimately than do husbands and wives of the working class.

SOCIOLOGY AND EVERYDAY LIFE 10.1
Women and Work in Three Socialist Societies

Here we look at inequality between men and women in the world of work in three socialist societies, and at the efforts of those societies to change that situation.

THE SOVIET UNION

In the years following the 1917 Communist Revolution, the drive toward rapid industrialization, combined with the World War I manpower shortage, led to major efforts to bring women into jobs traditionally held by men.

Women became aviators, factory managers, government officials, diplomats—as well as construction workers and field hands. In World War II, a women's bomber squadron served with distinction. Other females fought as partisans behind the German lines. In the 1980s, 69 percent of the nation's doctors and a predominant proportion of secondary-school staffs are females (Daniloff, p. 54).

Even though Soviet women are legally guaranteed equality with men, most of them are not actually equal to men in the world of work:

A great deal of women's discontent springs from the fact that economic necessity and Soviet custom require everyone to hold a job. Even the labor law states that "he who does not work, does not eat." Nursing mothers and the pensioned are exempt.

Wives and divorced mothers, as a result, spend 8 hours a day earning a livelihood and then more weary hours devoted to shopping and housework.

Sociologist V. D. Patrushev estimates that working women spend more than 30 hours a week on those two activities. And while husbands in their 20s and 30s are more willing to help at home than their own fathers were, a recent survey of the Russian Republic disclosed that on the average men spend only 15 hours a week on household chores. One explanation of why homemaking takes up so much time: Few Soviet families have labor-saving devices such as electric mixers, washers and dryers. Even in Moscow's outskirts, women are seen scrubbing clothes in ponds.

Women's need to attend to household duties often helps men enjoy huge advantages in the competition for good jobs. Directors of some enterprises admit they prefer to hire men because females are too distracted by domestic problems to perform efficiently on the job. The most common complaint by women is that they are shunted into low-paying work (Daniloff, p. 53).

CHINA

The People's Republic of China, which was established in 1949, is a socialist society that has adopted policies to bring women into the world of work. China has

stressed getting women out of the home and into "socially productive labor." Given that women rarely even left their homes before the communists came to power, much less worked outside the home, the change has been extraordinarily swift. In rural areas, where 80 percent of the Chinese population still live, virtually all women at some point in their lives work in the fields; in cities, although the situation is far from clear, it appears that better than half of urban women at present take part in labor. If men and women admittedly still do not participate equally in the work force, the improvement since 1949 has been impressive. There has been a desire to put women to work; a recognition that such a goal requires day care, communal mess halls, and other replacement services; and a definite, if sporadic, enthusiasm to establish these services. In rural areas, periodic campaigns have attacked the problem of equal pay for equal work, ameliorating if not solving it. And in the cities, women have been encouraged to move into nontraditional jobs as technicians, engineers, steel workers, and the like, which are, incidentally, also more highly paid (Adams and Winston, p. 7).

SWEDEN

Sweden is another socialist society that has tried to reduce inequality between men and women in the labor market. One report concludes that Sweden's policies are

formulated on the basis that each individual, irrespective of sex, should have the right to an education, to work, and to self support and that the responsibilities for the children and the upkeep of the home should be shared between the parents. The government should through youth and adult education, labor market policies, family support, public day care, and other measures, actively promote a division of labor built upon equality between the sexes. Everyone should be able to pursue a market career and still have a family life.

Women's problems in the labor market have been viewed as stemming from difficulties in combining market work and home responsibilities. Swedish labor market policies for women have therefore centered on the supply side of the market. The aim has been to remove the barriers that hinder women from becoming full fledged members of the labor force. The most important hindrance to which attention has been paid is child care, but there has also been an emphasis on education and vocational training. In this light one can also see the effort to remove laws and regulations in marriage, social welfare, and tax legislation that treat women unequally and provide a disincentive for women to earn their own living. . . .

Another principle behind Swedish policies is that sexual equality requires changing the role of men as well as the role of women. As long as men do not assume their share of the duties at home, women will not be able to compete in the market on equal conditions with men. This requires changing working life and child care patterns so that children no longer are costless to father while costing mother most of their advancement opportunities. Equality for women in the labor market requires an equal participation by men in work in the home (Jonung, pp. 34–35).

Sources: Nicholas Daniloff, "For Russia's Women, Worst of Both Worlds," *U.S. News & World Report* 92 (June 28, 1982): 53–54. Used by permission. Carolyn Teich Adams and Kathryn Teich Winston, *Mothers at Work: Public Policies in the United States, Sweden, and China.* New York: Longman, 1980; and Christina Jonung, "Sexual Equality in the Swedish Labor Market," *Monthly Labor Review* 101 (October 1978): 31–35.

Gender roles are socially created; they do not follow in any inevitable way from differences in sex. If sex did determine temperament and behavior, we would find that males and females would be expected to act in the same way in all societies at all times. Instead, we find much variation in gender-role behavior, whether we compare traditional and modern societies, socialist and capitalist societies, or even groups within a single society. However, in just about every society men have greater access than women to social rewards, such as property, prestige, and power. If gender roles are socially defined in such different ways among the societies of the world, why is there stratification by gender in all societies?

The Source of Gender Stratification

A search of the world's societies turns up few, if any, cases in which women control political power, hold more wealth, and earn higher incomes than men, or work at jobs with greater prestige than those held by men (Blumberg, 1978). In addition, we find other signs of male dominance; for example, the fact that males touch females more than females touch males reflects position in the social hierarchy, because the power to initiate physical contact is linked to dominance (Henley, 1973). The question of why men are dominant in almost every society is not easy to answer, and it is one that has caused much controversy.

IS ANATOMY DESTINY?

We have seen that males and females differ genetically, anatomically, and hormonally. In addition, more male than female fetuses die in the womb; more males than females die before they reach the age of one; males have higher death rates than females at every age; and several inherited disorders are found only in males. In spite of these differences, it remains unclear to what extent physical differences between the sexes account for differences in behavior, as in aggressiveness or sociability.

The only significant biological differences between the sexes that we can say for certain influence behavior are the reproductive and sexual functions (Money, 1977, 1980): Females menstruate, get pregnant, and nurse infants; and males impregnate females. Also, males must be sexually aroused to have intercourse and make a female pregnant; females do not need to be sexually aroused to get pregnant, although their arousal does increase the frequency of intercourse and make conception more likely.

Aside from these differences in reproductive and sexual functioning, we can say that differences might exist in predispositions between the sexes. For example, men are larger than women, on the average; also men are generally stronger in tasks that require exertion over a short period of time, although women show more strength at tasks that require endurance. What is important to recognize, however, is that these and other differences between males and females are differences in medians or means. If the average height of men is 5' 10" and the average height of women is 5' 4", we can say than men are, on the average, taller than women. However, we would make many mistakes if we interpreted this to mean that men are always taller than women. Clearly, there is much variation in height among men and among women. Many women are, in fact, taller than many men. This is typical of differences between the sexes; even when men and women differ in a median or a mean on some trait, there is usually much variation within each sex on that trait. For example, women show a greater ability than men to tolerate pain (Weitz, 1977); however, many individual men are better able to tolerate pain than many women, even though as a group women are superior to men in this respect.

Differences in hormonal balance between the sexes might account for some very general differences in predispositions between males and females. For example, hormonal balance predisposes males to aggressiveness. If a female is injected with certain male hormones, she is likely to become more aggressive; males who are given injections of additional male hormones also become more aggressive (Brody, 1981). Hormones do have general effects on behavior and emotions, but they do not determine behavior; rather, they may predispose one sex to act in ways that differ, on the average, from the ways that the opposite sex behaves (Money, 1977; Weitz, 1977). What is of much greater interest to sociologists, however, is the way that these predispositions are channeled or even extinguished through socialization. Thus, a male's predisposition toward aggressiveness might be channeled into a life of violent crime, a job as a professional athlete, or a career as an ambitious business executive; if his parents punished him for aggressive behavior, he might well have a career that does not require him to be aggressive in any way.

FUNCTIONALISM VERSUS CONFLICT THEORY

The importance of innate differences for gender stratification—the hierarchical ranking of men above women in nearly every society—has been hotly debated. Functionalists (Parsons, 1954; Parsons and Bales, 1955) have suggested that differences in gender roles originally developed because of the woman's role in reproduction. They have suggested that because women are often pregnant or nursing, especially in preindustrial societies where the birth rate is high, a division of labor developed in which women stayed at home where they could care for the children. It then became efficient for them to tend the house as well. Men, on the other hand, were relatively more free to plow the fields or work in a factory, because they were not tied to children the way that women were. Functionalists have suggested that this "efficient" division of tasks between the sexes became institutionalized in the family and became the basis of traditional gender roles that were passed from generation to generation through socialization. Eventually, this separation of tasks between men and women was thought to be "natural." We can see, however, in Table 10.1 that work is actually divided between men and women in very different ways, even in preindustrial or traditional societies.

The functionalist position sees the "nuclear family"—husband, wife, and their children—as essential to the smooth functioning of industrial societies (Parsons and Bales, 1955) (see Chapter 11). Traditional differences between gender roles are seen as complementary, with each sex performing tasks for the family. The female's gender role is expressive; she nurtures, comforts, and supports other members of the family. This role develops "naturally" from the woman's reproductive and nursing functions, which tie her to the home. The male role, which complements the female's, is instrumental or task-oriented; men work outside the home to provide money for their families.

Critics of this functionalist explanation of gender-role differences claim that it is a conservative position that supports male dominance (Friedan, 1963). The functionalist position also assumes that gender roles must be based on differences between the sexes. This implication that gender roles and gender stratification are in some way inevitable simply does not fit with the tremendous variation that we find from society to society. In addition, cross-cultural research finds no evidence that male

TABLE 10.1

Division of Labor Between Men and Women in Preindustrial Societies

	Number of societies in which each activity was performed		
Activity	*Always or usually by men*	*Equally by either sex*	*Always or usually by women*
Hunting	179	0	0
Fishing	132	19	7
Clearing the land for agriculture	95	17	18
Preparing and planting the soil	54	33	57
Construction of shelter	16	5	28
Tending and harvesting crops	25	35	83
Making and tending fires	24	25	84
Carrying loads	18	33	77
Gathering fruits, berries, and nuts	15	15	76
Gathering fuel	23	10	108
Preserving meat and fish	10	10	88
Cooking	6	9	186
Carrying water	7	5	126

Source: Adapted from George P. Murdock, "Comparative Data on the Division of Labor by Sex," *Social Forces* 15 (May 1937): 551–553. © The University of North Carolina Press.

and female roles are specialized along an instrumental–expressive dimension, as functionalists have asserted (Crano and Aronoff, 1978).

Critics of the functionalists assert that industrial societies can be quite flexible in assigning tasks to males and females, and that anatomy is not destiny. We can see this in Sweden's efforts to alter gender stratification (see SEL 10.1). The functionalist position was most clearly spelled out by American sociologists in the 1950s, an era when the culture as a whole fostered a "man at work, woman at home" model of gender roles. This division of tasks may be functional for some members of society, but we have seen that it is by no means the only way that gender roles can be defined. Indeed, increased life expectancy and declining birth rates in advanced industrial societies have made this traditional model of gender roles dysfunctional in many ways, as we see later in this chapter (Giele, 1978).

Differences between men and women in reproductive functioning, in hormonal balance, and in physical strength may be relevant in some general way to the initial development of differences in gender roles, although the gender roles that these differences produce vary greatly from society to society. Conflict theorists have focused on the ways that gender stratification is perpetuated once inequality between men and women has emerged (Collins, 1974: 228–259; Blumberg, 1978; Sokoloff, 1980). The assignment of the economic function to men gives them greater access to property and prestige, and political power often follows from control of these resources. Men then develop institutions that justify and reinforce this inequality. For example, they develop organizations to strengthen differences between masculine and feminine gender roles. The way that the Boy Scouts of America has historically perpetuated traditional masculine behavior that has worked to the advantage of men is shown in SEL 10.2. Men also maintain inequality between the sexes through the law; for example, for many years, women were denied the right to own property and the right to vote.

SOCIOLOGY AND EVERYDAY LIFE 10.2
Masculinity and the Boy Scouts of America

Between 1870 and World War I, changes in the American economy reduced the number of jobs in which men owned the property with which they worked; fewer men were farmers at the end of this period, and fewer owned their own businesses. At the same time, the number of men working as "clerical workers, salespeople, government employees, technicians, and salaried professionals" increased substantially (p. 187). "The dependency, sedentariness, and even security of these middle-class positions clashed with the active mastery, independence, self-reliance, competitiveness, creativity, and risk-taking central to the traditional male ideal" (p. 187). Men sought validation of their masculinity that they did not find in the jobs they held.

As public education expanded, it became more important to find support for the gender roles in which men had been socialized. Adolescents were increasingly exposed to female teachers, and fear developed among some men of the "feminization" of young American males. In part this was a reaction to one product of industrialization, the stage in the life cycle that we call adolescence:

A cohort of men who had reached social maturity before the use and public acceptance of adolescence as an age category, who had experienced the rural transition to manhood at an early age, and who had fought as teenagers in the Civil War or knew those who had were confronted with a generation of boys whose major characteristics were dependency and inactivity (p. 187).

Still another social force that "raised the specter of feminization" (p. 188) was the increased entry of women into the marketplace. Women commonly took white-collar jobs, and the large number of men who worked in such positions feared the loss of work as a way to demonstrate their masculinity.

These factors combined to produce several changes in American society. Leisure pursuits became increasingly oriented toward the physical, as did tastes in reading and the worship of cultural heroes. "Football, baseball, hiking, and camping became popular and were defended for their contribution to the development of traditional masculine character" (p. 186). Along with this emphasis came a pressure on women to maintain their "traditional attributes of purity, passivity, and domesticity" (p. 186).

In 1910, the Boy Scouts of America was formed, and six years later the organization received a federal charter. Ten years after its formation, the Boy Scouts had about 350,000 members and about 15,000 scoutmasters. This organization served the needs of American men, for it helped them to validate their masculinity and reassure them that the new generation of males would continue to play traditional gender roles.

The 1914 annual report of this organization makes it clear that scouting was to provide an alternative to the frontier in the development of masculine traits:

The Wilderness is gone, the Buckskin Man is gone, the painted Indian has hit the trail over the Great Divide, the hardships and privations of pioneer life which did so much to develop sterling manhood are now but a legend in history, and we must depend upon the Boy Scout Movement to produce the MEN of the future (p. 189).

Scouting would help the typical American boy "be a real boy, not too much like his sister" (p. 189). Scouts were to be active, not dependent and passive. Their mastery of skills was symbolized by the awarding of badges. Their take-charge approach to life was reflected in the expectation that they do a good deed every day. A 1912 statement defined the ideal scout:

The REAL Boy Scout is not a "sissy." He is not a hothouse plant, like little Lord Fauntleroy. There is nothing "milk and water" about him; he is not afraid of the dark. He does not do bad things because he is afraid of being decent. Instead of being a puny, dull, or bookish lad, who dreams and does nothing, he is full of life, energy, enthusiasm, bubbling over with fun, full of ideas as to what he wants to do and knows how he wants to do it. He has many ideals and many heroes. He is not hitched to his mother's apronstrings. While he adores his mother, and would do anything to save her from suffering or discomfort, he is self-reliant, sturdy and full of vim (p. 191).

In addition to training the young to fit this traditional masculine gender role, scouting also provided men—especially those working at jobs they felt had become "feminized"—to assert their masculinity by training boys to become "real men." As one observer notes, "Scouting disproportionately attracted men who had borne longer the 'feminine' environment of the schools and now were in occupations whose sedentariness and dependence did not fit the traditional image of American manliness" (p. 192).

Source: Adapted from Jeffrey P. Hantover, "The Boy Scouts and the Validation of Masculinity," *Journal of Social Issues* 34 (No. 1, 1978): 184–195. Used by permission.

The Boy Scouts of America was founded in 1910 to help boys validate their masculinity and reinforce traditional gender roles.

Learning Gender Roles

Every culture includes norms that specify ideal male and female behavior. These gender roles are instilled through socialization, which perpetuates inequality between the sexes. In the contemporary United States, the major agents of socialization from which boys and girls learn appropriate gender behavior are parents, peers, teachers, and the mass media. In recent years, the feminist movement has had some success in changing traditional gender roles.

GENDER STEREOTYPES

Gender stereotypes—exaggerated and simplified ideas about how people of each sex should behave—often contain an explicit or an implicit assumption that people of one sex are innately superior to people of the opposite sex; this ideology is called *sexism. Institutional sexism* occurs when a pattern of discrimination and a set of beliefs are built into a society's institutions and policies, causing members of one sex to deny opportunities and rewards to members of the other sex. In most societies, sexism and institutional sexism take the form of practices and ideas that males are inherently better than females, although statements by some radical feminists in the United States in recent years have suggested the innate superiority of females over males. Also, the traditional practice of routinely awarding child custody to the mother in divorce cases is based on a sexist belief in the superiority of the mother as a parent.

Not all gender stereotypes assume that one sex is superior to the other; some of these stereotypes simply suggest that there are basic differences between the sexes and that these differences complement each other. For example, the idea that women are more expressive and that men are better at instrumental tasks overlooks considerable variation in personality traits and skills within each sex, but it does not necessarily imply that one sex is better than the other. Still, stereotypes such as these are commonly used to deny women access to property, prestige, and power.

Gender stereotypes in the United States have changed since the late 1960s. Before then—and even now, to a considerable degree—the gender-role behavior of males and females was seen in terms of stereotypes. Indeed, these stereotypes are somewhat accurate in describing existing differences between the sexes, for socialization encour-

ages children to develop traits and behavior that are consistent with those stereotypes. Males have traditionally been seen as more competent, hard working, competitive, achievement oriented, ambitious, independent, logical, dominant, sexually aggressive, and emotionally unexpressive. The traditional stereotype of the female describes her in opposite terms: sensitive, emotionally expressive, nurturing, passive, dependent, creative, unaggressive, and concerned with physical appearance (Broverman et al., 1972).

Some studies have found that when college students are asked to rate a piece of written work, both males and females rate it more highly if they think it is written by a male rather than by a female (Goldberg, 1968). However, in a more recent study, females rated works higher if they were attributed to female authors rather than to male authors (Levenson et al., 1975). Nevertheless, there remains a strong tendency in American society for both males and females to regard men as more competent at many tasks.

LEARNING GENDER ROLES THROUGH SOCIALIZATION

A comprehensive survey of research on differences between the sexes found no conclusive evidence that boys and girls differ in sociability, suggestibility, self-esteem, analytic ability, achievement motivation, or intelligence (Maccoby and Jacklin, 1974). Four sex differences were found, but only one of them—the greater physical and verbal aggressiveness of males—showed up before the age of eleven. The other differences, which appeared during adolescence, were that girls surpass boys in verbal ability and that boys surpass girls in visual–spatial ability and in mathematical ability. These differences could have some genetic basis, but the fact that they do not show up for years makes it much more likely that they are the product of how boys and girls are socialized. We now turn to the agents of socialization that influence the development of gender roles.

Socialization in the Family

In a sense, the differential treatment of boys and girls by their parents begins before birth. Expectant parents generally say they would prefer to have a boy, and parents who already have children are more likely to continue having children if they have only daughters (Hoffman, 1977).

Gender stereotypes influence the ways that parents perceive and treat their children (Weitz, 1977; Richardson, 1981). One study found that parents said they could detect differences between boy and girl infants who were only one day old, even though the infants did not differ in size and weight and even though psychologists and medical personnel could see no differences between the sexes. Parents described their girls as softer, smaller, and more fragile; they described their boys as more active and better able to withstand rough play (Rubin, Provenzano, and Luria, 1974).

The way that parents perceive their male and female babies influences how they behave toward them. Because parents' perceptions reflect cultural stereotypes, they give rise to child-rearing behavior that in turn reinforces those stereotypes. By the age of one year, girls are more dependent on their mothers, less likely to wander away, and more quiet while playing. Boys, on the other hand, are more independent, more likely to explore their environment, and more active in their play. These differences seem to be attributable to mothers' responses to their children in the first six months of life (Goldberg and Lewis, 1972). In part, these differences are a result of the way that parents play with their children; they tend to "roughhouse" with boys and to talk quietly and be more openly affectionate with their daughters (Maccoby and Jacklin, 1974; Condry and Condry, 1976; Parke, 1979; Richardson, 1981). In fact, even before children develop verbal skills, their parents may convey expectations about gender-role behavior to them through body posture and facial expressions. For example, a mother might react calmly to a boy's wandering away from her but become tense when her daughter begins to explore the area nearby. Nonverbal gestures and body language are observed by children and can reinforce or extinguish behavior at any early age.

Children are socialized into gender roles by subtle verbal and nonverbal rewards and punishments. They are given toys that are considered appropriate for their sex. Shirley Weitz (1977: 58) observes that

the selection of toys is premised on different adult life plans: trucks and soldiers are chosen for boys, dolls for girls. At the same time, these toys mark out different childhood roles for the two sexes: action and physical activity for boys, sedentary interests for girls.

Boys and girls are also dressed differently; "blue for boys" and "pink for girls" might be somewhat less characteristic of children's clothing today than in the past, but the pattern is still common. Parents expect their sons and daughters to behave in different ways. In the United States, parents seem more willing to accept "masculine" behavior from girls than to accept "feminine" behavior from boys. This is probably because the masculine gender role is associated with dominance and access to social rewards; consequently, girls have more to gain and boys more to lose by acting according to the gender roles of the opposite sex.

From socialization in the family, boys and girls develop self-concepts that are appropriate to their gender (Weitz, 1977; Richardson, 1981). They first learn to categorize everyone as "boy" or "girl" or "man" or "woman." Next they place themselves in one of these categories; this self-categorization is based largely on the reactions of others to them. We have seen that a child's gender identity can, in rare circumstances, be different from his or her sex if other people treat the child as belonging to the "wrong" sex (Money and Ehrhardt, 1972; Money, 1977; Money, 1980). After placing themselves in one gender or the other, children next learn the behavior that the culture defines as appropriate to their category. By the age of five or six, boys and girls have developed a gender identity. They have also learned by this age that males are dominant in the social world. Around the age of three, boys and girls often express the belief that their own sex is better, but a few years later the self-image of girls becomes more negative while that of boys remains positive (Kohlberg, 1966; Horner, 1969; Weston and Mednick, 1970; Richardson, 1981).

Socialization by Peers

Gender-role behavior is learned through interaction with boys and girls of the same age. Until adolescence, peer-group activity is typically limited to other members of the same sex, and these peer groups "accentuate stereotyped features of sex roles" (Weitz, 1977: 87). Groups of girls characteristically play with dolls, dress up, or jump rope. Boys are more likely to play war games or competitive sports. Popularity is important to children and to adolescents, and being popular means conforming to the expectations of peers. These expectations are, of course, reflections of what children have learned from their parents, relatives, neighbors, teachers, and the mass media. Organized peer-group activities, such as Little League or Boy Scouts (See Sel 10.2), can reinforce gender stereotypes by channeling behavior in specific directions.

One study found that the play activity of boys and girls might prepare them for adult roles in very different ways (Lever, 1976, 1978). Boys tend to play in larger groups than girls; also, boys are more likely to play outside, more likely to belong to a play group that includes a wide range of ages, and more apt to play in a competitive and goal-directed way. In addition, boys' games are more likely to include rules and to present situations in which disputes must be settled. Boys also play for longer periods of time than do girls. The play activities of boys seem to prepare them better for careers, because they learn in their play groups to be independent, organized, and willing to compromise to settle a conflict. Girls' play, on the other hand, seems to prepare them better for interaction in small groups, for staying indoors, and for less goal-directed activities.

Socialization in School

From kindergarten until their early years of high school, girls perform better than boys in their academic work. In high school, boys begin to surpass girls, especially in mathematics (Lewis, 1968; Tobias, 1978; Benbow and Stanley, 1980; Richardson, 1981). In American society, mathematics is seen as a "masculine" discipline because it is logical and problem oriented. As a result, many girls curb their performance in mathematics to avoid competing with boys, for this would be seen as inappropriate gender-role behavior.

The difference between boys' and girls' achievements in school is largely a product of the expectations of their teachers, although it also reflects the fact that parents sometimes encourage their sons to do well in school in order to make a good career possible and discourage their daughters from the same path. As they get older, boys are more likely than girls to be urged by their teachers to do well in school to improve their job opportunities. Teachers also pay more attention to boys and praise their creative efforts more. They often assume that academic success in boys is a result of talent, whereas they are more likely to attribute girls' success to luck or to extraordinarily hard work (Deaux, 1976).

Boys and girls are treated differently in school as early as nursery school or kindergarten. They are given different toys, books, and tasks, and this reinforces the gender stereotypes they have already learned at home and from the mass media. Increasingly, girls have been encouraged to play sports, but their athletic endeavors usually are given less attention than those of boys. Some courses in school are segregated by sex; girls are more often directed toward "business" or "commercial" courses that prepare them for secretarial or clerical work, and boys are channeled into "academic" programs that prepare them for college and a career. Boys are also directed toward shop courses that provide them with skills and a sense of mastery, and girls are encouraged to take home economics courses. In recent years, many school systems have encouraged both boys and girls to take home economics and shop courses, a change that might help to weaken gender stereotypes and provide both boys and girls with useful skills they were denied in the past.

Despite the fact that in recent years publishers have made efforts to combat sexism and racism by including stories and photos of women and minorities, stereotypes are still being reinforced by the reading materials used in many schools. Elementary school readers contain many more stories about boys and men than about girls and women (U'Ren, 1971). These books often portray white males as the people who work at rewarding careers; females and minority-group members are less often shown in these desirable jobs. One study found that of all characters in a sample of elementary school readers, 70 per cent were white males, 15 per cent were white females, 10 per cent were minority-group males, and 4 per cent were minority-group females (Britton, 1975). Children other than white males must search their books for characters with their own traits. In addition, males in these books are typically shown to be heroic, brave, skilled, and adventuresome. Girls, on the other hand, are pictured as passive, domestic, incompetent, and emotional. These books reinforce gender stereotypes and fail to provide girls with the role models and the traits that they need for success in the world of work. These books also have harmful consequences for boys; for example, they might convey to boys that they will only succeed if they are aggressive and unemotional (Women on Words and Images, 1972).

Socialization by the Mass Media

Children's books that are read for pleasure rather than for classroom instruction present gender stereotypes in much the same way as elementary school readers (Stewig and Knipfel, 1975). There are more male than female characters in these books; in fact, one study found eleven times as many males as females in prize-winning children's books, and one third of these books did not contain a single female character (Weitzman et al., 1972). The females who do appear in these books are usually shown in subordinate positions in the home, rather than as active participants who hold jobs outside the home, as about half of all women do today. Males are pictured as active, independent, and competent at a variety of tasks.

TELEVISION. During their teens, adolescents watch television for an average of six hours per day, and their exposure to gender stereotypes—both in programs and in commercials—reinforces the stereotypes they have learned from their parents, peers, and teachers. In fact, those who watch the most television have been found to hold the most stereotypical views of gender-role behavior (Frueh and McGhee, 1975). Feminists and others concerned with the influence of television, the most influential of the mass media today, have pressed for changes in the way that men and women are portrayed (Black, 1982). Today it is possible to find television shows and commercials that show women who are active and competent, and men who are vulnerable and emotional. Still, traditional gender stereotypes continue to dominate the mass media.

Men have about three times as many leading parts in television shows as do females. Women shown on television are usually concerned with their relationships with men; they have sexual, romantic, and family interests, and they rarely have a strong commitment to work and career. Men are more often shown at work, and those women who do work hold traditionally female jobs and usually have men as bosses. Women are portrayed as incompetent and inferior to men; they are "symbolically annihilated" in these roles (Tuchman, 1979). In addition, women are pictured as young and attractive, setting a standard for viewers to emulate or to feel inadequate by comparison (Sternglanz and Serbin, 1974; Busby, 1975; Miles, 1975; Sprafkin and Liebert, 1978).

NEWSPAPERS. Newspapers also create and reinforce stereotypes of the genders in the way they present the news and in their advertisements. Public opinion polls that ask people who are "the most admired women" usually find that those who are named are "satellites to public male figures" (Richardson, 1981: 85). Relatively few women make the list on the strength of their own efforts; those who do are typically in fields traditionally reserved for women, such as nursing and the arts. One woman who regularly makes the "most admired" list is the First Lady, largely because she is given abundant attention on the front pages of newspapers. Women who succeed on their own in the business world are often relegated to the business pages or the "woman's pages"; the wife of the President, on the other hand, typically makes the front page, even when the "news" only concerns her clothing, a trip, or a ribbon-cutting ceremony. This kind of news and the "most admired women" list strengthen the stereotype of women as appendages to men.

MAGAZINES. Men's magazines typically focus on finance and sex, and women's magazines usually emphasize relationships with men. As the number of women who are single and the number of women who are part of the labor force have increased, some traditional magazines have modified their emphasis on home and marriage by adding features to appeal to those audiences. In addition, new magazines have emerged to appeal to working women, but these magazines usually assume that women will continue to care for children and home as well as hold a job. Women's magazines—whether traditional or new—imply that any solution to the problems that a woman encounters in combining work and family roles will be a personal solution—such as better budgeting of time or convincing her husband to help her. For the most part, these magazines do not propose social policies such as better funding of day-care facilities or more flexible work schedules that would alleviate the role conflict that develops from trying to work and have a family at the same time (Tuchman, Daniels, and Benét, 1978; Richardson, 1981).

ADVERTISING. Commercial advertisements on television, in newspapers, and in magazines also reinforce gender stereotypes; "selling products, in part, depends upon selling those stereotypes" (Richardson, 1981: 90). The importance of traditional gender-role stereotypes in advertising is astutely shown by Laurel Walum Richardson:

Look, if you will, at an advertisement in any magazine or newspaper. In your imagination, change the sex of the model(s). Does the picture still make sense and appear natural? Chances are the advertisement you have imaginatively recreated will seem inappropriate and strange. The reason is that the photo has been carefully constructed to display cultural understandings about the differences, and the relationships, between men and women (Richardson, 1981: 90).

Erving Goffman (1976) has investigated and illustrated the use of "genderisms," those subtle and not-so-subtle aspects of advertising that are used to reinforce gender stereotypes. For example, he finds that, compared to the women who appear in ads in the mass media, men are more likely to be shown as disproportionately larger than in real life, more likely to be portrayed as assertive and in charge, and more apt to be pictured as protective of other members of their families.

Another way that the subordinate status of women is reinforced is by the use of men rather than women to do the "voice-overs" on television and radio commercials. One study found that 90 per cent of the voices of the announcers on daytime television commercials were men, and 92 per cent of the voices in evening commercials were men. Both of these percentages are higher than a decade earlier. One researcher says, "Men today almost always are the voice-overs, even when the commercial is entirely female and is directed toward women. Men even announce feminine care products" (cited in Klemesrud, 1981b: A16). This use of male voices of authority "supports the automatic assumption that women can never be authorities and will always be subservient, and second in command" (cited in Klemesrud, 1981b: A16).

Gender Roles in the United States

Women have some of the characteristics of minority groups (Hacker, 1951). They are not treated as equals by men, who rank higher in all aspects of the stratification system. As with racial minorities, women are a physically distinct group, and that makes them easy targets for discrimination. Increasingly, women define themselves as a category that is systematically mistreated by the dominant group. Women do, however, differ from racial and ethnic minorities in important ways. They are not residentially segregated from the dominant group, nor is their social distance from men great. Even though women are found at all levels of the stratification system, they are still systematically denied equal access to property, prestige, and power.

GENDER ROLES AND THE FAMILY

In 1900, American women were subordinate to their husbands in many ways: They could not own property, make wills, or determine the education or religion of their children. In addition, they were punished by their husbands when they displeased them. Even today, in most states a husband who forces his wife to engage in sexual intercourse has not committed the crime of rape. For the most part, however, women have now achieved legal rights equal to those of men, though they remain subordinate in many areas of social life.

Because women in industrial societies have few children and are not likely to nurse them for long, they are relatively free of the need to stay home to care for their children. Nevertheless, most married men and women in the United States feel that young children do need a full-time parent, and that parent is usually the mother (Komarovsky, 1976). Partly as a result of gender stratification in the world of work—the lower pay and the lack of access to prestigious positions—women are more often full-time parents than are their husbands. Because of the demands of the family, many women have a checkered work career, leaving a job when they have a child and later returning to work, or even staying out of the labor force from the time of first pregnancy until their last child enters school (Schlegel, 1977). During the years that a woman is out of the labor force, her status within the family is low because she has no economic power.

Husbands in families of all social classes have more influence over family decision making than do their wives, but this subordination of the wife seems to be greatest in the lower class and the working class. In the middle class and the upper-middle class, men often verbally agree that family decisions should be made jointly, but they still wield more influence than their wives, in part because many of the important family decisions concern their careers. At all levels of the class system, wives have more power within the family when they have held high-prestige, well-paying jobs for several years (Blood and Wolfe, 1960; Gillespie, 1971). Even when both men and women hold jobs outside the home, it is typically women who do most of the housework and child care. Increasingly men have helped with these tasks, but both they and their wives usually see them as "helping out" around the house rather than as sharing equally in housework and child care (Converse, 1972; Weitz, 1977).

GENDER ROLES AND WORK

About the same proportion of all men work in every society, but there is considerable variation from society to society in the proportion of women who hold jobs outside the home. This reflects both

Increasingly men are taking part in housework and child care, but both they and their wives often see this as just "helping out" rather than as sharing equally in these tasks.

the economic tasks that need to be performed and cultural norms about gender roles. Also, the occupations at which women work differ from one society to another. For example, about twice as many physicians are women in Great Britain, West Germany, France, and Sweden as in the United States.

In 1940 only 27.4 per cent of the total civilian labor force in the United States was female, but by 1981 this figure had increased to 43 per cent. A higher proportion of men than of women work. In 1981, 77 per cent of all men over the age of sixteen were in the civilian labor force, a figure somewhat less than the 83.3 per cent of all men who worked in 1960. However, over this same period the proportion of all women over the age of sixteen who were in the labor force increased from 37.7 per cent to 52.1 per cent. Single women are the most likely of all women to work; 62.3 per cent of them held paid jobs in 1981. In contrast, 41.9 per cent of divorced and widowed women, and 51 per cent of married women with a husband present in the home were working. The married women who were most likely to be working outside the home were those whose children were in school; 62.5 per cent of married women with husbands in the home and whose children were between the ages of six

and seventeen were in the labor force. In contrast, 47.8 per cent of women whose children were under the age of six worked outside the home (U.S. Bureau of the Census, 1982: 375, 377, 382, 383). The fact that nearly half of all married women with husbands in the home and preschool children worked outside the home is a major change from the past, when women in such situations were expected to stay home with their young children. In 1978, nearly three-fourths of all Americans approved of a married woman working outside the home, even if she had a husband who could support her (Cherlin and Walters, 1981). Men have become more accepting of women holding jobs at the same time that women have become more resistant to the idea of stopping work altogether until their children are grown (Komarovsky, 1981).

Women work for much the same reasons as men. Single, divorced, and widowed women work to support themselves, because they usually have no other sources of income. Many married women work because their husbands earn low incomes; the lower her husband's income, the more likely a wife is to hold a job. The belief that inflation has eroded the family's spending power in recent years might explain why some women have taken jobs to pay for basic necessities or for "extras," such as a new car or a vacation. Some women have probably taken jobs as a source of personal fulfillment, but most of the jobs that they hold are not especially fulfilling, as is true of most of the jobs at which men work. Men and women are about equally satisfied with their jobs, which is somewhat surprising because women work at jobs that pay less and have lower prestige (U.S. Bureau of the Census, 1981: 387).

Women are only slightly more likely than men to be unemployed; 7.9 per cent of women in the labor force and 7.4 per cent of men were unable to find a job in 1981. These figures probably underestimate female unemployment, for women may be more likely to give up searching for a job or never to begin looking in the first place because of the low pay and the low prestige of many of the jobs available to them.

Working women earn less than working men. The median income for men eighteen years old and over who worked full-time on a year-round basis in 1981 was $20,708; for females, the median income was only $12,461. Women who worked on a full-time basis throughout the year thus earned only 60 per cent as much as men, a proportion that remained virtually constant over the previous decade (U.S. Bureau of the Census, 1982: 438; U.S. Bureau of the Census, *Money Income and Poverty Status*, July 1982: 15).

Why Do Women Earn Less Than Men?

There are a variety of reasons that women are paid less than men, have less prestigious jobs, and hold less authority. One reason is blatant discrimination: Even with the same educational credentials and the same number of years of experience, women are paid less than men and are given less authority (Treiman and Terrell, 1975; Featherman and Hauser, 1976; U.S. Bureau of the Census, 1982: 146; Lyon et al., 1982). This is partly a result of a cultural belief that a man is the primary "breadwinner" in the family and that a woman's income merely supplements his income (Hoffman and Nye, 1974). Job discrimination also results from the expectation that men will have continuous careers, and that women will be moving into and out of the job market as they have children. These beliefs are used to justify higher pay for men, which of course gives them more financial incentive to stay in their jobs and discourages women from working. These beliefs are also used to limit wom-

en's access to supervisory positions, a restriction that can reduce their commitment to work (Wolf and Fligstein, 1979).

In addition, within occupational categories men and women are paid differently. Men are more likely to hold positions of authority in a company, and these higher positions carry with them higher salaries. The career opportunities of women are also limited because many people—both men and women—do not want to work for a female boss, because women commonly have difficulty developing relationships with mentors who will sponsor their careers, and because women are locked out of the "old-boy network" that is important in being hired for top positions (Kanter, 1977).

Another source of gender inequality in the world of work is job segregation, the concentration of men and women in certain kinds of jobs (Miller and Garrison, 1982). Table 10.2 shows the percentage of all workers who were female in different occupations in 1981. Some jobs are almost exclusively "women's work"; more than 90 per cent of all secretaries, child-care workers, bank tellers, telephone operators, and registered nurses are women. These and other predominantly female occupations usually have low incomes, low prestige, long working hours, and little opportunity for career mobility. In comparison, women constitute only 14.1 per cent of all lawyers and judges, 13.7 per cent of all physicians, and 4.6 per cent of all dentists; these high-prestige occupations provide some of the highest incomes in the country. However, since 1961 some occupations—such as insurance adjuster and real-estate agent—that were once male domains have become increasingly dominated by women (Prial, 1982).

Income inequality between men and women is also due to the loss of seniority by women who leave their jobs to have children and raise them. According to economist Lester Thurow (1981: F2):

The decade between 25 and 35 is when men either succeed or fail. It is the decade when lawyers become partners in the good firms, when business managers make it onto the "fast track," when academics get tenure at good universities, and when blue collar workers find the job opportunities that will lead to training opportunities and the skills that will generate high earnings. . . .

But the decade between 25 and 35 is precisely the decade when women are most apt to leave the labor force or become part-time workers to have children. When they do, the current system of promotion and skill acquisition will extract an enormous lifetime price.

TABLE 10.2
Persons Employed in Selected Occupations,
Percentage Female, 1981

Occupation	Percentage female
Secretaries	99.1
Child-care workers, except private household	95.5
Bank tellers	93.5
Telephone operators	92.9
Registered nurses, dietitians, and therapists	92.6
Waiters	89.3
Billing clerks	88.2
Cashiers	86.2
File clerks	83.8
Elementary school teachers	83.6
Librarians, archivists, and curators	82.8
Sales clerks, retail trade	71.2
Social and recreation workers	62.4
Secondary school teachers	51.3
Real-estate agents and brokers	49.8
Writers, artists, and entertainers	39.8
Bank officers and financial managers	37.5
College and university teachers	35.2
Computer specialists	27.1
Sales managers	26.5
Life and physical scientists	21.9
Stock and bond sales agents	17.0
Post-office mail carriers	15.7
Lawyers and judges	14.1
Physicians, medical and osteopathic	13.7
Precision machine operatives	12.8
Police and detectives	5.7
Dentists	4.6
Engineers	4.4
Truck drivers	2.7
Construction laborers, including carpenters' helpers	2.2
Carpenters	1.9
Electricians	1.6
Automobile mechanics	0.6
Plumbers and pipe fitters	0.4

Source: Adapted from U.S. Bureau of the Census, *Statistical Abstract of the United States, 1982–83.* Washington, D.C.: U.S. Government Printing Office, 1982, pp. 388–390.

Also, many women who reenter the job market after raising children, after a divorce, or after the death of a husband do not have the skills that are needed to get a good job; consequently, they sometimes have to take whatever job they can find, and this is often one with low pay and little prestige.

Because of family demands by both children and husbands, many women take only part-time work; this does not pay as well as a full-time job, nor does it offer benefits or much room for advancement. Part-time jobs and even much of the full-time work that is available to women can make a career an unattractive alternative to a family-centered life, further reinforcing gender inequality in the world of work.

GENDER ROLES AND EDUCATION

Until the 1970s, women had been losing ground relative to men in educational attainment for several decades; since then, they have improved their relative position. Except for the highest levels of education, women are now about equal to men in educational attainment. In spite of differences in the way that they are socialized, women today seem to have educational aspirations much like those of men (Rosen and Aneshensel, 1978), although fewer women actually seek admission to the advanced-degree programs that provide entry into high-paying and high-prestige fields such as medicine and the law (Baird, Clark, and Harnett, 1973; Epstein, 1981).

In 1981 the median number of years of education completed for people twenty-five years old and over was about the same for men and women: 12.6 years for men and 12.4 for women (U.S. Bureau of the Census, 1982: 145). There are also few differences between males and females in college enrollment: In 1981, 50.2 per cent of all college students were females, and 49.8 per cent were males. However, more males finish college and more of them go on to complete graduate degrees, even though the proportion of all master's degrees and doctorates awarded to women has increased since 1965. Also, the enrollment of women in medical schools and law schools has shown a dramatic increase, such that today about one-fourth of all medical students and about one-third of all law students are women. This increase in the enrollment of women in professional degree programs has already produced significant changes in the world of work, as we can see in SEL 10.3.

SOCIOLOGY AND EVERYDAY LIFE 10.3
Women in the Law

Women have made significant gains in recent years in the legal profession. In 1910, only 1.1 per cent of all lawyers were women; by 1970, that figure had climbed to 4.7 per cent. By 1980, however, 12.0 per cent of all lawyers—nearly one in eight—were women. The proportion of all tenure-track law professors who are women has also increased, from only 1.7 per cent in 1967 to 10.5 per cent in 1979. Women are still underrepresented in these jobs in proportion to their numbers in the population, but the steadily climbing numbers of women enrolled in law school promises even more dramatic gains in the near future. In 1963, only 3.8 per cent of all law school students were women, but by 1980 that figure was up to 33.5 per cent. With one law school student in three being a woman, the proportion of lawyers and law professors who are women will continue to increase steadily.

This greater representation of women in the law has come at a time when there is a rapidly increasing number of law school graduates of both sexes competing in a job market that is not expanding as fast as the number of people with law degrees. Many graduates have thus had to take jobs in solo practice rather than in law firms, in business, or for the government. Competition for the high-prestige, well-paid positions is even more intense today than in the past.

There continues to be much stratification by sex in the legal profession. Women are often assigned jobs "ancillary to the dominant and highly visible male legal roles" (p. 104). Women with law degrees often assist senior male lawyers, and they are less likely than men to appear in court. In addition, women are more likely to specialize in trusts, estates, and wills; domestic relations, including divorce and child custody; and real-estate law. These specialties are closely related to traditional gender roles, because they focus on family and home. These specialties are also less lucrative than fields related to business—such as taxation, contracts, and stocks and bonds.

Even those female lawyers who find good jobs as lawyers often encounter sexist attitudes and discriminatory treatment by their male colleagues and by the male judges before whom they appear in court. One lawyer comments:

Some judges call you "young ladies" and do not take you as seriously as they take male lawyers. There's nothing you can put your finger on and it's nothing where I can say I'm being mistreated, but the case may be coming out the wrong way because of it. It is a very unpleasant situation. What I've always found is that when the other people are not taking me seriously, it makes it that much harder for me to take myself seriously (p. 277).

Another female attorney observes:

If you're a woman, you have to make fewer mistakes. . . . A woman must put greater effort into her work . . . because if you make a fool of yourself, you're a damn fool woman instead of just a damn fool (p. 278).

Being treated differently because one is a representative of some larger category—in this case, women—is a common experience for people who must contend with discrimination to gain access to positions higher in the stratification system.

In 1970, female attorneys worked more hours, on the average, than women in other occupations, even though those lawyers worked fewer hours than male lawyers. Women averaged thirty-nine hours a week, and men averaged forty-six. Some of this difference was because women combined work as a lawyer with their role as a mother. The law provides somewhat more flexibility, especially for attorneys who work alone, than do other professions, but keep in mind that these female attorneys still worked a full week by the standards of most jobs. The effort to combine a law career with other roles such as mother or wife sometimes leads women to specialize in areas of the law that do not require courtroom appearances or their presence at the offices of large legal firms. This accounts in part for the lower salaries of female attorneys and for their underrepresentation in the best-paying, highest-prestige jobs. Women who try to combine work as a lawyer with the mother role often find themselves under great pressure:

None of my children was going to be raised by a baby sitter. So I make it my business to be home by three, unless something extraordinary happens. And I try not to go out at night. Of course, if I have to, like with small claims where you just can't fit it all into the day, I work at night. But I try to make it a practice that I work just as a teacher would: between nine and three (p. 365).

Another woman coped with the conflict between her work role and her mother role as follows:

"She rarely stays past 7:00 or 7:30, and then she'll take a cab home. Her baby was three months old when she started and she had a four-year-old. And she's pretty much told the head of her department that she wants to work 9:30 to 6:00, I mean, she's still nursing the baby so she has to be home at night—the baby's on a daytime bottle. But that's a tough schedule to maintain because there are times in most jobs that are demanding, when you do need to stick around—in law a lot more so than in others. But she has been holding so far. She has stayed nights. One night she came back and brought the baby with her."

  "How did they feel about that?"

  "It was funny, several people came to see her in the office, and she had the baby sitting there and they didn't notice it. The baby was sitting in one of those little baby chairs, and she sort of had it on the desk, [pointing] on that side, and she was talking here, and she realized they did not notice the baby. Because the baby was just sitting there being quiet, and I guess was off angle. But it was really funny. One person saw her in the library with the baby and thought she had a doll. Another said to her the next day, 'What were you doing with a doll in the library, Emily?' She said, 'That wasn't a doll, that was my baby.' 'Oh,' he said" (pp. 371–372).

The increased representation of women in the legal profession has important implications. It means that women are gaining access to a high-paying, high-prestige occupation, although the opportunity to become a lawyer is greater for women whose parents are highly educated and earn high incomes than for women from families lower in the stratification system. Many female lawyers have used their professional skills on behalf of other women. Some support the goals of the feminist movement and work to eradicate job discrimination, the unequal treatment of women who apply for loans or credit, and the failure of former husbands to pay child support and alimony. Legal change to equalize the way that men and women are treated will be more likely in the future because of the growing number of women who work as lawyers.

Source: Based on Cynthia Fuchs Epstein, *Women in Law*. New York: Basic Books, 1981.

Women with more education are more likely to work than women with less education; this is probably because higher-paying jobs are available to people who have had more schooling. Women with more education also earn more money than women with less education, even though educated women earn less than men with the same amount of education (see Table 8.3, page 188). Only with the elimination of gender discrimination in hiring, pay, and promotion can the gains of women in education be converted into economic gains.

GENDER ROLES AND POLITICS

Although women were not granted the right to vote until 1920, by 1980 they were very slightly more likely than men to register to vote and to go to the polls (U.S. Bureau of the Census, 1982: 492). In addition to increasing the political participation of women, changing gender roles have in recent years led to "a gender gap" in the party preferences and political attitudes of women and men (see SEL 14.1, page 333). By the late 1970s, women had not yet unified into a powerful voting bloc, but there was evidence that a "women's rights bloc" was a significant force in the 1980 presidential election (Baxter and Lansing, 1981; Friedan, 1981).

In recent years, the position of women in the political system has also improved. Sandra Day O'Connor became the first woman justice of the United States Supreme Court. In addition, more than twice as many women held state and local public offices in 1981 as had in 1975. However, even in 1981 only 12 per cent of all officeholders were women, considerably less than the 51.4 per cent of the population that is female (Baxter and Lansing, 1980; U.S. Bureau of the Census, 1982: 489). Still, there has been an increase in recent years in the willingness of both men and women to say that they would vote for a qualified woman for president, as we can see from Table 10.3. Somewhat surprisingly, the least support for a woman for president is among white women, although nearly four-fifths of them say they would vote for a qualified female for this office.

In recent years the position of women in the political system has improved somewhat, as indicated by the fact that in 1981 Sandra Day O'Connor became the first woman to sit on the U.S. Supreme Court.

TABLE 10.3
"If Your Party Nominated a Woman for President, Would You Vote for Her If She Were Qualified for the Job," Percentage Saying "Yes," 1972–1978

	1972	1978
White men	73%	83%
Black men	77%	82%
White women	72%	79%
Black women	83%	90%

Note: The percentage willing to vote for a woman for president rose slightly from 1937 until the 1950s, stayed about constant from that time until the late 1960s, then increased sharply from 1969 to 1974, and went up slightly from 1974 to 1978.

Source: Andrew Cherlin and Pamela Barnhouse Walters, "Trends in United States Men's and Women's Sex-Role Attitudes: 1972 to 1978," *American Sociological Review* 46 (August 1981): 454–455. Used by permission.

HOW WELL DO TRADITIONAL GENDER ROLES WORK?

Functionalists have emphasized the benefits for society of traditional gender roles, but in recent years feminists and others have argued that this pattern of male dominance and female subordination is dysfunctional for both women and men. Let us examine some of the functions and dysfunctions of traditional gender roles for both men and women.

Consequences of the Female Gender Role

One positive consequence of the traditional female gender role is that because women are expected to express their emotions, they may be less likely to suffer psychosomatic illnesses such as ulcers and high blood pressure. Traditional gender roles also give women some power in the home, such as spending the family's income and rearing the children.

Another benefit of the traditional female gender role is that women are usually protected by the courts in divorce cases. Relatively few men are awarded custody of their children if the mother wishes to keep them. Women are also provided with child support payments and sometimes with alimony from their former husbands, although many men violate court orders to make these payments. Divorce imposes a heavy financial and emotional burden on both men and women. Having custody of children consumes a great deal of the single parent's energy, especially if the person also holds a job. Not having custody causes emotional pain for the parent who is separated from the children. Divorce and separation are also responsible in large part for what has been called "the feminization of poverty" (Pearce, 1978; National Advisory Council on Economic Opportunity, 1980: 17) (see Chapter 8). In 1976, for the first time, more poor people lived in households headed by women than in households in which there was a man present. In that year, one in every three female-headed households was below the poverty level, compared to only one in every eighteen households with a man present. In fact, low pay and expensive child care meant that in 1977 more than one-third of all single mothers who had children under the age of six and who worked full time at some point during the year were still poor (National Advisory Council on Economic Opportunity, 1980: 18).

The traditional female gender role is dysfunctional for women in a variety of other ways. Even if married women do spend the income earned by their husbands, it is the men who have the power to deny their wives money. Women who do not work outside the home are often isolated and receive little positive feedback from others for their efforts to raise children and clean house. In addition, when their children are grown and gone from the home, women who have been invested in the mother role may no longer have a source of personal satisfaction if they do not hold a job. Women who behave according to traditional gender stereotypes are often passive and dependent, traits that can be associated with low self-esteem and a sense of incompetence. As a result, when they first work outside the home, many of these women settle for jobs for which they are overqualified and even then they sometimes lack confidence that they can perform as expected. Employment does, however, provide women with rewards that are missing from the traditional homemaker role; and work can alleviate some of the stress associated with the traditional female role and provide emotional benefits (Kessler and McRae, 1981, 1982; Albin, 1981).

When women are employed outside the home, their work is often seen by their husbands, their bosses, and even themselves as temporary and supplementary to the family budget, rather than as part of a long-term career to which they are committed. Highly educated women with career aspirations often find this attitude especially difficult to contend with. In addition, gender stereotypes cause some men to treat women in sexual terms; for instance, women might be hired and promoted partly on the basis of their attractiveness rather than their competence. This institutional sexism can even lead some women who succeed solely on the basis of merit to question the reasons for their success.

Consequences of the Male Gender Role

For men, the male gender role in American society has many positive consequences, as well as a number of costs. Men earn higher incomes than women with the same education, training, and experience; this means, however, that the total family income of two-worker households is less than it would be if there were no pay discrimination against women. Because men are more likely to work than women, they have more opportunities to receive positive evaluations from others about their skills and talents, but they are also more open to criticism by others. Men gain from having women available as a temporary and inexpensive source of labor. Married men benefit from traditional gender roles because their wives do most of the menial housework and child care, even if their wives are working. In addition, men hold most of the political offices in federal, state, and local governments.

There are also several dysfunctions, or negative aspects, to the traditional male role. Many jobs that men hold are not fulfilling, and are instead seen by them as drudgery and "just a way to make a living." When men lose a job or fail to get a promotion, they may lose self-esteem, for work is an important part of their gender identity. Men also experience stress because of the socially imposed responsibility to support their wives and children. Because their jobs are seen as essential rather than optional, any setback in the world of work can have profound consequences for their self-image.

Another dysfunction of the traditional male role is that men have less time to spend with their children and less influence in their children's socialization. Also, men are rarely given custody of their children in a divorce case, even though this can be seen as functional in permitting them to devote time and energy to their careers.

The male role is dysfunctional in still another way: Competitiveness and ambition can limit the opportunity for close friendships with other men, who are seen as potential rivals in the areas of work and romance (Lewis, 1978; Pleck and Brannon, 1978; Pleck, 1980). Because men are taught to conceal their emotions, they have fewer ways to express their feelings than do women. This is probably linked to the greater frequency of certain diseases among men than among women, including ulcers, heart disease, and cirrhosis of the liver (which is usually associated with alcoholism) (U.S. Bureau of the Census, 1982: 77). American men have higher rates of alcoholism and drug addiction than do American women, although women are probably addicted to prescription drugs such as barbiturates more often. Men also have a suicide rate that is about three times that of women, and they commit many more violent crimes.

Men have a lower life expectancy than women; in 1980, the average life expectancy of a newborn male was 69.8 years, compared to 77.5 for women (U.S. National Center for Health Statistics, 1981). Some of this difference can be attributed to biological factors, for men die younger than women in every society. However, differences in gender-role behavior are probably more important in accounting for this difference in life expectancy. In fact, one estimate is that "three-fourths of the difference in life expectancy can be accounted for by sex-role related behaviors which contribute to the greater mortality of men'' (Harrison, 1978: 81).

Men seem to need marriage more than women. Widowers are more likely to die within a few years of their wives' deaths than are men of the same age who remain married. Widowers who remarry tend to live longer, on the average, than widowers who do not remarry. Widows do not, however, show a greater tendency to die within a few years of their husbands' deaths than do women whose husbands remain alive. Apparently, men have more of a need for a spouse to maintain their quality of life and to remind them to seek medical care when they are ill (Greenberg, 1981). Other evidence suggests that men gain more in mental health from marriage and suffer more from the breakup of a marriage than do women (Gove and Tudor, 1973).

Recent changes in traditional gender roles have caused stress in both men and women. Access to a variety of models of gender roles, rather than the single traditional model that was dominant for years, has produced anxiety and confusion. Men are sometimes uncertain about how to respond to women. For instance, if a man holds open a door for a woman, some women might regard him as sexist; if he fails to hold open a door, more traditional women might regard him as rude (Walum, 1974). Some men complain that women expect them to be dominant and yet sensitive, strong and yet vulnerable. These contradictory expectations are confusing to some men, even though few of them are aware of the source of their confusion (Komarovsky, 1976). Anxiety over contradictory role expectations also exists among women. Changes in gender roles are often beneficial to women (as well as to men), but these changes may require women to take more individual responsibility for deciding how to act; in the past, it was more acceptable to rely on traditional gender roles and members of the opposite sex for guidance. Only change will reduce the dysfunctions of traditional gender roles, but the process of developing new gender roles can be stressful for both men and women.

Changing Gender Roles: The Feminist Movement

Equal rights for American women were first sought by the suffragette movement of the early twentieth century. The suffragettes were women who demanded citizenship rights equal to those of men; they did not seek broad changes in traditional gender roles. They won the right to vote in 1920, a half century after blacks were enfranchised.

During World War II, women for the first time took factory jobs in large numbers, replacing men who were in the military. After the war, most of these women quit their jobs and returned to the home. In the 1950s, the mass media—including television, women's magazines, and the movies—resocialized women to accept the traditional roles of wife and mother.

The possibility of equal rights for women caused anxiety as far back as a century ago—as we can see from this illustration that appeared in one 1868 issue of **Harper's Weekly.**

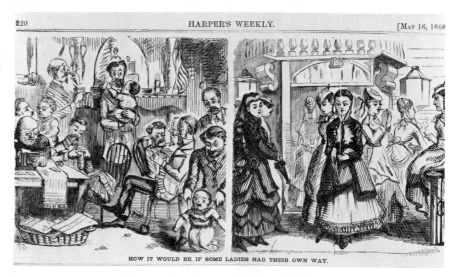

SOURCES OF THE FEMINIST MOVEMENT

Several changes during the 1960s spurred the development of the modern feminist movement, an organized effort to achieve a higher status for women. In 1961, the President's Commission on the Status of Women documented the subordinate status of women in the United States, focusing on the discrimination they suffered in the area of work. Soon after this report was made public, many states established similar investigative panels that also issued reports. All of this activity added to a growing public awareness of the disadvantaged position of women in the stratification system. These reports produced legislative change, including the Equal Pay Act of 1963 and the Civil Rights Act of 1964, which guaranteed equal employment opportunities to women as well as to minority groups. The federal and state commissions also gave the women who worked on them an opportunity to communicate directly, often for the first time, with other women who shared their commitment to social change.

The black civil rights movement of the 1950s and 1960s provided a model to follow in organizing for change. In addition, women who had been active in the civil rights movement applied their knowledge and skill at organizing to the feminist movement. Other factors also contributed to the emergence of this movement. The development of the birth-control pill opened the way for a public discussion of sexuality and led to a reevaluation of gender differences in sexuality. The pill's effectiveness as a method of birth control and other social forces lowered the birth rate, freeing many women from child-bearing and child-rearing, and causing them to search for new sources of personal satisfaction in the feminist movement and in the world of work (Mandle, 1979). During this period, a high divorce rate and a tendency to delay marriage until later in life provided additional impetuses for women to take jobs outside the home; their new work roles probably led many of them to become more concerned with feminist issues.

In 1966 the National Organization for Women (NOW) was formed; its goals included equal pay for equal work, childbirth leaves for working women, and nondiscriminatory hiring and promotion practices. Informal "consciousness-raising groups" were also formed in many communities across the country to give women a forum to share their experiences and to examine the effects of traditional gender roles on their lives. These groups took what had been perceived previously as personal problems and reconceptualized them as social issues (Freeman, 1973). These groups encouraged women to think of themselves as people with common interests that could be pursued through lobbying activities and legislative change. Participants in these consciousness-raising groups and members of NOW and similar organizations tended to be young, white, educated, middle- and upper-middle-class women who did not hold strong religious beliefs (Dempewolff, 1974).

EFFECTS OF THE FEMINIST MOVEMENT

One goal of the feminist movement has been to eliminate or to minimize gender stereotypes that are taught to boys and girls through the socialization process. Feminists have pointed to sexism in the mass media and have applied pressure to portray men and women in nonstereotypical ways, although gender stereotypes continue to dominate the media. Traditional gender roles have also been attacked by conscious efforts to alter the English language, which uses masculine pronouns to refer to both males and females and which uses masculine terms for occupations and roles—such as "fireman" and "chairman"—that may be filled by either men or women.

Feminists have focused attention on the physical abuse of women by men. They have drawn public attention to the pervasive use of violence by husbands against their wives. Shelters have been established to house battered wives who have been forced out of their homes. In addition, feminists have drawn the attention of the press and the public to rape. Rape is experienced by the victim as a brutal act of violence and domination, not as a sexual act, and feminists have brought that fact to light (Griffin, 1971; Brownmiller, 1975; Holmstrom and Burgess, 1983). Lobbying by feminists has changed rape laws in many states; one change has been to limit the defense attorney's right to question the rape victim about her past sexual behavior during the trial of an alleged rapist. Feminists have also been responsible for the development of support services for rape victims in hospitals and for more considerate treatment of these women by the police. Rape has been a major concern of feminists because they see it as having the effect of intimidating all women by keeping them in a continuous state of fear (Brownmiller, 1975: 15).

Gender discrimination in the world of work has been another major issue for the feminist move-

Many women worked for passage of the Equal Rights Amendment. However, others felt that it would deprive them of traditional privileges and protections such as alimony and exemption from military service.

ment. Legal action has been brought against employers for their unequal treatment of women, and a number of sizable awards have been won in these cases. Feminists have also been concerned with sexual harassment on the job. This usually takes the form of "blackmail" in which women are threatened with the loss of a job, a promotion, or pay if they do not engage in sex with a man who has authority over them. A few cases have also arisen of females harassing males in this way, but because men hold most of the positions of power in the economic system, the sexual harassment of women has been much more common.

The most ambitious effort at legal change was the Equal Rights Amendment to the Constitution, which was passed by Congress in 1972 but was finally defeated in 1982 when it fell three states short of ratification. This proposed Amendment stated: "Equality of rights under the law shall not be denied or abridged by the United States or by any State on account of sex." A sample of Americans that was asked about their attitudes toward this proposed Amendment shortly before its defeat favored it overwhelmingly: 73 per cent supported

it, 22 per cent opposed it, and 5 per cent were unsure (Harris poll, cited in *National NOW Times,* 1982). However, the proposed ERA encountered effective and organized opposition from groups that felt it would deprive women of certain privileges and protections, such as alimony and exemption from military service, and would erode the position of men in the stratification system.

Only since the early 1960s has a national policy on women been developed "to favor legal equality of rights and protection for men and women" (Richardson, 1981: 266). Today, women cannot legally be discriminated against in hiring or pay, or in eligibility for bank loans or credit. Gender discrimination in education has been prohibited by law since 1972; violations can result in the withholding of funds by the federal government. In 1973, the Supreme Court legalized abortion, although the right of a woman to terminate a pregnancy continues to be a source of controversy. In many other areas women have only recently been treated as equal to men: They became eligible for Rhodes scholarships in 1976, gained the right to have their name listed with their husband's in telephone books in 1977, became eligible to be astronauts in 1978, and gained the right to have pregnancy treated as a normal disability covered by workers' insurance in 1979 (O'Reilly, 1982).

Recently some feminists have suggested that continued change in gender roles will require the active effort of both men and women, and an increased attention to family roles as well as to work roles (Friedan, 1981, 1983). As one active supporter of the ERA observed shortly after the defeat of that proposed Amendment, "True equality will not occur until our sons, as well as our daughters, wonder how they can best manage to combine a career and family" (O'Reilly, 1982: 21).

Summary

Gender roles are a pervasive aspect of social life, and they are closely associated with the stratification of society. Although men tend to have greater access than women to the rewards of property, prestige, and power in all societies, the expectations of how males and females should behave are not linked to sex in the same way in all societies. Gender roles show considerable variation cross-culturally and over time within the same society. Indeed, consciously designed social policies have altered gender roles in significant ways over short periods of time in many industrial societies, including the United States.

Closely linked to gender roles are gender stereotypes, those exaggerated and simplified ideas about what constitutes masculine or feminine behavior. These stereotypes are part of a sexist ideology that is used to justify the dominant position of one sex in the stratification system. Gender stereotypes and gender roles are learned through socialization. This begins with the preference of expectant parents for boys, and it continues with their differential treatment of boys and girls. Parents play more roughly with their sons and are more openly affectionate with their daughters; they dress their children differently, and they give them toys and books that they think are "appropriate" for boys and girls.

Peer groups contribute to gender socialization, as do teachers who hold different expectations for boys and girls and praise them for gender-appropriate behavior. Throughout the life cycle, the mass media reinforce traditional gender stereotypes through fictional portrayals of men and women and through the use of "genderisms" to sell products.

One major change in gender roles in the United States in recent years has been a dramatic increase in the participation of women in the labor force. Women continue to earn less than men, however. They are discriminated against in hiring, pay, and promotion to positions of authority, despite federal laws to prohibit this. Women also do "women's work"—jobs that pay less, have lower prestige, and require longer hours of work than jobs in which most workers are men. Because of the expectations that women will care for young children, women are more likely than men to quit work and to stay home to raise children. This typically happens during those years when most workers are promoted to positions of authority and build up their salaries through seniority. Women have recently made some gains in advanced-degree educational programs such as medicine and the law, and they have been increasingly elected to public office. However, these gains still leave them behind men in their control of resources such as property, prestige, and power.

Traditional gender roles have both positive and negative consequences for men and women. The dysfunctions of traditional gender roles for women have been the basis of efforts by the feminist movement and others to press for change. American women have indeed gained greater equality under the law in recent years; but unless these legal rights are enforced, women and men will still not have equal access to social rewards, and gender stratification will continue to be an important aspect of society.

Important Terms

GENDER (221)
GENDER IDENTITY (221)
GENDER ROLE (221)

INSTITUTIONAL SEXISM (229)
SEX (221)
SEXISM (229)

Suggested Readings

Rae Lesser Blumberg. *Stratification: Socioeconomic and Sexual Inequality.* Dubuque, Iowa: William C. Brown, 1978. A brief but lucid treatment of gender stratification.

Rosabeth Moss Kanter. *Men and Women of the Corporation*. New York: Basic Books, 1977. An influential exploration of women and men in one kind of work setting.

Marcia Millman and Rosabeth Moss Kanter, eds. *Another Voice: Feminist Perspectives on Social Life and Social Science*. Garden City, N. Y.: Anchor Press/Doubleday, 1975. A collection of interesting papers on a variety of aspects of the sociology of gender roles.

Joseph H. Pleck and Robert Brannon, eds. "Male Roles and the Male Experience," a special issue of *Journal of Social Issues* 34 (No. 1, 1978). A wide-ranging collection of papers on various aspects of the changing male gender role in American society.

Laura Walum Richardson. *The Dynamics of Sex and Gender: A Sociological Perspective*, 2nd ed. Boston: Houghton Mifflin, 1981. A comprehensive and well-written textbook on the sociology of gender.

Jean Stockard and Miriam M. Johnson. *Sex Roles: Sex Inequality and Sex Role Development*. Englewood Cliffs, N. J.: Prentice-Hall, 1980. Another recent textbook covering aspects of gender stratification.

Gaye Tuchman, Arlene Kaplan Daniels, and James Benét, eds. *Health & Home: Images of Women in the Mass Media*. New York: Oxford University Press, 1978. A fascinating collection of papers on how women are presented on television, in magazines, and in newspapers.

Shirley Weitz. *Sex Roles: Biological, Psychological, and Social Foundations*. New York: Oxford University Press, 1977. A multidisciplinary review of research on gender roles.

part IV
MAJOR SOCIAL INSTITUTIONS

In an earlier section of the book, we looked at social structure and briefly at the institutions that are part of that structure. In the next six chapters, we focus on those institutions.

Chapter 11 deals with a universal social arrangement, the family. In every society the family fulfills basic social needs, even though interaction within families can be characterized by conflict. We look at the forms that the family takes in different societies and investigate marriage and divorce in the United States. This chapter also considers alternatives to the nuclear family.

Chapter 12 looks at elementary and secondary schools in the United States, focusing on the organization of the school, teacher–student interaction, and "grade inflation." This chapter also looks at higher education in two- and four-year colleges. The chapter concludes with an examination of the relationship between education and social inequality.

Chapter 13 deals with the components and functions of the institution of religion. Three contrasting interpretations of the relationship between religion and the economic system are presented. Then religious values and participation in religion in the United States are examined. The chapter concludes with a discussion of recent changes in religion.

The political system is the focus of Chapter 14. Power and the various sources of authority are explored, and the functionalist and conflict perspectives on the state are compared. Political participation in the United States is also examined. The chapter concludes by contrasting three models of political power.

Next we deal with the legal system. Chapter 15 looks at the social origins and consequences of the law, examining closely the police, lawyers, and the courts. Then the chapter compares four justifications for punishment—retribution, deterrence, incapacitation, and rehabilitation.

The final chapter in this section focuses on the economic system. We examine various kinds of economic systems, including those that rely on hunting animals for subsistence and those that have become postindustrial societies. Capitalism and socialism are compared, and the importance of corporations in the capitalist system is examined. In conclusion, we look at work and leisure in industrial societies.

THE FAMILY

In 1950, seven of every ten households in the United States were "Norman Rockwell families," consisting of a full-time working father, a stay-at-home mother, and at least one school-age child. Three decades later, only one household in seven fits this pattern (Yankelovich, 1981). This change was due to factors that we examine in this chapter, including increasing rates of divorce, illegitimacy, and later marriages by young adults. In addition, changes in the law and court actions have altered the American family in a variety of ways. In Connecticut, parents and their children can actually divorce each other; in 1980, more than one hundred parents and teenagers legally ended their family responsibilities to each other (Henry, 1981). A Pennsylvania judge allowed a twenty-three-year-old woman to change her family name and be adopted by a couple not related to her, in spite of objections by her parents. A New York City justice let one adult homosexual man legally adopt another. A woman in California won the right to prevent her husband from giving their children his surname. Grandparents in Pennsylvania won custody of a fourteen-year-old girl in a court fight with the girl's parents (Castillo, 1981). Although such cases are unusual, they show that family relationships are in a state of flux in the United States. Indeed, changes as significant as these even raise the question: What is a family?

What Is a Family?

In every society, social norms define a variety of relationships among people, and some of these relationships are socially recognized as family or kinship ties. A *family* is a socially defined set of relationships between at least two people who are related by birth, marriage, or adoption. We can think of a family as including several possible relationships, the most common being between husband and wife, between parents and children, and between people who are related to each other by birth (siblings, for example) or by marriage (a woman and her mother-in-law, perhaps). Family relationships are often defined by custom, such as the relationship between an infant and godparents, or by law, such as the adoption of a child.

The family is a social institution. Social norms define its relationships, even those that have some biological bond, such as between parent and child. The members of a family usually have mutual obligations and rights, and they enjoy intimacy not shared with outsiders. The members of a family often live together, or at least near each other. Husband and wife are usually expected to have sexual relations, and they typically look after and socialize their offspring. In most societies the family is also an economic unit involved in production, consumption, or both.

According to one survey of 250 societies, the institution of the family exists in all societies (Murdock, 1949). However, this conclusion has been challenged. The Nayar of India have households that typically consist of a man, his sister, and her children by various sexual partners. The woman is wed to a man before she has children, but this marriage lasts only a few days, after which she takes other partners. She lives with her brother, who cares for her children. This household unit differs from some conceptions of the family, because the adults do not have sexual relations and because socialization is done by the mother and her brother, rather than by the child's biological parents. Still, if we define the family as a union between a man and a woman and the children who are born to the woman, the family does exist among the Nayar (Gough, 1961).

Another commonly cited exception to the universality of the family is the Israeli *kibbutz*, a farming collective in which children live apart from their parents and are socialized by all the adults of the *kibbutz*. Children on the *kibbutz* visit regularly with their parents, and the family has remained strong in spite of some efforts to weaken it. Another effort to weaken family ties occurred in the Soviet Union after the Communist Revolution of 1917. The new government sought to lessen the influence of the family so as to free women for industrial work and to resocialize Russians to a new ideology. Child-care institutions were created, and the "bourgeois family" was attacked as an institution inappropriate to a socialist society. These efforts to weaken the family were abandoned after a while, and the family is a strong institution in the Soviet Union today.

The Nayar arrangement and the Israeli *kibbutz* do not disprove the claim that the institution of the family is present in every society, for these groups with "nontraditional" family relationships function within larger societies rather than as autonomous social systems. With the exception of the Nayar and a few other isolated tribal groups, the only societies without "traditional" families or with very weak families have been those that sought deliberately to eliminate the family. These planned efforts, which are usually based on an ideology that is incompatible with the continued existence of the family, have not succeeded over the long term, with a structure much like the traditional family eventually reemerging.

Functions of the Family

In preindustrial societies, the family serves a variety of functions. It is the basic economic unit of production and consumption; it socializes the young; it is the center of political power; it enforces norms and laws; and it is the source of religious beliefs. In industrial societies, the family surrenders some of these functions to the economic system, the school, the political system, the legal system, and organized religion. Even though the family serves fewer functions in modern societies, it still maintains a set of complex relationships with these other institutions. For example, parents influence the nature and quality of the education that their children receive in public schools. They also maintain links to the political system by voting and by being informed on public issues that affect family life, such as taxation policy and public assistance. In modern society, the family is not the all-encompassing institution that it is in traditional society, but it does retain certain basic functions.

REGULATION OF SEXUAL CONDUCT

All societies have norms that dictate the kinds of sexual behavior that are tolerated and expected. Married couples are generally expected to have sexual relations. Most societies also have norms that tolerate or even support premarital and extramarital sex under certain circumstances (Murdock, 1949). Premarital sex is tolerated in many societies to help the young prepare for marriage, to test the compatibility of potential spouses, and to determine fertility. In all societies sexual behavior is linked to marriage, because pregnancy out of wedlock confuses lines of descent, inheritance, and kinship relationships. Sex is commonly associated with reproduction, but sex can also be treated as a source of pleasure and not merely of offspring. The norms that link marital sex to reproduction are often reinforced by religious beliefs and by laws against adultery, premarital sex, and illegitimacy. In fact, in 1982 the Catholic Church for a time refused to marry a paralyzed man who was unable to have sexual intercourse; the man claimed that love and understanding were the essential components of marriage, but a priest felt that the absence of sex from a marriage violated "the law of nature" (S. Cohen, 1982).

REPRODUCTION

Although the expectation that married couples will produce children might be weakening in advanced industrial societies such as the United States, this norm still exists in most societies. Rules of legitimacy, which assign children to parents who have the responsibility to care for and socialize them, give reproduction—a biological fact—a social meaning (Malinowski, 1930, 1964). Children are usually regarded as legitimate if their biological parents are married by the time of their birth, but not necessarily at the time of their conception.

Because it provides a setting for reproduction to occur, the family ensures the survival of society. Most societies could not survive solely on the basis of immigration, the other major way to recruit new members. The reproductive function of the family is important everywhere, but it is somewhat less important in industrial societies than in traditional ones. The lower birth rate of industrial societies means that fewer children are born and that mar-

One of the functions of the family is to ensure the survival of the society through reproduction.

ried couples spend a smaller proportion of their lives raising children. Effective methods of birth control enable couples to determine the number and the timing of the children they have, making reproduction more and more a rationally planned event and less likely to be seen as beyond a couple's control. The low death rate in modern societies and the heavy use of the world's resources by the citizens of the world's industrial societies also make a low birth rate desirable (see Chapter 17). As a result, it is increasingly acceptable for a married couple in industrial society to have few children or even remain childless.

ASSIGNMENT OF STATUS

Another function of the family is to assign newborn children to a position in the social structure. This function is closely associated with the rules of legit-

imacy, because children are given a position that is based on the status of their parents. That is, children are socially recognized as members of their parents' ethnic group, religion, and social class. When they become adults, they may cease to identify with the ethnic group, change their religion, or move upward or downward in the class system, but they tend to carry into adulthood the traits they are assigned at birth, which influence their life chances and opportunities.

PROTECTION AND EMOTIONAL SUPPORT

Humans differ from other animals in that children are unable to survive apart from adults for several years, whereas the offspring of lower animals can live independently of their parents shortly after birth. Because of this extended period of dependence, the family serves the important function of caring for young children (Gough, 1971). Families provide the basic necessities of food, shelter, and clothing; care for the young when sick; and protect the young from harm by outsiders. They also look after the elderly and the infirm, although this function is less important in industrial societies than in preindustrial ones.

The family provides the physical closeness and enduring interaction needed to develop intimacy, the sense of being emotionally close to other people. Although the search for variety is one aspect of the sex drive, there is also a strong tendency to seek emotional attachment to a partner in a long-term relationship. There is a need to feel that another person cares and that one's life has a purpose greater than self-gratification. In the intimacy of family relationships, people support one another and share things they might conceal from strangers, casual acquaintances, or even friends. The family provides an emotional refuge from the outside world.

SOCIALIZATION

Parents are expected to transmit the culture of their society to their children and to make them fully socialized members of society. They are motivated to socialize their children because they have learned to see them as extensions of themselves and to feel that their children's behavior reflects on them as parents. Parents mold their children by interacting with them and by surveillance of their behavior. Children learn how to behave by being rewarded and punished for their behavior and by imitating their parents' behavior. For the young to be properly socialized, it is essential that their parents give them emotional support so that when they grow up they are able to have nurturing and loving relationships with others (Reiss, 1965).

THE ECONOMIC FUNCTION

The family is also a unit of economic production and consumption. In preindustrial societies, the family is relatively self-sufficient, performing all economic tasks necessary to its own survival. In complex, industrialized societies, the family shares its economic function with other institutions. In industrial society, production is relocated from the home to the factory, but the family remains important for the consumption of goods and services.

In every family there is a division of labor among the members so that certain tasks can be accomplished. In industrial societies, women have traditionally cared for the home and the young, men have worked outside the home, and children have usually performed no economically productive function, one reason why the birth rate tends to be lower in industrial societies. However, as we saw in Chapter 10, in many advanced industrial societies large numbers of women work outside the home, even though they usually continue to bear most of the responsibility for housework and child care.

Conflict in the Family

The family rarely runs as smoothly as suggested by a functionalist analysis of the institution. Conflict theorists suggest that patterns of dominance in the family—which they claim exploits women and children—mirror the social relationships of capitalist economies. In addition, studies of the family have drawn attention to problems such as spouse-beating and child abuse.

CONFLICT THEORY AND THE FAMILY

In *The Communist Manifesto* and later in a study of the origin of the family and private property, Marx and Engels (1848, 1967; 1884, 1972) attacked the family in capitalist society. They regarded the bourgeois family as based on private gain; they called for its elimination, and suggested that it would vanish when capitalism was overthrown by the proletariat. Marx and Engels pointed to the exploitation of children, especially working-class children, who were treated as "simple articles of commerce and instruments of labor" (Marx and Engels, 1848, 1967: 101). They claimed that the capitalist class treated women as property and used them as mere instruments of production. In addition, inequality in capitalist society was reinforced through the inheritance of wealth by children of capitalists (Engels, 1884, 1972; Collins, 1974).

In capitalist society the economy and the family are separate institutions, but conflict theorists suggest that the two institutions are closely intertwined. The rise of industrial capitalism separated factory work from the family and led to a search for personal identity outside the world of work. This heightened the oppression of women, who were assigned responsibility for maintaining the home as "a private refuge from an impersonal society" (Zaretsky, 1976: 10).

One conflict theorist (Sokoloff, 1980: 134–137) suggests that unpaid labor by women in the home is used against them when they enter the labor force. The value of their labor is reduced by the presumed prior claim on their efforts by their husbands and children. Employers sometimes assert that women are more likely to be late, absent, or unreliable because their family obligations take precedence over their obligations at work. Also, the jobs that women have tended to hold are sometimes seen as appropriate because of their similarity to domestic work, and so they are hired for "women's work" that does not pay well or have much prestige. In addition, the idea that men are the chief breadwinners of the family, and thus need the best jobs, is used to force women into low-paying, low-prestige jobs.

The separation of the family from the world of work produced the belief that the family would be a haven from the harsh reality of the economic system. However, in capitalist societies even the private realm of family life has not been free of capitalist enterprise, as Christopher Lasch (1979: xx–xxi) points out:

The history of modern society, from one point of view, is the assertion of social control over activities once left to individuals or their families. During the first stage of the industrial revolution, capitalists took production out of the household and collectivized it, under their own supervision, in the factory. Then they proceeded to appropriate the workers' skills and technical knowledge, by means of "scientific management," and to bring these skills together under managerial direction. Finally they extended their control over the worker's private life as well, as doctors, psychiatrists, teachers, child guidance experts, officers of the juvenile courts, and other specialists began to supervise child-rearing, formerly the business of the family.

Even leisure, formerly a private realm, became subject to the quest for profits as a large "leisure industry" emerged. Some institutions, such as the school and the government, actively sought to undo the effects of the family on children; for example, the schools in the United States tried to "Americanize" new immigrants. Between 1900 and 1930, "society in the guise of a 'nurturing mother' invaded the family . . . and took over many of its functions" (Lasch, 1979: 18). This ideology of social welfare undermined the ability of the family to provide for itself and justified the expansion of social services.

The opening paragraph of this chapter indicates just a few of the ways that another institution, the legal system, has intruded on the traditional family in recent years.

VIOLENCE IN THE FAMILY

Conflict in the family sometimes erupts into violence, and indeed most interpersonal violence in the United States occurs between family members (Straus, Gelles, and Steinmetz, 1979). Disputes often center on differences in authority between husband and wife and between parent and child. Although much of the violence is criminal, most of it is never recorded by the police because they have no access to the privacy of the home and because family members and neighbors do not report most assaults to the police.

Child Abuse

Child abuse is harm that parents or other caretakers inflict on children; it includes physical and emotional abuse, sexual abuse, neglect, and abandonment (Martin and Walters, 1982). Sometimes it is difficult to distinguish between child abuse and discipline; for instance, spanking a child can be seen as physical abuse, and sending a child to his or her room can be interpreted as emotional deprivation.

In most cases, child abuse is legally an assault, an aggravated assault if there is intent to cause bodily injury, or even murder or manslaughter if the child dies. However, few parents are prosecuted successfully in criminal court for child abuse, because it is difficult to prove criminal assault against a child. Often both parents will say that the harm was accidental, even if it was obviously inflicted; for example, a child with cigarette burns all over his or her body has clearly been abused and is not the victim of an accident. Laws now require professionals such as physicians, nurses, and social workers to report incidents of suspected child abuse to criminal justice agencies; these laws also protect professionals from legal action by the child's parents.

Child abuse not only harms children in the short run, but it can cause physical or emotional damage that lasts a lifetime. Children who are abused are more aggressive than children who are not. Abused children are also likely to grow up to be abusive parents, for they use the child-rearing practices they learned as children to deal with their own children (Owens and Straus, 1975; Reed, 1975; Straus, Gelles, and Steinmetz, 1979).

Violence against Spouses

Most murders and assaults occur between people who know each other. About one-sixth of all murders—nearly 4,000 deaths in the United States in 1981 (Webster, 1982)—are the result of family violence. There is no way to tell with any accuracy how many nonlethal assaults between spouses are not reported to the police. One study found that wives assaulted their husbands almost as often as husbands attacked wives, but that wives were more likely to be injured during such fights (Straus, 1978). In an effort to curb domestic violence, some police departments have specialized teams to answer calls about family arguments, with each officer on the team taking one spouse into a separate room for counseling (Bard, 1970).

One reason for the high rate of family violence is that intimate ties are emotionally intense. Because there is much interaction within the family, there is also much opportunity for interaction to turn violent; violence is uncommon between people who rarely interact. Because husbands and wives usually feel bound to each other, they may feel there is no escape from their problems. Indeed, serious violence is greatest against married women who are economically dependent on their husbands; in these families, women see few alternatives to marriage (Kalmuss and Straus, 1982).

Violence in the family is partly a product of the absence of effective external controls over domestic behavior. Neighbors tend not to interfere because they do not want to alienate one another and because they fear retaliation if they report domestic violence to the police. When the police are called to the scene of a family dispute by a spouse or a child, they often receive little cooperation; wives sometimes call the police but refuse to take legal action against their husbands. Men are less likely than women to call the police about family disputes, probably because of gender-role expectations that they should settle family arguments on their own.

The Structure of the Family

There are major differences in the way that the family is organized from one society to the next. One way that family systems differ is in the number of kin who are defined as members of the family. Another is that some family systems allow more than one husband or wife. Other sources of variation include the place where a newly married couple lives, how the line of descent is traced from one generation to the next, and who holds authority within the family.

FORMS OF THE FAMILY

An *extended family* consists of a husband and a wife, their children, the parents of one or both spouses, and possibly the brothers, sisters, nephews, and nieces of the spouses. An extended family includes members of more than two generations, and often they all live under one roof or very near one another. Extended families are based primarily on blood ties, although marriage does bring outsiders into the family. Extended families are functional in economic systems in which each additional person is an asset in a collective enterprise, for example, in fishing or agricultural societies.

The term "extended family" is applied to families that encompass more than a *nuclear family*, a unit composed of a married couple and their children. Nuclear families exist within a broader network of kinship ties, but in an extended family system the family itself is defined to include kin in addition to the husband, the wife, and their children. Nuclear families exist in very simple economic systems such as hunting and gathering societies, in which economic tasks require geographical mobility and individual initiative. Nuclear families are also typical of industrial societies, where mobility and initiative are valued (Nimkoff and Middleton, 1960; Winch and Blumberg, 1968).

When the nuclear family is the predominant form, a spouse's primary loyalty is to the other spouse rather than to blood relatives. The nuclear family that is created when a couple marries is referred to as the "family of procreation," suggesting that the married couple will produce children. In contrast, the "family of orientation" is the family into which a person is born and in which socialization takes place. Nuclear family systems stress the family of procreation; extended family systems place more emphasis on the family of orientation.

The Nuclear Family in Industrial Society

The structure of the typical family in industrial societies has changed over the past two centuries; the typical family is smaller than in preindustrial societies, and the nuclear family is the predominant form. Large families were more common in agricultural societies, and children helped with the farmwork at an early age. Because children do not serve as laborers in industrial societies, the average size of the family is smaller in these societies. In addition, industrialization has brought with it a lower death rate (see Chapter 17), which means that fewer children have had to be produced so that some survive to adulthood.

Actually, in many Western societies, most people have lived in nuclear families for the past few centuries. Because of high death rates in preindustrial societies, three-generation households were relatively uncommon even then, for people often died before their offspring could grow up and have children of their own. Furthermore, the relatively low standard of living in the past meant that many houses were too small to accommodate three generations. As far back as the sixteenth century most people in England, France, and the United States lived in nuclear families rather than in extended families (Coale et al., 1965; Laslett, 1972, 1973; Wells, 1974; Bane, 1976).

Industrialization weakens the family in several ways. Workers earn income from employment by a factory owner, rather than from land that is owned jointly by the family; as a result, individuals, rather than families as units, receive financial rewards. In addition, employers in industrial societies have little stake in the worker's family life, and this enables them to make demands on the worker's time and require a strong commitment to the job. Industrial employers commonly fail to help workers' families that are in crisis, ignore the wife's contribution at home, do not provide child care so that both spouses can work, and demand that a worker move in order to take a different job (Goode, 1982).

With industrialization have come new social institutions and a growth in the importance of existing institutions (Smelser, 1959; Goode, 1963). The emergence of institutions such as the school, the legal system, the state, and organized religion limits the functions of the family. Thus the family, having fewer functions to perform, has become simpler and smaller.

The nuclear family is compatible with industrial society, but the Industrial Revolution did not produce the nuclear family. It existed in Europe and North America well before industrialization, and it is common today in societies that have not yet industrialized. One effect of industrialization, however, has been to move work from the home to the factory, requiring at least one member of the family to take a job outside the home. Career advancement often requires workers to be geographically mobile. The simple family structure of the nuclear family is conducive to geographic mobility, in that it is easier to move with a spouse and children than to uproot an extended family. The nuclear family is well suited to an industrial economy that hires people on the basis of skills and educational credentials rather than on the basis of an ascribed status derived from their family of orientation. In an extended family system, obligations to kin might require that a particular person be hired, even if that person did not have the skills or the experience needed to do the job well.

Still, members of the nuclear family do not cut all ties with their relatives, for even in the most advanced industrial societies members of nuclear families maintain kinship ties by visiting, writing letters, and making telephone calls. Members of nuclear families commonly live close to their relatives, and this is especially true of the working class, for whom visiting relatives is an important leisure activity (Greeley, 1969). Mutual aid among relatives is also common. For instance, most middle-class families receive help from relatives in the form of direct financial assistance, needed appliances, babysitting, or care during an illness. This help is usually given by parents to their grown children, rather than by offspring to their parents (Sussman, 1959).

FORMS OF MARRIAGE

In most industrial societies the only accepted form of marriage is *monogamy*, the marriage of one husband and one wife. However, monogamy is not the ideal form of marriage in most of the world's societies.

Polygamy is any form of marriage that involves multiple spouses. There are three kinds of polygamy. One is "group marriage," which involves at least two husbands and at least two wives, all of whom are married to each other. Group marriage has never been the dominant form of marriage in any society. It has been tried on an experimental basis but has never endured for long.

A survey of 862 societies found that another form of polygamy called "polyandry" existed in only four societies (Murdock, 1967). This is the marriage of one wife to more than one husband. Polyandrous societies are usually poor societies that keep their birth rates low by having multiple husbands for each woman. This satisfies sexual desires without producing large numbers of children who would be hard to feed. Polyandry might

"Polygamy" describes any form of marriage that involves multiple spouses. The most common form of polygamy, however, is "polygyny"—the taking of multiple wives by one man.

also predominate when there is a shortage of women in a society, perhaps as a result of a cultural practice of female infanticide, or the killing of female babies. Polyandry sometimes involves the marriage of one woman to two or more brothers. The kinship bond between the husbands makes it less likely that jealousy and conflict will disrupt the family, and enables the brothers to keep a piece of land in the family rather than subdivide it.

The third form of polygamy is "polygyny," the taking of multiple wives by one husband. Murdock's (1967) survey of 862 societies found polygyny to be the preferred form of marriage in 83 per cent of the societies; monogamy was preferred in only 16 per cent of the societies. Polygyny is found in societies with a shortage of men, which might be a result of warfare or the hunting of dangerous game. Polygyny increases a society's rate of population growth because more than one woman can be pregnant by the same husband at the same time. This can be beneficial to societies in which children

have economic value, such as agricultural societies. The Mormons in the United States officially practiced polygyny until it was outlawed by the church in 1890; today a few dissident Mormons continue this practice, even though it violates both church doctrine and American law.

Most of the world's societies prefer polygyny as a form of marriage, but, for a variety of reasons—such as an equal number of men and women desiring spouses—many members of these societies have only one spouse. In addition, most of the societies that practice polygyny are small in total population. As a result, the overwhelming majority of the world's population actually lives in monogamous marriages. Of the women who do live in polygynous marriages, most are not dominated and exploited. They often share housework and child care, and they may be less isolated from contact with other adults than are women in monogamous nuclear families who do not work outside the home.

MARRIAGE AND MATE SELECTION

Few if any societies allow people to select a husband or a wife at random. In the United States and other industrial societies, the selection of a mate is largely up to the individual, but even in these societies there are formal and informal norms about mate selection. In Western societies people usually think of marriage as occurring between people who are "in love" with each other. However, in most societies love is not idealized in this way, and when love exists it is not necessarily seen as an appropriate basis for marriage. In many societies, marriage is regarded as a union between families for economic, political, or social purposes.

Defining the Eligible Mate

All societies have rules that define a pool of eligible marital partners for an individual. Rules of *endogamy* require that people marry within certain defined groups and categories. For example, members of a tribal society might be required to marry other members of the tribe, and in the United States people commonly marry others of the same race and religion. By limiting an individual's choice of marital partners, rules of endogamy help to ensure the continued existence of a group. If people married at random, group membership would decline as people left their own group for those of their spouses.

Rules of *exogamy* require people to marry outside a specific group or category. One rule of exogamy is the *incest taboo*, the rule that people cannot marry or have sexual relations with family members or kinfolk to whom they are closely related. Societies define incest in various ways, but most societies prohibit marriage and sexual relations between brothers and sisters and between parents and their children. A few societies have allowed certain people to marry and have sexual relations with other members of their family; this was so for Hawaiian and ancient Egyptian royalty.

In most societies, norms about mate selection produce *homogamy*, the selection of spouses with similar social characteristics (Carter and Glick, 1976). Groups also apply pressure on individual members to marry someone from the same kind of background. For example, family members urge people to marry someone with a class background and life style similar to that of the family. There is some evidence that similarity of educational attainment is even more important than similarity of class background in determining mate selection (Blau and Duncan, 1967). Pressure to marry someone with similar characteristics also comes from peers, religious organizations, and neighbors. The homogeneity of many communities means that people are likely to marry others of similar background, because people are most likely to meet and interact with those who live nearby (Kephart, 1981).

Arranged Marriages

One way for a society to ensure homogamy is to have a custom that older members of the family arrange the marriages of younger members. In many societies, boys and girls grow up expecting that their marriages will be arranged by their elders. Marriage is regarded as an economic or political alliance between families, rather than as a union based on romantic love. In extended family systems in which a husband or a wife moves into the household of the other spouse's parents, the members of the extended family who must receive the new spouse into the household have an interest in determining who that spouse will be. Families have traditionally ensured homogamy by restricting the interaction of young males and young females through the seclusion of females and the custom of chaperoning young people. These practices helped to inhibit the development of love and emotional attachment, which might conflict with the family's choice of a suitable mate (Blood, 1967; Shorter, 1977; Goode, 1982).

Romantic Love

The ideal of romantic love first developed in the courts of Europe during the eleventh and twelfth centuries. However, it was not until the eighteenth century that love first became linked to self-fulfillment in a way that altered the institution of marriage and the family. With the rise of capitalism came the development of individualism, which in turn was linked with the emergence of romantic love as a basis for marriage. People began to marry "for inclination and not for advantage"; they became "willing to sacrifice their pocketbooks for their affections" (Shorter, 1977: 150). Mate selection became freer of family control as the emphasis shifted to spontaneity, empathy, and the "completion" of oneself through romantic involvement with someone of the opposite sex (Swidler, 1980). The idea emerged that for each person there was one "right" person who could bring happiness in a marriage that would last a lifetime.

The ideal of romantic love fits well with the institution of the nuclear family (Goode, 1959; Shorter, 1977). Although the nuclear family in industrial society has been stripped of many of the functions it had in traditional times, it retains the important function of providing emotional support and mutual affection for the marital partners. This function is especially important because the members of the nuclear family are relatively isolated from other intimate attachments.

Idealized romantic love rarely survives the first few years of marriage. Daily life soon becomes routine and predictable, and romantic love thrives on mystery and uncertainty. People who are "in love" when they marry later come to care for each other, but the love that develops over time differs from the romantic feeling of being "in love." Romantic love thus motivates people to marry, but it is also associated with a high divorce rate because it can be a source of disappointment in marriage. Nevertheless, the belief in romantic love survives even divorce, because about 80 per cent of divorced Americans do remarry.

Dating and Marriage Rituals

In societies in which people are relatively free to select their own mates, dating and courtship practices give people considerable autonomy in forming relationships with members of the opposite sex. Dating and courtship allow people to determine if they have similar backgrounds, share common values, and have complementary needs. Because most people marry early in adulthood, dating is often associated with the young, but it has become increasingly common among older people who are divorced or widowed. These older people experience many of the same anxieties that younger people feel during dating: calling up a prospective date, worrying about rejection, wondering if a date will call again, thinking about how the last date went and how the next one might be, and how to handle a sexual relationship.

When people marry, there is usually a ceremony or a ritual to mark their union. This ceremony is often a religious ritual, but it can also be a civil ceremony with no religious significance. The mar-

Dating and courtship allow people to determine if they have similar backgrounds, share common values, and have complementary needs.

riage ceremony formally acknowledges the joining together of two people into a single family unit. After this ceremony, the couple is expected to live together, form one economic unit, and have children. As we shall see when we discuss alternatives to the nuclear family, some of these expectations have changed in recent years in the United States.

The American Family

The idealized form of the family in the United States is a nuclear family consisting of a husband, a wife, and their children. Many American families do not fit this description, but most Americans do live in a nuclear family at some time in their lives. The idealized American family is also monogamous, although the pattern of marriage, divorce, and remarriage has been called "serial monogamy," the taking of a new spouse after a divorce from a previous one. The usual residential pattern of American families is "neolocal," that is, couples usually live in a place different from that of either spouse's parents. Usually, however, the new location of the household established by the married couple is near the parents of one of the spouses. The line of descent of American families is "bilateral," meaning that the relatives of a child's mother and father have equal significance, except that children typically take the father's last name.

The pattern of authority in American families can be described as patriarchal (or male-dominated) with an egalitarian emphasis. One study of the images of families presented in magazine advertisements found an increasing emphasis on egalitarianism between 1920 and 1978; this change was especially notable in the portrayal of companionship and intimacy (Brown, 1981). There are also important differences by social class in authority patterns in the family; the lower class and working class are more patriarchal, and families of higher status tend to be more egalitarian.

MARRIAGE AND DIVORCE

Americans believe that their overall happiness depends more on their marital happiness than on satisfaction in any other area of life (Glenn and Weaver, 1981). It is therefore not surprising that the United States has one of the highest rates of marriage in the world. In 1981, there were 10.6 marriages for every 1,000 people in the country. About 95 per cent of all Americans get married at some time, and since 1960 the proportion of people

TABLE 11.1

Marital Status of People 18 Years Old and Over, 1965 and 1981

Marital status	Percentages	
	1965	*1981*
Single	14.9	20.5
Married	73.2	64.9
Widowed	9.0	7.9
Divorced	2.9	6.7
Total	100.0	100.0

Source: U.S. Bureau of the Census, *Statistical Abstract of the United States, 1982–83*. Washington, D.C.: U.S. Government Printing Office, 1982, p. 38.

over the age of sixty-five who have never been married has declined (U.S. Bureau of the Census, 1982: 41, 60).

One reason that the marriage rate is so high is that the United States also has one of the world's highest divorce rates. About 80 per cent of divorced Americans remarry, so the high marriage rate is partly accounted for by the many people who marry more than once.

In recent years, Americans have married at a slightly later age than they once did. Between 1950 and 1979, the median age at first marriage for men rose from 22.8 to 23.4, and the median age for women increased from 20.3 to 21.6 (U.S. Bureau of the Census, 1982: 82). Changes in the marital status of Americans between 1965 and 1981 are shown in Table 11.1.

PARENTHOOD

In 1981, nearly half of all American families included no children under the age of eighteen, either because they had not yet produced children, did not plan to have children, or had grown children who no longer lived at home (U.S. Bureau of the Census, 1982: 49). In recent years, people have had fewer children. As recently as 1970, 20.4 per cent of all families had three or more children under the age of eighteen, but by 1981 this figure had dropped to 11.5 per cent. In addition to this decline in family size, there has also been a trend for married couples to postpone child-bearing for several years. The number of first births to women in their thirties doubled during the 1970s, with

TABLE 11.2
*Changes in the Average Size of Family,
United States, 1940–1981*

Year	Average number of persons per family
1940	3.76
1950	3.54
1960	3.67
1970	3.58
1980	3.29
1981	3.27

Source: U.S. Bureau of the Census, *Statistical Abstract of the United States, 1982–83.* Washington, D.C.: U.S. Government Printing Office, 1982, p. 43.

most of this occurring among well-educated women (Hunter, 1982). The reduced size of families (see Table 11.2) and the delay in child-bearing are a result of better methods of birth control, the increased cost of raising children, changes in the educational and career aspirations of women, and an increased emphasis on self-fulfillment and marital satisfaction, which might suffer in the presence of children.

The Child-Rearing Stage

The birth of the first child changes the family in dramatic ways. Often the mother spends more time with the child than the father does, and there is less time for intimate interaction between husband and wife. Sometimes the husband becomes jealous at having less time alone with his wife, and the wife may resent spending so much time in child care. Living conditions in the home also become more crowded, unless the family moves to larger—and usually more expensive—quarters. If the mother worked before the birth of the child, the family might also suffer financial strain if she stops working to take care of the child. This increases the burden on the man, who might feel that he has become solely responsible for supporting the family.

With a child, a couple takes on a twenty-four-hour-a-day, seven-day-a-week job. They must arrange babysitters in order to be alone. Because of the relative isolation of the nuclear family, there is usually no reward or praise for parenting behavior. A woman's marital satisfaction is usually lowest during the child-rearing years; and men often complain about financial pressures, loss of friends, and reduced sexual activity after the birth of the first child (Russell, 1974). Overall, the presence of children in the family adversely affects marital happiness (Spanier and Lewis, 1980; Glenn and McLanahan, 1982). In addition, couples with few children report less stress, more comfort, and more happiness than couples with larger numbers of children. People adjust better to the parent role if they communicate well with their spouses, if their overall level of marital satisfaction is high, if they are strongly committed to the parent role, and if the mother's health and the infant's temperament are good (Russell, 1974).

SOCIOLOGY AND EVERYDAY LIFE   11.1
Marriage in the Working Class

The American family has a diversity of forms, and one source of this diversity is social class. Differences in financial resources influence the nature of family life in a variety of ways. In addition, the education of the husband and the wife, their childhood experiences, and traditions of child-rearing in the different classes all lead to significant differences between working-class and middle-class families. Lillian Breslow Rubin (1976) examined some of these differences in *Worlds of Pain*, a detailed portrait of fifty white working-class families that she compared with twenty-five white middle-class families.

REASONS FOR MARRYING

Members of the working class typically marry at a young age; in Rubin's sample the average age was eighteen for women, and twenty for husbands. These couples married for three major reasons: romance, pregnancy, and "chance." One woman who married at eighteen described the beginning of her courtship as follows: "We met at the coffee shop where some of us kids used to hang out. I guess we knew right away because we began to go steady right after. We just fell in love right away"

(p. 51). Her husband recounts their courtship in a different way: "We met at this place and I kind of liked her. She was cool and kind of fun to be with. Before I knew it, we were going steady. I don't exactly know how it happened" (p. 51).

Working-class wives seemed to marry because they were "in love"; their husbands expressed this feeling less often. More often, the husbands married because it seemed like the right thing at the time or because their friends expected them to marry. For them, the marriage seemed to "just happen," almost as if by accident.

The other major reason for marriage was pregnancy. Nearly half of the fifty working-class couples married for this reason. Some of these women said they had not used birth-control pills or other forms of contraception because only "bad girls" did that. They also believed that their bodies could be "given away" to their future husbands at the right moment. These beliefs—combined with their disapproval of abortion—often resulted in pregnancy and then marriage.

THE EARLY YEARS OF MARRIAGE

The working-class newlyweds found that marriage required a drastic adjustment in their expectations and their way of life. They had to compromise their hopes and take on new responsibilities, and all of this on a low income from a job that held few prospects for better times. One woman who married young described this as follows:

As you can see, that dream I had about getting married and having a storybook life didn't exactly work out. [That storybook life included] my own little family, in my own house, and everything pretty and shiny and new, like in magazine pictures. Life sure doesn't match the dreams, does it? Here I am living in this old, dumpy house and the furniture is a grubby mess. . . . Now I know we're lucky just to be able to keep up with the bills (p. 72).

Because many of these working-class women were pregnant at marriage, the first child arrived soon after marriage. In fact, the average time until the birth of the first child in these fifty working-class marriages was only nine months, compared to an average of three years for the middle-class couples. The working-class couples had less education and fewer job skills with which to earn an income, and the birth of the first child soon after marriage meant that they had little time to establish a financial cushion.

The combination of low income and young children sometimes created a sense of lost freedom, even lost youth, for working-class couples. One husband remarked: "I had just turned twenty and, all of a sudden, I had a wife and a kid. You couldn't just go out anymore when you felt like it. If you wanted to go anyplace, you had to take the kid" (p. 81).

CONFLICT WITH IN-LAWS

One of the other frustrations of early marriage is conflict with the in-laws, most often between the wife and her mother-in-law. This conflict is common among the working class, because they are more likely to settle near their parents than are newly married middle-class couples. Because many working-class husbands were young when they married, they had not become independent of their parents, and as a result some of the wives complained that they were expected to act like their husbands' mothers:

His mother was like a maid in the house, and he wanted me to do the same kinds of things and be like her. I know it's my job to keep the house up, but wouldn't you think he could hang up his own clothes? Or maybe once in a while—just once in a while—help clear the table? (pp. 89–90)

In contrast, middle-class couples more often have a period of transition during the college years to become independent of their parents and to learn to fend for themselves. They are also more likely to take their first jobs at some distance from the homes of their parents. As a result, when they do marry, their ties to their parents are weaker than are those of working-class couples, and they are better able to care for themselves.

Source: Based on *Worlds of Pain: Life in the Working-Class Family* by Lillian Breslow Rubin. © 1976 by Lillian Breslow Rubin. Used by permission of Basic Books, Inc., New York, N.Y.

"The Empty Nest"

As we have seen, child-rearing takes up a smaller proportion of people's lives today than it did in the past. The time of "the empty nest"—that period after children have left home—has traditionally been seen as a very difficult period for women, because many of them spend much time raising children and therefore suffer a loss of identity when that task is completed. However, this may be changing as women become more and more economically independent and gain a sense of identity outside of the mother/housewife role. In addition, marital satisfaction actually increases after children leave home, and children often remain a source of happiness to their parents even after they have grown up and moved away (Luckey and Bain, 1970; Borland, 1982).

THE TWO-CAREER FAMILY

In recent years, a growing number of married women, even those with young children, have taken jobs outside the home. In the past, a working wife was seen as an indication of her husband's inability to provide for the family. Although women with husbands who earn low incomes are still the most likely to work, women now work for a variety of reasons that are not related to their husband's ability to provide for the family. Women increasingly contribute financially to the family, and their authority in family decision making has risen as a result.

A *two-career family* is one in which the husband and the wife both work at jobs that have a career path and that they expect to work at for many years (Holmstrom, 1972; Rapoport and Rapoport, 1976; Hunt and Hunt, 1982). This contrasts with a pattern in which both spouses work and each expects that the wife will quit her job to bear and raise children. In two-career families, there must be good communication between the spouses in order to accommodate the many demands on their time, such as child-rearing, leisure activities, friendships, and time alone as a couple. Difficulties often arise from employers' expectations that each worker will be fully committed to the career, will work overtime, or will even move to another city.

A relatively uncommon form of the two-career family is the "commuter marriage," in which husband and wife live in different communities in order to pursue their own careers. This separation might be temporary, or it might be a relatively permanent arrangement in which the couple only sees each other on weekends (Gross, 1980). Although there may be romance and autonomy in this way of life, it is often associated with loneliness, the life style of a single person, and sexual infidelity (Gerstell, 1977).

Some employers have begun to respond to the needs of the two-career family because they believe that a failure to meet those needs "could affect recruiting, employee morale, productivity and ulti-

mately corporate profits" (Klemesrud, 1981a: 21). In one study, about three-fourths of the questionnaires returned by 374 corporations indicated concern with the problems of two-career families. However, nearly half of the respondents said that these problems had not yet affected their operations. Efforts to provide for the needs of two-career families include more flexible work hours, financial support for child-care facilities, more flexible benefits packages, and assistance to the spouses of workers who are forced to relocate.

THE ELDERLY IN THE FAMILY

Many elderly people in the United States do not live in a family setting. About two-thirds of all women seventy-five years old and over are widows, and about one-fourth of men that age are widowers. It is uncommon for elderly people to live in the same household with their married offspring and grandchildren; only one American household in twelve has three or more generations living together. However, about a third of the elderly do live with their grown children in two-generation households. In addition, many of the elderly live near to relatives, so they are less socially isolated than their living situations might suggest (Riley and Foner, 1968). There is also some evidence that interaction with relatives does not demonstrably improve the emotional well-being of the elderly anyway (Lee and Ellithorpe, 1982).

Rarely are the elderly thrown out of a home. Instead, the neolocal pattern of residence of the American nuclear family means that grown offspring who marry establish a home separate from that of their parents. Children who never marry—only about 5 per cent of the population—sometimes move away from their parents to take a job, live with another person, or live alone. Thus parents and their offspring usually separate when the grown child leaves home. Later, as parents age and one of them dies, the married children must deal with the issue of whether to bring the elderly parent into the household, and sometimes this is a source of conflict between spouses.

Alternatives to the Nuclear Family

Not only do relatively few Americans actually live in a nuclear family consisting of a working father, a stay-at-home mother, and young children, but the proportion of Americans living in this situation has also declined over the years (Yankelovich, 1981).

More mothers are working; the birth rate has declined; life expectancy has increased; divorce is more common; and the illegitimacy rate has risen. As a result, there is now a greater diversity of living arrangements and family structures than there was even a few years ago.

SINGLEHOOD

Between 1970 and 1981 there was a 75 per cent increase in households with only one person, a much faster rate of increase than was true of the total number of households in the country. This change is a result of people getting married later than they once did, living alone for several years after they finish their education and before they marry, or even choosing not to marry at all (Adam, 1976; Libby, 1978; Stein, 1981). In addition, increased gay rights activism in recent years may have made it easier for people to accept their homosexuality. In the past, some homosexuals married heterosexual partners to demonstrate their "respectability" to the world, and this could be less common today.

COHABITATION

Cohabitation is a situation in which people who define themselves as a couple live together but do not marry (Cole, 1977; Clayton and Voss, 1977; Macklin, 1978). In 1970 there were about 500,000 households consisting of two unmarried people of the opposite sex, and by 1981 this figure had more than tripled. Still, only 2 to 3 per cent of all households are of this variety. A study using 1975 data found that somewhat more than half of the people in these living arrangements had been married previously (Glick and Spanier, 1980). In 1981, nearly two-thirds of these cohabiting couples included a man and a woman who were both under the age of thirty-five (U.S. Bureau of the Census, 1982: 42). In addition to households of members of the opposite sex who live together while unmarried, there are also an undetermined number of homosexual couples who live together (Bell and Weinberg, 1978).

Some people see cohabitation as an alternative to marriage, and others see it as a "trial marriage." Living together can be the final stage in the selection of a mate, a time when a couple "tries on" the role of marital partner (Murstein, 1970). However, there is no evidence that cohabitation necessarily makes people more satisfied when they do marry or that it reduces the chance that they will divorce later (Macklin, 1978; Newcomb, 1979).

Cohabiting couples rarely have children without marrying first. Most states do not have laws to govern cohabitation, and this creates confusion and anger when these couples end their relationships. Without a marriage contract, the law does not provide for the division of property, alimony payments, or a formal end to the relationship. California does permit a division of community property for cohabiting couples, and some states recognize a "common-law marriage" of couples who have lived together for a specified length of time without getting married. Also, there have been a few well-publicized "palimony" cases in which one person has sued someone with whom he or she lived in an attempt to secure property that might have been received in a divorce settlement if they had been married.

CHILDLESS MARRIAGES

Another alternative to the traditional nuclear family is to marry and have no children. Whereas some married couples simply delay the birth of children, others do remain childless. The number of married couples today who will remain childless is uncertain, because even the spoken intention to do so does not guarantee that minds will not be changed or birth-control measures prove ineffective. However, some sociologists speculate that if current trends continue, as many as 25 to 30 per cent of women might remain childless (Gulino, 1981).

One study found that about a third of couples who remained childless had decided to do so before they were married; the rest repeatedly postponed the birth of children until they felt it was too late or not desirable (Veevers, 1973). Couples often see economic or social advantages to remaining childless. Childlessness is less expensive; and it enables couples to travel, see their friends, and go out in the evenings.

Childless married couples tend to live in large metropolitan areas, where both spouses work and have access to the cultural and social resources of the city. Because they commonly have two incomes and no children to support, these couples are often of relatively high social status (Gustavus and Henley, 1971).

SINGLE PARENTHOOD

Between 1970 and 1981, the number of one-parent families in the United States doubled. A major reason for this was the rising rate of divorce; the death of a spouse is another source of single-parent families, but this factor has not been responsible for the increase in such families in recent years.

Another major reason for the increase in one-parent families is a rise in the rate of illegitimacy. During the 1970s, premarital intercourse gradually became more socially acceptable (Singh, 1980).

Although abortion became legally available in 1973, by 1978 attitudes toward abortion had become more conservative (Ebaugh and Haney, 1980). These and other factors (see SEL 11.2) have produced increased numbers of births out of wedlock in recent years.

SOCIOLOGY AND EVERYDAY LIFE 11.2
Teenage Mothers

Increasing numbers of pregnant teenagers "without husbands, job prospects or steady incomes" (p. 1) are bearing and raising their children, rather than terminating a pregnancy with an abortion or putting a baby up for adoption. By one estimate, more than 40 per cent of American teenagers who become pregnant are now choosing to have their babies, and about 95 per cent of these young mothers keep their children. A variety of factors have caused this situation. Some states have laws that require minors to get parental permission for an abortion, and as a result some pregnant teenagers feel that their only choice is to have the baby. In addition, attitudes toward premarital intercourse, pregnancy, abortion, and motherhood have changed, as the director of a Boston shelter for pregnant teenagers observes:

Today, getting pregnant is OK among a girl's peers, but giving up a baby for adoption is not cool. . . . In one sense, it's wonderful that the stigma of pregnancy is lessening, but it can also be tragic, because a teenager's notions of motherhood are so unrealistic. . . . They have this fantasy that they can get on welfare and live happily ever after, but it doesn't work that way (p. 16).

Shortly after delivering a healthy daughter, one sixteen-year-old who had stayed at this shelter during her pregnancy spoke of her plans for the baby, whom she planned to raise in a foster home where she had been sent:

My mother and I weren't getting along. I was on probation from the courts. When I found out I was pregnant, I was so happy. I wanted a little girl to give my attention to, the way I never had it. . . . It's going to be different for her. I'm going to make sure she always has someone to talk to (p. 1).

This young mother was still in touch with the child's father, but she did not want to marry him. She said, "I'm too young. I saw how my mother and father were, and I don't want to take any chances. I can raise her better by myself" (p. 1). Although this young mother's plans to become a computer technician became less of a priority after the birth of her child, she did seem confident that she could raise the child: "We'll do OK. I've grown up a lot in the past nine months" (p. 1).

Many mothers start out with high expectations, but reality is often quite different. Many leave school and barely survive on welfare payments. About 15 per cent become pregnant again within a year. There are some programs to help these young mothers adjust to their new roles. One controversial approach has been to provide them with contraceptives. A more conventional policy is to have them attend classes on health, parenting, job skills, and career planning. This can ease some of their difficulties in adjusting to their new lives with children, but it also has a more subtle effect. By raising their self-esteem and self-confidence, these classes can help young mothers to find fulfillment in ways other than bearing children. Counselors who work with these mothers find that "[m]any girls from low-income or broken homes . . . see mothering as their only chance for fulfillment in a life that seems without hope for happiness, education or career. A girl may not plan to conceive, but once pregnant she feels her life at last has meaning" (p. 16).

Source: Adapted from Pamela Constable, "More Teens Keeping Their Babies without Husbands, Jobs, Incomes," *The Boston Globe*, December 13, 1982, pp. 1, 16. Used courtesy of *The Boston Globe*.

The single-parent family is often a transitional stage, both for unwed mothers and for divorced parents (Ross and Sawhill, 1975; Weiss, 1979). Because some mothers of illegitimate children later marry and because most divorced parents remarry within a few years, many single-parent families last for only a short time. Nevertheless, this kind of family has been on the rise in recent years.

COMMUNES

A *commune* is a household that includes at least three adults and can also include children. In a sense, communes are self-defined. Three roommates will not necessarily call themselves a commune, but three other people who are living together might choose to define themselves in this way. For young people in the late 1960s and early 1970s, communes were an alternative to marriage and the traditional nuclear family. Members pooled their resources and divided household tasks among themselves (Stein, Polk, and Polk, 1975). However, as time went on, most of these communes dissolved because of internal tensions about the proper allocation of work or the sharing of resources—problems that also plague the nuclear family—or because members left to form nuclear families (Berger, Hackett, and Millar, 1972).

One form of the commune that has lasted over time is the Israeli *kibbutz*. About 3 per cent of the population of Israel lives in these communal agricultural settlements, where all property, except for small personal items, is owned collectively and where profits are shared by all. In many ways the *kibbutz* performs the functions of a large extended family. Children live apart from their parents, and members of the commune are assigned to care for the children. The organization of the *kibbutz* reduces the authority of parents over their children, and husbands over their wives. However, the emotional bonds between parents and children and between husbands and wives remain important. Work on the *kibbutz* is still divided between the sexes; for instance, women usually stop work to bear and nurse children, and they often fill traditional female roles such as cook and teacher. However, men and women are roughly equal in political power on the committees that make important decisions for the *kibbutz* (Talmon, 1965; Rabin, 1970; Tiger and Shepher, 1975; Schlesinger, 1977).

One form of the commune that has lasted over time is the Israeli **kibbutz.** *Here the members of a* **kibbutz** *share a meal in their common dining room.*

Divorce

A society's rate of *divorce*—the formal termination of the legal contract of marriage—has sometimes been used as an indicator of marital satisfaction and the stability of the family, but the divorce rate does not provide direct evidence of satisfaction and stability. Unhappy marriages can end in desertion, separation, or even murder and not show up in the divorce statistics. Divorce rates can be low if the law prohibits divorce or makes it difficult or expensive. In addition, families could remain intact but be "empty-shell families" that are unbroken but have much internal conflict and unhappiness.

A society's divorce rate can be calculated in a variety of ways (Crosby, 1980). One measure is the number of divorces for every 1,000 people in a society, but the problem with this indicator is that not everyone is an eligible candidate for divorce, because many people are not even married. Another indicator is the proportion of all existing marriages that end in divorce each year, a figure that now stands at about 2 per cent for the United States. Perhaps the best way to measure divorce is to keep track of a group of married people over their lifetimes. Recent evidence shows that about 38 per cent of first marriages now end in divorce, but about four-fifths of those people eventually remarry; about 44 per cent of those second marriages later end in divorce (Population Reference Bureau, 1978; Woodward et al., 1978; Glick and Norton, 1979). Regardless of which measure is used, it is clear that divorce rates have increased in recent years.

CAUSES OF DIVORCE

A variety of social factors are associated with the high and rising divorce rate in the United States (Weiss, 1975; Carter and Glick, 1976; Booth and White, 1980; Goode, 1982). Divorce is more common among people who marry when they are young; the recent increase in the average age at marriage could bring about a drop in the divorce rate over the long run (Glick and Norton, 1979; Yoder and Nichols, 1980). People who know each other for only a short time before they marry are more likely to divorce, as are couples who have been married before. Divorce rates are also higher in large cities than they are in small towns and rural communities.

Social Class

The less educated are more likely to divorce than people who have completed more schooling. This might be because the more educated are better able to articulate their marital problems with one another and have the means to consult professional counselors, thus enabling them to make the adjustments that allow their marriages to continue. In addition, the more educated have higher average incomes, and this reduces financial strain on the marriage.

Divorce is most common among people of the lower and the working classes. Couples of higher class standing who do divorce are likely to do so for psychological and emotional reasons; lower-class couples more often divorce because of financial problems or physical abuse (Kephart, 1981; Goode, 1982). Low-income families cannot afford household help, babysitters, and child care, nor can they afford professional counseling, vacations, and leisure activities that might relieve marital tension. These financial difficulties can lead to divorce, although it might be safer to say that divorce occurs when people's expectations exceed their resources. Divorce rates are not as high in many societies that have lower standards of living than the United States, and rates in the United States were not as high when the standard of living was lower than what it is today.

Changing Gender Roles

The divorce rate has probably increased in part because of changes in traditional gender roles, especially the increased employment of women outside the home. However, the increased participation of women in the labor force is also a *result* of the high divorce rate: Divorced women need to work to support themselves and their children.

Working outside the home probably increases the chance of divorce. Women who work often realize that they can support themselves without their husbands' help, and if the marriage is unsatisfactory this source of income might free them to seek a divorce (Weiss, 1975). In addition, working wives sometimes become frustrated when they find that their husbands expect them to contribute their income to the family budget but will not help with the housework or the child care (Walker, 1970; Pendleton, Paloma, and Garland, 1980; Huber and Spitze, 1980). Those women who do work outside the home also have more authority in making family decisions, and this can cause their husbands to become confused and angry.

Social Background

Divorce is more common among people who marry without their families' approval, and this disapproval often stems from differences in the social backgrounds of the partners (Goode, 1982). Differences in race and ethnicity, religion, education, and social class increase the likelihood of divorce, as do differences in personal habits and personality. One study that compared divorced women and married women found that more of the divorced women came from a higher class background than their husbands; divorced women were also more likely to be dissatisfied with their husband's job and income (Scanzoni, 1968).

Sexuality and Personal Fulfillment

Another reason for divorce is sexual incompatibility, a factor that has reportedly become more common as traditional gender roles have changed. Adultery is also commonly cited as a reason for divorce, but it is more likely to be a symptom of marital difficulties than the cause of a breakup. In the first studies on the topic more than thirty years ago, Kinsey (1948, 1953) found that substantial proportions of married men and women had engaged in extramarital sex, but divorce was uncommon then. Adultery is only slightly more common today, but the divorce rate is much higher, suggesting that other factors have caused the high divorce rate.

The high divorce rate is associated with cultural expectations of personal fulfillment. The 1970s, known as the "me decade," were a time when people emphasized personal development and happiness, and love and marriage were important parts of this search for satisfaction. These expectations were a heavy burden on many marriages, and were the cause of many divorces, as a growing number of people stated they could not "find happiness" with their partner or felt that they "had grown at a different rate than their spouse." Many people chose to search for a more suitable partner rather than continue an unsatisfactory marriage. Because romantic love generally diminishes over the course of a marriage, for many people divorce is an opportunity to find romantic love once again.

Legal Changes

It is easier to get a divorce today than it was a few years ago. This change is partly a result of rising divorce rates—which apply pressure on the law to make it easier to end marriage—but once the legal system makes divorce simpler there is an incentive for unhappily married couples to divorce rather than merely to separate or live together unhappily. All but a few states now have some form of "no-fault" divorce that does not require either partner to show that the other one is legally to blame for the failure of the marriage (Melville, 1980). Also, most states that lack no-fault laws or limit the use of those laws have broadened the legal grounds for divorce in recent years, thus reducing the number of obstacles to ending a marriage.

The rising divorce rate has probably reduced the stigma of being divorced, and so made it easier to terminate a marriage. The increased number of divorced people means that there are more eligible people from whom to select a new mate. When the divorce rate is low, divorced people may feel alone and without options for remarriage—a situation that tends to make people stay married rather than get a divorce. When the divorce rate is high, there is less disapproval of divorced people and more opportunities for them to make friends, date, and remarry.

EFFECTS OF DIVORCE ON CHILDREN

One consequence of the high divorce rate in the United States is that many children now live with only one parent, usually the mother. The proportion of children living with only one parent increased from 11.8 per cent in 1970 to 20 per cent in 1981 (U.S. Bureau of the Census, 1982: 52).

Divorce is very painful for children. Even in conflict-ridden families, children rarely feel that the dissolution of the marriage is the best thing. In the aftermath of the separation, children spend much time distraught or angry at their parents, and they often harbor fantasies of their parents' reuniting. Children of a divorce might not, however, be much worse off in the long run than children raised in intact families (Kurdek and Siesky, 1980; Greenberg and Nay, 1982). According to one longitudinal study, although almost every child experienced divorce as deeply upsetting, by one year after the breakup more than half of the children seemed undamaged by the experience, and some were even better off than they were before the divorce (Wallerstein and Kelly, 1980). Young children who were well cared for by the custodial parent showed the best adjustment, as did adolescents who had brothers and sisters, or friends to turn to for support. A continuing and close relationship with the parent who had left home—usually the father—was also important to the adjustment of children after divorce. However, according to other research, one lasting effect of divorce seems to be that the children of divorced parents are more likely to get divorced themselves when they grow up, even though as children they might vow that it will never happen to them (Pope and Mueller, 1976; Mueller and Pope, 1977; Yoder and Nichols, 1980; Greenberg and Nay, 1982).

EFFECTS OF DIVORCE ON SPOUSES

Even when a husband and a wife wish to end their marriage, the actual separation is often difficult for both partners (Weiss, 1975; Chiriboga and Cutler, 1977). They commonly feel isolated when the actual breakup occurs, and many of their subsequent interactions tend to be characterized by anger and blame. Each person typically provides an "account" of the divorce to explain what went wrong, as SEL 11.3 illustrates.

SOCIOLOGY AND EVERYDAY LIFE 11.3
Accounting for Divorce

Husbands and wives who divorce often feel a need to explain "what went wrong" to their relatives, friends, and co-workers. They develop "accounts," explanations of why their marriages failed. Often the accounts of the husband and the wife are very different, because they interpret the same events in different ways and attribute the end of their marriage to different factors. An outsider who was given several husbands' accounts and an equal number of wives' accounts might well be unable to match the husbands and the wives. Robert Weiss provides one example:

In one instance the wife complained that her husband had tried to stop her from improving herself by taking college courses and had attacked her love of books. She talked about how little tolerance her husband had for her studies. Her husband, she said, could not comprehend her wanting to stay up to work on a paper or to finish a book. But her husband complained not about her studiousness nor about her passion for literature but rather about her flirtatiousness. He said that whenever they went to a party there were men around or, worse, a single other man. He said that he was constantly competing for her attention and that sometimes he lost the competition. None of the events significant to him appeared in her account, nor were any of the events significant for her included in his account (p. 15).

Weiss, who has done extensive work with divorced and divorcing couples, notes that several themes recur in their accounts. He lists six major reasons that couples use to explain the failure of their marriages:

1. The marriage was "wrong from the start" (p. 16). A man in his late twenties states:

The few months before the day we were married weren't that good. Differences already had come up and there were problems and we weren't as happy as we were before. But the wheels of marriage had already started working and we were already buying silverware and dishes and it was too late. . . .
   After being married a couple of months, at least subconsciously we realized that we were too different to be living together or even to be going out together. But divorce never really crossed our minds because we had just gotten married and sent out thank-you notes. You know, we couldn't very well say, "Thanks for the money. By the way, we are not married any more" (p. 16).

2. Each spouse wanted different things from life. A woman in her early thirties describes the cause of her divorce as follows:

I think what happened was that our interests were growing in different ways. I don't know, you'd think at this point I could put my finger on exactly what it was. He had this dream, everybody having a community with each other. He wanted to form a commune with some friends. And I realized that I just did not want that (p. 18).

3. One spouse found it impossible to live with some chronic failing of the other partner. These failings included alcoholism, gambling, stinginess, sexual inadequacy, and inattention.

4. One spouse was seriously depressed. A woman in her late twenties found herself increasingly unable to tolerate her husband's depression:

> My husband had lost a series of jobs and was very depressed. He just couldn't keep a job. He had a job for a couple of years, and that ended, and then he had another for a year, and that ended, and then he had another. And then he was really depressed, and he saw a social worker, but it didn't seem to be helping. And he was sleeping a lot. And I think one day I just came to the end of the line with his sleeping. I think I went out one night and came back and he hadn't even been able to get out of bed to put the children to bed. I left them watching television and there they were when I came back. The next day I asked him to leave. Very forcefully (p. 19).

5. The couple had gradually lost the ability to talk with each other over the years.

6. One partner was sexually unfaithful. Sexual infidelity was a cause of conflict and di-

vorce, but almost as important in some instances was the duplicity that went along with the extramarital involvement. A women in her mid-thirties reports:

> The last few years were just terrible. I couldn't do anything right. When he was home, which wasn't very often, he just sat in front of the television set and stared at it. I knew there was something wrong, but you don't realize. It happens so gradually. Then I found out that for over a year he had a little honey stashed away who was treated royally, who was wined and dined. He'd call me at night and say he had to work overtime.
>
> I was really broken up. I'd sit at work and the tears would come. I'd run in the washroom and cry. I lost so much weight I didn't have any clothes to wear. Finally I said, "See you later. Off you go" (p. 21).

Source: Adapted from *Marital Separation* by Robert S. Weiss. © 1975 by Basic Books, Inc. Used by permission of the publisher.

One way to look at divorce—especially when children are involved—is as a change in the relationship of a man and a woman, rather than as an end to their relationship. Former marital partners continue to interact, although less frequently and less intimately (Weiss, 1975). Sometimes their interaction is marked by disagreements over the arrangement of visits with the noncustodial parent or by complaints about how the children are being cared for by the other parent. Financial matters are another source of conflict. The majority of fathers—some estimate the figure to be as high as 90 per cent—either discontinue child-support payments or fail to make those payments on time (Brooks, 1982). The courts have been ineffective in enforcing divorce agreements that require these payments, and so many one-parent families live in poverty.

REMARRIAGE

Most divorced people eventually remarry. More men than women remarry, probably because the cultural pattern of men marrying younger women gives men a larger pool of potential mates from which to choose. Men are most likely to remarry if they are young at the time of divorce and if their income is relatively high.

"Reconstituted Families"

Remarriage creates new and often complex family structures that have some of the characteristics of extended families (Duberman, 1975; Norman, 1980). If a couple with two children divorces, and if both the man and the woman remarry spouses who also have two children from previous marriages, the original couple will each have relationships with four different children—their two natural children and their two stepchildren. Each of the two children from the original family will have two stepbrothers or stepsisters. The situation becomes even more complex when people divorce and remarry more than once.

The family structure also becomes complicated if a remarried couple then has children of their own. For example, the remarried man from the original couple might then be the father of two children who live with his first wife, as well as the stepfather of two children born to his second wife by her first marriage, and the father of any additional children he has with his second wife. As you can see, the terminology to describe this web of relationships is inadequate. The term "stepparent" has traditionally had negative connotations, although that image is beginning to change in some children's literature (Collins, 1982). Perhaps the increase in the number of these "reconstituted families" will give rise to new terms for the complicated set of kin ties created by divorce and remarriage.

The Future of the Family

In her book, *The Future of Marriage,* Jessie Bernard asks if marriage has a future. She answers her own question as follows: "Not only does marriage have a future, it has many futures" (Bernard, 1972: 270). The same can be said of the family; it is evolving rather than dissolving, and it is not in danger of extinction (Levitan and Balous, 1981). There is evidence that the family is strong, possibly stronger than it has been in the past (Bane, 1976). However, in the future the family will take a variety of forms in addition to that of the traditional nuclear family.

The long-term trend seems to be toward a lower rate of marriage, a higher rate of divorce, and a lower birth rate. There will also be a slight decrease in households of married couples, as some of the alternatives to the nuclear family that we have explored become more common. There might also be a drop in the number of households without children, although there is evidence of a recent increase in births among women in their thirties. Compared to the past, more women will work outside the home on a full-time and continuous basis, and will make greater contributions to family incomes. More and more people will have a variety of family experiences during their lifetimes (Bane, 1983). These new kinds of living arrangements "are likely to change the face of the cities, create markets for quite different kinds of houses and consumer goods and place new demands on public programs. They will create unprecedented challenges for the economy, the community and the government—challenges that the society must prepare to meet" (Masnick and Bane, 1980: 10).

Summary

The family serves a variety of functions for society. It regulates sexual conduct, ensures the replacement of the members of the society through reproduction, gives newborns a place in the stratification system, protects and emotionally supports the young, and acts as an economic unit of production and consumption.

The family is also a source of conflict and even violence, in forms such as child abuse and spouse-beating. The family can perpetuate social inequality; it reinforces class differences and is the locus of exploitation of women and children. The separation of the family from the economic system has caused workers to turn to the family for personal fulfillment, and the pressure this places on the family can prove disruptive. Also, the economic system has increasingly intruded on the formerly private sphere of the family; the leisure industry and the helping professions are examples of the spread of control over the family by outside agencies.

The family has taken many forms. The nuclear family of husband, wife, and their children is well-suited to industrial society, but it also exists in hunting and gathering societies. The extended family consists of the nuclear family plus a variety of other kinfolk; this system is better suited to an agricultural society in which each additional pair of hands increases productivity. Family systems differ in the number of spouses a person can have, but most of the world's population lives in monogamous families. Other sources of variation in family structures include where a newly married couple will establish residence and who has authority within the family.

Every society limits the choice of potential marriage partners in some way, and the rules that do this typically produce homogamous marriages. The incest taboo is a universal rule that limits marriage to those outside a socially defined set of family members. One way to ensure homogamy is through arranged marriages, a method that in many societies has given way to marriage based on romantic love. The idea of romantic love is well suited to industrial societies and to the nuclear family system, but is conducive to marital dissatisfaction because romantic love rarely endures beyond a brief period when the couple is first marrried.

Americans have a high rate of marriage, in part because they have a high rate of divorce and remarriage. However, the American family has grown smaller in recent years, as the birth rate has declined. Couples often have difficulty adjusting to the birth of children. Marital satisfaction is relatively low when there are young children at home, and it rises when the children have grown and left home. This suggests that the "empty-nest syndrome" might be a less serious problem for women today than it was once thought to be, because the increased participation of women in the labor force means that they do not need to rely on the mother/wife role as their sole source of identity. Usually the elderly do not live with their grown children, and these older people are less isolated from others than is commonly believed.

There are presently many alternatives to the traditional nuclear family in American society. In recent years, singlehood has become more popular, as people have delayed marriage or chosen to remain unmarried. Some single people cohabit with another person of the opposite sex, either in a "trial marriage" or as an alternative to marriage. Another option is to marry but remain childless. Other families are one-parent households, either because of the breakup of a marriage or because of illegitimacy. Communes are also an alternative to the nuclear family, and in the recent past this alternative has been a transitional stage between singlehood and marriage for young adults in the United States.

A variety of factors are associated with the high and rising divorce rate of recent years. Divorce is more common among people who marry young, people who have already been married, residents of large cities, the less educated, and the lower classes. Changes in gender roles have caused some people to consider divorce as more of a possibility. In addition, spouses from different social backgrounds are especially likely to divorce. The rising rate of divorce can also be attributed to the search for personal happiness, to changes in divorce laws, and to the reduced stigma of being divorced. Divorce is traumatic for children, but most of them are well-adjusted a year later. Divorce also causes anger, confusion, and loneliness in adults, with each of the former marital partners usually developing a very different account of what went wrong with the marriage. Most divorced people remarry, and the relationships in their reconstituted families are often quite complex.

The future pattern will be a diversity of family types, rather than the simple model of a traditional nuclear family. The size of households will continue to shrink, more women will work full time, divorce rates will remain high, birth rates will probably stay relatively low, and more people will live in different kinds of families during their lifetimes.

Important Terms

CHILD ABUSE **(253)**
COHABITATION **(263)**
COMMUNE **(265)**
DIVORCE **(266)**
ENDOGAMY **(257)**
EXOGAMY **(257)**
EXTENDED FAMILY **(254)**

FAMILY **(249)**
HOMOGAMY **(257)**
INCEST TABOO **(257)**
MONOGAMY **(255)**
NUCLEAR FAMILY **(254)**
POLYGAMY **(255)**
TWO-CAREER FAMILY **(262)**

Suggested Readings

Mary Jo Bane. *Here to Stay*. New York: Basic Books, 1976. A well-written examination of recent changes in the American family.

Theodore Caplow et al. *Middletown Families: Fifty Years of Change and Conformity*. Minneapolis, Minn.: University of Minnesota Press, 1982. A study of the long-term changes and continuity in families in "Middletown" (Muncie, Indiana).

William J. Goode. *The Family*, 2nd ed. Englewood Cliffs, N.J.: Prentice-Hall, 1982. A brief examination of the sociology of the family, with attention to the family in industrial society.

Christopher Lasch. *Haven in a Heartless World: The Family Besieged*. New York: Basic Books, 1979. A historical study of the relationship between the family and capitalism, focusing on the family in the United States in the nineteenth and twentieth centuries.

George Masnick and Mary Jo Bane. *The Nation's Families: 1960–1990*. Cambridge, Mass.: The Joint Center for Urban Studies of M.I.T. and Harvard University, 1980. A study of recent changes in the American family, with projections about its future.

Lillian Breslow Rubin. *Worlds of Pain: Life in the Working-Class Family*. New York: Basic Books, 1976. A fascinating exploration of married life in American society, with emphasis on younger members of the working class.

Peter J. Stein. *Single Life: Unmarried Adults in Social Context*. New York: St. Martin's Press, 1981. An examination of one alternative to the traditional nuclear family.

Murray A. Straus, Richard J. Gelles, and Suzanne K. Steinmetz. *Behind Closed Doors: Violence in the American Family*. Garden City, N. Y.: Anchor Press/Doubleday, 1979. A comprehensive account of conflict in the family, including child abuse and violence between spouses.

EDUCATION

A few years ago, a Navy recruit who was unable to read a repair manual caused $250,000 worth of damage to equipment (Kozol, 1980). Not long ago a worker in a Chicago feed lot killed a herd of cattle when he misread a package label and fed them poison rather than food (McGowan, 1982). In the United States today, there is widespread inability to do even relatively simple jobs, much less the complex work required in a high-technology economy. According to a 1979 report by the Ford Foundation, 25 million Americans cannot read at all and another 35 million lack the language skills to deal with the routine tasks of daily life (McGowan, 1982). *Functional illiteracy* is the inability to read and write well enough to be an effective (or functioning) member of society. Functional illiteracy is a major problem in the United States, where more money is spent on education than in any other nation. In the 1950s, the United States ranked eighteenth among nations in the proportion of its population that could read and write, but by the early 1980s the country had dropped to forty-ninth in its rate of literacy (Gaiter, 1982).

A 1975 survey found that 16 per cent of whites, 44 per cent of blacks, and 56 per cent of Hispanics in the United States were "functionally incompetent" at a variety of adult tasks. For example:

- 13 per cent of the sample could not address an envelope in a way that would guarantee it would get to its intended destination;
- 14 per cent could not fill out a check so that it would be sure to clear a bank; and
- 28 per cent could not figure out how much change they should get from a twenty-dollar bill after paying for something (Kozol, 1980: 2).

Functional illiteracy of this sort is costly to society: People have to pay others to do routine tasks such as filing income tax returns; employers must provide remedial education for their workers (Teltsch,

1983); jail and prison costs are high because people who cannot find work sometimes turn to crime; and welfare payments are high because many people lack the basic skills needed to hold jobs.

The rate of functional literacy measures how well a society's schools prepare its people for daily life. In order to create a functionally literate population, industrial societies have created systems of compulsory education in which everyone is required to attend school until a certain age. Universal and compulsory education of this sort has produced relatively high literacy rates in industrial societies, but because more skills and knowledge are needed to be functionally literate in industrial societies than in preindustrial societies, even industrial societies that have universal and compulsory education must deal with the problem of continually upgrading their population to meet the changing demands of daily life.

The Functions of Education

All forms of socialization are education in the broadest sense of the word, but in this chapter we consider *education* as the formal process by which people are systematically taught knowledge, skills, and values. Education in schools serves several functions: It socializes the young, integrates the society, creates new knowledge, trains people for work, and develops personal skills. Schools also have a variety of latent or hidden functions, some of which have negative consequences for society.

SOCIALIZATION AND SOCIAL CONTROL

Because it transmits the values, skills, and knowledge of a culture to a society's new members, including the young and immigrants, education perpetuates culture. Students learn from their teachers

273

and peers to behave in socially acceptable ways, so the educational process also acts as a type of social control. In fact, attending school gives many students their first opportunity to develop loyalties outside the family, something they will later do in the world of work. In this way, they learn how to behave in secondary groups after spending their early years in primary groups.

At home, children are treated according to their personal needs and tastes and according to their personal relationships with other members of the family. In school, however, children are treated and evaluated by their performance rather than according to their personal characteristics. The schools use a grading system based on standardized criteria, and students learn that their performance in school is being assessed and will have consequences for their future educational and work careers. In general, they learn to see their academic success or failure as a product of their own abilities, rather than as a consequence of luck or some ascribed social trait. Schools theoretically treat and evaluate all students according to standards that are applied to everyone in the same way, but in fact students of different genders, classes, and ethnic groups are often treated less objectively.

The "Hidden Curriculum"

Along with their coursework, children learn behavior that is conducive to the smooth functioning of the school and the society at large. This important part of the socialization process instills in children a set of values and norms that has been referred to as a *hidden curriculum* (Jackson, 1968). One observer has even compared kindergarten to a military "boot camp" where new recruits are taught to obey orders (Gracey, 1967). Children, it is said, learn to please their teachers, and so are instilled with an unquestioning willingness to submit to authority. However, many parents today feel that the schools do not teach students to be orderly, quiet, and attentive (Gallup Opinion Index, 1978).

SOCIAL INTEGRATION

Education integrates a society by teaching people a common language and a common way of seeing the world, thereby making it easier for them to communicate and interact. In many societies, including ours, the school is the only public institution that serves to assimilate new immigrants into the society and unite different racial and ethnic groups. By learning patriotic values and the na-

tion's history, all students are taught to identify with the nation-state, and the legitimacy of the political system is reinforced.

Critics of the integrative process claim that the schools have traditionally treated ethnic diversity as a problem to be overcome through the "Americanization" of students. Until recently, there had been a growing tolerance of racial and ethnic diversity in the schools. One result was the introduction of new courses in black history, and another was bilingual education—especially for Hispanic Americans. In 1983, however, a return to "Americanization" seemed imminent when an influential private research firm recommended that federal support for the teaching of courses such as science and mathematics in languages other than English should be abandoned (Daley, 1983).

CREATION OF NEW KNOWLEDGE

Education is an important source of new knowledge and technology. Research done in colleges and universities, and by people educated in those schools, helps society to adapt to changing conditions and to accomplish tasks more efficiently. For this reason, college and university research is often sponsored by the government, the institution that defines societal goals. Research is also supported by private interests, such as corporations, that intend to use new discoveries and inventions to increase profits.

TRAINING FOR WORK

One of the most important functions of education for society is to train workers to fill existing jobs and to work at jobs that will exist in the future. Literacy is essential for the performance of most jobs in an industrial society. Schools also teach work-related skills beyond reading, writing, and arithmetic; for instance, high schools teach carpentry and secretarial skills, colleges and universities train engineers and accountants, and graduate programs educate physicians and lawyers.

Conflict theorists have a different view of the relationship between the educational system and the economic system (Bowles and Gintis, 1976). In the nineteenth century, American industrialists treated public education as a way to convert new immigrants into productive factory workers. As the needs of the capitalist economy changed during the twentieth century, educational requirements were upgraded to provide employers with workers who had the skills necessary to do new kinds of work.

Education helps students develop personal skills. For example, these students are learning to cooperate in accomplishing group goals while they are putting together their school yearbook.

Conflict theorists suggest that capitalists have a vested interest in workers who have more education than they need to do their jobs. This gives employers flexibility in hiring and firing workers, by making available to them a large and educated labor pool from which to recruit new employees.

DEVELOPMENT OF PERSONAL SKILLS

Through education, students develop personal skills, attitudes, and interests that are not always directly related to their future careers. They learn to make friends and cooperate in accomplishing group goals, perhaps by participating on a sports team or on a prom committee. These experiences, which create a network of school friends, might help them later to find jobs, or to work on a corporate "team." Personal skills also enrich one's life outside the workplace, for friendships and participation in community activities are important parts of many adults' lives. In the future, changes in the economic system might provide people with even more leisure time than they now have, and education will help people to use this leisure time in more fulfilling ways. Education develops the ability

to find new sources of information on a topic and the skills to absorb new material on that subject without the direct supervision of a teacher. As a result, an educated person might pursue a subject of personal interest, such as Civil War, or read about how to plant an herb garden or build a patio.

Moreover, educated people are better able to understand and interpret new ideas and information. Compared to people with less schooling, educated people are more likely to express opinions on current social issues; they are more introspective and aware of their own motives; and they are more likely to seek new knowledge and tolerate diversity (Feldman and Newcomb, 1969; Hyman, Wright, and Reed, 1975; Hyman and Wright, 1979).

THE LATENT FUNCTIONS OF EDUCATION

The manifest, or intended, functions of education are socialization, social integration, the creation of new knowledge, training for work, and the development of personal skills. However, the educational system also has a variety of latent, or unintended, consequences.

One latent function of the schools is to weaken parental control over their children (Lasch, 1979). In school, students learn values, knowledge, and skills that their parents cannot supply, and sometimes what is learned in school contradicts what is learned at home. This can cause conflict between parents and schools, as it has in communities where schools have introduced sex education or taught scientific theories such as evolution that are incompatible with the religious beliefs of parents.

Schools also provide daytime custodial care for children for almost ten months of the year, permitting both parents to hold jobs or do other things during the day. Schools keep children off the streets and supervise them until they graduate or are old enough to quit school. In this way, the schools control the behavior of the young, although the high truancy rates of some schools minimize this supervisory function. Compulsory school attendance also keeps young people out of the labor market and thereby reduces competition for scarce jobs.

Separating the young in schools increases the chance that a youth counterculture will develop (see Chapter 3). The age segregation of students gives them an opportunity to interact with one another and develop values and norms that differ from those of the dominant culture. In addition, schools place students in a protected environment where they can try out behavior that might be too risky outside the school. For example, many people who actively demonstrated against the Vietnam War were college students who were able to protest American involvement without being expelled, losing a job, or developing a criminal record that might endanger future employment.

By providing a setting in which students can interact with peers, the school enables young people to develop close relationships outside their families for the first time. However, because most schools are located in homogeneous communities, these relationships are usually among people of similar social backgrounds; in this way, the school perpetuates existing barriers among people from different classes, races, and ethnic groups.

Elementary and Secondary Education in the United States

In most states, education is now compulsory until the age of sixteen. Education is also "free" in the sense that the public schools are supported by property taxes rather than by tuition paid by the students. The American system of universal and compulsory education has, however, developed only during the last century. In 1875, most Americans did not even complete primary school. By the end of the nineteenth century there was universal public education at the lower grades, although only 7 per cent of Americans had completed high school in 1900. By 1981, however, 69.8 per cent of everyone twenty-five and older had finished high school, 17.1 per cent had completed four or more years of college, and the median number of years of school was 12.5 (U.S. Bureau of the Census, 1982: 143).

Between 1970 and 1981 there was a decline in the number of students in elementary schools, as a result of the passing of "the tidal wave of the baby-boom generation" (Sawyer, 1981: 5). This decline has affected high school enrollments and is now starting to have an impact on college and university enrollments. The decline in elementary school enrollments created a surplus of schools and classrooms during the 1970s and 1980s; some schools were closed and converted into housing for the elderly, condominiums, and office buildings—often over the sharp protest of parents in the community. In addition, teachers were laid off, a painful experience for those who thought their jobs were secure and who were unable to find other positions. An exception to this trend is the recent effort to hire more teachers in mathematics and the sciences. In response to the higher salaries offered by private industry to people with these skills, there have been proposals to subsidize the education of science and math teachers or even to pay them more than teachers in other fields (Maeroff, 1982c).

Even with declines in the absolute number of students in elementary schools, a large proportion of all Americans do attend school. In 1981, for instance, about one American in every four—roughly 58 million people—was enrolled in some school, from nursery school to a university graduate program. This reflects the relative wealth of an American economy that can afford to support so many people in the economically nonproductive role of student. It also reflects American pragmatism, the belief that education is useful for people who want to improve their position in the stratification system. Pragmatism has also led to efforts to solve social problems such as inequality between racial groups and lack of knowledge about sex through the educational system.

THE FUNDING OF PUBLIC EDUCATION

The funding and control of American public schools—which enroll about 90 per cent of all elementary and secondary school students—are more decentralized than they are in most industrial societies. In the Soviet Union, for example, the national government determines the organization of the schools, their administrative regulations, the courses that are offered, the books that are read, and the training and assignment of teachers (Banks, 1968). In contrast, in the United States, these matters are decided at the local level.

For the most part, public education in the United States is funded by local sources such as property taxes (43.4 per cent of all school funds in 1980) and by state funds (46.8 per cent of the total). Federal money—which supports some school programs, such as the purchase of textbooks and the construction of school buildings—is a relatively small part of the total operating budget, only 9.8 per cent in 1980 (U.S. Bureau of the Census, 1982: 154). However, this money has been used to bring about changes such as school desegregation and better access for the handicapped. The federal contribution to public education declined during the Reagan administration, which reduced federal efforts to help the disadvantaged, the handicapped, and students who do not speak English.

The amount spent on education varies considerably from state to state. For example, in 1980 Tennessee spent only $460 per capita on education and Florida spent only $461 per capita. At the other end of the scale, Alaska spent $1,812 per capita—a figure that reflects the affluence resulting from the energy boom in that state—and Wyoming spent $914 per capita on education (U.S. Bureau of the Census, 1982: 285). The amount spent on education also varies from one community to another. Suburbs usually spend more than the cities; and as a result children who live in relatively well-to-do communities attend schools that have better facilities, a better-educated teaching staff, and a wider variety of extracurricular activities than the schools attended by children who live in poorer communities.

THE BUREAUCRATIC STRUCTURE OF THE SCHOOL

The school is a bureaucracy—a formal organization with specific rules and procedures that determine relationships among a board of education, administrators, teachers, and students. The school bureaucracy allocates authority and defines the behavior expected of each member of the organization. Bureaucratized schools deal less personally with students than more informally run schools, but bureaucratic schools may minimize the arbitrary treatment of students through the fair enforcement of written rules.

At the top of the school bureaucracy there is usually an elected board of education that appoints a superintendent of schools, establishes general educational policy, decides on a budget, and sets the staff's salaries (Rich, 1974). The board of education depends on the school superintendent for information about the actual daily operation of the schools. Information flows upward from the superintendent, who usually administers more than one school, to the board of education. Each school has a principal who is responsible for the details of school business and the supervision of the teachers.

Teachers instruct and supervise the students. Although teachers report regularly to the heads of their departments, they have considerable autonomy in planning and doing their work. Teachers are licensed by the state, but are hired and assigned by the local board of education and the superintendent. Some states have responded to the recent charge that poor quality teaching is the source of declining academic performance by students by requiring teachers to take competency tests, as well as to have a degree and certification in education, before hiring them (Maeroff, 1982b).

Students occupy the lowest position in the school bureaucracy, but it is the position for which the entire organization supposedly exists. In fact, the school bureaucracy can become self-serving, with the needs and interests of the board of education, the superintendent, the principal, and the teachers taking precedence over the educational and occupational goals of the students. From many students' point of view, the school is a total institution (see Chapter 7)—a regimented organization that they cannot leave before a certain age (Goffman, 1961; Jackson, 1968). Students sometimes complain that they are treated as "cases" by other members of the school organization, rather than as individuals who have their own needs and goals. The regulation of students by the school bureaucracy can limit their opportunities for self-expression, and sometimes this can produce hostility toward teachers and administrators or the emergence of an adolescent counterculture in which personal needs can be expressed more freely.

The Open Classroom

One effort to tailor the school to the individual needs of students is the *open classroom* (Silberman, 1970). This approach tries to minimize the formality and impersonality of the school bureaucracy by adapting seating patterns and the structure of the classroom to the educational and expressive needs of students rather than to the needs of the school's administrators and teachers. The open classroom is based on the idea that schools should respond to the interests of the students and adapt to the pace at which students learn. Students become involved in the learning process, and teachers are defined as resources to which students have access rather than as instructors who convey information. This system is demanding for teachers, because they must overcome the lack of structure and discipline and respond to the very different needs and interests of their students.

There are several problems in running an open classroom. Students sometimes lack the knowledge to know exactly what their educational needs are. Teachers have difficulty keeping order while maintaining the needed flexibility. Students sometimes fail to learn essential skills such as reading, writing, and arithmetic, causing some parents to demand a "return to the basics" (Lerner, 1982). There is, in fact, some recent evidence that schools in which the learning environment is more orderly and discipline stricter prepare their students better for jobs and for acceptance into colleges and universities (Coleman, Hoffer, and Kilgore, 1982a, 1982b). These factors have caused the open classroom to fall into some disfavor in recent years, and fewer schools now teach their students in these unstructured environments.

INTERACTION BETWEEN TEACHERS AND STUDENTS

Because of the difference in authority between teachers and students and because students are compelled to attend school until a certain age, interaction between teachers and students is filled with potential conflict. Usually the interaction proceeds smoothly, although it is formal and impersonal, as is characteristic of a bureaucracy. Teachers control the interaction among students in the classroom, maintain discipline, supply materials, and make sure that activities occur on schedule. Some critics of the use of computers in the classroom (see SEL 12.1) worry that the introduction of these machines as learning tools could undermine the authority of the teacher.

SOCIOLOGY AND EVERYDAY LIFE 12.1
Computers in the Classroom

In 1982, at least 15 per cent of all elementary and secondary schools in the United States were using computers in the classroom. The number will grow rapidly in the future, with a dramatic impact on the educational process. Some even predict that the effect of computers on learning will be as profound as the invention of writing.

"Jonathan is already 4, and he can't do the computer," remarked a 5-year-old student in a private school in Dallas (p. 1). This view may be atypical, but it underscores the increased use of computers in the early years of elementary school, or even before that at home. Computers now enable teachers to introduce very young students to geometry, to the skills needed for reading, and to new ways to solve problems. In addition, some colleges and universities have started to require "computer literacy" of their students, assuming that such skills are part of a well-rounded education and essential to a growing number of jobs.

In some classrooms, students might know more about computers than their teachers do. Computers alter traditional patterns of authority in the classroom, as students sometimes help their teachers over a rough spot in a computer program, and some teachers have felt threatened. Others, however, do not react in this way; for instance, one teacher says, "I work with third graders, and most of them are already beyond me. I think it is nice at that age to be able to tell an adult something and be right" (p. 42).

The computer has also changed peer relationships. Computers have not isolated students from one another, as some educators had feared, but rather seem to encourage cooperation and the sharing of techniques, especially if machines are clustered together in ways that

The number of schools that have computers in the classroom is already quite large, and statistics suggest that this number will grow rapidly in the future.

promote interaction. Sometimes students who do not do well in other academic subjects excel at the computer and are able to gain acceptance into peer groups because they can help others master computer skills.

By requiring students to break complex problems into a number of specific and manageable tasks, computers alter the way that students think. From their experiences with computers, students discover that there are often different ways to solve a problem. They also learn a precise and orderly approach to problem-solving; for example, correcting an error in a computer program requires close attention to detail. In addition, computers can even help to demystify mathematics by making the procedures of calculation and problem-solving more concrete. One mathematician suggests, "The fact that mathematics is an abstract discipline is a cultural construction rooted in the fact that it developed under limited technologies like pencil and paper. The computer can make the most abstract things concrete" (p. 42).

Computers are not, however, without critics. Some educators fear that they might undermine the traditional authority structure of the classroom by changing patterns of interaction among students and between students and teachers. Others suggest that computers can cause their users to think that the only problems worth solving are those that can be quantified. As one professor of computer science observes, "Abraham Maslow once said that to him who has only a hammer, the whole world looks like a nail. To him who has only a computer, the world looks like a computable domain" (p. 42).

The educational system will be changed in important ways by the introduction of the computer. We probably cannot even envision some of those changes, for it is now too early to determine the full impact of computers on the schools. As one university provost says, "It's like a community with five telephones. You can't judge the full effects till everyone has it" (p. 42).

Source: Adapted from Edward B. Fiske, "Computers Alter Lives of Pupils and Teachers," *The New York Times*, April 4, 1982, pp. 1, 42.

Teachers' treatment of their students can actually elicit the very behavior that teachers expect; sociologists call this the "self-fulfilling prophecy." In one classic experiment, researchers told teachers that certain students in their classes would improve markedly in academic performance during the year. In fact, these students did not differ from other students in the class in any way that might suggest that they would actually improve more during the year. However, the teachers treated those students whom they expected to do well in ways that elicited significant improvements in their classroom performance and their IQ test scores. Students of equal ability who were not designated as likely to improve did not show similar gains (Rosenthal and Jacobson, 1968). Another study found that teachers who were told that certain students had great ability tried to teach those students more material. As a result, those students learned more than other students who were not classified as having great ability, even though there was no real difference between the two groups in academic potential (Berg, 1970). These and other studies (Brookover and Erickson, 1975) indicate that teacher expectations affect student performance. However, there are studies that have failed to support this conclusion, and so the exact relationship between the expectations of teachers and the academic success of their students remains unclear (Elashoff and Snow, 1971; Fiedler, Cohen, and Feeney, 1971; Fleming and Anttonen, 1971; Brophy and Good, 1974; Boocock, 1978).

GRADES AND COMPETITION

Most schools use a restricted range of five or six grades to evaluate students. Reducing evaluations of academic performance to so few grades conceals important information about students—such as the extent to which they use their potential, their work habits, and their interest in different subjects. Pass–fail grading systems—which are used in some colleges and universities but in few elementary and secondary schools—provide even less information than a traditional A–B–C–D–F system. As a result, pass–fail grades must often be supplemented with detailed letters of recommendation.

Although the schools' use of a grading system is an effort to maintain some kind of standardized criteria for evaluating students, grading encourages students to compete with one another. This probably leads many to work hard and to learn, but it can also discourage students who earn low grades,

and thus develop poor self-concepts and even drop out of school. In the American educational system grades are earned through competition among individuals, but this is not a necessary aspect of the learning process. In the Soviet Union, for example, students compete for grades in teams; this instills in students a sense of cooperation rather than competition (Bronfenbrenner, 1970). Cooperation among Russian students is regarded as necessary for the development of a socialist society; in the United States, such cooperation would be defined as cheating. Competition for grades among American students fits in well with the culture's emphasis on individualism and the economic system's emphasis on competition. American education thus reflects and reinforces the capitalist economic system, just as the Soviet Union's system of education reflects and reinforces its economic system (Bowles and Gintis, 1976).

GRADE INFLATION AND DECLINING ACADEMIC SKILLS

The American educational system has been characterized by an apparent paradox since the 1960s: SAT (Scholastic Aptitude Test) scores have declined—indicating a drop in verbal and mathematical skills—but the grades awarded by schools have risen. This has been called *grade inflation,* because the As and Bs awarded in recent years seem to be worth less in terms of actual academic achievement than they were in the past.

The decline in SAT scores began around 1963. From about 1963 until about 1970, the drop in scores seemed to be largely a result of an increase in the proportion of all high school students who took the test. Poorer students who in the past would not have taken the SATs began to do so in the 1960s, and the result was a lowering of the average SAT scores. The number of students taking the SATs stabilized around 1970, but scores continued to decline in the following decade. This decline in the 1970s was apparently caused by a real drop in students' abilities rather than simply by a change in the kind of students taking the test. In 1981, test scores remained steady, and in 1982 they rose very slightly, possibly signaling a reversal of the trend (M. Cohen, 1982).

The reasons for the long-term decline in SAT scores are still unclear, but several possible explanations have been offered (Fiske; 1976; Fields, 1977). Some observers suggest their test scores might have dropped as a result of television viewing, which can take time away from homework, reduce students' attention spans, cause students to "tune out" uninteresting information, and lead students to expect school to be entertaining (Feinberg, 1977). Although television watching and aptitude test scores are correlated, there is no evidence that television watching *causes* aptitude test scores to fall (Mancusi, 1980).

Others have attributed the decline in test scores to the schools' deemphasis on teaching the "basics" (reading, writing, and arithmetic) that are tested on SATs, and their increased emphasis on "relevant" and "interesting" courses such as drug and sex education, black history, and women's studies. Still another possibility is that the decreased emphasis placed on memorization in the schools, and the increased emphasis on the process of learning and conceptualization, might not be reflected in the material that is included on SATs.

The declining quality of teaching is another factor sometimes cited as the cause of lower SAT scores. Salaries for teachers have not kept pace with pay in other occupations; as a consequence, some of the best college students who might have gone into teaching in the past have entered other areas of work. The college students who do enter elementary and secondary school teaching have SAT scores that are actually lower than the average for all students who take those tests. As a result, the best students now in school are being taught by teachers who scored lower on their SATs than the students themselves will score when they take the examination. The teachers are, however, better acquainted with the specific material that they are teaching.

Higher Education in the United States

In 1900, colleges and universities in the United States granted 30,000 degrees. In 1981, American colleges and universities awarded more than 1.3 million degrees, including 1,007,000 bachelor's degrees, 297,000 master's degrees, and 33,000 doctorates (U.S. Bureau of the Census, 1982: 166). There were about 12 million students enrolled in programs of higher learning in the United States in 1981.

A university differs from a college in that it provides graduate and professional education as well as a four-year bachelor's degree. About half of all colleges and universities in the United States are private, and the other half are publicly funded; however, roughly 80 per cent of all college and university students attend publicly funded schools. In addition to state funds, colleges and universities are supported by alumni contributions and student tuition and by federal funds in the form of research grants, construction money, and student aid.

THE COLLEGE EXPERIENCE

Why do people go to college? High school graduates attend colleges and universities to secure credentials for a good job, to gain a better sense of themselves and their goals in life, and to learn for learning's sake. Some students go on to college without clearly articulating their reasons for doing so; the expectations of families, teachers, guidance counselors, and peers sometimes push them into it.

In the first year of college, students must make major adjustments in their way of life. They are relatively free of adult supervision for the first time, and they interact more with their peers. As a result, they are more likely to turn to friends rather than to adults for advice and support. In their newly acquired autonomy, college students must decide what programs to pursue, what courses to take, and how much to study. Many students continue to depend on their parents for financial support, but the management of that money is often left to the student. Some students become disillusioned during the first year of college because classes seem too large and contact with professors too limited (Chickering, 1969; Goodman and Feldman, 1975; Dullea, 1982).

At the end of their college years, students are sometimes as uncertain about their career goals and their future lives as they were when they began. They will have gained knowledge and skills and changed their attitudes and behavior, but many have not been prepared for specific careers during this time (Katz et al., 1968). Recently, however, there have been efforts to bring traditionally nonvocational and nonprofessional programs such as liberal arts into line with the world of work (Green and Salem, 1981).

Effects of a College Education

Between their freshman year and graduation, college students make many changes. Table 12.1 shows the most important benefits of a college education as perceived by one sample of juniors and seniors. In addition to these benefits, a college edu-

In their newly acquired autonomy, first-year college students must decide what programs to pursue, what courses to take, and how much to study.

cation also increases participation in clubs and organizations and in political activities, and promotes openness to new experiences; it decreases racial prejudice, altruism, and interest in religion and athletics (Astin, 1972, 1977).

In general, these changes are greatest for students who attend small and highly regarded col-

TABLE 12.1
Benefits of College Perceived by Juniors and Seniors

Type of benefit	Percentage reporting "very much" or "quite a bit" of benefit
Personal development	84
Tolerance	78
Individuality	76
Social development	75
Friendships	74
Critical thinking	72
Specialized skills	71
Philosophy, cultures	69
Vocabulary, facts	69

Source: Howard R. Bowen, *Investment in Learning.* San Francisco: Jossey-Bass, 1977, pp. 228–229.

leges where they reside during their school years; changes are less significant for students who commute from their homes to large universities. Some of these alterations in attitudes and behavior are due to normal maturation over the four years, but comparisons of college students with people of similar ages who do not attend college show that these changes are also a direct result of a college education itself (Feldman and Newcomb, 1969). The possibility remains that students who choose to attend college differ from those who choose not to attend; for example, those who decide to go to college might be more open-minded and thus more susceptible to outside influences on their attitudes and behavior.

The increasing tolerance, flexibility, and openness among the college-educated does not continue in professional school—including medical, dental, and law schools. Students who enroll in these programs usually narrow their thinking along professional lines. The heavy work load that these students carry isolates them from outside influences to some extent, but these professional programs are also deliberately designed to socialize— or resocialize—students by exposing them to certain kinds of material and by imparting a distinctive perspective on the world (Van Loon, 1970; Pavalko, 1976; Wegner, 1976; Turow, 1977).

College Peer Groups

An important agent of socialization during the college years is the peer group. One kind of peer group found on many college and university campuses emphasizes parties, dating, and sports. Another type places a high value on learning. A third type is the vocational peer group, which sees the college years as a time to prepare for a career. A fourth is the nonconformist group, which has included bohemians, hippies, and political activists who oppose existing institutions and policies (Clark and Trow, 1966; Katz et al., 1968). The group that is dominant on any given college campus varies from time to time, and the relative significance of each group also varies from campus to campus. In the late 1960s and early 1970s, some campuses were dominated by a nonconformist group of antiwar activists; but in the 1980s the vocational group became relatively more important as high unemployment rates focused students' attention on preparing for jobs that pay well.

Academic performance is stressed more in college peer groups than in high school peer groups, primarily because college attendance is voluntary and high school attendance is compulsory until a certain age. Nevertheless, peer groups on college and university campuses do apply some pressure to downplay academic performance. Some students try to maintain an active social life and good grades while still creating an impression that they do not have to work very hard to get those grades. Some undergraduates try to get good grades with minimal effort by taking easy courses, by looking for teachers who are lenient in assignments, by reading only the material they expect to be tested on, by cramming, and by relying on files of tests given in the past (Becker, Geer, and Hughes, 1968). One study of medical school students found that they too developed ways to get acceptable grades with the least possible effort. Peer groups among medical students established group norms about how much of the assigned work they would actually turn in, thereby minimizing the risk of poor grades if they did not do all the assigned work (Hughes, Becker, and Geer, 1962).

TWO-YEAR COLLEGES

Junior colleges and community colleges are two-year schools that originally developed to educate people who could not attend four-year colleges and universities because of poor academic performance in high school or because of financial hardship. In 1960, there were 521 junior colleges in the United States with a total enrollment of 451,000 students. By 1980, the number of such schools had risen to 1,274, and total enrollments had reached 4,526,000, a tenfold increase (U.S. Bureau of the Census, 1982: 159).

Who Goes to a Two-Year College and Why?

Students who attend two-year colleges differ from those at four-year colleges and universities in that many have postponed college for some time after finishing high school. As a result, two-year students tend to be older than those at four-year schools. Two-year students are also more likely to be married and to be members of minority groups, and they are more likely to be working and attending school part time (Maeroff, 1982a).

Some junior-college and community-college students enroll in nondegree programs and take courses for personal interest, but most of these students are trying to improve themselves occupationally by completing the requirements for certification at a job (such as laboratory technician) or by finishing coursework that will help them gain admission to a four-year college or university (Maeroff, 1982a). About half of all two-year students go on to four-year schools. Some sociologists, however, have been critical of two-year colleges, arguing that they educate the lower social classes for vocational and technical jobs and thus do not give them a real opportunity to move into the middle class (Karabel, 1977). In addition, many students who attend two-year colleges to improve their job prospects cannot find work in their chosen field after finishing a program (Pincus, 1980).

Teaching in a Two-Year College

Junior-college and community-college faculty members are not expected to do research and publish articles and books, as are the faculty members of four-year colleges and universities. They spend more hours in classroom instruction, and they have less control over hiring, curriculum design, and text assignments than do the faculty at four-year schools. Some faculty members at two-year colleges regard their jobs as careers, and some see them as temporary stops on the way to four-year schools. Others work there to support outside pursuits such as writing and art. About half of junior-college and community-college faculty members prefer to be working where they are, and the rest would rather have a job in a four-year school or work full time at something else (Nolan and Swift, 1976).

SPECIAL ISSUES IN HIGHER EDUCATION

Two issues in higher education that have been widely discussed in recent years are tenure and academic freedom for professors and the value of degrees for college graduates.

Tenure and Academic Freedom

The autonomy of college professors from outside political, economic, and social pressures is guaranteed by *tenure*, a lifetime contract that is contingent on competent job performance; the university guarantees to retain the services of the professor, but the professor is free to leave for a position elsewhere. Tenure is designed to guarantee *academic freedom*, the opportunity to conduct the search for truth without external pressure to produce results that support particular interests.

Professors teach, serve on committees, contribute to the community outside the university, do research, and write books and articles (see SEL 1.1). In tenure decisions at colleges and universities, research and publication are given heavy emphasis; they are seen by the academic community as evidence that professors will keep abreast of the latest developments in their disciplines, will teach students the latest findings in their fields, and will bring money to the university in the form of research grants (which help to keep tuition lower than it would otherwise be).

Time limitations can pressure some faculty members—especially younger ones who are seeking tenure—to favor research and writing over teaching and advising students. However, because professors typically spend only six to twelve hours a week in classroom instruction—much less than the thirty to thirty-five hours per week spent in the classroom by elementary and secondary school teachers—time is available to do research and write. There is no reason to believe that research and writing detract from the education of students; in fact, they probably contribute to that education, because professors who spend much time in research and writing are often highly regarded as classroom instructors as well. In addition, the publications of professors contribute to the education of both undergraduate and graduate students; for example, this book relies heavily on the published work of hundreds of other sociologists.

Credentialism

By the 1970s, the number of people with college degrees exceeded the number of jobs that required those degrees. College graduates in the 1970s had to look for jobs that would pay well, in contrast to the 1960s, when jobs almost seemed to seek college graduates (Freeman, 1976). About half of all college graduates in the mid-1970s were underemployed; that is, they found jobs for which they were overqualified (Berg, Freedman, and Freeman, 1978). Even low-level jobs that have not historically required a college degree have recently come to require that credential. This condition of an overeducated and underemployed work force has been called "the great training robbery," because people who have pursued higher education find that after they have earned their degrees there are no jobs available in which they can use the knowledge and skills they have acquired in college (Berg, 1970). This situation has also been called *credentialism*, the requirement that a worker have a degree that is not actually necessary for the performance of a job.

In 1974, the payoff for a college degree was less than it was only five years earlier. In 1969, college graduates earned about 50 per cent more than workers with only a high school degree; by 1974, college graduates earned only 35 per cent more than high school graduates (Freeman, 1976). The high cost of a college education, the income that students forgo while in school, and the diminishing payoff in lifetime income of a college degree led some observers to conclude that a college education does not pay for itself (Bird, 1975). However, a report by the U.S. Bureau of the Census in 1983 estimated that the lifetime income of an eighteen-year-old man who earned a bachelor's degree would be $1,190,000, compared to $861,000 for a man with only a high school diploma and $601,000 for a man who failed to finish high school (*The New York Times*, March 14, 1983, p. A12). Completing a college degree would thus produce about $329,000 more in lifetime earnings, considerably more than the cost of a college education and the income not earned while in college. Women also earned more if they completed college, but the differences were smaller.

College has other benefits than greater lifetime earnings; it also produces an enriched way of life, more curiosity about the world, an interest in the arts, a better self-image, more self-awareness, more job satisfaction, and more skill in dealing with other people (Solmon and Taubman, 1973; Bowen, 1977; Astin, 1977; Drew, 1978).

One explanation that has been offered for credentialism is that keeping the educational requirements for jobs high is a way to recruit good workers. Employers can demand workers with more education for a job than is really needed if there are more highly educated people than there are jobs available. However, there is no evidence that better-educated workers are more productive, and there is even some evidence that they might be less productive in certain jobs (Berg, 1970; Collins, 1971; Harrison, 1972). In addition, grades in school do not predict very well how good a teacher, a lawyer, a physician, or a corporate exec-

utive a person may turn out to be (Gintis, 1971; Collins, 1979).

Credentialism is a product of "status competition," the effort by people relatively low in the stratification system—such as minority groups and women—to improve their positions through education. However, as these people gain more education, people higher in the stratification system respond by increasing their own education (Hurn, 1978). The population as a whole becomes more educated, but the relative position of different groups in the stratification system does not change much. In other words, credentialism is more a product of using the educational system to expand the opportunity for upward mobility than a result of changes in the knowledge and skills required by the economic system (Collins, 1971, 1979; Freeman, 1976).

SOCIOLOGY AND EVERYDAY LIFE 12.2
Credentialism and the Ph.D.

Changes in higher education during the 1960s and 1970s have left a ballooning number of Ph.D.s with few job opportunities in higher education, the place where they have historically found work. One factor reducing the number of academic positions for these new Ph.D.s was that undergraduate enrollments had stopped expanding and were even dropping at some colleges and universities. This decline was a consequence of a change in the age structure of the American population, the passing of the "baby boom" generation of the post–World War II years that had caused higher education to expand during the 1960s and 1970s. A related factor was that many of the young faculty members hired to teach these students had been granted tenure and would not retire for many years, and so there were few openings due to retirement. Because of a fear of being overstaffed with tenured professors, some schools even instituted tenure "freezes," which caused some Ph.D.s with teaching experience to look elsewhere for employment. In addition, the salaries of professors did not rise as fast as those of other occupations during the 1970s, and so academic work became less attractive to some potential employees.

As a result of these social factors, many people with a Ph.D. degree have taken jobs that do not in fact require this degree. In response to

this problem, a number of universities—for example, Harvard University, the University of Pennsylvania, New York University, UCLA, the University of Virginia, and the University of Texas—have developed intensive courses in business management to "retool" Ph.D.s for jobs in industry; these schools also provide assistance in finding such employment. The courses offered students in these programs include accounting, marketing, finance, and economics; N.Y.U., for example, gives their students the courses typically taken by first-year students in their M.B.A. program.

Some Ph.D.s have been skeptical of these retraining programs, fearing that their age or widely held stereotypes of intellectuals might disqualify them from work in industry. However, a former business executive who teaches in the Harvard Business School program for Ph.D.s said that he felt that business recruiters would be "pleasantly surprised by the maturity and the practical orientation of these people. They do not fit the stereotype of the impractical intellectual" (p. E7). He added that "the analysis they put out is better than that of students at regular M.B.A. programs or in company executive management programs" (p. E7). The results of the Harvard program bear out his confidence: Thirty-four of the forty-seven people completing the program in 1980 found work in industry, and only seven remained in academic positions. About 90 per cent of those who have taken the N.Y.U. program have taken positions in business.

Nevertheless, people with Ph.D.s who take these intensive courses in business management are an example of credentialism; they have degrees that make them "overqualified" for the work they do in industry, because their Ph.D.s are more advanced degrees than are needed for the positions they occupy.

Sources: Based on Fox Butterfield, "Harvard Offers Cramming for a Corporate Future," *The New York Times*, July 18, 1982, p. E7. Quotations are from this article. Also, Elizabeth M. Fowler, "N.Y.U. Was the Pioneer," *The New York Times*, July 18, 1982, p. E7.

THE FUTURE OF HIGHER EDUCATION

From now until the year 2000, the number of Americans who are in the age group from which colleges and universities have traditionally drawn their students will diminish (Carnegie Council on Policy Studies in Higher Education, 1980). This will force colleges and universities to develop new and more flexible programs—such as part-time degree programs and night schools—that will appeal to age groups that have not previously been the source of most college students. Some four-year schools have already begun to admit more students who have the characteristics of today's junior-college and community-college students—people who are older, members of minority groups, married people, and working people (Chira, 1982). More colleges and universities will compete for these kinds of students in the near future, and those that do not attract enough students may be forced to shut down. This is most likely to happen to schools of marginal academic quality, schools in undesirable geographic locations, and schools that have little financial support from their graduates.

Education and Inequality

In itself, educational attainment is a source of prestige, but Americans see education more in terms of its value in finding a good job than for its intrinsic worth (Coleman and Rainwater, 1978). Indeed, research shows that education is important for upward social mobility; a son's movement up the social ladder from his father's position can be attributed primarily to greater educational attainment by the son (Blau and Duncan, 1967).

According to conflict theorists, education is an institution that reflects and perpetuates a society's economic system. They claim that the schools serve the ruling class by maintaining social inequality (Bowles and Gintis, 1976; Bowles, 1977; Persell, 1977). The educational system is conservative; it preserves the status quo instead of encouraging students to alter the basic structure of society. The schools perpetuate inequalities of class, race, and sex by limiting opportunities for people lower in the stratification system to move up (DeLone, 1979). The conflict perspective suggests that social change—such as racial integration or the redistribution of wealth—cannot be achieved by the schools alone, because the schools are controlled by people who benefit from racial and economic inequality (Bowles and Gintis, 1976).

EDUCATION AND SOCIAL CLASS

The relationship between social class and academic ability is closely associated with the family environment and childhood experiences of students (Mercy and Steelman, 1982). For instance, middle-class and upper-class children are more likely than those from the lower classes to be exposed at an early age to books and educational toys that encourage learning. Because their parents are likely to have attained a higher level of education, children from these classes are more apt to value education, both for its own sake and for pragmatic reasons.

"Tracking"

Tracking is the placement of students in different educational programs—such as college-preparatory, business, and general studies—according to their academic skills and their career interests, or at least according to the way that teachers and administrators perceive those skills and interests. Functionalists explain tracking as necessary to train people of different abilities for the great variety of work that needs to be done. The goal of the American educational system in its ideal form is to develop basic skills in all students in the early years and then sort those students into different tracks through the use of grades, aptitude tests, and teachers' evaluations. By about ninth grade, most American students have been assigned to a track; students in Western European societies are usually assigned to tracks even earlier. At least in theory, tracking does not prevent a student from later switching, say from a business to a college-preparatory track; in practice, switching tracks is discouraged and uncommon (Rosenbaum, 1978).

According to functionalists, tracking permits brighter students to work at their own pace without being slowed down by less intelligent peers, and it enables slower students to take courses that they can manage and that will prepare them for the jobs for which administrators and teachers feel they are suited. One recent piece of research that is consistent with the functionalist perspective found that track placements were governed primarily by traditional academic criteria rather than by factors such as class background, racial group, or sex (Alexander and Cook, 1982). However, this study also found that track placement was a complex process that possibly was influenced by forces set in motion in the primary grades and that tracking might have less effect on academic achievement than earlier studies had shown.

Conflict theorists regard tracking as a way to channel people from the lower classes, minority groups, and "deprived" cultural backgrounds into educational programs that limit their access to jobs that pay well and have high prestige (Bowles and Gintis, 1976; Gintis, 1977). Conflict theorists argue that class background is closely associated with track placement, with middle-class students more likely than working-class students to be assigned to a college track. Job opportunities are thus limited for those students not assigned to a college track. Their schoolwork is often belittled, and they are sometimes even graded on a different scale than college-track students (Rosenbaum, 1978, 1980). Tracking takes what are relatively small differences among students in elementary school and junior high school and reinforces them through tracking in high school. This strengthens the existing stratification system and the social inequality intrinsic to it (Schafer, Olexa, and Polk, 1970).

Class and College Education

For a variety of reasons, the higher the family income, the more likely it is that a high school graduate will attend college (see Table 12.2). Students from the lower class and the working class sometimes lack even the most basic information about college; some are unaware that it is necessary to apply in advance for admission to colleges and universities (Rosenbaum, 1978, 1980). Teachers and guidance counselors are unlikely to furnish this information to these students unless they ask, for the teachers and guidance counselors are apt to assume that students from the lower social classes—especially those in tracks other than college preparatory, as most of them are—will not continue their education after high school. Even if they were encouraged to pursue their education, many of these students would not be able to afford the high and increasing cost of a college education.

TABLE 12.2
Percentage of 18-to-24-Year-Old Dependent Family Members Enrolled in College, by Family Income, 1981

Family income	Percentage of 18-to-24-year-olds enrolled in college
Under $10,000	28.5
$10,000 to $14,999	36.5
$15,000 to $19,999	38.3
$20,000 to $24,999	43.0
$25,000 and over	52.9
All income levels	44.3

Source: U.S. Bureau of the Census, *Statistical Abstract of the United States, 1982–83.* Washington, D.C.: U.S. Government Printing Office, 1982, p. 160.

Students from the higher social classes are also more likely to attend college because they do better academically in high school and score higher on the SAT tests that many colleges and universities use to admit students. Their better academic performance, as compared to students from the lower and working classes, is due to such factors as parental and peer pressures to do well in school, teachers' expectations of academic success, and the learning environment in the schools they attend. Students from well-off families are also more likely to attend college because their parents are better able to afford the costs of tuition, room, and board. However, as Table 12.2 shows, not all college students, by any means, are economically advantaged. Many students from the middle- and lower-incomes brackets do manage to get a college education.

WOMEN IN HIGHER EDUCATION

In 1960, only 17.8 per cent of female high school graduates enrolled in college, compared to 30.3 per cent of male high school graduates. However, by 1981, the proportion of female high school graduates enrolled in college (30.4 per cent) was almost equal to the proportion of male graduates (34.7 per cent) (U.S. Bureau of the Census, 1982: 159). In 1981, women made up about half of all full-time undergraduates and 45 per cent of all graduate students. Because women were in the majority among part-time students and junior-college and community-college students, they actually outnumbered men among all college students in 1981. In that year, there were 108 women in college for every 100 men, compared to only seventy-four women for every 100 men in 1972 (*The New York Times*, March 21, 1983, p. A13).

EDUCATION AND RACIAL GROUPS

Racial and ethnic groups in the United States have traditionally regarded the educational system as their path to success, but minorities have not been well served by American schools, with the exception of Asian Americans and Jewish Americans. In fact, blacks and whites were legally separated from

With the exception of Asian Americans and Jewish Americans, minorities have not been well served by American schools.

each other in public schools until the 1954 Supreme Court decision, *Brown* v. *Board of Education of Topeka, Kansas.* Since then, schools in areas that had *de jure* (by law) segregation—mainly in the Southern states—have been desegregated faster than schools in areas with *de facto* (in fact) segregation, which is based on residential patterns rather than the law. Only when schools are fully desegregated will all groups have equal access to the credentials required by employers. In addition, schools provide students with the social contacts and the information needed to find good jobs. For example, one study found that blacks who had attended desegregated schools were more likely to have jobs that blacks had not traditionally held; they also had higher incomes and better information about the labor market than blacks who had attended segregated schools (Crain, 1970).

Since 1960, blacks have become more similar to whites in educational attainment. In 1960, the median number of years of school completed by blacks was 8, nearly three years less than the years for whites. By 1981, the median number for blacks was 12.1 and for whites, 12.6—a gap of only half a year (U.S. Bureau of the Census, 1982: 143). In spite of this progress, differences in educational attainment persist. In 1975, blacks and whites who graduated from high school were equally likely to enroll in college, but by 1981 a difference between the groups had reemerged, with 28 per cent of black high school graduates and 32.5 per cent of whites enrolling in college (U.S. Bureau of the Census, 1982: 159).

The IQ Test Controversy

In spite of recent changes in the educational attainment of blacks, there is still evidence that blacks and whites differ in terms of average IQ (intelligence quotient) test scores. Possible explanations of this difference have provoked a storm of controversy in recent years.

One of the best known and most widely attacked proponents of the idea that there are real and significant racial differences in problem-solving ability (a common way to define intelligence) is Arthur R. Jensen (1969, 1980, 1981). Jensen argues that the difference in IQ test scores between blacks and whites does not reflect class differences alone, nor does it reflect cultural differences between the groups. Jensen speculates that the difference might well be due to genetic, or innate, differences between blacks and whites, though he does acknowl-

edge that there is as yet no scientifically satisfactory explanation for black–white differences in IQ test scores (Jensen, 1981: 202).

Jensen's position has elicited strong criticism from sociologists and other social scientists. One criticism is that IQ tests are based on an idea of intelligence that is held by the people who design the tests, and that in the United States it has usually been members of the white middle class who write these tests. Some critics even claim that IQ tests are so culture-bound as to be useless; thus a person who did well on an IQ test constructed for use in an industrial society might do poorly on one designed to measure problem-solving ability in an agricultural society. Intelligence, in other words, is a concept that has no clear and universal meaning.

Another criticism of Jensen is that he does not give enough attention to the large variation in test scores *within* each racial group. The difference between the average score for blacks and the average score for whites is about fifteen points (with 100 as an overall median score), but there is a range of scores among blacks and among whites that is much greater than fifteen points. In other words, a significant number of blacks score better on IQ tests than do many whites who take them. Jensen (1980, 1981) acknowledges this; indeed, he cautions against misusing IQ tests to treat individuals differently simply because they belong to a group with a high or a low average score. Nevertheless, he has spent considerable effort searching for an explanation of group differences in IQ scores.

One pertinent criticism of Jensen's suggestion that intelligence is inherited is that he and others have so far failed to pinpoint the exact way that problem-solving ability is genetically transmitted from parent to offspring. People seem to be born with a very broad "range of potential"—that is, the capacity to score well or score poorly on IQ tests when they are older. The cultural and social environment in which people are socialized makes a great deal of difference in how they will do on those tests (Blau, 1981). Most sociologists reject Jensen's speculation that the variation in IQ test scores from one group to another is due to inherited traits, suggesting instead that this variation can be attributed largely to environmental differences among groups. The fact that an individual's score on an IQ test can be raised substantially in a short time through coaching and cultural enrichment suggests that environmental factors do play a major part in determining how an individual will perform on an IQ test.

EQUALITY OF EDUCATIONAL OPPORTUNITY

The search for an understanding of the sources of social inequality in the American school system led James Coleman to conduct an important study in which data were gathered from 570,000 students and 60,000 teachers in 4,000 schools. Coleman found that public schools were segregated by race and that blacks, on the average, did not attend schools of as high a quality as those attended by whites. However, the difference in school quality between the two racial groups was less than anyone had anticipated, including Coleman. The schools attended by blacks and by whites did not differ much in money spent per student, age of the building, quality of the library, class size, and other measures. More importantly, the quality of a school was not closely related to the academic performance of its students. This surprised many people, especially educational experts who had long assumed that money spent on school improvements would benefit students academically. The Coleman report concluded that the poor academic performance of lower-class and minority students was not primarily a result of the quality· of the schools they attended.

What, then, did cause variations in academic performance among students? Coleman (1966: 22) found that differences in achievement were due mainly to the "educational backgrounds and aspirations of the other students in the school," and that these factors were in turn linked to the class background of the students. Family background of the students and characteristics of the residents of the neighborhood in which the school was located were the most important influences on educational achievement. Black students did better in schools in which the student body was composed of different racial groups and different social classes than they did in schools that were segregated by race and by class. Whites in desegregated schools did not do any less well academically than they did in segregated schools.

In the 1960s, the idea developed—partly as a result of Coleman's findings—that social policies should be developed to provide equal educational *results* for all students rather than simply try to provide all students with equal educational *opportunities*. As a result, policies were developed to reduce educational inequality. Some of these are compensatory education, busing, and the use of vouchers and tuition tax credits to encourage students to enroll in private schools.

Compensatory Education

The policy of creating intensive educational progams for disadvantaged students to bring them up to the the level of other students became federal law in 1965. This policy of *compensatory education* was intended to help the poor (rather than specific minority groups) to improve their academic performance through specially designed programs that included new textbooks, individual tutoring, and learning machines (Tyler, 1974).

The underlying assumption of compensatory education is that "culturally deprived" students come from homes in which they do not develop the skills they need to perform well in an academic setting. One program to remedy this is Project Head Start, begun in the 1960s and continuing today, which helps pre-school children develop academic skills and enthusiasm for learning. Some evidence shows that Project Head Start and other compensatory programs can raise academic performance and improve IQ test scores in the short run, but that these effects often disappear within a few years (Stearns, 1971; Hurn, 1978; Zigler and Valentine, 1979; Jensen, 1981; Tatel, 1983). Extending compensatory education through the later years in school might prolong the beneficial effects of these programs. During the 1970s, some of these programs came under attack for being condescending and for providing little lasting impact. In the 1980s, federal cutbacks in aid to education and assistance to the disadvantaged significantly reduced the money spent on compensatory education.

Busing

One controversial policy to reduce social inequality through school desegregation is the *busing* of children from one neighborhood to a school in a different community. Usually, though not always, black children are bused to schools in white neighborhoods, rather than whites being bused to predominantly black schools. This policy has been supported by Coleman's finding that blacks gain and whites do not lose from desegregation.

White Americans favor school desegregation, but they oppose busing to achieve that result. In fact, whites are two-and-a-half times as likely as blacks to oppose busing to desegregate schools (Rist, 1978, 1979; Gallup, 1982). Whites give several

Project Head Start is one of the compensatory programs designed to provide equal educational results for all students.

reasons for their opposition to busing. They claim that riding a bus is tiring for young children, creates the risk of getting lost in a strange neighborhood, reduces contacts between teachers and parents, and limits students' activities after school. In addition, some people oppose busing as a form of government interference in the neighborhood school, which has long been a tradition in the United States.

Another criticism of busing is that not all the research shows that blacks who have been bused to schools in white communities have actually improved their academic performance (Dentler, 1967; Armor, 1973; St. John, 1975; Rist, 1979). In fact, some critics of busing say that it can harm the self-image of black students and reduce their confidence and educational aspirations when they have

to compete with better-prepared white students. This kind of competitive atmosphere can also create conflict between blacks and whites. The general conclusion seems to be that desegregation does not always improve the academic performance of blacks, but it sometimes has this effect and it rarely reduces their performance. If busing were supplemented by continuing compensatory programs, there might be significant gains in the academic achievement of blacks.

Another often-heard argument against busing is that it is a cause of *"white flight,"* the migration of whites from the cities to the suburbs. It has been suggested that one result of desegregation is to accelerate white flight, especially in large school districts with more than 20 per cent minority enrollments and with nearby white suburbs (Armor,

1980). However, others suggest that the migration of whites to the suburbs is part of a long-term trend toward suburbanization that is not necessarily associated with school desegregation (Pettigrew and Green, 1976). Still another position is that the migration of whites to the suburbs is motivated by a desire by the middle class to escape the lower classes, regardless of the race of the people involved. High crime rates in the central city have also been pointed to as a factor in the flight of whites to the suburbs.

Although busing does have several disadvantages for both parents and children, students were riding buses to school long before it was proposed as a method of desegregating schools. Some of the opposition to busing appears to be a result of racial prejudice and discrimination, but there are other sources as well. The residential segregation of racial groups in American communities leaves few workable alternatives other than busing to achieve school desegregation. One alternative that has been discussed is to give parents a financial incentive to send their children to desegregated schools.

Vouchers and Tax Credits

A proposal that has been widely debated in the 1980s would change the American educational system by giving parents a financial incentive to find the school for which they feel their children are best suited. Parents would be given a *voucher* that they could use to pay the tuition at any school. The school would then redeem the voucher for government funds, which would come from the taxes that now support public schools. Another proposed method would give an income tax rebate to parents who pay tuition at Catholic or private schools.

ARE SOME SCHOOLS BETTER THAN OTHERS? The voucher and tax rebate proposals require some schools to be relatively more successful than others in educating students. Coleman's (1966) study of educational opportunity concluded that what went on in the school was less important in determining academic performance than was the social background of the students, but two major studies in recent years—including a new one by Coleman—have found that some schools do provide a better education. A study done in London showed that academic performance was better in schools in which teachers stressed homework and punctuality, carefully evaluated the work of their students, and enforced disciplinary standards (Rutter, 1979).

The conclusions of this London study are supported by recent work by Coleman (1981; Coleman, Hoffer, and Kilgore, 1982a, 1982b; Fiske, 1981; Cohen, 1981). This study of 58,728 high school sophomores and seniors from 1,015 public and private schools found that students in Catholic and other private schools performed better—especially in vocabulary and in mathematics—than public school students. Also, there was more improvement from sophomore to senior year among Catholic and private school students, and minority students in nonpublic schools did better than minorities in public schools. Coleman concluded that students did better in Catholic and private schools because those schools had the conditions most closely associated with academic success: an orderly social environment, rigorous academic demands, strict discipline, less class-cutting, and better attendance.

PUBLIC AND PRIVATE SCHOOLS: THE POLICY IMPLICATIONS. The results of Coleman's recent study have been used to support a policy of tuition tax credits or vouchers to encourage the transfer of students from public schools to Catholic and other private schools, although Coleman and his colleagues state that their work is not evidence on the actual effects of those policies (Coleman, Kilgore, and Hoffer, 1982b: 184). Supporters claim that tuition tax credits or vouchers would improve the quality of American education—both for students who are able to transfer to better schools and for students who stay in public schools that would have to improve to keep from losing students to private schools. Tuition tax credits and vouchers might also reduce the segregation of racial and ethnic groups as minority students transferred to Catholic and private schools.

Critics of Coleman's study claim that Catholic and private schools are more effective than public schools in educating students because they are more selective in admitting students (McPartland and McDill, 1982). Coleman has responded that there is actually little difference in the social background of students in public schools and those in Catholic and private schools, and that students in the Catholic and private schools do better academically when they are compared to students of similar social backgrounds in public schools (Coleman, Hoffer, and Kilgore, 1982a, 1982b).

Another criticism of Coleman's study is that there are simply not enough Catholic and private schools to have a major effect on the American educational system. Only about 10 per cent of elementary and secondary students attend nonpublic schools. Coleman has suggested that conditions in the public schools might be made more like those that produce academic success in Catholic and private schools. Another possibility is the development of new Catholic and private schools in response to the availability of voucher funds. This possibility has led some critics—especially the National Educational Association—to oppose vouchers and tax credits for fear of the demise of public education. However, the overall proportion of American children enrolled in private schools has declined since the early 1960s. In 1959–1960, 14.4 per cent of elementary school students attended private schools; by 1979–1980, this figure had declined to 11.2 per cent. Over these two decades the proportion of high school students enrolled in private schools dropped from 11.1 per cent to 7.4 per cent (Herbers, 1982d).

Parents who send their children to private schools often claim that they are forced to carry a double financial burden: They pay property taxes to support public education, and they also pay tuition to educate their own children in private schools. They and their supporters argue that this burden should be alleviated through vouchers or tax credits. Their critics fear that such plans would provide much larger tax benefits to the middle class and the upper class than they would to the lower classes. Critics also claim that vouchers and tax credits would favor the opening of new private schools and the expansion of existing ones, and that this might increase, rather than decrease, segregation by race, class, and religion.

EDUCATION AND SOCIAL CHANGE

Americans have long believed that the public school can bring about social change. In recent years, that belief has been eroded by opposition to desegregation, a sense that public education is declining in quality, and the development of plans to encourage the transfer of students from public schools to private ones. In addition, research suggests that education is limited in its ability to reduce income inequality among groups. Jencks and his associates (Jencks et al., 1972; Jencks et al., 1979) suggest that if Americans want to create greater equality of income, they should redistribute wealth from the rich to the poor in a direct way, rather than rely on the schools to provide the education and the credentials that will lead to better jobs and higher incomes. Highly educated people do earn more than people with less education, but many

other factors distinguish the rich from the poor. Schools reflect and reinforce social inequality in various ways, and it is too much to expect the schools to reduce that inequality without the full support of other institutions.

Summary

People who live in complex industrial societies need skills and knowledge that they cannot easily acquire from their families; the institution of education meets those needs. In addition to providing the literacy needed to work in an industrial economy, schools socialize young people and immigrants to the ways of the culture. Students learn a hidden curriculum, a set of values and norms that includes punctuality, obedience, and other habits required by their future employers. In addition to their manifest functions, schools have several latent functions, such as "babysitting" students while their parents work and keeping young people out of the labor force.

Over the last century, American education has undergone a dramatic transformation: Today most adults have completed high school, but a century ago most had not even finished elementary school. About one-fourth of all Americans are now enrolled in some kind of school, although changes in the age of the population have caused the number of students in elementary and secondary schools to decline. These schools are run by local communities and are funded primarily by local property taxes and by state money. The school itself is a bureaucratic organization—a formal structure that includes a board of education, administrators, teachers, and students. One effort to reduce the impersonality of the school bureaucracy is the open classroom, a program that fits the structure of the learning environment to students' needs.

The American educational system is based on competition among individual students for grades. In recent years, this system has awarded more As and Bs, even though declining SAT scores indicate that academic skills have fallen rather than improved. Several explanations have been offered for this drop in SAT scores, but none has yet been conclusively supported by research.

Higher education in the United States has also expanded greatly in the twentieth century; in fact, the number of Ph.D.s awarded in 1980 was more than the number of bachelor's degrees awarded in 1900. Students make major adjustments during their first year of college, especially if they do not live at home. By the end of four years, many students still have not set career goals, but they do change their attitudes and behavior during that time. For instance, they become more tolerant of diversity and less interested in religion and athletics during this time. Peer groups are a major source of socialization for college students, and the influence of different kinds of peer groups varies over time and by campus.

Colleges and universities are bureaucratic organizations that are funded by the state, by churches, or by contributions from graduates. The federal government has also been an important source of money for higher education, although in recent years its assistance has declined. College professors are awarded tenure after a number of years as a way to ensure academic freedom, the right to search for knowledge without external pressure to produce results that support particular interests.

Two-year colleges expanded tenfold in enrollment between 1960 and 1980. They offer educational opportunities to students who are, on the average, older and more likely to be married, working, and members of minority groups. Many of these students are trying to improve themselves occupationally. Critics of these schools claim that they do not fulfill their implied promise of upward mobility into the middle class and instead perpetuate the working-class status of their students.

In the 1970s, people with college degrees began having difficulty finding jobs in which they could use the skills and knowledge they had acquired in school. Many jobs required college degrees that were not really necessary for the work, a situation that has been called "the great training robbery," or credentialism. This situation has affected those who hold doctorates as well as those with bachelor's degrees, for the number of jobs available in colleges and universities has not expanded as fast as the number of Ph.D.s.

Conflict theorists claim that the educational system perpetuates social inequality, an idea that contradicts the American belief in education as the path to higher social positions. Tracking and differential treatment by teachers make it difficult for students from lower-class and working-class families to obtain the educational credentials needed to enter the middle class. In addition, racial segregation in the schools perpetuates inequality between blacks and whites. The suggestion that differences in IQ test scores between racial groups are due to genetic factors has no scientific support, and the fact that coaching and cultural enrichment can raise these scores in a short time suggests that differences in IQ scores can be attributed to environmental factors.

Efforts to provide equal education for all groups have produced several different policies in recent years. One that has not had a major impact over time is compensatory education. Another policy is busing students to schools outside their neighborhoods to achieve racial desegregation. This policy does not seem to have improved blacks' academic performance markedly, but it has aroused much opposition among whites. The policy discussed most recently is the use of vouchers or tuition tax credits to encourage parents to send their children to schools of their own choice. Evidence indicates that students now enrolled in private schools are better educated than those who attend public schools, but it is not clear that those private schools could expand enough to accommodate all the students who would transfer to them under the proposed voucher or tax credit plans.

Social policies can reduce inequality in educational opportunity, but there is reason to think that these changes would not significantly affect income inequality in the United States. There are many sources of inequality of income among groups, but education does not seem to be the primary one. Income inequality could better be reduced through a direct redistribution of income, rather than by providing people with the educational credentials that might lead to better jobs and higher incomes.

Important Terms

ACADEMIC FREEDOM (284)

BUSING (290)

COMPENSATORY EDUCATION (290)

CREDENTIALISM (284)

EDUCATION (273)

FUNCTIONAL ILLITERACY (273)

GRADE INFLATION (280)

HIDDEN CURRICULUM (274)

OPEN CLASSROOM (278)

TENURE (284)

TRACKING (286)

VOUCHER (292)

"WHITE FLIGHT" (291)

Suggested Readings

Samuel Bowles and Herbert Gintis. *Schooling in Capitalist America: Educational Reform and the Contradictions of Economic Life*. New York: Basic Books, 1976. A conflict perspective on education in American society.

James S. Coleman, Thomas Hoffer, and Sally Kilgore. *High School Achievement: Public, Catholic, and Private Schools Compared*. New York: Basic Books, 1982. A widely discussed study of the school characteristics that are associated with academic performance.

Randall Collins. *The Credential Society: An Historical Sociology of Education and Stratification*. New York: Academic Press, 1979. A study of credentialism and the part that education plays in the stratification of American society.

Christopher J. Hurn. *The Limits and Possibilities of Schooling: An Introduction to the Sociology of Education*. Boston: Allyn and Bacon, 1978. A good introduction to the sociology of education.

Herbert H. Hyman and Charles R. Wright. *Education's Lasting Influence on Values*. Chicago: University of Chicago Press, 1979. The authors examine several surveys and find that the number of years of schooling is associated with attitudes on civil liberties, on the right to privacy, and on minority-group rights.

Gene I. Maeroff. *Don't Blame the Kids: The Trouble with America's Public Schools*. New York: McGraw-Hill, 1982. A lucid account of some of the problems facing the schools today: school finance, ensuring minimum competency for students, public and private school education, and inner-city schools.

Ann Parker Parelius and Robert J. Parelius. *The Sociology of Education*. Englewood Cliffs, N.J.: Prentice-Hall, 1978. A textbook that explores both functionalist and conflict perspectives on education.

Caroline Hodges Persell. *Education and Inequality: The Roots and Results of Stratification in America's Schools*. New York: Free Press, 1977. A look at the ways that schools reinforce inequality in the United States.

Walter G. Stephan and Joe R. Feagin, eds. *School Desegregation: Past, Present, and Future*. New York: Plenum, 1980. A collection of articles on many aspects of school desegregation, including "white flight" and the history of desegregation efforts.

RELIGION 13

People everywhere question the meaning of life, their place in the natural world, and whether there is a supernatural force that controls events. The beliefs and practices that develop to deal with these "ultimate questions" take many forms. Some reveal a belief in life after death, and others treat death as the final stage of existence. In some societies, people regard a tree or a bear as holy, whereas in other societies a cross inspires awe. Regardless of the exact form, the beliefs and practices that deal with the ultimate questions are a source of comfort in the face of uncertainty, a basis of social order, and a way to mark important changes of status during a lifetime.

These systems of beliefs and practices are called religions. Specifically, a *religion* is a stable and shared set of beliefs, symbols, and rituals that focus on the *sacred* (Durkheim, 1912, 1947; Glock and Stark, 1965; Berger, 1967). By stability, we mean that religion is an institution that endures beyond the lifetimes of its adherents at any given time. For example, the Catholic Church is recognizable as the same institution that it was a century ago, even though it has undergone some changes in content—that is, beliefs, symbols, and rituals—and a complete turnover in Church members during that time. Our definition of religion also emphasizes that the content is shared; a personal belief system or an individual "philosophy of life" cannot qualify as a religion because it is not shared with others. In this chapter we will look at the content of religion, but first we must turn our attention to the central focus of religion—the sacred.

Emile Durkheim (1912, 1947) defined the sacred as the ideal and the supernatural that are not observable and that stand apart from daily life. One contemporary sociologist who has written extensively on religion says that the sacred "sticks out" from normal routine life (Berger, 1967: 26). Although the sacred is extraordinary and awe-inspiring, mysterious and potentially dangerous, it can be harnessed to human needs. The sacred is a superhuman force, but it resides in natural and artificial objects, in animals, or in people; it is the quality of the "otherness" of those things. Different religions define the sacred in very different ways, and it is not clear why something is defined as sacred in one belief system but not in another. A Hindu defines a cow as sacred, but most Christians would see the cow as a source of food. However, many of these Christians would regard a thin wafer used in the ritual of communion as sacred whereas Hindus might see the wafer simply as food. Religious beliefs—and the rituals based on those beliefs—define the sacred; it is not a trait that is intrinsic to an object.

The sacred is often contrasted with the *profane*, the everyday and routine. The profane is commonplace and is subject to empirical study; the sacred, on the other hand, is transcendant—it goes beyond the everyday. Sacredness has also been seen as the opposite of chaos, because sacredness suggests an order to the universe that is missing when chaos prevails (Berger, 1967).

It is not the job of sociologists to study the validity or the accuracy of religious ideas; rather, they seek to understand the social origins and the social consequences of religion. Durkheim (1912, 1947), for example, saw religion as an institution that strengthens social bonds. He suggested that whenever people worship gods, spirits, or sacred objects, they are actually worshipping a cultural representation of their own society. In fact, the types and the numbers of gods in a religion are directly associated with a society's organization and its means of economic subsistence (Swanson, 1960; Simpson, 1979). For example, ancestors are worshipped in societies in which older people have high social standing, and religions in societies marked by significant social inequality often justify the accumulation of wealth.

Sociologists treat religion as one institution in a complex web of institutions that form a society. Changes in religion affect the rest of society. For instance, the Moral Majority—an organized movement of fundamentalist Christians—has tried to influence the choice of school textbooks and has supported political candidates sympathetic to its beliefs. Changes in the rest of society also influence religion. For example, the civil rights movement of the 1950s and 1960s prompted several churches to social activism, a change with consequences that we look at later in this chapter.

The Functions of Religion

The fact that religion is present in all societies suggests that it serves essential functions for individuals and for society as a whole. Religion gives meaning to life and a sense of security, and it establishes standards of judgment and norms of behavior. One important consequence of religion is social integration; from the individual's perspective, religion is a source of sociability and connection to other people. Religious rituals also mark important transitions between the various stages of the life cycle.

PROVIDING MEANING AND COMFORT

Religions develop to answer questions about the meaning of life; for example, a belief in the hereafter helps people to deal with impending death (Weber, 1922, 1963). Religious belief systems include a world view—a perspective on the world and the place of people in it. Sometimes this takes the form of an "origin myth," a socially accepted tale about the origin of a society. One dysfunction of religion is that by providing answers to questions that might be accessible to empirical study, it may curb free inquiry and inhibit the pursuit of scientific knowledge. For instance, a belief in the power of ritual to bring rain might inhibit the development of a modern system of irrigation.

Religious beliefs help people to make sense of a world that they often find to be frightening and threatening; in doing so, it provides them with comfort, support, and consolation. Religion puts everyday troubles into perspective by reminding people of the existence of something more significant than their mundane concerns (Berger, 1967, 1979). Because nature and human behavior sometimes seem unpredictable, people need to be reassured that things happen for a reason and that there is an order to the universe.

ESTABLISHING NORMS

Another important consequence of religion is the development of norms or standards that are used to judge the world and the behavior of individuals. Religion often reinforces the social norms of the profane world, leading believers to obey abstract rules rather than act in their narrow self-interest. "Thou shalt not steal," one of the Ten Commandments, reinforces the legal system's prohibition on the theft of property. Religion also increases social conformity, maintains a group's heritage, and lends legitimacy to the social, political, and economic institutions of the larger society. Legitimacy—the belief that something is appropriate and worth supporting—is a result of religion's locating social institutions within a sacred and cosmic frame of reference for believers (Berger, 1967: 33).

On the other hand, religion may inhibit people from developing their own standards by encouraging them to accept those of the religion. This is not to suggest that religious believers do not think for themselves, but merely to point out that religion is an important agent of socialization that affects thought processes and behavior. By establishing standards, religion has another dysfunction in that it often supports the existing social order. By supporting the status quo, religion may impede social reform and perpetuate injustice. Reformers are faced, then, with the need not only to alter existing social conditions, but also to deal with religious support for those conditions.

STRENGTHENING SOCIAL BONDS

From his study of primitive Australian religion, Durkheim concluded that a major consequence of religion is to strengthen ties among believers. His theory that commitment to a religion is a form of commitment to society is probably best taken to mean that attachment to a religion binds people to a group of believers. If that group is the whole society, as it is in a religiously homogeneous society such as Italy, religion will reinforce social solidarity. However, in societies where there are a variety of religions there tends to be conflict among their

Emile Durkheim saw religion as an institution that strengthens social bonds.

adherents; Lebanon, for instance, has been torn by strife between Christians and Moslems. The large number of religious groups in the United States has not led to divisiveness, as it has in Lebanon, for reasons that we will discuss later in this chapter.

Religious rituals give people a sense of belonging to a group and thus counteract the feeling of being alone in the world. In his study of suicide, Durkheim (1897, 1951) found that rates were lowest among people who were most attached to a religious group. This sociability function of religion has also been important to immigrants to the United States; their churches have been centers of social activity and sources of ethnic identity.

Some critics have suggested that religion in the United States might be even more important as a source of social identity than as a source of beliefs and practices dealing with the sacred. In this view, many Americans participate in religion more to find a place in society than because of their convictions. To be a good American means that one must belong to some religious group, but not necessarily be very religious (Herberg, 1960). As a result,

churches and synagogues often become social centers as well as places of worship.

MARKING CHANGES IN STATUS

Another important function of religion is to mark passages from one stage in the life cycle to another. Religious rituals celebrate a birth with baptism, announce a new member of the church, publicly sanction a marriage, and mark the death of a member with a funeral rite. These rites of passage recognize changes in status while maintaining the individual's attachment to the group. Sometimes these transitions are stressful, and a formalized and therefore predictable ritual eases the change in status. The public nature of these rituals helps to minimize confused social relationships by announcing the new status; a marriage, for example, gives public notice that the partners are no longer available for dating. Rituals surrounding death remind the living that others will miss them when they die, and also demonstrate that the group will remain intact in spite of the loss of a member.

THE UNIQUENESS OF RELIGION

Many of the functions once served almost entirely by religion are now served by or shared with other institutions and social practices. For instance, in many societies a change in status from the single to the married life is marked by a civil ceremony; the Soviet Union, in particular, has deliberately created "socialist rites" to replace religious rituals that once marked all births, marriages, and deaths (Schmemann, 1983). Social movements such as feminism and civil rights help people feel connected to one another, as does participation in a religious service. Moreover, ultimate questions about the meaning of life are sometimes dealt with by personal philosophies or by secular philosophies such as Marxism. What distinguishes religion from these alternative ways to fulfill the same functions is its emphasis on the sacred. In other words, religion serves these social functions by bringing to bear on worldly activities the force of a mysterious, awe-inspiring, and otherworldly power in which a group of people believe.

Components of Religion

We have defined religion as a set of beliefs, symbols, and rituals that deal with the sacred. Let us now look at each of these three components.

BELIEFS

As we have seen, religious beliefs deal with matters such as the nature of the universe, the origin of the world and its people, the purpose of life, and existence after death. Because many of these beliefs deal with a nonempirical world, they cannot be tested for their validity; for instance, there is no scientific way to test a belief in reincarnation. There is much variety in the beliefs of the world's religions, in part because different questions are of concern to different groups of people. These beliefs include faith in gods, spirits, ghosts, or a set of principles. Many religions believe in supernatural beings that have human traits; these beings get angry and punish people, enjoy praise, and protect the faithful from harm.

One kind of religious belief is a *myth*, a story that defines the relationship of believers to their ancestors, to nature, or to life after death. These stories deal with the sacred by telling about the activities of divine beings or about moral principles enunci-

ated by holy people. They also explain the origin of the world and its people, the meaning of life, and the nature of good and evil. Myths have symbolic meaning; in other words, they have meanings that go beyond the apparent surface simplicity of the tales (Wallace, 1966).

Theology is a more elaborate set of doctrines, teachings, and philosophical speculations about religious matters. These ideas are often written down, argued about, and spelled out in religious texts or scriptures. The theology of a religion often includes a code of ethics that prescribes certain behavior; one example is the Ten Commandments, which form a part of the theology of Judaism and Christianity.

Types of Belief Systems

Religions vary considerably in the content of their beliefs. Some reflect a faith in impersonal forces of good and evil that are located in specific objects. Other belief systems include good and evil spirits and ghosts that are active in the world and have human traits, but are not worshipped as deities. Still another kind of religious belief system involves abstract ethical ideals, a holy way of thought and behavior rather than a god or gods; Buddhism, Confucianism, and Taoism are examples of major religions that define spiritual fulfillment in this way.

In contrast to these kinds of belief systems is *theism*, a belief system that includes a god or gods who are more powerful than humans and who should be worshipped. Theistic religions are highly organized, with a set of scriptures and a priest class or a clergy that leads worship services. Some theistic systems include a belief in the supremacy of a single god; these "monotheistic" religions include Christianity, Islam, and Judaism—religions with some of the largest memberships in the world today. Theistic systems that believe in more than one god are called "polytheistic"; Hinduism is the largest religion of this sort.

Table 13.1 shows the approximate number of adherents of the world's major religions. The largest religion is Christianity, followed by Islam and then Hinduism. Religious affiliations are listed for only slightly more than half of the world's population because organized religion is discouraged in large communist nations such as China and the Soviet Union, which do not make figures available on the actual beliefs and practices of their populations.

TABLE 13.1
Estimated Number of Adherents of Major World Religions

Religion	Estimated number of members*
Christianity	998,000,000
Roman Catholic	580,000,000
Protestant	341,000,000
Eastern Orthodox	76,000,000
Islam (Muslim)	589,000,000
Hindu	478,000,000
Buddhist	255,000,000
Confucian	156,000,000
Shinto	57,000,000
Taoist	31,000,000
Jewish	14,000,000
Total	2,578,000,000
Total world population	4,415,000,000

*Rounded to the nearest million.

Source: Reprinted with permission from the *1981 Britannica Book of the Year.* Copyright 1981 Encyclopaedia Britannica, Inc. Chicago, Illinois. p. 604 (Rounded off).

SYMBOLS

A symbol is something that stands for something else; it has a meaning for people socialized in the same culture. One kind of sacred symbol is a *totem*, an object worshipped by a community of believers. Animals, plants, and objects often have totemic significance in the religions of preindustrial societies. Sacred symbols—such as the cross, which symbolizes the Resurrection of Jesus Christ to Christians—acquire their holiness from the beliefs shared by a group of adherents. To Christians, communion symbolizes the body and blood of Jesus Christ with a wafer and with wine. These symbols play an important part in the religion's ritual practices, which in turn reinforce shared beliefs.

RITUALS

Rituals are traditional and stylized practices that define the relationship of believers to the sacred. Prayer meetings, baptisms, and weddings are examples of rituals. These practices reenact the myths of a religion, reinforce beliefs, and unite people through their collective participation in worship. They also help people to cope with strain and un-

certainty, and are used to mark changes in status in the life cycle. Marriage, for instance, commonly takes place in the church; one unusual marriage ritual was the simultaneous wedding of 2,074 couples in Reverend Sun Myung Moon's Unification Church on July 1, 1982.

Rituals can take the form of asking divine beings for something, but other practices are designed to appease sacred beings or to thank them for benefits that have been conferred. Prayer is one ritual that often takes place alone. Some rituals involve a single believer and a member of the clergy, such as confession in the Catholic Church. Other rituals are conducted in the presence of many believers, such as worship services or religious feasts. These rituals evoke emotions in participants, enable people to express their beliefs and demonstrate their commitment to the religion, and bind worshippers closer together.

Magic is one ritualistic practice that is often distinguished from religion, although it is closely related to it. Magic is a technique for manipulating and controlling matters that seem to be beyond human control and that often involve danger and uncertainty. Whereas magic is a means to an end, religion is usually an end in itself, although the

Symbols are an important part of religious practice. One kind of sacred symbol is a totem, which can be an animal, a plant, or an object.

practice of prayer can be seen as utilitarian when a believer asks a deity for some personal benefit. For the most part, however, religion serves to unify a group of believers, and magic is designed to help the individual who uses it (Malinowski, 1954).

Religious Organizations

Religion has both a cultural aspect—its beliefs, symbols, and rituals—and a structural aspect—its social organization. Only because they are organized can religions endure over time by recruiting new adherents, by uniting believers in rituals that are often led by clergy, and by coping with the external social environment.

In tribal societies, religion is not usually distinct from other social institutions; for instance, the religious leader is often the head of the family. In other preindustrial societies, an individual called a "shaman" or witch doctor is designated to perform religious rituals. Religion emerges as a distinct and more highly organized institution in industrial societies. A clergy develops to specialize in sacred matters, raise money for the construction of facilities, and maintain relations with the rest of society. Sometimes the clergy seeks to hold on to its own authority through the creation of a bureaucracy.

Religions are organized in various ways—some are highly structured bureaucracies, and others are spontaneous gatherings of believers. We examine religious organizations by distinguishing among churches, sects, and cults. Each has different features, and each can develop into one of the other forms over time (Troeltsch, 1931; Yinger, 1970; Johnstone, 1975).

CHURCHES

A *church* is a religious organization with a relatively large number of members who worship regularly in formal rituals. These people often join the church because their family has been affiliated with it, rather than because they have converted to the religion as a result of their personal beliefs. Churches usually do not make extensive demands on the time of their members, and participation in worship services follows established rituals rather than being spontaneous.

Churches are formal organizations with trained clergies who comfort and support members of the congregation but who also challenge them on occasion. The relationship between clergy and church members varies from one religion to another; so too does the way that the clergy are selected, trained, and assigned. In some churches the members play an important role in choosing the clergy, and in other churches the clergy are selected and assigned by those at the top of a church hierarchy. All churches have a hierarchy of authority, but they differ in the extent to which they are bureaucratized. Bureaucratized churches are structurally similar; internally they confront routine problems in the same way, and externally they engage in public relations, lobbying, fund-raising, and investment in similar fashion (Berger, 1967).

Churches are "of the social world"; that is, they commonly support the existing social, political, and economic systems, in contrast to sects and cults that oppose or withdraw from the social world (Stark and Bainbridge, 1979). Some churches are officially recognized by the state. In contrast to officially recognized churches are *denominations*, branches of a church that coexist on a more or less equal basis. In the United States, for instance, the three largest churches are Catholic, Protestant, and Jewish, but there are many Protestant denominations, including Baptists, Methodists, Lutherans, Episcopalians, and Presbyterians.

SECTS

A *sect* is a relatively small religious organization that recruits its members through conversion rather than by birth into a family that is already affiliated with the religion. The worship practices of sects are less formal and more emotional than those of churches. Their religious leaders are part-time rather than professional clergy, with members of the sect often leading religious services. Sects are less bureaucratized than churches, even though they can endure for long periods of time. They oppose the secular world, focusing instead on life after death and otherworldly matters. Some sects encompass the entire lives of their members by requiring strict adherence to a code of ethics that denies certain worldly pleasures such as sexual relations; adherence to this code is made easier because many sects isolate their members from secular society.

Sects typically begin by splitting off from a church. This usually happens when a group of church members becomes unhappy with the bureaucratization of the religion and feels that the church has become too concerned with worldly matters and too little concerned with the spiritual needs of its members. In addition, sects can also arise when lower-class members become dissatisfied and come to feel that the church organization has been taken over by middle-class members (Johnstone, 1975). Sects develop to "purify" the religion's beliefs and practices by returning to a traditional interpretation of the scriptures; sometimes, a result is intolerance of religions that do not share the sect's reading of the texts. However, established churches usually tolerate sects because they are too small to constitute a real threat.

By cutting themselves off from the external social environment, sects can inhibit their growth because they lack access to potential recruits (Stark and Bainbridge, 1981). Some sects remain stable even though they are socially and geographically isolated from the secular world; an example is the Amish group that originally broke away from the Mennonites and continues today as a thriving sect. Other sects grow and even evolve into churches; when this happens, they tend to become less isolated from the social environment and compromise the purity of their beliefs in order to attract new members. As a sect grows, it can become bureaucratized as a formal division of authority is established, a professional clergy is trained, lines of succession to positions of leadership are defined, and methods to raise financial resources are developed.

CULTS

Religious groups that emphasize a specific belief or practice and that are led by a charismatic individual—that is, one who has extraordinary personal qualities—are called *cults* (see SEL 13.1 for one example). Unlike sects, cults provide their members with a new religious alternative rather than try to purify the religion of a church; in other words, cults are not part of another religion before their formation. Members of cults seek salvation through total commitment to a leader whom they see as a prophet. They are enthusiastic and emotional in their religious participation, and they generally do not adhere to an intellectualized theology. Cultic beliefs and practices include direct contact with the sacred, witchcraft, the development of psychic powers, and faith in the impending transformation of the social order (Stark, Bainbridge, and Doyle, 1979). Because cult members profess loyalty to a leader rather than to a set of religious principles that require them to remain uncontaminated by opposing beliefs, they are usually tolerant of other religious groups.

Religion or Therapy?

This selection examines Wingsong, a group in Oakland, California. Because the leader's inspiration for this organization was divine, we can treat it as a religious cult. However, as with a number of quasi-religions, this cult also has characteristics of a secular form of psychotherapy, like other groups in the "human potential movement," such as est and Scientology.

The young woman sitting in a workshop with 23 people passed around the latest Mercedes-Benz catalogue, pointed at a 300SD Turbodiesel model in chocolate brown, priced at $38,000, and said loudly, "That's the one I want to manifest right now."

Manifesting is the notion that one can acquire a new car, wealth, a new relationship or anything, simply by wishing for it. The theory is one of 13 taught at Wingsong, a therapy business founded here two years ago by Lisa de Longchamps.

Miss de Longchamps asserts that she has successfully sold to "thousands upon thousands" of people what she calls her "divine plan of opulence," which was communicated to her, she says, "through channelings from my divine guides."

The divine plan, which costs $815 and consists of four one- or two-day workshops, represents a new movement on the far fringes of therapy in the Bay Area, where a dazzling array of techniques on how to become assertive, rich and happy are available.

Wingsong also offers a two-day workshop on relationships for $275; participants are taught how to attract "their inner twin flames."

Miss de Longchamps said she had a degree in humanistic psychology and worked in real estate before she founded Wingsong. She said she thought of the divine plan of opulence when she was riding on a bus and heard voices that told her to spend a year in silence and seclusion.

In that year, which she spent in Los Angeles, the voices instructed her in the teachings of the divine plan, which she wrote down and now reads to her students in a high, tremulous voice.

"Manifesting is simply making real in your experience all your superficial needs," she said. "Once people get past their superficial desires, everyone wants the same thing, an end to grievance and separation in their world."

She declined to discuss Wingsong's profits but said she gave away 85 to 95 percent of her income.

"Most of us have been brought up to believe that money is evil and the rich are wicked," said Iris Jackson, a protégé of Miss de Longchamps. "Manifesting is about getting rid of all that junk in our consciousness so that we can join the rich.". . .

Few Wingsong participants believe they are overcharged.

"The cost of the classes doesn't matter to me at all—I would spend my last dime on them," said Toby Clark, 44 years old, a Wingsong participant since February.

Mr. Clark, who has been through est, "rebirthing" and 14 enlightenment "intensives," added, "Life is just a workshop."

Source: "Coast Group's Novel Theory: Wishing Can Make It So," *The New York Times*, March 11, 1982, p. B11. © 1982 by the New York Times Company. Reprinted by permission.

Religions based on loyalty to charismatic leaders eventually confront a problem of how to continue after that leader dies. Sometimes the leadership of the charismatic figure is institutionalized in a religious organization through a process called the *routinization of charisma* (Weber, 1922, 1963). This involves the establishment of worship rituals and the emergence of a clergy that preaches the principles enunciated by the leader. It also requires the development of a theology composed of beliefs that are consistent and that have philosophical support. The routinization of charisma takes the emotional and personal aspects of leadership and transforms them into an organization that has established roles and patterns of authority.

Recruiting Cult Members

Cults are not usually very concerned with the secular world; they neither reject that world in an active way nor seek to establish strong ties to social institutions. Although cults typically prefer to be ignored by the rest of society, they must bridge the gap between themselves and secular society in order to raise money. One way that some cults, such as the Unification Church and the Hare Krishnas, have solved this problem is to elevate the act of public solicitation of funds to the level of a sacred ritual that serves the religion (Bromley and Shupe, 1978, 1979).

Cults must also deal with the secular world in order to recruit new members; those that cut themselves off from sources of potential recruits will fail to grow and might even disappear when members leave the group or die (Stark and Bainbridge, 1981; Rochford, 1982). People who join cults usually have a close tie to a member of the cult and weakened attachments to other people (Lofland and Stark, 1965; Glock and Bellah, 1976; Cox, 1977; Stark and Bainbridge, 1980; Downton, 1980). One study of conversion to the Nichiren Shoshu Buddhist movement in the United States found that intensive interaction between a potential recruit and a convert was the critical factor in recruitment to the cult; personal motives for joining and commitment to the cult developed from this interaction rather than from a preexisting set of religious beliefs (Snow and Phillips, 1980).

The enthusiasm and total commitment of cult members sometimes lead outsiders to suspect that they have been brainwashed, because many members undergo a radical change in behavior and beliefs after joining a cult. In recent years cult membership has been treated as a "medicalized" form of deviance (See Chapter 5); cult members have been defined by their parents and by therapists as people who need psychiatric treatment to restore them to mental health (Robbins and Anthony, 1982). Some parents have hired "deprogrammers" who physically remove—many would say kidnap—their children from the cult (Patrick, 1976; Shupe and Bromley, 1980; Robbins and Anthony, 1982). Parents understandably wish to protect their children from what they see as coercion and brainwashing, but the forcible removal of their children from cults infringes on their civil rights, especially when they are legally adults. Parents and mental health workers sometimes respond that there is no civil liberties question involved because the cult members have been brainwashed and therefore lack free will.

Religion and the Economic System

The complex relationship between religion and the economic system has been studied by both Karl Marx and Max Weber and more recently by Peter

L. Berger. In simple terms, Marx emphasized the impact of the economic system on religious beliefs and practices, and Weber stressed the way that religion influenced the economic system. Both, however, recognized the complex interplay between religion and economy. Berger has looked at the different ways in which religions respond to the process of economic and social change.

MARX: RELIGION AS A REFLECTION OF THE ECONOMIC SYSTEM

Marx saw religion as a source of alienation. He claimed that people project or externalize aspects of themselves and their society, create a God or gods that represent their own traits and ideals, and then stand in awe of their deities. In this way, religion alienates people from themselves by creating a supernatural manifestation of society that is regarded as beyond human control.

According to Marx, the dominant religion in any society reflects the interests of that society's privileged classes. This religion—which is based on the economic system—justifies social inequality and the advantages enjoyed by those at the top of the stratification system. For example, religion was used to support American slavery; it was part of a conscious effort by slaveholders to instill obedience and discipline in plantation slaves (Stampp, 1956: 158–159).

Marx (1844, 1964: 42) referred to religion as the "opium of the people," implying that both opium and religion can lull people into a passive and comfortable state. For Marx, religion was a form of "false consciousness," an erroneous belief that the position of each group in the stratification system is inevitable and even beneficial to it. Marx saw religion as supporting the status quo and the inequality that is part of the status quo. For example, the search for witches in Europe during the Middle Ages strengthened the dominance of nobility and clergy by diverting the attention of peasants from the real causes of problems such as food shortages and natural disasters (Harris, 1974). In some preindustrial societies, oppressed and uprooted people who have suffered a plague, a war, or great poverty are attracted to "millenarian" or "messianic" cults whose leaders promise a sudden and radical transformation of the social order that will compensate believers for their past hardships with a much better life (Cohn, 1962; Lanternari, 1963).

In capitalist societies, according to Marx, the working class is taught to believe in a religion that justifies existing social conditions and promises rewards in the hereafter; this minimizes the chance that they will try to change society through revolution. Capitalists, on the other hand, often believe in a religion that supports their control of economic wealth and political power. For example, the industrialist John D. Rockefeller regarded the exploitative behavior of nineteenth-century "robber barons" not as socially harmful but as "the working-out of a law of nature and a law of God" (cited in Hofstadter, 1955: 45).

Does Religion Retard Social Change?

One study of religion and protest among black Americans found that the most religious members of churches that had otherworldly concerns were the least militant in pressing for social change in the area of civil rights. However, members of black churches that were oriented toward life on earth were more favorably disposed to social change and more active in working for civil rights when they were very religious (G. Marx, 1967). Religion thus keeps some black Americans from protesting their subordinate status, but it inspires others to work for change.

Religion is a source of intergroup conflict and social change when it becomes the basis for interest-group activity. The temperance movement that culminated in the Prohibition Amendment that made the sale of alcoholic beverages illegal in the United States between 1920 and 1933 was based on religious beliefs. Debates over abortion and homosexual rights also regularly invoke religious beliefs. In cases such as these, religion can be used by different interest groups both to support the status quo and to bring about change.

The conflict perspective, including the work of Karl Marx, focuses on the way that religion perpetuates social inequality and the way that it leads to conflict among groups. In some situations, however, religion leads to social change rather than support for the status quo. The leaders of social movements—such as the civil rights movement—sometimes point to religious principles to pressure clergy and church members to act in accordance with their beliefs. Mohandas K. Gandhi brought about change in India in this way, and so did the Reverend Martin Luther King, Jr., in the United States. By looking at Latin America, we can see that there is no simple or constant relationship between religion and the economic system. For centuries the Catholic Church and its clergy supported or at least tolerated military regimes that oppressed

the poor, but since the late 1960s members of the clergy in several Latin American countries have opposed the government and pressed for changes that would benefit the poor (Beaulac, 1981; Novak, 1982).

WEBER: THE PROTESTANT ETHIC AND MODERN CAPITALISM

From his studies of religion in European, Middle Eastern, and Eastern societies, Weber concluded that modern capitalism—an economic system based on profit, acquisition, and investment—developed in Europe in the sixteenth century before it emerged elsewhere. Furthermore, modern capitalism developed in the areas of Europe that were predominantly Protestant, and many of the early capitalists were Protestants rather than Catholics. These observations caused Weber to ask why capitalism was historically linked to Protestantism. He tentatively concluded that the link between capitalism and Protestantism was the value system, or the *Protestant ethic*, that was inherent in the religious beliefs of Calvinism, a Protestant denomination (Weber, 1904, 1958).

Calvinists believed in "predestination," the idea that God had determined before people were born whether they would be saved and go to Heaven, or be damned and go to Hell. People did not gain or lose salvation by their worldly activities; predestination meant that human efforts did not affect life after death. Predestination was the source of much anxiety among Calvinists, because they could not change their fate. Everyday behavior thus took on religious significance as people sought "signs of grace," usually in the form of material wealth, that would indicate that they were among the saved. However, because Calvinism also included a belief in "worldly asceticism"—the idea that people should not seek or enjoy pleasure—the only thing for Calvinists to do with their wealth was to reinvest it. With its emphasis on the acquisition and reinvestment of wealth in the material world, Calvinism was better suited to the development of modern capitalism than was Catholicism, which emphasized rewards in the hereafter.

Weber did not claim that modern capitalism was caused by Calvinism alone; rather, he suggested that the Protestant ethic was one important factor in the emergence of this economic system. This claim has been disputed. An alternative interpretation of the historical evidence is that changes in the economic system in the sixteenth century *produced* a change in religious beliefs, including the development of Calvinism as a religion that could justify the behavior of capitalists (Tawney, 1926). This position—that economic change preceded a change in religious beliefs—is compatible with Marx's interpretation of the relationship between religion and the economic system. Another criticism of Weber's theory is that religion is a belief system that does not necessarily influence economic behavior, even if both the beliefs and the economic behavior exist in a society at the same time.

BERGER: RELIGION AND ECONOMIC CHANGE

Peter L. Berger (1979) suggests three possible ways for organized religion to respond to the transition from a traditional and preindustrialized society to one that is modern and industrialized. One way is for religion to reaffirm beliefs and practices that developed in the distant past and so oppose the modernization process. This provides continuity with the past but can retard economic development and social change. The establishment of an Islamic government in Iran headed by the Ayatollah Khomeini is one example of a religion asserting control over the process of modernization. This government even tried to reverse the modernization process rather than simply maintain the status quo; for example, popular music was banned, and women returned to wearing the traditional veil.

Berger suggests two additional ways that religion can respond to the process of social change. One way is to adapt its beliefs to the secular world, deemphasizing the sacred by becoming more ''relevant.'' The Protestant ethic is one example of this response, with the secularization of the belief in

An example of a religion asserting control over the process of modernization was the 1979 establishment of an Islamic government in Iran, headed by the Ayatollah Khomeini.

predestination spurring the development of modern capitalism. The third kind of response to change is for a religion to try to maintain traditional beliefs and practices while still applying them to modern society. This has been the characteristic pattern of fundamentalism in the United States since the 1960s and especially since the late 1970s; we examine this fundamentalist revival later in the chapter.

Religion in the United States

In comparison to people who live in Western European nations, a higher proportion of Americans—about 95 per cent—profess a belief in God. In addition, Americans seem to attend religious services more regularly than do people in other industrial societies. On the basis of this evidence, Americans have been called the "most religious people in the world among industrial nations" (Gallup Opinion Index, 1976: 1). This conclusion has been questioned by others who note that American churches are relatively free of theological content and often seem more like voluntary associations than religious organizations. Some critics also point out that religion plays a small part in the daily lives of most Americans.

A DENOMINATIONAL SOCIETY

Many early immigrants to the United States came here searching for asylum from the religious persecution they had encountered in their homelands. Their experiences with religious intolerance and the variety of religious groups in the United States prevented a single religion from establishing dominance. Indeed, the First Amendment to the Constitution states that "Congress shall make no law respecting an establishment of religion, or prohibiting the free exercise thereof."

Today, a multitude of denominations, sects, and cults flourish in the United States; one survey lists nearly twelve hundred such groups (Melton, 1979). Membership in American religions varies from a handful of people in some sects and cults to the fifty million members of the Roman Catholic Church. It is often difficult to define membership in a religious organization: It can be measured by formal membership, regular attendance at worship services, personal beliefs, or family affiliation. Religious groups count their members in different ways, and some might exaggerate their numbers. As a result, it is not easy to compare the relative size of different religions.

The largest single religious organization in the United States in 1980 was the Roman Catholic Church, with 50,450,000 members. However, this figure is smaller than the combined membership of all Protestant denominations, about 73,479,000 (U.S. Bureau of the Census, 1982: 55). The largest of these Protestant denominations are the Southern Baptist Convention (13,600,000 members in 1980), the United Methodist Church (9,585,000), and the Lutheran Church in America (2,923,000) (*The New York Times*, June 15, 1982, p. A8). In 1980, the size of the Jewish community—including nonbelievers who regard themselves as ethnically Jewish, as well as members of Reformed, Conservative, and Orthodox synagogues or temples—was 5,920,000 (U.S. Bureau of the Census, 1982: 55). We can see in Table 13.2 that the proportion of all

TABLE 13.2
Membership of Churches, 1950 to 1980

Church	1950	1980
Protestant	58.8%	54.5%
Roman Catholic	33.0%	37.4%
Jewish	5.8%	4.4%
Other religions	2.4%	3.7%
Total	100.0%	100.0%

Source: U.S. Bureau of the Census, *Statistical Abstract of the United States, 1982–83.* Washington, D.C.: U.S. Government Printing Office, 1982, p. 55.

church members who were Jewish declined somewhat from 1950 to 1980, as did the proportion who belonged to the various Protestant denominations. Catholics and members of "other religions" increased in proportion to the total number of church members over this time.

Most Americans follow their parents in choosing a religion. This might suggest that people do not select a religion on the basis of personal beliefs or theological preferences, but it can also mean that socialization by the family creates in children needs that are much like those of their parents and that can thus best be met by the same religion. Americans who occupy positions in the stratification system that are similar to those of their parents might also be expected to have the same religion. In fact, people whose social position differs from that of their parents are more likely to be affiliated with a different religious group (Newport, 1979). We examine the effect of social mobility on religious affiliation later in this chapter.

BASIC RELIGIOUS VALUES

Religion is an important part of American culture. The Constitution reflects the culture's value of tolerance of religious diversity and the expectation that religion will be free of government control. In the United States there is also a norm that everyone will proclaim some religious preference, even if it is not associated with active participation in a group. In addition, everyone is expected to believe in certain tenets of a "civil religion" that supports the political system.

Separation of Church and State

Many industrial societies do not require separation of religion and the state; for example, public schools in West Germany give religious instruction to Protestant and Catholic students. Long ago, Alexis de Tocqueville (1831, 1945) noted that the legal requirement that church and state remain separate contributed to the strength of religion in the United States by preventing a close alliance between the churches and the government that would have given the state the power to destroy or weaken religion. However, the exact meaning of the separation of church and state is unclear and has changed over time. For instance, it was only in 1925 that American children were allowed to attend parochial schools rather than public ones. Since then, the law has evolved to permit certain

kinds of government assistance—but not other kinds—to church-affiliated schools:

The Supreme Court decided at various times in the 1970s that transporting parochial students to and from school at public expense is constitutional but transporting them on field trips is unconstitutional; that the loan of public school textbooks to a parochial school is constitutional but the loan of audio-visual material is unconstitutional; that a state may provide guidance counseling for parochial students in a mobile unit but not on their school grounds. It became difficult to tell what the principle of separation between church and state meant in a particular case without resorting to litigation (Caplow, 1982b: 81).

Perhaps the most heatedly debated issue in recent years concerning the separation of church and state is school prayer. Several court decisions—most notably, the United States Supreme Court's 1963 decision in *School District of Abington Township v. Schempp*—have prohibited the saying of school prayers and the reading of the Bible in public schools. Many parents and teachers have criticized these decisions, arguing that such religious practices are not linked to any specific denomination and that they are an important part of the socialization of the young. They also point out that school prayer was constitutional for nearly two centuries, that Congress begins each day with a prayer, that the United States military employs chaplains, and that the Constitution prohibits only the establishment of a state religion or the preference of one religion over others. Some states have passed or considered laws to permit school prayer, and the federal government has considered a similar Constitutional Amendment; but so far, school prayer remains unconstitutional. Opponents of school prayer argue that students would feel compelled to join in the prayer even if they held no religious beliefs, and that this is a form of coercion prohibited by the First Amendment.

Peter L. Berger (1977: 151) points out that the doctrine of separation of church and state does not imply that "the state must be antiseptically clean of all religious qualities—only that the state must not give unfair advantage to one denomination over another." Berger goes on to say that a "militant secularism" would deny churches the right to influence public policy in accordance with religious morality. Indeed, there has been much debate over the proper role of churches in the legislative process in recent years. For instance, the Catholic Church has lobbied to have abortion made illegal since a 1973 Supreme Court decision legalized it under certain circumstances. The Church argues that abortion is a type of murder and that the prevention of murder is in the public interest rather than in the narrow interest of any particular religion. Those who favor legalized abortion claim that the Catholic Church should register as a lobbyist and even be denied tax-exempt status because of its efforts to make abortion illegal. So far, the legal system has found that the Church's efforts are consistent with its tax-exempt status and do not violate the principle of separation of church and state. However, recent laws that require public schools to teach a creationist view of the origin of life along with the theory of evolution have been found by the courts to violate the principle of separation of church and state, as we can see in SEL 13.2.

SOCIOLOGY AND EVERYDAY LIFE 13.2
Creationism: Science or Religion?

In recent years, some states have passed or considered legislation that would require public schools to give students a "balanced treatment" of the origins of human beings by presenting "creationism" or "creation science" along with evolutionary theory. Such laws were passed by Louisiana and Arkansas in 1981, but were overturned by the courts in 1982.

Evolutionary theory proposes the slow emergence of one species from others in a complex process that takes millions of years. According to this theory, humans developed from other species, most recently apes. This theory runs counter to Christian fundamentalism, which interprets the events in the Bible in literal terms. Some supporters of creation science claim that evolutionary theory is a belief rather than a proven theory, and that their beliefs be given "equal time" in the classroom. Other creationists assert that their position is indeed a science, even though most scientists feel that it fails to meet the criteria of science—that is, proposing and testing hypotheses and rejecting those that do not fit the evidence.

The Arkansas law defined creation science as the scientific evidence and related inferences that indicate:

(1) Sudden creation of the universe, energy, and life from nothing; (2) The insufficiency of mutation and natural selection in bringing about development of all living kinds from a single organism; (3) Changes only within fixed limits of originally created kinds of plants and animals; (4) Separate ancestry for man and apes; (5) Explanation of the earth's geology by catastrophism, including the occurrence of a worldwide flood; and (6) A relatively recent inception of the earth and living kinds.

This law did not specifically state that the religious views of fundamentalists must be taught.

However, the definition of creation science did conform closely to a literal interpretation of the events in the Book of Genesis, and the judicial decision that found this law unconstitutional concluded that it did in fact require the public schools to teach a partisan religious position.

Critics of creationism—and of the laws that mandate classroom instruction in it—point out that evolutionary theory explains evidence that is simply ignored by the creationists. In fact, creationism directly contradicts extensive scientific evidence that the Earth was never entirely engulfed by a great flood and that the Earth was not created recently. Critics of creationism fear that it will have harmful effects beyond the introduction of religion into the schools. They fear that textbooks might be written to dilute the explanatory value of evolutionary theory and to elevate the questionable theory of creationism to the level of a science. School districts located in states that do not require the teaching of creationism might then have to choose only from textbooks that present a "balance" of the two theories.

The American Association for the Advancement of Science sees creation science laws as "a real and present threat to the integrity of education and the teaching of science"; it rejects creationism as having "no scientific validity." However, a 1982 Associated Press poll found that three-fourths of all Americans favor the teaching in school of the biblical theory of the origin of life. A 1982 Gallup Poll found that 44 per cent of Americans agreed that "God created man pretty much in his present form at one time within the last 10,000 years," even though an Episcopal bishop states that he was not aware of a single reputable biblical scholar who agreed with that statement. Forty-seven per cent of those polled believed in some form of evolution; most felt that God played an important guiding role in that process.

So far the courts have upheld the critics of creation science, finding that laws requiring the teaching of this theory violate the Constitutional requirement of separation of church and state. Some legislators, caught in the crossfire between court rulings and public pressure to pass creationism laws, have voted for such laws, even though they know that the courts will not allow those laws to be implemented.

Sources: Based on a special issue of *Academe* on "Creationism and the Classroom," March–April 1982, pp. 7–36; Stephen Jay Gould, "Creationism: Genesis vs. Geology," *Atlantic Monthly* 250 (September 1982): 10–17; and Richard Severo, "Poll Finds Americans Split on Creation Idea," *The New York Times*, August 29, 1982, p. 22. Used by permission.

Tolerance of Diversity

In the United States each religious group is expected to respect the right of all other groups to practice their faith. This norm of tolerance for religious diversity sustains a large number of religions with relatively little overt conflict among them, and it stops any one group from dominating the others.

One consequence, however, of the large number of religions in the United States is competition for new members. This can lead to a missionizing orientation that threatens religious tolerance, but the large number of religions and the tradition of tolerance usually prevent such competition from having harmful consequences. Competition for members sometimes requires religions to adapt to the needs of their members to keep from losing them; to some extent, religion must be marketed (Berger, 1967: 144; Caplow, 1982b). This is one reason for the limited emphasis on theology in American religion, which tends to focus on ethics rather than on philosophical arguments.

Religious tolerance is an American value, but the history of the nation has been marred by intolerance. The Ku Klux Klan, usually associated with its violence toward blacks, also opposes Catholics and Jews. Recently, Jews, Catholics, and Protestants in New York City joined together to fight what were referred to as "destructive cults" (Montgomery, 1982). Anti-Semitism also has a long history in the United States, although it is no longer as virulent and open as it was in the 1920s, 1930s, and early 1940s. Today there is little support for discrimination against Jews in employment or in housing, but there is still discrimination against them by private clubs and in intermarriage. Anti-Semitism is least common among people with more education, and the long-term trend toward greater educational attainment among Americans is partly responsible for the decline in anti-Semitism (Quinley and Glock, 1979).

The Need for Some Religion

Most Americans see religion as important, even if they themselves rarely attend services and hold no deep religious convictions. They seem to feel that religion is a good thing in itself; affiliation with some religion—preferably Protestantism, Catholicism, or Judaism—is seen as part of the "American way of life" (Herberg, 1960). Americans are sometimes suspicious of people who are not religious; more than half would prevent a person who did not believe in God from holding public office or from teaching in a public school (Stark and Glock, 1969). Religion is seen as a way to define a person's place in society; it thus influences those with whom people will interact and thereby affects the selection of marital partners.

Civil Religion

All Americans are expected to believe in certain ideals, symbols, and rituals that commit them to the support of society and its political system. This "underlying culture-religion" (Herberg, 1960) that celebrates "the American way" has been called *civil religion*, a belief system that elevates aspects of the secular world to the status of the sacred and interprets national history in terms of a transcendant reality (Bellah, 1967, 1975, 1978; Bellah and Hammond, 1980). Civil religion is not an organized religion, but the largest and most influential religious organizations in the country do agree with its general beliefs. The beliefs of the civil religion have been summarized as follows: "(1) There is a God (2) whose will can be known through democratic procedures; therefore (3) democratic

Faith in the American political system is sustained by civil ceremonies that make general references to God. Every President, except George Washington at his second inauguration, has mentioned God in his inaugural speech.

America has been God's primary agent in history, and (4) for Americans the nation has been their chief source of identity" (Hammond, in Bellah and Hammond, 1980: 41–42). This use of religious beliefs to support the political system is apparent in the following justification of the annexation of the Philippines by the United States, given by Senator Arthur J. Beveridge in 1900:

God has not been preparing the English-speaking and Teutonic peoples for a thousand years for nothing but vain and idle self-contemplation and self-admiration. No. He made us master organizers of the world to establish system where chaos reigned. He has given us the spirit of progress to overwhelm the forces of reaction throughout the earth. He has made us adept in government that we may administer government among savage and senile peoples. Were it not for such a force as this the world would relapse into barbarism and night. And of all our race He has marked the American people as His chosen nation to finally lead in the redemption of the world (cited in Bellah, 1975: 38).

Faith in the American political system is sustained by political ceremonies that make general references to God. Every President has mentioned God in his inaugural speech, with the exception of George Washington in a brief speech at his second inauguration. Recital of the pledge of allegiance, which includes the phrase "one Nation under God," teaches civil religion to the young (Smidt, 1980). National holidays such as Thanksgiving and Memorial Day invoke the will of God, although Memorial Day has less religious significance today than it once did (Warner, 1961). Indeed, some have claimed that since the mid-1960s the civil religion has become trivialized and corrupted and attribute "the explosion of cults" since then to the search by young people for the certitude that cults promise (Hammond, in Bellah and Hammond, 1980: 193).

One dysfunction of the civil religion is that it has in the past been used to rationalize injustice in the name of religion. Genocide against Native Americans in the nineteenth century was seen as the will of God and as necessary to spread "civilization" across the continent. The enslavement of blacks was also rationalized as God's will. In addition, sects and cults that do not share the beliefs of the civil religion have sometimes been treated with intolerance.

RELIGIOUS PARTICIPATION

People are involved in religion in many ways. Some attend worship services only on major holidays and hold no deep religious convictions. Others see the church as a voluntary association that provides them with social contacts and friends. Still others have strong beliefs that influence all aspects of their daily lives (Lenski, 1963).

The nature and extent of religious participation are related to a variety of factors (Demerath and Roof, 1976). Adherence to beliefs and involvement in rituals reflect the way that people have been socialized; they learn that it is "right" to attend services, and they sometimes do so because others expect them to. Participation is also related to personal involvement in other activities that compete for an individual's time; for example, someone who holds a job that requires working long hours and who lives in a large city with many available cultural opportunities might be less religiously active than a person who does not work and who lives in a small town where there is little to do.

Church membership is one measure of religious participation. Since 1850 there has been a long-term increase in the proportion of Americans who claim membership in a religious organization, even though there does not seem to have been any increase in the proportion of Americans professing strong religious beliefs over that time (Demerath and Hammond, 1969). More recently, there was an increase in church membership from 1950 to 1959, a decline during the 1960s, and a leveling off in the early 1970s. By 1980, somewhat less than 60 per cent of all Americans were affiliated with a church.

In recent years, there has been an increase in the proportion of all Americans who claim to believe in no religion. Some of them have never been members of any religion, and others have left religious organizations to which they once belonged. The people who are the most likely to leave a church have the following traits: They are male, young, highly educated, from relatively high social classes, and live in the West and the Northeast. Defections from the Catholic Church have been especially common among young adults, especially after the 1968 papal encyclical called *Humanae Vitae* reaffirmed the Church's opposition to artificial methods of birth control (Greeley, McCready, and McCourt, 1976; Greeley, 1977). Today, the use of birth control measures by Catholics is not different from that of non-Catholics in any major way, in spite of the fact that such practices are still against Church doctrine. This convergence of the contraceptive practices of Catholics and non-Catholics began before World War II (Westoff, 1979).

RELIGION, ETHNICITY, AND CLASS

In the United States religion has been historically linked to ethnic identity. Immigrants to the country often turned first to the church, because it was one source of continuity with life in the "old country." In these ethnic churches the new immigrants could associate with people from their homeland who had been in the United States longer; this helped them to adjust to life in the new society (Greeley, 1972). Sometimes these ethnic churches adapted to the changing needs of members as they improved their social standing; for example, worship services that were once conducted in the members' native language might begin to use English.

Religious preferences vary markedly with position in the stratification system. Indeed, one theologian concluded that social class is more important than religious doctrine in determining an American's denominational affiliation (Niebuhr, 1929, 1957). Americans higher in the stratification system are more likely than people from the lower classes to join a church and attend worship services, prayer meetings, and other church activities. People from the lower and working classes are more likely to mistrust social organizations in general and to avoid active participation in a religion. The middle and upper classes also have more knowledge of theological issues than do people from less socially advantaged groups. On the other hand, the middle and upper classes are less intense and less expressive in their involvement in religious rituals; their participation tends to be more formal and more intellectual than that of the lower classes (Fukuyama, 1961; Glock and Stark, 1965; Demerath, 1965).

Churches and denominations can be ranked by their members' income, education, and occupational prestige (Gallup Opinion Index, 1981). Ideally, Catholics of different ethnic groups and Protestants of various denominations and races should be looked at separately, because the categories Catholic and Protestant include many different groups; however, this information is not available. Comparing the three major churches, we find that Jews rank highest in average income, occupational prestige, and educational attainment. Catholics outrank Protestants in income and occupational prestige, and the two groups are similar in education. SEL 13.3 provides a more detailed portrait of American Catholics.

SOCIOLOGY AND EVERYDAY LIFE 13.3
Portrait of the American Catholic

Andrew M. Greeley is a sociologist and Catholic priest who has written extensively on Catholics and white ethnic groups in the United States, as well as being the author of best-selling novels. This selection is taken from his introduction to a book in which he examines the characteristics of American Catholics.

Let us begin with a series of paragraphs describing the American Catholic:

1. Catholics tend to be blue-collar workers and belong to the lower-middle class. Educationally and financially they do not compare with their Protestant counterparts. A Catholic background makes it less likely that a young person will choose an academic career or, should he choose one, do well in it. Those Catholics who do become successful academics will leave the church. Irish Catholics, who have been in the United States longer than other ethnic groups, have achieved a certain amount of modest respectability, but they have not made the most of their opportunities in the new world—perhaps because of their religion, or their family structure, or their drinking habits.

2. While they have traditionally voted Democratic, Catholic ethnics are conservative. They are more likely to be racist, less likely to support civil liberties, more likely to take a punitive attitude toward the counterculture. They were stronger supporters of the Vietnam war than other Americans and voted heavily for Wallace in 1968. As many of them moved into the suburbs and became more affluent, they began to drift away from the Democratic party in both affiliation and voting behavior.

3. Most Catholic priests are not happy in their vocations. Those who have left the priesthood are the best and the most talented. The commitment to celibacy makes it impossible for a man to develop capacities of openness, intimacy, and sympathy with human frailty. Most Catholic clergy would marry given the chance.

4. While Catholics are more likely than Protestants to be against abortion, the opening up of the church in the Second Vatican Council has caused a notable decline in Catholic religious practice. The encyclical letter *Humanae Vitae* on birth control, however, caused serious moral anguish for large numbers of American Catholics.

5. Catholic support for their schools is declining, mostly because Catholics now realize that in the suburbs where they now live the public schools are better. There is little willingness in the Catholic population to make the financial sacrifices required to keep parochial schools in operation. In any event, there is no evidence that parochial schools make their graduates any more religious than they would have been had they gone to public schools. Parochial school graduates are more likely to have hostile attitudes toward blacks and Jews, and less likely to be well equipped for success in American society.

All five of the above paragraphs seem unexceptionable. They are a fair portrait of what everyone knows to be true about certain aspects of American Catholicism. Why would one waste time, effort, and money to collect social science data to support such obviously true statements?

In fact, every single one of the above propositions is demonstrably false. There exists empirical evidence to demonstrate that each one is not true, and that in many cases the opposite is true. For example: The Irish are the most successful gentile group in the United States both financially and educationally. Support for Catholic schools has not declined in the last ten years, and there is considerable willingness to provide them with financial support—and this is as true for Catholics in their twenties as it is for those in the older age cohorts. Catholics did not support Wallace in any appreciable numbers. They have not drifted to the right politically, and they have not left the Democratic party. Catholics are no longer disproportionately blue-collar workers. On the contrary, they are more likely than Protestants to be members of the middle class (taking into account race, region of the country, and urbanism). Most Catholic priests are happy in their work, and only a minority would marry if they were free to do so. Psychological testing does not show them to be deficient in their capacity for intimacy. I could go on.

Source: From *The American Catholic: A Social Portrait* by Andrew M. Greeley. © 1977 by Andrew M. Greeley. Used by permission of Basic Books, Inc.

One-third or more of all Americans switch religious affiliation at some time (Newport, 1979; Roof and Hadway, 1979). In most cases, they give up religion altogether or change to the religion of their spouse. Much "religious switching" is among the various Protestant denominations; changing from one of the three major churches to another one is relatively uncommon. Changing religious affiliation is often associated with social mobility, with upwardly mobile people often switching to a religion that includes people who are of higher social standing than the members of the church to which they once belonged. This kind of switching reflects a desire to enhance personal prestige by associating with a high-status group rather than any change in personal religious beliefs (Stark and Glock, 1968).

Recent Changes in American Religion

Valuable insights into changes in American religion since the 1920s have been gained from a recent study of Muncie, Indiana. This medium-sized city—originally called "Middletown" when it was first studied by sociologists Robert and Helen Lynd in 1924–1925 and again in 1935—was the subject of an intensive research project carried out in 1976–1978. Over this half-century several changes in religion were evident. It became more acceptable to change religious affiliations, and interfaith marriages became more common. The different congregations became more similar in average incomes and educational attainment over this time. Attendance at religious services became less of a duty and more a source of pleasure. There was no evidence that attachment to religion or participation in church activities declined; if anything, people attended church more often than when the first study was done (Bahr, 1982). Religion also became less puritanical, and religions were more tolerant of one another (Caplow, 1982b). The churches had grown more responsive to "consumer preferences" by the 1970s; they had dropped long sermons and mandatory fasts that were common in the 1920s. In addition, new forms of religion had developed—including "televised services, gospel music concerts, home prayer groups, coffee house ministries, retreat centers, and charismatic conferences" (Caplow, 1982b: 85).

It is not easy to judge whether these changes are also characteristic of the rest of the nation, because other areas have not been subjected to such careful study over a long period of time. However, significant changes have occurred in American religion in recent decades. The 1950s were a quiescent stage in the United States, and religion reflected this. In the 1960s, the civil rights movement and the Vietnam War drew many members of the clergy into social activism. These people were instrumental in changing national policies, but in doing so they alienated some members of their congregations who were more conservative on these issues (Caplow, 1982b). The decline in church membership and contributions in the late 1960s and the 1970s has been attributed by some to the churches' involvement in social activism, but others have suggested that these changes were a result of the churches' failure to recruit new members to replace an aging congregation and the country's lowered birth rate (*The New York Times*, June 15, 1982, p. A8). Since the late 1970s, the churches have retreated from social activism to a large extent—with some notable exceptions such as the antinuclear movement. Today there is more emphasis on traditional beliefs and practices, and there is some evidence that the decline in church membership of the last two decades might be about to reverse itself (*The New York Times*, June 15, 1982, p. A8; Austin, 1983).

In recent years, American society has been marked by several apparently contradictory changes in religion. On the one hand, there has been a trend toward cooperation among different churches and denominations. On the other hand, there has been a growth in intense involvement in fundamentalist and evangelical religions and in Eastern sects and cults. This growth in religious commitment has occurred in spite of what many sociologists feel has been a long-term trend toward a reduced influence of religion over other aspects of social life.

ECUMENISM

The pervasive influence of civil religion in American society and the limited emphasis on theology in American religion have contributed to *ecumenism*, a movement to achieve harmony among various religious groups by emphasizing what they have in common rather than stressing their doctrinal differences in a competition for new members. One force behind the ecumenical movement has been a common search for ways to reduce declining church memberships and declining contributions suffered by many churches and denominations. In addition, changes in the Catholic Church resulting from the Second Vatican Council of 1962—such as the use of English rather than Latin for masses—have opened the way for closer relations among the churches.

Ecumenism has led to conferences in which members of different religions share their views and their strategies for enlarging the role of religion in American society. Different denominations sometimes discuss which one of them will establish a new church in a community, and they also work together to provide social services. In some cases, different denominations have even merged, thereby reducing the overhead costs associated with maintaining separate organizations. Cooperative efforts of this sort are most likely to succeed when the denominations involved have similar beliefs and practices and when their members come from similar social backgrounds.

THE EXPLOSION OF CULTS AND SECTS

Another change in American religion since the 1960s has been a large increase in the number of new cults and sects. These groups are highly concentrated on the West Coast, and the United States as a whole does not have an especially high per capita rate of cults and sects, at least when compared to Africa. One study of 417 American-born sects found that most of them were quite small and that few were growing rapidly; in fact, a third of them had not grown since their formation (Stark and Bainbridge, 1981). These cults and sects are puzzling and esoteric to many Americans, but many of these religious groups are compatible with the Protestant ethic in their emphasis on individual effort to control one's own destiny (Wuthnow and Glock, 1974; Robbins and Anthony, 1979).

Personal-Growth Groups

One study in the San Francisco area—where more than one hundred "new religions" were born between the mid-1960s and the late 1970s—distinguished three major types of sects and cults (Wuthnow, 1976, 1978; Glock and Wuthnow, 1979). One kind—the personal-growth groups such as Scientology, est, and NLP (Neuro-Linguistic Programming)—is not religion because it does not emphasize the sacred. However, these groups do serve some of the same functions as religion in that they address ultimate questions and provide members with a sense of fulfillment and meaning in life. In addition, these personal-growth groups

often draw on religious teachings and divine inspiration (see SEL 13.1).

Neo-Christian Groups

Neo-Christian groups, such as the Christian World Liberation Front, Jews for Jesus, and other evangelical religions, are a second type of "new religion." One such neo-Christian group is the Catholic Charismatic Renewal, which first emerged at Duquesne University in Pittsburgh in 1967 and later spread throughout the country (Lane, 1976). This movement is a Pentecostal, or charismatic, religion, which means that it believes in the immediate presence of the Holy Spirit during prayer meetings and worship services. Pentecostal groups such as this one participate enthusiastically in religious rituals; sometimes they engage in "glossolalia" or speaking in tongues, the utterance of sounds that cannot be understood as language but are believed to be inspired by the presence of a sacred being.

Countercultural Religions

A third type of new religion is countercultural. These religions, which are usually imported from Eastern societies, include Zen Buddhism, yoga, Hare Krishna, and the Unification Church (or "Moonies"). Members of the Hare Krishna group, who chant and solicit contributions on the streets of many American cities, remain celibate and oppose social authority and modern science (Judah, 1974). The Moonies follow Reverend Sun Myung Moon, a Korean industrialist who claims to be Christ reincarnated. Followers of the Reverend Moon turn over all personal property to the Church when they join, and they spend much time soliciting money for the group; the poverty of the individual members contrasts sharply with the wealth of the Church and its leader.

Who Is Most Likely to Join the New Religions?

One study found that experimenters with Eastern or countercultural religions were better educated and more intellectually sophisticated than other residents of their community. They were also less likely to have social attachments to a conventional way of life, and they tended to be young, single, and geographically mobile. They also placed great

"*You go on home without me, Irene. I'm going to join this man's cult.*"

Drawing by Chas. Addams; © 1982 The New Yorker Magazine, Inc.

value on novelty, and their lack of social ties left them free to experiment with new things. Many were college students whose flexible schedules left more time for such experimentation than they would have had if they had been working at a full-time job to support a family. Some were experiencing work-related stress, and many were searching for meaning in life. Because some of these factors have become more common in American society in recent years—such as increases in the numbers of people attending college and remaining single for longer—these religions have grown in membership (Wuthnow, 1978). Eastern religions are chosen by these people because they meet needs that are not fulfilled by traditional Western religions. In addition to finding friends in these groups, adherents are attracted to the emotional religious experience provided by these sects and cults. These religions are also appealing because they focus on the nonmaterial world, fulfill a need to submit to a charismatic leader, avoid the male domination that sometimes characterizes Western religions, and emphasize health and ecology (Cox, 1977).

Members of countercultural religions and members of personal-growth groups are often politically radical and unconventional, but members of neo-Christian groups are more likely to be politically conservative and conventional in life style. It is not clear whether these new religions will grow in size over time; some of their members might eventually be absorbed into mainstream religions or give up religion altogether. Glock and Wuthnow (1979) suggest that non-Western religions could become a more important part of American religion in the future, but Berger (1977) argues that any important religious movements in the United States will develop from the Judeo-Christian tradition rather than from Eastern religions. Indeed, the recent resurgence of Christian fundamentalism and evangelicalism, which involve far larger numbers of people than the new religions, is an example of a return to traditional beliefs and practices.

THE RETURN TO TRADITIONAL RELIGION

One dramatic change in American religion since the 1960s has been a resurgence of traditional or conservative forms of Protestantism. A 1977–1978 survey found that one-third of adult Americans had had a "born-again experience" in which they had committed their life to Christ, and about one American in five had experienced a spontaneous spiritual rebirth and sought to convert others to his or her beliefs. The typical born-again Christian is a white woman over fifty who lives in a small Southern town; nevertheless, large numbers of young people have also converted to conservative forms of Christianity in recent years (Gallup Opinion Index, 1977). Many of these converts come from the middle and upper-middle classes, in contrast to the past when born-again Christians were more commonly drawn from the lower classes. One reason for the rapid growth in conservative Christianity is that the intense commitment of these believers makes them less likely to leave their churches than is true for members of other religions (Bibby, 1978).

There is much variety within Protestant denominations. Religiously liberal Protestants do not hold an absolutist position on such issues as the Second Coming of Christ and the physical Resurrection of Christ. This group has controlled the bureaucracies of these denominations for years, but it is being increasingly challenged by more conservative groups. These more conservative Protestants include both evangelicals and fundamentalists, two distinct groups that are often lumped together as "fundamentalists" or "born-again Christians" (Briggs, 1982).

Evangelicals

In recent years, there has been a significant increase in the number of evangelicals, who are perhaps most visibly represented by the Reverend Billy Graham. They stress personal commitment to Jesus Christ and actively seek converts through "testifying" to their beliefs. They criticize liberals for their doubts and fundamentalists for their absolutism. Evangelicals rely on the Bible as the highest authority, but they do not interpret every passage as literal truth. They own a number of thriving publishing firms and run colleges such as the College Church of Wheaton in Illinois and Fuller Seminary in California. Nonsectarian colleges have also been

the scene of an explosion of evangelical enthusiasm in recent years. *Christianity Today*, the most widely read religious journal in the nation, is an evangelical publication.

In addition, a number of liberal seminaries—such as those at Harvard, Yale, and Princeton—have recently added evangelical professors and admitted increasing numbers of evangelical students. Evangelicals have tried to wrest control of denominational organizations from liberals, and they have sought to distinguish themselves from fundamentalists. Many support politically liberal causes such as social justice for the poor, nuclear disarmament, and a cleaner environment. Most oppose abortion on principle, but many support the right of women to choose to have an abortion. Evangelicals are receptive to science and favor alternatives to the creationist theory of the development of life on Earth (Briggs, 1982).

Fundamentalists

Fundamentalists, on the other hand, interpret the Scriptures literally; for example, they believe that God created the world in six days and that a great flood engulfed the entire world. Fundamentalists participate intensely and frequently in worship services, prayer meetings, and other activities; these activities often take up a considerable portion of their lives. They are expected to show a high commitment to the faith before joining the church and later to strengthen their commitment through interaction with others in the congregation and through religious instruction (McGaw, 1979).

The Influence of Fundamentalists and Evangelicals

Since 1979 there has been much discussion about the part that conservative Christians, particularly fundamentalists, play or might play in American politics. Groups of the "religious right"—such as the Moral Majority, Christian Voice, and the Religious Roundtable—have taken credit for the defeat of liberal congressional candidates and for the election in 1980 of President Ronald Reagan. These groups point to their extensive mailing lists and their ability to mobilize support at the polls. However, their claims of political influence have so far proved to be exaggerated. In fact, conservative Christians did not vote for Reagan in 1980 much more often than voters with other religious beliefs (Johnson and Tamney, 1982). These conservative

Christians differ from other voters on only a few issues—such as school prayer and allowing homosexuals to teach in public schools—and many people do not vote for or against a candidate solely on the basis of these issues.

Fundamentalists and evangelicals have astutely recognized the influence of the mass media on religious beliefs and everyday behavior. Fundamentalist groups have sought to ban "objectionable" books from school and public libraries, and they have called for a boycott of companies who sponsor television programs that portray sex and violence. Evangelicals and fundamentalists own several radio and television stations that feature religious programming. This programming serves a dual purpose: It brings new converts to the religion, and it raises money for the organization. Both radio and television programs of this sort appeal frequently for direct contributions and offer the audience the chance to buy religious articles such as records, books, and pictures (Mariani, 1979). The overall audience for syndicated religious programs on television increased substantially from 9.8 million in 1970 to 22.5 million in 1978, but by 1980 it had dropped a bit to 20.5 million (Hadden and Swann, 1981: 55). These figures are, however, less than the total audiences for some of the network programs that fundamentalists would like to banish from television.

THE SECULARIZATION OF SOCIETY

The recent upsurge of interest in both traditional Christianity and the "new religions" has taken place in the context of a long-term decline in religious influence over the family, education, and the political system in industrial societies. This process by which other institutions become increasingly separated from religion is called *secularization*. In secularized societies, religion is less likely to be reflected in the arts, literature, and philosophy than was the case in earlier times. Secularization also means that individuals are less likely to see the world and their own lives from a religious perspective (Berger, 1967, 1977; Acquaviva, 1966, 1979; J. Wilson, 1978).

One aspect of secularization is that churches often modify their doctrines and practices in response to the changing needs of their members and in response to changes in society. For example, in 1976 the Episcopal Church of the United States first officially allowed women to become priests, in response to pressure by the feminist movement and by women in the Church; by 1982 more than five hundred women were Episcopal priests (Barthelme, 1982). Secularization also influences the content of religious beliefs; in so doing it may lead to the development of sects that want to return to a more traditional theology. The long-term decline in the emphasis on theological issues by American religions, and the accompanying increase in attention to public issues, has meant that the sacred has become relatively less important and the profane relatively more important. Today religion is often seen as a way to strengthen the family, insure mental health, and improve society rather than as a way to worship the supernatural (Berger, 1969).

Secularization is the product of changes in society. Modern science and advanced technology lead people to think that problems can be solved by applying human reason and effort. Religion in industrial society often comes to reflect this emphasis on pragmatism, and in doing so it sometimes moves away from faith in the power of the supernatural. The rise of the nation-state and the growth of government have caused the state to take over some of the functions traditionally performed by religion, such as providing help for the poor. In addition, secularization is a result of the growing size of religious organizations; bureaucratized churches divert the attention of the clergy from theological issues to secular matters such as fundraising and the construction of facilities (B. Wilson, 1966; J. Wilson, 1978).

The religious institution is a less pervasive influence in modern societies than in preindustrial societies. Nevertheless, religion continues to serve important functions in meeting individual needs and enhancing social solidarity. Religion does have a more restricted domain in industrial societies, but the intense commitment of large numbers of people to churches, sects, and cults in those societies indicates that religion is unlikely to disappear in the foreseeable future.

Summary

In every society we find religions, or belief systems that try to answer ultimate questions about the meaning of life. These belief systems differ from personal philosophies of life in their emphasis on the sacred—the awe-inspiring quality of the supernatural—and in the collective aspect of their beliefs, symbols, and rituals.

Religion serves a variety of functions for individuals and for society as a whole. It helps people to cope with the uncertainty of life and what awaits them after death. Religion also socializes people in norms and values that characteristically support the social system. Religion strengthens social bonds; indeed, Durkheim felt that religion was itself a cultural representation of the society. The passage from one stage of the life cycle to another is often eased by religious ritual. These functions are sometimes served by other social institutions too, but these alternative ways to meet the same needs are not distinguished by an emphasis on the sacred.

Beliefs are a major component of all religions. They take the form of myths or an elaborate theology that reflects faith in gods, spirits, ghosts, impersonal forces of good and evil, or abstract ethical principles. Religious symbols such as the cross are often a part of rituals that both reflect and strengthen these beliefs. These rituals define the relationship of believers to the sacred through traditional and stylized practices.

There are various kinds of religious organizations. One is the church, a large organization of many members who worship together in formal rituals. Churches are closely associated with the secular world and often take the form of a bureaucracy. Sects, on the other hand, are smaller groups with looser structures that have often split off from a church to "purify" a theology. They sometimes cut themselves off from the secular world, although this creates problems in recruiting members and raising funds. Cults are small religious groups that stress a specific belief or practice and that are led by charismatic leaders. Only if they find a way to routinize this charisma in a formal organization will they endure over time.

Marx, Weber, and Berger have all explored the relationship of religion to the larger society, especially its economic system. Marx treated religion as an institution that was used to reinforce the advantages of the dominant group in the economic system. He felt that religion alienated people and inhibited the development of socialism and communism. Weber, on the other hand, focused more on religion as a source of economic change. He argued that the Protestant ethic inherent in Calvinism was a major source of modern capitalism, for it impelled people to work hard and reinvest the fruits of their labor.

Berger sees a complex interrelationship of religion and the economic system, suggesting that religion can respond to the process of modernization in a variety of ways.

In the United States we find that most people profess a belief in God, and many are suspicious of those who claim to have no religion. The multitude of churches, sects, and cults in the United States and the Constitutional protection of the freedom of religion are closely associated with a norm of tolerance for religious diversity. However, American society has been marred by religious intolerance from time to time. In addition, the separation of church and state is an unclear principle that is still being interpreted by the courts, as we can see from the recent debates over school prayer and creation science. Civil religion is a belief system that supports the existing political system by elevating aspects of the secular world to the status of the sacred.

In recent years there has been a slight increase in the proportion of Americans who claim to have no religion, but most Americans believe in God and most are affiliated with a church. Affiliation differs for various ethnic groups and social classes; indeed, it is possible to rank religions by the average income, occupational prestige, and education of their members. There is a significant amount of religious switching among Americans; some of this is related to upward mobility, but much of it involves changing to a spouse's religion or giving up religion altogether.

American religion has undergone significant changes since the 1960s. Ecumenism—the movement toward increased cooperation among churches and denominations—has grown since then. There has also been an explosion in the number of cults and sects, although this trend does not involve most Americans. These "new religions" include personal-growth groups, neo-Christian groups, and countercultural groups that are often based on Eastern religions. Another major trend since the 1960s has been the growing strength of evangelical and fundamentalist Christianity, although the political influence of the "religious right" has so far been exaggerated. There is a long-term trend toward the secularization of society—that is, the reduced influence of religion on the rest of society. However, religion remains a major force in industrial societies such as the United States and seems to be in no danger of disappearing.

Important Terms

CHURCH (302)	RELIGION (297)
CIVIL RELIGION (311)	RITUAL (301)
CULT (303)	ROUTINIZATION OF CHA-
DENOMINATION (303)	RISMA (304)
ECUMENISM (315)	SACRED (297)
MAGIC (301)	SECT (303)
MYTH (300)	SECULARIZATION (319)
PROFANE (297)	THEISM (300)
PROTESTANT ETHIC	THEOLOGY (300)
(306)	TOTEM (301)

Suggested Readings

Robert N. Bellah and Phillip E. Hammond. *Varieties of Civil Religion.* San Francisco: Harper & Row, 1980. An examination of the civil religion from a historical, comparative and contemporary perspective.

Peter L. Berger. *The Sacred Canopy: Elements of a Sociological Theory of Religion.* Garden City, N.Y.: Doubleday, 1967. A good introduction to the sociology of religion.

Jackson W. Carroll, Douglas W. Johnson, and Martin E. Marty. *Religion in America: 1950 to the Present.* San Francisco: Harper & Row, 1979. A well-documented study of changes in American religion over three decades.

Charles Y. Glock and Robert N. Bellah, eds. *The New Religious Consciousness.* Berkeley, Calif.: University of California Press, 1976. A wide-ranging collection of essays on "new religions."

Andrew M. Greeley. *The American Catholic: A Social Portrait.* New York: Basic Books, 1977. An empirical study of Catholics in American society.

Jeffrey K. Hadden and Charles E. Swann. *Prime Time Preachers: The Rising Power of Televangelism.* Reading, Mass.: Addison-Wesley, 1981. An in-depth examination of religious programming on American television.

Max Weber. *The Protestant Ethic and the Spirit of Capitalism,* trans. by Talcott Parsons. New York: Scribner's, 1904, 1958. A classic study of the influence of Calvinist beliefs on the emergence of modern capitalism.

John Wilson. *Religion in American Society: The Effective Presence.* Englewood Cliffs, N.J.: Prentice-Hall, 1978. A thorough examination of the sociology of religion.

THE POLITICAL SYSTEM 14

In August 1974, Richard M. Nixon became the first American president to resign from office. At the time, it seemed inevitable that he would be removed from office by the process of impeachment, in which the Senate conducts a trial on charges that have been voted by the House of Representatives. Mr. Nixon did not give up the reins of power easily, for he had devoted his life to the contest for governmental power that we call politics. He had been elected to the most powerful office in the nation—some would say the world—by a large margin of victory in 1972, shortly after the discovery of the burglary at the Democratic party's headquarters at Watergate, the crime that eventually was his undoing.

The Nixon presidency illustrates several key aspects of the *political system*—the institution that meets society's needs for internal order, protection from external enemies, resolution of group differences, and the definition and pursuit of societal goals. Mr. Nixon's career was characterized by the seeking of power—a scarce resource whose possession enables people to impose their will on others and that is often associated with prestige and wealth. Nixon was part of the national *government*—the group of people who hold office at a given time—having served as Senator, Vice President, and President. His fall from power was caused by a sharp decline in public trust as a result of "Watergate"—both the burglary and his involvement in a conspiracy to conceal it from the public and from law-enforcement officials—and other actions such as his failure to pay more than $400,000 in taxes one year. These and other incidents undermined his *legitimacy* in the eyes of many Americans; in other words, people felt that it was no longer appropriate for him to hold power. When Mr. Nixon reluctantly resigned, he attributed his fall to a hostile press and to Congressional opposition. In other words, he continued to see power as a resource that was won or lost in a contest between opposing forces; in contrast, most observers viewed his resignation as a result of a severe decline in his legitimacy—something far more disastrous to a political leader than simple unpopularity or sharp criticism.

Power, Legitimacy, and Authority

Because power is basic to organized social life, political relationships are present in all societies, except perhaps for a few communal societies that have very simple economic systems. However, it is only since the fifteenth century that the *state* has emerged as a centralized and strong institution distinct from the rest of society. The state is an organization that has a monopoly on the legitimate use of physical force within a defined territory (Weber, 1918, 1949: 78).

Political systems can be described in part by the relationship between officials and citizens. Officials are members of the government who are expected to make and to implement decisions that help to achieve societal goals. These decisions are binding on all citizens, those people who are expected to meet obligations such as voting, abiding by the law, and being loyal to the state. People are socialized into the citizen role by parents, teachers, peers, and the mass media; we examine this process of political socialization later in the chapter.

POWER

Max Weber (1925, 1947: 152) defined power as "the probability that one actor within a social relationship will be in a position to carry out his own will despite resistance." Power is thus a form of domination, an unequal relationship between people who interact with each other within the same social system. Except in cases of physically violent domination, both parties to the interaction generally wield a reciprocal influence, because to exert power an individual needs people with less power who will eventually comply (Wrong, 1979).

One source of power is physical force, the infliction of pain or suffering either to encourage compliance with a command or to encourage avoidance of particular actions. Power is also derived from the ability to provide or withhold things that people want. Those who can give or withhold money, praise, or prestige have power over people who desire those rewards. Another source of power is a personality trait that enables certain individuals to persuade or inspire others, as in the case of charismatic leaders. Expertise can also be a source of power; people with special skills or with access to technical knowledge and information have power over those who lack such abilities and knowledge.

LEGITIMACY

When those who are subject to the commands of others believe that those others have the right to exercise power, we say that those with power have legitimacy. The legitimate or appropriate use of power is often called authority. Officials maintain their legitimacy as long as they behave within certain limits set by their subjects. Usually rulers are aware of those limits, but sometimes they test them by seeing how far they can go without losing legitimacy (Moore, 1978: 18; Wrong, 1979). President Nixon, for example, was able to maintain enough legitimacy to stay in office for about two years after the discovery of the Watergate burglary, but eventually public awareness of his involvement in a conspiracy to cover up the burglary undermined his legitimacy and forced him to resign.

The illegitimate use of power—such as obstruction of justice (one of the charges against Nixon) or demanding a bribe from someone seeking personal favors—is regarded as an improper exercise of authority. Power can also be used illegitimately by people who are not political officials; for example, gangsters extort "protection money" from shopkeepers, and robbers steal from banks. Illegitimate uses of power to force compliance are called "coercion." When most citizens believe that a leader's authority is legitimate, the exercise of power will be stable; just the opposite is true of coercion, which

does not rely on popular consensus. For instance, Idi Amin ruled Uganda during the 1970s through coercion, by the arbitrary application of force; in one incident, he had a cabinet minister executed for picking his nose during the filming of the documentary, *Idi Amin Dada*. Ultimately Idi Amin fell from power because his rule was not regarded as legitimate by his people, by other members of government, and by foreign governments.

THE SOURCES OF LEGITIMACY

Authority, or legitimate power, stems from a variety of sources. Max Weber proposed three distinct types of authority, each having a different source: traditional authority, charismatic authority, and rational–legal authority. Actual political leaders often hold more than one of these kinds of authority.

Traditional Authority

Sometimes a ruler's authority is based on a widely shared idea that existing power arrangements are natural or inevitable. The authority of chiefs, kings, queens, and priests is often based on customs and long-standing practices rather than on specific skills or on victory in an election. This *traditional authority* elicits loyalty from subjects that is based on their devotion to both the leader and the status that the leader occupies. The Queen of England is one example of a ruler holding traditional authority.

Charismatic Authority

Charismatic authority is a type of moral authority that is derived from a person's unique vision, inspiration, or sense of destiny. Originally, this term referred to religious leaders, but today it is regularly used—perhaps even overused—to characterize political leaders who inspire loyalty and excitement because of their "magnetic personalities" rather than because of the offices they hold. The use of the mass media in industrial societies to create a public image for a candidate through public relations and advertising has sometimes produced "pseudo-charisma" rather than a true inspirational quality in candidates for office (Bensman and Rosenberg, 1976; Marger, 1981).

Charismatic leaders such as Mao Zedong and Adolf Hitler sometimes emerge during crises to challenge the existing political institutions and to

Traditional authority such as that exercised by Queen Elizabeth of Britain, elicits loyalty among subjects that is based on both devotion to the leader and recognition of the status the leader occupies.

provide an alternative kind of leadership. A charismatic leader can bring about social change; an example of this is the Iranian revolution of 1979, when the Ayatollah Khomeini came to power after the Shah was overthrown; Khomeini undertook to create a revolutionary Islamic society. Hitler's rise to power was related to the economic depression and the lack of effective political leadership in Germany after World War I. Thus, to understand the emergence of charismatic leaders, both the social context and the individual characteristics of the leader must be examined.

Many charismatic leaders face a problem that Weber called "the routinization of charisma" (see Chapter 13). Because it is based on personal qualities that cannot easily be transmitted from one leader to another, charisma is an inherently un-

stable form of authority. As a result, charismatic leaders must shift to a traditional or a rational–legal basis of authority if their goals are to be pursued effectively after their death. Whether leaders such as the Ayatollah Khomeini can manage to shift the basis of authority and bring about permanent political change is always open to question.

Rational–Legal Authority

Power that is based on the formally defined rights and obligations of people who occupy the status of official is called *rational–legal authority*. Under this form of authority, citizens are loyal to a set of abstract principles and rules rather than to the specific individual who holds office at a given time. For instance, occupying the office of President of the

United States is often enough to influence American public opinion; a presidential speech can shift opinion in the President's direction, even if the President is not an especially popular leader.

Rational–legal authority is based on laws and formal rules that are designed to achieve goals efficiently. These laws and rules are usually written down, and both leaders and subjects can point to them if the leader's obligations or rights are in question. In addition to defining the obligations and rights of political officials, this type of authority is also the basis for bureaucratic organizations such as profit-making corporations, universities, and social service agencies.

Weber's three kinds of authority are ideal types. Many political leaders actually rely on some combination of the three. For example, President John F. Kennedy had personal charisma that was enhanced by his effective use of the mass media, but he also derived traditional authority and rational–legal authority from the office of President of the United States. The Ayatollah Khomeini's power is derived from personal charisma, the traditional authority of Islamic religious leader, and the rational–legal authority of head of the government. Kings and queens hold traditional authority, but if they are loved by their subjects they can also develop charismatic authority.

The State

In the fifteenth century, autonomous city-states in Europe began to consolidate into larger political units. Increased trade and improved transportation and communication gradually led to the diffusion of culture and made possible a common identity among people who lived far apart. The states that emerged were sovereign, meaning that they were self-governing and legally equal to other states in the international community. These centralized political systems guaranteed rights to their citizens, but they also had the power to protect the narrow interests of a rising class of merchants, who were one of the forces behind the development of the state.

THE FUNCTIONALIST PERSPECTIVE ON THE STATE

Functionalists see political power as essential to the accomplishment of societal goals. They suggest that for chaos to be avoided authority must be delegated to leaders who can coordinate policy making and implementation. For instance, in order to ensure that there is adequate production of goods and services to meet society's needs, there must be a framework to manage the efficient use and development of resources. One role of the state is to provide this framework for a society's economic system. Functionalists, then, see the state as essential to the maintenance of social order, and inequality of power as an inevitable outcome of the need to assign certain tasks to officials.

Maintaining Internal Order

One function of the state is to maintain internal order by giving a society a sense of overall direction and by establishing and enforcing certain rules of behavior. One way that this is done is through the legal system, which is discussed in Chapter 15. For instance, the criminal law deters some behavior that lawmakers have defined as harmful to the social order or to the interests of certain groups. The aim of civil sanctions that require a blameworthy party to pay damages is to restore the injured party to his or her prior condition; thus a drunken driver might be required to pay medical expenses to an injured pedestrian. The civil law also regulates the economy through agencies that control the practices of industry. Moreover, the law defines the rights and obligations of people in certain social relationships; for example, both partners in a marriage can legally end their relationship under certain conditions such as adultery or alcoholism.

Sometimes the state maintains internal order by the use of force, over which it has a monopoly. The police might be used to control behavior defined as detrimental to the general welfare or to the narrow interests of a special group. For instance, the "police riot" in Chicago during the Democratic party's national convention in 1968 was designed to crush a protest against the Vietnam War. The militia or the armed forces are also used to quell popular disturbances, such as the urban riots that broke out in black ghettos of American cities during the mid-1960s. Actions that political leaders see as necessary to maintain internal order may be seen by others as oppression and coercion to enhance the power of those officials.

Strengthening National Identity

Closely related to the function of maintaining internal order are the state's efforts to establish, maintain, and strengthen a national identity. A sense of common purpose is often a product of such efforts, which can require citizens to make personal sacrifices in the name of national interests; for instance, without a sense of loyalty to the state, it would be difficult to raise armed forces during wartime. Sometimes national identity is enhanced by conflict between nations. War and other international hostilities—such as the taking of American hostages by militant Iranian students in 1979—often strengthen a sense of common identity, as was evident in the celebrations that followed the return of those hostages to the United States.

Political campaigns in democratic nations are one occasion for the strengthening of national identity. Often, the candidates' rhetoric supports the state while attacking officials who are part of the existing government. Even the concession speeches made by losing candidates commonly serve to strengthen national identity by praising the political system. Other ways that this identity is reinforced include the pledge of allegiance in school, the singing of the national anthem at athletic events, and the display of the flag on public buildings.

Dealing With Other Nations

One important function of the state is to maintain relations with other nations. This is done through alliances, trade agreements, and diplomatic exchanges. Nations that are political adversaries on some issues might nevertheless engage in trade. For instance, even though there were political differences between the United States and the Soviet Union in the early 1980s over the Soviet invasion of Afghanistan and Soviet support for the military regime in Poland, the United States government still sold wheat to the Soviet Union, although efforts were made to prevent the sale of gas pipeline equipment to the Russians. Sanctions against South Africa for its racist policies have reduced that country's ties to the international community, but its production of gold and diamonds has kept many channels of trade open.

In the event of an outbreak of hostilities between nations, the state acts to protect its citizens from external threat. To do this, most states maintain a military force. Often citizens disagree as to how much of a society's resources should be spent on the military, as well as over how and when the armed forces should be used. Some people have criticized President Reagan for requesting increased military appropriations, but others argue that this is required by the relative weakness of the American armed forces in comparison to those of the Soviet Union.

Policy Making

Another important function of the state is to make and implement policies that influence the use of scarce resources. States vary in the degree to which they control the allocation of goods and services. Some adopt a laissez-faire, or hands-off, policy that allows people to keep most of what they earn and inherit; others use taxation and government regulation to redistribute income from the wealthy to the poor, or from private uses to public uses. There was no federal income tax until 1913, but since then Americans have paid a significant portion of their earnings to the federal government in taxes, even though the proportion of total personal income paid in taxes is less in the United States than in Western European nations. Tax revenues are then redistributed to those who meet certain criteria of eligibility; benefits in the United States include aid for the dependent children of the poor, unemployment compensation, and social security payments for the elderly. The state also uses tax revenues for purposes such as the construction of schools and hospitals, the building and maintenance of highways, and the establishment of public health measures.

THE CONFLICT PERSPECTIVE ON THE STATE

In contrast to the functionalists, conflict theorists regard the state as a tool used by certain groups for their own advantage. Rejecting the functionalists' claim that the authority of the state is based on a belief in its legitimacy that citizens share, Marxists and other conflict theorists see the state as organized coercion (Miliband, 1969, 1977). Lenin, for example, saw the military and the police as the basis of state power. For conflict theorists, then, revolution occurs only when the state's monopoly on force breaks down; functionalists, on the other hand, see revolution as occurring when the state has lost legitimacy (Skocpol, 1979).

Karl Marx and Friedrich Engels (1848, 1967) claimed that the state serves the interests of the dominant class in the economic system. As we discussed in Chapters 1 and 8, this means that in a capitalist economic system the bourgeoisie, or capitalists, will control and use state power to protect their property and the economic system that serves them well. Marx stopped short of asserting that capitalists completely control the state, acknowledging that the state often provides benefits for the population as a whole.

Until recently, Marxists usually treated the state as an instrument of power controlled by the dominant class, rather than as an autonomous institution with its own interests to serve. Lately, however, Marxists have examined the "relative autonomy of the state" (Miliband, 1969, 1977; Skocpol, 1979). In other words, they have found that the state sometimes acts independently of the dominant class, often to preserve the economic system but at other times to serve the more narrow interests of government officials and bureaucrats.

Marx and Engels (1848, 1967) predicted that inherent flaws or contradictions in the capitalist system would eventually lead to a revolution by workers who would take control of the means of production as well as the state itself. The first step in the revolution would be *socialism*, a society in which property was publicly owned and there was a "dictatorship of the proletariat." Next would come *communism*, a classless society in which property was communally owned and, at least according to Engels, the state would begin to "wither away." In fact, no society has yet moved from capitalism through socialism to communism, and there have been no signs that the state withers away after a workers' revolution.

FORMS OF THE STATE

Since the end of World War II, there has been a rapid increase in the formation of new states, particularly in Africa and Asia. The breakdown of colonial rule by nations such as Great Britain and France has resulted from rebellion by indigenous populations (as in Zimbabwe, formerly Rhodesia, and in Algeria) and from pressure by indigenous populations on rulers to turn over the reins of power to them (as in India). The decline of colonialism has often produced a stronger sense of national identity among people who historically had regarded themselves as members of distinct tribal groups; however, in some nations, such as Nigeria, tribal loyalties have hindered the emergence of a shared sense of nationhood.

In recent years, states have grown larger because of increasing populations and because technological advances have made it possible to unite larger numbers of people through improved communication and transportation. These changes have led to more reliance on rational–legal authority, because traditional authority does not adapt as quickly to the rapid transformation of society. Also, because domestic and international economic systems have become so complex, the state has come to play a larger role in regulating industry and commerce in order to achieve societal goals. As a result of these changes, the state has become more bureaucratized and has exerted greater control over the daily lives of its citizens. For instance, the United States government is now the single largest employer in the country, with nearly three million civilian employees and about two million military personnel. Efforts to reduce the size of this federal work force, much of which works in bureaucratic organizations, have so far achieved few significant results.

Totalitarianism

Totalitarianism is a centralized state that is relatively intolerant of opposition and that manipulates its citizens through its control of basic institutions such as the family, the school, the church, labor unions, and the mass media. Citizens in totalitarian states are accountable to their rulers; this is the opposite of democracies, where rulers—at least in the ideal type of democracy—are accountable to citizens. In totalitarian states, power is concentrated in the hands of government officials rather than diffused among a variety of groups and institutions.

Many totalitarian states have emerged from unstable social and economic conditions, such as the severe economic depression and social dislocation in post-World War I Germany that led to Hitler's rise to power. Totalitarianism is especially common in poor societies that lack a sizable middle class; a number of Latin American nations are examples of this. Because the government has absolute control over the economy in a totalitarian state, rapid industrialization is at least theoretically possible, by carefully planning the use of resources and mobilizing the people for work; in reality, however, totalitarian states have faced many obstacles in their efforts to industrialize.

In some totalitarian states, such as the Soviet Union and the People's Republic of China, government officials are members of a single political party that is equated with the state. Citizens may vote in periodic elections, as they do in the Soviet Union, but they have no real choice among candidates. In other totalitarian regimes, the military controls power; this is especially common in Latin America and in Africa. Sometimes religious leaders exercise totalitarian control over the state, as the Ayatollah Khomeini does in Iran.

Because totalitarian states monopolize force, they are able to minimize the threat of violent revolution by discontented citizens. Lack of weapons is one reason why black South Africans have not yet mounted a real challenge to their white rulers, even though blacks outnumber whites by more than three to one. Some totalitarian governments control their citizens through terror, the use of violence to instill fear and cause people to behave in certain ways (Walter, 1969). Stalin's rule in the Soviet Union, which included the widespread killing of real and imagined opponents both inside and outside government, is one example of terror in a totalitarian state.

FASCISM. One form of totalitarianism is *fascism*, a one-party dictatorship headed by a charismatic leader, such as Hitler or Mussolini. Fascism is fervently nationalistic and hostile to communism. Fascist states maintain repressive control over their citizens; they allow people to have private property but exercise considerable control over the economy. Citizens have no effective way to change the government in fascist states; instead, they are controlled by the state through its domination of the family, the school, the mass media, and business. Every institution is used to further the state's goals; for instance, children might be encouraged to inform on their parents if they act contrary to the interests of the state (Friedrich and Brzezinski, 1965).

One form of totalitarianism is "fascism," a one-party dictatorship headed by a charismatic leader such as Hitler or Mussolini.

COMMUNISM. Another form of totalitarianism is *communism*. The main difference between communist and fascist states is that communists place greater emphasis on public property than on private property. Also, in most communist states a single political party is usually more important than a charismatic leader, although there have been notable exceptions such as Stalin in the Soviet Union and Mao Zedong in China.

States that we commonly call "communist"— such as the Soviet Union and China—might be described more accurately as socialist totalitarian states dominated by a Communist party. These states do not fit Marx and Engels's definition of communism, a society with no classes and with a weak or nonexistent state. In Poland—a country we often call communist—workers' efforts to unionize in the early 1980s led to military repression backed by the Communist parties of Poland and the Soviet Union. These events indicate that social classes do exist in Poland, and that the state is still strong there. Poland therefore does not fit the Marxist definition of communism; indeed, the repression of workers indicates that it may not even be correct to call Poland a socialist state in Marxist terms, because the workers do not control the state.

Democracy

Democracy, the form of the state in which authority is vested in the people, is relatively rare because certain conditions are needed for it to emerge and flourish. Usually democracy requires an affluent economy with an advanced technology, although democracy can exist under other conditions, as it does in India. For the most part, democracy needs a literate and informed middle class that will support a stable government and take an active role in the political process. For such a class to exist, a society must have the resources to develop a good educational system and must have reached a level of economic development that permits large numbers of people to spend their adolescence and even their early adulthood in school (Lipset, 1959).

The diffusion of power among a variety of groups is also conducive to democracy, although these groups must share an underlying belief in the legitimacy of the political system and be tolerant of dissent. In addition, the state must allow citizens to remain loyal to their families and their religions, rather than demand absolute loyalty from them. People who owe allegiance to a variety of groups and organizations are more likely to feel the "cross-pressure" of competing loyalties and are thus less likely to become intensely committed to their position in bitter and disruptive conflicts with members of other groups.

Democracy and totalitarianism are ideal types; real political systems often have aspects of each. Totalitarian states often lack full control over their citizens, and leaders in such systems are restrained by a need to maintain legitimacy in the eyes of the people (Moore, 1978). In contrast, democratic states rely on the consent of the governed, but real power is often concentrated in small groups of wealthy individuals, as we will see later in this chapter. In addition, democratic governments sometimes attempt to manipulate public opinion, regulate the information available to people, and control the lives of their citizens in various ways, even though that control is less complete than in totalitarian states.

Political Behavior in the United States

There are a variety of ways for people to participate in the political system. In democracies, they vote in elections, join political parties, contribute to campaigns, and organize to influence policy making. In totalitarian states, they support their leaders and comply with officials' commands. People's views of their political system and their role in the political process are related to the form of the state itself, but their socialization experiences also affect their political attitudes and behavior.

POLITICAL SOCIALIZATION

The status of citizen is associated with certain attitudes and behavior; for instance, citizens are expected to support their government actively and to abide by the law willingly. The process through which people learn political attitudes and behavior is called *political socialization* (Jennings and Niemi, 1974; Sears, 1975; Niemi and Sobieszek, 1977; Lorence and Mortimer, 1979; Marger, 1981). This process involves learning the cultural expectations of the role of citizen and developing a belief in the legitimacy of the state.

The ages from nine to thirteen are especially important in political socialization. Children of nine or ten typically see the government in individualistic terms, identifying the state with the president (Hess and Torney, 1967). During this stage, they begin to trust the government and its officials and institutions. Between eleven and thirteen they start to see the government in institutional terms; they learn that the presidency or the legislature will endure after the people currently holding office change. About this time, children also learn about voting and the political decision-making process. By the age of thirteen, most of them have a relatively low level of specific political knowledge, but they are aware of aspects of citizenship such as obedience to the law and participation in civic affairs (Jennings and Niemi, 1974; Renshon, 1977). In addition, by early adolescence many have developed a preference for a political party. The beliefs that have been formed by the end of adolescence usually remain relatively stable over the course of a lifetime (Sears, 1975; Lorence and Mortimer, 1979). However, adult experiences—such as work or amassing considerable wealth—influence political behavior and beliefs among adults to some degree (Niemi and Sobieszek, 1977; Lorence and Mortimer, 1979).

In some political systems—especially totalitarian ones—children are subjected to a more formal and more intensive political socialization by their family, by state-run child-care centers and schools, and by the mass media. Criticism by peers is sometimes used to encourage conformity to norms approved by the state; eventually this process of criticism is internalized (or learned) and people in a sense police themselves. Through this process a shared national identity is created and individuals are subordinated to the collectivity (Bronfenbrenner, 1962, 1970).

In the United States, political socialization is a result of efforts by the family and the peer group, which are relatively free of state control, and by the schools, which are under local rather than national control. The family provides children with membership in a social class, an ethnic group, a religion, and other groups that are likely to be associated with particular kinds of political beliefs and behavior. From interactions with their parents, children develop a basic trust—or mistrust—of the political system, its officials, and its institutions. Their knowledge of politics and their party preferences tend to follow their parents' quite closely. School reinforces what children have learned from their parents and instills patriotic beliefs by presenting the nation's history in a certain way and through symbolic ceremonies such as the pledge of allegiance. Schools also give children their first experience with an impersonal authority whose commands they must obey, an experience that influences their attitudes toward the state itself. The importance of the school as an agent of political socialization was made clear during the early 1950s, with the "Red scare" of the McCarthy era, when some states required teachers to take a "loyalty oath" to show that they were not "un-American" and sympathetic to communism.

POLITICAL PARTICIPATION

Citizens engage in many kinds of political behavior—including voting in elections, running for office, and trying to influence the decision making of officials (Alford and Friedland, 1975; Kourvetaris and Dobratz, 1982). American citizens have the legal right to participate in politics, but they are not required to participate. As a result, many choose not to play certain roles of the citizen.

Voting

Participation in American presidential elections has declined in recent years from about 60 per cent of the voting age population for the elections between 1952 and 1968 to about 54 per cent for the elections between 1972 and 1980 (U.S. Bureau of the Census, 1982: 489). These figures are well below those for elections in other nations, for a variety of reasons. Unlike citizens in some democracies, Americans are not automatically registered as voters, nor are they required to vote. In addition, elections are more numerous in the United States than in many other countries; and American elections are held on weekdays rather than on weekends, as they are in Europe, making it more difficult for some Americans to get to the polls (Dionne, 1983).

Participation in American elections has probably declined in recent years because of the influx of new voters into the electorate. The Constitutional Amendment that lowered the voting age from twenty-one to eighteen had its first impact on a national election in 1972, and the percentage of people voting that year was much lower than in 1968, the year of the previous presidential election. Young people are less likely than older people to register to vote and less likely to vote if they are registered. The effect of low voter turnout can be to reduce the legitimacy of the government: President Reagan won the 1980 election by a "landslide" with the votes of only 27 per cent of all Americans of voting age, and even fewer people cast ballots in "off-year" elections. For example, only 34.9 per cent of the voting age population cast ballots for U.S. Representatives in 1978, compared to 47.4 per cent of the voting age population voting for representatives in the presidential election year of 1980 (U.S. Bureau of the Census, 1982: 489).

Why do so many Americans fail to vote? One reason that is commonly given is that citizens do not care about the outcome of elections or feel that their votes will not have any real effect on their lives or on the outcome of an election (Ladd, 1978; Hadley, 1978). This might reflect a belief that all candidates are equally qualified for office and that all will do an equally good job if elected. However, it could also reflect the belief that none of the candidates will do a good job or improve matters much for the average citizen. Although it might seem plausible that alienated people—those who feel powerless to influence the course of their lives through political participation—would be the least likely to vote, research indicates that the alienated vote as often as people who are not alienated (Citrin, 1978; Wolfinger and Rosenstone, 1980).

WHO VOTES? One study of those who vote found that the two most important variables determining participation in elections were educational attainment and age (Wolfinger and Rosenstone, 1980). The more educated were more likely to vote, apparently because they had more of the skills needed to learn about politics and public issues and because they found it easier to register and to vote. Voting also increased with age, even into the years after retirement. This suggests that a common explanation for nonvoting—the illness and infirmity of the elderly—is probably overrated as an explanation for the failure to cast ballots. Age seemed to be associated with voting because older people were better able to understand political issues as they matured, felt more responsible for civic matters as they grew older, and developed the habit of voting over time. One interesting conclusion of this study was that although nonvoting might reduce the legitimacy of the government, it could be less important than some people think, because voters and nonvoters actually differ relatively little in their attitudes on public issues. In other words, those who go to the polls seem to be a fairly representative selection of the population of all people who are eligible to vote.

People are more likely to go to the polls if they

"You've got my vote, sir. But I'm poor, and poor people are notorious for not registering and voting."

Drawing by Dana Fradon; © 1982 The New Yorker Magazine, Inc.

are pressured by a reference group to vote in a particular way. However, if they are "cross-pressured" by different groups to vote in different ways, they might not vote at all (Lipset et al., 1954; Lipset, 1963a; Orum, 1983). For example, Catholic business executives who are pressured by Catholic friends to vote for a Democratic candidate but who are also pressured by colleagues at work to vote for a Republican candidate might stay away from the polls on election day. Cross-pressures can reduce political participation, but they can also contribute to political stability by weakening the intensity of political feelings that might threaten the social order.

Voting and other forms of political participation are related to an individual's social standing. In the United States, people with higher incomes, more prestigious jobs, and more education are more likely than people of lower status to register, to vote, and to join a political party (Campbell et al., 1964; Verba and Nie, 1972; Alford and Friedland, 1975; Wolfinger and Rosenstone, 1980; U.S. Bureau of the Census, 1982: 493). People who have recently won the right to vote—such as women in the earlier part of this century—are less likely to participate in politics than groups that have had citizenship rights longer. Ethnicity is also related to voting behavior: Whites are more likely than blacks to register and to vote, and blacks are more likely than Hispanics to participate in politics (U.S. Bureau of the Census, 1982: 493).

Most studies of voting that were done in the 1940s and 1950s found that social characteristics and group memberships were fairly accurate indicators of electoral behavior. Many people voted on the basis of traditional party loyalties, and there was a strong correlation between party affiliation and class. The working class typically voted Democratic, and the middle and upper classes characteristically voted Republican. A study of "Middletown" (Muncie, Indiana) found that class voting had not declined—and perhaps had even increased, especially among blacks—between 1936 and 1976 (Guterbock, 1980). Class voting is especially important when economic issues dominate a contest for office. As SEL 14.1 illustrates, gender has emerged recently as another important dimension of voting behavior.

SOCIOLOGY AND EVERYDAY LIFE 14.1
Voting: "The Gender Gap"

Surveys done in the early 1980s showed a growing "gender gap" in the political activities and preferences of men and women. Women were considerably more likely to register as Democrats than as Republicans, and women were also more critical of President Reagan. What are the sources and implications of this gender gap for American politics?

Women were enfranchised in 1920, but they were slow to enter the ranks of voters. By 1964, women outnumbered male voters, largely because the female population was larger than the male population in all age brackets of potential voters. However, 1980 was the first election year—other than 1944, when many men were abroad in the armed forces—when higher proportions of women than of men registered to vote and actually cast ballots. Perhaps more importantly, in recent years the gap between men and women has been greatest among the young, suggesting that in the future women might gain even more power at the polls.

Another difference between men and women has been emerging—in party preferences and attitudes on the issues. If men and women had similar feelings about important issues and preferred each of the major parties equally, the growing participation of women in elections would make little difference. However, women are more favorably disposed than men toward the Democratic party. For instance, a *New York Times*/CBS News Poll found that in the 1982 elections 56 per cent of women voted Democratic and only 40 per cent Republican; men voted Democratic over Republican by a smaller margin, 53 to 43 per cent.

Some observers have suggested that the difference between men and women in party preference simply reflects the relative unpopularity of President Reagan among women, rather than an aversion to the Republican party itself. If this is so, women's attitudes toward the Republican party might change when Reagan leaves office. However, others suggest that the difference in party preference is due to growing differences between men and women in political attitudes. Republicans have not traditionally supported feminist issues, and the "women's rights bloc" was a force in the 1980 election and seems to have cost the Republicans a few victories in 1982 as well.

Until the mid-1970s, gender was not considered a significant variable in voting studies, because men and women had similar party preferences and attitudes on the issues. The exception was the "war and peace" issue: Women have historically been more opposed than men to the use of force. This has been true since 1952, and it showed up in the earlier and stronger opposition of women to the Vietnam War. Opposition among women to Reagan has been attributed by some to their perception that he is likely to involve the United States in another war.

Women are also critical of Reagan's economic policies, which favor the well-to-do. As we saw in Chapter 10, women tend to rank lower than men in income and occupational prestige. Women seem to be more critical of Reagan for the extravagant life style of him and his advisors. In addition, women oppose Reagan because of his administration's weak environmental protection policies; polls find that women are more concerned than men with protecting the natural environment. Efforts to cut social security benefits have elicited additional opposition from women, who, because they live longer than men, on the average, are more likely than men to depend on this as a source of income.

The Republican party has made some efforts to attract more female voters. It has used more women in political advertisements, stressed President Reagan's arms control plan, and emphasized his appointment of women to office. Some Republicans feel that the party should develop a "compassion issue" that would attract more female voters, and others have pressed the party to support feminist issues. Whether these efforts—which critics see as cynical attempts to woo voters rather than as sincere efforts—can reduce the "gender gap" so that the sex variable again becomes irrelevant to electoral politics is something to watch for in future elections.

Sources: Based on Sandra Baxter and Marjorie Lansing, *Women and Politics: The Invisible Majority*. Ann Arbor, Mich.: University of Michigan Press, 1980; Adam Clymer, "Doubt on Reagan Plan Spurred Voters, Polls Show," *The New York Times*, November 8, 1982, p. B11; Betty Friedan, "Feminism's Next Step," *The New York Times Magazine*, July 5, 1981, pp. 13–15, 32–35; and "Rating on Reagan Lags at Midterm," *The New York Times*, January 16, 1983, p. 14.

There is, however, some evidence that when there is a clear choice on noneconomic issues, voting today might be less likely to follow traditional patterns of class or party affiliation than was true in the 1940s and 1950s. In the 1960s and 1970s, the political beliefs of voters became somewhat more ideologically structured, which means that voters increasingly made connections among issues such as war, welfare, and school integration (Pomper and Lederman, 1980: 70). As a result, in recent elections voting choices have been made more on the basis of attitudes toward issues that are significant to voters than on the basis of social characteristics, group memberships, or party affiliations (Nie, Verba, and Petrocik, 1976; Kourvetaris and Dobratz, 1982).

Running for Office

Relatively few citizens in a democracy ever run for elective office. To do so requires substantial financial resources, interest, and time to campaign and hold office if elected. For example, in 1982 the median campaign expenditures for those elected to the United States Senate totaled $1,746,230, and a median of $214,767 was spent by those winning seats in the House of Representatives (Clymer, 1983a).

Private contributions to campaigns are legal, but because strict limits have been placed on direct corporate contributions, political action committees have emerged in recent years. These PACS, which numbered 3,371 in 1982, are funded by private contributions that are then given to candidates favorably disposed to the interests of the contributors. As one U.S. Representative remarked, "You don't buy a United States Congressman with a contribution, of course, but you buy access and access is the name of the game" (Synar, cited in Clymer, 1983b: A20). In the 1979–1980 presidential race, PACs accounted for nearly two-thirds of all campaign funds (Weaver, 1982); and in 1982 contests for seats in the House of Representatives PACs contributed 35 per cent of the winners' campaign funds (Clymer, 1983b). During the 1979–1980 presidential race, Republicans spent nearly five times as much as the Democrats. This inequality between the parties was much greater than in the previous presidential election, when the Republicans outspent the Democrats by about two to one. Much of this money was spent on advertising in the mass media, especially television and the newspapers; in 1980, for example, $26.7 million was spent on political advertising in the newspapers (U.S. Bureau of the Census, 1982: 568). The spending differential between the parties in this campaign paid off handsomely for the Republicans, who won the Presidency easily, gained control of the Senate, made gains in the House of Representatives, and won many state and local contests as well (Weaver, 1982).

In the United States today, most office-holders are married white men who are older and wealthier than the average citizen. As Table 14.1 illustrates, almost all members of the United States Senate and House of Representatives are white males, although there was a tiny increase in females and nonwhites between 1971 and 1982. The table indicates that over this period, the proportion of senators and representatives who were single, widowed, or divorced rose, and as a group they became somewhat younger. In addition, at the federal, state, and local levels, between 1970 and 1981, there was an increase in the number of black and female office-holders, although many of these officials held positions in city or county government or on school boards rather than in the state or federal government (U.S. Bureau of the Census, 1982: 488–489).

TABLE 14.1
Selected Characteristics of Members of the United States Congress, 1971 and 1982

Characteristics	1971	1982
Percentage male	97.6	96.1
Percentage white	96.8	95.7
Percentage married	94.6	82.8
Percentage age 50 and over	62.3	47.3

Source: Based on U.S. Bureau of the Census, *Statistical Abstract of the United States, 1982–83.* Washington, D.C.: U.S. Government Printing Office, 1982, p. 485.

POLITICAL PARTIES

One important organization that is intermediary between government officials and the mass of unorganized citizens is the *political party*, a formal organization that mobilizes resources and voter support in order to win power. Usually these organizations are led by a small group that either co-opts power for itself or is appointed by party officials (Michels, 1915, 1962; Duverger, 1959). Parties develop policies, educate potential voters, transmit public opinion to officials, select candidates for office, and integrate different regions and social groups into one organization (Dowse and Hughes, 1972; Burnham, 1975). One critic suggests that American parties are largely restricted to the last two of these activities (Domhoff, 1978a).

In totalitarian states, elections are often mere endorsements of a single official party. Democracies have at least two, and often more, political parties. Today, the United States has one of the few two-party systems in the world; other democratic states have multiple parties. These multiple-party systems may represent the full range of political views in the society better than a two-party system, but multiple-party systems can have unstable governments because dividing votes among a large number of parties often means that no one party wins a majority. In order to rule, parties must form coalitions, and these coalitions can dissolve over specific issues, forcing new elections or new coalitions (Duverger, 1959; Lipset, 1963a).

Occasionally the American political system gives birth to a third political party with some strength, as it did in 1968 with George C. Wallace's American Independent party and again in 1980 with John B. Anderson's campaign as an independent candidate. However, the system is still best characterized as a two-party system because few third parties have mounted a serious challenge to the dominance of the Democrats and the Republicans in recent years. These two parties are organized more weakly at the national level than are political parties in many nations. They are important mainly at election time, although they seem to be of declining significance even then because of primaries and because of direct appeals to voters through the mass media, especially television. American parties are less ideological and have vaguer platforms than parties in most other political systems, partly because the two parties have aimed for the center of the political spectrum and designed their platforms to appeal to the largest possible number of voters.

Political parties seem less important to the American political system today than in the past. Party identification declined from 75 per cent in the period from 1952 to 1964 to 63 per cent in 1976 (Clymer, 1981). New voters who entered the electorate in the late 1970s and early 1980s were more likely than older voters to define themselves as independents, and voters did not show a tendency to change from independence to a partisan affiliation as they got older.

Political parties in the United States have declined because they have lost their earlier monopoly over resources, methods of recruiting candidates, and information about voter preferences. Today the party is only one of several groups and associations that participate in the electoral process; it has taken its place among professional associations, labor unions, political action committees, and other interest groups (Pomper, 1977). Recently, some political scientists have suggested that the emergence of stronger national party organizations with large staffs, large budgets, and the expertise to help candidates might reverse the long-term decline of political parties, but so far there is little evidence that this has happened (Pomper, 1980; Clymer, 1981).

INTEREST GROUPS

Citizens sometimes participate in the political process as members of *interest groups*—groups that attempt to influence decision making by elected officials and government bureaucrats in ways that are favorable to group members. Interest groups such as the AFL-CIO or the National Association of Manufacturers might seek changes in government policies that would bring economic gains to their members. Other interest groups work for measures that will support a particular moral standard or strengthen their position in society; examples include the temperance forces that pushed through Prohibition, groups that oppose or favor legalized abortion, and groups that oppose or favor equal rights for homosexuals. Interest groups are effective when they are able to mobilize resources such as money, time, and the involvement of their members. Business groups such as the U.S. Chamber of Commerce, which has a staff of 1,200 and an annual budget of $30 million, can translate wealth into power.

Organized interest groups use a tactic called *lobbying* to pressure lawmakers and agency officials. This includes letter-writing, petitioning, advertising, demonstrating in public, and raising campaign funds in order to influence officials who make and implement policies. Interest groups also take issues to the courts; for example, the National Association for the Advancement of Colored People (NAACP) has used this strategy effectively to improve the social and legal standing of black Americans.

Because American lawmakers vote as individuals rather than according to a strict party line, interest groups and public opinion can influence the actions of elected officials (Welsh, 1979). Some research indicates that most state legislators feel that they should vote according to their own best judgment, rather than strictly according to their constituents' views. Smaller numbers of legislators feel that they were elected to represent directly the views of the voters. Another group thinks that they should vote as their constituents wish whenever possible, but that they should use their own best judgment on many issues (Wahlke et al., 1962). When constituents have strong views on an issue, those views are likely to influence their representatives. When constituents are indifferent, however, lawmakers can respond to their own consciences or to pressures from other legislators to compromise on an issue. There is some evidence that "policy outcomes conform to public opinion on issues the public cares about" (Burstein, 1981: 308).

Members of interest groups are able to exercise more power as a group than they could as unorganized individuals. They can use this influence between elections, as well as at the polls. Interest groups help to define issues, educate the public, and force people to take sides. However, these groups have been criticized as undemocratic. This is because powerful interest groups can mobilize support and financial resources that can lead to the election of officials and to the development of policies that favor the narrow interests of some people over the best interests of the whole society.

One example is the powerful National Rifle Association (NRA), an organization of about two million people that spends millions of dollars each year to convince lawmakers to oppose passage of restrictive gun-control laws. The NRA uses professional lobbyists and encourages its members to flood lawmakers with letters expressing their opposition to gun control. Because many members of this organization are one-issue voters who will oppose a legislator simply because he or she supports tighter gun control, this interest group has been able to thwart the passage of significant gun-control measures at the state and federal levels, even though polls consistently show that a majority of the American public favors such legislation

Pictured here are the emblems of four interest groups, which line up on either side of the gun-control issue.

(Schumann and Presser, 1978; *The New York Times,* June 20, 1983, p. A16).

"Lobbying in the Streets"

Another form of political participation is organized protest through public demonstrations. This "lobbying in the streets" requires the mobilization of large numbers of people who are committed to common beliefs and goals. These people must elicit the sympathy of others, counteract efforts by defenders of existing policies to preserve the status quo, and organize for strategic protest (Gamson, 1975). Protests are often effective in generating free publicity in the news media, although a reduced interest by newspapers and television in repeated demonstrations can provide an incentive for more dramatic and possibly violent protests in order to attract the attention of the media and the public (Eisinger, 1974: 606). We examine these forms of collective action in more detail in Chapter 19.

Power in the United States

The central question in the sociological study of the political system is: "Who has power and how do they use it?" (Marger, 1981). Sociologists agree that in the United States power is not dispersed equally among all citizens; the "one man, one vote" principle spelled out by the Supreme Court does not describe the reality of everyday politics. Sociologists have proposed different explanations of the actual distribution of power in American society. Here we describe three models of power, following Martin Marger's (1981) typology, and examine research on the exercise of power at both the local and the national levels.

THREE MODELS OF POWER

The *pluralist model* of power in the American political system sees society as composed of multiple and competing groups. A second model suggests that any institution—the political system or the economic system, for instance—is controlled by a small group of leaders who are more skilled or more ambitious than other members of the organization; this is the *elite model*. Similar to the elite model in some ways is the *class model*, which treats one particular elite—the dominant class in the economic system—as a ruling class that is capable of exercising control over all sectors of society. Table 14.2 shows the major components of these three models of the power structure.

TABLE 14.2
Three Models of the Power Structure

	The pluralist model	The elite model	The class model
Major source of power	Various political resources, including wealth, authority, and votes	Control of key institutions, primarily the corporation and the executive branch of the federal government	Control of society's productive resources (wealth)
Key power group(s)	Elective political officials; interest groups and their leaders	Relatively cohesive power elite, made up of top corporate and government leaders	Ruling class (owners and controllers of the corporate system)
Role of masses	Indirectly control elites through competitive elections and interest-group pressures	Manipulated and exploited by the power elite	Manipulated and exploited by the ruling class
Function of state	Referee the arena of interest groups; create political consensus	Protect interests of dominant elites and their institutions	Protect capitalist class interests; perpetuate class system

Source: Adapted from *Elites and Masses: An Introduction to Political Sociology* by Martin N. Marger. © 1981 by Litton Educational Publishing, Inc. Reprinted by permission of Wadsworth Publishing Company, Belmont, California 94002.

The Pluralist Model

Functionalists have usually favored a pluralist model of power in the United States that emphasizes consensus on the "rules of the game" and the positive consequences of competition among groups with access to financial resources and popular support (Dahl, 1961; Rose, 1967; Wolfinger, 1974; Dahl and Lindblom, 1976; Dahl, 1982). Pluralists suggest that the masses exercise some power through their election of officials and through their participation in interest groups. These groups—including business associations, labor unions, and consumer organizations—are specialized by issues, relatively decentralized in their operations, and more or less free of direct control by the government (Wolfinger, 1974).

In the pluralist model, power is "fragmented and diffuse, deriving from many sources" (Marger, 1981: 36). There is no single and well-integrated elite in this model. Instead, there are multiple centers of power that each have their own elite, a set of leaders who are relatively autonomous of other elites in different organizations and institutions. These different elites commonly disagree with one another, and indeed there is often disagreement within the elite in any given organization.

In a pluralist system, there are multiple sources of authority (Dahl and Lindblom, 1976; Dahl, 1982). Sometimes a group can effectively prevent opposing groups from realizing their goals, even if the first group lacks the power to get its own policies implemented; for this reason, the competing groups in a pluralist system have been called "veto groups" (Riesman, 1950). Because no group has the resources to achieve its goals on every issue, alliances and compromises are necessary to form coalitions and make agreements to accomplish political objectives. One disadvantage of pluralist systems is that stalemates in the "politics of confrontation" among these multiple power centers can prevent the development of policies essential to the public interest unless each veto group can be satisfied in some way (Thurow, 1980; Dahl, 1982).

EVALUATING THE PLURALIST MODEL. Pluralists have been accused of failing to see the large discrepancy in the actual resources—especially the economic resources—that are available to different organized groups. As a result, the pluralist model of many groups competing with each other on a more or less equal basis might not describe the political process very accurately. In fact, many citizens belong to no organized interest group, and others who do belong cannot control the group's leaders or the policies they espouse.

The pluralist model has also been criticized for minimizing the importance of elite power and for failing to see the way that different elites interlock to form a single ruling class (Domhoff, 1978a, 1978b). Moreover, these critics allege, pluralists who study power in local communities usually overlook the impact of a national ruling class on defining what issues are considered, how those issues are dealt with, and what decisions are eventually reached (Domhoff, 1978b). Others claim that pluralists pay too much attention to political power and too little attention to the way that economic power held by large corporations affects the course of society (Marger, 1981).

One of the foremost pluralist theorists, the political scientist Robert A. Dahl (1961, 1982), has recently taken into account some of these criticisms of earlier formulations of the pluralist model. Dahl notes several flaws in democratic pluralism: Organized interest groups can reinforce social inequality, harm the public welfare by promoting their own narrow interests, and distort the public agenda by defining which issues are to be considered. At the national level, debate and compromise among competing interest groups have proved incapable of achieving a stable economy, slum clearance, and a good system of medical care (Dahl and Lindblom, 1976; Thurow, 1980; Dahl, 1982). Yet Dahl assumes that a pluralist system can minimize the power of the central government, create mutual restraints by organized interests on each other, and achieve the public good (Dahl, 1982).

The Elite Model

Vilfredo Pareto, Gaetano Mosca, and Robert Michels were among the first social theorists to propose that all organizations—including the state, political parties, and the economic system—are inevitably controlled by small groups of talented, expert, or ambitious leaders. Sometimes well-qualified members of the masses enter the elite, and occasionally a group emerges within the organization to challenge the elite that holds power. These theorists suggest, however, that at any given time power is controlled by a small group. Once it has attained power, this elite seeks to preserve its control and the advantages associated with it, and to

pass them on to its hand-picked successors. Michels calls this the "iron law of oligarchy" (see Chapter 7) and sees it as an undemocratic aspect of all organizations, even those political parties that are dedicated to democratic principles.

In contrast to the classical elite model of Pareto, Mosca, and Michels is contemporary "radical elitism" (Marger, 1981: 78–85). Radical elitism sees power relations as characterized by the manipulation and exploitation of the masses by a self-serving elite. For radical elitists, this situation is not inevitable, as it was for classical elitists who saw the masses as unable or unwilling to rule themselves. Radical elitists claim that members of the elite come from the upper class, though occasionally talented individuals of lower standing are co-opted into the elite. These individuals are selected and socialized in ways that lead them to support rather than challenge the dominance of the existing elite.

One important radical elite theorist, C. Wright Mills (1956), claims that a "power elite" of corporate executives, military officers, and political officials make all decisions of national significance—including decisions on war, trade, and economic policy. These leaders are not part of a conspiracy, nor do they constitute a highly integrated ruling class; instead, they cooperate in a loose coalition based on similarity of interests and common social background. They circulate freely between business and the government, and between the military and business. This "job interchange" gives them knowledge of how people operate in different spheres of power, and it personally acquaints them with the leaders in these different sectors. Most members of this power elite wield power outside the formal political system and are therefore not accountable to the voters.

In 1960, President Dwight D. Eisenhower told the American public in his farewell speech: "In the councils of government we must guard against the acquisition of unwarranted influence, whether sought or unsought, by the military-industrial complex. The potential for the disastrous rise of misplaced power exists and will persist" (cited in Melman, 1970: 10). Coming from a former general who became president, this warning was especially significant. The elite Eisenhower warned of is a group of interlocking military leaders and corporate executives who are concerned with maximizing the size of the nation's military budget and increasing private profits through the manufacture of armaments. During World War II, private industry that had been designed for the production of consumer goods was converted to the production of military equipment. After the war, many of these factories continued to manufacture armaments and to pursue federal contracts; often they hired former military officers to help them secure these contracts.

Industry and the military are two parts of Mills's power elite; the third part consists of elected officials and government bureaucrats. Below these three elite groups is a middle level of power that includes Congress and interest groups such as labor unions and professional associations. Organizations in this middle level more or less "rubber-stamp" decisions already made by the power elite, because, according to Mills, decisions at the middle level can only be made within the limits set by the power elite. Below the middle level are the masses, a relatively powerless and disorganized voting public manipulated by the power elite, often through the mass media.

EVALUATING THE ELITE MODEL. Elite theory explains the alienation of the masses from the government and helps us to understand why the political system is so slow to change. This model also helps us to see social reforms in a different light: Many of them are designed to keep the masses happy but leave the power structure intact. The existence of people who hold great power is indisputable, but critics suggest that powerful individuals do not necessarily constitute an elite—a "cohesive, self-sustaining, and self-serving" group (Marger, 1981: 81). Elite theory pays too little attention to the lack of coordination among people in elite positions; often they disagree bitterly among themselves about what is the best policy or what strategy should be used to influence decision making.

Elite theory also slights democratic trends in industrial societies, such as workers' control of factories in Sweden and efforts to return revenue to local communities. In addition, this model minimizes the power that the electorate does wield, and it neglects the close attention that political officials pay to public opinion polls. Pluralists have criticized elite theorists for making so sharp a distinction between the rulers and the masses, because this overlooks the contributions of intermediate organized groups to many kinds of decision making (Dahl, 1961; Rose, 1967).

The Class Model

The class model of power is closely related to the elite model, for both point to the rule of the few and the relative powerlessness of the masses. What distinguishes the two is that elite theorists claim that power is the result of control of *some* key institution, whereas class theorists argue that power results from position in the economic system. In societies such as the United States that are characterized by industrial capitalism, power is the product of the control of corporate wealth. The state is regarded as a tool that capitalists use to protect their interests and maintain their dominant social position (Miliband 1969, 1977; Syzmanski, 1978).

Karl Marx saw political power as part of the "superstructure" that is based on a society's system of economic production; in other words, the ruling class in any political system is the dominant class in the economic system. As Marx and Engels stated in *The Communist Manifesto* (1848, 1967: 82): "The executive of the modern State is but a committee for managing the common affairs of the whole bourgeoisie."

Today, class theorists still claim that the economic system is the basis of political power, but they acknowledge that there is often a complex relationship between the state and the economic system. The state establishes the conditions that make the accumulation of capital possible; this can cause large amounts of tax revenue to be spent on military equipment or even lead to military action to guarantee peace in nations that are important markets for corporations. Sometimes the state directly subsidizes industry, as it did in 1979, when the ailing Chrysler Corporation received a federally guaranteed loan. Such "welfare for the rich" binds the state and the economic system closely together.

EVALUATING THE CLASS MODEL. According to its critics, one flaw of the class model is the lack of attention it pays to noneconomic variables. Class is certainly an important dimension of politics, but so are religious beliefs, sexual preferences, and social prestige. Conflict over abortion, gay rights, and school prayer—issues hotly debated in the political arena in recent years—cannot easily be accounted for strictly in terms of class. Because the class model at times overstates the impact of the economic system on the political system, some Marxists have recently suggested that more attention be paid to the relative autonomy of the state from the economic system (Skocpol, 1979).

Another criticism of the class model is its implication—sometimes stated as an assumption—that a society can be built in which there is no ruling class. An industrial society probably requires a ruling class of some sort, and the prospect of the state's declining in size and influence as Engels suggested seems remote. Even in socialist states run by Communist parties we find support for Michels's iron law of oligarchy, both in the organization of the political party and in the bureaucratic apparatus of the state.

RESEARCH ON THE POWER STRUCTURE

Which of these three models best fits what we know about the American political system? Research on the power structure of local communities has proved somewhat easier than research on the national power structure, and so we examine it first. Then we turn to recent studies of what has been called a national "ruling class" and the way that it exercises power.

Power in the Local Community

Sociologists and political scientists have studied decision making in a variety of local communities (Clark, 1975). Two that have been researched intensively for many years are New Haven, Connecticut, and Atlanta, Georgia.

The systematic study of power relations in New Haven began in the 1950s, when Robert A. Dahl and a team of researchers examined the way that policies were made on local issues such as urban renewal (Dahl, 1961; Wolfinger, 1974; Polsby,

1980). Their work generally supported the pluralist model. Various competing groups—or more accurately, the leaders of various groups—tried to influence the making of political decisions, but no single group was able to dominate because many groups had the money, the expertise, and the popular support to argue their cases effectively. Business leaders were an influential group, but they did not control policy making.

A later study of decision making in New Haven arrived at quite different conclusions. Domhoff (1978a) challenged Dahl's pluralist theory, claiming on the basis of a variety of evidence that between 1940 and 1960—the period that Dahl also studied—there was a network of business executives, bankers, corporate lawyers, and Yale University trustees and administrators who did indeed form a ruling class. Moreover, argued Domhoff, this ruling class had close ties to a national ruling class. The ruling class in New Haven supported urban renewal and helped to implement it, contrary to Dahl's interpretation that they were reluctant to change the face of the city and were overruled by government officials favorable to such change. Members of the ruling class lived mostly in the suburbs, but they were greatly concerned with the health of the city, where corporate headquarters, universities, and cultural organizations were located.

The ruling class theory suggests that the leading business citizens in a community hold power over political decisions.

Another study that identified a cohesive business group capable of thwarting a variety of public organizations focused on five political campaigns on transportation issues in California. The business community was of one mind on the issues in each campaign, even though its position changed from one campaign to another. This business group was highly organized and able to raise large sums of money to influence the public's views on transportation policies (Whitt, 1980).

A classic study of community decision making in Atlanta by Floyd Hunter (1953) produced results that were consistent with the evidence for a business-led ruling class in New Haven and in California. Hunter found a small and cohesive group of corporate executives and bankers who transmitted their policy recommendations to elected officials, who in turn usually acceded to their demands. This ruling class operated independently of the voters and made decisions informally, often over lunch. They had common interests and similar social backgrounds, enjoyed high social standing, and interacted with each other on a regular basis.

Years later, Hunter (1980) returned to Atlanta and was still able to identify a ruling class. The previously all-white power structure had admitted a few black business leaders during the 1960s and 1970s. Some new groups were represented among the ruling class, including real-estate developers and insurance company executives. In spite of shifts of personnel in the ruling class, "the steeply pyramided structure" of community decision making remained intact (Hunter, 1980: 163). Indeed, the same businesses and associations generated leaders and the same families still provided members of the ruling class.

Power at the National Level

In recent years, the thrust of sociological research on the national power structure has pointed to the existence of a ruling class that is based on the control of economic resources. Pluralists, on the other hand, have provided less evidence that multiple interest groups can effectively compete with each other or veto the policies supported by dominant economic groups.

The pluralist position on the national power structure is presented by Arnold M. Rose (1967) in his response to C. Wright Mills's *The Power Elite*. Rose acknowledges that every organized activity in American society has a power structure. However, Rose asserts that there is less coordination among

different elites than Mills suggests, even though Mills actually sees less coordination among various elites than has been suggested by recent class theorists such as Domhoff. Rose claims that many pressure groups wield considerable power at the national level, and he describes the power structure of the United States as complex, diversified, and more or less democratic. He also claims that the political elite of elected leaders is ascendant over the economic elite rather than subordinate to it.

The class model of national power has received considerable support from the research of G. William Domhoff (1967, 1971, 1974, 1978a, 1978b, 1980) and others (G. Moore, 1979; Useem, 1978, 1979, 1980a, 1980b). Domhoff has meticulously listed people who hold influential positions; he shows that they have similar backgrounds and are often listed in the *Social Register*, frequently marry other members of the ruling class, sit together on the same boards of directors, and interact informally in resort areas and exclusive private clubs. Domhoff claims that there is an American ruling class that constitutes about 0.5 per cent of the population, but which holds about one-fourth of all privately controlled wealth in the nation. This class is the source of the leading executives and directors of the largest corporations and banks in the country. It also includes corporate lawyers who work in prestigious firms, public relations and advertising executives, stock brokers and management consultants, academicians (especially economists, political scientists, historians, and scientists), newspaper correspondents and editors, museum directors, and foundation executives (Domhoff, 1974).

Domhoff (1978b) claims that the ruling class translates its interests into actual policies through four processes. One process is lobbying in order to gain tax breaks, neutralize onerous government regulations, and secure other favors. A second method is the "policy-formation process" (Alpert and Markusen, 1980): Policy groups and think tanks such as the Council on Foreign Relations, the Committee for Economic Development, the Conference Board, the Business Roundtable, and the Trilateral Commission (see SEL 14.2) develop positions on key issues that are presented as objective analyses. The "expertise" of these groups influences public opinion and the course of debate on these issues. A third method of influencing policy, according to Domhoff, is to use campaign contributions and personal contact with political party officials to affect the choice of candidates for office. The fourth way that the ruling class carries out its wishes is by influencing schools, churches, voluntary associations, and other public institutions. The ruling class has ties to these organizations through membership on school boards, church governing boards, and the executive committees of voluntary associations. It also shapes the public's sense of what is important through "public interest" advertising in the mass media, business association awards to community leaders, and corporate contributions to charities.

SOCIOLOGY AND EVERYDAY LIFE 14.2
The Trilateral Commission

The Trilateral Commission is one of several groups that advise the executive branch and its agencies on a variety of policy matters that might affect business. Eighteen top officials of the Carter administration—including President Carter himself—had been members of the Trilateral Commission. Only two Reagan administration officials—one being Vice President Bush—have belonged to this group.

What is this elite organization, and how does it influence policy making by the federal government? The Commission was formed in 1973 by David Rockefeller, chairman of Chase Manhattan Bank, the third largest financial firm in the country. According to George S. Franklin, coordinator and administrative head of the Commission in 1981—and college roommate of Rockefeller at Harvard University in the 1930s—the Commission was formed to help the industrial democracies of North America, Western Europe, and Japan unify on political, economic, and social issues. Each of these three regions is a "semiautonomous" branch with its own chairperson, and overall the Commission has about three hundred business leaders, political officials, and academicians as members. Rockefeller is head of the North American branch and the source of about 10 per cent of the Commission's annual budget. Some of the largest and best-known American corporations—such as Coca-Cola, Exxon, and IBM—also make large contributions to the Commission.

What exactly does the Trilateral Commission do? Its task forces produce policy reports, and it publishes a periodical called *Trialogue*. On the surface, the Commission appears to be simply a "think tank" that collects and analyzes information on topics such as nuclear proliferation, detente, and international trade. Issues are thrashed out in secret plenary sessions held each year. Critics see this secrecy as evidence of a conspiracy, but Franklin says that a closed session is needed to promote the free sharing of ideas without the pressure of publicity. The results of the Commission's activities are made public in the form of policy papers at no charge. The Commission is open about its membership list and its sources of funds, but its efforts to translate its recommendations into actual policies through influence with political officials are less open to public scrutiny.

Critics of both the left and the right allege that the Trilateral Commission has an unhealthy influence on the political system of the United States and on the world system of nations. The John Birch Society, a right-wing organization, accuses the Commission of being an international Marxist conspiracy aimed at controlling American government. The charge of being Marxist is not credible, because the members of the Commission include many business leaders who would be regarded by most Marxists as exploitative capitalists rather than friends of workers. However, the Commission has supported internationalism over domestic sovereignty as a way to strengthen world capitalism; for instance, it has supported free trade, changes in the world's monetary system, and international economic integration.

Leftists have criticized the Commission as a conspiracy of powerful business leaders who want to control governmental policy making for their own financial gain. Although Commission members who take positions in government are required to resign from the Commission, they continue to have informal ties to members of the Commission and might be expected to act in ways that support the interests of those people. The left claims that the Commission's foreign policies are designed to achieve the narrow interests of capitalists and multinational corporations, and that these policies harm workers in modern capitalist societies and all people in the Third World nations that are just beginning to industrialize.

Sources: Based on Richard D. Carreno, "A Who's Who of World Clout," *The Boston Globe*, April 19, 1981, pp. A27, A29; and Alan Wolfe, *The Limits of Legitimacy: Political Contradictions of Contemporary Capitalism.* New York: Free Press, 1977, pp. 325–330.

Class theorists such as Domhoff have identified an upper class in American society and suggested some ways that this class dominates the political system. Further study of competition among various interest groups in the formulation of actual policies might find that this upper class does indeed achieve its objectives regularly, but before we can draw this conclusion sociologists must do more detailed studies of the way that a variety of actual political decisions are made.

Summary

Politics is the contest for the right to impose one's will on others. Officials in the political system control legitimate power, or authority; this authority is based on charisma, tradition, formal rules, or some combination of these sources. Rational–legal authority based on formal rules is usually the most important source of power in industrial societies.

In these modern societies, the state is a distinct institution that has a monopoly over the legitimate use of force. Functionalists see political power as necessary to the fulfillment of essential societal tasks such as maintaining internal order, stengthening national identity, dealing with other nations, and making policy. Conflict theorists, on the other hand, see the state as organized coercion. They regard the political system as a tool used by the dominant class in the economic system to foster its own interests through the exploitation of subordinate classes.

Totalitarianism and democracy are two different forms of the state, even though actual political systems often incorporate characteristics of each type. Totalitarian states are centralized, intolerant of dissent, and manipulative of many aspects of their citizens' lives. Fascism is totalitarianism with a one-party dictatorship headed by a charismatic leader; the state is nationalistic and retains private property while still controlling the economy. Another form of totalitarianism is communism, a one-party system that emphasizes public property. In totalitarian states, citizens are accountable to the government, whereas in democracies the government is accountable to the citizens through regular elections. Certain conditions are usually needed for democracy to develop: relative affluence, an educated middle class, tolerance for dissent, and a diversity of social groups.

Citizens learn a variety of attitudes and behavior through political socialization by parents, teachers, peers, and the mass media. The most extensive form of political participation in the United States today is voting, even though the proportion of Americans who vote is lower today than a few years ago and is lower than the proportions that go to the polls in Western European democracies. Americans are more likely to vote if they are older, more educated, and not subject to cross-pressures from different reference groups. In addition, groups higher in the stratification system are more likely to vote, except that women are now slightly more likely than men to vote. Because of the expense and the time involved, relatively few Americans ever run for political office; those who do hold office are for the most part white males who are older and wealthier than the average citizen.

Parties are less important in the American political system than they were in the recent past. Television, public opinion polls, political action committees, and organized interest groups have all taken over some of the functions that parties have traditionally served: candidate selection, voter education, transmission of voter opinion to officials, policy formation, and the integration of diverse groups into one organization. The American political system is essentially a two-party system; this provides for a more stable government than often exists in multiple-party systems, but it may offer voters little real choice because the two parties design their platforms to appeal to the mass of voters in the middle of the political spectrum. An important organization in the American political system is the interest group; well-financed interest groups and those whose members are willing to vote for or against candidates because of their position on a single issue are especially influential.

We examined three models of the power structure of the United States. The pluralist model proposes a competition among a variety of organized groups and their leaders. No one group is all-powerful, and the relative importance of groups varies with the issue under consideration and with the group's resources and support. Early studies of decision making in New Haven supported the pluralist model. The elite model proposes that all organizations give rise to a small group of talented or ambitious leaders.

This model proposes a variety of elites—for example, business executives, military officers, and government officials—that have common interests but do not form a tightly integrated ruling class. Somewhat similar to the elite model is the class model, which emphasizes the importance of one particular elite—the dominant class in the economic system. Class theorists have identified politically influential individuals in studies of New Haven and Atlanta, and they have listed a ruling class for the nation as a whole. These theorists argue that this class dominates the political system through four processes: special interests, policy formation, candidate selection, and ideology. However, pluralists claim that these theorists have not yet shown how potentially powerful people control the making of actual political decisions. Combining a study of members of the upper class with a study of how real decisions are made might make it possible to integrate the pluralist, elite, and class models into a single theory of the power structure.

Important Terms

CHARISMATIC AUTHORITY (324)
CLASS MODEL (337)
COMMUNISM (328), (330)
DEMOCRACY (330)
ELITE MODEL (337)
FASCISM (329)
GOVERNMENT (323)
INTEREST GROUP (336)
LEGITIMACY (323)
LOBBYING (336)

PLURALIST MODEL (337)
POLITICAL PARTY (335)
POLITICAL SOCIALIZATION (330)
POLITICAL SYSTEM (323)
RATIONAL—LEGAL AUTHORITY (325)
SOCIALISM (328)
STATE (323)
TOTALITARIANISM (328)
TRADITIONAL AUTHORITY (324)

Suggested Readings

Sandra Baxter and Marjorie Lansing. *Women and Politics: The Invisible Majority*. Ann Arbor, Mich.: University of Michigan Press, 1980. A careful examination of changes in political participation by women since they won the vote; special attention is paid to the black woman as a voter.

Robert A. Dahl. *Dilemmas of Pluralist Democracy: Autonomy vs. Control*. New Haven, Conn.: Yale University Press, 1982. A reconsideration of the author's earlier work; the emphasis here is on the problems of pluralism and reforms that might improve the working of the political system.

G. William Domhoff. *The Powers That Be: Processes of Ruling-Class Domination in America*. New York: Random House, 1978. An examination of the methods by which the upper class controls the process of political decision making.

Martin N. Marger. *Elites and Masses: An Introduction to Political Sociology*. New York: Van Nostrand, 1981. An outstanding textbook that carefully examines the pluralist, elite, and class models of the power structure and reviews research on each model.

Ralph Miliband. *Marxism and Politics*. New York: Oxford University Press, 1977. A thorough treatment of Marx's theory of the state and some of the important issues raised by the class model of the power structure.

Anthony M. Orum. *Introduction to Political Sociology: The Social Anatomy of the Body Politic*, 2nd ed. Englewood Cliffs, N.J.: Prentice-Hall, 1983. A comprehensive textbook that deals with theories of the political system, models of the power structure, political participation, and political change.

William A. Welsh. *Leaders and Elites*. New York: Holt, Rinehart and Winston, 1979. An examination of elite behavior in cross-cultural perspective that also looks at methodological problems in the study of political leadership.

Raymond E. Wolfinger and Steven J. Rosenstone. *Who Votes?* New Haven, Conn.: Yale University Press, 1980. A well-documented study of who votes in the American political system.

THE LEGAL SYSTEM

A visitor to the United States who tried to learn about the legal system from television and the movies would leave with a distorted picture of how the police, the courts, and the prisons operate. The visitor would conclude that the police spend most of their time "fighting crime"—investigating serious violations of the law, "shooting it out" with offenders, and, when they inevitably solve the crimes, arresting the suspects. From the media's portrayal of the legal system, our visitor would assume that the police regularly coerce confessions, carry out searches without warrants, and refuse to provide lawyers for the suspects they take into custody (Arons and Katsh, 1979). Television and the movies would also suggest that criminal lawyers typically help their clients go free by figuring out who really committed the crime of which their client has been falsely accused; for example, Perry Mason often got someone else to make a last-minute confession in court. The mass media also imply that convictions are frequently obtained by fingerprints and other scientific evidence, even though this is relatively uncommon in real criminal cases (Siegel, 1980). Because the mass media usually show a culprit being brought to justice, it would also be easy to conclude that the legal system efficiently punishes the guilty.

In fact, our visitor would have a mistaken view on several counts. The police spend relatively little time dealing with serious crime, and they solve only one-fifth of the offenses reported to them. Most defendants are actually guilty, and most plead guilty without a jury trial; usually they are induced to plead guilty in return for a lighter sentence than they might receive if they insisted on a jury trial. Lawyers rarely act as Perry Mason and save their clients in court, and evidence such as fingerprints is rarely decisive in securing a conviction. The American legal system is shrouded in myth; in this chapter, we examine the organization of that system.

Law and Society

More than 150 years ago, one visitor to the United States, a Frenchman named Alexis de Tocqueville (vol. 1, 1831, 1945: 290), concluded from careful first-hand observation of the legal system that "scarcely any political question arises in the United States that is not resolved, sooner or later, into a judicial question." This statement is probably even truer today than it was then. Issues as diverse as the quality of the environment, birth and death, parent–child relations, and school prayer are treated by the legal system. In fact, so many social issues have become legal issues that one eminent lawyer has spoken of "legal pollution" (Ehrlich, 1976).

The central component of the legal system is the law, a set of norms that have been formalized by the political system and that define an obligation to behave in certain ways. Unlike informal norms, laws are enforced according to well-defined procedures and can involve the loss of liberty or property for those who are found guilty of violating them. In contrast, norms that are nonlegal are enforced by informal means such as social pressure or banishment from a group.

The laws with the most legitimacy correspond closely to informal norms. Efforts to enact and enforce laws that conflict with the expectations of people often fail. Thus, the effort to eliminate the sale and consumption of alcoholic beverages during Prohibition failed because people wanted to drink and found illegal sources of alcoholic beverages. The law was widely violated; the government's enforcement of it was unsuccessful, costly,

Prohibition laws were difficult to enforce because they did not correspond closely to informal norms. Pictured here are some federal agents engaged in "wine dumping."

and caused great public resentment. This law also provided organized crime with a highly profitable activity (bootlegging) that led to the consolidation and growth of criminal gangs that still flourish today (Gusfield, 1963).

When a country has been colonized by foreign rulers, there is a tendency for the law to lack legitimacy. The colonial government has usually imposed its laws on indigenous groups, each of which already had laws of its own before being conquered. The informal norms and laws of the indigenous groups have typically conflicted with the imposed laws of the colonial regime. For example, some tribal norms support killing people, witches, for instance, whose supernatural powers are considered threatening. However, the laws of the colonial government have regarded this behavior as simple murder that should be punished as a crime, rather than as behavior to be excused in light of tribal norms (Lewin, 1947; Seidman, 1965).

FUNCTIONALISM AND THE LAW

Functionalists have characteristically interpreted the law as reflecting societal consensus (Evan, 1980: 60–90). This view—which is based on the assumptions of the pluralist model of the power structure—treats the law as the product of compromises among competing groups who eventually arrive at a consensus on each issue. For functionalists, the legal system acquires legitimacy by incorporating the values and norms that are shared by members of the society.

Functionalists point to the many positive consequences of the law for the social system (Friedman, 1977). It helps to maintain social order and resolve disputes among groups. Laws distinguish acceptable behavior from behavior that is prohibited and will be punished. The law vests authority in people who occupy certain positions, thereby defining the rights and the obligations of officials and citizens.

When parties to a dispute resort to the law and formalize their differences, hostilities can fade. The legal system also educates people about the norms of their culture; through enactment and enforcement of the law, social norms are clarified and made public. The law defines societal goals and establishes policies to achieve those goals. Welfare legislation, for instance, aims to relieve poverty by providing benefits to those who are eligible. Still another function of the legal system is to store information; events such as births, marriages, real-estate transactions, and deaths are recorded in legal documents.

CONFLICT THEORY AND THE LAW

Marx regarded the law as part of society's super-structure; in other words, the legal system was an outgrowth of the economic system. Marx claimed that in capitalist systems the bourgeoisie controlled the enactment and the enforcement of the law to maintain the economic system and the advantages it gained from that system (Marx and Engels, 1848, 1967; Kelsen, 1955; Beirne and Quinney, 1982). However, recent examinations of a variety of laws—including Prohibition, the development of juvenile courts, narcotics legislation, and laws concerning sexual psychopathology—have concluded that although business groups often seek to influence legislation, they do not always predominate over other interest groups (Berk, Brackman, and Lesser, 1977; Hagan, 1980).

Modern conflict theorists do not restrict their views to such a narrow economic determinism. Rather, they see the legal system as an arena in which various groups compete with each other (Gusfield, 1963; Quinney, 1979; Chambliss and Seidman, 1982). Prohibition, abortion, gay rights, and school prayer are just a few of the many issues that have been fought over by interest groups that are not defined primarily by their relationship to the economic system. Modern conflict theorists do share with more traditional Marxists the view that the law is the product of one group's victory over other groups in a contest to define what behavior is acceptable. Crime is behavior that is punished because it threatens the dominant group in a society; for instance, theft threatens property-owners, and the legalization of homosexuality would threaten many heterosexuals. Conflict theorists thus see the law as a tool by which one group dominates others; unlike the functionalists, they do not believe that the law reflects societal consensus.

RECONCILING CONFLICT THEORY AND FUNCTIONALISM

Daniel Glaser (1978) has suggested that both the conflict perspective and functionalism might accurately describe significant aspects of the legal system. He proposes that many laws are initially the product of one group's victory over others in a contest to define the law. However, laws that result from conflict may in the long run achieve wide-spread support and reflect a societal consensus. For example, the law against theft was originally a product of the growth of trade and the narrow economic interests of merchants (Hall, 1952), but today all members of society, even most thieves, agree that the theft of property should be punished. Even controversial laws such as the law establishing social security in the United States often gain widespread support with time.

Origins and Consequences of the Law

Americans usually stop for red lights, and most of them pay their income taxes by April 15. However, many Americans do violate the law; millions use illegal drugs, and each year hundreds of thousands steal property and assault other people. Why do some laws seem more effective than others in preventing behavior? Before answering this question, we must ask a more basic one: Why do societies have the laws that they do? To address this question, sociologists have looked at the social sources of the law.

SOCIAL ORIGINS OF THE LAW

Many social conditions affect the content of a society's laws and the form of its legal system. Advances in technology produce changes that sometimes require new laws or modifications of old laws (See SEL 15.1). For instance, industrialization led to pollution of the air and the water, and this in turn has produced laws designed to clean up the environment; also, the invention of the automobile led to laws to regulate drivers, traffic patterns, and car safety.

One example of how a variety of social conditions affect the law is the emergence of workers' compensation boards—state administrative agencies that use employers' contributions to pay workers for injuries that they suffer on the job.

In the first half of the nineteenth century, workers' injuries were dealt with in civil courts according to the "fellow-servant rule," a law that allowed workers who were injured on the job to collect damages (hospital expenses and lost wages, for example) from negligent co-workers. Workers could collect money from an employer only if they could show that the employer's misconduct had directly caused the injury. Because this was difficult to demonstrate, workers were rarely paid much for their losses; the employers held the wealth but could not be shown to be the direct cause of most injuries, and negligent co-workers usually were not wealthy enough to be worth suing.

Several changes altered this system. The courts gradually made exceptions to the fellow-servant rule, requiring employers to pay damages in certain circumstances. The possibility of winning a case in court prompted more workers to sue their employers. The courts became overburdened with cases, and judges sought an alternative to the fellow-servant rule. Court actions also increased because the number of industrial accidents rose dramatically between 1875 and 1900 as a result of the rapid industrialization of the American economy, the greater complexity of machinery, and the expanded size of the work force. Another change that caused more and more cases to be brought to court was the development of the contingent fee system by which attorneys took cases to court in return for a percentage (usually 30 to 40 per cent) of the monetary award to the injured worker. Because the worker did not have to pay a fee if the case was lost, there was little expense in suing an employer. Increased litigation was costly to employers, however, for they had to pay their own lawyers and make an increasing number of expensive settlements.

Another force behind the change in the law of industrial accidents was the growing militancy of organized labor. Along with better pay and shorter hours, workers also demanded safer working conditions and the assurance of compensation for on-the-job injuries.

In the early twentieth century, in response to all these changes and to reports by investigative commissons that documented the extent and the seriousness of injuries at work, the states slowly formed workers' compensation boards modeled on those used in some European countries. Wisconsin's board, established in 1911, was the first to be upheld by the courts; Mississippi was the last state to create a board in 1948. This change from the fellow-servant rule to the workers' compensation board was a shift from litigation in civil court to routine administration by a government agency.

Sources: Based on Lawrence M. Friedman and Jack Ladinsky, "Social Change and the Law of Industrial Accidents," *Columbia Law Review* 67 (January 1967): 50–82; and William Chambliss and Robert Seidman, *Law, Order, & Power*, 2nd ed. Reading, Mass.: Addison-Wesley, 1982, pp. 159–163.

One social change that has affected the legal system is population growth. The German sociologist Georg Simmel (1950) suggests that in small societies a common set of standards can be enforced by informal group pressure, but that larger societies need formal legal procedures because direct social pressure is less likely to create conformity. A study of two Israeli settlements found that the degree of face-to-face interaction is indeed important in determining the kind of legal system that a community will have. In one farming collective in which people worked, ate, and lived together as a unit, there was no legal system to enforce norms because this could be accomplished through informal pressure. However, in another farming community in which each family worked, ate, and lived apart from other families, a formal legal system was needed to enforce the rules in the absence of face-to-face interaction (Schwartz, 1954; Shapiro, 1976; Schwartz, 1976). This study suggests that the method of norm enforcement might be determined more by the structure of interpersonal relations in a community than by the size of the community, because both Israeli settlements were about the same size.

The structure and size of a society both influence the form of its legal system. Within that society, several forces affect the content of specific laws and how those laws are enforced. Those influences include public opinion, interest groups, and expert evidence.

Public Opinion

Democratic political systems are based on the principle that the consent of the governed is the primary source of authority. Consequently, lawmakers try to assess public opinion before passing new laws; this both enhances the legitimacy of the law and makes it easier to enforce. Legislators sometimes assess public opinion by the letters they receive from their constituents, even though the people who write these letters are apt to be more concerned about an issue, more literate, and less alienated than the general public. Opinion polls give a better representation of the views of the entire public.

Surveys have been used to measure people's attitudes toward specific laws. One study that compared laws defining parental authority over children with people's attitudes toward those laws found that there was substantial disagreement between public opinion and the law (Cohen, Robson, and Bates, 1958). The difficulty with such research is that people might give quick responses to certain questions—such as whether parents should be allowed to disinherit children who are minors—without considering the complex consequences of a change in the law or how a new law might be enforced. Because it is easy to get people to express opinions about the law ("there oughta be a law") without their fully understanding the legal system, lawmakers often find that public opinion polls are of limited usefulness in helping them write the laws. For instance, knowing that the public disapproves of parents' right to determine their children's religious affiliation does not tell lawmakers how to write and enforce a law giving children the right to choose their own religion.

Interest Groups

In Chapter 14 we saw how interest groups try to control political power. By hiring attorneys or former government officials to present their views to legislative committees or regulatory commissions, interest groups also try to influence the enactment and the enforcement of laws. Because these groups want to achieve specific goals that improve or maintain their advantages, they sometimes try to mold public opinion so that people will either support their position or at least will not oppose their efforts to influence the legal system. For instance, one consequence of rising oil prices during the 1970s and early 1980s was the oil companies' use of television advertisements aimed at convincing the public that oil companies were deeply concerned with the discovery of new petroleum reserves and were not directly responsible for rising gasoline prices or environmental pollution. These advertisements were meant to "soften up" the public and undermine pressures for government regulation of the oil industry.

LICENSING A PROFESSION. Occupational groups sometimes use the law to further their interests by getting the government to license them as a profession. Usually the licensing of a professional group comes at the suggestion of the group itself rather than as a result of public pressure, although the group usually claims that licensing and regulation are needed to protect the public from unqualified practitioners. Before 1900, only two occupations were regularly licensed by the states: physicians and attorneys. Today there are probably more than one hundred such groups.

One reason for the rise is the increased specialization of occupations and the resulting change in the knowledge and the training needed to do a job. However, other factors are also important. Licensing gives an occupation more prestige and enhances the standing of people in that occupation in the eyes of the public. This in turn can lead to increased business or be used to justify higher fees. Licensing limits the number of people who can enter a certain field. Restricted entry reduces competition and is another way to maintain or increase the salaries of those already in the "profession" (Gellhorn, 1977).

REGULATORY AGENCIES. One important way that organized interest groups influence the enforcement of the law is through their contact with federal regulatory agencies. Many of these agencies were originally created to serve the public interest, but some were created because of pressure by specific interest groups who hoped to improve their economic position by winning the support and protection of a federal agency. One example is the Civil Aeronautics Board, which was formed in

1938 as a result of pressure by the airline industry. For years, this agency—with the support of the airline industry—restricted competition from new airlines and helped to keep fares higher than they would have been with open competition. Many other regulatory commissions are controlled by those they are intended to control. Reports by Ralph Nader's research group that were critical of various regulatory agencies were attacked by the industries that were being "regulated," rather than by the agencies themselves. The industries did not like "their" regulatory agencies being criticized because those agencies had served them so well.

Interest groups influence regulatory commissions in many ways (Fellmeth, 1970). One way is through social contacts. Another way is by consulting with the agency's formal advisory committees; these committees are ostensibly open to discussion with any interested party, but in fact they usually consult with members of the industry that is being regulated rather than with the general public.

The enforcement of regulations is also influenced through "job interchange" between the agencies and industry. Sometimes lawyers take jobs with these agencies, only to leave them after a few years for well-paying jobs in the industry that they were regulating. Their personal contacts and expertise make them attractive to firms that wish to influence governmental regulation. One effect of this job interchange is that lawyers working for the agency might try not to antagonize those who are being regulated, lest they sacrifice a possible job offer in that industry. Job interchange also occurs at the highest levels of these agencies, with commissioners selected from and later returning to jobs in the same industry they are to regulate. For example, William Ruckelshaus went from being head of the Environmental Protection Agency in the Nixon administration to working for the polyvinyl chloride industry (which manufactures a toxic chemical that causes liver cancer), and then back to head the EPA in 1983 in the Reagan administration.

Expert Evidence

Besides public opinion and interest groups, a third influence on the enactment and the enforcement of the law is evidence provided by experts who claim scientific validity for their data or opinions. There is considerable debate over exactly who is an expert; psychiatrists, for instance, feel that only they are competent to give testimony about the psychological condition of a criminal defendant, but social workers and psychologists argue that they too have the skills to make such assessments. Even when there is general agreement about who are experts, judges and lawyers are often reluctant to cede

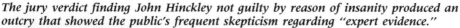

The jury verdict finding John Hinckley not guilty by reason of insanity produced an outcry that showed the public's frequent skepticism regarding "expert evidence."

power to them. Moreover, the public is sometimes skeptical of experts. For instance, in 1982 John Hinckley was tried for attempting to assassinate President Reagan. The jury verdict that found him not guilty by reason of insanity produced an outcry from the general public and from lawmakers to curtail sharply the use of the insanity defense and psychiatric testimony, even though relatively few criminal trials employ either.

On several occasions in recent years the legal system has turned to sociologists, psychologists, and economists for scientific evidence. In the Supreme Court's 1954 school desegregation decision, research was cited to show the negative effects of segregation on children. The 1966 Coleman Report influenced lawmakers and judges to try to reduce school desegregation through busing. In the 1970s, the courts used statistical evidence to assess the impact on the quality of education of the long-standing practice of financing public schools with property taxes. Social science research has been introduced in other cases as well, including evidence on racial discrimination in the administration of the death penalty and studies of the impact on jury decisions of having juries of fewer than twelve members (Collins, 1978; Tanke and Tanke, 1979). In SEL 15.2 (see page 361) we see how sociological research has been used in the jury selection process.

THE EFFECTS OF THE LAW ON BEHAVIOR

The law is intended to discourage behavior (such as murder) or to encourage behavior (such as paying taxes). Sometimes, however, the law has unintended effects. As we have seen, Prohibition failed to stop the consumption of alcoholic beverages, even though it did reduce consumption somewhat. One of its unintended effects was to provide great profits for criminal gangs; another was the violent deaths of federal agents, bootleggers, and innocent bystanders (Gusfield, 1963).

One general unintended effect of the law is the *crime tariff* (Packer, 1968). This means that if a good or a service is made illegal and some people continue to supply it to those who demand it, the price of that good or service will rise to cover the increased costs and risks to those who supply it illegally. For example, the illegality of heroin in the United States makes it much more expensive than it is in Great Britain, where heroin is supplied to registered addicts at a low cost.

Another unintended effect of the law is that harsh penalties can backfire if judges or juries refuse to administer them to people who are actually guilty. In early nineteenth-century Great Britain there were more than two hundred crimes for which people could be executed, but juries often acquitted obviously guilty people rather than send them to the gallows for stealing a loaf of bread (Kalven and Zeisel, 1966). Lawmakers often assume that stiffer penalties will deter more people from certain kinds of behavior, but research shows that judges and juries sometimes refuse to impose harsh penalties when they seem unjust (Campbell and Ross, 1968; Joint Committee on New York Drug Law Evaluation, 1978).

The law often has a didactic or educative effect. It both reflects and reinforces the society's values, and it is one aspect of the culture that people learn through socialization. Lawmakers might be reluctant to repeal a law lest this convey to people that behavior that was once illegal has become acceptable; for example, the widespread use of marijuana has not yet led to its legalization, partly because legislators fear that such an action would encourage nonusers to smoke marijuana.

The law has its greatest effect on socialization when it is supported by values and norms that people learn from their parents, teachers, peers, and the mass media. However, the law can induce conformity even when it conflicts with group norms: The threat of federal sanctions prompted the desegregation of schools even in communities where informal norms did not support it. Often the law is less effective in changing attitudes than in changing actual behavior, but attitudes frequently change after people have been required to change their behavior.

The Police

All industrial societies have a police force. The *police* are a formal organization designed to preserve order and to provide public service. Clear evidence of the order-preserving function of the police is the fact that in 1970—at the end of a decade of ghetto riots and antiwar protests—those cities with the most economic inequality and the largest black populations also had the largest police forces (Jacobs, 1979). This fact is consistent with the conflict perspective's argument that the police are used to control the poor and minority groups and to strengthen the position of the propertied classes and the dominant racial group.

Modern police organizations are bureaucracies in which authority has a rational–legal basis (see Chapter 14). Rules and procedures are carefully spelled out. Police officers are authorized to enforce the law, but in reality they exercise considerable discretion in deciding whom to arrest. If the police actually arrested everyone who violated a law, the courts and the prisons would be overburdened to the breaking point. As a result, the police must decide which laws to enforce rigorously and which violations to overlook. Rules and procedures are passed from those at the top of the police department down to others in the organization, but the actual implementation of the law is determined by the way that individual officers on the street exercise judgment. Because these officers operate as individuals or in teams of two and do not have their daily contacts with the public directly monitored by those of higher rank, there are few formal checks on their behavior.

Police officers develop a "working personality" that is a product of the dangers they face in their daily work and the authority they have (Skolnick, 1975). They are suspicious of "symbolic assailants," people whose clothing, hair style, language, or gestures signify potential danger. The police are attentive to street-life; their suspiciousness and their authority to investigate whatever makes them suspicious can create public hostility and isolate them from the community. One consequence of the danger faced by the police is solidarity among officers; this is illustrated by their rapid response to an officer's call for assistance.

THE POLICE AND THE COMMUNITY

In societies without a police force, the members of the community often take responsibility for apprehending and even punishing offenders. When the police develop as a formal organization, people turn over much of this responsibility for law enforcement to them. Sometimes the creation of a police force leads people to withdraw altogether from the law-enforcement process. They fail to report crimes, with the justification that the police are solely responsible for dealing with violations of the law (Conklin, 1975).

Hostility between the police and the community is common. In black ghettos a predominantly white police force is often regarded as an invading army that oppresses disadvantaged minorities in order to protect those who control wealth and power. In these communities, the police sometimes receive little cooperation from citizens; crimes might not be reported and offenders might be protected. This lack of cooperation causes crime in the community to increase, and the police are then blamed for the high crime rate. Community hostility toward the police is often returned in kind by the police, who may be reluctant to answer calls for help and may respond to perceived challenges to their authority with brutality or discourtesy. As a result of these problems, many police departments have created police–community relations programs to ease this mutual hostility (Radelet, 1973; Cohn and Viano, 1976).

Hostility toward the police sometimes derives from their "proactive" stance toward crime, that is, a policy of actively patrolling the streets and aggressively seeking information about violations of the law. Because much social activity takes place on the streets of urban communities, particularly in warm weather, the police are often seen as invaders of privacy. This problem is less common in wealthier suburban communities, where the police are more likely to take a "reactive" stance toward crime; in other words, they wait until someone calls them to the scene of a crime. Also, social activity in the suburbs is more likely to occur in the home than on the streets, and the police lack access to private homes. For these and other reasons, such as the greater respect the police show to people of higher social standing, the police are viewed with less hostility in the suburbs than they are in urban communities (Stinchcombe, 1963; J. Wilson, 1963, 1975; Reiss and Bordua, 1967; Reiss, 1971).

The duties assigned to the police guarantee that many of their contacts with the public will generate hostility. No one appreciates getting a parking ticket or being cited for speeding. The police are called to the scene of many "domestic disputes," which they often have difficulty settling without angering one or both of the contentious parties. Arresting the offending spouse might elicit anger, but so can the failure to make an arrest. The police try to use their best judgment in these circumstances, but their actions and even their presence in the home often cause anxiety, embarrassment, and hostility (Bard, 1970; Berk and Loseke, 1980–1981).

Table 15.1 shows the results of a study of police behavior. Most of the calls received by the police dealt with matters other than law enforcement and the apprehension of criminal suspects. In fact, the police only solve one-fifth of all the serious crimes they learn about. They have a relatively easy time solving crimes such as murder and rape because

TABLE 15.1
Citizen Complaints Received by Radio Patrol Vehicles, Syracuse,
New York, Police Department, June 3–9, 1966

Type of call	Percentage of calls
Information gathering (book and check; get a report)	22.1
Service (accidents, illnesses, ambulance calls; animals; assist a person; drunk person; escort vehicle; fire, power line, or tree down; lost or found person or property; property damage)	37.5
Order maintenance (gang disturbance; family trouble; assault, fight; investigation; neighbor trouble)	30.1
Law enforcement (burglary in progress; check a car; open door, window; prowler; make an arrest)	10.3
Total number of calls received	312

Source: James Q. Wilson, *Varieties of Police Behavior: The Management of Law and Order in Eight Communities.* Cambridge, Mass.: Harvard University Press, 1968, p. 18. Reprinted by permission.

the victims are often closely associated with the offenders. Crimes against property such as burglary and theft are not solved as easily because victims are less likely to be able to identify the offender and because there is rarely any evidence such as fingerprints to point to the culprit.

ABUSES OF AUTHORITY

The police are a subculture with a distinctive set of values and norms that differ in important ways from those of the larger society (Skolnick, 1975). During their training as new recruits, the police learn to be suspicious, to act so as to maintain public respect for the police, and to protect other officers from danger. Under some circumstances, these lessons lead to the abuse of authority.

Sometimes the police abuse their authority by engaging in brutality, harassing suspects, or even planting evidence and then making an arrest. Some police officers take bribes in return for not making an arrest; this tends most to occur when the crime has no complaining victim and the police do proactive work, as in prostitution and drug dealing (*Knapp Commission Report on Police Corruption*, 1973; Sherman, 1974).

Another police abuse of authority involves racial prejudice. As we saw in Chapter 9, prejudice is a negative attitude toward a group or category of people, and discrimination is behavior that treats those people differently. Although there is some

evidence that the police are prejudiced toward blacks, it is less clear that they actually discriminate against blacks (Reiss, 1971). A study of police shootings of civilians in Chicago found that a white suspect in a serious crime actually had a greater chance of being shot than a black or a Hispanic suspect in a serious crime (Geller and Karales, 1981). However, a study of police shootings in Memphis, Tennessee, found that black suspects were more likely to be shot than were white suspects (Fyfe, 1982). The use of police violence might well vary with the characteristics of a community's population, the exposure of different groups to police action because of their involvement in crime, and the official policy of the local police department regarding the use of force.

Lawyers

Another important part of the American legal system is the *lawyer,* a trained specialist in legal rules and procedures. The United States probably has more lawyers per capita than any other nation, and its legislatures have more lawyers than any other law-making bodies in the world. In 1980, there were about 240 attorneys for every 100,000 Americans, compared to a ratio of about 9 lawyers per 100,000 people in Japan (Lohr, 1982b).

Lawyers are employed by the government, sit in state and federal legislatures, and work in private

Lawyers engage in a variety of activities. Here a lawyer advises his client at a district courthouse.

industry as in-house counsel to advise corporate executives. However, most attorneys work for themselves or for law firms, which can be big enough to have the characteristics of a bureaucracy. These lawyers advise their clients about how to use the legal system to their best advantage. They handle personal injury suits, do tax work, carry out real-estate transactions, and represent clients in divorce actions and custody cases. Attorneys who work for large firms often specialize in one kind of law, most commonly business law or probate (wills and estates). Those who work alone or with one or two partners are more likely to take whatever cases they can find.

THE TRAINING OF LAWYERS

Admission to American law schools has become based increasingly on standards that are nonpersonal and that anyone can theoretically meet; in the past admission was more often influenced by factors such as social class, ethnicity, and personal relationships. Now admission is based largely on an applicant's grades as an undergraduate and on performance on the Law School Admission Test (LSAT). Letters of recommendation, extracurricular activities, and personal interviews count to some extent, but admission is determined mostly by grades and test scores.

The primary method of teaching in most law schools is the *case method,* an intensive analysis of decisions that have been written by judges. Students carefully dissect these cases to learn about legal reasoning and the principles of the law. In class, law students are called on to recite the relevant facts in a case and are then questioned by their professors about the fine points of the decision. This approach, which Harvard Law School pioneered in 1870, is designed to teach students how to ''think like a lawyer,'' which is the major change that law students say that they undergo in law school (Erlanger and Klegon, 1978). This method of teaching pays little attention to any possible contributions by the social sciences to an understanding of the issues with which the law deals. The case method has also been criticized for its conservative style of examining only past decisions rather than considering innovative solutions to problems.

LAWYERS' INCOMES

As a group, American lawyers have an average income that ranks only below that of physicians. However, the salaries of attorneys vary over a wide range. Senior partners in large law firms can earn more than $250,000 a year, but many lawyers who work on their own have to struggle to provide even a minimal standard of living for themselves and their families. Lawyers who work in large firms usually have higher incomes and higher prestige than do lawyers who work in small firms or on their own. Few attorneys who begin a career on their own or in a small firm move into the better-paying, higher-prestige positions in large firms. Many who begin their careers in large firms do not become partners in those firms; after a few years they move into smaller firms or go to work on their own (Carlin, 1966; Taylor, 1982).

In recent years, many young attorneys have taken jobs in which they do not use their legal training. This is because the increase in law school graduates has outpaced the growth in new positions for lawyers. There are now about 550,000 lawyers in the United States, and that number is growing each year as more come out of law school than retire from the profession.

LAWYERS' ETHICS

A profession is distinguished from other occupations in part by the fact that professionals are expected to learn and to act according to a code of behavior. The code for lawyers that developed in the nineteenth century increased the prestige of that profession. Today, the standards of behavior are formally stated in the American Bar Association's Code of Professional Responsibility, which has been adopted in modified form by state bar associations. This code is necessary because of the monopoly over access to the courts that the states grant to lawyers. States allow lawyers to regulate themselves because legal work is confidential and cannot be assessed publicly, because clients lack the expertise to evaluate how well their attorneys have done for them, and because so much is often at stake in legal cases. State bar associations can also punish lawyers who violate the code with a warning, suspension, or even dismissal from the legal profession.

One of the few studies of the sources of unethical behavior by lawyers was done in New York City by Jerome Carlin (1966), a sociologist who also has a law degree. Carlin found that unethical behavior was most common among attorneys who served clients on a "one-shot" basis. For example, exploitation of criminal defendants, couples getting divorces, and home buyers was relatively common because lawyers did not expect any repeat business from them. In addition, attorneys who practiced before the lower courts and before local rather than federal agencies were most likely to violate ethical standards. A third important factor was the attorney's colleagues: Lawyers who worked in large firms were more likely to be subjected to peer pressure to behave ethically than were lawyers who worked alone or with a few partners.

Formal controls over lawyers by state bar associations seem to be relatively ineffective in preventing unethical behavior. Carlin (1966) estimated that in any one year in New York City, fewer than 2 per cent of all lawyers who violated those ethical standards that were accepted by all members of the bar were dealt with by the bar association's grievance committee; and only about 1 per cent of those dealt with by that committee were actually punished. Only the most widely publicized violations were punished, and sanctions seemed to be aimed more at maintaining a good public image for lawyers than at controlling unethical behavior.

Unethical behavior and incompetence by lawyers might be an even greater problem today than when Carlin did his research in the 1960s, because now there are more lawyers who work alone and more who compete for a limited number of clients. One study estimated that perhaps 10 per cent of the lawyers in Massachusetts lacked the basic skills and techniques needed to practice the law competently. They were unqualified to interview witnesses, work on behalf of clients, set fees, or handle wills and estates. A panel of lawyers, legal scholars, and law school deans recommended mandatory training in legal skills for all new attorneys, remedial programs for incompetent lawyers, the assignment of a mentor to every new lawyer, and the creation of a board to oversee the proficiency of the bar (N. King, 1982).

PUBLIC DEFENDERS AND LEGAL AID SOCIETIES

The high cost of lawyers has resulted in federal and state efforts to provide adequate legal assistance for the poor. Supreme Court decisions in 1963 (*Gideon* v. *Wainwright*) and in 1972 (*Argersinger* v. *Hamlin*) required the states to provide lawyers for poor criminal defendants who could be imprisoned if found guilty. Public defenders have been accused of being unconcerned with their clients and with procedural fairness. They have also been called inexperienced, incompetent, and poorly prepared. Often these attorneys are overloaded with cases and therefore try to get their clients the best "deal" possible through plea bargaining (see below); they assume that their clients are guilty and simply try to minimize the punishment.

In the 1960s, the federal government began financial support of local legal aid societies that assisted the poor in disputes with private parties such as landlords and merchants. Originally these legal aid societies were designed by local bar associations and funded by the now-defunct Office of Economic Opportunity (OEO), which required as much participation by the poor as possible in setting policy for these legal aid societies. The purpose was to make these societies reform oriented, rather than to have them simply handle each client on an individual basis. This program, which had the support of the American Bar Association, came under attack in the 1970s by political leaders—including Richard Nixon, Spiro Agnew, and Ronald Reagan—who felt that federal money was supporting efforts by the poor to attack the policies of the federal and state governments.

The OEO legal aid program was replaced in 1975 by the Legal Services Corporation, an organization whose directors and funds are approved by the federal government. Participation of the poor in this organization has been minimal. Several controversial issues have been declared off-limits to legal aid programs supported by the Legal Services Corporation; these issues include abortion, draft and military desertion, school desegregation, assistance to aliens, and homosexuality. Today, legal aid programs deal with routine matters such as divorces, landlord–tenant problems, welfare and social security benefits, and consumer problems. The Reagan administration tried but failed to abolish all government support of legal aid, although it has reduced funding for this program. Reagan favors voluntary public assistance by practicing attorneys, even though most observers claim that this could not make up for losses in legal aid for the poor if federal funds were eliminated. Even with federal funding, in 1981 only 15 to 20 per cent of the legal needs of the poor were met by legal aid programs (Drew, 1982).

The Courts

Courts are formal organizations that resolve disputes and determine how a society's idea of justice will be implemented. Civil courts mediate disputes between private parties; they handle divorces and custody cases, breaches of contract, personal injuries in accidents, and the probating of wills. Criminal courts resolve charges brought by the state against individuals accused of committing acts for which they can be punished. Civil actions and criminal cases are usually resolved at the lowest court level, but a few cases are appealed all the way to the Supreme Court.

DELAY IN THE COURTS

A major problem in the courts of the United States is the long delay before disputes are eventually resolved. Some personal injury cases arising from car accidents are not settled for five years. Criminal cases are also delayed through "continuances" (formal delays granted by a judge at the request of the defense attorney or the prosecutor), clogged court calendars, and unavailable witnesses. Thus the selection of a jury to try black activist Bobby Seale in Connecticut took five months, and the murder trial of Charles Manson in California took nine months. In contrast, the longest murder trial in England took only twenty-one days (Fleming, 1973).

Delay occurs for many reasons. A guilty criminal defendant gains nothing from a quick verdict but might benefit if the verdict is delayed. In civil cases, one party may gain from delay because the money that will eventually be paid in damages can be invested until the case is resolved. Lawyers profit from delay because they can justify charging higher fees and take on more cases. By allowing all parties to a case as much time as they want before the trial, judges reduce the chance that their decisions will be overturned on appeal because the parties were not allowed enough time for preparation (Fleming, 1973).

Delay can have advantages for various participants in the court system, but it is costly in other ways. For example, as the time between the crime and the eventual punishment lengthens, the likelihood that the punishment will prevent the offender from committing the crime again may be reduced; deterrence requires prompt punishment. Sometimes delay is financially ruinous for parties in civil actions because they need the money to pay medical bills or to replace wages lost due to an accident.

Various solutions for this problem have been proposed (Zeisel, Kalven, and Buchholz, 1959; Fleming, 1973). Judges, for example, might control their court's calendar more effectively. Another solution is to create a mechanism whereby the parties in a civil action can agree on a settlement without going to trial; for instance, the use of an impartial panel of medical experts might facilitate the settlement of accident claims. A shift from jury trials to trials before judges would also save time, but there is a constitutional right to a jury trial in criminal cases. Delay could also be minimized by increasing either the number of judges or the number of hours that judges work.

Plea Bargaining

One practice that has developed to speed court verdicts is *plea bargaining*, a process in which the prosecuting attorney, the defense attorney, the defendant, and the judge agree on the charge to which the defendant will plead guilty and the sentence that the defendant will receive (Rosett and Cressey, 1976; *Law and Society Review*, 1979; Langbein, 1980). Plea bargaining usually begins between the prosecutor and the defense attorney. After they tentatively agree on an appropriate charge and penalty, the defendant is asked if he or she will plead guilty to that charge in return for a specific punishment. If the defendant agrees, the prosecutor presents the proposed "bargain" to the judge in court; usually the judge accepts the guilty plea and metes out the agreed-upon penalty.

Plea bargaining has been criticized for its leniency. A defendant charged with forcible rape might be allowed to plead guilty to a reduced charge of simple assault and receive a one-year jail sentence; if he had been convicted of forcible rape by a jury, he might have been sentenced to ten years in prison. Although plea bargaining produces penalties well below the maximum allowed by law, it saves the court's time and guarantees that criminals will be punished to some extent.

However, one problem with plea bargaining is that, to avoid the possiblity of a long sentence, defendants who are actually innocent but who face serious charges may be encouraged to plead guilty to a crime they did not commit. The criminal justice system is formally an "adversary system" in which prosecutors and defense attorneys battle it out in court to arrive at the "truth." In reality, defense attorneys often encourage their clients to plead guilty (Neubauer, 1974; Blumberg, 1979). Judges try to avoid having innocent or unwilling defendants plead guilty by asking them in court if they are

"If the larceny charge can be dropped, my client is prepared to plead guilty to the lesser charge of creating a climate of larceny."

Drawing by Handelsman; © 1978 The New Yorker Magazine, Inc.

in fact guilty, but this question might well be answered untruthfully to avoid a long sentence. The less educated may be the most susceptible to pleading guilty without full knowledge of the consequences, and the poor may be pressured to plead guilty by the public defenders who represent them.

JUDICIAL BEHAVIOR AND SENTENCE DISPARITY

State laws usually establish a range of penalties for people convicted of a specific crime; for example, armed robbery might carry a penalty of one to twenty years in prison. Because judges are free to give a convicted offender any penalty within the range established by the legislature, there is a problem of *sentence disparity* among judges. Whereas one judge might feel that an appropriate penalty for robbery is five years in prison, another might feel that every convicted robber should spend the maximum of twenty years in prison. Injustice results when two people with the same criminal record are punished differently for the same crime. This can cause bitterness among prisoners when they compare their sentences, which could make rehabilitation difficult (Irwin, 1970). The rationale for allowing a range of punishments rather than a single fixed penalty for each crime is that individual offenders and the circumstances surrounding their crimes are different and warrant some flexibility in sentencing. However, the disparity of sentences seems more to reflect variations in the preferences of judges than variations in the characteristics of offenders and their crimes (Ostrow, 1982).

One significant kind of sentence disparity is the administration of more severe penalties to members of minority groups. Discrimination of this sort is especially serious because it brings the power of the state to bear against people with a particular ascribed status. Not all research shows that the courts do discriminate by race. Although one recent study found that black men received harsher sentences than white men, the black offenders had more serious criminal records and had been charged with more serious offenses. However, this study did find evidence that the poor received harsher punishments than defendants of higher economic standing, and blacks are more likely than whites to be poor. This study also found that convicted white offenders were more likely than convicted blacks to be placed on probation (supervised release) and that blacks were more likely than whites to be sent to prison (Spohn, Gruhl, and Welch, 1981–1982). Other studies, however, find less evidence of racial discrimination in the sentencing of offenders (Hagan, 1974).

One suggestion that has been made to reduce sentence disparity is a commission on sentencing that would recommend penalties for certain kinds of offenders who are convicted of particular crimes. These commissions might help to standardize penalties by reviewing and commenting on the actual sentences that judges give to offenders (Frankel, 1973). Another suggestion is "presumptive sentences" that are recommended by law for certain offenses and offenders; judges who deviate from those presumptive sentences would have to justify their actions in written reports. "Fixed sentences" that a judge could not modify also might be required by state law as a way to reduce sentence disparity.

JURIES

A jury is a group of people chosen from a community to hear a criminal or civil case and reach a verdict. Even though an estimated 80 per cent of the world's jury trials take place in the United States, only a relatively small percentage (perhaps 5 per cent) of all serious crimes are eventually tried before a jury in this country. Most cases are disposed of by guilty pleas that are often induced by plea bargaining (Kalven and Zeisel, 1966; Baldwin and McConville, 1980).

By law, American juries must be composed of the defendant's peers. Yet research and court decisions indicate that juries are often unrepresentative of the community from which they are drawn:

> Despite recent gains, in most courts in the United States significant segments of the population are still not included on juries as often as they would be in a completely random system aimed at impaneling a representative cross-section. Blue-collar workers, nonwhites, the young, the elderly, and women are the groups most widely underrepresented on juries, and in many jurisdictions, the underrepresentation of these groups is substantial and dramatic (Van Dyke, 1977: 24).

This underrepresentation is a result of the way that jurors are picked from the pool of those who are eligible. Some people are routinely excused from jury duty—for instance, the mothers of preschool children—and others are excluded by lawyers during the process of selecting a jury to hear a particular case (Baldwin and McConville, 1980). In a few cases, social science evidence is used to screen jurors to secure an impartial or even a favorably biased jury (see SEL 15.2).

SOCIOLOGY AND EVERYDAY LIFE 15.2
Using Social Science to Pick a Jury

The 1971–1972 trial of Father Philip F. Berrigan and other anti-Vietnam War protesters in Harrisburg, Pennsylvania, was the first major case in which social science research was used to aid in the selection of a jury. Jay Schulman, an antiwar activist and former professor, decided that he could use his training in the social sciences to help his friends, whom he thought would face a hostile jury. Schulman, a colleague, and a group of graduate students designed a survey that was carried out with volunteer interviewers.

Jury researchers such as Schulman survey a sample that is representative of the population from which jurors are to be drawn. These researchers look for variables such as sex, race, age, and education that are associated with attitudes and beliefs, which in turn seem likely to predict the kind of decisions that similar people would reach if they sat on a jury. Lawyers have always used their hunches about what factors will make jurors sympathetic to their position, but jury researchers test those hunches with empirical data. Schulman explains some of the results of his Harrisburg survey as follows:

"For instance, we discovered that Catholics would be O.K. on the issue of social protest. This was Harrisburg, not New York, and it was in this area that the Molly Maguires were hanged a century ago. Also, contrary to what our lawyers expected, college-educated people were not likely to be liberal in Harrisburg. Liberal college graduates, it seems, leave Harrisburg for other places, and those who stay support conservative norms" (pp. 78, 82).

Jury researchers use other strategies besides the survey. Social psychologists have interpreted the meaning of prospective jurors' body language for lawyers. Research on small groups has been employed to pick juries that will form cliques, interact, and assign authority in ways that will produce desired verdicts. Recently, some lawyers have staged make-believe trials before mock juries composed of people with the characteristics that surveys have found beneficial to their clients. These "jurors" are paid for their participation in these experiments, which enable lawyers to test a variety of strategies in presenting their cases and then choose the best approach for the actual trial.

The services of sociologists, psychologists, and market-research firms that aid in the jury selection process are expensive and therefore rarely used. The head of one firm says, "If it isn't worth spending $50,000 for jury research for your case, forget it. And a full-scale workup can run as much as $500,000" (p. 72). Consequently, these consultants have been employed primarily by large corporations facing civil suits or criminal prosecution. Dissidents such as Berrigan and Angela Davis, who can enlist the aid of enthusiastic sympathizers or the National Jury Project—an organization of consultants formed in 1975 by Schulman and his colleagues—have also been the beneficiaries of this expertise.

The use of social science to select jurors raises important questions about the fairness of trials. Juries are supposed to represent a cross section of the community, but critics charge that jury researchers enable their clients to "stack the deck" by choosing jurors favorably disposed to them. Jury researchers answer that their techniques are simply used to select an impartial jury. Nevertheless, defense attorneys probably prefer juries that will acquit their clients, rather than juries that are totally unbiased. Perhaps in the future there will be a legal requirement that if one party in a case uses jury selection experts, the state will have to pay for experts for the other side, too.

Source: Based on Morton Hunt, "Putting Juries on the Couch," *The New York Times Magazine*, November 28, 1982, pp. 70–72, 78–88.

THE JUVENILE COURT

We saw in Chapter 4 that the stage in the life cycle called adolescence developed only with industrialization. The legal system responded slowly to this change, and the first juvenile court in the United States was established in Illinois in 1899. The rationale for separate juvenile courts and correctional facilities was that adolescent offenders should be treated as people who need assistance rather than punishment (Platt, 1977). As a consequence, juvenile courts avoided the formality of adult criminal courts until the Supreme Court's 1967 decision *in re Gault*. This decision guaranteed juveniles faced with serious charges a variety of legal rights, including the right to an attorney and the right to be informed of the charges against them. This formalization of juvenile court procedures protects young offenders from some of the abuses of an informal system, but it may also make it more difficult to provide them with social services.

The realization that labeling by the juvenile courts might only drive young people deeper into crime has prompted efforts to divert adolescents—especially first offenders—from the juvenile justice system (Lemert, 1971; Schur, 1973; Klemke, 1978; Empey, 1982). However, diverting young offenders who have committed relatively trivial offenses into community programs has resulted in competition among agencies for these clients. These agencies sometimes provide long-term treatment that apparently has no beneficial effects on the young offenders (Rojek and Erickson, 1981–1982).

Punishment and Corrections

Ideas about how people who violate social norms should be sanctioned are a part of every culture. A sanction administered by a legitimate authority—such as a chief of a tribe or the state in an industrial society—is *punishment*. Cultures justify punishment on different grounds; indeed, we even find a variety of such justifications in American culture. One rationale for punishment is *retribution*, the idea that people who have done wrong deserve to suffer. Other justifications are more utilitarian—that is, they try to accomplish some good for society by punishing offenders. One utilitarian justification is *deterrence*, the notion that punishment, by instilling fear, can prevent crime. Another is *incapacitation*, the use of prison to prevent crime by keeping offenders off the streets. A third is *rehabilitation*, trying to change offenders so that they will give up their criminal activities.

RETRIBUTION

Retribution requires offenders to be punished in proportion to the harm they have done to their victims or to society. The ancient principle of "an eye for an eye, a tooth for a tooth" expresses the idea that punishment should be proportional to the harm inflicted. To develop a system of retribution, it is necessary to rank different crimes by their relative seriousness, rank penalties by their relative harshness, and then link offenses with different degrees of seriousness to penalties of different severity. Some research provides a partial basis for such a system of what has been called "just deserts," but much work remains to be done (Von

Hirsch, 1976; Hamilton and Rotkin, 1976; Kellogg, 1977; Erickson and Gibbs, 1979).

When they write laws that assign penalties to certain acts, lawmakers are guided by the principle of retribution; they give the more serious offenses the more severe penalties. Judges are also guided by this principle when they mete out harsher punishments to offenders they consider more dangerous, either because of the crime of which they have been convicted or because of their criminal record. Judges may disagree about what constitutes an appropriate penalty for a particular offender who has committed a certain crime, but each judge tries to reserve the harshest punishments for the most serious offenders. The decisions of parole boards, which are state agencies that decide when prisoners are to be released, are also based in part on retributive considerations. Prisoners who have committed the most serious offenses and those who are regarded as the most dangerous to society will not be released until they have served most or all of their maximum sentence.

DETERRENCE

Deterrence justifies punishment with the assumption that people commit crimes only after rationally considering the costs (or risks) and the benefits (or rewards) of their actions. This perspective assumes that increasing the negative consequences of harmful behavior can turn people away from that behavior (see SEL 15.3).

Deterrence seems to work best for "instrumental" crimes, those that are directed toward a specific goal such as the theft of property. Crimes that are "expressive," or based on personal needs—such as rape committed on the spur of the moment—are less likely to be deterred. People who respond to their emotional needs with criminal behavior are less likely to consider the risks and rewards of their actions than are people who carefully weigh the advantages and disadvantages of a particular course of action. Moreover, people who are highly committed to a life of crime are not as apt to be deterred by punishment as people less committed to crime (Chambliss, 1969).

Lawmakers often behave as if the severity of a penalty were the most important aspect of the law; they raise the punishment for a crime in the hope that it will have a greater deterrent effect. However, the certainty of being detected and punished may be more important as a deterrent than the harshness of the penalty (Schwartz, 1968; Antunes and Hunt, 1973). A high probability that an offender will have to serve a year in prison could be a better

SOCIOLOGY AND EVERYDAY LIFE 15.3
The Death Penalty: Deterrent or "Just Deserts"?

Between 1930 and 1967, nearly 4,000 Americans were executed as criminals; no one was put to death between 1968 and 1977; but about one execution a year took place between 1978 and 1982. Since 1972, when the United States Supreme Court struck down capital punishment laws, about three-fourths of the states have re-enacted death penalty statutes to meet the objections of the Court in *Furman* v. *Georgia*. In 1983, there were more than 1,100 prisoners on Death Row across the country, and there is reason to believe that some of them will be put to death. Recent public opinion polls find that Americans support the death penalty by a ratio of two to one.

The usual justification for the death penalty is that it is an effective deterrent to murder; the fear of being executed is supposed to stop potential murderers from killing. Another justification is that murderers deserve to die. Because it seems to violate a cultural norm that human life should be valued, this retributive, or "just deserts," argument for capital punishment is heard less often than the deterrence argument. Deterrence, on the other hand, fits well with American culture's emphasis on pragmatism.

Does the death penalty deter crime? This is a difficult question to answer definitively. First, the real question is whether the death penalty deters some crimes that would not be deterred if the penalty were "only" life or a very long time in prison; the alternative to execution is a long prison sentence rather than freedom from any punishment. Second, we need to ask if the death penalty deters those crimes for which it is used. The crime for which most Americans have been executed is murder. (Some have also been put to death for rape—usually black men convicted of raping white women—but a 1977 Supreme Court decision ruled out execution for rape alone.) Because most murders—perhaps as many as four out of five—are crimes of passion rather than premeditated acts, it would be surprising if capital punishment deterred murder, for most killers do not consider the possible consequences of their actions. On the other hand, capital punishment might deter premeditated murders such as gangland killings by "hit men."

Despite much evidence to the contrary, many Americans continue to support the death penalty as a deterrent. Many also say they would support capital punishment even if conclusive evidence were found that there was no deterrent effect, claiming that murderers deserve to lose their own lives in return for taking those of others. Retribution of this sort has also been justified as a reasonable expression of a community's anger against those who have violated the norm that it holds most strongly. Critics reply to the retributive argument by pointing to the negative effects on the public of seeing the state take a human life and to the irreversibility of execution in the event of a miscarriage of justice.

Sources: Based on Hugo Adam Bedau, ed., *The Death Penalty in America*, 3rd ed. New York: Oxford University Press, 1982, Walter Berns, *For Capital Punishment: Crime and the Morality of the Death Penalty*. New York: Basic Books, 1979; and Peter Ross Range, "Will He Be The First?" *The New York Times Magazine*, March 11, 1979, pp. 29, 72–82.

deterrent than a small chance that the offender will have to serve five years in prison. Crime may also be more easily deterred if a penalty is administered promptly (Chambliss, 1969; Zimring and Hawkins, 1973; Andenaes, 1974; Gibbs, 1975; Blumstein, Cohen, and Nagin, 1978; Cook, 1980).

INCAPACITATION

Considerable attention has been given to incapacitation, the policy of preventing crime by locking up offenders for a period of time; during that time at least they cannot commit crimes against the public.

It is difficult to determine the exact incapacitative effect of the law because that would require knowledge of precisely how many crimes particular offenders commit when they are on the street for a given period. Not enough research has been done on criminal activity to estimate the impact on the crime rate of incarcerating more offenders or imprisoning inmates for longer times. Studies that have used different estimates of the number of crimes committed during a criminal's career have come to different conclusions about the effects of a policy of incapacitation (Clarke, 1974; Greenberg, 1975; Shinnar and Shinnar, 1975; Cohen, 1978).

REHABILITATION

Rehabilitation is a utilitarian perspective that assumes that, through treatment, human behavior can be altered so that offenders will turn away from crime in the future. Because each offender must change in different ways and may take a different amount of time to change, the idea of rehabilitation is used to tailor penalties to the individual needs of offenders. Consequently, offenders who have committed the same kinds of crime might be given different penalties.

Rehabilitation includes individual and group therapy, vocational training, and educational programs. It assumes that there is a model of acceptable and law-abiding behavior that offenders should be changed to fit. Some critics regard this view as demeaning to offenders, who might freely have chosen to violate the law and pay for their crime (Kittrie, 1971; Lewis, 1971; Von Hirsch, 1976).

Judges consider the rehabilitation programs that are available in the prisons and in the community before they sentence an offender, although their options are often quite limited. The goal of rehabilitation led to the introduction at the end of the nineteenth century of the *indeterminate sentence*, which allows judges to sentence offenders to inexact periods of time in custody—such as one year to life, or five to ten years. Offenders are released from prison only when they are considered to have been rehabilitated. If they refuse to change or if existing treatment methods are ineffective, they may serve the maximum sentence.

The effects of treatment are usually assessed by comparing a group of prisoners who are subjected to a particular kind of treatment with another group of prisoners who do not receive the same treatment. Relatively few prison treatment programs have been evaluated systematically, but those that have been seem to have no significant impact on the rate at which released prisoners ''go straight.'' For instance, a study in a California prison found that inmates who were given group counseling returned to prison at the same rate as inmates who did not receive group counseling (Kassebaum, Ward, and Wilner, 1971). Comprehensive reviews of treatment programs have concluded that few if any affect the rate at which released offenders stay away from criminal activity (Lipton, Martinson, and Wilks, 1975; Sechrest, White, and Brown, 1979; James Wilson, 1980). Consequently, the rehabilitative justification for punishment has lost some favor in recent years, and greater attention has been paid to deterring crime, incapacitating offenders, and creating a system of just punishment.

Summary

The law defines permissible behavior, assigns legitimate authority to certain people, settles conflicts between groups, defines societal goals, and maintains the social order. Laws have the greatest legitimacy when they are consistent with informal norms, which often is not the case in countries run by colonial governments. Conflict theorists claim that the law reflects the interests of the dominant class in the economic system and see the legal system as another institution used to exploit the workers in a capitalist system. Some laws that are initially the result of conflicts among groups do eventually gain the support of the whole community.

Public opinion influences the law in societies in which power is derived from the consent of the governed. Interest groups that are organized to achieve specific goals also affect the enactment and enforcement of the law. People working in the same occupation sometimes form interest groups that pressure lawmakers to license and regulate their profession; this enhances prestige, restricts the entry of new workers, and increases wages. Interest groups also bring pressure to bear on regulatory agencies that often serve those they are supposed to regulate rather than the public interest. The law is also affected at times by scientific research and the opinions of recognized experts.

The law sometimes has an unintended consequence or no effect at all. One unintended effect is the crime tariff, which causes the price of illegal goods and services to rise, thereby providing illegal suppliers with high profits. Another is that harsh penalties can backfire if judges or juries refuse to impose them.

The police are a formal organization with rational–legal authority that seeks to preserve order, enforce the law, and provide public service. Police officers exercise discretion in their enforcement of the law; they do not arrest everyone who violates a law. Often there is hostility between the police and the community, especially in urban ghettos. The police spend more time doing routine tasks and preserving public order than fighting crime. In the United States, they only solve about one-fifth of all serious crimes. It is unclear whether police prejudice is translated into actual discriminatory behavior.

Lawyers are advocates who have specialized knowledge of legal rules and procedures. One change over the last two decades has been the provision of legal assistance to the poor in both criminal and civil matters. In law school, students learn legal reasoning through intensive analysis of judicial decisions. As lawyers, they are guided by a code of behavior. The ethical behavior of lawyers is closely linked to their relationship with their clients, the courts and agencies before which they practice, and the colleagues with whom they work.

Courts resolve disputes between individual parties in civil cases and between the state and individuals in criminal cases. A major problem in the American court system is delay, which occurs because different parties gain by prolonging the eventual verdict. Plea bargaining has developed to speed up the legal process; defendants agree to plead guilty to reduced charges in return for lighter sentences than they might have received after a trial. The flexibility of criminal sentences creates considerable variation from one judge to another in the penalties meted out for similar crimes committed by offenders with similar criminal records. Most jury trials in the world occur in the United States, but relatively few convictions are actually the result of a trial before a jury. Many juries are unrepresentative of the community from which they are selected, even though the Constitution requires that defendants have a jury of their peers. Juvenile courts developed at the turn of the century to provide service rather than punishment to adolescents who violated the law; in recent years, these courts have become more formalized, as juveniles have been granted legal rights.

Punishment is a state-administered sanction for a person convicted of violating a criminal law. One justification for punishment is retribution, the idea that those who do wrong deserve to be punished in proportion to the harm they have caused. Another justification is deterrence, the utilitarian idea that punishment can reduce crime by increasing the costs of socially harmful behavior. Another utilitarian justification for punishment is incapacitation, the idea that the imprisonment of offenders will prevent crime during the time that they are off the street. Rehabilita-

tion is a third utilitarian justification; it suggests that crime can be reduced by reforming convicted offenders. Most research on treatment programs has concluded that they have no significant effect in reducing the rate at which offenders return to crime.

Important Terms

CASE METHOD (356) PLEA BARGAINING (359)
COURT (358) POLICE (353)
CRIME TARIFF (353) PUNISHMENT (362)
DETERRENCE (362) REHABILITATION (362)
INCAPACITATION (362) RETRIBUTION (362)
INDETERMINATE SEN- SENTENCE DISPARITY
TENCE (364) (360)
LAWYER (355)

Suggested Readings

Piers Beirne and Richard Quinney, eds. *Marxism and Law.* New York: Wiley, 1982. A collection of papers on the Marxist theory of the legal system that focus on crime, the state, ideology, and socialist societies.

Abraham S. Blumberg. *Criminal Justice: Issues & Ironies,* 2nd ed. New York: New Viewpoints, 1979. A fine introduction to the criminal justice system, especially as it describes the way that the courts operate.

William J. Chambliss and Robert Seidman. *Law, Order, & Power,* 2nd ed. Reading, Mass.: Addison-Wesley, 1982. A textbook on the sociology of law, with emphasis on the conflict perspective.

Lawrence M. Friedman and Stewart Macaulay, eds. *Law and the Behavioral Sciences,* 2nd ed. Indianapolis: Bobbs-Merrill, 1977. A comprehensive collection of journal articles, legal cases, and commentary on the sociology of law.

James M. Inverarity, Pat Lauderdale, and Barry C. Feld. *Law and Society: Sociological Perspectives on Criminal Law.* Boston: Little, Brown, 1983. A textbook that examines contributions by Marx, Weber, and Durkheim to the sociology of law, and that also explores the creation and enforcement of the law.

Arthur Rosett and Donald R. Cressey. *Justice by Consent: Plea Bargains in the American Courthouse.* Philadelphia: Lippincott, 1976. A study of one instance of plea bargaining viewed from the perspective of various parties to the "deal."

Jerome H. Skolnick. *Justice without Trial: Law Enforcement in Democratic Society,* 2nd ed. New York: Wiley, 1975. A good introduction to police behavior based on the author's firsthand observations.

Scott Turow. *One L.* New York: Putnam's, 1977. A popular account of the experiences of a first-year student at Harvard Law School.

THE ECONOMIC SYSTEM 16

Have you ever donated a pint of blood to a hospital or to the American Red Cross? Perhaps you have sold your blood; about half of all donors in the United States are paid. In Great Britain blood donors are not paid, though in Japan nearly everyone who gives blood is compensated (Titmuss, 1971). Blood is distributed differently in different societies: It can be made available by appealing to a humanitarian urge to help others or by offering money to donors. Goods such as blood are made available through the *economic system*, which also produces and distributes services such as education and legal assistance.

Economists study the process of supply and demand—the way that producers create goods and services in response to the needs and desires of consumers, and the way that these users of goods and services get others to provide things for them. Sociologists are also interested in the economic system, but they are more likely than economists to examine the social context within which economic forces operate. Unlike most economists, sociologists do not assume that economic behavior is rational and carefully planned; rather, they focus on the effects of values and norms on economic behavior. Economists, on the other hand, usually assume that economic behavior is influenced by considerations of the price and the usefulness of goods and services. Whereas an economist would regard work as a way to earn income, a sociologist would be apt to look at other functions of work—such as providing people with an identity or integrating them into groups.

Aspects of the Economic System

The essential need for food, shelter, and clothing is rooted in human biology, but the fulfillment of basic needs is influenced by culture and social structure. People in cold climates need clothing to protect themselves, but industrial economics in cold climates manufacture a range of clothing that is aesthetically pleasing and provides symbolic evidence of wealth, as well as offering warmth. Besides the basic needs, people are socialized to have various desires; they *need* a winter coat, but they learn to *want* a fashionable and attractive coat. Essential needs are limited; human desires may be unlimited.

Every society develops a mode of subsistence—an economic system that ensures survival by using scarce resources such as land, capital, and labor to produce goods and services that meet human needs and desires. The economic system determines what goods and services are produced, how many of each is produced, the methods used to produce them, and the way they are distributed among the members of the society. The way these decisions are made is closely linked to norms about property, modes of economic exchange, the division of labor, and the process of economic socialization.

PROPERTY

In every culture there are norms about property— the rights and obligations attached to scarce and valued things. Property is best conceptualized as a socially acknowledged right rather than as a material object. Property involves the right of ownership, which differs from simple possession of an item and differs from the item itself; for instance, a robber might possess a victim's watch but does not legally own it. Norms about property give people the confidence to enter into economic exchanges such as the purchase of food or clothing; without property norms, people would be reluctant to pay money for something that another person did not clearly have the right to sell.

ECONOMIC EXCHANGE

As we saw in Chapter 6, one form of social exchange is *economic exchange*—the process by which individuals and organizations give each other valuable goods and services in return for different goods and services. A written contract between a manufacturer and a supplier to deliver raw materials for a certain price is one kind of economic exchange. Other forms of economic exchange, such as depositing a dime in a public telephone or purchasing a magazine, do not involve written contracts. Working for pay is an economic exchange, and so are all purchases made with money or credit cards.

An economic exchange that is common in preindustrial economies is "gift exchange" (Mauss, 1925, 1954). By giving gifts, people create a general obligation to help and support one another in time of need, but they do not expect immediate reciprocation; the voluntary donation of blood is one example (Titmuss, 1971). Gifts sometimes symbolize and strengthen social relationships; if you send a Christmas card or give a birthday present to someone but receive none in return for a few years, you might well assume that the social bond with that person has been broken.

Another common form of economic exchange in preindustrial economies is "barter," the direct exchange of goods and services. In the marketplace, farmers who have grown more potatoes than their families can eat will trade their surplus for different kinds of food that others have in excess. Barter limits economic exchange because a person with a surplus must find someone else who wants the specific item and who can also provide a good or service that the first person wants.

In "money economies," items that have little or no intrinsic value—such as the wampum or shells once used by Native Americans or the paper bills they use today—are defined in the culture as a standard of general value that can be used to complete economic transactions. Money facilitates exchange because it enables people to measure the worth of goods and services; it is easier to buy a number of potatoes for a dollar than to bargain with a farmer over how many potatoes can be traded for a certain number of apples.

Advanced money economies sometimes evolve into "finance economies" in which money is treated as a commodity with a value of its own. The interest rate charged on a loan is the price paid for the use of money. In financial exchange, money is used to make more money through interest charges or through capital investment and growth. Finance economies are characterized by an increased use of credit and a decreased use of cash.

THE DIVISION OF LABOR

In all economic systems, tasks are specialized and there is interdependence among various statuses and roles. Simple economies are often specialized by sex and by age; for instance, men and women perform different jobs (see Table 10.1), and the young carry out different economic functions than do the elderly. Industrial economies, on the other hand, rely more on educational credentials, skills, and talents to assign tasks.

One of the earliest discussions of the division of labor was Adam Smith's *The Wealth of Nations* (1776, 1937). Smith argued that the source of a nation's wealth is its productivity—the capacity to use the factors of production to make things that others regard as valuable. He claimed that productivity is increased by the specialization of tasks through the division of labor (see Chapter 7). Specialization generally increases efficiency because people can do a single task more efficiently than they can do several different tasks, even though the boredom that sometimes comes from repetition of the same task can lead to dissatisfaction and eventual inefficiency. For an economic system to work, many specialized jobs must be coordinated into productive enterprises.

Emile Durkheim (1893, 1933) also examined the division of labor, treating it as a general feature of social life rather than simply as a characteristic of an economic system. He claimed that preindustrial societies are held together by the similarity of their members, but that complex industrial societies are united instead by differences among their members. According to Durkheim, in modern societies the interdependence of many people who perform different social and economic functions is the basis of solidarity; interdependence acts as a kind of "social glue" that allows complex societies to endure.

ECONOMIC SOCIALIZATION

Through *economic socialization* people learn to regard the economic system as legitimate and learn the values and behavior needed to fill positions in the division of labor. Russian and Chinese students learn cooperation in school, and this fits with their collectivist economic systems (Bronfenbrenner, 1970). In the United States, students learn values that support a capitalist economy (Bowles and Gintis, 1976; Cummings and Taebel, 1978). They learn from their parents and teachers that inequality is inevitable, a value that neo-Marxists see as intrinsic to capitalism. American students also learn to favor private ownership of the means of production, individual initiative, differential rewards, and a government "hands-off" approach to the economy. Moreover, through socialization they learn negative attitudes toward socialism and toward labor unions. These procapitalist and antisocialist attitudes become more common as children pass from the third through the twelfth grades (Cummings and Taebel, 1978).

Types of Economic Systems

The mode of subsistence is so basic that some sociologists have classified entire societies by the primary way that the economic system meets human needs and desires (Lenski and Lenski, 1982). This approach, which treats technology as a primary determinant of social relations, shares with Marx the view that social institutions are part of a superstructure based on the economic means of production; but it differs from Marx in emphasizing technological developments rather than class conflict as the source of social change.

PREINDUSTRIAL SOCIETIES

Societies that have not developed mechanical sources of energy depend on human or animal efforts to provide food, clothing, and shelter. These preindustrial societies differ in their modes of subsistence and in their complexity.

Hunting–Gathering Societies

Societies that rely for food primarily on the hunting of animals and the gathering of food that grows in the natural environment are called *hunting–gathering societies*. Because the environment cannot sup-

Societies that rely for food primarily on the hunting of animals and the gathering of food that grows in the natural environment are called hunting-gathering societies.

port large numbers of people, these societies are usually quite small. They lack political institutions and their members are roughly equal in status, although some hunting–gathering tribes do have leaders. Kinship ties are the most important basis of social organization in these societies. Tasks are specialized by age and by sex rather than by expertise in particular kinds of work. People wander about to find new food supplies, and because of their nomadic behavior they have few material possessions. Leisure time is often plentiful because the gathering of food usually occupies only a few hours each day.

Pastoral Societies

Pastoral societies develop in areas with little rainfall, a short growing season, or mountainous terrain, where farming is not possible, but animals can be domesticated and used for food. This mode of subsistence enables people to produce more food than they need. The size of a person's herd becomes a basis of social inequality and a source of power. Differences in authority emerge, and form the basis of a rudimentary political system. Material possessions are limited to what can be transported easily. Pastoralists wander about in search of new grazing land for their livestock. This nomadic behavior fosters both trade and warfare with other societies.

Horticultural Societies

Horticultural societies are those that raise plants by farming that is based mainly on human labor. These societies are less nomadic than societies that employ simpler technologies. Land is cleared and crops are raised until the land is depleted, and then horticulturalists move on in search of more fertile lands, for productive soil is needed to produce an adequate food supply and a surplus to trade. Occupational specialization develops, and differences in wealth emerge as some people accumulate more than others. Tools and weapons are more common than in hunting–gathering or pastoral societies, and trade and commerce are more widespread. A growing surplus of food makes it possible for these societies to become relatively large, necessitating the development of a political system to maintain internal order and pursue shared goals.

Agrarian Societies

Agrarian societies employ the plow to increase the fertility of the soil. Animals are used to help people farm large fields, and this results in greater produc-

tivity. Tasks become highly specialized, and distinct social classes based on differences in accumulated wealth become common. Population growth and urbanization are made possible by food surpluses, which enable some people to perform economic functions other than growing food and then exchange their own goods or services for the food grown by others. In agrarian societies, the state becomes a separate institution, a money economy develops, and trade becomes commonplace.

INDUSTRIAL SOCIETIES

Industrialization is the process by which an economy based primarily on energy supplied by animals and humans changes to one based mainly on mechanical sources of energy such as the steam engine and electricity. *Industrial societies* use science and advanced technology to produce goods and services. Their division of labor is highly specialized; for instance, the *Dictionary of Occupational Titles* for the United States lists over 20,000 different jobs, including 142 that involve the manufacture and repair of clocks and watches (U.S. Department of Labor, 1977).

One effect of industrialization is the movement of work out of the home and into the factory. As a result, the family is less important as an economic unit than in preindustrial societies; its functions, except for the role of the breadwinner, become limited to consumption, rather than including both production and consumption. In many industrial societies, the average family is quite small, because each additional child is an extra mouth to feed rather than an extra pair of hands to work the fields. Education becomes more important in industrial societies because literacy and skills are needed to do complex tasks. Bureaucracies increasingly become the setting for work, and growth and bigness are prized. In addition, the need for a large number of workers in one place encourages urbanization; the development of trade leads to improvements in transportation and communication; and national economies become more highly integrated (Toffler, 1980).

In industrial societies, unskilled and semiskilled workers are sometimes displaced by machines, because work must be more carefully synchronized and products made more standard. This process of *automation*—or the mechanization of production—is the result of the use of an advanced technology to do jobs once performed by people. One result is that fewer workers are needed for fewer hours to produce the same goods. This can increase available leisure time and accelerate the growth of the recreation and entertainment industry. Because most jobs that become automated are repetitive and simple tasks that hold little real interest, automation might eliminate the most boring jobs and reduce overall worker dissatisfaction. However, automation often requires people to work closely with machines, and this creates an impersonal work environment and forces employees to work at a pace set by machines. Automation has cost some workers their jobs, but it has also upgraded other jobs for those with the necessary training, skills, and supervisory abilities (Serrin, 1982b). Automation does require the retraining of displaced workers and people who wish to find jobs that require new skills. It is estimated that by 1992 there will be a shortage of more than 500,000 computer operators and technicians in the United States, a number that cannot be supplied by the entry of new workers into the labor force but that will instead require extensive retraining of those already holding jobs (Oreskes, 1982).

Industrial economies have produced high standards of living. The productivity of any economic system can be measured by its *gross national product* (GNP), a monetary measure of the total value of goods and services produced in a given year. A society's standard of living—the goods and services that people can afford—can then be measured by dividing the total GNP by the number of people in the society. Per capita GNP does not tell us about the distribution of goods and services among the members of a society, but it does indicate the relative wealth of different societies. Table 16.1 shows

the per capita GNP of the ten wealthiest nations in 1978. The United States ranks sixth, a decline from first place in 1972. Kuwait is the only one of the ten wealthiest nations that is not fully industrialized, and its high per capita GNP conceals a very uneven distribution of wealth between rich oil producers and the poor masses.

POSTINDUSTRIAL SOCIETIES

All economic systems can be characterized by the way that goods and services are produced. Production is divided among three basic sectors of the economy. The "primary sector" produces or extracts raw materials by farming, mining, lumbering, and fishing; this sector is the only source of goods in preindustrial societies. The "secondary sector" converts raw materials into finished products through manufacturing and construction. Services such as finance, trade, transportation, medicine, the law, education, and recreation form the "tertiary sector."

The process of industrialization shifts an economic system's emphasis from the primary sector to the secondary sector. Today, however, more than three-fifths of American workers hold jobs in the tertiary sector (Rossides, 1976; U.S. Bureau of the Census, 1982). This might be the highest proportion working in the service sector of any economic system in the world. As a result, some observers have called the United States a *postindustrial society* (Bell, 1973).

In postindustrial societies, scientific and professional workers are very important and consultants are increasingly used to solve technical problems. Change is planned in a rational way, and computer projections of possible "scenarios" may be used in the decision-making process. Advanced education in technical matters becomes more important, as people are taught how to learn, rather than being taught specific knowledge that may soon be obsolete because of the rapid pace of technological change. In addition, postindustrial societies are characterized by growth in the power of the state over the private sector, an increased availability of leisure time, and more emphasis on personal fulfillment (Bell, 1973).

Alvin Toffler (1980) has described postindustrial society as a "Third Wave" civilization that will differ dramatically from the "First Wave" of agricultural societies and the "Second Wave" of industrial societies. According to Toffler, the Third Wave will have the following characteristics: decentralization of production, the use of renewable energy,

TABLE 16.1
Per Capita GNP of Ten Wealthiest Nations, 1978

Nation	Per capita income
1. Kuwait	$15,970
2. Switzerland	12,990
3. Denmark	10,580
4. Sweden	10,540
5. West Germany	10,300
6. United States	9,770
7. Belgium	9,700
8. Norway	9,560
9. Netherlands	9,200
10. France	8,880

Source: Jim Anderson, "U.S. Drops to No. 6 in Income per Head," *The Boston Globe*, April 19, 1981, p. 21.

deurbanization, work in the home, and merging of the roles of producer and consumer. Moreover, according to Toffler, this Third Wave civilization will be marked by the rapid growth of four new industries: the space industry, industry in the depths of the oceans, genetic engineering, and the electronics industry.

High-Technology Industry and Computerization

The electronics, or high-technology, industry has flourished in two regions of the United States: the Route 128 area outside Boston and the Silicon Valley area south of San Francisco. One study found that a variety of factors accounted for the rapid development of these two areas:

- a close association between a major research university and new electronics firms;
- a cultural climate or geographical setting that attracted young engineers;
- a group of entrepreneurs willing to provide guidance and funds for investment;
- managers who treated their workers as allies and rewarded them for productive work; and
- a "critical mass" of companies that permitted the development of new firms by innovative and ambitious workers (Butterfield, 1982).

High-technology industry has already revolutionized American life in several ways. Electronic equipment has eliminated some clerical and white-collar jobs because menial clerical tasks such as billing, bookkeeping, and typing can be performed more efficiently with computers and word processors. However, this equipment requires op-

erators, programmers, and service technicians—all of whom do skilled jobs created by modern technology. A more subtle way that computers and high technology can affect work is to polarize the labor force into two groups—a small group of skilled and well-paid workers and a large group of people who hold menial jobs that do not pay well (Serrin, 1982b). However, computerization does facilitate decision making and, by increasing the speed and efficiency with which information is processed, frees some workers for more interesting jobs.

It is difficult to foresee how computers will alter social life, but it is clear that the changes will be far-reaching. Crime might be curbed and economic transactions monitored more carefully by replacing cash with computerized accounts (Lederman, 1981). It may not be long before many homes will have a centralized computer that provides security from burglars, conserves energy by turning off lights, prepares meals in advance, and pays the bills. Leisure activities have already been affected in major ways by modern technology; home video games and special effects in the movies are just two examples.

Modern Economic Systems

So far, we have classified economic systems by their primary mode of subsistence and their level of technological development. A somewhat different way to categorize economies is by their dominant means of production and their class systems. Marx distinguished among what he called primitive com-

Reprinted by permission: Tribune Company Syndicate, Inc.

munism, in which property was jointly owned and social classes were absent; slavery, in which workers were owned as property by their masters; and feudalism, in which workers were bound to landowners and nobility. In *capitalism,* the next stage in Marx's scheme, a bourgeoisie or capitalist class owns factories, machinery, and raw materials and pays workers or the proletariat less than the full value of their labor to convert raw materials into finished goods. Marx claimed that class conflict, the oppression of workers, and declining profits would lead to a revolution in which workers took control of the means of production and shared the profits. This stage of socialism would next evolve into communism, an economic system in which all property is once again jointly owned and all classes disappear.

Today sociologists usually focus their attention on the distinction between capitalism and socialism, because the most powerful societies can be described as capitalist or socialist—or more often as mixed systems with characteristics of each type. Capitalism and socialism are distinguished by the amount of political control over the economy. In capitalist systems there is relatively little control by the state, and in socialist systems the state plans the economy to a greater degree. Another difference is that consumers are given more influence over economic decision making in capitalist systems, and government officials wield more power in socialist systems (Lindblom, 1977). Socialist economies exist in totalitarian states such as the Soviet Union; democratic states such as Sweden have also adopted aspects of socialism. Likewise, capitalism exists in democratic systems such as the United States and in Latin American dictatorships as well.

CAPITALISM

For centuries there has been much disagreement over the characteristics and the consequences of capitalism. One useful way to highlight some of these differences is to contrast the views of one of capitalism's staunchest defenders, Adam Smith, and one of its harshest critics, Karl Marx.

Adam Smith's Capitalism

In *The Wealth of Nations* (1776, 1937), Adam Smith described a pure capitalist economy—one in which raw materials, equipment, and money are combined by entrepreneurs to produce profits from the labor of workers. In this system, producers and consumers make economic decisions, free of government control. The market—that is, the "natural" forces of supply and demand—establishes the prices of goods and services and the amount and types of things that are produced. Profits—the result of charging more for goods and services than they cost to produce—are the incentive for capitalists to risk investing in factories and equipment. These profits can be accumulated as personal wealth or spent on consumption items, but the crux of capitalism is accumulation—the use of capital to create more capital through reinvestment (Heilbroner, 1982). Smith believed that the pursuit of individual self-interest—whether the goal is a fair profit or a good wage—produces the greatest good for the whole society, as long as the state allows the market forces of supply and demand to operate in an unrestricted way. This is the concept of *laissez-faire*.

Karl Marx's Capitalism

Capitalist economies initially developed through the exploitation of workers. The low wages and long hours demanded of workers during the Industrial Revolution of the eighteenth and nineteenth centuries yielded huge profits that were reinvested, making possible the rapid industrialization of Western Europe and North America. Writing during this period, Marx argued that capitalism contained the seeds of its own destruction. The course of economic development in capitalist systems contradicts Marx's predictions. Modern Marxists have elaborated on his ideas to present more accurate descriptions of modern capitalist systems, but here we are contrasting two distinct views of capitalism.

Contrary to Marx, workers in capitalist systems have not become poorer; rather, their standard of living has improved significantly. Labor unions and state regulation of the economy have protected workers and given them rights that Marx thought could come only from revolution. Marx did not foresee how capitalists would expand their use of machines to raise profits without increasing the exploitation of workers. The development of the mass media has enabled capitalists to stimulate consumer demand and then meet that demand through increased production, which in turn provides workers with more income to spend on goods and services. Moreover, capitalists have maintained their profits by extracting raw materials from foreign nations and by selling their products abroad; this result was predicted by Lenin, in his elaboration on Marx's analysis of capitalism.

SOCIALISM

Socialism is an economic system characterized by public property; the means of production and distribution are owned by the state rather than by private individuals and organizations. Economic decisions are in the hands of state planning boards rather than determined by the market forces of supply and demand, although socialist systems vary considerably in the extent to which the state controls the economy. In socialist societies, the government aims to influence the economic system so that wealth and income are distributed more equally.

The socialist economy of the Soviet Union that was created after the 1917 Communist Revolution now includes collective farms, industrial cooperatives, and consumer cooperatives. People still own private property such as homes and personal items, but the state limits the production of consumer goods, which are quite expensive. Soviet citizens cannot own capital that yields a profit from the labor of others; the state owns all means of production. National resources are invested in the military and in heavy industry; so far, the Soviet Union has not developed a high-technology industry. The state guarantees every citizen an education, a job, health care, and other basic necessities. Centralized state planning has not, however, guaranteed a sound Soviet economy. In recent years, it has fallen short of its agricultural goals; suffered declines in industrial productivity, output, and worker morale; and accumulated substantial debts (M. Goldman, 1982).

In the socialist democracies of Western Europe the means of production are often privately owned but regulated by the state; for instance, more than 90 per cent of the Swedish economy is in private hands. In welfare states such as Great Britain and Denmark, social services are provided by the government; health insurance, child care, and housing are subsidized by tax revenues and distributed so as to minimize inequality. Cross-national data support the goal of state planning; where there is direct state involvement in the economy, there tends to be less income inequality, because state planning facilitates full employment (Stack, 1978).

MIXED ECONOMIES

Capitalism and socialism are ideal types; most economic systems have some characteristics of each type. *Convergence theory* proposes that capitalist systems and socialist systems might gradually evolve toward a middle ground that includes certain common elements (Hollander, 1973; Meyer, Boli-Bennett, and Chase-Dunn, 1975). Such convergence is not inevitable, but industrialization does have similar effects on both capitalism and socialism (Form, 1979). In both kinds of economies, industrialization gives rise to increasingly large and bureaucratic organizations, and in turn state regulation sometimes emerges to restrain the economic power of these organizations. Industrial economies—whether capitalist or socialist—stress science, rational planning, and efficiency. Also, because industrial economies try to make the most productive use of workers, tasks are often assigned on the basis of skills rather than on the basis of ascribed traits such as sex or age. The use of differential rewards of money and prestige to motivate workers in an industrial economy can stimulate competition and materialism in socialist as well as in capitalist economies.

Modern Industrial Capitalism

Capitalism does not exist today in the pure form described by Adam Smith. Instead of a system of open competition, companies are more likely to try to eliminate or thwart their competitors. Growth often replaces profits as a corporate goal. The increasing domination of certain industries—such as the automobile and steel industries in the United States—by a small number of companies has led to more state regulation in capitalist systems. As we saw in Chapter 14, one function of the state is to pursue societal goals; when the economic system does not perform in ways that meet those goals, the state sometimes intervenes.

In some cases the state actually owns business enterprises; this is relatively rare in the United States—one exception is the United States Government Printing Office—but it is common in Western European democracies. What is common in capitalist systems is state regulation of the economy. Federal wage and price controls during and after World War II and again on a more limited basis in the 1970s violated Adam Smith's dictum that wages and prices should be determined by the market forces of supply and demand. Increased state planning of the American economy occurred during and after the Great Depression of the 1930s, when programs such as the Civilian Conservation Corps were designed to create jobs. In 1982, even the conservative President Reagan proposed a massive national effort to repair roads and bridges by adding a 5¢ tax to each gallon of gasoline; a law to do this was passed and took effect in 1983.

Another example of government intervention in the American economy is "welfare for corporations," the use of government-guaranteed loans or tax breaks to help ailing corporations that are important to the economy because of the jobs they provide or because of their production of military equipment. In recent years, the federal government has helped corporations such as Lockheed and Chrysler in this way. This would have shocked Adam Smith, for in his system of pure capitalism Lockheed and Chrysler would have been allowed to go out of business if they could not compete effectively in an unregulated market. Today few large corporations fully support the idea of laissez-faire. More often they seek the state's assistance, while complaining about burdensome federal regulations that limit their freedom to pursue profits.

"THE FISCAL CRISIS OF THE STATE." One way that the state regulates the economy is through monetary policy—the manipulation of the money supply and interest rates; in the United States, the Federal Reserve Board plays a major role in setting monetary policy. Congress is influential in determining fiscal policy—the sale of government bonds (Treasury bills) and the use of taxation to raise revenue. Beginning in the 1970s, rising rates of unemployment and inflation and a diminishing rate of economic growth reduced state revenues and produced what some have called "the fiscal crisis of the state" (O'Connor, 1973; Flacks and Turkel, 1978; Block, 1981; Kohl, 1981). The state has tried to maintain or increase its share of the GNP by tax increases and by deficit spending, but citizens have applied pressure to reduce government spending and taxes; Proposition 13 in California and Proposition $2\frac{1}{2}$ in Massachusetts are two examples of "taxpayer revolts."

President Reagan and his advisors have favored reduced government expenditures. One risk of such budget cuts is a loss of legitimacy for the state if people feel they are getting too few services and benefits for their taxes. The furor over proposed reductions in social security benefits is one example of this. Following the theory of "supply-side economics," Reagan has reduced both government spending and personal income taxes, a policy that threatens an even greater loss of revenue for the state. Coupled with less government regulation of business and more tax breaks for corporations,

"Reaganomics" is designed to provide incentives for personal savings and business investments. Theoretically, cuts in benefits for the poor would encourage them to work and cuts in taxes would stimulate harder work, at least by people with jobs (Bell, 1982).

How well has this economic approach worked? In the first year and a half there was no consistent increase in personal savings (Arenson, 1982). There was, however, a growth in the gap between people with higher incomes and the working poor, as well as a widening of the gap between states in the Northeast and Midwest (which suffered most from cuts in social services) and states in the West and Southwest (which gained most from increases in military spending) (Kurtz, 1982). Inflation rates decreased significantly in the first two years of the Reagan administration, but unemployment rates rose to their highest levels since the Great Depression.

Modern Industrial Socialism

Today, socialist systems also have many characteristics of a mixed economy. No industrial socialist economy has yet behaved as Marx predicted and evolved into a communist system. On the contrary, modern socialist systems have often introduced elements of capitalism. Incentives such as better housing and the use of cars are offered to attract people to political positions (Davies and Shaw, 1978). Leaders in China have begun to encourage private business in the cities and to allow farmers and factories more freedom to choose what to produce (Sterba, 1981; Wren, 1981). Stimulating production by the profit motive, self-interest, and competition would make the Chinese economy more like a capitalist system than a pure socialist economy. The head of China's State Planning Commission recognized this when he said that the government would "regulate the economy according to the pressures of supply and demand in the market, within the state plan. Where necessary, administrative measures should be used to control market forces so as to avoid economic anarchy" (cited in Sterba, 1981: 1).

Convergence?

Capitalist economics emphasize private property and a free market, and socialist systems stress public property and state planning. With time, the two systems have taken on some of the traits of each other as they have industrialized. Capitalist systems have been subjected to state planning, and market forces and the profit motive have been introduced into socialist economies. Another factor that could produce convergence is the growing economic interdependence of the nations of the world. This might result from the increasing power of multinational corporations or from extensive trade relations among countries. However, if different economic systems play different and unequal roles in the international economy—such as supplier of raw materials or exploiter of other nations' resources—divergence could be the result. Some sociologists see the convergence or divergence of economic systems to be the product of changes in the world's economy, rather than the result of any inevitable change of different national economies toward one kind of system (Meyer, Boli-Bennett, and Chase-Dunn, 1975).

Corporations in a Capitalist Economy

During the nineteenth century, the economic systems of Great Britain and the United States more or less fit Adam Smith's model of capitalism—individual entrepreneurs competing with each other in a relatively unregulated market. However, by the end of the nineteenth century, the large corporation had become the basic unit of American capitalism.

Corporations are organizations that are chartered by the state and have a legal existence apart from their directors, managers, stockholders, and lower-level employees. The part that each group plays in these formal organizations has been examined by both sociologists and economists. In the corporation, ownership is separated from control over decision making, with investors formally owning the corporation but directors and managers making the important decisions (Berle and Means, 1932, 1968). Directors have the power to dismiss and appoint managers, but management personnel have the technical expertise and the authority to control the firm's lower-level employees. These managers work to increase the corporation's profits and public reputation, and they try to stimulate corporate growth and show others that they are dynamic leaders who can contribute to the firm's success (Berg and Zald, 1978). Because managers are concerned with narrowly defined and prag-

matic matters, they sometimes "display a significant sense of unconnectedness with the world outside of business" (Cox, 1982: 383). Lower-level employees are less powerful than the managers, but they can impede the implementation of decisions made by others higher in the corporate bureaucracy.

THE CONCENTRATION OF CORPORATE WEALTH

The public can purchase shares in most American corporations, but the ownership of this stock is actually concentrated in a small proportion of the population. About 50 per cent of all corporate stock is held by 0.5 per cent of the total population, one of the most striking examples of inequality in the United States (U.S. Bureau of the Census, 1982: 449). In many large firms, a few people or organizations own substantial blocks of stock and the rest is owned by a large number of people who are rarely organized enough to influence corporate policy.

Inequality in the class structure of the United States is also a product of *interlocking directorates*, or boards of directors of different firms that include many of the same individuals (Allen, 1974; Mintz and Schwartz, 1981; Roy, 1983). When the same people sit on the boards of several companies in the same industry, they can influence wages and prices in that industry and thus control scarce resources. This is especially true when the industry is run by a small number of companies, because then a few firms or a few individuals can affect the market in significant ways. For instance, in 1973 and 1974 domestic oil companies restricted their output of petroleum products at the same time that foreign imports were curtailed, thereby increasing the price of gasoline and heating oil beyond the level that would have resulted from the Middle Eastern oil embargo alone (Zwerdling, 1979).

In industries dominated by a few firms, competition is kept to a minimum and there is no need to improve products or lower prices to attract buyers. For example, in the American automobile industry, great sums of money are spent to attract buyers by distinguishing basically similar cars from one another. The cost of the advertising to do this is passed on to customers in higher prices. The auto industry has long been criticized for "planned obsolescence," the production of cars that are built to last a short time and designed to go out of style quickly. As a result, there has been a steady erosion of sales of domestic cars by foreign car manufactur-

The auto industry has long been criticized for "planned obsolescence," the production of cars that are built to last a short time and quickly pass out of style.

ers, especially Japanese firms, that make cars that seem to many buyers to be of higher quality, lower price, and greater fuel efficiency (see SEL 16.1). Exhortations to "Buy American" will probably be ineffective in cutting into the 30 per cent of the market now controlled by foreign car manufacturers unless American producers can build cars that actually offer better value than they do now.

SOCIOLOGY AND EVERYDAY LIFE 16.1
The Japanese Corporation

In recent years, American corporations have frequently been compared to their Japanese counterparts, and the more efficient Japanese firms have tended to come out on top. For instance, one comparison of the average automobile manufacturing plant in the two countries found that the typical Japanese factory:

- *operated with a smaller work force;*
- *had a lower rate of absenteeism;*
- *built a small car in about half as many hours;*
- *made nearly twice as many parts per hour; and*
- *changed a die in five minutes rather than the four to six hours it took in American plants (Lohr, 1982a).*

In the following selection, Ezra F. Vogel compares Japanese and American firms in an effort to understand their differences.

After touring automobile assembly lines in both countries, a visitor observed, "The American factory seems almost like an armed camp. Foremen stand guard to make sure workers do not slack off. Workers grumble at foremen, and foremen are cross with workers. In the Japanese factory, employees seem to work even without the foremen watching. Workers do not appear angry at superiors and actually seem to hope their company succeeds."

Japanese workers' pride in their work and loyalty to their company are reflected in their capacity to produce goods that are not only competitive in price but reliable in quality. Some workers, especially younger workers in small plants, may be alienated from their company, but compared to Americans, they are absent less, strike less, and are willing to work overtime and refrain from using all their allotted vacation time without any immediate monetary benefit. The average Japanese laborer may accomplish no more that a loyal hard-working American counterpart in a comparable factory, but loyalty to the company is typically higher and hard work more common. Many an American businessman, after touring a Japanese company and inspecting figures on time lost from absenteeism and strikes, has expressed the wish that he had such a labor force. . . .

[The Japanese company has a] system of permanent employment whereby an ordinary employee remains in the firm from the time he first enters after leaving school until he retires, which in most firms averages about fifty-seven or fifty-eight. The firm is committed to the employee and provides a sense of belonging, personal support, welfare and retirement benefits, and increased salary and rank with age. Barring serious long-term depression, the employee expects that he will never be laid off, and even if the company were to disband or be absorbed by another company, he expects that a new job elsewhere will be arranged. . . .

Because an employee has job security and knows his salary will rise with seniority, he is willing to accept moderately low wages during his first few years in the company. Also, since retirement age is normally in the late fifties, salary increments can go up fairly rapidly without a company's worrying about having very high-paid elderly employees for many years. . . .

The seniority system in the company works much as in the bureaucracy. Although there are pay differentials later in the career based on performance and responsibility, these are small compared to those accounted for by seniority pay. Responsible executives consciously try to keep pay distinctions among those with the same seniority no larger than, and if anything smaller than, what most employees consider appropriate. New employees ordinarily receive precisely the same pay for the first several years in the company; when differentials begin to appear later, they are minor, having more psychological than monetary significance. Equal pay tends to dampen competition and strengthen camaraderie among peers during their early years. . . .

When asked to describe a Japanese company, most Japanese managers list as one characteristic the practice of "bottom up" rather than "top down." The lowly section, within its sphere, does not await executive orders but takes the initiatives. It identifies problems, gathers information, consults with relevant parts of the company, calls issues to the attention of higher officials, and draws up documents. Of course the section acts within the context of the wishes of higher officials and is in constant communication with them. . . . Section people take great pride in their work because of their initiatives and because they have a chance to develop their leadership and carry great weight within the company on matters relating to their sphere. . . .

For this system to work effectively, leading section personnel need to know and to identify with company purposes to a higher degree than persons in an American firm. They achieve this through long experience and years of discussion with others at all levels. Company aims are not canonized into documents but continue to fluctuate with the changing environment, and therefore section leaders must avoid being locked into a specific list of aims but rather adapt to overall opportunities for the company as a whole. Section leaders are sufficiently tuned to this overall thinking of the company for them to in fact achieve this, and they are given the leeway to act accordingly because higher officials know that section leaders are thoroughly committed to their company, where they will remain until retirement. . . .

The most important single criterion for assessing quality for regular term promotions is the capacity to work well with others. The person who rises more rapidly is not the one with the original ideas but the one who can cooperate with others in finding a conclusion satisfactory to everyone. Personal achievement cannot be separated from the capacity to work effectively in groups. . . . In an American company without a strong group spirit and without expectations of permanent employment, an employee might come to feel that the only significant reward is salary and position, which in his view ought to be finely tuned to match performance. In the Japanese view, this custom, like tipping which they still avoid, cheapens the sense of service and contributes to contentiousness. In a Japanese company with strong group spirit and a long time frame, the really significant reward, the thing an employee strives for, is the esteem of his colleagues.

Source: Reprinted by permission of the author and the publishers from *Japan as Number One: Lessons for America* by Ezra F. Vogel, Cambridge, Mass.: Harvard University Press, © 1979 by the President and Fellows of Harvard College. pp. 131–150 (excerpts).

The growth of American corporations has accelerated since the end of World War II (U.S. Bureau of the Census, 1982: 535). Sometimes corporations grow by absorbing competitors in the same industry, and other times companies in different industries merge into a single conglomerate. Large size gives firms a better opportunity to influence prices and prevent new firms from entering the market. Because they determine the rate at which profits are reinvested and control the development and use of new technology, large firms can also affect a nation's economic development (Kaysen, 1966).

CORPORATIONS AND THE POLITICAL SYSTEM

Modern corporations are more likely to establish close ties to the political system than to espouse Adam Smith's laissez-faire philosophy. Corporations want a stable economic system that offers incentives for investment, and they often solicit the help of public officials to establish those conditions. Today corporations also depend on the government for contracts, especially in the armaments industry. Firms that supply the government with vital goods and services sometimes turn to the state to bail them out with taxpayers' money or loan guarantees when they suffer financial setbacks due to poor decision making and inefficiency.

As we saw in Chapter 14, corporations exercise political influence by contributing to political action committees (PACs) that support candidates who are sympathetic to corporate goals. Firms also employ lobbyists to change laws and regulations and to gain tax concessions from Congress. One lobbying tactic often used at the state and local level is the threat to relocate a factory to another state or even to another country unless the corporation's demands are met. Relocation of industry disrupts the local community, increases unemployment rates, and decreases tax revenue (Bluestone and Harrison, 1982).

One consequence of recent cuts in federal and state aid for cities, social service agencies, cultural organizations, and other programs has been an increased pressure on business firms to support these activities. In 1981 and 1982, the annual philanthropic contributions of American corporations totalled about $3 billion. According to a 1982 estimate, between 1982 and 1985 the nation's 300,000 nonprofit organizations will lose an estimated $33 billion in federal assistance, an amount that private industry cannot easily make up

(Teltsch, 1982). One important result of federal cuts is that decisions about which private programs will be funded have been shifted from the public sector of government to the private sector of business (Freedman, 1982).

MULTINATIONAL CORPORATIONS

A *multinational corporation* is a firm based in one nation that buys, produces, and sells goods and services in other nations. These firms often have large annual incomes and substantial assets, and foreign business accounts for a significant proportion of their total sales (Barnet and Müller, 1974; Evans, 1981). Today, multinational corporations account for at least one-fourth of the total production of the world's economy, and by the year 2000 that proportion might be as much as one half (Heilbroner, 1976). Therefore, these corporations have, and will continue to have, a strong influence on the lives of the world's citizens. By investing in foreign economies, these firms are able to use cheap domestic labor and raw materials to produce goods that are sold in that country or exported for sale elsewhere. This has caused plants to relocate in foreign countries where manufacturing costs are lower; this "disinvestment" has hurt a number of American communities (Bluestone and Harrison, 1982).

Multinational corporations also threaten the state in those societies in which they operate because these firms are often wealthier than the state itself. For example, about 130 different countries have a national budget less than the annual sales revenues of General Motors. Indeed, about half of the world's largest economic units are not nations, but multinational corporations. Multinational firms can contribute to economic development in the short run, but they often create technical dependence that adversely affects economic development in the long run (Bornschier and Hoby, 1981). Foreign investment can undermine the local economy if the high wages paid by a multinational corporation increase local wages beyond what domestic firms can afford to pay. In addition, foreign investment in industrializing societies produces a larger income gap between the poor and those higher in the stratification system (Bornschier, Chase-Dunn, and Rubinson, 1978; Bornschier and Ballmer-Cao, 1979; Evans and Timberlake, 1980).

Even though the executives of multinational corporations are not elected by the citizens of the countries in which they operate, they exercise great power nonetheless by bribing officials, threatening to withdraw business if favors are not granted, interfering in local elections, and even assassinating officials who oppose them. The leaders of multinational corporations sometimes see their organizations as sovereign powers that must overcome the impediment of state sovereignty to maximize profits and to expand into new markets (Kindleberger, 1969; Barnet and Müller, 1974; Fatemi, Williams, and de Saint-Phalle, 1976). The wealth of multinational corporations is now growing at about twice the rate at which the world's GNP is growing, a fact that suggests that wealth and power are increasingly being concentrated in a small number of firms that operate in many nations.

Work in an Industrial Economy

The nature of work undergoes distinct changes during industrialization and the shift to a postindustrial economy. As technology becomes more complex, occupations become more specialized, and specialization requires higher levels of education and training. Specialization can cause worker dissatisfaction, which may lead to the organization of labor unions to raise wages, increase prestige, and improve working conditions. Moreover, the mass media in industrial society contribute to worker discontent by presenting a limited perspective on the kinds of jobs that people do (see SEL 16.2).

SOCIOLOGY AND EVERYDAY LIFE   16.2
Work and the Mass Media

In this passage, Pauline Kael, widely regarded as one of the best contemporary American film critics, examines the way that work is portrayed in the movies and on television.

Movies set up these glamorized occupations. When people find they are waitresses, they feel degraded. No kid says I want to be a waiter, I want to run a cleaning establishment. There is a tendency in movies to degrade people if they don't have white-collar professions. So people form a low self-image of themselves, because their lives can never match the way Americans live—on the screen.

I consider myself one of the lucky ones because I really enjoy what I do. I love my occupation. But I've spent most of my life working at jobs I hated. I've worked at boring office jobs. I never felt they were demeaning, but they exhausted my energy and spirit. I do think most people work at jobs that mechanize them and depersonalize them.

The occasional satisfaction in work is never shown on the screen, say, of the actor or the writer. The people doing drudge jobs enjoy these others because they think they make a lot of money. What they should envy them for is that they take pleasure in their work. Society plays that down. I think enormous harm has been done by the television commercial telling ghetto children they should go to school because their earning capacity would be higher.

They never suggest that if you're educated you may go into fields where your work is satisfying, where you may be useful, where you can really do something that can help other people.

When I worked at drudge jobs to support the family I used to have headaches all the time, feeling rotten at the end of the day. I don't think I've taken an aspirin or a pill in the last twenty years. The one thing that disturbs me on television is the housewife, who's always in need of a headache remedy from tension and strain. This is an incredible image of the American woman. Something terrible must be going on inside her if she's in that shape. Of course, she's become a compulsive maniac about scrubbing and polishing and cleaning—in that commercial.

Housewives in the movies and on television are mindless. Now it takes a lot of intelligence to handle children and it's a fascinating process watching kids grow up. Being involved with kids may be much more creative than what their husbands do at drudge jobs.

To show accurate pictures, you're going to outrage industry. In the news recently we've learned of the closing of industrial plants—and the men, who've worked for twenty years, losing out on their pensions. Are you going to see this in a movie? It's going to have to be a very tough muckraking film maker to show us how industry discards people. Are you going to have a movie that shows us how stewardesses are discarded at a certain age? And violate the beautiful pact that the airlines have with the movie companies, where they jointly advertise one another?

We now have conglomerate ownership of the movie industry. Are they going to show us how these industries really dehumanize their workers?* Muckraking was possible when the movie companies were independent of big industry. Now that Gulf & Western, AVCA, Trans-America, these people own the movie compa-

nies, this is very tough. Are you going to do muckraking about the record industry, when the record from the movie grosses more than the film itself?

It's a long time since we've had a movie about a strike, isn't it? You get something about the Molly Maguires, which is set in the past, but you don't see how the working relationship is now. I'd be interested in seeing a film on Lordstown.

*Of course, from time to time there have been films that deal with the problems of workers. Recent examples include *Norma Rae* and *9 to 5.*

Source: From *Working: People Talk About What They Do All Day and How They Feel About What They Do,* by Studs Terkel. © 1972, 1974 by Studs Terkel. Reprinted by permission of Pantheon Books, a Division of Random House, Inc., pp. 155–156.

OCCUPATIONAL SPECIALIZATION

For many people, their jobs are a primary source of identity. The importance of work to an individual's sense of self is suggested by the fact that most workers say they would continue to work even if they had enough money to support themselves for the rest of their lives (Morse and Weiss, 1955; Tauskey, 1969). Some people who say this claim that they do not know what else they would do with their time, but most who say they would continue to work give more positive reasons: the challenge of the job, social contacts at work, the need for a source of identity, and the importance of remaining active. One indication of the high value placed on work in modern societies is the widely held view that people who are content to live either on accumulated wealth or on welfare assistance are immoral, lazy, or unmotivated.

In industrial economies, acquired skills are the most important basis of occupational specialization. However, credentialism—the requirement that a worker have experience or education that is not really needed for performance of a job—can create employee dissatisfaction. Harry Braverman (1974) claims that some jobs have been improperly labeled "skilled" and that work now requires fewer skills than it did in the past. White-collar jobs are generally considered to have higher prestige than blue-collar jobs, but some white-collar occupations such as file clerk or computer operator actually require less skill than some blue-collar occupations such as plumber or electrician. It therefore may be unfounded to assume that an increase in white-

collar jobs with industrialization represents an upgrading of work. Also, farm work that is often treated as relatively unskilled blue-collar work has in fact become increasingly mechanized and technical, and is probably a more skilled occupation than some white-collar jobs.

ALIENATION AND JOB SATISFACTION

For Karl Marx (1844, 1961), industrial capitalism is an inevitable source of worker dissatisfaction. Marx saw capitalism as a system of economic exchange in which workers are treated as commodities that can be bought and sold. *Alienation* is a consequence of the separation of workers from the products they make; the fruits of their labor are taken from them and sold for profit by capitalists, and the workers are paid only part of the total value they have created. Because they do not control the products of their labor and because their work is highly specialized and fragmented, workers in a capitalist system derive no real satisfaction from their jobs, in Marx's view. Their work does not give them a sense of mastery, but rather forces them to adapt passively to the economic system of which they are part. Jobs are alienating because those who do them are not allowed to fulfill their human potential (Marx, 1844, 1961; Giddens, 1971; Bell, 1972; Seeman, 1975).

In industrial economies, technology influences the division of labor and along with it a variety of job characteristics such as the repetitiveness and the pace of work; these in turn affect workers' behavior and job satisfaction (Blauner, 1964; Shepard, 1977). Assembly lines on which each worker performs a small task toward the completion of a product such as a car cause a sense of powerlessness and meaninglessness and a feeling that each individual contributes little to the overall productive process. Automated plants isolate workers from each other because noise and the fast pace of the work make interaction difficult and inhibit the formation of work groups (Blauner, 1964). Working with machines rather than with other people can also be dehumanizing, as one spot-welder on a Ford assembly line observes:

You really begin to wonder. What price do they put on me? Look at the price they put on the machine. If that machine breaks down, there's somebody out there to fix it right away. If I break down, I'm just pushed over to the other side till another man takes my place. The only thing they have on their mind is to keep that line running (cited in Terkel, 1974: 160–161).

Worker alienation is a reality in industrial economies, but it might be less a result of capitalism, as Marx suggested, than a result of industrialization itself. Moreover, we have no evidence that searching the forests for game or plowing the fields in a preindustrial society is any less alienating than factory work.

Job Satisfaction in the United States

Although job dissatisfaction among American workers seems to have increased slightly in recent years, most surveys find that the overall level of job satisfaction is quite high (Ritzer, 1977; Quinn and Staines, 1979; Staines and Quinn, 1979; Katzell, 1979; Converse et al., 1980). One 1980 survey found that 84 per cent of all workers were satisfied with their jobs (U.S. Bureau of the Census, 1981: 387). However, fewer blue-collar workers than white-collar workers would enter the same line of work if they had it to do over again (*Work in America*, 1973: 15–16; Gruenberg, 1980).

Job satisfaction seems to be related more to working conditions than to the worker's social background or psychological makeup. Evidence that job satisfaction is more closely associated with basic features of the job itself—such as the chance to learn and use new skills or the opportunity to mix with other workers—than with extrinsic rewards such as wages or job security suggests that alienation and dissatisfaction might be reduced by enriching jobs and by altering working conditions (Gruenberg, 1980; Converse et al., 1980).

Workers sometimes combat job dissatisfaction by trying to "beat the system"; they may steal from the company, subvert rules against interacting with other workers, or limit their output (Chinoy, 1955; Roy, 1954, 1959–1960; Horning, 1970; Jaspan, 1974). Workers in low-prestige jobs sometimes emphasize the good aspects of their jobs—such as security, high pay, flexible hours, or fringe benefits—or try to make relatively meaningless work more important by creating new job titles or by claiming that their work is critical to meeting organizational goals.

Some efforts have been made to change working conditions in order to reduce alienation and dissatisfaction (*Work in America*, 1973; Rothschild-Whitt, 1981; Lindenfeld and Rothschild-Whitt, 1982). Many of these changes have been limited to small work groups rather than encompassing whole factories or industries. In some cases, workers have been given or have bought stock in the company, and in other situations they have sat on boards of directors or consulted with managers about changes in the company. Some work groups have been given more autonomy in working on a product at different stages of the manufacturing process or in maintaining the area where they work. Giving work groups more autonomy sometimes means giving them new information that is needed to reach decisions on their own, and it may also mean giving workers more supervisory powers. Workers become more satisfied with their jobs if they have been rewarded for learning and doing a variety of tasks; encouraging them to become generalists rather than specialists increases their flexibility and makes their jobs more interesting. Job satisfaction can also be enhanced by allowing workplace rules, such as the timing of coffee breaks, to evolve from the experiences of employees rather than imposing those rules arbitrarily on workers. These changes in working conditions have had the following effects:

- higher profits and sales
- higher output
- the need for fewer levels of management
- less waste of raw materials
- fewer plant shutdowns
- fewer job complaints
- more worker involvement in the outside community (*Work in America*, 1973; Simmons and Mares, 1982).

These reforms have not yet been applied extensively in the United States, but they do show that job dissatisfaction can be reduced as productivity is being enhanced.

UNIONIZATION

One response of workers to the low wages, dangerous working conditions, and long hours they experienced during the early years of industrialization was to form labor unions that demanded change. The first unions were formed in Great Britain in the early nineteenth century; unions developed in the United States later in that century. Unions have been most effective in gaining concessions during times when the economy is flourishing, and they have been less successful in periods of economic decline.

During the 1970s, the percentage of American workers in the private sector who belonged to unions declined somewhat, but the proportion of workers in the public sector who joined labor unions increased significantly (Raskin, 1981). White-collar workers such as teachers and government workers have unionized in recent years, but other high-prestige jobs in the growing tertiary sector have been harder to organize. Female officeworkers have proved difficult to organize, but lately there has been an increase in the percentage of all union members who are women. There has also been some increase in the unionization of minority

groups in recent years, although data from 1947 to 1974 show that unions did not have much success in reducing income inequality between blacks and whites (Beck, 1980).

Labor unions engage in *collective bargaining*—a peaceful form of conflict in which representatives of a union and representatives of management negotiate wages, hours, working conditions, and fringe benefits such as health insurance and retirement pensions. From time to time employees hold strikes, during which they refuse to work, but these are more carefully planned and less violent today than they were earlier in the century.

Unions are often led by an elite that tries to maintain its own power within the organization while still accomplishing the goals of the membership. Some union leaders—the late George Meany was a prime example—have grown so powerful that many consider them to be part of the ruling class. Unions and their leaders are less antagonistic toward employers today than they once were, often sharing with management the desire for economic prosperity so that they can improve wages and working conditions. In the early 1980s, the United Auto Workers actually gave up increases in wages and benefits to keep ailing car manufactur-

Strikes are one tactic that unions use to get management to meet their demands. Here a group of white-collar workers demonstrate at a rally in Boston.

ers from bankruptcy. Critics contend that the union accepted management's definition of corporate difficulties too readily, did not demand sufficient concessions, and weakened its bargaining power through these "givebacks." Others suggest, however, that the companies made concessions to the union in the form of more participation in corporate decision making, greater access to information about the firm, job security, and guarantees not to close plants (Serrin, 1982a).

UNEMPLOYMENT

In every industrial economy some workers are out of work at any given time. An unemployment rate of 2 or 3 per cent of the labor force is often considered full employment, because there are always some people who are switching jobs and others who have not yet found jobs after completing their educations. During the Great Depression the unemployment rate reached 25 per cent. Since the end of World War II the rate has fluctuated between about 3.5 per cent and 10.8 per cent, the latter being the rate in late 1982 and early 1983.

Figure 16.1 shows changes in the unemployment rate between 1925 and 1982.

Figure 16.1 is based on unemployment rates that actually conceal much higher rates for certain categories of people. For instance, black teenagers have had unemployment rates about five times as high as the whole population in recent years. Blue-collar workers and young workers also have unemployment rates that are higher than average (Robbins, 1982). In addition, people who abandon the search for a job are not counted as unemployed; these "discouraged workers" are calculated by the Bureau of Labor Statistics but are not included among the unemployed—a category that includes only those people who did not work at all in the week before being questioned but had tried to find work in the previous four weeks (S. King, 1982). Part-time employees who want to work full time are also not counted as unemployed.

Unemployment has a multitude of social costs. Interaction with friends and relatives can be embarrassing and awkward for the unemployed person because of the high value that Americans place on work. The unemployed are often bored at having nothing productive to do with their time,

FIGURE 16.1
Unemployment Rates in the United States, 1925-1982

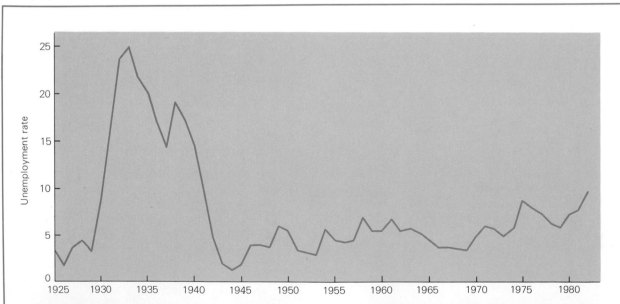

Source: U.S. Bureau of the Census, *Historical Statistics of the United States: Colonial Times to 1970*, Part 1. Washington, D.C.: U.S. Government Printing Office, 1975, p. 135; U.S. Bureau of the Census, *Statistical Abstract of the United States*, 1982-83. Washington, D.C.: U.S. Government Printing Office, 1982, p. 375.

for work structures the day and provides opportunities for social contacts. Unemployment is also linked to high rates of suicide, homicide, alcoholism, child abuse, marital discord, mental disorders, and physical disease. Because health insurance in the United States is usually tied to a job, the unemployed commonly lack the money to have these problems treated. These consequences of unemployment can lead the unemployed to accept low-paying jobs for which they are overqualified, and this can impede career development over the long run (Brody, 1982b; Pines, 1982).

Figure 16.1 shows that unemployment rates in the United states were higher in the 1970s and the early 1980s than they were in the 1960s. One reason is that an increased number of people began to enter the job market in the late 1960s as a result of the post-World War II "baby boom" (see Chapter 17). Later in the 1980s the number of young people entering the labor force will decline, because of a decline in birth rates that began in the early 1960s; this should cause unemployment rates to drop to somewhat lower levels (Linden, 1982). Another factor contributing to the recent increase in unemployment rates is the increased number of women who have sought full-time work in recent years. In 1950, only 31.4 per cent of all women were in the labor force, but by 1981 that figure had reached 52.1 per cent. During this period, there was a large increase in the number of women looking for work, as well as an increase in the size of the labor force due to changes in the age structure.

Consumption and Leisure

Neither the market forces of capitalism nor the state-planned economy of socialism can always guarantee consumers an adequate supply of goods and services at affordable prices. Price increases that exceed increases in income can reduce the standard of living for consumers. In capitalist systems, dissatisfied consumers have organized to ensure the quality and safety of the goods and services they buy. Another significant long-term change in the consumption patterns of industrial economies has been an increase in expenditures for leisure activities.

INFLATION

Inflation is a continuing increase in the general level of prices for goods and services. Sometimes prices rise because wages increase faster than worker pro-ductivity. The demand for goods and services might then exceed the goods and services that are available, and this boosts prices. Increases in the cost of natural resources also cause prices to rise; for instance, the Arab oil boycott of 1973 raised prices for both industrial producers and individual consumers. Other factors such as the failure to raise taxes to pay for the Vietnam War and a wheat shortage caused by a large grain sale to the Soviet Union also led to dramatic increases in prices in the United States during the 1970s. In addition, lobbying by different groups seeking to reduce their own economic insecurity contributed to inflation. Price supports for farmers, increased social security benefits for the elderly, and an increased minimum wage all fueled inflation in the 1970s (Thurow, 1980).

During the 1950s, the average rate of inflation in the United States was 2.2 per cent, and in the 1960s the average rate was 2.5 per cent. During the 1970s, however, the average annual rate of inflation was 7.1 per cent. The rate reached 13.5 per cent in 1980, and then dropped to 10.4 per cent in 1981 and 6.1 per cent in 1982 (Mehegan, 1981; U.S. Bureau of the Census, 1982: 461). Even the high rates of the late 1970s and early 1980s are relatively low compared to those experienced by some nations. For instance, both Israel and Brazil have recently suffered 100 per cent inflation rates in a single year, meaning that prices doubled in a mere twelve months; and in Argentina prices tripled in 1982. Even more dramatically, inflation in post-World War I Germany was so rampant that by 1923 a postage stamp cost 40 billion marks, the face value of all property in the country before the war. Inflation and the more general collapse of the German economy paved the way for Hitler's rise to power (Fergusson, 1975; Mehegan, 1981).

The Consequences of Inflation

Inflation has far-reaching effects. People might buy goods in the present rather than wait until the future when prices will be higher. This causes more dollars to compete for goods and services in the present, and contributes to additional price increases. Inflation also encourages buying on credit because money that is repaid in the future is worth less than money spent in the present.

People might also be reluctant to save money if they think that their money will lose value over time; money earning 5 per cent in a savings account actually declines in value when the inflation rate exceeds 5 per cent. The failure to save reduces the funds available to banks for home mortgages and business loans, and thereby raises the interest rates charged for loans.

Not everyone is hurt in the same way by inflation. When the price of a product rises faster than people's incomes, those who buy the more expensive product will find that the real value of their incomes has decreased, but those who sell the product will find that their real incomes have risen. Because some lose and others gain from inflation, one of its effects can be to redistribute real income—the actual goods and services that people can buy with their money (Thurow, 1980; Vidich, 1980). The distributional effects of inflation in the United States since 1970 have been debated. Some evidence indicates that the poor have suffered the most from inflation (Caplovitz, 1979). However, other evidence suggests that inflation has not hurt any one group more than others. Each fifth of the American population, based on annual money income, earned about the same percentage of the total income in 1981 as in 1970 (U.S. Bureau of the Census, 1982: 435). Cost-of-living increases were about the same for different social classes during the 1970s. Blacks, the elderly, farmers, and the young did not seem to lose ground relative to other groups as a result of inflation, at least in the 1970s (Thurow, 1980). However, people who live on fixed incomes such as social security benefits, pensions, and savings do suffer when their benefits and incomes are not adjusted upward. Inflation and a changing age structure that includes more elderly people have severely strained the social security system, necessitating increased payroll deductions over time and leading to reforms in the system in 1983.

CONSUMERISM

In 1936, Consumers Union, the publisher of *Consumer Reports,* was formed to protect the consuming public. However, it was the 1960s that gave birth to modern *consumerism*—an organized moral, economic, and legal effort to improve the lot of people who buy and use goods and services (Evans, 1980b). One landmark was President John F. Kennedy's 1962 statement that it was the consumer's right to be safe, to be informed, to choose, and to be heard. More recently, this "bill of rights" has been expanded to include the right to have claims settled fairly and the right to have a physical environment that maximizes the quality of life (Aaker and Day, 1982). Another landmark in the development of the consumer movement was the

publication in 1965 of *Unsafe at Any Speed,* Ralph Nader's critical study of car safety. This and subsequent reports by Nader's researchers have received extensive media coverage and have shown how organized action can check abuses by private industry.

What are the sources of the consumer movement? As consumers in a postindustrial society, we are faced with a myriad of goods and services from which to choose. The growth of bureaucracy has depersonalized the producers and distributors of these goods and services, and consumerism has arisen as an effort to focus responsibility and communicate with industry. In addition, advertising in which producers "puff their wares" has heightened expectations about how products should perform; the dissatisfaction that results when these goods fail to measure up to advertising claims is an underlying reason for the consumer movement. The widely held perception that real income has been eroded substantially by inflation over the years might be another source of consumers' demands for more value for their money. Moreover, certain disadvantaged groups—such as the poor, the elderly, and the very young—face special problems as consumers and need legal protection from abuses by industry (Aaker and Day, 1982).

The consumer movement seemed to have peaked in intensity in the late 1970s, but a 1983 poll found public concern with consumer issues to be on the rise (Hinds, 1983). Federal, state, and municipal agencies now exist to help consumers. The mass media educate the public; television stations often have consumer specialists, and some advertising even takes an educational approach. In response to consumer pressures, more and more businesses have established complaint procedures, quality-control measures, product information, and sometimes even in-house consumer advocates. In addition, some business trade associations have developed methods of self-regulation—although these associations are primarily established to serve the interests of their members (Evans, 1980a).

Pressure from consumers has brought about the mandatory installation of seat belts in cars, the recall and repair of unsafe cars at the manufacturer's expense, safer toys and clothing for children, limitations on cigarette advertising, truth-in-lending laws, and pricing information to help shoppers buy more rationally in grocery stores. Consumers have also extended their influence to issues such as environmental pollution and nuclear power. Critics of consumerism note, however, that the movement has been a mixed blessing; they point to the costly regulations imposed on business, the large sums of money spent by business in lobbying against what it sees as excessive consumer demands, and conflicts among industry, the government, and consumers (Evans, 1980a).

The consumer movement has also affected the socialization process. Today, consumers are more skeptical and less willing to accept the claims made for goods and services than they once were. They increasingly believe that they can influence producers and advertisers, and they have become a force that restrains industry in ways not foreseen by Adam Smith more than two centuries ago. Smith felt that competition among buyers would ensure quality and keep prices low; today cooperation among buyers performs those functions.

LEISURE

In preindustrial societies, work is often integrated with other daily activities; only when remunerated work develops does the idea of leisure emerge. In industrial societies, leisure, or free-time activities, often take place outside the home. Specialized settings such as movie theaters, night clubs, athletic clubs, and restaurants separate leisure activity from the home, even though many popular activities such as television viewing and visiting with friends and relatives occur at home (Cheek and Burch, 1976).

As technology has increased productivity and labor unions have won their demands for shorter work hours, workers have gained more free time (Dumazedier, 1974). The average hours worked each week by Americans have fallen from about 62 in 1890 to about 35 in 1982 (Kreps and Spengler, 1966; U.S. Bureau of the Census, 1982: 394). Hours have also become more flexible; for instance, some federal agencies permit their employees to choose their own hours as long as they are on the job during a certain period in the middle of the day. These and other changes, such as longer life expectancy, have increased the total amount of time available for leisure activities.

---

and the chairman of Atari sees a time in the near future when half of all homes will have video game systems. For many people, video games have become an even more important use for their television sets than the reception of network programs. Videodisks and cable television are other developments that have extended the use of a television technology that became a source of leisure activity just a few decades ago.

Listening to music is another leisure activity that has undergone major changes recently. In 1982, the sale of prerecorded cassettes surpassed the sale of disks for the first time; the year before, records outsold tapes by a ratio of five to three. Cassettes were invented in the late 1960s as a dictating device, but three major changes in the last few years have increased the sale of taped music. One was the introduction in 1979 of the Walkman, a portable cassette player. Another was the increased use of cassettes in car stereo systems at about the same time. The third change was a marked improvement in the sound quality of cassettes. These cassettes had a flexibility that disks did not have; they could be used in the home, in the car, and on foot.

In recent years some of these leisure industries have become integrated with each other. Record stores have begun to sell home video game cartridges. Manufacturers compete for licenses to make home video games that are based on successful movies such as *E.T., Raiders of the Lost Ark,* and *Return of the Jedi.* Some film companies have entered the arcade and home video game markets; for example, Walt Disney Productions now markets the arcade game TRON, which is based on the movie of the same name. Moreover, the soundtracks of successful films are often a source of revenue for both the movie business and the record industry. One unusual combination of leisure industries is Coleco, a company that for years built and sold swimming pools but turned to home video games in 1982.

Sources: Based on John Culhane, "Special Effects Are Revolutionizing Film," *The New York Times,* July 4, 1982, pp. H1, H13; Hans Fantel, "An Era Ends as Cassettes Surpass Disks in Popularity," *The New York Times,* November 21, 1982, pp. 19, 23; and Aljean Harmetz, "Home Video Games Nearly as Profitable as Movie Business," *The New York Times,* October 4, 1982, pp. A1, C15.

The technology of industrial and postindustrial societies has changed the form of leisure activities, as we can see from SEL 16.3. Television broadcasts athletic events and devotes about five minutes of its local news programs to the day's sports activities. Leisure activities also receive much coverage in newspaper sports pages, movie and theater sections, and book reviews. Many "how-to" books are published each year for the leisure market, and other books are read during free time. Magazines are directed at audiences interested in specific leisure pursuits such as hunting, running, television viewing, and listening to music; and those magazines not specializing in a leisure activity are read during leisure time.

The five leisure activities that Americans most often engage in are all passive: eating, watching television, listening to the radio, reading books, and listening to music at home. Smaller proportions engage in activities such as fixing up the home, dancing, hiking, fishing, hunting, and boating (ABC News–Harris Survey, 1979). Leisure pursuits vary with social characteristics such as income, education, ethnicity, and region of the country. For example, wealthier and better-educated people are more likely to attend museums, classical music concerts, the theater, the opera, and the ballet. Lower-income and less-educated people are more likely to spend their time watching television or visiting friends and relatives (Cheek and Burch, 1976; U.S. Bureau of the Census, 1980: 537–540).

Sociologists have paid more attention to work than to leisure, but in recent years they have started to examine the ways that people use their free time (Cheek and Burch, 1976; John Wilson, 1980). Since the early 1960s, the idea of leisure education or leisure counseling has developed, based on the idea that people need to learn how to use opportunities for leisure, how to vary their off-the-job activities, and how to express themselves and develop their potential (Epperson, Witt, and Hitzhusen, 1977). These questions, and the difficult one of how to integrate work with leisure, will become even more important in the future as technological advances provide more free time for workers.

Modern technology has changed the forms of leisure activity. The people pictured here are using a "running machine" in order to do some exercise.

Summary

The economic system determines which goods and services are produced and how they are distributed among the members of society. In all cultures, property norms define the rights and obligations attached to scarce and valued things. Economic exchange is the process by which valuable goods and services are given and received by individuals and organizations. Economic exchange takes the forms of gift exchange, barter, money exchange, and financial transactions. We learn these and other aspects of the economic system through economic socialization by our parents, teachers, peers, and the mass media.

Entire societies can be classified by their primary mode of subsistence. Level of technological development determines what kind of a society people will live in: hunting–gathering, pastoral, horticultural, agrarian, industrial, or postindustrial. Industrial societies employ mechanical sources of energy rather than human and animal sources. In postindustrial societies such as the contemporary United States, a large proportion of the workers are employed in the tertiary or service sector and a small proportion work in the primary sector. Automation is characteristic of both industrial and postindustrial societies, and computerization becomes an important force in postindustrial societies.

Capitalism is an economic system based on private ownership of the means of production and the market forces of supply and demand. In a capitalist economy, competition theoretically produces fair profits, reasonable prices, and good wages. In contrast, in socialist economic systems the means of production are publicly owned and the state regulates the economy to achieve greater equality of income. Most economic systems include characteristics of both capitalism and socialism; most economies are controlled by the government to some degree, and most rely to some extent on the forces of supply and demand to set prices and wages. The growing interdependence of the world's economic systems might lead to further convergence of capitalist and socialist societies.

Corporations are enterprises that are chartered by the state and that have a legal existence apart from their directors, managers, stockholders, and lower-level employees. The ownership of corporations is separated from control over their daily functioning; control is by boards of directors and managers rather than by the stockholders who own the corporation. Corporate wealth in the United States is highly concentrated; a small proportion of the population owns most corporate stock. The concentration of corporate wealth is also a result of interlocking directorates, boards of directors of different companies that include the same individuals. Multinational corporations—organizations that have branches in different countries—account for a large and growing proportion of the world's total production. In many foreign nations, these multinational corporations wield great influence over the local economic and political systems by paying high wages, bribing officials, and interfering in domestic politics.

With industrialization, occupations become more specialized, as distinct jobs develop and technology becomes more complex, although some sociologists doubt that work has actually become more skilled with time. Industrial economies—and, according to Marx, particularly capitalist ones—cause alienation among workers. This includes a sense of being separated from the product of one's labor, self-estrangement, a lack of fulfillment, a sense of powerlessness, and isolation from other workers. Today most American workers seem to be relatively satisfied with their jobs, but satisfaction does vary with working conditions. Workers have formed labor unions to improve their working conditions. In industrial economies, some workers are always looking for work but unable to find it; unemployment creates various problems for them.

Consumers in many industrial societies confront inflation, the continuing increase in the general level of prices for goods and services. Inflation has important social consequences; it leads to spending in the present rather than to saving, and it encourages buying on credit. Inflation can redistribute income among social groups, especially those who live on fixed incomes that are not adjusted to price increases. Consumerism is an organized effort to counteract the power of private industry and improve the situation of people who buy and use goods and services. One area of consumer spending is leisure pursuits. Modern technology has changed the forms of leisure activity. Today most Americans spend their free time in relatively passive activities such as watching television, listening to music, and reading.

Important Terms

AGRARIAN SOCIETY (370)
ALIENATION (381)
AUTOMATION (370)
CAPITALISM (373)
COLLECTIVE BARGAINING (383)
CONSUMERISM (386)
CONVERGENCE THEORY (374)
CORPORATION (376)
ECONOMIC EXCHANGE (368)
ECONOMIC SOCIALIZATION (368)
ECONOMIC SYSTEM (367)
GROSS NATIONAL PRODUCT (GNP) (371)
HORTICULTURAL SOCIETY (370)
HUNTING–GATHERING SOCIETY (369)
INDUSTRIAL SOCIETY (370)
INDUSTRIALIZATION (370)
INFLATION (385)
INTERLOCKING DIRECTORATE (376)
LAISSEZ-FAIRE (373)
MULTINATIONAL CORPORATION (379)
PASTORAL SOCIETY (370)
POSTINDUSTRIAL SOCIETY (371)

Suggested Readings

David A. Aaker and George S. Day, eds. *Consumerism: Search for the Consumer Interest,* 4th ed. New York: Free Press, 1982. A comprehensive collection of articles on the consumer movement.

Robert Blauner. *Alienation and Freedom: The Factory Worker and His Factory.* Chicago: University of Chicago Press, 1964. A major study of job dissatisfaction and alienation in different industries.

Harry Braverman. *Labor and Monopoly Capital: The Degradation of Work in the Twentieth Century.* New York:

Monthly Review Press, 1974. A landmark study of the working class, occupations, and factory conditions in a modern capitalist economy.

Neil H. Cheek, Jr., and William R. Burch, Jr. *The Social Organization of Leisure in Human Society*. New York: Harper & Row, 1976. A thorough examination of theory and research on what people do in their free time.

Clark Kerr and Jerome M. Rosow, eds. *Work in America: The Decade Ahead*. New York: Van Nostrand Reinhold, 1979. A wide-ranging collection of papers on impending changes in the world of work.

Gerhard Lenski and Jean Lenski. *Human Societies,* 4th ed. New York: McGraw-Hill, 1982. An influential examination of technology and society that classifies economic systems by their primary mode of subsistence.

Neil J. Smelser. *The Sociology of Economic Life,* 2nd ed. Englewood Cliffs, N.J.: Prentice-Hall, 1976. A brief introduction to the sociological perspective on the economic system.

Studs Terkel. *Working: People Talk about What They Do All Day and How They Feel about What They Do*. New York: Pantheon, 1974. A series of first-hand accounts of American workers talking about their jobs.

Alvin Toffler. *The Third Wave*. New York: Morrow, 1980. A popular and controversial examination of the future of Western society.

part V
PROCESSES
OF SOCIAL CHANGE

The last four chapters deal with broad processes of social change that alter social institutions and daily life in myriad ways.

In Chapter 17, which deals with population and the ecosystem, we introduce three processes that affect population structure: fertility, mortality, and migration. We show how an imbalance among these elements can lead to overpopulation. Next we examine human population in the broader context of the ecosystem, the network of all living and nonliving things.

Chapter 18 deals with urbanization and city life. Population movement from small towns and rural areas to larger communities has sparked some of the greatest social change of the twentieth century. After a brief discussion of cities in preindustrial and developing societies, this chapter focuses on the modern metropolis. Different models of the structure of cities are compared. Three theoretical perspectives that attempt to explain the quality of life in the city are examined. Finally, we look at efforts to deal with urban decline.

Another source of social change is collective behavior and social movements. In Chapter 19 we look at some forms of relatively unorganized, large-scale behavior such as mass hysteria, public opinion, crazes, fads, and fashions. We explore various theories of crowds. The chapter concludes with a close look at resource-mobilization theory, a recent theory that explains how social movements and organizations develop to produce change in the structure and ideology of a society.

The last chapter deals with theories that try to explain long-term trends in entire societies. First we explore some sources of social change. Then we examine evolutionary theories, which see change as a gradual process leading to the progressive improvement of societies; cyclical theories, which propose that all societies rise and fall; equilibrium theories, which treat change as a movement from one integrated social system to another; and conflict theories, which regard competition for scarce resources as the basis of change. We conclude the chapter, and the book, with another look at postindustrial societies, and at the contribution of sociology to an understanding of the future.

POPULATION AND THE ECOSYSTEM

In 1798, Reverend Thomas Robert Malthus published in England his *Essay on the Principle of Population*. In his controversial work Malthus predicted that the world's population would soon outgrow the food supply. He claimed that population increases in a geometric, or exponential, fashion—1, 2, 4, 8, 16, and so on—because each increase in population is based on past increases; any additional children born today will grow up to have more children of their own. On the other hand, food supply increases in an arithmetic, or additive, fashion—1, 2, 3, 4, 5, and so on—because the amount of land to be farmed is limited and can only be increased a small amount at a time. Malthus predicted disaster, because he could not see how the food supply could be increased enough to feed a burgeoning population, and he felt that methods to curb population growth were unlikely to solve the problem. According to Malthus, births might be reduced by the postponement of marriage, sexual abstinence, birth control, or abortion. He disapproved of birth control and abortion and urged delaying marriage and practicing sexual abstinence (though he felt that the sex drive was too strong to be checked). As a result, Malthus pessimistically concluded that only war, disease, infanticide, or starvation would keep the population in line with the food supply.

For a variety of reasons that we explore in this chapter, Malthus's predictions have not yet proved correct. However, a more recent forecast, made in 1981 by the Council on Environmental Quality and the Department of State, somewhat confirms Malthus's predictions. This report concluded that by the year 2000 the world's population would be about 6.35 billion, up 50 per cent from what it was in 1975. There would be a slight increase in the per capita amount of food available, but most or all of that increase would go to people in industrialized nations; the residents of preindustrial and industrializing nations would scarcely improve their intake of food and might even have less food available. The less developed countries would also face declining energy resources, a scarce water supply, and deteriorating soil.

Both Malthus and the Council on Environmental Quality were talking about the subject of *human ecology*—the study of the relationship of people to other living and nonliving things in the ecosystem. The ecosystem is a complex and self-sustaining system of people, the lower animals and organisms, the water and the air, the food supply, chemicals, and raw materials that are present in a particular area (Ehrlich, Ehrlich, and Holdren, 1977; Clapham, 1981). Because these components are intricately connected, a change in one part of the ecosystem often has important ramifications for other parts. For instance, human efforts to dominate the environment by clearing forests or building industrial plants affect the water, the air, and the wildlife in the ecosystem. Because humans are the dominant species ecologically, the study of *population*—the number of people living in an area at a given time—plays a central role in research on the ecosystem (Nam, 1982: 362).

The Size and Structure of Populations

The study of population is called *demography*. Demographers look at changes in populations over time, the social and cultural sources of those changes, and the various consequences for society and for the environment. They study the absolute size of populations and the way they grow or shrink. In addition, demographers study population structure or composition. There are a variety of ways to describe the structure of a population, but one way to do this is to look at the age and sex of its members.

COUNTING PEOPLE

The size, composition, and distribution of a population are systematically measured in a *census*. It is expensive to take a census, which also requires technical skills to design, implement, and analyze. As a result, many nations do not conduct censuses on a regular basis. Population counts for many African nations have been characterized as "made up of equal parts inaccurate local counts, cumbrous mathematical formulas, and wishful thinking" (Petersen, 1982: 39). In 1982, China took its first census in eighteen years (see SEL 17.1). The Constitution of the United States requires a census every ten years. The results are used to apportion Congressional representatives, define state legislative districts, construct or demolish schools, develop new social programs, and assess the overall quality of life in the society.

The information gathered by the U.S. Bureau of the Census includes more than a simple count of

---

SOCIOLOGY AND EVERYDAY LIFE 17.1
Counting the Population of China

In 1982, the population of China was counted for the first time since 1964. The 1,008,175,288 Chinese make up nearly a fourth of the world's population. Despite the remarkable strides China has made in recent years toward reducing the growth of its population, one baby is added to its population every two seconds.

To conduct the 1982 census was a prodigious undertaking. Over five million census-takers—a number greater than China's armed forces—spent four months traveling around the country by bicycle and on foot to count the people. The official cost of the census was $200 million, but the actual cost was probably several times that amount. Banners, posters, newspapers, magazines, postage stamps, and speeches by government officials all proclaimed the need for public cooperation. The stated aim of the census was to collect accurate information that could be used to feed and clothe the people and close the gap between China and the industrial West. At least two years will be spent analyzing the results of the census. This process will employ 100,000 data coders and technicians and twenty-nine computers, a marked contrast to the use of abacuses in the 1953 and 1964 censuses.

The census form used in China asked nineteen questions about name, age, sex, nationality, education, occupation, marital status, and actual and expected number of children. More than earlier censuses, the questions focused on the number of children a couple planned to have; this was in line with the government's efforts to curb population growth.

The Chinese government had to surmount several obstacles to enumerating the population. Deaths are sometimes concealed so that a family can continue to use the deceased person's ration card to meet their own needs for food and clothing. The official policy that married couples should have only one child has caused some people to underreport the number of children they have. Between the 1964 and 1982 censuses, Peking relied on local leaders to report on population, but official pressure to keep population growth at low levels often yielded low estimates that were designed to please government officials. China seems to have a less geographically mobile population than many societies, but some people return illegally to the cities from rural areas to which they were sent during the Cultural Revolution, and some peasants migrate illegally to the cities. The official policy to correct these and other irregularities discovered while taking the census might have added an obstacle to getting a precise count of the Chinese population, although the government claims that its final count of just over one billion people is highly accurate.

Sources: Based on Christopher S. Wren, "China Counts Its Quarter of the World's Noses," *The New York Times*, July 6, 1982, pp. A1, A6; and "China, Pop. 1,008,175,288, Has 4th of World's People," *The New York Times*, October 28, 1982, p. 1.

the number of people in the country. Questionnaires administered by mail and by door-to-door census-takers require everyone to provide basic information such as age, sex, race, and place of residence. In 1980, a sample of 20 per cent of all households received long questionnaires that asked for additional information, such as marital histories. Censuses are supplemented with monthly surveys that update the information gathered every decade. In addition, the states provide the federal government with vital statistics on births, deaths, marriages, divorces, and immigration.

The Bureau of the Census faces several obstacles to obtaining an accurate count of the population. Often people do not believe that their answers will actually remain confidential, even though they are promised that this is so. This is one source of undercounting illegal immigrants, and it probably also means that people wanted by the law will fail to show up in census figures. In addition, some questions are difficult to design and ask; for instance, it is difficult to classify people as belonging to one ethnic group if their parents are from different groups. There are also various ways to categorize people as Hispanics—by family heritage, by language spoken at home, or by surname—and none of these measures seems to be intrinsically better than the others (Siegel and Passel, 1979).

In recent years, the Bureau of the Census has been criticized and even sued for undercounting certain categories of people—especially blacks, illegal immigrants, and the homeless. Undercounting not only misrepresents the total population, but it also means that some cities or states are given smaller amounts of federal revenue than they should receive. According to one estimate, about 7.6 per cent of all blacks—a total of 1.9 million people—were left uncounted in 1970 (Coale and Rives, 1973). To ensure a fuller count in 1980 the Bureau of the Census made use of extensive advertising and local committees, and emphasized the confidentiality of results. Nevertheless, the Bureau estimates that it still missed 1.3 million blacks, or 4.8 per cent of the country's black population (*The New York Times*, April 5, 1982, p. A18).

The first United States census in 1790 counted 3.9 million people. By 1900, that figure had climbed to 76 million, and by 1970 it had reached 203.3 million. The 1980 census counted 226.5 million people, an increase of 11 per cent over the 1970 count (U.S. Bureau of the Census, 1982: 6). The Bureau of the Census projects that the population of the United States will reach 309 million by 2050, and thereafter it will begin to decline somewhat (Pear, 1982c).

POPULATION STRUCTURE

The characteristics of a society's population influence the behavior and the needs of its members. A society with a high proportion of people under age eighteen will have to invest heavily in schools, and a society with a high proportion of people over sixty-five will have to use its resources to care for the elderly.

Age and sex are two variables that demographers often use to describe the structure or the form of a population, although populations can also be described by variables such as marital status, income, education, race and ethnicity, and place of residence. The age and sex composition of a population influences the number of people who will be born and die, the number who will marry, the number available for employment, and many other aspects of social life. Figure 17.1 shows the structure of the population of the United States in 1980 in terms of age and sex. In this diagram, called a *population pyramid*, each horizontal bar represents the number of people in the country in a particular *age cohort*, or group of people born in a specified period of time. For example, everyone born between 1951 and 1955 would be in the twenty-five-to-twenty-nine-year-old age cohort in 1980. The part of the horizontal bar to the left of the vertical line in Figure 17.1 represents the number of males in an age cohort, and the part of the horizontal bar to the right of the vertical line represents the number of females in that age group.

Although Figure 17.1 does not look like a real pyramid, the United States had in the past, as many other societies have today, an age composition that forms a pyramid (or more accurately, a triangle) when portrayed pictorially. A triangular population pyramid is characteristic of societies in which the largest age cohorts are in the youngest years and the smallest age cohorts are in the oldest years. This occurs when many babies are born but large numbers of them do not survive until old age. In 1980, the United States did not have this type of age structure, because many Americans do survive until old age and because many married couples limit the number of children they have.

Figure 17.1 shows certain "bulges" in the population structure of the United States. For example, the large age cohorts between fifteen and nineteen

FIGURE 17.1
*Population Pyramid
of the United States,
1980*

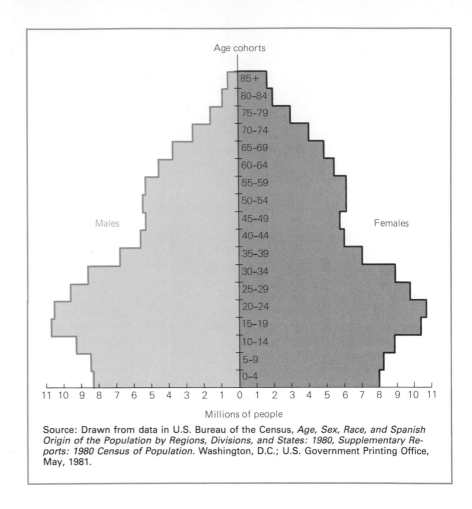

Source: Drawn from data in U.S. Bureau of the Census, *Age, Sex, Race, and Spanish Origin of the Population by Regions, Divisions, and States: 1980, Supplementary Reports: 1980 Census of Population.* Washington, D.C.; U.S. Government Printing Office, May, 1981.

and between twenty and twenty-four were born between 1956 and 1965. In the 1980s this group will be entering the age range when people usually marry for the first time; by the 1990s, they might be producing large numbers of children. In this way, population pyramids can be used to forecast future trends, although predictions must be made cautiously because small changes in the basic demographic processes of fertility, mortality, and migration (which we examine in the next section) can change the structure of a population in major ways.

The size of the age cohort to which an individual belongs influences personal welfare and life chances in important ways. According to one demographer (Easterlin, 1980a: 4), people who belong to a "baby boom" generation—that is, one with a large number of members—are likely to confront some of the following problems:

- difficulty in finding jobs and advancing in their careers,
- pressure to delay marriage and having children, and
- a high probability of marital strain and divorce.

Age

A useful summary statistic that tells us something about the age composition of a population but does not provide details about the size of each age cohort is the median age. A population's median age is the age that half of the population falls above and half falls below. Between 1820 and 1950, the median age of the United States population rose, as a result of people living longer and the migration of adults to the country from abroad. From 1950 to 1971, the median age declined, mainly because of

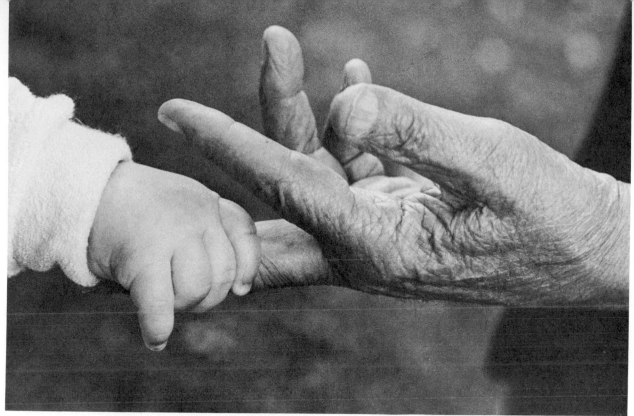

A society is said to have a high dependency ratio if it is made up of many people under the age of fifteen and over the age of sixty-five who are dependent upon a few economically productive people.

the large number of children born after World War II. Between 1971 and 1981 the median age of the American population rose somewhat; in 1981, it was 30.3 (U.S. Bureau of the Census, 1982: 26).

The *dependency ratio* is another useful statistic that describes the age structure of a population. Demographers usually consider as economically dependent children under the age of fifteen who have not yet begun to work and elderly people over the age of sixty-five who have stopped working. The dependency ratio is then calculated by dividing the number of economically dependent people— the young and the old—by the number of economically productive people between fifteen and sixty-five. A society with a high dependency ratio will have a relatively small number of active workers to support the economically dependent young and old.

Societies that are industrializing often have very high dependency ratios because their populations include many people under the age of fifteen. In these societies, working people support large numbers of dependents, even though many dependents actually make significant economic contributions by helping with agricultural work. In industrialized societies such as the United States, the dependency ratio is lower than it is in preindustrial or industrializing nations, because the number of young children in technologically advanced societies is a relatively small part of the total population. However, industrialized societies often face another problem—how the economically productive members of the society are to support a large and growing number of dependent elderly people.

THE ELDERLY IN THE UNITED STATES. Americans sixty-five and over today make up an increasingly large proportion of the population. In 1970, this age cohort was 9.8 per cent of the population; by 1981, the elderly were 11.4 per cent of the population, about twice the proportion they were in 1900. The Bureau of the Census predicts that the elderly will grow to 13.1 per cent of the population by 2000 and to 21.7 per cent by 2050 (U.S. Bureau of the Census, 1982: 27; Pear, 1982c). The United States is not alone in this "graying" of the population; by 2000, Japan will have one of the world's oldest populations (Knox, 1982).

The aging of a population has several important ramifications for society. Its culture might become less youth oriented, even to the point of conflict between the generations. For instance, in Florida, where the elderly are now a large proportion of the population, the elderly have pressured the state legislature to punish juvenile delinquents more harshly and have opposed raising taxes to pay for the public schools (Herbers, 1981a).

A major problem now being faced by many industrial societies is how to support the dependent elderly. The elderly are already such a drain on the Japanese economy that some observers have spoken of "aging pollution" (Knox, 1982). In the United States, social security benefits have become a major concern of lawmakers and their constituents. Even though major reforms were introduced in 1983, many Americans doubt that the system can avoid bankruptcy until they reach retirement age. This is because increasing numbers of elderly people will have to depend on a shrinking work force for the money to pay their social security benefits.

Sex

The balance between the number of males and the number of females in a population influences the chances of marriage, and this in turn affects the number of births in the society. For instance, during a war when many men are overseas, the number of marriages is usually low and few children are born. When the balance between males and females is more equal, as it is when men return home from war, marriages increase and births become more common. There was a dramatic shift of this sort in the United States after World War II, as we can see in Figure 17.1: The large age cohort born between 1946 and 1950 was between thirty and thirty-four in 1980. When a nation experiences the death of many men during a war, as did the Soviet Union in World Wars I and II, the number of marriages and births is affected for generations.

The balance between males and females in a population is called the *sex ratio*. Specifically, the sex ratio is the number of males in a population for every 100 females in that population. In the United States, more males than females are born; the sex ratio of newborns is 105, meaning that 105 male babies are born for every 100 females. However, males are more likely to die at every age than females, and so the overall sex ratio in 1981 was only 95. The sex ratio for Americans sixty-five and over in that year was only 67, a result of the fact that women live longer than men on the average (U.S. Bureau of the Census, 1982: 27).

Sex ratios vary from time to time. In 1910, the overall sex ratio in the United States was 106, but by 1981 it had dropped to 95. The sex ratio declined for a variety of reasons: the death of large numbers of men in war, a decline in immigration between the 1920s and the 1960s (which reduced the sex ratio because men are more likely than women to migrate), a decrease in the rate at which women die during childbirth, and larger increases in the average age at death for women than for men.

Demographic Processes: Fertility, Mortality, and Migration

The growth or decline of a population is a product of changes in fertility (the rate at which people are born), mortality (the rate at which people die), and migration (the rate at which people move into or out of a society). These three basic demographic processes determine the size, composition, and distribution of a population and the ways that it changes over time.

FERTILITY

The reproductive potential of women, or their *fecundity*, varies with their health, diet, and age. Because women do not have as many children as they are biologically capable of having, demographers use measures of *fertility*—the actual number of births—rather than measures of fecundity. In all societies, fertility is less than fecundity because social practices as well as biological factors affect the reproductive process.

The *crude birth rate* is the annual number of live births for every 1,000 people in a population. In 1981, the crude birth rate for the United States was 15.9 per 1,000 people, about one-half the birth rate for Mexico and about one-third the rate for Nigeria (U.S. Bureau of the Census, 1982: 60, 861). The crude birth rate is a useful measure of the overall rate at which people are born into a population, but it does not indicate that some groups are more likely than others to produce children. A consequence of group differences is that a society's social composition affects its crude birth rate. For instance, a society in which a high proportion of the population is elderly will probably have a lower crude birth rate than a society in which a large proportion of the population is between fifteen and thirty-four.

The birth rate is affected by many factors in addition to the age structure of a population. A sex ratio that differs much from 100 can reduce opportunities for marriage and thereby decrease fertility. Norms that discourage premarital sexual intercourse or sexual relations between married couples who have recently had a child can depress the birth rate. The availability and acceptability of effective birth control measures—including sterilization and abortion—can also reduce fertility. In addition, a practice of delaying marriage until the twenties or later can lower a society's birth rate, as would a high divorce rate that leaves large numbers of people single for extended periods during their reproductive years. Increased opportunities for women to become educated and to work might delay marriage, increase the divorce rate, or lead to a desire for fewer children or no children at all. Still another source of low birth rates is inadequate medical care and poor maternal health; these factors are sometimes associated with a high rate of sterility due to diseases such as gonorrhea, a high rate of miscarriages, and a high rate of maternal and infant mortality.

Familism

The value that encourages people to marry and bear children is called *familism*. Sometimes national ideologies favor large families as a way to grow and gain power in the international community, even though a policy of population growth often makes it difficult for nations to industrialize. Mao Zedong encouraged the Chinese to have large families, but the next generation of leaders has made every effort to curb population growth. Another source of familism is religion, which can encourage a high birth rate by prohibiting contraception and abortion and by enjoining believers to "be fruitful and multiply."

Familism is especially important in societies where it is advantageous for parents to have large numbers of children. In an agricultural society, each additional child means another productive worker in the fields, and so there is an economic reason for large families. The lack of retirement benefits and adequate housing for the elderly can encourage parents to have many children to ensure that they will be supported when they grow old.

Economic factors sometimes reduce the impact of familism. Birth rates may be low if married couples wish to improve their own standard of living rather than have a large number of children, or if

they have few children so that they can provide more for each one. The increased educational and employment opportunities for women that often accompany industrialization can also reduce the birth rate, as nonfamily roles for women acquire more prestige and less emphasis is placed on marriage and child-rearing.

Fertility in the United States

Over the past two centuries, the United States has experienced a long-term downward trend in its crude birth rate, even though the rate has occasionally increased for brief periods. The number of births per 1,000 people fell from 30.1 in 1910 to 18.7 in 1934, rose slightly to 20.4 in 1945, and then increased dramatically to 25 in 1955. The high birth rate during the decade from 1945 to 1955 is often referred to as the postwar "baby boom." Since 1955, the birth rate dropped to an all-time low of 14.8 in 1975 and 1976 and then increased slightly to 15.9 in 1981 (U.S. Bureau of the Census, 1982: 60) (See Figure 17.2).

Married women in the United States now produce about 1.9 children, on the average. This figure is lower than the average of 2.1 that is needed to replace the existing population. However, the large age cohorts of women now in their child-bearing years (see Figure 17.1) means that the population of the United States will not actually stop growing for a number of years, and then it will only do so if the crude birth rate remains low.

Even though the trend for married couples has been toward smaller numbers of children, relatively few married people say they expect to have no children or would prefer to remain childless. In 1980, only 6 per cent of married white women and only 4 per cent of married black women said that they did not expect to have any children. These figures are low, but they are somewhat higher than they were in 1967 and in 1975 (see Table 17.1).

One study of childless couples found that one-third of them had decided before they were married not to have children, and the other two-thirds decided after they were married to remain childless (Veevers, 1973). Couples who decided before marriage to remain childless usually based their decisions on the women's preferences; these women did not want to bear children because their own mothers had been unhappy, because they had doubts about how good a mother they would be, or because they had experienced "parenting" as adolescents who took care of younger siblings and did

FIGURE 17.2
Crude Death Rates and Crude Birth Rates, Per 1,000 People, 1910 to 1980*

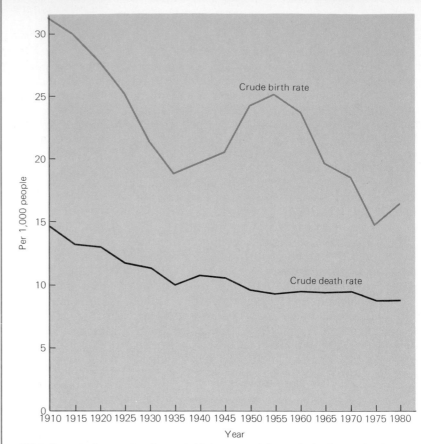

* This figure is drawn using the crude birth rates and the crude death rates for the United States at five-year intervals.

Source: U.S. Bureau of the Census, *Statistical Abstract of the United States, 1982-83*. Washington, D.C.: U.S. Government Printing Office, 1982, p. 7.

TABLE 17.1
Lifetime Births Expected by Married Women, 18 to 34 Years Old, Whites and Blacks, 1967 To 1980, Percentages*

Number of births expected	1967		1975		1980	
	Whites	*Blacks*	*Whites*	*Blacks*	*Whites*	*Blacks*
None	2.2%	3.0%	4.9%	3.0%	6.0%	4.0%
One	5.5	8.1	10.8	10.7	13.2	14.4
Two	31.4	24.9	49.8	40.0	51.5	45.3
Three or more	60.9	64.1	34.4	46.4	29.2	36.4
Total percentage	100.0%	100.1%	99.9%	100.1%	99.9%	100.1%

*Column percentages do not always add to 100% because of rounding errors.

Source: U.S. Bureau of the Census, *Statistical Abstract of the United States, 1982–83*. Washington, D.C.: U.S. Government Printing Office, 1982, p. 64.

not want to do so again. Those couples who decided after marriage to remain childless had often intended to have children when "the time was right" but kept postponing it because the "right time" never arrived. Social pressure and criticism often caused them to deny for many years that they had actually decided to remain childless.

MORTALITY

Mortality, or the number of deaths in a population, is usually measured by the *crude death rate*—the annual number of deaths for every 1,000 people. This rate is closely associated with the age structure of a population because the highest rates of death are usually among the elderly, although the rate of death of newborns can also be high. Mortality is also affected by the sex ratio of a population because females usually live longer than males, on the average. In 1981, the crude death rate for the United States was 8.7 per 1,000, compared to 6 per 1,000 for Mexico and about 18 per 1,000 for Nigeria (U.S. Bureau of the Census, 1982: 60, 861). Figure 17.2 shows that the overall death rate in the United States dropped between 1910 and 1935 but has changed little since then.

Infant Mortality

The annual number of deaths of children in the first year of life for every 1,000 live births in a population is called the *infant mortality rate*. This rate tells us the chance that newborns will survive the first year, a time when they are especially vulnerable to disease and infection. In 1940, the infant mortality rate of the United States was 47 per 1,000 live births and by 1981 it had fallen to 11.7 per 1,000 (U.S. Bureau of the Census, 1982: 60). During the twentieth century, improved medical care, better diets, and more sanitary living conditions have reduced infant mortality rates throughout the world, but the rates in preindustrial societies are still much higher than they are in industrial societies. For example, India's infant mortality rate is more than ten times the rate for the United States (U.S. Bureau of the Census, 1982: 861).

Among industrial societies, the United States ranks about ninth in infant mortality rates. In spite of the high per capita income for the country as a whole, there are groups and areas within the nation that receive inadequate medical care. In 1979, black infants were nearly twice as likely as white babies to die before the age of one (U.S. Bureau of the Census, 1982: 75). Washington, D.C., where

70 per cent of the population is black, has one of the highest infant mortality rates in the nation—a rate higher than rates in much poorer countries such as Jamaica, Cuba, and Costa Rica. Lack of medical facilities could be one explanation for this high infant mortality rate, but at least one city official attributes it more to a lack of awareness on the part of pregnant women—many of whom are poor, unmarried, young, and uneducated—about what medical care they need during pregnancy. Other causes of the high infant mortality rate in Washington include alcohol and drug abuse and smoking, which are associated with lower birth weights that make the death of a newborn more likely (*The New York Times*, December 13, 1981, p. 37).

Life Expectancy

The average number of years of life that a person of a particular age can expect to live is called *life expectancy*. This variable is often expressed as the number of years that a newborn child is expected to live. Much of the substantial increase in life expectancy that has occurred in the United States and elsewhere during this century is a result of reductions in infant mortality rather than any increase in the number of additional years that adults can expect to live. Life expectancy differs from *life span*— the maximum number of years that people might live. The human life span is about 115 to 120 years, a figure that probably has not changed much since the Stone Age because neither the genetic basis of the aging process nor the degenerative diseases that often afflict the elderly are yet fully understood or controllable (Schmeck, 1981).

In the United States, life expectancy differs for males and females and for whites and blacks. More males are born than females, but from birth through old age more males than females of every age die each year. In 1980, the average life expectancy of a newborn white female was 78.1 years, compared to an average life expectancy of 70.5 for white males. Black females had an average life expectancy of 74, and black males could expect to live for 65.3 years (U.S. National Center for Health Statistics, 1981). The differences between the sexes can be attributed to some combination of biological differences in the aging process and social differences in gender roles and life experiences. The lower life expectancy of blacks is a result of differences between the racial groups in income, housing, jobs, diets, and medical care. Poorer Americans of both races have lower life expectancies than people of higher economic standing.

Mortality is also related to marital status. Death rates are lowest for married people, higher for those who have never married, and highest for those who are divorced or widowed (Thompson and Lewis, 1965). These differences could be due to the regularity of behavior and diet that accompany married life or to the presence of another person to attend to one's physical and emotional needs. It is also possible that married people are healthier to begin with and therefore more likely than unhealthy people to be selected as marital partners.

Causes of Death

In preindustrial societies, death is commonly a result of infectious and parasitic diseases such as typhoid, diphtheria, malaria, influenza, pneumonia, tuberculosis, and diarrheal diseases (Preston, 1980). Nutritional problems such as protein deficiency are also a major cause of death. These problems especially affect the young and cause high rates of infant mortality in preindustrial societies.

In industrial societies, relatively few people die from infectious and parasitic diseases, but chronic and degenerative diseases such as heart conditions and cancer are comparatively more important. In 1900, the two leading causes of death in the United States were tuberculosis and pneumonia, which accounted for about one-fifth of all deaths in that year but only 2.4 per cent of all deaths in 1979. The two leading causes of death in 1979 were diseases of the heart and cancer; they accounted for 59.4 per cent of all deaths in that year, although they were not among the three leading causes of death in 1900 (Wrong, 1977: 42; U.S. Bureau of the Census, 1982: 76).

The leading causes of death in industrial societies are those associated with the aging process. Better diet, cleaner water, improved housing, and changes in sanitation and sewage disposal have made it possible to control the major causes of death in preindustrial societies. Vaccinations, antibiotics, anesthesia, and other improvements in medicine have also reduced the incidence of smallpox and malaria, which had been major causes of death. Today, death in industrial societies is associated primarily with poor diet, lack of exercise, stress, and environmental pollution. These causes of death can be controlled by individual attention to personal health and by social policies that educate people about health and curb pollution.

MIGRATION

In addition to fertility and mortality, a third demographic process that affects the size, composition, and distribution of a population is *migration*—the movement of people from one area to another. Immigration is movement into an area, and emigration is movement out of an area. The *net migration rate* is the difference between immigration and emigration, expressed as a net number of people per 1,000 in a population who enter or leave an area during one year. Migration is important for several reasons: It can relieve population pressure in an overpopulated area, spread culture from one society to another, bring groups into contact and sometimes into conflict, and create problems of adjustment for people who are uprooted from their homes.

International Migration

The movement of people from one country to another is called *international migration*. Many nations limit immigration and emigration. They might restrict entry into the country by people who are likely to impose a financial burden on the state, people who are culturally different from the native population, or people with few skills to contribute to the society. Underpopulated nations sometimes encourage immigration by imposing no restrictions or even by offering financial incentives or free land; Australia has offered such incentives to immigrants. Some nations such as the Soviet Union have limited the emigration of their people out of fear of losing people to countries that promise an improved standard of living or greater religious or political freedom.

The United States was open to immigrants until 1921, when Congress set a ceiling that was designed to limit the entry of Orientals. Between 1929 and 1968, immigration was restricted by quotas based on the national origins of Americans. In 1968, those quotas were abolished, but numerical limitations were set to give people in different countries an equal chance to move to the United States. Between 1968 and 1979, an average of 420,000 people settled in the United States each year; this number does not include illegal immigrants (U.S. Bureau of the Census, 1982: 86). Immigrants to the United States today are more likely to come from Asia or the Western Hemisphere than from Europe, which historically has been the source of most settlers. In addition, since

Before 1921, the United States was open to immigrants from all nations. Here a group docks at Ellis Island in the port of New York.

1968 immigrants have been more similar to the rest of the population in age, sex, and marital status than was the case in the past (Massey, 1981).

Today, there are between three and twelve million illegal aliens in the United States (Massey, 1981). Some have sneaked into the country, others have overstayed their visas, and some have arranged false marriages to Americans. One of the few national surveys of illegal immigrants found that about 60 per cent came from Mexico, 30 per cent came from Western Europe, and 5 per cent came from Asiatic nations (North and Houstoun, 1976). Some people claim that these illegal aliens have taken jobs away from Americans and thereby increased the nation's unemployment rate. Others point out that few unemployed Americans would take the low-paying, menial jobs that illegal immigrants usually hold (Petersen, 1978).

How well have immigrants to the United States done in recent years? One study finds that as a group they have contributed more in taxes than they have used in public services. Moreover, within a decade of their arrival they earn more than native-born Americans, and their children overtake native-born children in educational attainment within a few years. However, immigrants from some countries have enjoyed greater economic success in the United States than have people from other countries. For instance, the Japanese, the Chinese, and non-Hispanic whites have all done better economically than have Mexicans and Filipinos (Pear, 1980).

Since the 1960s, there has been a trend in international migration for workers to move from countries with low incomes and high unemployment rates to nations with better job prospects (Ritchey, 1976; Massey, 1981). For example, the nations of West Germany, Switzerland, and France have filled some jobs with "guest workers" from Mediterranean countries. These temporary immigrants contribute to the economy of the country in which they work, even though they can place a strain on that society's schools, social services, and housing (Petersen, 1978). Another form of international immigration is the movement of highly educated and technically skilled workers from one country to another that offers better pay, greater opportunities for career advancement, or modern research facilities. This "brain drain" often benefits the country to which these skilled workers move, but it can harm the economy of their homeland (Petersen, 1978).

Internal Migration

Population movement from one area to another within the same country is called *internal migration.* Industrializing societies experience internal migration from villages and rural areas to large cities; we examine this process of urbanization in the next chapter. Another form of internal migration is found in the United States today—the movement of people from large cities to the suburbs and to rural areas and small towns. Still another kind of internal migration is movement from region to region; in SEL 17.2 we look at the recent migration of Americans to the Sun Belt.

SOCIOLOGY AND EVERYDAY LIFE 17.2
Moving to the Sun Belt

In every census since 1790 the population center of the United States has moved westward, and since 1910 it has gradually shifted southward too. The population center, which is shown for each census in the map on the next page, is "that point at which an imaginary flat, weightless, and rigid map of the United States would balance if weights of identical value were placed on it so that each weight represented the location of one person" (U.S. Bureau of the Census, 1982: 7).

The southwestwardly shift of population is made even clearer in the census figures for 1970 and 1980. During this decade the population of the nation increased by 11.4 per cent. However, the population of the Sun Belt states from Virginia to Florida and westward to southern California increased by 22.5 per cent, while the remainder of the nation increased by only 5.9 per cent.

Why did the population shift so dramatically to the South and the West, and will this trend continue? Decay and congestion in the cities of the Northeast and the Midwest, rising unemployment rates in those areas, and increased heating fuel costs all pushed people out of communities in the Northeast and Midwest. On the other hand, the Sun Belt's tradition of unbounded opportunity, its relaxed and outdoor style of living, and its warm climate attracted these people.

Of the five major subregions in the Sun Belt, the Southwest (Arizona and New Mexico) grew the fastest between 1970 and 1980, increasing in population by 44.6 per cent. This area has attracted people seeking a warm, dry climate because they have respiratory problems and similar illnesses, although some of the cities in this area have begun to experience severe environmental pollution. The high-technology industry in this area has drawn many young techni-cal and professional workers; for example, 38 per cent of the manufacturing sector in Arizona is high technology, compared with about 7 per cent for the nation as a whole. In some ways, the Southwest is a prototype of a postindustrial society.

Another rapid-growth area is Florida, where population grew by 43.4 per cent between 1970 and 1980. This was a result of the settlement of retired people from other regions and an influx of immigrants from the Caribbean and Latin America. Florida has experienced social unrest in recent years—including riot activity in Miami, hostility between blacks and Cuban-Americans, and conflict between the young and the elderly. Florida's rapid growth has also destroyed some of its wilderness areas and beaches to make room for industry, housing, and resort hotels.

A somewhat slower rate of growth occurred in the "Oil Patch"—Texas, Oklahoma, and Louisiana. The population of this area rose by 23.3 per cent during the decade, largely as a result of the exploration and production of oil and gas. Some immigrants from the North have returned home, however, after being unable to locate jobs in this part of the Sun Belt and after finding that welfare benefits there are either low or unavailable.

Southern California's population increased by 18.7 per cent between 1970 and 1980, largely because of its appealing climate and its job opportunities. The growth of this subregion's population has started to slow down from its rapid pace of the last two decades, and southern California is now experiencing some of the problems of the old cities of the Northeast and the Midwest.

The slowest growth rate of the five subregions of the Sun Belt is in the Southeast—Virginia, North Carolina, South Carolina, Georgia, Alabama, Mississippi, Tennessee, and Arkansas.

However, even here, population rose by 16.4 per cent during the last decade. In the 1960s and 1970s, this area attracted industry from the Northeast and the Midwest because of the Southeast's low wages, lack of labor unions, and low heating costs. As the country has shifted from an industrial economy to a postindustrial one, however, manufacturing has proved a less stable economic base than service industries and high technology. As a consequence, the Southeast's rate of growth has abated.

Ninety per cent of the increase in population of the country in the fifteen months after the 1980 census was taken has occurred in the Sun Belt. There is reason to think that this rapid growth might slow down as unemployment rates rise and people living elsewhere learn of the problems associated with growth. However, population projections indicate that the Sun Belt will still gain population faster than the rest of the country between 1980 and 1990. One consequence will be a further redistribution of political power to states in the South and the West. Twelve seats were moved from other regions to the Sun Belt states in 1980, and more will probably be reapportioned to that region in 1990. This will have important effects on the political system; indeed, the last four elected Presidents have all come from Sun Belt states—Reagan, Carter, Nixon, and Johnson.

Source: Based on William K. Stevens, "Sun Belt Having Difficulty Living up to Its Promise," *The New York Times*, July 5, 1982, pp. 1, 7.

FIGURE 17.3
Population Center of the United States, 1790-1980

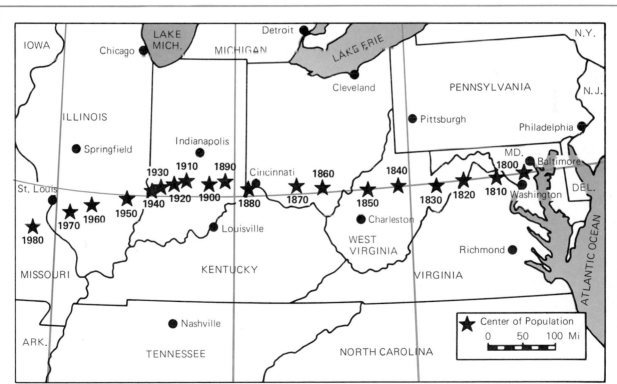

Source: U.S. Bureau of the Census, *Statistical Abstract of the United States, 1982-83*. Washington, D.C.: U.S. Government Printing Office, 1982, p. 7.

Push and Pull Factors

Both internal migration and international migration are the results of push and pull factors (Lee, 1966; Ritchey, 1976). A *push factor* is something that induces people to move from a country or an area. Push factors that drive people out of an area include political persecution, religious intolerance, racial discrimination, overpopulation, famine, harsh climate, and conquest during war. The Pilgrims came to North America in the seventeenth century because of religious persecution, and many Jews left Europe in the 1930s and 1940s for a similar reason. The Irish came to the United States in the mid-1800s because of a potato famine in their homeland. More recently, 107,000 Vietnamese settled in the United States in 1978 and 1979 after leaving their country because of war and political conflict (U.S. Bureau of the Census, 1982: 89).

International and internal migration are also influenced by *pull factors*—those forces that induce people to move to another area. Pull factors include political freedom, religious tolerance, a favorable climate, economic opportunity, educational opportunity, a high standard of living, and the previous settlement in the area of people from the same country. Pull factors draw people to a new place to improve their lot in life, in contrast to push factors, which lead people to move in order to escape from something. The balance of push and pull factors influences shifts of population from country to country and from region to region within the same country; we can see in SEL 17.2 how some of these factors have caused Americans to move to the Sun Belt.

POPULATION GROWTH

One way to measure population growth is by the *rate of natural increase*—the difference between the crude birth rate and the crude death rate. This rate is usually expressed as an annual net gain or net loss per 1,000 people in the population. Graphically, this is represented by the gap between the crude birth rate line and the crude death rate line in Figures 17.2 and 17.4. The rate of natural increase for the United States in 1981 was 7.2 per 1,000 people, the difference between the crude birth rate of 15.9 and the crude death rate of 8.7.

The *net growth rate* of any nation's population is its rate of natural increase plus its net migration rate. Populations grow when more people are born than die and when more people immigrate than emigrate. Because many nations have net migration rates close to zero, their rates of natural increase are about the same as their net growth rates. Sometimes net growth rates are expressed as a percentage. For instance, in 1979 the net growth rate of the United States was 0.93 per cent or 9.3 per 1,000. Most industrialized nations have net growth rates of 1 per cent or less, and preindustrial and industrializing nations typically have net growth rates between 1 and 4 per cent. Because most of the world's people live in societies that are not fully industrialized, the net growth rate for the world's population is relatively high. The current net growth rate for the world's population—which is the same as its rate of natural increase because the net migration rate for the world is zero—is 17 per 1,000 or 1.7 per cent, nearly twice the rate for the United States (U.S. Bureau of the Census, 1982: 856).

The concept of *doubling time* is one useful way to look at rates of population growth. Doubling time is the number of years that it will take a population to become twice its current size, given its current rate of growth. Even small differences in the rate of natural increase greatly affect the number of years that it takes for a population to double (Van der Tak, Haub, and Murphy, 1979: 5):

Annual rate of natural increase	Number of years to double in population
1%	69
2%	35
3%	23
4%	17

The population of the world doubled between 1650 and 1850, a period of 200 years. It doubled again from 1850 to 1930, a period of only eighty years. The world's population doubled once again in the forty-seven years from 1930 to 1977, and at its 1982 rate of growth it will double yet again in forty-one years. The population of the world in 1982 was about 4.7 billion; by the year 2000 it will be around 6.35 billion (Council on Environmental Quality and the Department of State, 1981; Petersen, 1982). Today, about 9 per cent of all people who have ever lived are alive (Wilford, 1981).

Zero population growth (ZPG) describes a population with a rate of natural increase that is zero; in other words, the crude birth rate and the crude death rate are the same. Because some children do not live to become adults and because some adults do not bear children, 2.1 children must be born to an average couple to achieve zero population growth. Even with a rate of reproduction this low it might take years to achieve a condition of no overall growth in a population if there is a disproportionately large number of people in the child-bearing years between fifteen and forty-four. Also, if a society acquires new members through net migration, its population will increase even if its crude birth rate equals its crude death rate.

The Demographic Transition

Population grows with industrialization because modern societies can support more people than societies based on simpler technologies. Industrial societies also produce the knowledge and the methods needed to reduce mortality dramatically in a short time. Moreover, social conditions in industrial societies encourage people to limit the size of their families, as we will see. These changes over time in fertility, mortality, and population growth rates are called the *demographic transition*, a model of population change that is shown in Figure 17.4.

In the first phase of the demographic transition, both the crude birth rate and the crude death rate are high, resulting in relatively stable populations. Death rates are high because of a low standard of living and inadequate medical care. High birth rates compensate for the high rate of infant mortality; they also add hands to the family to work the fields, and they yield offspring who can support their parents when they grow old. This first stage is characteristic of preindustrial societies.

The second stage in the demographic transition is the stage of transitional growth, usually found in the early stages of industrialization. Death rates drop with improved living conditions and advances in medicine. Birth rates remain high for some time because people adjust slowly to the increased chance that their children will survive until adulthood. The rate of population growth is high during this second stage because births greatly exceed deaths. However, many European nations did not experience a high rate of population growth as they industrialized because (1) both death rates and birth rates declined slowly at about the same time and (2) because many Europeans, perhaps as much as one-fourth of the population, emigrated from the continent between 1820 and 1930 (Van der Tak, Haub, and Murphy, 1979: 9; Petersen, 1982). Death rates declined slowly in Europe as improved agricultural productivity increased the food supply, housing conditions improved, clothing became more adequate, water was purified, and sewage disposal systems were built. The role of medical breakthroughs in reducing Europe's mortality rate has been the subject of some disagreement among scholars (McKeown and Brown, 1955; McKeown and Record, 1962; Razzell, 1969; Preston, 1977; Van der Tak, Haub, and Murphy, 1979).

The third stage in the demographic transition is the stage of incipient decline, which occurs in the later stages of industrialization. This phase is characterized by a low death rate and a low birth rate that combine to produce a low rate of natural increase or even zero population growth. In reality, nations in this stage often experience short-term fluctuations in fertility from time to time (Easterlin, 1980b; Petersen, 1982). The reason that birth rates

FIGURE 17.4
The Demographic Transition

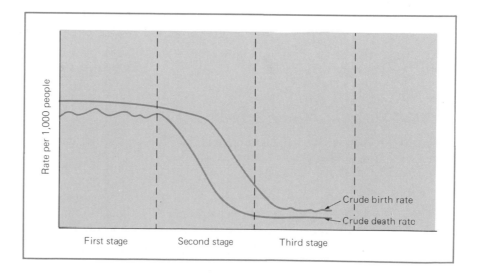

eventually fall in this third stage is that children are expensive to bear, educate, and raise in industrial societies. Compulsory education means that children must spend years in school acquiring the skills needed in a modern society, and during these years children are of little economic value to their parents (Lindert, 1980). Fertility also declines because the lowered death rate means that parents do not have to produce large numbers of children to have a few survive until adulthood, and the development of national social security systems makes it less necessary for parents to rely on their children for support in old age.

Some demographers doubt that today's preindustrial and industrializing societies will all pass through the three stages of the demographic transition—as have the United States, Canada, Australia, Japan, and European nations. Many societies, as they industrialize, experience rapid declines in death rates when they adopt modern medical technology and public health measures. For instance, Sri Lanka (formerly Ceylon) saw its life expectancy at birth rise from forty-three years in 1946 to fifty-two years in 1947, an increase that took half a century to achieve in Western Europe (Newman, 1977; Petersen, 1982).

Because fertility has not declined as rapidly as mortality in today's less developed countries, rates of population increase have been high—often considerably higher than those experienced in European nations during industrialization. Over 90 per cent of the projected increase in the world's population by the year 2000 will occur in these preindustrial and industrializing nations (Council on Environmental Quality and the Department of State, 1981: 9). Industrialization might eventually lead to lower birth rates, but as we will see in the next section it is not clear that there are enough natural resources on the Earth to allow every nation to become fully industrialized.

Population and Human Ecology

If you have ever flown over the continental United States, you might have been struck by the vast stretches of uninhabited land. How can this planet be overpopulated when one of its most populous nations has so much empty space? Overpopulation is less a matter of population density—the number of people per square mile—than of the *carrying capacity* of the Earth. Carrying capacity refers to the number of people who can be sustained by the eco-

system. Each person takes up a certain amount of space, and each also needs food, clear air, fresh water, and fuel. Some people, particularly those who live in technologically advanced societies, use disproportionately large amounts of the world's resources. They have a much greater impact on the environment than a similar number of people living in a less economically developed society.

Demographers disagree about the planet's carrying capacity. Most think that the Earth is overpopulated relative to its natural resources, and that population controls are needed to maintain a decent standard of living for everyone (Brown, 1978, 1983). Others take the more unorthodox view that overpopulation and resource depletion are short-term problems and that in the long run people will be creative enough to solve environmental problems (Simon, 1981). What is important but difficult to measure precisely is the relationship of people to their environment. Technology can alter some aspects of the ecosystem, such as creating and cleaning up industrial pollution, and it can provide substitutes for depleted resources, such as plastic to use in place of wood or rubber. However, other aspects of the ecosystem are difficult to alter; for instance, long-term changes in the temperature of the atmosphere might be possible only if the process of industrialization is halted.

Studying the ecosystem is a complex undertaking that requires an understanding of both the social sciences and the natural sciences. Here we look at some of the major components of the ecosystem that affect human population—water, the atmosphere, land, energy resources, and food supply.

WATER

For many societies, fish is an important source of food. In recent years, the world's fish catch has declined somewhat. This has resulted from overfishing, which makes it difficult for fish to regenerate fast enough to maintain past levels of food supply; from pollution of the waters; and from the construction of canals that interfere with the natural environment (Brown, 1978; Clapham, 1981). A recent report concludes that the world's fish catch will not increase much by the end of this century and that population growth may mean that fish will contribute even less protein per capita than they do today (Council on Environmental Quality and the Department of State, 1981).

Another problem is a decline in the supply of fresh water. One reason for this is that modern agriculture requires irrigation, which makes water unavailable for other uses. The water shortage is also caused by deforestation and desertification of the land; both affect the water table and lead to soil erosion. Preindustrial and industrializing societies are now the most severely affected by the water shortage, and their problems will become even worse by the year 2000 unless current practices are changed (Council on Environmental Quality and the Department of State, 1981). In the future, nations will compete and may even go to war for water rights. Indeed, this has already happened; India and Bangladesh disputed the use of the Ganges River in 1976, and the United States and Mexico have argued for some time over the waters of the Colorado River (Brown, 1978).

Pollution poses a great risk of destroying aquatic life and reducing the water supply available for human consumption and irrigation. Pesticides used in agriculture pollute the waters, as do industrial pollutants that are poured into rivers and lakes or buried in chemical waste dumps. Sometimes fish are contaminated with mercury and other poisons and cannot be eaten safely. Pollution of the waters can reach extreme proportions; for instance, the Cuyahoga River in Ohio must occasionally be "put out" by firefighters when its pollutants catch fire.

THE ATMOSPHERE

The emission of industrial pollutants into the atmosphere affects human health; for example, emphysema and other fatal or debilitating diseases are associated with unclean air. These emmissions have also altered the climate; from 1880 to 1940, the temperature of the atmosphere rose, but it has fallen steadily since then (Clapham, 1981). Fluorocarbons from aerosol cans, nitrogenous fertilizers, and other impurities in the atmosphere have partially destroyed the ozone layer. Some feel that this is a cause of skin cancer, because more of the sun's ultraviolet rays pass through a thinner atmosphere (Brown, 1978). The "acid rain" produced by the burning of sulfur-based fuels can damage crops, forests, and lakes, and in the long run this may reduce the world's food supply. Burning fossil fuels such as petroleum and coal has also polluted the atmosphere. These pollutants have changed the Earth's atmosphere, caused disease and death, damaged crops, extinguished species, and caused the deterioration of buildings and clothing.

Another kind of atmospheric pollution is noise pollution. The sounds of an industrialized and urbanized society—airplanes, cars, trains, factory machinery, and loud music—all take their toll. At least ten million Americans are subjected to harmful amounts of noise that can cause high blood pressure, ulcers, fatigue, irritability, and aggression (Brody, 1982a). Noise has also been found to hurt the performance of students who attend schools near airports, railroads, subways, and highways (A. Goldman, 1982).

LAND

Human behavior alters the uses of the world's lands. Wilderness areas might be preserved if people were to recognize the advantages of those areas for recreation, scientific research, and water supply (Clapham, 1981). However, the wilderness is often destroyed in the name of progress; it is converted into cropland or the suburbs of expanding cities. Often the only reminders of the wilderness in a modern city are a few small parks.

Forests provide people with lumber, paper, and chemicals. Good management of the forests can make them a renewable resource, but today there is a trend toward deforestation, as a result of the harvesting of trees and the clearing of land to grow crops. One study predicts that the world's growing stock of trees will be reduced by about 47 per cent by the year 2000; almost all of this decline will be in preindustrial and industrializing nations (Council on Environmental Quality and the Department of State, 1981). This deforestation will reduce the supply of wood and raise its price; it will have similar effects on the chemicals and paper products made from trees. A particularly serious problem is the depletion of firewood, a major source of heat in societies that cannot afford the high cost of fossil fuels. Deforestation also reduces agricultural productivity because it leads to soil erosion, flooding, and depletion of the water supply.

A related problem in the conversion of land usage is the desertification of the world—that is, the creation of desert out of formerly usable land. The world's deserts are now expanding to the extent that an area about the size of the state of Maine is lost to desert each year. At this rate, by the end of the century there will be about 20 per cent more desert land than now exists (Council on Environmental Quality and the Department of State, 1981).

Arable land—land that can be productively cultivated—will increase by only 4 per cent by the year 2000. Most of any increase in food supply by

412

An area about the size of Maine is lost to desert each year.

that time will come from higher yields on land that is already farmed (Council on Environmental Quality and the Department of State, 1981). An additional problem is overgrazing by livestock, occurring when animals consume grasses beyond the regenerative capacity of the soil and the climate. This could strain the economies of societies that depend heavily on animals for energy to plow the land, for food, and for leather and wool for clothing (Brown, 1978).

ENERGY RESOURCES

Ultimately, our only sources of energy are the sun, gravity, and the atomic nucleus (Clapham, 1981). Wood and fossil fuels, such as petroleum and coal, are stored solar energy. The forests can be renewed with proper care, but fossil fuels are finite in supply because of the extraordinarily long time that it takes for them to be produced.

The production of oil will soon approach geologists' current estimates of the world's supply. Industrial societies will probably be able to meet their energy needs until about 1990, but less developed countries will have difficulty meeting their needs as supplies dwindle and prices rise (Council on Envi-

ronmental Quality and the Department of State, 1981). Long-term increases in the price of petroleum will have important consequences: Fishing fleets will find it less profitable to travel to marginally productive waters, and the cost of gasoline used by farmers will raise the price of food.

Other sources of energy pose different problems. Natural gas is clean and relatively easy to supply, but reserves are limited and not increasing as fast as the demand. Coal, which is now in plentiful supply, is dangerous to mine and dirty to burn; careless strip-mining practices have also caused soil erosion and affected the water table. Nuclear energy poses several problems. One is the disposal of nuclear waste, which remains dangerously radioactive for centuries. The far-reaching and disastrous consequences of nuclear power plant accidents also make this a hazardous source of energy. Every year the Nuclear Regulatory Commission reports thousands of cases of malfunctions in nuclear power plants in the United States; the near-catastrophe at Three Mile Island in Pennsylvania in 1979 was the most widely publicized of these breakdowns.

A less expensive alternative to gasoline that has been proposed as fuel for cars—and used to a limited extent—is gasohol, a mixture of petroleum and alcohol distilled from farm crops. This proposed solution to the energy crisis illustrates how various components of the ecosystem are intricately interwoven. Cropland can be used to produce food, or it can be used to raise crops for other purposes such as the manufacture of gasohol. In the future, the dwindling supply of petroleum could lead to conflict over the use of cropland between the relatively wealthy few who own cars that need fuel and the masses of the world who need more food (Brown, 1980).

THE FOOD SUPPLY

Earlier we saw that nearly two centuries ago Thomas Malthus predicted mass starvation for the people of the world. To support his pessimistic conclusion, Malthus focused on one particular aspect of the ecosystem: the relationship between human population and food supply. Since he wrote, two major changes have at least postponed the most dire of the consequences Malthus predicted. One change was a decline in the birth rate as many societies industrialized. A second was a significant increase in agricultural productivity and a better worldwide distribution of food. However, today food supply again threatens to cause some of the problems foreseen by Malthus.

Estimating the actual supply of food in the world is not easy. Often there are no government records of food that is grown and consumed by individuals on their own. There is probably enough grain in the world today to provide everyone with enough calories to keep them healthy, if not well fed, but this supply of food is distributed unevenly. Malnourishment, or the lack of sufficient nutrients in the diet, is linked to a variety of diseases that result from protein, vitamin, or mineral deficiency. The Food and Agricultural Organization of the United Nations estimates that about 11 per cent of the world's population is malnourished. Each year, about ten million of these people, many of them children, die of starvation or from diseases that would not have been fatal if they had been fed properly (Clapham, 1981).

Although there is enough food to provide everyone with a decent diet, that food is not always available to the people who need it. Famines are less the result of an inadequate supply of food in the world than a product of the inability of some people to command food in the international economy (Sen, 1981). Also, much of the world's grain is fed to livestock, an inefficient and costly source of nutrition, and in some nations such as the United States substantial amounts of food are fed to household pets. Food output is also restricted by governments and by multinational "agribusiness" corporations to keep prices as high as possible.

During the 1960s, the *"green revolution"*—a major change in agricultural technology—gave rise to the hope that the world's food supply could be increased to the point where everyone could be well fed. The green revolution was the result of the development by plant geneticists of new dwarf varieties of wheat and rice that could double or triple yields on the same amount of land. These new plant varieties were the primary cause of a 50 per cent increase in the world's production of food and feed grains between 1965 and 1981 (King, 1981). Figure 17.5 shows how the output of wheat in India increased between 1950 and 1981; the surge in production between 1966 and 1972 was a direct and immediate result of the green revolution. Today, however, there is reason to believe that these high-yield grains have reached their limit as a source of increased productivity. These grains require much water, fertilizer, and pesticide to grow, posing problems for the ecosystem. Another limiting factor in the use of high-yield grains is that they have proved susceptible to insects, diseases, and floods. In addition, the high cost of raising these new varieties of wheat and rice has led to increased investment in farming by large corporations. As a result, agribusiness has become a more important force in farming around the world, and it has sometimes used its power to reduce the food supply in order to maximize profits.

There is uncertainty about the future of efforts to feed the world's people. The Council on Environmental Quality and the Department of State forecasts that by the year 2000 there will be 90 per cent more food than there was in 1970. However, because of rapid increases in population, the average diet of people in less developed countries will probably not improve much, if at all, by the end of the century. Advances in genetics could eventually lead to a second green revolution, but that now seems to be in the distant future. As Lester R. Brown, director of an international food and resource research organization called Worldwatch, has said: "There may be other important breakthroughs down the road if the scientists do find the key to increasing photosynthesis. But the gains from those discoveries would also be only time buying if population increases aren't checked" (cited in King, 1981: E24).

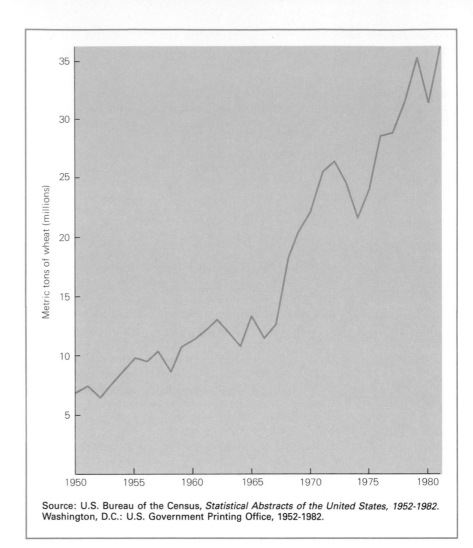

FIGURE 17.5
Wheat Production in India, 1950-1981, in Millions of Metric Tons

Source: U.S. Bureau of the Census, *Statistical Abstracts of the United States, 1952-1982.* Washington, D.C.: U.S. Government Printing Office, 1952-1982.

Coping with the Population Problem

A large and rapidly growing world population is increasingly straining the carrying capacity of the ecosystem. Resources are being depleted, the air and the water are being polluted, and food is in short supply for many people. Population growth also has consequences for society. Economic development is slowed, as resources needed to feed and clothe people are made unavailable for investment. Unemployment rises, as the number of people increases faster than the number of jobs. Cities become overcrowded and public services such as roads and sewers deteriorate from overuse. These problems can sometimes be solved in the short run with technological breakthroughs or emergency measures, but in the long run, as Lester R. Brown suggests, only a reduction in the rate at which the world's population is growing will avert disaster. How can population growth be checked?

Historically, industrialization has been associated with a slower rate of population growth as the birth rate declines to close to the level of the death rate. One way to avoid a Malthusian future might be to encourage industrial development. However, this is an unlikely solution to the population problem. Dwindling resources—especially fossil fuels—will limit industrial growth in the future. Even if new resources were discovered or technological advances produced substitutes for depleted resources, industrialization would continue to pollute the environment. This would pose an increased danger to human health and to wildlife, and it would harm crops and increase malnourishment and starvation (Meadows et al., 1974). Even if the world's population remained at its current level of 4.7 billion, industrial growth would have to proceed more slowly for severe damage to the ecosystem and the human population to be averted.

CONTROLLING FERTILITY

The only long-term solution to the population problem is to curb the rate of natural increase. Because the value placed on human life makes it impossible to raise the death rate, the remaining option is to reduce the birth rate (Brown, 1983). This will require government intervention rather than reliance on continued industrial growth.

Family Planning

One policy that has been used as a way to reduce fertility is *family planning,* the conscious decision making by married couples to have only as many children as they want to have. The goal of family planning is to reduce unplanned and unwanted children. Even in the United States, where effective measures of birth control are widely available and extensively used, one study found that 14 per cent of all children born between 1966 and 1970 were both unplanned and unwanted, and another 29 per cent were unplanned but wanted (Westoff, 1976).

The difficulty with family planning is that married couples might have as many children as they want and only then use birth-control measures. In a society in which familism is a strongly held value, a couple might successfully plan their family and have five or even ten children. Of course, by planning their family this way, they would contribute nothing to efforts to reduce population growth.

To reduce population growth, family planning must be accompanied by an antinatal policy—that is, one that encourages people to have small numbers of children. In contrast, many governments have adopted pronatal policies that directly or indirectly encourage high birth rates. East Germany, for instance, has given cash bonuses to couples who marry and have children (Presser and Salsberg,

1975). Pronatalism is also a result of laws against abortion, policies that discourage sterilization, and tax laws that provide equal and substantial deductions for each additional child. Religions also strengthen pronatalism by prohibiting birth control and abortion and by instructing believers to "be fruitful and multiply."

Birth Control

A variety of birth-control devices are available for controlling fertility. Historically, people have limited births by delaying the age at marriage, abstaining from sex after the birth of a child, abortion, and even infanticide (although this is technically not "birth" control); these measures have kept fertility well below women's potential for reproduction (Van de Walle and Knodel, 1980). More recently, effective contraceptive measures such as the pill, the intrauterine device (IUD), condoms, the diaphragm, and jellies and foams have become available. Sterilization has also become more widely used; about three-fourths of the couples in India who practice birth control have been sterilized (Nortman, 1977). Another effective measure to reduce the birth rate is abortion; Japan cut its birth rate in half from 1947 to 1957 largely as a result of widespread abortions, and Romania's birth rate rose from 14.3 per 1,000 in 1966 to 40 per 1,000 in 1967, after abortion was made illegal (Taeuber, 1960; Tietze and Dawson, 1977).

For these measures to work, they must be compatible with people's values, available, effective, and used regularly (Coale, 1973). Although abortion is now legally available to about two-thirds of the world's population, it still violates many people's familistic values and religious beliefs. The 1973 United States Supreme Court decision of *Roe* v. *Wade* prohibited states from preventing abortion in the first three months of pregnancy, allowed states to regulate the conditions under which abortions could be performed during the second trimester, and permitted the states to make abortion illegal altogether in the last three months. Since that decision, there has been widespread disagreement over abortion in the United States. Those who favor legalized abortion claim that women have the right to control their bodies, that the fetus cannot live outside the womb on its own during the first six months after conception, that children should be wanted by their parents, and that for many women the alternative to a legal abortion is a dangerous illegal abortion. Opponents of legal abortion argue that it is murder of a living being and that easy access to abortion will encourage promiscuity and weaken or destroy the family.

The Chinese "Success Story"

One nation that has been remarkably successful in cutting its birth rate in a short period of time is China, where the birth rate fell from 34 per 1,000 in 1970 to only 18 per 1,000 in 1979. This reduction is particularly important because China's population is one-fourth of the world's total. The Chinese have used family planning, birth control, and government pressure and incentives to limit couples to a single child. The fact that China's population is quite young (the median age is about twenty-one) means that large numbers of children will probably be born in the near future in spite of a low birth rate.

The Chinese government's efforts to limit couples to one child have met with resistance. Husbands and grandparents often place wives under considerable pressure to produce a son who will continue the family's name; there have even been reports of abortions after medical tests have shown that the fetus is female. If the abortion of female fetuses or even female infanticide became common practice, this would upset the sex ratio in ways that in the long run could reduce marriages and affect the birth rate. The government has taken several steps to make the Chinese people content with a single child. Girls are allowed to take their mother's surname and to inherit their father's factory job when he retires. Daughters are now legally responsible for the support of their elderly parents, whereas until recently sons alone had this duty; this undercuts the motive to have many children so that parents will be supported when they grow old (Wren, 1982a, 1982c).

The Chinese government urges couples to use birth control—especially sterilization—after their first child and encourages abortion for women who get pregnant a second time. According to the constitution adopted in 1982, each man and woman is required to practice family planning. The Chinese have relied on a community-based birth-control program that uses teams of trained local people to work with couples to meet a government-established birth quota for the community. More than half of all married Chinese couples have pledged to have only one child. Those who take this pledge are entitled to many benefits: priority in housing and jobs, a monthly bonus, medical care, a larger food allowance, and free nursery school care. However, if a couple has a second child, they are denied these benefits for three years and can even be required to reimburse the government for the bonuses they have received (Wren, 1982a; McLaughlin, 1982). Couples who continue to have children have been punished by dismissal from a job, reduction in wages, expulsion from the Communist party, shutting off their electricity or water, and confiscation of the family bicycle or television set. These economic penalties have not always been effective in rural communities, where some families realize that they can gain more in increased output from an additional worker in the fields than they will lose in penalties imposed by the state (Wren, 1982a).

Reducing the Birth Rate

China's policy of using strong government pressure—some would say coercion—to limit population growth is a radical way of reducing the birth rate, but it is not clear that birth-control policies can be effective without some coercion by the government. The Gandhi government fell in India in 1977 largely because of public opposition to forced sterilization, and the new Gandhi government in 1980 chose voluntarism over coercion as a way to curb population growth (Petersen, 1982). Realizing the ineffectiveness of voluntary measures, the government of Bangladesh—the world's most densely populated country—announced in 1982 that to cut the birth rate from 29.5 per 1,000 to 15 per 1,000 by 1985 1.4 million people would be sterilized within two years; at the time of the announcement, only 20 per cent of the people were using birth-control measures (*The Boston Globe,* December 3, 1982, p. 12).

A few small nations with stable governments, such as Singapore and Hong Kong, have managed to use government action successfully to reduce fertility. Birth rates also declined dramatically in Taiwan and South Korea, but this may have been associated more with their relatively high levels of economic development than with government efforts to implement a birth-control policy. The use of community-based efforts similar to those used in China has also reduced birth rates in rural Thailand and on the island of Bali, Indonesia (Van der Tak, Haub, and Murphy, 1979).

Probably the most effective way of reducing the birth rate is through a variety of strategies, rather than a single approach. One way is population education—demonstrating to people that they can plan the arrival of children and showing them that the quality of their lives will improve with a smaller family. This resocialization process also includes efforts to alter values about the ideal number of children in a family, the use of birth-control measures, and the appropriate age for marriage (Nam, 1982: 370). Universal education is an important part of "population socialization," because people learn in school about alternative kinds of family organization. Education has another important consequence: It opens up new opportunities for women. As women become more integrated into society, especially by taking jobs outside the home, they are likely to delay marriage and to have fewer children when they do marry. Greater opportunities for women and more education in general also increase material aspirations and thereby provide an additional incentive to have fewer children.

A variety of legal changes can help to reduce fertility. A society can increase the minimum age at marriage so as to reduce the number of years that couples have to bear children. Another strategy is to limit the number of maternity leaves from work that women can take or to charge higher delivery fees for later children; Singapore has used both of these policies successfully to reduce its birth rate (Kee and Lee, 1973). Tax incentives can be offered to motivate couples to have fewer children; Singapore, for example, permits only three tax deductions for children. In the United States today, each child gives parents an additional $1,000 tax deduction. Limiting the number of deductions to two or three, and even providing a larger deduction for the first child than for the second and third ones, might reduce the birth rate. The disadvantage of such a plan is that those who could least afford to pay increased taxes would be placed under an even greater financial burden. Other financial incentives have also been used to reduce fertility; for example, Indonesia has provided water and roads to communities that reduce their birth rates (Van der Tak, Haub, and Murphy, 1979).

The availability of a wide array of birth-control measures is another important part of any effective policy to curb population growth. China and Singapore have had success in using local workers to help couples plan their families; government-run clinics have been less effective. These local workers can educate people about a variety of methods of birth control, including abortion and sterilization. Because of resistance to certain methods, choice is an important part of a workable plan to reduce the birth rate.

An improved standard of living—including higher incomes, better diets, more literacy, and more education—can reduce the rate of population growth. Reductions in infant mortality that come with higher standards of living can reduce the birth rate, because parents have to produce fewer children to have some survive to adulthood. However, the limitations imposed by the ecosystem will make it difficult for many nations to reach the level of economic and social well-being necessary to cause birth rates to fall to the point of little or no population growth. Technological advances in agriculture may delay the future that Malthus predicted, but in the long run efforts to control fertility seem the most likely way to avert ecological disaster.

Hunger like that experienced by this child is frequently the result of overpopulation. Efforts to control fertility seem the most likely way to deal with this problem.

Summary

Human population is an important component of the complex, self-sustaining set of relationships among living and nonliving things called the ecosystem. People are the dominant species ecologically; today, they threaten to destroy the ecosystem by overpopulation and abuse of the environment. Human ecology is the study of the relationship of people to their environment; demography focuses more specifically on the processes of fertility, mortality, and migration that affect the size, composition, and distribution of populations.

Censuses enumerate the size and the characteristics of a population. In the United States, censuses are taken every ten years, but in many nations they are conducted less regularly. Many obstacles are confronted in counting accurately the number of people in a country. Undercounting can have serious ramifications; for example, in the United States it can result in an incorrect apportionment of Congressional seats or inadequate federal funding of a community's social programs.

The population of any country can be represented in a population pyramid that depicts the number of males and females in each age group, or age cohort. The size of an age cohort has a major impact on the life chances of the members of that cohort; for example, people who belong to a large cohort experience more competition for jobs. Age is also important in determining a society's dependency ratio, or the number of economically dependent members of the society divided by the number of economically productive members. Rising proportions of elderly people in industrial societies such as the United States and Japan have put retirement benefit programs under considerable strain.

Fertility is usually measured by the crude birth rate—the number of births for every 1,000 people in a population. Birth rates are high in societies that place a high value on familism. This is especially true of preindustrial and industrializing societies, where additional children can help out in the fields and support their parents when they grow old.

Mortality is usually measured by the crude death rate—the number of deaths for every 1,000 people in a population. In many preindustrial and industrializing societies, the rate of infant mortality is high. The United States ranks about ninth among nations in infant mortality, but some groups and areas of the country have infant mortality rates much like those of less developed nations. Life expectancy—the average number of additional years people of a particular age can expect to live—is markedly higher in industrial societies than in less economically developed ones. In the United States, life expectancy is higher for women than for men and higher for whites than for blacks. The causes of death change as a society industrializes; infectious and parasitic diseases become less common, and diseases of the heart and cancer become relatively more important.

Migration is a third important demographic process. People move from one nation to another (international migration) and from region to region within the same nation (internal migration). Migration is a product of factors that push people out of one country or area and factors that pull them to another country or area.

Population growth results from more births than deaths and from more immigration than emigration. One way to measure it is by net growth rate, the net gain in population per 1,000 people; another way is by doubling time, the number of years that it will take a population to become twice its present size if it continues to grow at its current rate. Zero population growth occurs when the crude birth rate and the crude death rate are the same, assuming there is a net migration rate of zero. The demographic transition model describes a process by which populations pass from a situation of a high birth rate and a high death rate to a stage in which the death rate falls but the birth rate remains relatively high, and finally to a stage in which the birth rate falls to about the same low level as the death rate. Most of the world's population now lives in countries that have not yet entered the third stage, and the limits placed on industrial growth by the ecosystem make it doubtful that all countries will enter this third stage.

The water is an important part of the ecosystem that has become a dwindling resource due to overfishing and pollution. In addition, fresh water has become less plentiful, and this threatens the food supply because it is needed for irrigation. The air is increasingly polluted, resulting in a variety of debilitating and fatal diseases. Pollution of the air has changed the atmosphere's temperature and threatened the ozone layer that protects living things from the sun's rays. The lands of the Earth have been increasingly devastated; deforestation and desertification have reduced the water supply, eroded the soil, and reduced agricultural productivity. Energy resources have been depleted; fossil fuels are already in short supply, and a firewood shortage threatens preindustrial and industrializing societies. Alternative sources of renewable energy are needed, but they have not yet been fully developed.

Half a billion people are malnourished, and about ten million die each year from this problem. The inability to buy or grow food, rather than an absolute shortage of food, is the crux of this problem. The "green revolution" of the 1960s greatly increased agricultural productivity, but continued population growth has left many people hungry. Further technological advances in agriculture are possible, but in the long run it will be necessary to reduce the rate of population growth to preserve the ecosystem.

The only long-term solution to ecological problems is to reduce the birth rate. This requires a combination of family planning and an antinatal policy; in other words, couples must begin to plan to have fewer children. This can be done by educating people about how a smaller family would improve their standard of living and by providing them with access to a choice of birth-control measures. The Chinese have successfully reduced fertility in a short time through measures that some regard as coercive. Other nations have used financial incentives, persuasion by the government, community-based workers, legalized abortion, and sterilization to reduce their birth rates. In the long run, economic development might reduce the birth rate, but the limits imposed by the ecosystem make continued industrialization an unlikely prospect and therefore require that attention be turned to reducing the birth rate.

Important Terms

AGE COHORT (397)
CARRYING CAPACITY (410)
CENSUS (396)
CRUDE BIRTH RATE (400)
CRUDE DEATH RATE (403)
DEMOGRAPHIC TRANSITION (409)
DEMOGRAPHY (395)
DEPENDENCY RATIO (399)
DOUBLING TIME (408)
FAMILISM (401)
FAMILY PLANNING (415)
FECUNDITY (400)
FERTILITY (400)
"GREEN REVOLUTION" (413)
HUMAN ECOLOGY (395)
INFANT MORTALITY RATE (403)
INTERNAL MIGRATION (406)
INTERNATIONAL MIGRATION (404)
LIFE EXPECTANCY (403)
LIFE SPAN (403)
MIGRATION (404)
MORTALITY (403)
NET GROWTH RATE (408)
NET MIGRATION RATE (404)
POPULATION (395)
POPULATION PYRAMID (397)
PULL FACTOR (408)
PUSH FACTOR (408)
RATE OF NATURAL INCREASE (408)
SEX RATIO (400)
ZERO POPULATION GROWTH (ZPG) (408)

Suggested Readings

Lester R. Brown. *The Twenty-Ninth Day: Accommodating Human Needs and Numbers to the Earth's Resources.* New York: Norton, 1978. A well-written and comprehensive look at population growth, energy resources, food supply, and the economic factors that affect the future prospects of the planet.

W. B. Clapham, Jr. *Human Ecosystems.* New York: Macmillan, 1981. A textbook that presents a thorough treatment of environmental issues and includes a useful chapter on population.

The Council on Environmental Quality and the Department of State. *The Global 2000 Report to the President: Entering the Twenty-First Century,* Vol. 1. Washington, D.C.: U.S. Government Printing Office, 1981. A brief summary of a longer study that offers projections about population, food, and the environment until the end of the century; special attention is paid to differences between industrialized societies and less developed ones.

Richard A. Easterlin. *Birth and Fortune: The Impact of Numbers on Personal Welfare.* New York: Basic Books, 1980. A fascinating account of the different life chances of people who are part of large or small birth cohorts.

Donella H. Meadows, Dennis L. Meadows, Jørgen Randers, and William W. Behrens, III, *The Limits to Growth: A Report for the Club of Rome's Project on the Predicament on Mankind,* 2nd ed. New York: Universe Books, 1974. A widely discussed and pessimistic study of population growth, resource depletion, and world starvation.

Jan Van der Tak, Carl Haub, and Elaine Murphy. "Our Population Predicament: A New Look," *Population Bulletin* 34 (December 1979): 1–48. A long article on a variety of important population issues, including the demographic transition and the experiences of different countries with family planning and birth control.

Dennis H. Wrong. *Population and Society,* 4th ed. New York: Random House, 1977. A good introduction to the study of population.

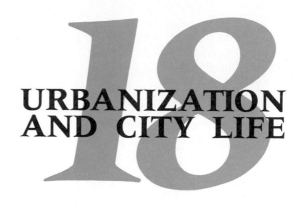

URBANIZATION AND CITY LIFE

In 1975, a United States Senator gave the following reason for Congress's reluctance to help New York City solve its financial problems: "Cities are viewed as the seed of corruption and duplicity, and New York is the biggest city" (cited in Tolchin, 1975, p. 1). Are we to assume, then, that the fifteen million people who live in the New York City metropolitan area are corrupt and duplicitous? Of course not, for New Yorkers lead daily lives much like those of other Americans, work at similar jobs, and watch the same television programs. Many people who live in the New York City area would not want to live anywhere else. They enjoy fine museums, a wide choice of movies and plays, and countless stores and shops. However, some New Yorkers would like to move out of the center of the city, at least to the suburbs and perhaps to the countryside. At the same time, they want access to the city's resources. This ambivalence toward cities is deeply ingrained in American culture; the vast majority of people in the United States live in or near cities, and yet many harbor dreams of "a little place in the country."

American attitudes toward the city—and toward suburbs, small towns, and rural areas as well—are mixed, but they include an assumption that a person's place of residence has an important effect on social behavior. Later in this chapter we examine differences in types of *communities,* which are relatively permanent groups of people who interact to meet common goals and needs and who live in one location (Schnore, 1973). Communities vary in size from a few families living in huts to the fifteen million residents of the New York City area. Communities also differ in population density, which is usually measured by the number of people per square mile. Some communities are more heterogeneous than others; that is, the residents differ in age, race, ethnicity, class, and other characteristics.

These three aspects of communities—size, population density, and heterogeneity (or diversity)—distinguish the *city* from smaller communities. Cities are large, densely populated, and heterogeneous communities. In contrast, small towns and rural areas have fewer residents, are less densely packed, and are more homogeneous. Some sociologists claim that these three characteristics make life in the city very different from life in smaller communities; we will examine this and contrasting viewpoints later in the chapter, when we look at urbanism as a way of life.

Urbanization

Cities have existed for five or six thousand years, but the rate of *urbanization*—that is, the process by which societies become "citified" as people move from small communities to large cities—has accelerated over the past two centuries. For example, in 1850, about 2 per cent of the world's people lived in cities with populations greater than 100,000; only London had a population of more than one million. Today, there are more than a hundred cities with populations of one million or more, and about one-fourth of all people live in cities with more than 100,000 people (Fischer, 1976; United Nations, 1979).

One reason for rapid urbanization is that while the death rate has fallen, fertility has failed to decline as quickly, giving rise to a high rate of natural increase that has expanded urban populations (see Chapter 17). Another factor is migration from rural areas and small towns to large cities. Some of this is a product of the "pull" of the city; many people are drawn to the city by economic opportunities. Migration is also a product of "push" factors; for instance, people leave rural areas because of high agricultural density (that is, a large number of farmers per acre of land) and because plantation systems of agriculture deny ownership of the land to them (Firebaugh, 1979).

THE PREINDUSTRIAL CITY

Historically, cities emerged only after advances in the domestication of plants, the irrigation of fields, and the application of metallurgy to the plow made it possible for farmers to grow more food than they could eat. This food surplus was needed to support nonagricultural workers in the city. Indeed, some sociologists have even defined the city by its dependence on food grown in other places.

The first recognizable cities developed about 3000 or 4000 B.C. in the fertile valleys of the Tigrus–Euphrates, the Nile, the Indus, and the Yellow Rivers. Rarely did these cities grow to populations of more than 10,000. Their small size was due to inefficient agricultural techniques that could not produce enough surplus food to support more people.

Preindustrial cities were largely organized around kinship ties, but economic functions became increasingly important as the basis for interaction among city dwellers. Political institutions became more complex in the preindustrial city, and a small elite typically held power. Work was usually done in the home or in craft shops rather than in factories, which did not develop until many centuries later. Often, specific occupational groups inhabited identifiable areas of the city. The poor usually lived on the outskirts of the city, and the political elite and the wealthy tradespeople typically lived in the center of the city (Sjoberg, 1960; Gist and Fava, 1974; Palen, 1975).

Preindustrial cities existed in ancient Rome and Greece. Athens was a city with concentrated wealth and power and a complex division of labor. At its peak, its population was between 120,000 and 180,000, not large by modern standards. Rome was a large city by ancient standards, although its population was probably only half a million (Palen, 1975). Most of the population of the Roman Empire lived in small villages and rural areas some distance from the city. After the fall of the Empire that began in the fifth century A.D., cities did not reemerge until after 1100 (Gist and Fava, 1974). The absence of an advanced technology—especially for transportation and communication, the building blocks of a unified and extended community—limited cities in the Middle Ages to populations of about 80,000 (Palen, 1975: 28). Moreover,

the lack of modern sanitation and sewage disposal meant that the death rate in these cities was high, especially during epidemics such as the Black Death (1348–1350), which decimated about one-fourth of Europe's population and more than half of the people who lived in the cities.

INDUSTRIALIZATION AND THE CITY

Large cities as we know them today developed only with industrialization. The Industrial Revolution of the eighteenth and nineteenth centuries replaced hand tools with machines, animate sources of energy with inanimate ones, and work at home with labor in the factory. Advances in agricultural technology, such as the mechanization of farming, made it possible for the population to include larger numbers of people who did no farming. Public health measures such as sewage disposal systems cut the death rate in cities, and the organization of police forces and firefighters made city life safer.

Today, in some preindustrial and industrializing nations, less than 10 per cent of the population lives in cities; most of these countries are quite small in total population, such as Yemen, Chad, and Nepal. At the other extreme, in many highly industrialized nations, more than 70 per cent of the population lives in cities. Countries such as Australia and Belgium are nearly 90 per cent urbanized, and in 1980 73.7 per cent of all Americans lived in a city or one of its suburbs (U.S. Bureau of the Census, 1982: 20). Most of the countries in the world fall between these extremes; moderate levels of urbanization characterize most of southern and eastern Europe, most of Latin America, and the nations of the Middle East (Gist and Fava, 1974: 108–109).

Primate Cities and Overurbanization

Even though a comparatively small proportion of people live in cities in those societies that are still industrializing, the rate at which the population of those countries is becoming urbanized is often quite high. Many of these societies have one "primate city," a large urban community that might be the only recognizable city in the whole country. These cities act as magnets for people who want to escape unfavorable economic conditions in rural areas and fulfill dreams arising from a "revolution of rising expectations," which is often a product of exposure to the mass media.

Overurbanized cities in developing nations often have a squatter shantytown on the outskirts of the city.

Many preindustrial and industrializing societies face the problem of "overurbanization," meaning that more people live in the city than there are available jobs or facilities for. These overurbanized cities do not have adequate housing, electricity, transportation, sewage disposal, and social services for everyone. On the outskirts of many of these cities, there are squatter shantytowns where poverty-stricken migrants from rural areas live in unplanned and often illegal communities. Their housing is built from scrap metal, cardboard boxes, or discarded lumber. Because of congestion and unsanitary living conditions, these shantytowns have very high rates of illness and death (Peattie and Aldrete-Haas, 1981).

THE MODERN METROPOLIS

Urban communities in industrial societies include central cities that are used for business, entertainment, and residence. They also include suburbs that lie outside the political boundaries of the city; these communities are used primarily for residence and increasingly for business and entertainment. In addition, rural areas and small towns are often connected to the central city in various ways. A central city, its suburbs, and the surrounding towns and rural areas that are socially and economically linked together are called a *metropolis* or, in the technical language of the U.S. Bureau of the Census, a *Standard Metropolitan Statistical Area* (SMSA). An SMSA is an area that includes a city of at least 50,000 people and the adjacent counties with urban populations that are economically and socially integrated with the city. About three-fourths of the nation's population lives in the 318 SMSAs defined by the Census Bureau, even though those SMSAs cover only one-sixth of the nation's land area. In 1980, 30 per cent of Americans lived in central cities, 44.8 per cent in metropolitan areas outside central cities, and 25.2 per cent in small towns and rural areas outside metropolitan areas (U.S. Bureau of the Census, 1982: 15).

Metropolitan growth occurs as urban communities expand from their center and incorporate outlying towns and rural areas into their social and economic network. This process of growth often obscures distinctions among the central city, the suburb, the small town, and rural areas. Metropolitan growth has been encouraged by the policies of

TABLE 18.1
*Sixteen Standard Consolidated
Statistical Areas, 1980*

SCSA	1980 Population
New York–Newark–Jersey City, N.Y.–N.J.–Conn.	16,122,000
Los Angeles–Long Beach–Anaheim, Calif.	11,498,000
Chicago–Gary–Kenosha, Ill.–Ind.–Wis.	7,870,000
Philadelphia–Wilmington–Trenton, Pa.–Del.–N.J.–Md.	5,548,000
San Francisco–Oakland–San Jose, Calif.	5,180,000
Detroit–Ann Arbor, Mich.	4,618,000
Boston–Lawrence–Lowell, Mass.–N.H.	3,448,000
Houston–Galveston, Tex.	3,101,000
Cleveland–Akron–Lorain, Ohio	2,834,000
Miami–Fort Lauderdale, Fla.	2,644,000
Seattle–Tacoma, Wash.	2,093,000
Cincinnati–Hamilton, Ohio–Ky.–Ind.	1,660,000
Milwaukee–Racine, Wis.	1,570,000
Indianapolis–Anderson, Ind.	1,306,000
Providence–Fall River, R.I.–Mass.	1,096,000
Dayton–Springfield, Ohio	1,014,000

Source: U.S. Bureau of the Census, *Statistical Abstract of the United States, 1982–83.* Washington, D.C.: U.S. Government Printing Office, 1982, p. 904.

the United States government, including its support for the construction of highways and schools outside the central city.

Urban growth sometimes connects cities that are near each other. Two or more contiguous, or adjoining, SMSAs that are integrated with each other socially and economically are called a *Standard Consolidated Statistical Area* (SCSA) by the Bureau of the Census. Table 18.1 shows the populations of the sixteen SCSAs defined by the Bureau in 1980; together, the population of these SCSAs is about one-third of the country's total.

When a number of metropolitan areas become connected by urban, semiurban, or suburban areas to form a more or less continuous urban community, it is called a *megalopolis*. These extended communities have no one central city; instead they have a series of central cities that are loosely joined together. Megalopolises exist in Great Britain, Japan, and West Germany, but perhaps the most notable example of such urban sprawl is the agglomeration of cities and suburbs that extends from southern New Hampshire through the Boston area, Connecticut, the New York City area, New Jersey, the Philadelphia and Washington, D.C., areas, into northern Virginia. About one-fifth of Americans live in this megalopolis.

Megalopolises are socially and economically integrated but politically fragmented. Because they include many different political jurisdictions, it is difficult for them to develop a coherent plan for the whole region. Consequently, the use of the land is wasteful, open areas and agricultural land are infringed upon by developers who hurt the ecosystem, and there is costly duplication of facilities and services.

The Central City

The core of a metropolitan area—the *central city*—is usually characterized by large size, high population density, and diversity. Moreover, this kind of community has a culture that distinguishes it from the traditional culture of small towns and rural areas. In the United States, several phenomena specific to the central city arose during the nineteenth century and transformed urban culture in important ways. Five of these urban phenomena—the apartment building, the metropolitan press, the department store, the ballpark, and the vaudeville house—are examined in SEL 18.1.

In recent years, American central cities have lost people to the surrounding suburbs, and beginning

SOCIOLOGY AND EVERYDAY LIFE 18.1
The Culture of the City

During the nineteenth century, five new phenomena arose in American cities that served to help foreign immigrants, migrants from rural areas and small towns, and long-term city dwellers develop a common culture. Unlike the church and the school, the apartment building, the metropolitan press, the department store, the ballpark, and the vaudeville house all emerged in the city. These five phenomena helped city residents find "privacy, identity, and happiness" (p. 4).

The apartment house altered living conditions by providing privacy in a crowded city, by reducing the congestion common to tenements and boarding houses, and by providing cleaner and better-heated quarters. The construction of apartment houses, which began in the 1860s, provided jobs for the people who built and maintained them and caused land values to rise in many urban neighborhoods.

A second important phenomenon that changed urban culture was the metropolitan press. Technological advances in printing, changes in management techniques, and new ways of increasing circulation (such as the newsboy) all changed the newspaper business between the 1830s and the 1890s. The telegraph and the telephone made it possible to transmit news from city to city, and the formation of news associations such as the Associated Press in 1848 helped newspapers report recent events that had occurred miles away. The urban press was important in creating a common identity among the city's people. It provided information that helped people adjust to daily life in a strange environment. In a sense, the newspaper replaced the gossip and first-hand experiences more common to small towns and rural areas; the fast pace of city life reduced opportunities for idle talk, and the large size of the city made gossip an inefficient way to gather information. The press also had important economic ramifications. Its advertisements encouraged workers to earn and to spend. It also educated consumers about how to spend their money and how to get a good bargain by being selective in their purchases.

One source of advertising for the metropolitan press was the department store, another important phenomenon that emerged during the nineteenth century. In the nineteenth century, men typically held paying jobs outside the home and women spent most of the family's income on food, clothing, home furnishings, and other merchandise. Department stores developed to attract these women as customers, which was possible because of the development of improved transportation systems such as the horsecar and the trolley. The department store brought women out of their homes and to the center of the city; for many women this was "a form of real emancipation" (p. 129):

Most women welcomed the adventure of downtown shopping, which for many was not only a fashionable activity but also a truly urban one. They went window-shopping, strolled through the stores, gazed at the displays and each other, chatted with friends, listened to clerks' explanations, assessed the articles and other shoppers, bought something they considered a bargain, and under fortunate circumstances went home with the feeling that they had not only done something women were supposed to do, but had actually enjoyed doing it. This experience, repeated almost daily, intensified their identity as modern urban women (pp. 144–145).

The position of clerk in these stores was often filled by women, because most of the customers with whom the clerks dealt were women.

Spectator sports also emerged as an important part of city life during the nineteenth century. At first, horse racing and boxing were especially popular. During the middle of the century, baseball became popular, and by 1900 organized leagues of professional teams had been formed. The ballpark itself became a bit of greenery in the middle of the city, a reminder of the rural areas that many people had left behind. Spectators became conscious of the ways that rules regulated their daily lives by watching the ordered activity of a game, and, by watching the contest, they learned the value of competition. Of course, baseball was also a business; tickets were sold to spectators, and sporting equipment was sold to people who enjoyed playing the game or aspired to become professionals. The games themselves were scheduled around work hours, usually in the evenings during the week and during the day on weekends. Baseball provided the urban press with readers, because fans turned to the papers for the results and descriptions of the games they did not attend. In addition, baseball teams became a source of civic pride, a way to identify with the city in the competition with teams from other cities.

Still another important phenomenon of the city in the nineteenth century was the vaudeville house, where variety shows of songs, juggling, gymnastics, dancing, and comedy sketches entertained entire families. These shows helped to create a sense of common humanity and social harmony. They served as guides for urban living by focusing on everyday problems, especially the search for economic success. Vaudeville shows usually maintained people's optimism by conveying a message that was uplifting and exalting.

The apartment building, the metropolitan press, the department store, the ballpark, and the vaudeville house all changed the physical appearance of the city because they were housed in new or renovated buildings. They also helped to socialize new residents of the city to the values of American culture: privacy, materialism, competition, and tolerance.

Source: Based on Gunther Barth, *City People: The Rise of Modern City Culture in Nineteenth-Century America.* New York: Oxford University Press, 1980.

in the 1970s they lost population to small towns and rural areas as well. Those who are most likely to leave the central city for the suburbs are commonly the most skilled, the best educated, and the wealthiest of the city's residents. As a result of this selective migration, those who remain behind in the central city tend, on the average, to be of lower social standing. This makes it difficult for city governments to raise the tax revenue needed to pay schoolteachers, police officers, and firefighters. It limits the funds available for welfare benefits. Necessary repairs to municipal buildings, streets, and sidewalks may be postponed because of the lack of public funds. With their declining resources, cities have come close to bankruptcy in their efforts to maintain even minimum standards.

The financial problems of central cities are compounded by the fact that many of their services—such as the police and the mass transit system—are used regularly by people who live outside the central city but travel into the city to work, shop, dine, and be entertained. Because the central city is a political jurisdiction distinct from the surrounding suburbs, people who live outside the city cannot be taxed to pay for these services. Financial problems of this sort are especially serious for the older cities of the Northeast and the Midwest, because they have been losing people to the Sun Belt (see SEL 17.2) at the same time that their aging buildings, streets, and transportation systems have been deteriorating. In the last section of this chapter we consider some proposals to deal with this urban decline.

The Suburb

One way that Americans have resolved their ambivalence toward the central city is to live outside the central city in communities with open space and quiet and with access to the economic and cultural opportunities of the city. The *suburb*—a community outside the central city but within the metropolitan area—has a smaller population, a lower population density, and less diversity than the central city.

Suburbs first developed in the United States at the end of the nineteenth century (Palen, 1975). People were able to live near the central city but outside it only after systems of transportation such as the train and the streetcar had been developed. The first phase of suburban development in the late 1800s was followed by a second phase in the 1920s, when mass ownership of cars made it possible for more Americans to move out of the central city. Cars provide greater flexibility in the choice of housing, but dependence on the car causes problems. Traffic congestion frustrates commuters and wastes fuel and time. Inadequate parking facilities in the city discourage travel from the suburbs to the city to shop, dine, or be entertained. Mass transportation is less flexible than the car, and even the higher gasoline prices of recent years have not turned commuters from their cars to trains and buses. In fact, from 1970 to 1980, a period when gasoline prices rose significantly, the percentage of American workers who commuted by mass transit systems actually fell from 9 per cent to 6 per cent (Herbers, 1983). The relatively small proportion of commuters' incomes paid for gasoline makes it unlikely that this factor will significantly affect suburban growth (Bradbury, Downs, and Small, 1982).

The third phase of suburban growth in the United States began in the late 1940s. The pent-up demand for housing caused by the Great Depression and by World War II, along with federal policies designed to encourage suburban development, caused a rapid growth in communities outside the central city. Federally subsidized highways provided easier access to the city for suburbanites during the 1950s. Those who had served in the military were eligible for low-interest loans, and the banks brought home ownership within the means of many Americans by providing low-interest mortgage loans with a small down payment. The relative inexpensiveness of land and houses in the suburbs also attracted people. Moreover, the federal policy of allowing tax deductions for interest payments on mortgage loans and for property taxes provided a strong financial incentive to own rather than rent housing. In 1980, 70.9 per cent of housing units in the suburbs were occupied by their owners, but only 49.5 per cent of units in the central city were owner occupied (U.S. Bureau of the Census, 1982: 751).

The growth of the suburbs was also spurred by the importance placed on the value of familism (see Chapter 17) in the years after World War II. Many married couples were reunited after the war, and other people married once the sex ratio returned to normal when soldiers came home. The marked increase in the birth rate after World War II was closely associated with a rising demand for housing in communities where children could attend good schools and be raised safely. The suburbs grew to meet the demand for a family-centered and home-oriented community (Gans, 1967).

Originally, many suburbs were "bedroom communities" from which people commuted to jobs in the city. In recent years, however, jobs and services have followed people to the suburbs. Today, these communities commonly include light and high-technology industries, malls that provide shopping opportunities as good or even better than those found in the city, restaurants, and movie theaters. Many people who live in the suburbs rarely travel to the city, even though they may like the idea of having access to it if they wish.

Many suburbanites rarely need to travel to the city because in recent years jobs and services—such as those provided in this shopping mall—have followed people to the suburbs.

Some critics claim that life in the suburbs is more oriented toward conformity than is life in the city. Behavior in the suburbs is probably more visible to neighbors and therefore more subject to social control than is behavior in the city, where neighbors are more likely to be strangers. However, people who move to the suburbs might be more conventional to begin with and might be well aware of what their neighbors will expect of them before they move to the suburbs. "Voluntary conformity" is probably more common in the suburbs than "involuntary conformity," which results from strong pressure to give up one's individuality (Gans, 1967). For the most part, suburban residents are satisfied with their houses, the outdoor living, and their easy access to people with whom they feel comfortable. However, the smaller size, lower population density, and greater homogeneity of the suburbs could make it difficult for residents who differ from their neighbors to find enough people similar to themselves to form social groups (Gans, 1967; Fischer, 1976).

In recent years, it has become apparent that suburban living is not without its problems. The inner ring of suburbs around the central city has become run down; and in many suburbs crime rates have risen. Poor planning of the buildings in some suburbs has resulted in flash flooding and sewage pollution. Housing has become more expensive, and the cost of traveling to work has risen (Kowinski, 1980). All of these changes have required adjustments in suburban communities and in the expectations of those who live there.

Small Towns and Rural Areas

At the outset of this chapter we described the antiurban bias among some Americans who characterize cities as artificial communities filled with vice, strangeness, individualism, and rapid change. Small towns, on the other hand, have often been characterized by virtue, naturalness, familiarity, group loyalty, and tradition (Fischer, 1976). Of course, these perceptions oversimplify the actual differences between large cities and smaller communities. Even in the nineteenth century, small towns and rural areas had their share of problems such as arson by tramps who were refused food and shelter, suicides, mental illness, and poverty (Lesy, 1973).

Traditionally, rural areas have had an agricultural rather than an industrial economic system, and small towns have acted as marketing centers for farmers' produce. Today, however, there are few counties in the United States that rely primarily on agriculture. The economies of most rural areas and small towns now rely on light manufacturing, mining, education, or services instead of farming (Herbers, 1982b). The increased productivity of agriculture in recent years has made it possible for the labor of a few farmers to feed large numbers of people, and this has reduced the number of workers engaged in agriculture. In 1930, about one-fourth of all American workers were farmers, but in 1981 that proportion had dropped to only 2.6 per cent (U.S. Bureau of the Census, 1982: 649).

During the 1970s, there was an important turnabout in a demographic trend that had existed for the previous 150 years: More Americans began to leave the central cities for small towns and rural areas than were migrating to the cities from those communities (Herbers, 1981d, 1982b). Although this trend will probably not "deurbanize" American society significantly, it does seem to be a trend that will continue in spite of recessions and cutbacks in federal funds. In part this trend is due to the spillover of people from metropolitan areas into nearby counties that have not yet been absorbed into the SMSA. Low-cost housing, cheap land, low property taxes, and job openings have drawn people to these smaller communities. In addition, growing numbers of elderly people are retiring to small towns and rural areas. As these communities grow, they will either be redefined as urban areas or will become part of nearby SMSAs. This growth of rural areas and small towns poses problems for society: the conservation of farmland that is threatened by developers, the maintenance of highways, and the shortage of water that often accompanies the rapid growth of a new community (Herbers, 1981c; Kneeland, 1981).

In the past, the geographic isolation of rural areas and small towns created and reinforced cultural differences between people living in those communities and people living in cities. Today, however, the mass media expose people who live in even the most isolated areas to a common culture. As a result, the values and norms of all members of the society have become increasingly similar. The major difference between rural areas and large cities in the United States is now occupational rather than cultural, and even occupational differences are declining as the number of farmworkers shrinks and service industries develop in smaller communities.

Urban Ecology

One specialized branch of human ecology (see Chapter 17) is *urban ecology,* the study of the relationship of people to each other and to their environment in an urban setting. Urban ecologists examine the relationship of the central city to the suburbs, small towns, and rural areas that surround it. They look at the ways that the physical location of a city influences its growth and structure; for example, a nearby waterway might provide easy transportation and make trade possible. In addition, urban ecologists study the ways that behavior varies from one community to another within the city.

ECOLOGICAL PROCESSES

Different ecological processes influence the structure of urban communities (Park, Burgess, and McKenzie, 1925). "Concentration," the clustering of people and activities in one area, occurs when a city is formed and grows. The opposite process is "dispersion," the scattering of people and activities away from a central location. Moving to the suburbs is one form of dispersion, and so is the recent growth of small towns and rural areas.

Concentration is closely associated with the ecological process of "centralization," in which economic, recreational, political, and educational activities are concentrated in a location to which people have easy access. The land values tend to be high in these central locations, which are also crossroads of transportation and communications. "Decentralization" is an ecological process through which different centers of activity develop within a city or a metropolitan area. This is often the result of the search for cheaper land, lower rent, lower taxes, and easier access to workers.

"Specialization" in urban areas creates a variety of smaller communities and neighborhoods that have been called "natural areas." Differences in land values and differences in access to transportation and communications give urban neighborhoods special qualities that are functional for the whole city. For example, a city might include a financial district, a shopping area, and a "red-light" district. Each area is differentiated from other areas. Even though these area are usually not the result of conscious planning, the people who live there and their activities give the neighborhood a distinct identity. Differences in urban neighborhoods can fragment a city because people may need to travel

from one place to another for some purpose, but these areas are often functionally integrated into a single urban community. In other words, each area has different consequences for the city as a whole, and the areas are knit together in ways that give the city a coherent structure.

Another ecological process is "segregation," the tendency of groups with similar characteristics such as ethnicity, class, or age to live separately in the same communities. Segregation can occur by choice, as when new immigrants settle in a neighborhood where people from their country already live; or it can be imposed, as when realtors and banks discriminate against black Americans who try to buy a house in a "white neighborhood." "Invasion" is the ecological process that occurs when people with certain social characteristics move into a community already occupied by people with different characteristics. Usually this involves a low-status group moving into an area occupied by people of higher standing. "Succession" has occurred when the new residents have replaced the old. Invasion and succession are most common when people of one racial or ethnic group take over a residential area from a different group; for example, neighborhoods in the Roxbury and Dorchester areas of Boston that were once occupied primarily by Jews are now primarily black communities.

MODELS OF THE CITY

Ecological processes give cities an identifiable pattern and structure, although differences in geography and history mean that the results of these processes vary from city to city. Urban ecologists have used three major models to describe certain tendencies in the organization of urban communities.

Concentric-Zone Model

Urban ecology began during the 1920s with research by sociologists at the University of Chicago, who used Chicago to develop a model of the city that is called the *concentric-zone model* (Park, Burgess, and McKenzie, 1925). This model—one version of which is diagrammed in Figure 18.1A—portrays the city as a series of circles within circles, with each circle or zone differing in the way land is used. At the center of the circles is the "central business district," an area used for commerce, business, banking, government, shopping, and entertainment. Land here is quite expensive and so rents are high. Next to the central business district is an

FIGURE 18.1
Ecological Models of the City

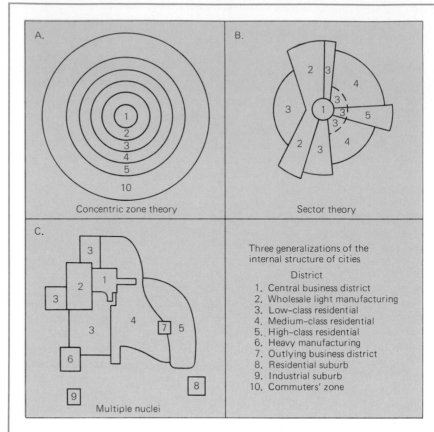

A. Concentric zone theory

B. Sector theory

C. Multiple nuclei

Three generalizations of the internal structure of cities

District
1. Central business district
2. Wholesale light manufacturing
3. Low-class residential
4. Medium-class residential
5. High-class residential
6. Heavy manufacturing
7. Outlying business district
8. Residential suburb
9. Industrial suburb
10. Commuters' zone

area of "wholesale light manufacturing." Outside this zone is the "low-class residential" area, or "zone of transition." This area of run-down buildings occupied by the poor, minorities, and recent immigrants is usually in the process of invasion and succession. The outward expansion of the first two zones drives up land values and rents and forces residents of this area to move farther from the center of the city. The next zone is "medium-class residential"; this area is also called the "zone of working-class homes" and contains many two- and three-family houses that are occupied by blue-collar workers. Outside this circle is the "high-class residential" area or "zone of middle-class homes," a community of single-family houses where people live and from which they commute to the center of the city for work, shopping, and entertainment. Most distant from the central busi-

ness district is the "commuters' zone," an area of single-family houses occupied by the relatively well-to-do.

This concentric-zone model fit Chicago relatively well during the 1920s and 1930s, although the presence of Lake Michigan meant that full circles did not exist around the central business district. This model fits best cities with a single center that grew up in the United States in the early twentieth century as a result of immigration. The model does not fit preindustrial cities very well, because in those cities the rich often lived at the center of the city and the poor on the outskirts (Sjoberg, 1960). Today, the suburbs of some cities in industrial societies, such as the Soviet Union and Japan, also have suburbs occupied by people who are poorer than many residents of the central city (Morton, 1977). The concentric-zone model also fails to describe fully those cities that have developed since the introduction of the automobile, because the mobility provided by the car has led to decentralization and dispersion. Moreover, this model does not describe very well those cities that grew up near waterways and mountains. Even those cities that fit the model quite well contain exceptions to the concentric-zone pattern, such as expensive apartments near the business district or industry on the periphery of the city. Despite these shortcomings, this model does alert us to important ecological processes.

Sector Model

A different model of the city was developed by Homer Hoyt (1939, 1943), based on his study of American cities. Hoyt proposed that because of the way that transportation paths in urban areas are laid out, certain patterns of land use are repeated along waterways, railroad lines, and highways farther from the center of the city. Industry often develops along such transportation routes, and this affects the use of nearby land. Hoyt suggested that one type of land use, such as for industry or for residence, will expand outward in sectors shaped like pieces of pie until some natural or artificial boundary is reached. This *sector model*, pictured in Figure 18.1B, is another idealized picture of the city that does not fully describe any one city in every detail; it does describe the shape of some cities, such as San Francisco, quite well.

Multiple-Nuclei Model

A third ecological model of the city, which is depicted in Figure 18.1C, was developed by Chauncy D. Harris and Edward L. Ullman (1945). The *multiple-nuclei model* shows cities as having different centers that affect land use and rents in surrounding neighborhoods. The first nucleus of a city often develops around a port, a mine, or a retail district. Later, other nuclei develop because some activities require certain facilities nearby: some activities gain from being close to each other (for example, several small "specialty" shops); some activities are disadvantageous to each other (such as luxury apartment buildings and heavy industry); and some activities cannot afford the high rents in particular neighborhoods. These requirements produce multiple nuclei rather than the single one suggested by the concentric-zone model. This model fits cities that were formed by the merger of smaller cities, and it also describes cities that developed multiple centers for specific historical and

geographical reasons. Boston is one city that this model describes quite well.

Beyond Ecology

Urban ecologists focus on the processes that structure the city. They traditionally have emphasized economic forces, particularly the competition for land that determines its use and rental value. However, this approach often overlooks or slights the cultural and political forces that shape cities in important ways. For instance, the value placed on open land leads to the preservation of parks in the city, even though this is a "noneconomical" use of the land. Also, political decisions such as zoning restrictions that limit the use of certain urban lands affect the location of factories in the city and determine what kinds of people can afford to live in different neighborhoods (Shlay and Rossi, 1981). The shape of cities is also affected by state and federal legislatures that appropriate funds for the construction of highways through certain neighborhoods and around others. Even the decisions about where to place exit and entrance ramps to those roads influence the form that a city takes.

Urbanism as a Way of Life: Three Perspectives

In a classic essay published in 1938, Louis Wirth, a member of the Chicago school of sociology, proposed that three aspects of urban ecology—size, population density, and heterogeneity (or diversity)—produced a special way of life in the city that he called *urbanism*. Not all sociologists accept Wirth's conclusions about the differences in values and behavior between city dwellers and people who live in small towns and rural areas. Some claim that the kind of people who live in the city, and not the ecology of the city itself, accounts for these differences in values and behavior (Gans, 1962, 1982). Another position is that both the urban environment and the traits of the people who live there combine to create a variety of groups or subcultures that do not exist in smaller, less densely populated, and more homogeneous communities (Fischer, 1976). Let us take a look at these three approaches to urbanism.

THE DETERMINIST PERSPECTIVE

Louis Wirth's (1938) paper on urbanism—which was based on an earlier essay by the German sociologist Georg Simmel (1905, 1950)—was critical of the city. His position has been called a *determinist perspective*, because it assumes that life in the city is a direct outcome of the size, density, and diversity of the community. According to Wirth, interpersonal relations in the city are superficial and impersonal because people cannot interact on a personal level with everyone with whom they come in contact. Consequently, people in the city typically limit their dealings with others to the specific roles those other people play. For instance, a city dweller would only be interested in paying for food at a grocery store's check-out counter, but a resident of a small town might engage the clerk at the counter in a personal conversation.

Because urban residents are continually stimulated by inputs from their environment—the talk of passersby on the sidewalk, the sounds of industry, and the movement of cars—they need to screen out some of these stimuli to prevent "sensory overload" (Simmel, 1905, 1950; Milgram, 1970). This screening of inputs takes a variety of forms, as we see in SEL 18.2, and it often gives rise to "norms of noninvolvement," or expectations that people will ignore each other.

SOCIOLOGY AND EVERYDAY LIFE 18.2
Coping with Sensory Overload in the City

In a perceptive and influential essay on city life, Stanley Milgram looks at some of the ways that people screen out inputs from their environment so as to avoid sensory overload.

In 1903 Georg Simmel pointed out that, since urban dwellers come into contact with vast numbers of people each day, they conserve psychic energy by becoming acquainted with a far smaller proportion of people than their rural counterparts do, and by maintaining more superficial relationships even with these acquaintances. Wirth points specifically to "the superficiality, the anonymity, and the transitory character of urban social relations."

One adaptive response to overload, therefore, is the allocation of less time to each input. A second adaptive mechanism is disregard of low-priority inputs. Principles of selectivity are formulated such that investment of time and energy are reserved for carefully defined inputs (the urbanite disregards the drunk sick on the street as he purposefully navigates through the crowd). Third, boundaries are redrawn in certain social transactions so that the overloaded system can shift the burden to the other party in the exchange; thus, harried New York bus drivers once made change for customers, but now this responsibility has been shifted to the client, who must have the exact fare ready. Fourth, reception is blocked off prior to entrance into a system; city dwellers increasingly use unlisted telephone numbers to prevent individuals from calling them, and a small but growing number resort to keeping the telephone off the hook to prevent incoming calls. More subtly, a city dweller blocks inputs by assuming an unfriendly countenance, which discourages others from initiating contact. Additionally, social screening devices are interposed between the individual and environmental inputs (in a town of 5000 anyone can drop in to chat with the mayor, but in the metropolis organizational screening devices deflect inputs to other destinations). Fifth, the intensity of inputs is diminished by filtering devices, so that only weak and relatively superficial forms of involvement with others are allowed. Sixth, specialized institutions are created to absorb inputs that would otherwise swamp the individual (welfare departments handle the financial needs of a million individuals in New York City, who would otherwise create an array of mendicants continuously importuning the pedestrian). The interposition of institutions between the individual and the social world, a characteristic of all modern society, and most notably of the large metropolis, has its negative side. It deprives the individual of a sense of direct contact and spontaneous integration in the life around him. It simultaneously protects and estranges the individual from his social environment.

Source: Stanley Milgram, "The Experience of Living in Cities: A Psychological Analysis," *Science* 167 (March 13, 1970): 1461–1468. © 1970 by the American Association for the Advancement of Science.

Wirth claimed that cities reduce the significance of primary groups such as the family, friends, and neighbors. Rather, social relations in the city are characterized by membership in secondary groups; for example, many people work in large bureaucracies or belong to labor unions. According to

FIGURE 18.2
Urbanman

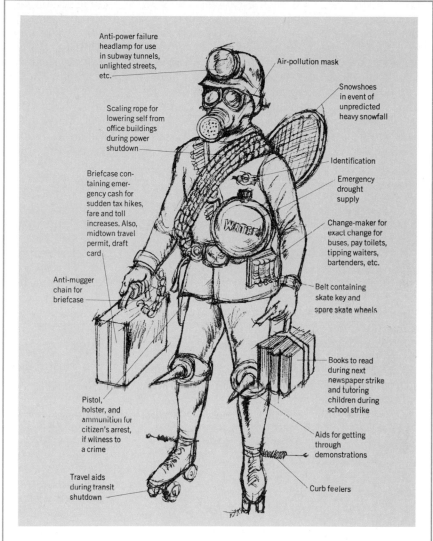

Anti-power failure headlamp for use in subway tunnels, unlighted streets, etc.

Air-pollution mask

Scaling rope for lowering self from office buildings during power shutdown

Snowshoes in event of unpredicted heavy snowfall

Identification

Briefcase containing emergency cash for sudden tax hikes, fare and toll increases. Also, midtown travel permit, draft card

Emergency drought supply

Change-maker for exact change for buses, pay toilets, tipping waiters, bartenders, etc.

Anti-mugger chain for briefcase

Belt containing skate key and spare skate wheels

Pistol, holster, and ammunition for citizen's arrest, if witness to a crime

Books to read during next newspaper strike and tutoring children during school strike

Aids for getting through demonstrations

Travel aids during transit shutdown

Curb feelers

Source: *Urbanman: The Psychology of Urban Survival* by John Helmes and Neil A. Eddington. New York: The Free Press, a Division of Macmillan Publishing Company, 1973.

Wirth, the relative insignificance of primary groups in the city means that the people who live there will lack guidance in everyday life. This creates anomie, or a state of normlessness, which in turn leads to social and personality disorders such as crime and mental illness. This is an outcome of the large size and the diversity of the city, which weaken primary groups and make value consensus difficult.

There are some problems with Wirth's view of city life. It does not describe life in preindustrial cities very well, because those cities usually manage to preserve extensive primary group ties (Morris, 1968). Even in cities in industrial societies there is little conclusive evidence that high population density alone leads to pathologies such as high crime rates or high mortality rates (Freedman, 1975; Fischer, 1976; Choldin, 1978). High density does seem to be associated with somewhat less favorable attitudes toward one's community, but high density can also be associated with easier access to work and to cultural opportunities that in turn produce more satisfaction with the community (Christenson, 1979).

Because Wirth's view of the city inevitably reflected his observations of Chicago during the 1930s, a time of economic depression and large-scale immigration, it fits some cities and groups better than others. Many urban neighborhoods do have the characteristics of primary groups. Similar occupations, a shared ethnic identity, and long-term residence all contribute to a sense of community in many areas of the city (Suttles, 1968; Kasarda and Janowitz, 1974). A study of an Italian working-class slum in Boston's West End found that primary groups such as the family and friends were very important; the author depicted this "nonurban" quality of the residents' way of life by referring to them as "urban villagers" (Gans, 1962, 1982).

Critics of Wirth's determinist position claim that the characteristics that he outlined for city life are aspects of life in a modern industrial society rather than aspects of cities as such (Dewey, 1960). These critics claim that anonymity is best seen as a consequence of the large size and the complex division of labor required by industrialization, that heterogeneity is best regarded as a product of migration to cities because of the employment opportunities there, and that the impersonality of urban life is best treated as a result of the task orientation and the instrumental behavior required by an advanced technology. In addition, in modern industrial societies rural life has become more like urban life as the mass media and the extensive economic ties between farm and city have created a more homogeneous culture in all communities.

THE COMPOSITIONAL PERSPECTIVE

The *compositional perspective* downplays the impact of ecological factors and instead emphasizes the ways that aspects of a population's composition such as income, age, ethnicity, and occupation influence life in the city (Gans, 1962, 1982). In other words, there are differences in the values and behavior of city dwellers and small-town residents because different kinds of people are drawn to these areas. Compared to people who live in smaller communities, urban residents are younger, less likely to be married, and more likely to do bureaucratic or professional work (Fischer, 1976: 95–96). Urban populations are also more heterogeneous, and both the compositional perspective and the determinist perspective see this diversity as having an important influence on life in the city.

Instead of the single form of urbanism suggested by Wirth, Herbert J. Gans (1962) proposes that there are at least five different styles of urban life. "Cosmopolites" are intellectuals and professionals who live in the city to enjoy its cultural and entertainment activities. The "unmarried or childless" work in the city and like the easy access to cultural resources and to their friends. Some of them move to the suburbs when they marry and have children, but others live in the city all their lives. A third identifiable urban life style is that of the "ethnic villagers" who live in a Chinatown or a Little Italy where the traditions of one nationality are preserved. The "deprived" are people who are disadvantaged by poverty, race, ethnicity, mental illness, or physical disability; they live in the city because it provides relatively good welfare benefits, low rents, and many jobs that require few skills. The "trapped" are people who cannot afford to leave the city because of their declining economic fortunes; some are elderly people who live on fixed incomes and have been attached to one neighborhood for years.

THE SUBCULTURAL PERSPECTIVE

A third position on city life is the *subcultural perspective*. This approach regards the size, density, and diversity of the city as conducive to the formation of primary group ties, rather than destructive of those ties, as Wirth asserted. According to Claude S. Fischer (1976, 1981a, 1981b), these ecological characteristics of the city make it possible for almost anyone to find other people who share similar interests, needs, and ways of life. The city provides the variety of people needed to form many different subcultures or groups, and the large size of urban communities provides the "critical mass" required for these groups to form:

For example, let us suppose that one in every thousand persons is intensely interested in moden dance. In a small town of 5,000 that means there would be, on the average, five such persons, enough to do little else than engage in conversation and dance. But in a city of one million, there would be a thousand— enough to support studios, occasional ballet performances, local meeting places, and a special social milieu. Their activity would probably draw other people beyond the original thousand into the subculture (those quintets of dance-lovers migrating from the small towns). The same general process of critical mass operates for artists, academics, bohemians, corporate executives, criminals, computer programers— as well as for ethnic and racial minorities (Fischer, 1976: 37).

Rather than being communities in which people lack close ties to others, cities are places where people belong to various groups based on friendship, occupation, ethnicity, stage in the life cycle, recreational interests, or even deviant pursuits such as drug use or prostitution. Urban people do have primary-group ties. They see their relatives as often as do people who live elsewhere. In fact, except for the elderly and the residents of skid row, urban dwellers have even more friends than do people living in small towns and rural areas. The friends of urban dwellers are likely to come from different backgrounds and likely to be scattered throughout the city, whereas the friends of people living in nonurban communities are more likely to be from the same social background and more likely to live nearby. Life in the city is not associated with estrangement from relatives, friends, and neighbors. However, it sometimes leads to estrangement from people who are not known, who are from different backgrounds, or who seem to pose a threat (Fischer, 1981a, 1981b).

Housing in Urban America

Ecological processes affect the cost and the quality of the housing that urban residents can find. Expansion of the central business district often reduces the available supply of houses and apartments and thereby increases rents. The high population density of the city is associated with overcrowded neighborhoods and congested living conditions within apartments and houses. The segregation of minority groups limits their choice of housing to the least desirable neighborhoods.

Housing is important for more than just shelter. People who rent an apartment or buy a house also take into account "health, security, privacy, neighborhood and social relations, status, community facilities and services, access to jobs, and control over the environment" (Pynoos, Schafer, and Hartman, 1980: 1). Inadequate housing deprives people in many ways: They may lack indoor plumbing, be cold in the winter, live in crowded quarters, have their budgets strained by high rents, or live in dangerous neighborhoods (Frieden et al., 1977).

The housing market in the United States is characterized by a "trickle-down process": People with relatively high incomes improve their living environment by purchasing new and desirable housing, and people with lower incomes settle for the older and the less desirable housing abandoned by the more affluent (Foley, 1980). Fewer than 4 per cent of all American households occupy public housing;

as a result, most of the poor rely on the private housing market rather than subsidized housing (Downs, 1977; Heumann, 1979; Foley, 1980).

SLUMS

A *slum* is an area with high population density and run-down housing that is occupied by the poor. In the United States, slums are usually located in the central city, but there are also rural slums—communities with dilapidated housing and inadequate plumbing. Many rural slums have a low population density in terms of people per square mile, but in most cases living conditions within houses are congested.

A slum is defined by the low income of the residents rather than the age of the buildings. Old buildings can actually be desirable housing, as in fashionable districts such as Back Bay in Boston or Society Hill in Philadelphia. Slums develop when living conditions within buildings become crowded and when owners fail to maintain buildings (Muth, 1969). Slums are not only the product of neglectful slumlords who live outside the slum, but also result from the inability of relatively poor people who own their homes to keep up with rising property taxes and essential repairs (Sternlieb and Burchell, 1973).

Life in slum housing is unpleasant and even dangerous. Residents must cope with rats and cockroaches, potential poisoning from lead-based paint, the threat of fire from frayed electrical wiring, cold when heating systems break down, inadequately protected roofs and fire escapes, and potential injury from broken glass on the streets and in the halls (Rainwater, 1972). Crime is relatively common in slum communities, and rates of mortality and disease are also high.

Although outsiders often portray slums as disorganized communities, these neighborhoods usually have a well-defined social structure (Liebow, 1967; Suttles, 1968, 1972; Whyte, 1943, 1981; Gans, 1962, 1982). Residents have a sense of "turf," a notion of their community's boundaries that they protect from intruders. A set of values and norms that differs somewhat from the dominant culture commonly develops among slum residents as a result of their poverty, lack of political power, and racial and ethnic traditions.

RESIDENTIAL SEGREGATION

Blacks in the United States are more likely than whites to live in the central city. In 1980, 57.8 per cent of all blacks and only 25 per cent of all whites lived in central cities. In that same year, 23.3 per cent of blacks and 48.3 per cent of whites lived in the suburbs. Nonmetropolitan communities contained 18.9 per cent of all blacks and 26.7 per cent of all whites (U.S. Bureau of the Census, 1982: 15). In addition to being more concentrated in central cities than are whites, blacks are also segregated within certain neighborhoods in those cities.

A significant trend during the 1970s was that the populations of many central cities became increasingly black; some cities became more than 50 per cent black for the first time. This was largely because whites left these central cities faster than did blacks during this period. In Chapter 12, we mentioned that some sociologists attribute this to "white flight"—migration that results from whites' fears that the changing racial composition of the city will cause property values and educational quality to fall, and crime rates to rise. However, there are also factors that pull people to the suburbs. Suburbs typically have lower property taxes than cities, and job opportunities in the suburbs have increased in recent years. Moreover, housing is better and more readily available in communities outside the city's limits. Because of income inequality between blacks and whites, and because of discriminatory practices by realtors and banks, whites have historically been more likely than blacks to move to the suburbs.

In spite of the fact that many cities became increasingly black during the 1970s, there was a small increase in the proportion of all suburban residents who were black, from 4.8 per cent in 1970 to 6.1 per cent in 1980. There are two different interpretations of this change. One is that the movement of blacks to the suburbs has increased racial integration there and enhanced the opportunities of some blacks to find better jobs and to own their own houses. A different view is that the suburbanization of blacks is just a "spillover" or expansion of the city into communities just outside its boundaries. This inner ring of suburbs often takes on some of the characteristics of the city itself rather than offering blacks the kind of life usually associated with the suburbs. These suburbs have become more densely populated, more filled with poor people, and increasingly used for nonresidential purposes. Consequently, many blacks who moved to the suburbs during the 1970s experienced little or no upward mobility relative to whites. Suburban residence does not necessarily mean middle-class status; in fact, nearly one-fourth of the blacks who live in the suburbs have incomes below the poverty line. This spillover explanation

of black suburbanization seems to fit the metropolitan areas of Cleveland, Chicago, and Detroit. In other metropolitan areas—such as Philadelphia, St. Louis, and Washington, D. C.—there has been some growth in the black population of those suburbs lying outside the communities that immediately surround the central city (Pear, 1982a).

CHANGING PATTERNS OF URBAN HOUSING

Between 1970 and 1981 the population of the United States increased by 12 per cent, but the number of households in the nation rose by 29.9 per cent. Over this period, the proportion of all households composed of just one person rose from 17 per cent to 23 per cent, and the average number of people in each household dropped from 3.14 to 2.73 (U.S. Bureau of the Census, 1982: 42–44). A variety of factors caused these changes, all of which affected housing in the United States. During this period, more people delayed marriage and lived alone before they married, and those who did marry produced fewer children. In addition, an increased divorce rate meant that what was formerly a household of two adults became two households with one adult each. These changes have altered the living conditions of Americans and are associated with the development of alternatives to apartments and single-family houses.

Gentrification

Gentrification describes the movement of middle-class and upper-class people into the city from the suburbs and the permanent settlement in the city of middle-class and upper-class people who in the past probably would have moved to the suburbs. Gentrification is accompanied by the renovation of old buildings in the central city. This can increase property values, raise the amount of taxes the city collects, and reverse the deterioration of urban neighborhoods. Gentrification can also help a city achieve a mix of classes and ethnic groups, although this can produce conflict between people who have lived in a neighborhood for years and people of higher social standing who adopt that neighborhood as their own. Another cost of gentrification is that minority groups, students, and other people with relatively low incomes may be pushed out of the community as property values and rents rise beyond their means. This uproots people from their communities and applies pressure on the housing market throughout the city, perhaps increasing rents outside the gentrified community.

What effect has gentrification had on American cities so far? The President's Commission for a National Agenda for the Eighties (1980a) found that this "urban renaissance" has actually been on a very small scale so far. There has been no mass return of the middle and upper classes to the city; in fact, more than 70 per cent of those who live in the revitalized areas moved there from other neighborhoods in the city. There has been no extensive renovation of urban housing either. A few neighborhoods have been restored, but between 1968 and 1979 only 0.5 per cent of the nearly 20 million housing units in American cities were affected by these revitalization efforts. Overall, concluded the Commission, urban housing conditions have deteriorated rather than improved in recent years.

Condominium Conversion

Another recent change in urban housing is the conversion of buildings into condominiums, living units owned by individuals but managed by others. People who buy a condominium own part of a building and are responsible for paying for the up-keep of the building and for a portion of the property taxes. Today, condominiums constitute only 5 per cent of all housing units in the country, but in some communities the proportion is much higher.

The recent increase in condominium conversion is partly a result of rising property taxes and maintenance costs in many cities, which have led the owners of some apartment buildings to convert apartments into condominiums and sell them as individual units. This often displaces renters who cannot afford to buy the unit or do not wish to invest in the property, and this in turn can raise rents in the city by reducing the total number of rental units available. When local ordinances prevent apartment building owners from evicting their tenants for purposes of condominium conversion, arson sometimes becomes a way to drive tenants out, gut the buildings, and raise insurance money for the conversion into condominiums (McNamara and Klibanoff, 1981).

Urban Homesteading

Buildings that have been abandoned because of unpaid property taxes, arson, or disrepair are often taken over by the city government. Because the

One solution to the problem of abandonment of buildings has been "urban homesteading," a policy whereby these buildings are given or sold for small amounts to people who agree to pay overdue property taxes, to repair the buildings, and to live in them for a designated period of time.

municipal government rarely has the funds to renovate these buildings, they often stand empty, become more dilapidated, and provide targets for arsonists and vandals. One solution to this problem is *urban homesteading*, a policy of giving these buildings or selling them for small amounts to people who agree to pay overdue property taxes, repair the buildings with low-interest loans, and live in the buildings for a certain period. This both improves the physical condition of the building and provides relatively poor people with homes.

Rent Control

In recent years, rents for urban housing have increased because of the expansion of business districts, higher property taxes brought about by the flight to the suburbs of the middle class, and the processes of gentrification and condominium conversion. In reaction to rising rents, some communities have passed rent-control laws that fix rent at a low level and limit the amount that a building owner can raise rents. Rent control protects tenants from large increases in rent, but it can also make it unprofitable to own and maintain buildings. This can lead to the abandonment of buildings or to the conversion of apartments into condominiums. If rent control reduces the number of housing units available in a community in those ways, its long-run effect may be to increase the rents charged for the remaining units.

Planning the Future of the City

Urban planning is the rational effort to design, build, and change a city. Urban planners assume that the ecological processes we have examined do not inevitably determine the organization of the city but can be shaped to serve specific human needs.

Early reformers tried to make cities similar to rural areas. They took a negative view of cities: Cities were too large, too crowded, too dangerous, and too dirty. These planners wanted to improve housing, eradicate slums, and create more open space; in doing so, they often paid little attention to the ways that urban residents used the city to meet their needs. Some modern planners who work with maps, charts, and statistics also neglect the positive consequences of urban communities as

they are and the negative effects that proposed changes would have for residents.

Before World War II, many urban planners developed comprehensive plans for the development of a city. Since then, they have focused on more limited goals and timetables. Today, planners consult a variety of experts—including architects, community agency workers, social scientists, and organized interest groups such as tenants—to help them develop workable plans to meet specific needs. Planners are now more likely than they once were to focus on the specific needs of small neighborhoods, rather than on the needs of the city as a whole. As a result, they commonly emphasize small changes over a short period of time rather than quick and drastic changes.

URBAN RENEWAL

Urban planning that tries to improve the city by tearing down old buildings and constructing new ones is called *urban renewal.* Urban renewal began in the United States in the 1930s, and in 1949 the federal government started to provide public funds for the purchase, clearance, and improvement of urban areas. In some cases this led to the destruction of desirable aspects of old communities; and in many instances it produced new buildings that had negative consequences for the city's people. In practice, urban renewal often meant that more housing units were destroyed than were built, that the poor and minority groups were displaced from their neighborhoods to housing projects more distant from the center of the city, and that rents increased. For example, Boston's West End was destroyed between 1958 and 1960 because it was seen as a run-down urban area, and in its place were built luxury high-rise apartment buildings and government office buildings. The community that this project destroyed was, however, more than a slum; it was a tightly structured ethnic community to which people felt strong attachment. When their community was demolished, they were dispersed throughout the metropolitan area. Many grieved for their lost homes in much the same way that people grieve for a lost relative (Gans, 1962, 1982; Fried, 1963).

Since the 1960s, the emphasis in urban renewal has been less on slum clearance than on improving the overall quality of urban life. In practice, this has resulted in the development of entertainment districts, shopping facilities, and convention centers. Projects such as Quincy Market in Boston and

Ghirardelli Square in San Francisco attract both city dwellers and suburbanites, but have little or no effect in improving the life of the urban poor.

Jane Jacobs (1961) has argued that urban renewal can succeed only if it produces a community that has a diversity of uses, including residence, shopping, entertainment, and dining. Jacobs claims that to maintain such diversity a neighborhood must have both old and new buildings, because new buildings usually have high rents that make it unprofitable for certain activities to be undertaken there. Thriving urban neighborhoods require a concentration of people to use the various facilities in the area; these neighborhoods also require a large number of buildings in a small geographic area to create a diversity of uses for the land. A variety of activities will draw people to the streets, and this human traffic in turn makes the streets safer by increasing the informal control of behavior.

NEW TOWNS

A radical type of urban planning is the construction of *new towns,* planned and largely self-contained communities that are often built on open land. The hope is that a new community will not have the problems that old cities do, but will have all the advantages offered by modern technology, architecture, and social science.

The Englishman Ebenezer Howard (1902) first proposed the construction of new towns—or "garden cities," as he called them—which were to be autonomous towns of about 30,000 people who would live, work, go to school, and enjoy their leisure time in the community. Letchworth, the first English town based on Howard's suggestions, encountered a number of problems: Its site was poor, it did not attract many investors, and it failed to draw industry to it. A second town, Welwyn Garden City, also had financial difficulties but recovered and is now a thriving town of 44,000 people (Palen, 1975).

The United States government has never had a policy to subsidize new towns, but some have been built with private funds. Most are within major metropolitan areas, and a number are retirement communities. Reston, Virginia, an upper-middle-class community near Washington, D. C., is a new town that has had less success in attracting industry than has Columbia, Maryland, a new town close to Baltimore. The initial expense of developing new towns is large, and it is unlikely that these commu-

nities will provide alternative places of residence for many Americans in the future (Palen, 1975). Instead, efforts will probably be concentrated on changing existing cities.

URBAN DECLINE

In recent years, the problems of American cities have reached crisis proportions. Fiscal problems, rising rents, deteriorating buildings and facilities, the flight of the middle class to the suburbs, large numbers of people on welfare assistance, increasing crime rates, and dangerous levels of pollution have all precipitated urban decline and led to various proposals to deal with it.

A controversial report by the President's Commission for a National Agenda for the Eighties (1980a: 65–66) suggested that the government should try to moderate the harsh consequences of urban decline for individuals but should not try to "preserve [cities] under glass" by trying to reverse trends such as the migration to the Sun Belt and the movement from central cities to the suburbs, small towns, and rural areas. The Commission (1980a: 65, 69) noted that "cities are not permanent" and "growth and decline are integral parts of the same dynamic process in urban life." The panel argued for a federal urban policy that was people-oriented rather than place-oriented. It proposed to assist people who were willing to move to communities where jobs were plentiful, even though this might lead to the demise of certain cities. It discouraged efforts to keep a city's population from shrinking and efforts to revitalize obsolete industries. The Commission argued that these cities are being transformed rather than dying, and federal policies should help them adjust to smaller populations and different economic systems. The Commission suggested that some urban decline is simply a result of a shift to a postindustrial society, one in which heavy manufacturing is replaced by finance, education, the professions, and management.

The Commission's report has provoked controversy. Political officials in the Northeast and the Midwest have attacked it for encouraging continued migration to the Sun Belt, which will cause further deterioration of the aging cities in their regions. The Commission's assumption that places and people can be separated is also questionable; a policy that helps people move where there are jobs will cause problems associated with being uprooted from a community and adjusting to a new one.

SOCIOLOGY AND EVERYDAY LIFE 18.3
The Streets of San Francisco

Why are the streets of one city clean, and those of another city dirty? The answer lies in a combination of factors that include the values of the residents, the money spent on street cleaning, and the age of the city. In this selection, we see how these and other differences account for the immaculate condition of San Francisco's streets and the relative filth of Boston's.

Don Brown abandoned Boston after the Blizzard of 1978 and came to San Francisco. One of the first things he noticed was the clean streets.

"I used to tell people back in Boston that at 6 in the morning [here], somebody vacuums the whole city, and at 6:30, they bleach it," he said.

Brown pays a lot of attention to how spiffy the streets look here because he works on a litter survey at San Francisco State University.

He and other participants in the study, led by geography professor John Westfall, assign numbers to the streets they travel. A "1" goes to streets inside walks that are absolutely clean. A "5" designates a place where "it's so dirty you have to walk around it."

All the information is plotted on a map and fed into a computer, then shared with the San Francisco Department of Public Works.

Jeffrey Lee, the city's public works director, thinks the ongoing litter survey is a big help and is just one reason why, in Brown's opinion, San Francisco "is much, much cleaner than almost any other city in the country."

Whether [to] a surveyor or a casual visitor, this city indeed seems to keep its face well scrubbed. From the Embarcadero up and over the hills to the Sunset district, from Fishermen's Wharf to the Fillmore district, San Francisco fairly gleams.

For Brown, the contrast with Boston is considerable. He remembered one of his last days in Boston, standing at the corner of Newbury and Berkeley streets. He was surrounded by blowing litter, swirling more than two stories above him. "It was a garbage storm," he said.

Boston and San Francisco are similar in population size, and both cities are in states where popular ballot measures slashed property taxes and thus cut revenues to local governments. And yet San Francisco's 900 miles of streets are cleaner than Boston's 750 miles. The difference can be explained in part by how the two cities pay for their street-cleaning services, by the weather, by the age of the cities and, perhaps, by a stronger cleanliness ethic in California than in Massachusetts.

In Boston, the city's public works budget for 1981 was reduced by 40 percent on the heels of the passage of Proposition 2½. But in the four budget years since the passage of California's Proposition 13, San Francisco's public works budget has not undergone a similar financial trauma, largely because street cleaning is not funded by property-tax revenues, but by a percentage of the state tax on gasoline. . . .

[San Francisco] concentrates its street cleaning efforts in the heavily traveled downtown and commercial areas. During the week, the average commercial street is cleaned twice on one side and three times on the other (which is usually the windward side where more trash collects). Residential sections are cleaned once a week.

Parking bans on street-cleaning days are strictly enforced. Some 35 parking-control officers work ahead of the sweepers, tagging violators with $10 tickets. Sgt. Edgar Eimil of the San Francisco Police Department's parking enforcement division said the public's observance of the bans "is pretty good," but could be improved. The department currently issues between 2000 and 3000 parking citations a day, he said.

San Francisco State's Brown said the weather appears to be a factor in the city's cleanliness. Moisture from the fog keeps the dust down in drier months, and because there is no snow, debris has no place to hide. The streets are also in better condition than in Boston and are thus easier to keep clean because there is no severe variation in the weather. And San Francisco is younger than Boston, Brown added.

Then there is the human factor. "There seems to be more vigilance out here" about litter, Brown said.

That fact might be proven by one statistic. Boston collected more than 75,000 tons of litter during fiscal 1980. Last year, San Francisco swept up just 20,000 tons.

Source: James R. Carroll, "The Streets of San Francisco," *The Boston Globe,* February 24, 1982, p. 2. Used by permission of the author.

A good street-cleaning system and the relative vigilance of the residents regarding litter seem to be two good reasons for the cleanliness of San Francisco's streets.

Also, the Commission fails to pay much attention to "the process of abandonment, decay, and arson that has haunted the poor as they have moved from one neighborhood deserted by the middle class to another" (Herbers, 1981b: A17). This Commission was appointed by President Carter, but its recommendations are in many ways compatible with President Reagan's emphasis on local control of the economy and an increased role for private money in the development of the cities. However, it has become clear in recent years that private industry, the states, and the cities will not be able to make up for the reduction in federal assistance to the cities that began in 1978 (Herbers, 1982a). In fact, representatives of about half of seventy-nine municipalities contacted in late 1982 had cut their work force in that year and planned to do so again in 1983 (*The New York Times*, January 3, 1983, p. A15).

A recent study of urban decline concludes that continuing population declines in most large U. S. cities seem irreversible, at least in the near future. Hence public policies should not seek to reverse or even to halt such declines, but should aim at helping city governments and residents adjust to lower levels of population and activity, and at counteracting or offsetting any serious negative impacts of decline—especially upon the poor (Bradbury, Downs, and Small, 1982: 12).

The authors recommend that federal policies that favor new construction outside the central city rather than revitalization of the city should be changed. In addition, attention should be paid to the possible effects of federal policies on the redistribution of population from one region to another. Bradbury, Downs, and Small also suggest empowering people to find goods and services for themselves in the market by creating jobs, retraining the unemployed, guaranteeing an annual income, and building low-income housing in communities throughout the metropolitan area.

On their own, cities cannot solve their problems, because the migration of the middle class to the suburbs and the rapid deterioration of facilities in the central city quickly exhaust a city's capacity to maintain past standards, much less improve itself. In Texas, cities can annex nearby suburbs, but annexation seems an unlikely solution to urban decline because the residents of the suburbs have both the political power and the wealth to thwart efforts by cities to adopt a metropolitan solution to the problems of central cities.

The movement of Americans from central cities to surrounding suburbs and to small towns and rural areas will continue to change the kind of communities in which millions of people live. Historically, the city has given rise to a variety of new phenomena that have become part of American society, and it has been associated with a distinct way of life called urbanism that has permeated nonurban communities as well. In the future, as Americans change the kind of communities in which they live, new phenomena and new ways of life will emerge.

Summary

Over the past two centuries, societies throughout the world have urbanized at a rapid rate; in other words, larger and larger proportions of their people have come to live in communities that are large, densely populated, and diverse. This movement into the cities is associated with factors pushing people out of rural areas and factors pulling them to urban areas. Economic opportunity is a major attraction of the city, and urbanization has increased with industrialization, although some overurbanized cities draw more people than they have jobs and facilities for.

The modern metropolis includes a central city and its surrounding suburbs, as well as towns and rural areas that are linked to it socially and economically. When metropolitan areas merge with each other in a continuous urban sprawl, the result is called a megalopolis. For many years, the suburbs of large metropolitan areas in the United States have increased in size faster than the central cities; during the 1970s, small towns and rural areas began to grow somewhat faster than metropolitan areas. People have left the central cities for what they see as better jobs, homes, and schools in the outlying areas, and this has reduced tax revenues for the deteriorating central cities.

Urban ecologists have described the patterns of cities in various ways. Their models of the city—concentric zone, sector, or multiple nuclei—describe the results of certain ecological processes such as concentration and dispersion, centralization and decentralization, specialization, segregation, and invasion and succession. These models do not describe every city in all its details, but they help us to understand how different kinds of urban communities are organized. Cultural values and political forces often intrude on the operation of ecological forces to influence the structure of the city.

In a 1938 essay, Louis Wirth argued that size, density, and heterogeneity influence the way of life that he called urbanism. He saw these ecological factors as responsible for weakened family and neighborhood ties and for higher rates of crime, mental illness, and other kinds of behavior that he found undesirable. In contrast to Wirth's determinist position, the compositional approach sees city life as a product of the kinds of people who live there; the class, ethnicity, and age of residents affects the way of life in a community, according to this position. The subcultural position is that the ecological factors common to cities influence life there by giving rise to groups, rather than destroying groups; large size and diversity make possible the formation of a variety of subcultures in the city.

The housing in metropolitan areas ranges from dilapidated slum buildings to luxury high-rise apartment complexes, and from buildings with hundreds of units to mansions on spacious grounds. Housing affects people's health, safety, privacy, and sense of well-being. Consequently, residential segregation affects the life chances of minority groups. Between 1970 and 1980, blacks became an increasing proportion of the population living in many cities as whites moved to the suburbs, small towns, and rural areas. Blacks have become slightly more suburbanized in recent years, but in many metropolitan areas they have moved to an inner ring of suburbs that have the characteristics of cities rather than the traits usually associated with suburban living.

Changing patterns of urban housing—such as gentrification, condominium conversion, and urban homesteading—have not yet affected large numbers of urban Americans. The construction of new towns on open land is another innovative type of community that has also affected few Americans.

Purposeful efforts to change the city are called urban planning. Between the 1930s and the early 1960s this often took the form of urban renewal—the destruction of the old and the construction of the new. Often this "unslumming," as Jane Jacobs has called it, displaced poor people to less desirable communities and to more costly housing.

The central cities in the United States are now in decline, and most observers feel that they will continue to lose population and jobs for years to come. Two recent reports favor allowing this decline to continue until cities readjust to fewer people and fewer jobs. However, these reports also recommend federal, state, and local efforts to help the residents of the cities adjust to these changes by retraining them for available jobs, helping them to move where there is work, and empowering them in various ways to meet their needs. The poor make up a growing proportion of the population of these deteriorating cities, and they will need the most help in adapting to the declining fortunes of their communities.

Important Terms

CENTRAL CITY (424)
CITY (421)
COMMUNITY (421)
COMPOSITIONAL PER-
SPECTIVE (434)
CONCENTRIC-ZONE
MODEL (429)
DETERMINIST PERSPEC-
TIVE (432)
GENTRIFICATION (436)
MEGALOPOLIS (424)
METROPOLIS (423)
MULTIPLE-NUCLEI
MODEL (431)
NEW TOWN (439)
SECTOR MODEL (431)
SLUM (435)
STANDARD CONSOLI-
DATED STATISTICAL
AREA (SCSA) (424)
STANDARD METROPOLI-
TAN STATISTICAL AREA
(SMSA) (423)
SUBCULTURAL PERSPEC-
TIVE (434)
SUBURB (426)
URBAN ECOLOGY (429)
URBAN HOMESTEADING
(438)
URBAN PLANNING (438)
URBAN RENEWAL (438)
URBANISM (431)
URBANIZATION (421)

Suggested Readings

Mark Abrahamson. *Urban Sociology*, 2nd ed. Englewood Cliffs, N. J.: Prentice-Hall, 1980. A useful textbook on urban sociology.

Edward C. Banfield. *The Unheavenly City Revisited*. Boston: Little, Brown, 1974. A controversial analysis of urban problems and social policies to solve them.

Katharine Bradbury, Anthony Downs, and Kenneth A. Small. *Urban Decline and the Future of American Cities*. Washington, D. C.: Brookings Institution, 1982. A fact-filled study of urban decline that describes its extent, causes, and remedies.

Claude S. Fischer. *The Urban Experience*. New York: Harcourt Brace Jovanovich, 1976. A well-written and illuminating introduction to the sociology of the city that includes a discussion of the determinist, compositional, and subcultural perspectives on urbanism.

Herbert J. Gans. *The Urban Villagers*, updated and expanded ed. New York: Free Press, 1962, 1982. A classic study of a community destroyed by an urban renewal project in Boston's West End; the author, who takes a compositional perspective, has added an introduction and some material to several chapters in this new edition.

Jon Pynoos, Robert Schafer, and Chester W. Hartman, eds. *Housing Urban America*, 2nd ed. Hawthorne, N. Y. Aldine, 1980. A useful collection of papers on the problems that Americans have in finding suitable places to live.

Catharine R. Stimpson et al., eds. *Women and the American City*. Chicago: University of Chicago Press, 1981. An exploration of some of the special problems of being a woman in the city.

Gerald D. Suttles. *The Social Order of the Slum: Ethnicity and Territory in the Inner City*. Chicago: University of Chicago Press, 1968. An important study of the social organization of a slum community in Chicago.

William K. Tabb and Larry Sawers, eds., *Marxism and the Metropolis: New Perspectives in Urban Political Economy*. New York: Oxford University Press, 1978. A good collection of essays by Marxist scholars that deal with urban growth and redevelopment, the fiscal problems of cities, and urbanization in socialist societies.

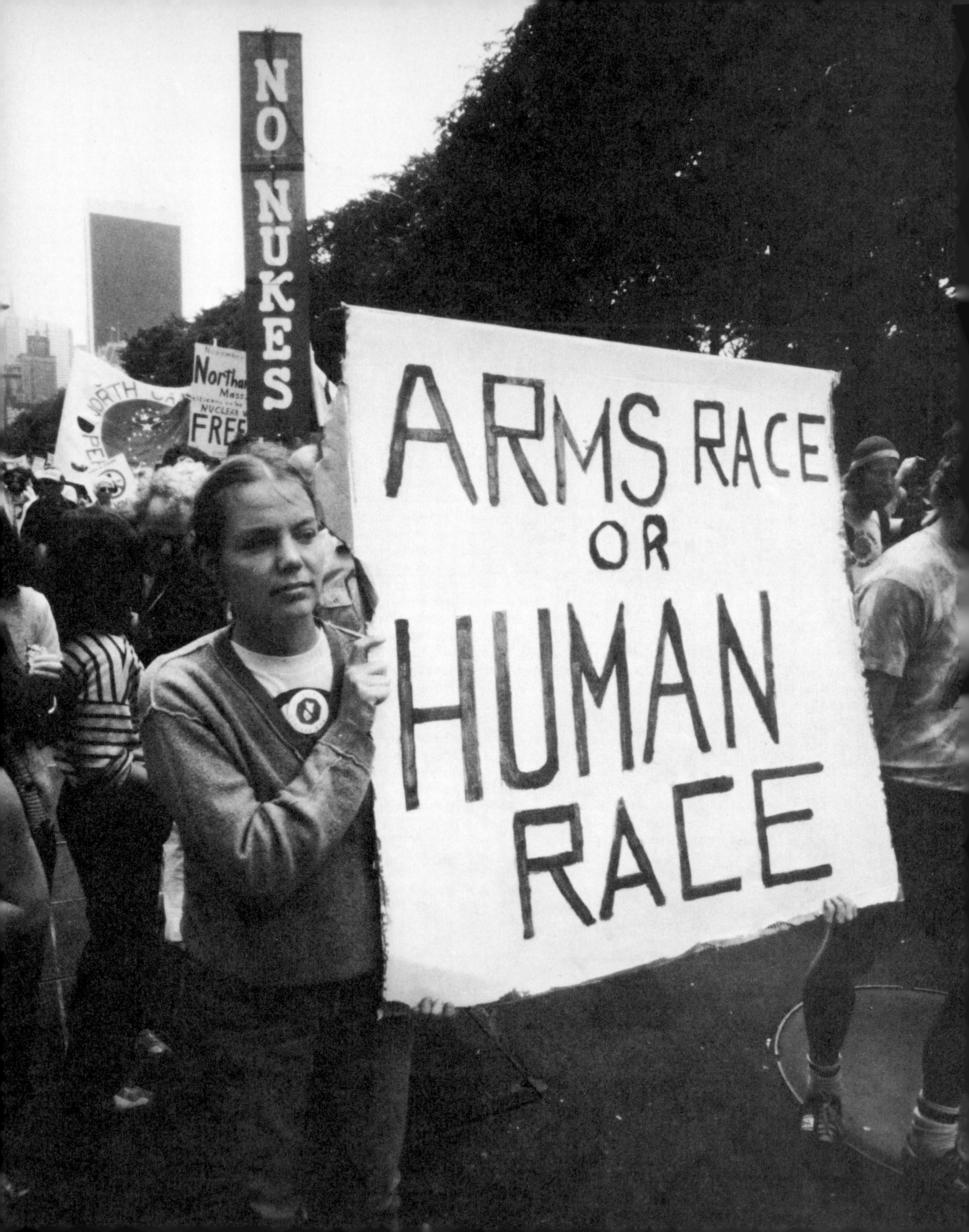
NO NUKES
ARMS RACE OR HUMAN RACE

COLLECTIVE BEHAVIOR AND SOCIAL MOVEMENTS

In December 1979 about 20,000 people waited at the doors of an auditorium in Cincinnati, Ohio, where the rock group The Who was to perform. These fans had unreserved seats, and so a good vantage point for the concert depended on a quick dash to the front of the hall. As the doors started to open, the crowd rushed forward. Eleven people were trampled to death, and many others were injured seriously (Thomas, 1979). A few months later in the African nation of Zaire, Pope John Paul II was to say an outdoor Mass for 1.5 million people. As the iron gates to the plaza opened, the crowd pushed forward, crushing seven women and two children to death and injuring others (*The New York Times*, May 5, 1980, pp. A1, A7).

These tragic events elicited different reactions from the American press. Relatively little was made of the deaths in Zaire, probably because they occurred abroad and because attendance at a religious service is seen as a worthy activity that rarely has disastrous results. The press paid more attention to the deaths at the Cincinnati rock concert, perhaps because the event took place within the country and because it involved a recurring activity that might pose a future threat to young people. Hostility toward young people—their loud music, drug use, and general rowdiness—caused some observers to condemn rock fans as a group. However, a later investigation found that the deaths could have been avoided if reserved seats had been used instead of general admission, for this would have eliminated the fans' need to push forward as soon as the doors opened.

The events in Cincinnati and Zaire are examples of *collective behavior*—spontaneous, unstructured, and temporary action by a large number of people who interact with each other or respond to a common stimulus (Blumer, 1957, 1969a; Turner and Killian, 1972). Collective behavior, though not

always as frenzied as in these two events, is less organized than the kinds of behavior we examined in earlier chapters. For example, the employees of a bureaucratic organization behave quite predictably every day, and so does a committee that is led by a chairperson and follows a specific agenda. On the other hand, collective behavior such as mass hysteria, public opinion, rumors, and crowd activity is less structured and less permanent, and so it is harder to predict.

Collective behavior often has a dramatic appeal. It makes good news for the mass media because it takes place in a brief span of time and involves large numbers of people acting in ways that evoke human emotions. Sociologists, however, are interested in collective behavior less for its dramatic appeal than as a way to study how relatively unorganized groups make sense of the world and arrive at a common solution to a shared problem.

The sociological study of collective behavior is difficult for a variety of reasons. Because collective behavior is often temporary and unstructured, it is not easy to use standard research methods to study it, and because it is often destructive it cannot be studied through controlled experimentation. It is not easy to interview participants and nonparticipants during the course of a riot or a disaster. These people can be interviewed when the collective behavior has ended, but their responses may be distorted in some way by hindsight. Sociologists often must rely on recapitulations of collective behavior by participants, eyewitnesses, reporters, and police officers. Any one of these sources might introduce distortions into the re-creation of events, but the use of multiple sources helps sociologists zero in on what really happened.

When the collective actions of people become structured and orderly, they sometimes develop into a *social movement*—a set of attitudes and self-conscious actions by people who seek to change society's structure or ideology (Ash, 1972). Social movements are relatively organized collective efforts to establish or maintain a particular social order, whether a return to an idealized past, maintenance of the status quo, minor reforms in the social system, or full-scale revolution.

Sociologists disagree about whether to treat social movements as highly structured forms of collective behavior or as something else altogether. Incidents of collective behavior often accompany large-scale social movements, especially in their early stages. For example, protests and parades have been a part of both the civil rights movement and the feminist movement. Also, both collective behavior and social movements occur outside the institutional framework of everyday life.

However, collective behavior and social movements have some important differences. Social movements have specific goals and strategies; they are systematic efforts to change social institutions, unlike some forms of collective behavior such as mass hysteria and panics. Unlike collective behavior, social movements have some characteristics of formal organizations; for example, many social movements have elected leaders, methods of recruitment, a division of labor, and continuity over time. Those who participate in social movements also have a sense of destiny and common purpose that is missing from many kinds of collective behavior (Traugott, 1978).

Masses, Publics, and Crazes

Some kinds of collective behavior involve people who are not in physical proximity to each other but who do respond to the same events, issues, or people. Two such collectivities are masses and publics.

MASSES

A *mass* is a large and heterogeneous number of people who are not in the same physical location but who all react to a common stimulus. A mass does not respond as an organized group of interacting individuals; the physical detachment of the members of a mass from each other means that they react independently, even though their reactions are often quite similar. Masses are most common in industrial societies because the concentration of people in cities and their common exposure to the mass media are conducive to the development of a mass out of a diverse population. By providing people with common information and by arousing in them similar emotions, the mass media can also set the stage for other forms of collective behavior such as fads, fashions, and riots.

Mass Hysteria

The response by physically dispersed individuals to a common perception that they face a great and unpreventable threat is called *mass hysteria*. It involves irrational and sometimes compulsive beliefs and behavior that spread among people, frequently with the help of the mass media. Mass hysteria is not always focused on the real source of people's anxiety, which is often ambiguous. Not everyone is equally available to participate in mass hysteria, but those who are caught up in it commonly fail to exercise critical judgment in their efforts to explain unusual experiences and events. They seek scapegoats, or targets that they can blame for their predicament. For instance, the threat of Communism that Americans perceived after World War II led to McCarthyism in the 1950s. Senator Joseph McCarthy and his supporters—who never outnumbered their detractors—found it easier to investigate Americans they thought were Communists or "Communist sympathizers" than to deal directly with Communists in the international arena. This "witch hunt" ruined hundreds of reputations and careers (Lipset, 1963b, 1963c).

Another form of mass hysteria occurred in Seattle in 1954, when people began to notice the "pitting" of their car windshields. They attributed this damage to a variety of sources, but the most popular explanation was fallout from H-bomb tests. Lack of information about the effects of nuclear testing created uncertainty and anxiety, prompting many to search for evidence of its effects on their daily lives. The pitting of the windshields seemed to validate their fears, and it made it possible for them to take action to protect their property, such as covering their cars to protect them from fallout. In fact, the pitting was caused by the natural effects of the weather on aging cars rather than by fallout. The pitting had always been there, but fear of nuclear testing led people to look for signs of damage to their property (Medalia and Larsen, 1958). Another instance of mass hysteria is examined in SEL 19.1.

SOCIOLOGY AND EVERYDAY LIFE 19.1
Invasion from Mars

On Halloween night, 1938, about six million people across the United States listened to a radio dramatization of H. G. Wells's *War of the Worlds* presented by Orson Welles and his Mercury Theatre on the Air. This story of an invasion from Mars left an estimated 1.2 million people frightened or disturbed. Thousands took action by

. . . praying, crying, fleeing frantically to escape death from the Martians. Some ran to rescue loved ones. Others telephoned farewells or warnings, hurried to inform neighbors, sought information from newspapers or radio stations, summoned ambulances or police cars (p. 47).

For a few horrible hours people from Maine to California thought that hideous monsters armed with death rays were destroying all armed resistance sent against them; that there was simply no escape from disaster; that the end of the world was near (p. 3).

What accounted for this mass hysteria, and could it happen again today? Hadley Cantril set out to discover why so many people had been so gullible. He interviewed a nonrandom but broadly representative selection of 135 residents of New Jersey, the area where the fictional attack from Mars had begun. More than 100 of these people reported that they had been upset by the broadcast.

The radio show they had heard began with the announcement, "The Columbia Broadcasting System and its affiliated stations present Orson Welles and the Mercury Theatre on the Air in *War of the Worlds* by H. G. Wells" (p. 4). However, 42 per cent of a sample interviewed in a CBS survey a week later said they had tuned in late to the show. Those who tuned in late were more likely to accept the broadcast as news of a real invasion from Mars than were listeners who had been with the show from the start.

Orson Welles was then introduced, and he spoke briefly about how people on Earth were being watched by superior beings in space. After this, the broadcast moved to a weather report and then to an announcement of a program of music from a New York City hotel. Anyone tuning in at this point would be unaware that *War of the Worlds* was on the air. Soon after, an announcer interrupted the music to read a bulletin about an astronomer's observation of "several explosions of incandescent

gas, occurring at regular intervals on the planet Mars" (p. 6). The broadcast returned to the music, and there soon followed another interruption for an interview with an astronomer about the planet Mars. A later bulletin announced a "shock of almost earthquake intensity occurring within a radius of twenty miles of Princeton" (pp. 9–10). The "invasion" was under way. "Reporters" later described the spaceship and a Martian that incinerated people and buildings with a deadly ray:

A humped shape is rising out of the pit. I can make out a small beam of light against a mirror. What's that? There's a jet of flame springing from that mirror, and it leaps right at the advancing men. It strikes them head on! Good Lord, they're turning into flame! (SCREAMS AND UNEARTHLY SHRIEKS)
    Now the whole field's caught fire. (Explosion) The woods . . . the barns . . . the gas tanks of automobiles . . . it's spreading everywhere. It's coming this way. About twenty yards to my right. . . .
(CRASH OF MICROPHONE . . . THEN DEAD SILENCE . . .) (p. 18).

Eventually the Martians were destroyed by bacteria against which they had no immunity. Orson Welles closed with "if your doorbell rings and nobody's there, that was no Martian . . it's Halloween" (p. 43). An announcer then told the audience again what it had been listening to and what the program would be the following week.

The format of this show was partly responsible for its credibility. Americans were accustomed to the radio as a source of important information, and the bulletin format was a common way to report significant events as they happened. The fact that Europe was about to break out in war sensitized people to the possibility of sudden violence, and the backdrop of the Great Depression heightened insecurities. The radio broadcast was a well-done drama with professional actors; shortly thereafter, Orson Welles directed *Citizen Kane*, a movie that some critics think is the best American movie ever made. In addition, the prestige of the "experts" interviewed on the show—an "astronomer," a "professor," and a "military officer"—gave the broadcast credibility. "Reporters" described events in everyday language, and often these events occurred in places well known to listeners. At first the

Orson Welles (with hands raised) directs a rehearsal of one of his radio plays.

events were believable, such as the exploding gases on Mars, and only gradually did the show build to incredible occurrences. The announcers expressed disbelief throughout the show, reflecting listeners' skepticism and drawing them in to the show.

Listeners reacted to the drama in a variety of ways. Some could tell from the show itself that it was a play; they knew Orson Welles's voice or H. G. Wells's story, or they thought the story sounded like science fiction. Others checked the broadcast against other information and learned that it was only a play; they turned to other stations or looked at the radio listings in the newspaper. Few of those who successfully checked on the show were frightened.

Some listeners tried to check on the show's veracity but nevertheless continued to believe it was news of a real event. Their efforts involved unreliable methods; one person later said, "I looked out of the window and everything looked the same as usual *so I thought it hadn't reached our section yet*" (p. 93). Still others did not even try to check on the truth of the broadcast. They were too frightened to do so, never thought to check, stopped listening out of fear, or became resigned to their fate. Some tried to escape immediately. Of those who did not check or were unsuccessful in their efforts to check, about two-thirds were frightened by the show and the rest were disturbed to a lesser extent.

The better-educated listeners were the most likely to check the truth of the story or disbelieve it from the start. They had more critical ability and were less likely to have blind faith in what they heard on the radio. The social context in which people listened was also important. People who had been told to turn on their radios by frightened friends and relatives were prepared for danger and were more likely to be frightened by the show. Those who were cut off from their families and those who listened in public places where they observed signs of mass hysteria (such as traffic jams) were more apt to believe that an invasion was in progress.

Mass hysteria of this sort would probably not occur today. Television now presents visual images of events that would make it difficult to fabricate an invasion from Mars, although special-effects technology might make this possible. Radio leaves much to the imagination, and Orson Welles used this to create a credible scenario. In addition, today there is more responsibility by the mass media to avoid shows that

might create such mass hysteria; some of this is a direct result of public response to the *War of the Worlds* broadcast. Moreover, people are now more knowledgeable about astronomy and the possibility of life on nearby planets. Still, hundreds of people report sightings of unidentified flying objects (UFOs) each year, even though there is so far no tangible proof of their existence.

Source: Adapted from Hadley Cantril, *The Invasion from Mars: A Study in the Psychology of Panic*. New York: Harper & Row, 1940, 1966.

PUBLICS

A *public* is a large number of people who share a common sentiment on some issue. Publics are more organized than masses because they have a common attitude toward a particular topic, idea, or individual; they also exercise more critical judgment than masses do. Publics exist in large and complex societies; in small and simple societies there are too few issues or too few people to have the diversity of views needed to form publics.

Any given person can be a member of many publics. For example, one individual could be part of the public favoring legalized abortion, the public opposing the death penalty, and the public supporting the efforts of Ralph Nader. The membership of individuals in multiple publics prevents any single issue from tearing society apart and thereby knits society together.

The members of a public adopt a common position on an issue. For other people in the society that particular issue may be insignificant. For example, one public might support equal rights for women, and another public might oppose equal rights. A third category of people might not belong to any public on this issue, feeling that the legal equality of men and women is of no direct concern to them.

Public Opinion

Public opinion is the actual attitude or position on an issue that is held by the members of a public. Public opinion is a collective response to an issue; it develops from direct interaction with others and from information gathered from the mass media. Sometimes opinions are changed through efforts

by social movements; for instance, the feminist movement has forced many Americans to take a position for or against issues such as equal pay for men and women and legalized abortion.

Because it is closely related to a specific situation, public opinion often changes as social conditions change. Knowing the attitude of the public on a given issue at one time does not necessarily indicate what its opinion on that issue will be in the future. For example, support for the death penalty in the United States fell from 62 per cent in 1936 to 42 per cent in 1966, and then it increased steadily to about 67 per cent in the late 1970s (Bedau, 1982). One possible reason for the change since 1966 was the rise in crime rates that began in the mid-1960s, which may have led many Americans to turn to capital punishment to deter potential offenders (SEL 15.3 on page 363).

People's views often reflect those of their reference groups, the significant others to whom they look for guidance and support. In fact, people might be more likely to change their views in response to their reference groups than they are to fit their views to the law (Berkowitz and Walker, 1967). Also important in the formation of public opinion are "opinion leaders," intermediaries between the mass media and the general public, who transmit and interpret information. Opinion leaders are better informed on current issues than is the average person, and because these opinion leaders are of relatively high status they tend to have a significant impact on the formation of public opinion (Katz and Lazarsfeld, 1955). The influence of these opinion leaders may have been diluted by television and its newscasters and celebrities who adopt a personal approach to their audiences.

Publics can emerge from an undifferentiated mass when that mass is exposed to information from the media and takes a position around an issue. One important kind of information presented in the mass media is the public opinion poll, which tells the audience what others think. The polls presented in newspapers and on television sometimes present distorted results, because they rely on unrepresentative samples such as those picked from a telephone book. Another flaw in these polls is that the views of all respondents are given even though many people offer opinions on issues about which they know little or nothing.

MANIPULATING PUBLIC OPINION. Public opinion can be manipulated by *censorship*, or the restriction of information. The government sometimes denies people information that is harmful to a position it supports, thereby reducing the likelihood that publics opposed to its interests will develop. Most governments engage in censorship by classifying information that could be detrimental to the society if it were revealed. In 1971, *The New York Times* published the Pentagon Papers, a set of documents about American policy in Southeast Asia, in spite of the government's claim that doing so would endanger national security. The Supreme Court upheld the right of the newspaper to publish these documents. This case involved a conflict between the government's right to censor information that might harm the national interest or embarrass its officials, and newspapers' right to be free of government interference. A press free of all restrictions is an important check on abuses of government power, but it can also be argued that the public is better served by having decisions about what information can be printed made by elected officials rather than by reporters and editors.

Public opinion can also be manipulated through *propaganda*, the deliberate and calculated presentation of distorted, one-sided, and selective information to the public in order to change its opinion in a desired way. Propagandists use a variety of methods. Often they associate their own position with other more widely held ideas, hiding their true intentions in the process. Propagandists also try to arouse the public's fears, and then show people how those fears can be alleviated by supporting the propagandist. Another technique is to convey a sense of their own strength by announcing the support that they have from powerful groups, famous people, or a large segment of the population. The Reverend Jim Jones of the Peoples Temple (see SEL 19.3) used many of these methods. He befriended

politically influential people, including Rosalynn Carter and Mayor George Moscone of San Francisco. He convinced his followers that others were out to destroy the cult. He presented the cult as a Christian church intent on social justice, while concealing a personal quest for power and wealth (Reiterman, with Jacobs, 1982). The result of Jim Jones's use of propaganda was a generally favorable opinion among most residents of San Francisco and many of its political leaders, an opinion that changed abruptly with the mass suicide of 913 members of the Peoples Temple in Jonestown, Guyana, in 1978.

Propagandists face several obstacles to the easy manipulation of public opinion. In many modern societies, there is competition among a variety of sources of information; for every group that presents one point of view, there are others that present opposing perspectives on the same issue. Sometimes this confuses the public, but it also forces people to use critical judgment in forming their views. Propaganda may also be ineffective if the source of information has little credibility; credibility can be undermined if the public learns that the source's self-interest is being served by the information it is conveying. Propaganda is also less effective when the target group is well informed. Thus, a literate and well-educated public is probably less subject to manipulation by propagandists than an illiterate and uneducated public, even though the literate and well-educated population is likely to live in an industrial society where the mass media can be powerful tools of propaganda.

CRAZES

A *craze* is action by people who share an unquestioned belief that something will be rewarding to them. Crazes include fads and fashions; speculative booms in land, securities, or even tulip bulbs (in seventeenth-century Holland); a bandwagon effect for a political candidate; and religious revivals (Smelser, 1962). Those who participate in a craze are a kind of public, because they have a common attitude toward the object of their desires. They also share with participants in mass hysteria a lack of critical ability and a degree of obsessiveness.

Fads

A *fad* is a new and relatively trivial activity that many people adopt quickly and enthusiastically; it is a craze that has expressive or emotional characteristics. Because most fads are short-lived, they tend to be viewed skeptically and negatively by many people. Fads allow people with developing identities, particularly young people who lack a defined place in the social structure, to show others that they are different. Fads are thus a form of status-seeking that involves novel behavior; when the fad loses its novelty, it is usually abandoned (Smelser, 1962; Klapp, 1969).

Examples of fads include the hula hoop, stuffing people into telephone booths, swallowing goldfish, streaking, owning pet rocks, and using slang expressions. The popularity of movies such as *Star Wars, The Empire Strikes Back, Return of the Jedi*, and *E.T.* has led to a fad of seeing these movies multiple times; prestige is conferred not by seeing the movie, which most people have, but rather by the number of times a person has seen it. Another fad inspired by films occurred in China in 1982, when the popular movie *Shaolin Temple*, which featured displays of *wushu*—a combination of boxing, fencing, and acrobatics—created a fad for the martial arts that led young Chinese to enroll in *wushu* courses, buy books on the martial arts, and even run away to a monastery where they mistakenly thought monks still gave instruction in *wushu* (*The New York Times*, September 12, 1982, p. 10).

Fashions

The term *fashion* usually refers to trends in clothing, but there are also fashions in art, literature, and music. Fashions are simply styles of appearance or behavior. In comparison to fads, fashions change slowly and they usually build on previous fashions rather than making sharp breaks with past styles. Change in fashion is slow partly because of the expense of adopting a new fashion. For example, a rapid change in clothing styles would force people to abandon their wardrobes and replace them with entirely new apparel. Because people might resist such radical changes, commercial enterprises usually introduce new fashions gradually in order to build public acceptance. Fashions often change in a cyclical way; for example, hemlines will rise and then fall, and neckties get narrower before getting wider.

Fashion is a product of the emphasis on progress in industrial societies. Change is equated with progress; the new is seen as better than the old. People do not want to be "out of date," which is the same as "out of fashion." Fashion is most common in class systems of stratification where it can be used to symbolize social status. Often, the up-wardly mobile change their mode of dress to show others that they belong in their newly attained social position. In caste systems, fashion is not needed to symbolize social standing, because differences among people are widely known and fixed, nor do communist systems require fashion to make social distinctions, because everyone is regarded as equal (Blumer, 1969a).

Fashion frequently diffuses throughout a class system when people try to adopt the styles of a different class. Much fashion diffuses downward in the stratification system, with the lower class and working class adopting the clothing styles and speech patterns of people with higher social standing. However, there are also examples of fashion diffusing from the lower classes to the higher classes; a recent example is the wearing of denim jeans, an upward diffusion of a style that originated among workers and farmers. Of course, a designer's label often distinguishes the jeans worn by the middle and upper classes from those worn by laborers, and this label confers prestige on the wearer.

Rumor

A *rumor* is a piece of unverified but not necessarily incorrect information that is transmitted from person to person relatively rapidly (Shibutani, 1966; Rosnow and Fine, 1976). Rumor is a collective attempt to develop a common understanding of a situation in order to determine an appropriate behavioral response. People pool their intellectual resources to find an acceptable explanation for an ambiguous event. In a sense, rumor is "improvised news"; people interact, watching each other's reaction to the "news," and then react to those responses (Shibutani, 1966). Rumors can also be seen as a kind of purposive social exchange in which people trade information for prestige, entertainment, power, or other information (Rosnow and Fine, 1976).

Rumors are usually transmitted by word of mouth, although they can also be conveyed by the mass media, books, and written information. Conspiracy theories that arise after political assassinations are often transmitted through books and articles and by television, and are then picked up and passed from person to person. In other cases, rumors are the conscious creation of propagandists who want to influence the public in a certain way. Sometimes rumors have no basis in fact at all (see SEL 19.2).

SOCIOLOGY AND EVERYDAY LIFE 19.2
Rumor in Orléans, France

A rumor that apparently had no factual basis spread throughout Orléans, France, in 1969. The story was that several young women had been injected with drugs while in the fitting rooms of six different dress shops, all of which were owned by Jews. These women were supposedly sent abroad where they were forced to become prostitutes.

This rumor, apparently started by adolescent girls, spread first in the schools and then to adults, even though it received no support from the press or the police and even though it was not based on any incident remotely like the story that was circulated. As time passed, the rumor became more elaborate. The dress shops were said to be connected by underground tunnels, and the press and the police were said to be silent because they had been bribed by Jewish residents of the city.

The rumor dissipated after the press discounted it by pointing out that there were no missing women and by suggesting that anti-Semitism and "Hitlerism" were behind the fabricated tale. Even then, many people insisted that something mysterious had actually been going on and had been hidden from the public.

Source: Based on Edgar Morin, *Rumour in Orléans,* trans. by Peter Green. New York: Pantheon, 1971.

Rumors spread through networks of people, but the transmission process is usually not as simple as in "pass it on," the game in which one person whispers a message to a second person, who in turn passes it to a third person and so on. Instead, people are likely to hear a rumor from several sources, and this often enables them to check one version against another for accuracy and consistency. Rumors are more likely to be accepted and transmitted when they fit with people's norms and values. When they conflict with those norms and values, people are apt to be skeptical and may try to verify the rumor. Often rumors prepare people for collective action such as a riot, and sometimes they develop after an event such as a lynching to explain what happened.

People play different roles in the process of rumor transmission. They can add to a story to show others that they have "inside information," because this confers prestige. They may be skeptical of the rumor and ask probing questions before passing it on. Other people in the network might deliberately lie or distort the rumor to further their personal interests. Some people simply relay the rumor or just listen to it without asking questions or changing it in any way. Others act on the rumor by mobilizing people to do whatever the story seems to require (Shibutani, 1966). Those who are more anxious and less tolerant of ambiguity are more likely to spread rumors than people who are calmer and better able to deal with uncertainty (Rosnow and Kimmel, 1979).

Rumors can be distorted in the transmission process. "Leveling" is the tendency of rumors to be shortened for easier understanding and simpler transmission. Rumors are also "sharpened" by selectively stressing certain aspects of the story and omitting other aspects so as to accentuate certain themes and minimize other elements. Another distorting process is "assimilation," the addition of new material to a rumor so that it will fit the interests and beliefs of the person who is transmitting it (Allport and Postman, 1947). Rumors are not always distorted in the transmission; if people have a personal stake in making sure that a story is correct, a rumor may become more accurate as it is passed from person to person (Schachter and Burdick, 1955). When distortion does occur, it is often a result of trying to develop understanding and consensus out of an ambiguous situation (Shibutani, 1966).

Crowd Behavior

The rock fans at The Who concert in Cincinnati and the people who gathered to hear the Pope in Zaire were examples of *crowds*—relatively large and temporary gatherings of people in one place who have a purpose and who are aware of each other (Blumer, 1957, 1969a). Crowds often lack organization in their early stages, but over time interaction leads to rapport and to the development of a social structure that includes leaders and participants. Many crowds have a core of dedicated participants, people on the periphery who may be mobilized for action, and a passive audience.

TYPES OF CROWDS

One way to classify crowds is by their purpose and organization. According to Blumer's (1969a) typology, crowds can be casual, conventional, expressive, or acting.

Some crowds have no clearly defined goals. Examples of such "casual crowds" include gatherings of people on the street, near a construction site, or in a park. These crowds often gather in an unplanned and random fashion. Participants are not emotionally aroused and usually lack a sense of unity, even though events such as a fire or a political speech can lead to interaction and some degree of common purpose. Casual crowds typically disband after a short time, and their participants are unlikely to interact again.

"Conventional crowds," on the other hand, are planned gatherings of people at specific events such as football games or movies. These crowds have a common focus of attention and are highly structured, in the sense that their behavior is quite predictable. Certain norms guide the behavior of conventional crowds. For instance, there is an expectation that people will not talk loudly during a movie, although some people violate that norm, whereas it is permissible to talk loudly and even to shout at a football game. Conventional crowds often interact with the performers by cheering at a basketball game, applauding after songs in a musical, or heckling a candidate at a political rally. Athletes, actors, and candidates are aware of the difference between a "good audience" and a "bad audience." A good audience that is enthusiastic can even elicit a better performance. "Claques" are sometimes hired to cheer or applaud the performers in order to stimulate enthusiasm in the rest of the audience; cheerleaders openly serve this purpose, but sometimes claques pose as members of the audience. "Canned laughter" is used in a similar way on television shows to stimulate viewers at

Crowds can be classified by their purpose and their organization. Here we see a "conventional crowd" gathered to cheer on their team at a professional baseball game.

home; however, these viewers are a mass rather than a conventional crowd because they are not present in the same place.

Another kind of crowd is an "expressive crowd," a gathering of people who seek to relieve tension and give vent to their emotions. One example is a rock show audience; indeed, sometimes the expression of emotions by these audiences seems more important than listening to the music, as was apparently the case at the Woodstock festival in 1969. Other examples of expressive crowds include the annual Mardi Gras celebration in New Orleans and pep rallies before athletic contests.

The type of crowd most often studied by sociologists is the "acting crowd," one that has a specific target and pursues its goals in an aggressive and sometimes violent manner. Underlying discontent often comes to the surface in an acting crowd when collective action is sparked by a dramatic event—such as a police beating of a suspect—that reinforces existing beliefs about the source of the participants' problems.

THE CROWD IN HISTORY

Collective action has taken different forms in preindustrial societies and in industrial societies (Rudé, 1964; Tilly, 1978, 1981). In eighteenth-century Europe, crowd behavior took the form of food riots, resistance to conscription, rebellion against tax collectors, and demands made at public festivals. Often, protesters wore costumes and hung their enemies in effigy.

Economic and political changes in Western Europe during the nineteenth century altered the form of collective action. The expansion of electoral politics rewarded those who could mobilize people for collective protest; displays of strength at public meetings and in protest marches were a threat to elected officials. The centralization of power in the state meant that the government was able to repress certain kinds of protest and tolerate or even encourage other types of action. Furthermore, the development of capitalism created conflict between owners and workers that gave rise to strikes and worker protests. The repertoire of crowds shifted from the eighteenth century's relatively spontaneous direct action on a small scale to a larger-scale, more structured show of strength in the nineteenth century. The forms of collective action typical of the nineteenth century continue to characterize crowd behavior and social movements today (Tilly, 1981).

VARIETIES OF CROWD BEHAVIOR

Crowd behavior includes various forms of collective action: panics, disaster behavior, mobs, and riots. The specific way that a gathering of people acts is closely related to their reasons for being in one place and to the specific circumstances they confront.

Panics

Sudden flight by a crowd that is responding to a belief about an ambiguous and uncontrollable threat is called a *panic* (Smelser, 1962; Schultz, 1964). During panics, people feel trapped when they think that escape routes are blocked. If people realize that there is no escape, as in a sinking submarine, resignation rather than panic may be the result. Panics often involve some communication among the members of the crowd, including rumors about the immediate threat they face, but communication is often faulty enough that people cannot agree on a plan of escape. Sometimes, sudden action by one person triggers similar behavior by others and causes a stampede. For instance, if someone frantically tries to break down a door in a burning theater, others might push against that door and trample each other. If one person plays the role of leader and orders people away from the door while someone with a key unlocks the door, and then that leader directs the crowd through the exit, panic might be averted.

The term panic is sometimes used to refer to collective behavior that does not involve a crowd. Financial panics, such as the sale of stock that people feel is worthless or the withdrawal of money from a bank thought to be insolvent, can create a self-fulfilling prophecy. In other words, the attempt to escape from a situation of potential financial loss can make that loss inevitable. For instance, banks collapsed during the Great Depression when many depositors tried to withdraw their money at the same time. Because banks do not keep enough cash in their vaults to pay off all depositors at the same time, this run on banks reduced public confidence in banks and forced many of them into bankruptcy. This kind of behavior is more like mass hysteria than panic, because people usually react as separate individuals to a rumor or a common perception, rather than behaving as a crowd gathered in one location. However, depositors gathered outside a bank before it opens can have their fears of financial ruin increased by the stories that others tell them.

Disasters

A *disaster* is a situation of collective stress and social disruption that is caused by human or natural means (Barton, 1970; Quarantelli and Dynes, 1977). Disasters often strike quickly, but they can also occur over a long period of time, as when industrial waste poisons a community's water supply. Some disasters happen with little warning, but others can be predicted in advance. Even when disaster is predicted, convincing the endangered people that they should act is often difficult. People usually behave in an orderly way to help each other after the initial shock of a disaster such as a flood or a forest fire; looting and other kinds of antisocial activity are relatively uncommon.

After first being stunned and disoriented by damage to their physical environment, people frequently experience a loss of their sense of community. The destruction of communal ties to friends and neighbors was a major consequence of the bursting of a dam that released millions of gallons of mud on the town of Buffalo Creek, West Virginia, in 1972 (Erikson, 1976). More recently, a flood in Times Beach, Missouri, drove 2,000 people from their homes. A few weeks later they were warned not to return to the town because the flood waters contained dioxin, one of the deadliest toxic chemicals known. Residents were ambivalent about abandoning their property and the community they had known for years, but most did so. Some organized to demand that the government pay them for their homes and the other possessions they had to abandon (*The New York Times*, January 1, 1983, pp. 1, 5).

Disaster behavior has been studied from the perspective of collective behavior, but recently there has been considerable attention paid to the part that formal organizations play in disasters. Established organizations such as the police, the fire department, and hospitals are usually the first to respond to disasters. Other organizations may be formed to deal with the disaster; for example, a community-wide agency to coordinate rescue activities could be created and then disbanded after the crisis passes (Quarantelli and Dynes, 1977).

Mobs

A *mob* is an emotional crowd that cooperates in striving for a common goal or in expressing a shared hostility with violence. One type of mob is a lynch mob, a crowd intent on punishing someone without relying on the criminal justice system. Lynch mobs in the United States, particularly in the South, were historically used to "keep blacks in their place." The leaders of these lynch mobs typically came from the white middle and upper classes, and the rank and file came from the white working class. Usually the police made little effort to protect the lower-class black victims from the white mobs.

Riots

When people band together in a relatively spontaneous, unplanned, and temporary way to act in an openly violent fashion against other people or their property, the result is called a *riot*. People in a riot are less goal oriented and less organized than a mob; if leaders emerge at all, it is usually some time after the crowd has gathered. Some riots are expressions of political grievances, but they are not widely recognized as a legitimate way to change society. Riots are rarely revolutionary in their goals, but they can lead to reforms by the government. This makes the riot an effective tool for eliciting attention and producing social change, particularly for the politically powerless. Other riots are not politically motivated, such as riots at soccer matches or rock concerts, although even these riots can signify discontent and alienation on the part of the participants.

The riots that have occurred in the black ghettos of American cities since 1965 commonly started after an encounter between a black person and a white police officer drew a crowd that eventually rioted. These riots were directed against property that symbolized white control of wealth and power. In contrast to riots earlier in the twentieth century, there was little violence between blacks and whites, other than that which occurred between black rioters and white police officers. Urban riots that have occurred in Great Britain in recent years have some of these same characteristics: They too involve minority groups, often immigrants from countries in the Commonwealth who have faced racial discrimination and high unemployment rates; an initial confrontation with the police; and the destruction of property.

EXPLANATIONS OF CROWD BEHAVIOR

Sociologists have formulated various theories to explain panics, disasters, mobs, and riots. Each of the theories we examine points to certain aspects of

During the New York City blackout of 1977, riots broke out in various parts of the city (aftermath shown here). Most of the rioting and looting was directed against storeowners.

collective behavior and fits some kinds of collective action better than others. One theory, the value-added approach, explains both organized social movements and the collective behavior of crowds.

Contagion

Gustave LeBon (1896, 1968) offered an early explanation of crowd behavior. LeBon was a conservative who deplored the part that crowds played during and after the French Revolution of 1789 in destroying a social order based on rule by an aristocracy. His explanation of crowd behavior has its flaws, but it does have some validity.

LeBon claimed that people in a crowd no longer behave as individuals but instead become submerged in a collectivity with a mind of its own. One characteristic of crowds is the anonymity of their members. According to LeBon, this anonymity weakens social control and makes people feel that their actions are free of any negative consequences. As a result, they behave more impulsively and more irrationally than they would if they reflected more critically on their actions. Another characteristic of a crowd is suggestibility. In other words, its members are easily influenced by other participants and are subject to manipulation by charismatic leaders. The suggestibility of crowds means that rumors often become a basis for collective action.

The anonymity and suggestibility of crowds are closely linked to *contagion*, the spread of behavior and beliefs among participants through interaction and imitation. A more recent theory refers to this as "circular reaction," the response of individuals in a crowd to each other's excitement and activity (Blumer, 1969a). Contagion occurs in crowds because there are no well-established norms to provide guidelines about appropriate behavior, and people turn to those near them for cues about how to act. The more uncertainty there is about how to behave and the more exposed people are to others in a similar predicament, the more likely they are to rely on each other as guides to appropriate behavior.

One aspect of circular reaction is "milling," a process by which people in one location move around and respond to each other's emotions and behavior. Milling, which usually occurs in the early stages of crowd development, intensifies feelings and reinforces agitation. As relatively passive onlookers are caught up in the excitement, milling and circular reaction draw new recruits into a crowd (Blumer, 1969a).

The contagion explanation of crowd behavior has been criticized on several grounds (Milgram and Toch, 1969; Brown and Goldin, 1973). The theory contains a negative judgment of crowds that treats them as more disorderly than they sometimes are. It also fails to make clear the exact conditions under which contagion develops. LeBon's assumption that crowds have a single mind or a common purpose is also incompatible with evidence that participants in a crowd sometimes have very different motives; they may want to protest social conditions, steal property, express frustration, or relieve boredom. Contagion theory also errs in suggesting that crowds are always irrational (Couch, 1968). For example, the black ghetto rioters behaved rationally in a way; because other channels of protest had proved ineffective in bringing about major social changes, the riots were a way to attract national attention. Furthermore, in burning the stores of exploitative white merchants while often leaving the stores of black merchants untouched, rioters showed that their actions were carefully considered.

In spite of its flaws, contagion theory is useful in drawing attention to the way that behavior spreads among the members of a crowd and the way that emotions and commitment intensify to create a common course of action. This theory is also helpful in pointing to the way that social control breaks down in a crowd to free people from certain constraints on their behavior.

Convergence

Contagion theory assumes that people gathered in the same location sometimes interact in ways that lead them to develop common perceptions and common behavior. In contrast, *convergence theory* suggests that crowds develop when people who have similar characteristics, attitudes, or needs before joining a crowd come together for collective action. In other words, convergence theory suggests that similar people are drawn together, and contagion theory proposes that even people with different dispositions may form a collectivity through interaction.

One version of convergence theory suggests that crowds are composed of "riffraff," the dregs of society who have little to lose from engaging in antisocial behavior. Another version is that people who have the same grievances but lack effective ways to change their situation turn to riots to improve their collective lot. Still another view is Eric Hoffer's (1951) position that some people have a personal need to join crowds or organized social movements; they might have a need to subordinate themselves to a leader or a need for the sense of camaraderie that comes from belonging to a group that is striving for a common purpose. Hoffer called people who are more interested in belonging to a group than in the actual content of that group's program "true believers," because they seem capable of total commitment to any of a number of causes. Some people seem to derive gratification from being part of a crowd or a social movement, but these true believers are probably a small proportion of all participants in most instances of collective action.

Explanations of crowd behavior that rely on the idea of convergence cannot explain why crowds often pass through a number of stages, from disorganized milling to organized action against specific targets. Changes in crowd behavior over time cannot be explained by participants' characteristics that do not change over time. However, the idea of convergence does direct researchers' attention to the motivations and predispositions of participants in collective action.

Research on the ghetto riots of the 1960s both supports and contradicts the idea of convergence. Blacks who participated were not "riffraff" or people from the lowest positions in the stratification system; their income was about the same as black residents of the community who did not take part in the riots. However, the idea of convergence is supported by evidence that the rioters had some traits in common with each other and did differ in some ways from the nonparticipants. The fact that the rioters were blacks directs attention to the grievances they shared before the riots. According to some research, compared to blacks who did not riot, those who participated in riots were more likely to have been born and raised in the community, more educated, more likely to express black pride, more apt to feel that they deserved better jobs, more likely to regard white racism as an obstacle to upward mobility, and more active in their community (McCone, 1965; National Advisory Commission on Civil Disorders, 1968; Fogelson and Hill, 1968). Shared grievances did underlie the riots, but convergence theory does not specify the social conditions that cause people with shared grievances to riot; for instance, it does not tell us why the riots occurred between 1965 and 1968 when the underlying grievances had existed for years.

Emergent Norms

Another explanation of crowd behavior is that new expectations and standards develop through interaction among the people gathered in one place (Turner, 1964; Turner and Killian, 1972). According to *emergent-norm theory*, people come to share the same views and develop a group structure that reflects specific norms and values. For example, when violence is directed against certain targets but not against others, the norm has "emerged" that random destruction is unacceptable to the members of the crowd. The theory of emergent norms does not consider the shared attitudes and common behavior of crowds to be a result of blind obedience to a "group mind," as contagion theory suggests, nor does it attribute them to the convergence of like-minded people. Rather, the shared norms and social structure of crowds are seen as emerging from social interaction in the same way that other organized forms of behavior develop. Crowd behavior is treated as a process by which people seek a shared interpretation of the reality they confront.

The idea of emergent norms implies that crowd members have different motives for participating in collective behavior. They develop common standards by observing and listening to each other, so that contagion plays a part in the development of the crowd's norms. Leaders play a role in the emergence of these norms by presenting to the crowd a particular interpretation of its predicament, but even crowds without leaders typically develop shared expectations about what behavior is appropriate.

Payoffs

Another way to look at crowd behavior is as rational activity that is designed to produce benefits for the participants. This approach is different from contagion theory's assumption that crowd behavior is irrational. Instead, the payoff explanation sees crowd action as a product of many individual decisions, which are based on available information that is used in a calculated way to maximize the payoffs or advantages for participants. According to this perspective, people try to predict the consequences of their actions and then behave according to their perceptions of those consequences. They try to maximize their gains, minimize their losses, and win as much social approval as they can (Berk, 1974a, 1974b).

Payoffs for behavior are often different in a crowd setting than they are on an individual basis. Looting can have a negative payoff for a thief who acts alone and is arrested, but the same behavior might have a positive payoff in a crowd if it allows the thief to win approval from friends and neighbors who are also rioting. Moreover, arrest and prosecution are probably less likely in a crowd because there is a kind of "safety in numbers."

Political Protest

One explanation of crowd behavior that combines elements of other theories proposes that crowd behavior is sometimes a form of political protest resulting from lack of access to other sources of power and influence. This approach suggests that crowd participants share needs and grievances that can be dealt with only by the political system; in this way, political-protest theory is similar to convergence theory. Political-protest theory shares with emergent-norm theory the idea that crowd members agree on appropriate targets for collective action. Like the idea of payoffs, the theory of political protest also assumes that crowd behavior is a rational response to existing social conditions.

One type of political-protest theory attributes crowd behavior to *relative deprivation*, the discrepancy between a group's expectations of what it is legitimately entitled to and the actual conditions that the group experiences or feels are possible within the existing social system (Gurr, 1970). Relative-deprivation theory suggests that discontent is greatest when the gap between expectations and capabilities is the largest. When alternative means to influence the political system are unavailable, crowd behavior and even political revolution can result. One study of revolutions found that they often occurred after a long period of economic gain followed by an abrupt economic setback; a decline in well-being combined with still-high expectations set the stage for political violence and revolution (Davies, 1962). However, research on the ghetto riots of the 1960s does not support this particular form of relative-deprivation theory (Miller, Bolce, and Halligan, 1977).

Value-added Theory

One comprehensive theory that explains both collective behavior and social movements is Smelser's (1962) *value-added theory*. This theory uses an idea borrowed from economics: the notion of value-added, that at each step in the production process value is added to the original raw materials. For example, iron ore has many possible uses but little intrinsic value as ore. The mining and extraction of iron from the ore add to its value. When manufactured into steel, the iron becomes even more valuable. The steel is then shaped in certain ways that give it more specific uses, such as for car parts. A car fender, for instance, is more valuable than iron ore, but it is also of more limited use, because it cannot be used to build a bridge or a skyscraper. At each stage of the manufacturing process, the raw material becomes more valuable but more specific in its use.

Using this value added approach as an analogy, Smelser developed a theory of collective behavior and social movements that includes six stages. At each stage "value" is added to the "raw material"—the social conditions underlying collective action—and at each stage the likelihood of a final "product" of collective behavior or a social movement becomes more inevitable. The possibilities at any one stage are limited by what has happened in the earlier stages.

STRUCTURAL CONDUCIVENESS. The first stage in value-added theory is "structural conduciveness," the social conditions that must be present before collective behavior or social movements can develop. For example, communication among people in a similar predicament and the right of those people to assemble for action are conducive to the emergence of collective behavior and social movements. Repressive governments can create conditions that are not conducive to collective action. The government of South Africa, for instance, requires blacks to carry identification cards and isolates them in certain regions of the country; these conditions inhibit organization for change. On the other hand, the antiwar movement in the United States during the 1960s and 1970s was made possible in part by the presence of potential draftees in universities where free speech was valued and protest demonstrations were tolerated.

STRUCTURAL STRAIN. If social conditions are conducive to the development of collective action, "structural strain," or hardships that produce discontent and unrest among people, may provide the next step in the development of collective behavior or a social movement. Structural strain can take the form of alienation, a vague sense of threat, a feeling of helplessness, or general dissatisfaction with the status quo. The presence of students on campus was conducive to the development of an antiwar movement, but it was the Vietnam War itself that posed an immediate threat of being drafted and heightened a sense of injustice. The gay liberation movement has been a result of an "intolerable reality" faced by homosexuals, including job and housing discrimination and police harassment (Humphreys, 1972).

GROWTH AND SPREAD OF A GENERALIZED BELIEF. Structural strain is focused by a "generalized belief" that defines a particular situation as a problem in need of a solution. This belief locates the sources of structural strain and suggests possible responses to the strain. Sometimes a well-developed ideology such as Marxism is used to explain a particular problem such as poverty or racial discrimination. The civil rights spelled out in the United States Constitution are another set of generalized beliefs that have contributed to the development of social movements such as black civil rights, feminism, and gay rights.

PRECIPITATING FACTORS. A "precipitating factor" is a specific, dramatic event that confirms the fears and sense of threat produced by the structural strain and defined by the generalized belief. This event might be specific action by the perceived source of the trouble, such as President Lyndon Johnson's extension of the war in Southeast Asia and expansion of the draft. It could also be a direct confrontation with authority by the discontented, such as a campus riot against the war or police brutality against a black in the ghetto. The gay liberation movement has been traced to a 1969 police raid on an after-hours gay bar in Greenwich Village called the Stonewall Inn. For four nights, gays and the police confronted each other; gays were clubbed, and responded by throwing things at the police and destroying property. Less than a month later, the Gay Liberation Front was organized (Humphreys, 1972: 5–7).

MOBILIZATION OF PARTICIPANTS FOR ACTION. Collective action often begins with a core of dedicated supporters for a cause. Only after a generalized belief has developed and spread and after precipitating factors have focused attention on an issue will other people join. This mobilization sometimes involves milling and contagion in a crowd setting. Leaders also play an important role in mobilizing participants; they define problems and provide participants with specific ways to deal with those problems. Sometimes collective behavior such as crowd activity or a protest demonstration focuses public attention on a problem and draws new recruits into a social movement, as the following example indicates:

In the summer of 1971, the owner of a credit agency on New York's 42nd Street was questioned about his agency's practice of informing employers of the suspected homosexual tendencies of prospective employees, as well as credit applicants. "If a man looks like a duck," he was quoted as saying, "walks like a duck, quacks like a duck, and associates with ducks, I'd say he is a duck." In a short time, a dozen [Gay Activists Alliance] members, dressed in duck costumes, were waddling around the sidewalk at the entrance to the credit agency, quacking and carrying picket signs (Humphreys, 1972: 126).

THE OPERATION OF SOCIAL CONTROL. Finally, the development of collective behavior or a social movement is influenced by the response of social-control agents, such as the police and the courts. Collective action can be curbed by a strong and hostile reaction from these institutions, but an inappropriate response can provoke anger, show that the generalized belief about the causes of the problem is correct, and mobilize new participants out of sympathy for the cause. Control agents can also cause precipitating events that contribute to the development of collective action; one example is police brutality against members of minority groups that has led to riots in both the United States and Great Britain.

ASSESSING VALUE-ADDED THEORY. Smelser's value-added theory organizes the causes of collective behavior and social movements in a logical sequence. Yet the theory has been criticized as vague and difficult to apply to real situations. In addition, in some kinds of collective action, all six stages are not found or do not occur in the sequence that Smelser specifies (Milgram and Toch, 1969). The theory does seem to incorporate the key conditions that underlie collective behavior such as crazes, panics, and riots and many kinds of social movements. It also makes it clear that collective action requires more than discontent and an effective leader (Marx and Wood, 1975).

Social Movements

Earlier we saw that sociologists disagree about the relationship between collective behavior, such as mass hysteria and riots, and organized social movements that endure over time. As we will see shortly, a rejection of traditional explanations of collective behavior has prompted some sociologists to develop a theory of social movements that emphasizes social organization and the mobilization of resources for action.

Social movements—which, as we pointed out at the beginning of the chapter, are sets of attitudes and self-conscious actions by people seeking to change society (Ash, 1972)—are sometimes very broad trends that develop over long periods of time. These general social movements include the gradual expansion of welfare rights during the twentieth century and the enfranchisement of different groups of citizens. Specific social movements, on the other hand, develop from general movements, and are highly organized and focused in the goals they pursue. They have formal leaders and a clearly defined membership (Blumer, 1969a). The gay liberation movement is a specific social movement that is related to the more general movement to extend civil rights to various groups.

A social movement often gives rise to several formal organizations that pursue similar goals, but by different means. The feminist movement, for instance, gave birth to the National Organization for Women (NOW) and many consciousness-raising groups. These and other organizations have pursued the goal of equal rights for women, but each has used different means: lobbying, political support of candidates, unionization of office workers, and group discussion.

Social movements can be classified by their goals and their orientation to the status quo:

1. Movements are reactionary if they want to turn back the clock to what is regarded as a better past. Often, the past envisioned by reactionary movements never existed in the form imagined. The Moral Majority is one example of a reactionary movement.

2. Conservative movements try to maintain the

status quo by resisting change (Lo, 1982). One example is the antibusing movement, which seeks to prevent the desegregation of schools.

3. Other movements are oriented toward reform of the existing social structure. They include the feminist movement and the gay liberation movement, both of which seek equal rights through lobbying, litigation, and influencing public opinion.

4. In contrast, revolutionary movements try to alter the very structure of society, especially its economic and political systems. Some revolutionary movements have clear ideas about the kind of new society they would build on the ruins of the old, but others seek to destroy the existing society without having a clear conception of what will replace it. We examine revolutionary movements in more detail in the next chapter.

5. Still other movements are utopian, striving to create an idealized social system among a small number of people in the hope that the new system will become a model for the rest of society to emulate. By its disastrous end in 1978, the Peoples Temple, which is described in SEL 19.3, had evolved into a utopian social movement.

SOCIOLOGY AND EVERYDAY LIFE 19.3
Revolutionary Suicide and the Peoples Temple

On November 18, 1978, in a small agricultural settlement in the jungle of Guyana, South America, 913 members of the Peoples Temple committed "revolutionary suicide." As interpreted by the Temple's leader, the Reverend Jim Jones, this concept meant that oppressed people could make an important statement to the world about inhumane social conditions and their commitment to socialism by choosing the time and place of their own death, rather than allowing their enemies to determine their fate. Actually, this extraordinary act of destruction included both suicide and murder, because some were unwilling to drink the poisoned fruit punch and had to be injected with potassium cyanide by the Temple's armed security staff. However, conditioned by Jones, pressured by other Temple members, and caught up in the contagion of the ritual suicide, most did take their own lives.

How can we interpret this collective act? It does not fit any category of collective behavior very well, because it was not a spontaneous and unplanned act by an unstructured gathering. Jones had begun to speak of mass suicide five years earlier, and once he had even held a "rehearsal"; he also prepared his followers for death in his sermons.

By 1978, the Peoples Temple had become a utopian social movement, but it began in Indiana in the 1950s as an evangelical sect. The difficulty in describing the Temple is evident in the following analysis by Tim Reiterman, a reporter who spent more than five years studying it:

In Indiana, the Temple was more of a church than a social movement or cult; in California, it was more of a social movement and cult than a utopian community; in Guyana, it would become a utopian community and in some ways the ultimate cult (p. 279).

In the early stages, Jim Jones preached evangelical Christianity with a strong emphasis on social justice. He was intent on creating a racially integrated church; he was white, but about 70 per cent of those who died in Guyana were black, mostly from the working class. Most of Jones's closest aides were white, however.

From the beginning, Jones used deception and manipulation to attract followers. He staged "healings" and "raised the dead" using fraudulent techniques that he explained to his aides by saying that the Temple's ends justified any means. Jones was able to combine approval with criticism in ways that tied followers to him and to the Temple. He was a charismatic figure, as both his followers and several political officials could attest. However, he never institutionalized his charisma, and so the Temple would not have survived his death if the Jonestown massacre had not occurred.

Feeling under attack by his enemies, most of whom were imaginary, Jones moved the Temple from Indiana to California. There it became a voice for the oppressed. It drew mostly blacks, because many of them had been exposed to his revivalist style of preaching, in which he often used black street dialect, and because he promised them a life free of discrimination. Blacks and others alienated from society were drawn to the Temple because it provided them with "pride in being part of a recognized group. For many, the collective identity helped erase lifelong feelings of powerlessness" (p. 167). Just before taking her life in Jonestown, one woman said, "I'd like to thank Dad [Jim Jones] because he's the only one who stood up for me" (p. 560).

In California, Jones supported socialism in his sermons; to outsiders, he presented himself as a moderate social reformer rather than as a revolutionary. He spoke to his followers of "the Promised Land" in Guyana, where he relocated most of them in 1973 and 1974. There he hoped to create a socialist utopia that would be a model for the world, but the hardships of the jungle and his own deteriorating psychological and physical state made that impossible. Jones had once been described by his psychiatrist as "paranoid with delusions of grandeur"; by the end, he had also become a heavy drug user.

Jones ran the Guyana commune with an iron hand. People were forced to work long hours. Those who complained were punished; some were isolated in an underground sensory-deprivation box, and others were drugged. All were isolated from the outside world, and they were carefully coached by Jones for their rare contacts with visitors from the United States. Jones was their only source of news, and he continually drilled into them the message that the Temple's enemies wanted to destroy all of them. When Representative Leo Ryan and a group of Americans visited Jonestown shortly before the mass suicide to check on conditions there for relatives back in the United States, a few Temple members defected with Ryan. Jones felt that the loss of even a single member was a personal affront and a threat to reveal what really went on in Jonestown. Fearing the worst from his enemies, Jones ordered Ryan and others murdered at a small airport at Port Kaituma, an act that spurred him to carry out his earlier threats of mass suicide.

An undated file photo of Jim Jones, leader of the Peoples Temple.

The act of revolutionary suicide was part of an unusual social movement led by a charismatic, manipulative man who was regarded by some of his followers as God. Jones bound members to the Temple in various ways, which included having them sign confessions that they had sexually abused their own children as a sign of loyalty to Jones. He also used beatings, sleep deprivation, taped conversations, self-renunciation, the destruction of family ties, and heterosexual and homosexual acts with himself to humiliate, reward, and control his followers. He presented himself to them as a sex object, and members of the Temple competed for his attention and approval.

Jones's unusual combination of tactics never succeeded in mobilizing much support. At the time of the Jonestown deaths there were no more than 1,200 active members, most of whom were in Jonestown and the rest in California. Even with these small numbers, Jones amassed more than $10 million by 1975 by asking members for sizable contributions, includ-

ing having the elderly sign over social security checks and donate the proceeds from the sale of their houses to the Temple. In California, Jones had learned that communal living was inexpensive and freed income for such contributions. The Jonestown settlement was expensive to build, but large sums of money remained in secret bank accounts at the time of the mass suicide. There was even some evidence that Jones might have planned to escape from Jonestown after the mass suicide to claim this money. As much as five years before the Jonestown massacre, Jones had claimed that he would need to remain behind after the act of revolutionary suicide to explain its meaning to the world.

Source: Based on Tim Reiterman, with John Jacobs, *Raven: The Untold Story of the Rev. Jim Jones and His People.* New York: Dutton, 1982.

RESOURCE-MOBILIZATION THEORY

In recent years, some sociologists have rejected such theories of collective behavior as contagion, convergence, and the value-added approach for *resource-mobilization theory*. The traditional theories treat collective behavior and social movements as products of shared grievances, the sources of which are not well understood by participants who often seem to behave erratically and irrationally (Gamson, 1975). Theories that emphasize personal needs or pathology, such as Hoffer's (1951) theory of the true believer, regard social movements as something distinct from routine political activity. Resource-mobilization theory, on the other hand, sees social movements as purposive activity that does not differ in any significant way from conventional politics by parties and interest groups. Resource-mobilization theorists see discontent or deprivation as just one component of social movements, and often a secondary component at that. Discontented people do not always engage in collective action, it is argued, and grievances and collective action do not seem to be closely associated at the national level (Snyder and Tilly, 1972; Miller, Bolce, and Halligan, 1977). Leaders and organizations often define, create, and manipulate

grievances rather than reflecting existing grievances (McCarthy and Zald, 1973, 1977; Zald and McCarthy, 1979; Tilly, 1981).

As we saw earlier, formal organizations became a more important part of collective action with the development of the modern state and capitalism. Beginning in the eighteenth and nineteenth centuries, the government and the owners of capital came to exercise considerable control over the political and economic systems. To counteract this power, the unorganized masses needed leaders to recruit supporters and to raise money with which to pursue their collective interests (Tilly, 1978, 1981). Resource-mobilization theory assumes that discontent will exist in any capitalist society and that collective action depends on the mobilization of that discontent by leaders and organizations.

The Resources of Social Movements

Some of the resources that must be mobilized to generate a social movement are: (1) a body of supporters; (2) financial resources; (3) legal talent; and (4) access to the news media.

One of the major resources is a body of supporters who have the time and the skills to press for change. University students have often been im-

One of the major resources needed to generate a social movement is a body of supporters. Here a group called Women United for Action demonstrates for lower food prices.

portant constituents of social movements because they have time available and are well educated. Students were important in the draft-resistance movement on American campuses in the 1960s and 1970s, in a revolutionary movement in France in 1968, and in the Islamic revolution in Iran in the late 1970s and early 1980s.

The recruitment of participants depends on social networks and communication between people who are already part of the movement and potential participants. The feminist movement began during the 1960s with contact among women who worked for state commissions on the status of women and in the student antiwar movement (Freeman, 1973, 1979). Active participants in Boston's antibusing movement had ties to friends and neighbors who shared their attitudes toward busing as a way to achieve school desegregation; socially isolated people were less likely to join the movement (Useem, 1980). Discontent alone does not lead to participation. To be recruited into a social movement, an individual must be in contact with someone in the movement and must be relatively free of conventional ties to a family, job, or community that would inhibit participation (Snow, Zurcher, and Ekland-Olson, 1980).

Resources other than participants are required to give birth to a social movement. Money is needed to publish newsletters, rent meeting halls, print news releases, pay for trips to demonstration sites, and hire lawyers. Legal talent is important for various reasons: It provides a defense when protest leads to arrest, and supports civil actions for damages and litigation to enforce constitutional rights. Legal action also provides publicity that can raise the public's awareness of an issue, strengthen a movement's legitimacy, and attract new recruits (Handler, 1978).

Access to the news media is another important resource that must be mobilized. Innovative actions such as the Gay Activists Alliance's parade in duck costumes can draw the attention of the press and increase public consciousness of a movement's grievances. The use of the media can in fact be a substitute for inadequate financial resources; news is free publicity and thus saves money that might otherwise be spent on posters or advertisements to announce meetings and rallies.

A variety of other resources can also generate or retard the development of a social movement. Lack of access to firearms has inhibited the development of a revolutionary movement among black South Africans, and the fact that they do not have the right to vote has meant that even a broad-based reform movement has not emerged among those oppressed people.

The Organization of Social Movements

Resource-mobilization theory treats social movements as organized action—patterned behavior that involves a formal structure with leaders and followers. Different kinds of leadership skills are needed at different stages of social movements. At first, agitators are needed to focus discontent on certain targets; charisma and rapport with the masses are important for agitators. Later a prophet who arouses emotions and predicts a better future is critical in mobilizing support. Reformers also emerge to clarify issues and develop specific methods to produce change. A statesmanlike leader may later become important in sustaining the movement's momentum by dealing with day-to-day political matters. Finally, as a social movement becomes more formally organized, an administrative leader comes forth to coordinate activities, raise funds, speak to the press, and maintain a cadre of dedicated workers (Dawson and Gettys, 1935).

Outsiders sometimes play an important role in mobilizing support for a movement. These are people who are not directly affected by the social conditions that lead others to join the movement. These outsiders are, however, sympathetic to the plight of the disadvantaged, and they are "disinterested" in that they do not stand to gain personally from the movement's success. Often outside leaders dedicate their time, money, and organizational skills to the movement out of a sense of moral outrage. The consumer movement, for instance, developed "from the top down" as a result of efforts by Ralph Nader and other professionals to create a social movement organization and mobilize mass support for its goals.

A study by William A. Gamson (1975) of fifty-three social movements that developed in the United States between 1800 and 1945 found that success in achieving a movement's goals was associated with "combat-readiness." Movements that were organized so as to maintain the commitment of their followers over a long period were most likely to achieve their goals. Movements that used violent means were also more likely to achieve their goals. A more recent evaluation of Gamson's research concluded that the attributes of social movement organizations—such as bureaucratization and centralization of power—were not relevant to a movement's success, but that the incidence of crises in the broader society determined whether a movement would achieve its goals. In other words, timing rather than organization seemed important to a movement's success (Goldstone, 1980).

Obstacles to Social Movements

Social movements confront various obstacles to reaching their goals. Freedom of speech or the right to assemble in public can be restricted by a repressive government, and access to resources such as the news media may be denied by a conspiracy to ignore a movement.

One problem movements face is how to appeal at the same time to various constituencies: participants, the news media, the general public, and the opposition (Lipsky, 1968; Barkan, 1979). Creating a good image with the press and the public can antagonize the more militant participants, but militant action might create an unfavorable public image, bring government repression, and cut off sources of potential recruits.

Social movements differ in their need for outside support. If they have sufficient funds and personnel, they might not need to appeal to the general public for these resources. However, movements that are small or vulnerable to reprisals often must turn to outside support. For instance, the protest movement against the construction and operation of nuclear power plants has so far been too small to pose a threat of disruption, and so it has had to focus on winning favorable publicity in order to attract support (Barkan, 1979).

An organizational problem faced by many social movements is "goal displacement," which occurs when leaders and participants lose sight of the movement's original goals and become more concerned with maintaining the social movement organization itself (Ash, 1972). Goal displacement is closely associated with Michels's iron law of oligarchy (see Chapter 7), the idea that even democratic movements give rise to a formal organization with entrenched leaders who seek to maintain their position and power. Resource-mobilization theorists have acknowledged the emergence of oligarchies in social movements, often attributing them to the need to remain "combat ready." These theorists claim that oligarchies do not necessarily lead to goal displacement, because an undemocratic organization can further a movement's goals (Gordon, 1971). For example, the oligarchical structure of the consumer movement has contributed in important ways to the general welfare of consumers. However, oligarchy and goal displacement do present recurring problems for many social movement organizations, and they can be harmful to the achievement of goals (Schwartz, Rosenthal, and Schwartz, 1981).

A Revision of Resource-Mobilization Theory

The theory of resource mobilization began by rejecting the idea that significant fluctuations in discontent explained the development of social protest movements. It was assumed instead that grievances were generally present and only needed to be mobilized (McCarthy and Zald, 1973, 1977; Zald and McCarthy, 1979; Jenkins and Perrow, 1977). Resource-mobilization theory was offered as a replacement for the social-psychological approach to collective behavior and social movements; the new theory placed greater emphasis on organization, structure, and resources.

Recently, research and theory have supported a revision of resource-mobilization theory that would reintroduce a social-psychological perspective. A study of Boston's antibusing movement found that although neighborhood organization and personal relationships were important in mobilizing support, relative deprivation also explained participation in the movement (Useem, 1980). A study of citizen protest over the Three Mile Island nuclear power plant accident in 1979 also found that grievances were important in the mobilization of support. Local organizations that had protested the existence of the plant had had little support before the accident, but they gained new adherents after the threat of a "meltdown." However, the presence of organizations opposed to nuclear power plants did make mobilization after the accident easier (Walsh, 1981).

William Gamson, who has criticized traditional social-psychological perspectives on collective behavior, recently charged that resource-mobilization theory has been weak on the role of ideas and political consciousness in shaping collective action and has paid too little attention to the role of face-to-face interaction in mobilizing support for social movements (Gamson, Fireman, and Rytina, 1982). He has suggested that resource-mobilization theories should look at "encounters" (Goffman, 1966), which are gatherings of people who have a single focus of attention and a heightened awareness of each other's behavior. Encounters—including recruitment meetings and interactions with reporters, allies, and antagonists—are often critical in building a social movement.

Resource-mobilization theory has contributed in a major way to the study of social movements as purposive and organized collective action. The theory would offer an even more powerful explanation of the emergence, organization, and consequences of social movements if it focused more on two factors: the role of grievances and discontent in mobilizing support, and interaction among movement participants and between participants and outsiders.

Summary

By studying collective behavior and social movements, sociologists learn about behavior that exists outside the institutional framework of society and that often changes that framework. Collective behavior is more unstructured and more spontaneous than social movements, but it often exists as part of a social movement that has focused goals.

Masses and publics are large numbers of people who are not in the same place at the same time but who respond to the same issues or events. When physically dispersed people react to a shared perception about a threat that they face, it is called mass hysteria; the *War of the Worlds* scare is a classic example. In contrast to masses, publics share a sentiment or attitude on an issue. Public opinion can be manipulated through censorship and propaganda, even though a diversity of sources of information and a modern educational system help to curb those who try to manipulate opinion.

Behavior by people who have an obsessive belief in the great value of something—such as land, securities, or even tulip bulbs—are called crazes. Fads are crazes that are new, relatively trivial, and short-lived. Styles of appearance and behavior that are more lasting but still change over time are called fashions. Fads and fashions serve important functions; for instance, they provide a sense of identity and symbolize distinctions among social groups.

Unverified but not necessarily incorrect information that spreads from person to person is called a rumor. Rumor is a collective effort to make sense of an ambiguous situation and develop an appropriate response. Individuals play different roles in the transmission of rumors, and social networks that link people are essential to the spread of such stories.

There are various kinds of crowds, which are

relatively large and temporary gatherings of people in one place who have a purpose and are aware of each other's presence. Crowds have been classified as casual, conventional, expressive, and acting. One type of acting crowd is a panic, a sudden flight by people who are reacting to a shared belief about an ambiguous and uncontrollable threat. Disaster behavior involves crowds responding to the collective stress and social disruption caused by human or natural means, and it also includes the reactions of formal organizations such as the police or the fire department. Mobs are hostile crowds that strive for a common goal; one example is a lynch mob. In comparison to mobs, riots are less goal-oriented and less unified.

Various explanations have been offered for crowd behavior. Some see crowds as having a group mind, a set of shared and irrational impulses that spread by contagion and circular reaction. Another approach suggests that people with similar needs converge to form crowds, and a different perspective proposes that norms about appropriate crowd behavior emerge from the interaction of participants. A crowd can also be seen as a gathering of people acting in a rational way to produce certain results or as a form of political protest, possibly based on relative deprivation. Smelser's value-added theory explains both collective behavior and social movements as action designed to understand and change social conditions; it specifies six sequential stages that generate such collective action.

In recent years, sociologists have used resource-mobilization theory to explain social movements. This theory rejects the social-psychological emphasis of traditional explanations for collective behavior in favor of an approach that stresses the organization of movements. Movements mobilize supporters and funds and develop ties to the news media, allies, and antagonists. Leadership skills are an important resource for social movements, and different skills are required at different stages of movements. Resource-mobilization theory also looks at obstacles faced in the mobilization of resources, such as the need to appeal to a variety of constituencies, goal displacement, and the iron law of oligarchy. More recently, some sociologists have suggested that resource-mobilization theory should incorporate discontent and grievances into the theory more explicitly by developing a social psychology that focuses on social interaction.

Important Terms

CENSORSHIP (450)
COLLECTIVE BEHAVIOR (445)
CONTAGION (456)
CONVERGENCE THEORY (457)
CRAZE (450)
CROWD (452)
DISASTER (455)
EMERGENT-NORM THEORY (458)
FAD (450)
FASHION (451)
MASS (446)
MASS HYSTERIA (446)
MOB (455)
PANIC (454)
PROPAGANDA (450)
PUBLIC (449)
PUBLIC OPINION (449)
RELATIVE DEPRIVATION (458)
RESOURCE-MOBILIZATION THEORY (463)
RIOT (455)
RUMOR (451)
SOCIAL MOVEMENT (445)
VALUE-ADDED THEORY (459)

Suggested Readings

Roberta Ash. *Social Movements in America*. Chicago: Markham, 1972. A sociological analysis of social movements from the Colonial Era to the present.

Richard A. Berk. *Collective Behavior*. Dubuque, Iowa: William C. Brown, 1974. A brief introduction to theories of collective behavior, including the author's examination of the payoff theory.

William A. Gamson. *The Strategy of Social Protest*. Homewood, Ill.: Dorsey Press, 1975. A study of fifty-three American social movements and the kinds of organization and tactics that made them succeed or fail.

Frances Fox Piven and Richard A. Cloward. *Poor People's Movements: Why They Succeed, How They Fail*. New York: Pantheon, 1977. A detailed exploration of four social movements and their organizations: unemployed workers during the Great Depression, industrial workers, civil rights, and welfare rights.

Ralph L. Rosnow and Gary Alan Fine. *Rumor and Gossip: The Social Psychology of Hearsay*. New York: Elsevier, 1976. A detailed study of research on rumors, including their role in collective behavior.

Neil J. Smelser. *Theory of Collective Behavior*. New York: Free Press, 1962. The classic presentation of the value-added theory of collective behavior and social movements.

Charles Tilly. *From Mobilization to Revolution*. Reading, Mass.: Addison-Wesley, 1978. A historical study of collective action that uses resource-mobilization theory.

Ralph H. Turner and Lewis N. Killian. *Collective Behavior*, 2nd ed. Englewood Cliffs, N.J.: Prentice-Hall, 1972. An influential introduction to the study of collective behavior.

Mayer N. Zald and John D. McCarthy, eds. *The Dynamics of Social Movements: Resource Mobilization, Social Control, and Tactics*. Cambridge, Mass.: Winthrop, 1979. An important collection of papers on the resource-mobilization theory of social movements.

SOCIAL CHANGE

Imagine daily life before the discovery of electricity. The arduous work of farm and factory had to be done by hand. Housework was also more time-consuming and tiring; clothes were cleaned with a washboard rather than in a washing machine, and cooking required a fire be started rather than simply turning on an oven. Lack of electricity affected leisure activities as well; people visited each other, sewed, and read, rather than watching television, listening to records, or playing video games. In addition, social interaction took different forms; telephone conversations were not possible, but letter-writing may have been more common. Clearly, even the apparently simple innovation of electricity, by now so well-integrated into our daily lives that we rarely stop to consider it, can profoundly alter the course of work and social activity.

Sociologists refer to the process by which whole societies, institutions, patterns of interaction, work and leisure activities, roles, and norms are altered over time as *social change*. Changes in society are often closely related to changes in the culture—such as the alteration of technology or the emergence of new values—so sociologists usually study social and cultural changes together. For instance, the discovery of electricity was a change in technology, a part of the culture, that was made possible by the social institution of science and that produced changes in the social organization of work and leisure.

Social change varies in its speed and its scope. Some changes occur rapidly, but others take a long time. The United States industrialized over many decades, but today's developing nations are trying to do so much more quickly. Social change also varies in scope. Sometimes it influences many aspects of society and disrupts the whole social system, as in the process of industrialization; but in other cases, such as the substitution of matches for rubbing sticks together to start a fire, it has a much narrower scope.

Social change means a change in the social structure rather than a change in the experiences of an individual. When people age, they move from one stage to another in the life cycle and perceive this as change. However, the stages in the life cycle are relatively stable over time for a society as a whole; in other words, as people age they usually face a situation similar to the one faced by their parents when they were old. Aging and other changes over the course of individuals' lives, such as marriage or enrollment in college, are not examples of social change. Social change refers to a broad transformation of the social structure itself. For example, the stage in the life cycle called adolescence emerged when societies industrialized. Also, the expansion of higher education in the United States in this century is a social change that has had ramifications for the stages in the life cycle through which individuals pass.

Another characteristic of social change is that it endures for a relatively long time by becoming institutionalized. Short-term responses to passing emergencies are not usually called social change. For instance, rationing during wartime is a response to a specific crisis, although not a basic change in the economic system; but a society that establishes rationing as a long-term policy effects change in a more fundamental way.

Today, most sociologists assume that change is a natural and inevitable part of life in every society. They see change as continuous and ever-present, even though a society at one time does resemble itself at an earlier time in many ways. However, as we will see in this chapter, there is no single theory of social change on which all sociologists agree. To develop one theory of social change would require a single theory of society on which everyone agrees, and we have seen throughout this book that sociologists take different theoretical perspectives. Before looking at some of the major theories that sociologists have used to explain social change, let us examine some of the sources of this change.

Sources of Social Change

Social change is usually the product of a complex interaction among many factors. Sociologists often have a difficult time sorting out the relative importance of each factor in producing change. They cannot experiment as a chemist or a psychologist might, but must instead rely on historical evidence or the study of contemporary societies. Because there are a limited number of societies to study and because each society differs from others in important ways, social patterns that might be useful to examine may not even exist.

Some sources of change are internal to the social structure, others are external, and often external sources interact with internal sources in a complicated way to produce change. For instance, the cars that Americans drive are different from those they drove twenty-five years ago. One source of this change is federal laws that have required the addition of safety measures such as seatbelts and the installation of pollution-control devices. However, other changes are due to external factors: Competition from foreign imports has led to smaller cars being produced in Detroit, and rising gasoline prices due in part to OPEC pricing policies have created a demand for more fuel-efficient cars.

Some theories of social change stress the role that people play in modifying the social structure. These voluntaristic theories suggest that people create and implement solutions to their problems, and these solutions then produce social change (Moore, 1974). Other theories of change are more deterministic; they emphasize the impact on society of forces beyond human control, such as natural disasters or inevitable developments in technology. Some theories combine voluntarism and determinism. For example, Marx saw technological change as largely outside human control, but he also claimed that classes had to become aware of their true interests before they would engage in revolutionary action.

One kind of voluntaristic theory that looks at the part played by influential leaders has been called the "great-man" theory of history. Most sociologists look at the social conditions that make it pos-

sible for certain leaders to wield power rather than at the personal characteristics of those leaders. Hitler, for example, was able to mobilize the German people after World War I largely because of the economic disaster caused by the war; and Churchill became a revered leader during World War II because his nation needed a strong leader while under siege. Sociological theories often attribute the changes produced by leaders such as Churchill and Hitler to the needs of a society, and they suggest that had those individuals not been available someone else would have emerged to fill the role of leader. Although difficult to prove, this might be true, but it can underestimate the importance of particular individuals who have unique traits and inspirational qualities—what Max Weber called charisma. Still, even a charismatic leader requires suitable social conditions to be effective; for instance, it is not likely that Hitler would attain power in the United States today, even with its high unemployment rate.

THE ENVIRONMENT

The physical environment in which people live can either place limits on social change or, in some cases, cause dramatic changes. Climatic conditions and natural resources influence the kind of society that can develop in a particular setting; large cities, for instance, rarely develop in inland areas with no nearby waterways. Usually the impact of environmental forces on social change is gradual. Thus the spread of the desert in some areas of the world has been a slow but measurable factor that has changed some societies' economic systems and social structures. Harsh environments, such as the desert or the arctic, can slow the development of an advanced technology or the emergence of certain kinds of culture (Lenski and Lenski, 1982). Even in such extreme settings, however, the limits to social change are unclear: Both the Mormons in Utah and the Israelis have successfully reclaimed desert lands for productive farming. Today, the opportunity to borrow from technologically advanced societies means that the physical environment sets fewer limits on social change than was once true.

Another geographic factor affecting social change is the physical location of a community in relation to other communities; communities that are geographically isolated are less likely to borrow cultural products and social patterns from one another. The most technologically backward societies in the world today are generally those without easy access to other cultures. Communities located at the crossroads of transportation, trade, and communication are more likely to experience social change because of their extensive contact with different societies.

Natural disasters such as floods, hurricanes, tidal waves, volcanic eruptions, and tornadoes can cause rapid social change, although societies with advanced technologies can prevent cataclysmic change to some extent. This may be done by predicting earthquakes with seismographs or by using the mass media to urge people to take refuge in sturdy shelters. Even when disasters are forecast, they can affect the economic and social system. For instance, a volcanic eruption such as that of Mount St. Helens in Washington can cover fertile farmland and hurt agricultural productivity. Also, hurricanes demolish factories, and floods disrupt social relationships by forcing people to flee from a community (Erikson, 1976).

Natural disasters that force people to move can also produce change when those people come into contact with others who have a different culture. Migration occurs for many reasons in addition to natural disasters, but, whatever the reason, it requires people to adapt to a new social, cultural, and physical environment. Irish farmers who migrated to the United States because of the potato famine in the nineteenth century had to adapt to the physical environment of large cities. One effect was a gradual change in family structure. In Ireland, many men did not marry until they owned land on which to raise the food to support a family, and thus they commonly delayed marriage until their thirties or forties. In the cities of the United States, other sources of work were available, and marriage was feasible at an earlier age. This had important consequences for the family, such as a smaller difference between the ages of parents and their children (Bales, 1962; Kammeyer, 1976).

Often human actions affect the physical environment, which in turn leads to social change. For example, pollution of the air and the water that is caused by industrialization affects the physical environment in which people live. Industrial pollution of a lake can destroy or contaminate fish, which can ruin the fishing industry in the towns on that lake, forcing people to migrate or enter new occupations and thereby changing the social structure of the community in significant ways.

POPULATION

Changes in the size and composition of a population can also lead to social change. Increased size alters the economic system by making more job specialization possible and by requiring more coordination among the tasks done by workers. By increasing the size of communities, population growth also causes problems that are associated with urbanization.

Changes in the structure of a population also lead to social change. The post-World War II "baby boom" in the United States produced a "bulge" in the population pyramid (see Chapter 17) that changed the society in profound ways (Easterlin, 1980a). More schools had to be built, and more teachers were hired. Later, the economic system had to absorb large numbers of young job-seekers, and this has contributed to high rates of unemployment in recent years.

Another important influence on social change is the balance between population size and natural resources. Some observers feel that growing population and dwindling resources make continued industrialization impossible (Meadows et al., 1974). Industrializing nations now have such large populations that any increased output must be used to meet the basic needs of food, clothing, and shelter and is therefore unavailable to reinvest in industry. After World War II, southern Italy was overpopulated relative to the region's resources that were available for economic development, but the migration of people from that area helped increase its rate of development (Lopreato, 1967). Migration will not, however, provide a solution to overpopulation in today's developing countries. Many experts think that only fertility control can curb population growth and raise the standard of living in these countries (Brown, 1983).

TECHNOLOGY

Another important cause of social change is technological advance. In Chapter 3 we noted that technological change is cumulative, in that it builds on past knowledge and methods. The more complex societies have more knowledge and methods available to recombine into new forms of technology, and so technological development and social change in general are more rapid in those societies.

One invention that has changed society in dramatic ways is the automobile, which has been called "a primary element in the moral and cultural revolution in Euro-American culture that took place earlier in this century" (Pelto and Müller-Wille, 1972: 166). Cars have spread culture by increasing interaction among people who live far from each other. For instance, easy access to the

One important cause of social change is technological advance. An invention that has changed society in dramatic ways is the automobile.

city by people who live in the suburbs, small towns, and rural areas has spread an urban way of life to nonurban communities. Automobiles enable people who live in outlying areas to work, shop, and dine in the city, and cars have thus changed patterns of residence in metropolitan areas. Cars are also the basis of a variety of large industries, including the production and maintenance of the cars, the manufacture of car stereo equipment, the insurance industry that replaces stolen cars and equipment, and forms of entertainment that depend on cars, such as drive-in theaters, stock-car racing, and browsing in shopping malls. A number of occupations depend in whole or in part on the car, including insurance salesperson, police officer, and highway construction worker. Automobiles have also changed leisure activities; people now travel farther on their vacations, and young people

find it easier to have privacy from their parents by riding around for fun or ''parking.'' Moreover, cars are status symbols among people of all ages, indicating the driver's income and taste, as television commercials for the latest models constantly remind us.

Other inventions have also changed society in significant ways. For instance, the snowmobile has altered the lives of arctic people, as we see in SEL 20.1. Another example is the bicycle, which increased mobility for women and changed their clothing fashions to make riding easier when it was introduced in the nineteenth century (Aronson, 1968). The invention of the telephone has made communication possible without face-to-face interaction and has created and maintained social networks as well as sped the transmission of information (Pool, 1977).

SOCIOLOGY AND EVERYDAY LIFE 20.1
Snowmobiles in the Arctic

Social change sometimes involves a complex intertwining of technology, social structure, and ecology. An excellent example of this is the impact that the snowmobile has had on the Lapps of Finland and the Eskimos of Canada. The introduction of this technological breakthrough in transportation that replaced travel by skis, snowshoes, and sleds has had a profound effect on the economic system, stratification system, patterns of social interaction, and ecology of these arctic peoples since the early 1960s.

INTRODUCTION OF THE SNOWMOBILE

Snowmobiles are expensive for most Lapps and Eskimos, but the speed and mobility they offer has led to their widespread adoption nevertheless. Lapps have sometimes sold their draft reindeer to finance the purchase of snowmobiles, and Eskimos have sold their sled dogs for the same reason. Installment buying has helped to make the purchase of these machines possible. Among both the Lapps and the Eskimos, the first people to buy snowmobiles often had regular jobs that paid wages or had some other available source of funds. These early owners of the machine gained advantages over others. In Lapland, they were hired to herd reindeer, and this enhanced or maintained their influence over decision making about herding activities. Other Lapps benefited from being hired to provide transportation. People who bought snowmobiles later gained less because there were more machines around and fewer people who needed their services.

THE ECONOMIC SYSTEM

The snowmobile affected the economic systems of the Lapps and the Eskimos. It made it easier to gather firewood, bring fresh water from distant lakes, and visit trading posts. The reindeer roundups that were essential to the Lapps' economy could be held with less advance planning and completed in shorter time. Lapps without snowmobiles were soon at a major disadvantage in the herding of reindeer and had to buy them just to keep up with their neighbors.

Because the Eskimos' economic system relies less on teamwork than does reindeer herding among the Lapps, and because Eskimo hunting and trapping are more individualistic enterprises, the early adoption of the snowmobile offered fewer advantages to the Eskimos. Nevertheless, snowmobiles have reduced Eskimos' losses from traps to predatory animals, because hunters can now check their traps more regularly. These machines have also extended the range that Eskimos can hunt or trap. Some Eskimos have had more time available for hunting and trapping because they no longer need to spend time maintaining a team of dogs for their sled, and others who are wage earners can hunt on weekends because it takes less time to get to the hunting grounds. The use of snowmobiles has increased output in some areas, but in at least one community it has led Eskimos to reduce the number of hours they hunt and trap rather than to increase their output by working the same number of hours with a snowmobile.

SOCIAL INTERACTION

Because it has increased the mobility of Lapps and Eskimos, the snowmobile has brought them into contact with new communities and made visiting with relatives and friends easier. In Lapland, attendance at movies and dances has increased because of the mobility afforded by the snowmobile, and competitive snowmobile racing has also brought people together. In at least one Lapp community the mechanic who services snowmobiles has become a focal point of social interaction. In addition, reindeer hunters are now more likely to stay in a nearby house than to sleep in the open, and this expands people's social networks.

In northern Canada, the Eskimos now use snowmobiles to visit people who live far away, sometimes as much as 400 miles. In one area, people have moved into two clustered settlements from more scattered homes because the snowmobile gives them access to distant hunting grounds. In some instances, the snowmobile has allowed Eskimos to maintain their traditions; for example, it has permitted wage earners to hunt in their spare time and then engage in the customary practice of reciprocal meat-sharing, a pattern of interaction that had fallen into disuse.

STRATIFICATION

In some situations, the snowmobile has changed the stratification system of arctic communities. In Lapland it has widened the gap between wealthy reindeer owners and others. Before the introduction of the snowmobile, roundups were egalitarian endeavors that included all sled owners, but now those who do not own snowmobiles are at a decided disadvantage.

The effect of the snowmobile on stratification is less uniform among the Eskimos. In some communities it is a status symbol, and thus a source of differences in prestige. However, because Eskimos earn their livelihoods more as individuals than as members of groups, they can still make a living with a sled instead of buying a snowmobile.

ECOLOGICAL EFFECTS

The full effect of the snowmobile on the environment of the arctic peoples is not yet clear. The bear population was nearly destroyed soon after the snowmobile was introduced to Finland, and this led to laws to curb such hunting. Lakes in Finland that were not fished before have become accessible since the introduction of the snowmobile. Another ecological effect of the snowmobile is noise pollution, although many animals do not fear this noise. So far, the snowmobile has increased the food supply for Lapps and Eskimos, especially the Eskimos who no longer need to hunt food for their dogs.

The effect of the snowmobile on these arctic societies is complex. It has changed their economic systems, altered their stratification systems, enhanced social interaction, and changed the environment. Each of these changes sets off others; for example, more social interaction leads to cooperation in new economic enterprises, and more stratification may reduce certain kinds of social interaction. The process of social change thus includes multiple variables in complex relationship to each other.

Source: Based on Pertti J. Pelto and Ludger Müller-Wille, "Snowmobiles: Technological Revolution in the Arctic," in H. Russell Bernard and Pertti J. Pelto, eds., *Technology and Social Change*. New York: Macmillan, 1972, pp. 166–199.

VALUES AND BELIEFS

Social change often alters values and beliefs, but new values and beliefs can also produce change or cause resistance to change. Sometimes it takes years to see the full implications of the values and beliefs that are part of a culture. Conflict over incompatible values and beliefs can be an important source of change. For example, the American values of individualism and private property sometimes clash with the value of equal opportunity, such as when a homeowner refuses to sell a house to a member of a minority group. The tension between values such as these is frequently resolved by the legal system; in the United States, for instance, the law now prohibits homeowners from refusing to sell houses to members of minority groups, although institutional racism still leaves most communities racially segregated.

Social change also results from conflict between values and existing social conditions; incompatibility between values and social conditions is often defined as a social problem that requires a solution. For example, sex discrimination in the United States is inconsistent with the value of equality. Rather than abandon this value, efforts have been made, although with mixed success, to guarantee women legal equality with men. Some of these efforts have been resisted by people who hold what they consider to be more important values. For example, Phyllis Schlafly and others organized to defeat the Equal Rights Amendment, which they saw as a threat to traditional relationships between men and women.

The process of social change is greatly affected by the value placed on change itself. Some cultures have no ideas of progress, but in many cultures progress is both desired and expected (Nisbet, 1979). In addition, values that support scientific research and education are conducive to change because they encourage independent thought rather than uncritical acceptance of traditional ways of doing things. Education exposes people to alternatives; sometimes this changes their expectations and leads them to alter social conditions to meet their new expectations.

According to Karl Marx and others, one possible source of resistance to change is religion and its values. In the United States, some Catholics and some fundamentalist Protestants have strongly opposed the 1973 Supreme Court decision legalizing abortion; their efforts to declare abortion illegal again continue more than a decade after the decision. However, religion is not always a source of resistance to change. As we saw in Chapter 13, Max Weber's theory that the Calvinist values of predestination and worldly asceticism were supportive of modern capitalism is a plausible and widely accepted explanation of how religious values can contribute to social change, even though this theory has its critics.

Secular or nonreligious ideologies such as communism and self-improvement philosophies are additional sources of values and beliefs that can lead to social change. Social movements espousing these secular ideologies gain strength and exposure in industrial societies when their ideas are disseminated by the mass media. These ideologies can develop from a movement that originates in a society, or they can be imported from other societies. For instance, self-help movements such as est and Scientology combine various ideas in one philosophy; they draw on sources as different as modern sales techniques and Eastern religions. Philosophies such as these, and political ideologies as well, can change the way that their adherents perceive the world and lead to action to achieve their social, economic, and political goals.

DIFFUSION

The spread, or *diffusion,* of values, ideas, and technology from one society to another is frequently an important source of change. Often, we can chart on a map the diffusion of an innovation from where it was produced to other societies that adopted it. This process enables societies to move rapidly from a technologically backward stage to a more advanced stage by borrowing from other cultures. Borrowing by societies with a modern technology from societies with a less advanced one does occur but is much less common.

Innovations spread in many ways. Diffusion sometimes results from face-to-face interaction between people from different societies, including missionaries, diplomats, explorers, conquerors, colonial officials, migrants, multinational corporation executives, and participants in international conferences. The education of members of the elite of less developed nations in the colleges and universities of technologically advanced societies is another source of diffusion. The mass media also convey information about other cultures, with the

radio being relatively more important in developing societies and television playing a major role in industrial societies.

All aspects of culture can be diffused, but nonmaterial culture—including religion, ideology, beliefs, values, literature, and the fine arts—is less likely to be transferred from one culture to another than is material culture such as technological developments. This is because differences in language often make it difficult to communicate new ideas and because it is often harder for people to see the advantages of changing their nonmaterial culture than to see the gains from adopting a technological innovation (Barnett, 1953). For instance, adopting a new religion would require people to abandon their old religion and substitute a new set of beliefs that do not seem intrinsically better than their traditional beliefs. On the other hand, the adoption of material culture in the form of a new tool or a system of sewage disposal requires a simple addition to material culture and does provide obvious benefits.

Certain conditions tend to cause diffusion of culture. It is most common when an innovation is compatible with existing values and beliefs (Arensberg and Niehoff, 1971). Changes that are easy to understand have an advantage in being adopted over those that are more complex; for example, television is relatively easy to adopt because it simply requires the owner to push a button to use it, even though the cost of television is prohibitively high for many who could use it. Also more readily diffused are innovations that can be tried on a limited basis before making a full-scale commitment to major change. Borrowing is most common when the financial and social costs of adopting a change are not too great. Diffusion is less likely if it conflicts with powerful vested interests; often, different classes selectively adopt innovations to enhance their advantage over others (Chirot, 1976). Changes that are first adopted by a leader or a person with high prestige are more apt to be accepted by others; fashion sometimes spreads in this way. In other cases, change is introduced by *change agents*, people committed to and informed about a particular innovation who try to get others to adopt it; new methods of agriculture are often introduced in this way (Rogers, 1962).

Some of the factors that determine whether a change will be adopted can be seen in the response of women in a small Peruvian town to efforts to convince them that boiling contaminated water would improve hygiene (Wellin, 1955; Rogers,

Diffusion of Western material culture is obvious throughout the world. One example is the purchase made for their child by this Saudi Arabian couple.

1962: 7–12). In spite of vigorous efforts by a change agent, only eleven women from the town's 200 families were persuaded to boil water. Why was such a simple procedure so widely rejected? Some did not want to talk with the change agent, seeing her as a "snooper" or simply lacking the time to do so. Others could make no sense of the microbe theory of disease, because it seemed to them that tiny germs must drown in water. In addition, the women could not understand how something as small as germs could harm them. Local traditions distinguished between "hot" and "cold" foods and their appropriate uses, and according to these beliefs only people who were already ill needed to boil their water. Other women were unwilling to boil their water because they did not have enough time to gather firewood or enough money to buy fuel for boiling water.

Theories of Social Change

Sociologists have used a variety of theories to explain social change. Some theories treat change as a gradual process that proceeds from one stage to the next most advanced one, and others see change as a process by which societies rise and fall. Another theory of social change proposes that all societies tend toward balance and integration, an assumption opposed by conflict theorists who treat change as intrinsic to societies because of competition among groups with different interests.

EVOLUTIONARY THEORY

Evolutionary theory regards social change as an orderly, gradual process that leads to greater complexity and the progressive improvement of societies. There are, however, some important differences between the early evolutionary theories of the nineteenth and early twentieth centuries, and the neoevolutionary theories of recent years.

Early Evolutionary Theories

Some of the early evolutionary theories of social change showed the profound influence on sociologists of Charles Darwin's *On the Origin of Species* (1859). These theories saw human societies as analogous to biological organisms (see Chapter 1), in that both required an interdependence of parts and the coordination of complex functions. Like biological organisms, societies also must adapt to the environment in order to survive and evolve.

These early evolutionary theories were often unilinear, meaning that societies were seen as evolving along one path through a rigid sequence of stages to the most advanced one, which had the characteristics of the western European societies in which the theorists lived. These theories resulted in part from the discovery and colonization of preindustrial societies, which many social scientists of the time assumed were more "primitive" because they differed from Western societies. These social scientists proposed that all societies could be arranged in order from the least evolved to the most evolved, and that the least evolved at any time were much like contemporary societies had been in the past.

AUGUSTE COMTE. One of the first theories of social change was that of Auguste Comte, who proposed that all societies evolve through three stages of thought. In the first stage, supernatural forces were perceived as the cause of events, and a priest class interpreted the will of the gods and the reasons that things happened as they did. In the next stage, people explained events by abstract forces that reflected the principles of a religion or a secular philosophy; clergy and lawyers were influential at this point. The third and most advanced stage, which Comte claimed began in Europe around 1800, was characterized by scientific explanations and by the influence of people with technical expertise. Comte suggested that all societies eventually pass through these stages to the highest one, but that only certain European societies had entered the most advanced stage at the time he wrote in the nineteenth century.

HERBERT SPENCER. Another sociologist who proposed an evolutionary theory of change was Herbert Spencer. Spencer's ideas were the basis of "social Darwinism," an effort to apply Darwin's biological work to human societies. Spencer argued that societies competed with each other, and he claimed that the principle of "survival of the fittest" determined which societies survived and evolved and which ones became extinct. He thought that social evolution was the product of natural forces and was not subject to human control. This view was popular in the United States in the late nineteenth and early twentieth century because it fit well with the laissez-faire, or hands-off, philosophy of government favored by the powerful entrepreneurs of the time (Hofstadter, 1955).

EMILE DURKHEIM. Comte and Spencer were relatively optimistic about the course of societal evolution, but other sociologists, such as Emile Durkheim, were less hopeful. Durkheim saw an inevitable change from simple societies united by the similarity of their members (what he called "mechanical solidarity") to complex societies based on specialization and the functional interdependence of their members (what he called "organic solidarity"). He was concerned with establishing greater social solidarity in complex societies, and much of his work dealt with the consequences of the change to organic solidarity, including the high rates of suicide and crime common to industrial societies.

Neoevolutionary Theories

Modern evolutionary theories—such as those developed by Gerhard Lenski (1966; Lenski and Lenski, 1982) and by Talcott Parsons (1966, 1971, 1977)—are more tentative than the evolutionary theories of Comte, Spencer, and Durkheim. These *neoevolutionary theories* do not assume that change is inevitable, nor do they propose that change invariably proceeds along the same path. They do suggest that there is a general trend toward a more complex technology and a more elaborate division of labor. Because the potential for rapid technological change is now present in all societies as a result of the ability to borrow from more advanced societies, it is possible for societies to "skip" stages in the evolutionary process. However, because of resistance to modern technology, this potential for change is not always fulfilled. The importance of rational decision making in modern societies also means that it is possible to halt evolution toward a more complex technology, although this has not yet occurred.

Neoevolutionary theories are culturally relativistic; in other words, they recognize that different cultures have different ideas about what constitutes "progress." Industrialization might represent progress in one culture, but in a different one it could be seen as destructive of valued traditions. Earlier evolutionary theorists tended to be more ethnocentric, with their views often reflecting the belief that the society in which they lived was the pinnacle of societal evolution and that other, less advanced societies would eventually progress to that stage.

GERHARD LENSKI. Gerhard Lenski (1966; Lenski and Lenski, 1982) proposes that evolution depends largely on changes in a society's mode of economic production and its level of technology. The change from simple to complex technology has consequences for all aspects of society, including the family, the political system, the division of labor, the size of the population, and the stratification system. Lenski describes the major kinds of societies in this evolutionary process as hunting–gathering, horticultural, agrarian, and industrial. More specialized "evolutionary bypaths" include herding (or pastoral) societies, fishing societies, and maritime societies.

TALCOTT PARSONS.   Another neoevolutionary theory was developed by the functionalist Talcott Parsons (1966, 1971, 1977), who during his earlier years had adopted an equilibrium theory that we will examine later in this chapter. Parsons's neoevolutionary theory distinguished among three major types of societies: primitive, intermediate, and modern. The transition from primitive society to the intermediate level results from the development of writing, a skill that allows a culture to be diffused and borrowed and that permits a society to record its history, thereby giving its people an identity and a sense of continuity. Writing also makes possible the accumulation of knowledge and provides people with the ability to learn and adapt to change. According to Parsons, the transition from the intermediate level to the modern stage is marked by the development of formal law. This enables people to protect themselves from the government, ensures individual freedom, and makes behavior more predictable (Parsons, 1966).

Early evolutionary theorists often did a better job of describing societies than they did of explaining why and how they changed, but neoevolutionary theorists have focused more on the processes of differentiation, specialization, coordination among statuses, and social disruption (Parsons, 1966, 1971, 1977; Smelser, 1976; Lenski and Lenski, 1982). *Differentiation* is the process by which a society becomes more specialized over time; the growth in the number of occupations that accompanies industrialization is one example. Differentiation results in "adaptive upgrading," meaning that a more specialized society can respond better to its people's needs and to environmental change. Differentiation is usually treated as a product of technological change, with societies that experience technological progress having more control over energy resources and thus being better able to grow larger and more complex. As a society becomes more differentiated, it needs to find new ways to integrate the great variety of specialized functions. The successful integration of various functions makes it possible for a society to become even more differentiated and complex.

Neoevolutionary theories are more sophisticated than the early evolutionary theories. They are less ethnocentric and less deterministic, and they recognize a tendency toward change without regarding that change as inevitable or unilinear. These neoevolutionary theories have been criticized for being too descriptive and for not explaining the causes of change, but they are better than the earlier theories at specifying the causes and processes of change. However, these neoevolutionary theories are sometimes quite general and offer few testable hypotheses and clear predictions about the exact conditions under which change occurs.

Modernization Theory

Modernization theory is closely associated with neoevolutionary theories, although it is not necessarily a neoevolutionary theory; for instance, a cyclical theory of the rise and fall of societies (see below) could incorporate modernization and eventual decline. *Modernization* is a change from a simple, preindustrial society to a complex, industrial one. However, societies can adopt some of the characteristics of a modern society without industrializing; for instance, they may urbanize, develop systems of mass education, and borrow modern modes of dress from technologically more advanced societies.

Some theories of modernization assume that the modern is better than the traditional. Indeed, tradition might even be seen as an obstacle to modernization. Some scholars, and many political leaders and residents of economically backward countries, have a preference for the modern that is largely the result of certain advantages that are associated with a modern society: a lower death rate, better health care, higher levels of consumption, better methods of communication, more rapid transportation, and more opportunities for self-expression. However, modernization is not an unmixed blessing, for it is also associated with industrial pollution, the depletion of resources, the disruption of extended families and small communities, secularization, and crowded cities.

Modernization today is quite different from what it was when societies such as Great Britain and the United States began to industrialize. The first nations to industrialize did so slowly, and as a result they did not have the sense of urgency that is common in developing countries now. One reason for this sense of urgency is that today's highly industrialized societies, by offering a model of what life can be like, produce a sense of dissatisfaction with a traditional way of life. Another factor that speeds up modernization today is that developing societies can borrow from societies that are already industrialized, rather than having to innovate for themselves. Nevertheless, these developing countries face problems not confronted by nations that industrialized in the past. Many are overpopulated, which reduces the resources available for investment. As we will see, conflict theorists also point out that today a world system of states inhibits the modernization of societies that have not yet industrialized.

CYCLICAL THEORIES

Evolutionary theories emphasize progress and change toward a better or more advanced society. In contrast, *cyclical theories* of change propose that societies rise and fall, grow and decline. They suggest that apparent trends often end and reverse themselves, but they share with evolutionary theories the assumption that there are regularities in the process of change. Cyclical theories cover long periods of history, but they often fail to specify what causes change, and instead attribute the rise and fall of societies to "destiny," "fate," or some other vague force. These theories typically deny that people can plan social change to avert the inevitable decline of their society.

Oswald Spengler

In *The Decline of the West* (1918, 1965), the German historian Oswald Spengler argued that all societies are destined to undergo a cycle of birth, growth, decline, and death, much as people do over the course of the life cycle. Spengler drew examples from different cultures to support his argument that societies are born, develop rapidly, experience a "golden age" of maturity, decline slowly, and then disintegrate and die. His historical examples were not evaluated with any degree of objectivity or rigor, but were instead chosen to support his theory. Spengler used this nonscientific method to show that is was not possible to prevent the decline and death of a society, any more than a middle-aged person could grow young again. Unlike the early evolutionary theorists, Spengler did not believe that progress was inevitable, even though it was characteristic of certain periods in a nation's history.

Arnold Toynbee

Another cyclical theory that questions the inevitability of progress is Arnold Toynbee's theory of challenge and response. Toynbee was a British historian whose theory of social change is presented in *A Study of History* (1946). From his study of how twenty-one societies began, developed, and disintegrated, Toynbee concluded that societies change in response to challenges presented by the physical and social environment (Nisbet and Perrin, 1977). If they do not overwhelm the society and if the society can respond creatively, these challenges stimulate growth. A successful response to a challenge releases energy for continued development, but an unsuccessful reaction leads to the decline or even the extinction of the society. Toynbee examined the part played by elites in responding to challenges, and he looked at the ways that societies borrowed from each other to meet challenges. However, he did not explain convincingly why societies met, or failed to meet, particular challenges successfully.

Pitirim Sorokin

The Russian-American sociologist Pitirim Sorokin (1937) has provided one of the most comprehensive theories of social change. He proposed that any period in world history can be characterized by a dominant and unifying cultural theme that can be found in the fine arts, literature, law, and other aspects of culture. One kind of cultural theme is what Sorokin calls the "ideational mentality." It is spiritual and otherworldly, emphasizes absolute moral standards, and values the search for the truth. Opposite to this perspective is the "sensate mentality," which stresses a morality determined by the immediate situation rather than one that is absolute and timeless. In a sensate culture, people are materialistic, and they rely on science rather than religion to explain events. The "idealistic mentality" is a mixture of the ideational and the sensate. It characterizes periods of transition as a culture moves from the ideational to the sensate, or from the sensate to the ideational; and its primary emphasis is on logic and rationality.

For Sorokin, historical change is the result of a movement toward an extreme form of either the sensate or the ideational culture. This causes certain basic social needs to be ignored, and groups then arise to reinstate the values of the opposite cultural mentality. This causes the dominant cultural mentalities to swing back and forth between the two extremes over many centuries. Sorokin does not adequately explain such changes, but he presents some empirical evidence that different periods can be characterized by dominant cultural themes.

EQUILIBRIUM THEORY

Equilibrium theory explains social change in functionalist terms. It sees society as a stable set of interlocking institutions that have consequences for each other and for the whole society (Parsons, 1951). According to this theory, at any given time a society is either in a state of balance or moving toward such an integrated condition. Disruptions to the status quo such as labor strikes and protest demonstrations are treated as temporary maladjustments rather than as basic to the structure of society. Because they seem to disapprove of such disruptions, equilibrium theorists have been criticized as conservatives who oppose change.

Today's functionalists usually regard social change as the movement of society from one balanced state to another. However, they pay relatively little attention to what causes a society to change or to what a society is like when it is in a state of disequilibrium. Instead, equilibrium theorists are more likely to acknowledge that societies do change and then to describe different states of equilibrium. As societies change, they adapt to the social and physical environment and adjust to new and "healthy" states of balance, although equilibrium theory is often vague about what constitutes "societal health." In response to these criticisms of equilibrium theory, Talcott Parsons developed the neoevolutionary theory of social change that we examined earlier.

Even though few sociologists today regard social change as negatively as some functionalists once did, many sociologists now employ one of the insights of equilibrium theory—the idea that various social institutions are interdependent and that a change in one part of society sets off a chain reaction in other parts. Because each aspect of a society can change at a somewhat different rate, the social system as a whole may be "out of balance" for some time.

Cultural Lag

William F. Ogburn's (1922, 1950, 1964) version of equilibrium theory proposes that cultural change is a result of four processes:

1. the invention of mechanical devices such as the car or television, social arrangements such as the United Nations, and cultural innovations such as the alphabet;
2. the accumulation of new elements in the culture that can be combined in new inventions, a process hastened by the development of writing;
3. the diffusion or spread of inventions; and
4. the adjustment of different parts of society to each other.

Cultural lag occurs when two parts of a culture that were once in adjustment with each other change at different rates and become incompatible with each other. The institution or practice that has changed more slowly is said to "lag" behind the other one. Ogburn's approach focuses on the way that nonmaterial culture often lags behind material culture. Material culture includes technology, the means of production, and the output of the economic system. Nonmaterial culture, on the other hand, includes values, beliefs, norms, and noneconomic institutions such as religion and the family. Ogburn claims that nonmaterial culture is "adaptive," meaning that it responds to changes in material culture. Cultural lag occurs when nonmaterial culture fails to change fast enough to keep up with technological change. An example of cultural lag would be an author who insists that writing books in longhand is "better" than composing them on a typewriter or a word processor; here, beliefs have not changed as fast as technology.

Ogburn's concept of cultural lag has been criticized. The division between material culture and nonmaterial culture is not always clear. In addition, the theory seems to be more applicable to industrial societies than to preindustrial ones, which sometimes experience change in their nonmaterial culture before their material culture changes. For example, a nuclear family structure or materialistic desires might develop before a society industrializes. Ogburn has also been criticized for disregarding the sources of resistance to changes in material culture. Moreover, he does not pay enough attention to the way that a new technology can actually strengthen traditional, nonmaterial culture under some circumstances. For instance, fundamentalist ministers often use television, including cable stations that

An example of cultural lag might be an author who believed that composing in longhand was "better" than using a typewriter or a word processor.

employ orbiting satellites, to convey beliefs and values that have existed for centuries.

CONFLICT THEORY

In contrast to equilibrium theory's assumption that all societies are integrated sets of social institutions that tend toward stability, conflict theory treats societies as undergoing continual change or at least having the potential for change. For conflict theorists, a temporary state of equilibrium is the result of domination by a privileged group that wants to protect its advantaged position; this differs from equilibrium theory's idea that social order rests on consensus among a society's members. Change is usually regarded favorably by conflict theorists, because it makes possible the alleviation of oppression and the improvement of social conditions. As Marx wrote, "Without conflict, no progress: this is the law which civilization has followed to the present day" (cited in Dahrendorf, 1959: 9).

Karl Marx and Class Conflict

Karl Marx's theory of social change, which we have examined in earlier chapters, proposes that all societies pass through a series of stages as technology alters the basic mode of production. Except in the first stage of primitive communism, technology is a source of social inequality; that is, some groups benefit more from their relationship to the means of production than do other groups. The struggle between classes, or groups of people who share the same relationship to the means of production, generates change from one economic system to another until the most advanced stage of communism is reached.

Marx shares with evolutionary theorists a belief that societies will inevitably pass through a number of stages until the "best" one is attained, but he is more specific than most evolutionary theorists in defining the cause of change—class conflict. Marx's theory also incorporates the idea of voluntarism: Classes must recognize what is in their own best interests before they will act to change the social system.

Marxist theory proposes that if a society fails to change, it is not because social arrangements are functional for everyone, but rather because powerful groups are able to prevent change. In a capitalist system, the bourgeoisie prevents change by exploiting and oppressing the proletariat. Marx claimed that capitalist society would eventually become polarized into two distinct classes, a bourgeoisie and a proletariat, and competition among capitalists would drive the unsuccessful ones into the ranks of the proletariat, thereby increasing its size and strength. Working conditions would become worse as capitalists tried to increase their profits by lengthening working hours, lowering wages, speeding up production, and replacing workers with machines. According to Marx, these events would increase unemployment, polarize the classes, lead to revolution, and produce a communist society.

Marx's predictions of social change in the capitalist system have proved wrong. Most socialist and communist revolutions have occurred in preindustrial societies rather than in advanced capitalist ones, and peasants rather than factory workers have usually been the source of support for revolutions led by an intellectual elite (Paige, 1975; Skocpol, 1979). The polarization of the classes has not occurred; in fact, the number of gradations between the classes has increased and social mobility has blurred class distinctions. Capitalism has also proved capable of self-regulation, as governments have introduced the minimum wage, unemployment compensation, job retraining programs, and legal protection for labor unions.

Ralf Dahrendorf and Authority Relationships

Ralf Dahrendorf (1959) has proposed that a theory of social conflict should apply to all authority relationships rather than just to class conflict, as does Marx's theory. Dahrendorf's theory is more general than Marx's, and it is therefore more useful for studying conflict between ethnic groups, interest groups, and status groups.

Dahrendorf looks at conflict within "imperatively coordinated associations," organizations characterized by a dimension of power and domination. Imperatively coordinated associations include factories, labor unions, schools, clubs, and entire societies. Social change results from the alteration of relationships between dominant groups and subordinate groups in these organizations. Usually one group tries to preserve its privileges by maintaining the status quo, and another group tries to usurp authority and the privileges that go with it. Dahrendorf suggests that conflict over authority within imperatively coordinated associations can

lead to gradual reform through peaceful means or to violent revolution as Marx predicted.

Revolution

A *revolution* is a basic and rapid change in a society's political, economic, and stratification systems. Revolution is a form of conflict, often of a violent sort, between classes and political groups that have mobilized for change (Tilly, 1978; Skocpol, 1979). Several of the theories of collective behavior and social movements that we examined in Chapter 19—especially relative-deprivation theory, the value-added approach, and resource-mobilization theory—have been used in the study of revolution. Here we look at revolution from the perspective of two different approaches: a "natural history" approach and a structural approach.

THE NATURAL HISTORY APPROACH. The natural history approach delineates a sequence of stages leading to revolution. Those revolutions studied most thoroughly by natural historians are the English Revolution of 1640, the American Revolution of 1776, the French Revolution of 1789, and the Russian Revolution of 1917 (Edwards, 1927; Pettee, 1938; Brinton, 1938, 1965). These major revolutions have some similar characteristics, which Jack A. Goldstone (1982: 189–192) summarizes as follows:

1. Prior to a great revolution, the bulk of the "intellectuals"—journalists, poets, playwrights, essayists, teachers, members of the clergy, lawyers, and trained members of the bureaucracy—cease to support the regime, writing condemnations and demanding major reforms. . . .
2. Just prior to the fall of the old regime, the state attempts to meet its sharpest criticism by undertaking major reforms. . . .
3. The actual fall of the regime begins with an acute political crisis brought on by the government's inability to deal with some economic, military, or political problem, rather than by the action of a revolutionary opposition. . . .
4. Even where the revolutionary opposition to the old regime was once united, the collapse of the old regime eventually reveals the conflicts within the revolutionary opposition. . . .
5. The first group to seize the reins of state are moderate reformers. . . .
6. While the moderates seek to reconstruct rule on the basis of moderate reform, often employing organizational forms left over from the old regime, alternative, more radical centers of mass mobilization spring up with new forms of organization. . . .

7. The great changes in the organization and ruling ideology of a society that follow successful revolutions occur not when the old regime first falls, but when the radical, alternative, mass-mobilizing organizations succeed in supplanting the moderates. . . .
8. The disorder brought by the revolution and the implementation of the radicals' control usually results in the forced imposition of order by coercive rule. . . .
9. The struggles between radicals and moderates, and between defenders of the revolution and external enemies, frequently allow military leaders to move from obscurity to commanding, even absolute, leadership. . . .
10. The radical phase of the revolution eventually gives way to a phase of pragmatism and moderate pursuit of progress within the new status quo.

This natural history approach has identified certain patterns that characterize many revolutions, but it does not explain other aspects. For example, the structural conditions under which revolutions are likely to occur and how opposition to political rulers is mobilized are not made clear. Moreover, because of economic and military pressures in the international arena today, this approach does not fit the experiences of contemporary societies as well as it fits the experiences of past societies.

STRUCTURAL THEORIES OF REVOLUTION. In recent years, sociologists have focused on the structural aspects of revolution, and particularly on the political and economic systems. For example, from her study of the French, Russian, and Chinese revolutions, Theda Skocpol (1979) concludes that class conflict was important in each case but that the state itself had a degree of autonomy or independence from the stratification system. This conclusion requires a modification of Marx's theory of revolution, which treated the state as a tool of the dominant class. Skocpol finds that it was the inability of the state to deal with political problems and class conflict that led to revolutionary upheavals. These problems and conflicts were not resolved until new administrative and military organizations were created. The revolutions that Skocpol studied generated more far-ranging changes in the organization of the state than in the stratification system. The state became more centralized, autonomous, bureaucratic, and powerful as a result of the revolution, and it was therefore better able to accelerate the society's rate of economic development.

Skocpol suggests that in order to understand revolution, attention must be paid to the way that states respond to international pressures as well as to domestic problems. She calls attention to the relationships among nations, pointing out that societies now confront circumstances different from those that led to the three revolutions she studied. For example, today's developing societies often lack autonomy because they depend on industrial societies for economic aid and because they are threatened by foreign military powers. Because of changes in international relations, warns Skocpol, we must be wary of generalizing from the experience of the French, Russian, and Chinese revolutions to contemporary societies, particularly those developing nations that rely on industrial societies. For instance, one study of the Cuban Revolution found that trade difficulties such as the embargo by the United States were at least partly responsible for a long-term decline in the rate of Cuba's economic growth (Lewis-Beck, 1979).

Sociologists who have looked at the structural causes of revolution have also found that it often occurs in preindustrial societies that are based on an agrarian mode of production; China, Cuba, and Vietnam are examples. In fact, the way that agriculture is organized influences the likelihood that a revolutionary social movement will emerge in rural areas. In his study of seventy states and colonies in the Third World, Jeffery M. Paige (1975) found that class-based agrarian revolution develops only in decentralized sharecropping systems. In these systems, there are incentives for cultivators to organize because they do not risk losing the land that other people own. In addition, the upper class bitterly resists any reforms, because its primary source of income is the land. In these societies, the upper class cannot fall back on industrial or financial capital to maintain its advantaged position, so it is unwilling to give up its land or the political power required to hold on to the land. In such a system of agriculture, an organized rural proletariat confronts an unyielding upper class that is weakened by its inability to control physically dispersed sharecroppers and by middlemen who control important parts of the economic system. This set of conditions, concludes Paige, is conducive to the development of a revolution.

World-System Theory

Both Skocpol and Paige concur that revolution cannot be understood without looking at the position of a nation in the international system of states. Their work incorporates the insights of *world-system theory,* which is also called "dependency theory" (Baran, 1957; Frank, 1967; Wallerstein, 1974, 1979, 1980; Chirot, 1977; Etzioni-Halevy, 1981; Chirot and Hall, 1982). This theory proposes that the capitalist West—the "core" states of the world system that rely on manufacturing, commercialized agriculture, skilled labor, and high rates of investment—has developed economically and maintained its dominance by exploiting the "periphery" of the system— the economically dependent states of the Third World. This has been done by extracting raw materials, exploiting cheap labor, withdrawing capital, and maintaining certain kinds of agricultural production (Etzioni-Halevy, 1981; Chirot and Hall, 1982). Military force, monopolistic trade relations, foreign aid, multinational corporations, and international bankers have all contributed to the exploitation of the periphery by the core. World-system theorists claim that this system accounts for the modernization of the West and the continued economic backwardness of the Third World.

One important implication of world-system theory is that in the peripheral states, social change— whether gradual economic development or sudden revolution—does not unfold according to any predetermined logic or evolutionary law. Marx's conflict theory and Parsons's and Lenski's neoevolutionary theories do not fully explain change in peripheral states because forces in the international arena affect the process of change in those societies. In addition, there is no inevitable trend toward modernization because economic, political, and military pressures from outside often keep preindustrial societies from developing.

World-system theory does have some shortcomings. It does not really explain whether dependence on the core states causes economic underdevelopment, or whether economic backwardness is the cause of dependence on the core states. Another difficulty is that it is not always useful or accurate to attribute the problems of communist nations and Third World nations exclusively to the actions of the capitalist core states; some of those problems are the result of internal factors. In addition, world-system theory has not yet shown what would replace the current system of states if a socialist revolution in that system occurred, as is sometimes predicted will happen (Chirot and Hall, 1982). In spite of these shortcomings, world-system theory is important in focusing attention on the fact that today, more than ever before, societies do not exist or act in isolation from the international community of states.

A Look to the Future

Some of the theories of change that we have examined imply or even claim outright that there is little we can do to affect the future course of society. Cyclical theories propose that all societies will rise and fall, evolutionary theories suggest that progress is inevitable, and equilibrium theories claim that all societies tend toward a stable condition. Some conflict theories leave room for social change through collective action, but world-system theory identifies forces that are not easily controlled by human action. The broadness of these theories can obscure processes of change over which people do have some control. In fact, the development of a postindustrial society, a trend related to evolutionary theory, is marked by increased control over technology and the direction that society will take.

POSTINDUSTRIAL SOCIETY

Postindustrial societies are characterized by a growth in the importance of the tertiary or service sector and a relative decline in the significance of the primary and secondary sectors (see Chapter 16). Theoretical and practical knowledge is increasingly used to solve technical problems and develop social policies. Higher education grows in significance in postindustrial societies, and learning how to learn rather than learning specific information become more important as the rate of change accelerates (Bell, 1973, 1980; Toffler, 1970, 1980).

Technology can help to cope with social problems. The industrial technology that has caused air and water pollution is also a source of methods to clean up the environment; emission-control devices on cars are one example. Technology can sometimes provide "shortcuts" to the solution of social problems. For instance, the synthetic drug methadone has been used to deal with the problems associated with heroin addiction, the drug antabuse has been used to help alcoholics, and breathalyzers have been employed to combat drunken driving and reduce traffic fatalities. None of these technological breakthroughs has eliminated the social problem, and the conditions underlying addiction, alcoholism, and drunken driving persist. However, these technological shortcuts help to reduce some of the personal and social costs associated with these problems (Etzioni and Remp, 1973).

In postindustrial societies, new problems are raised by changes in the technology of communications: how to "intermesh" telephones and computers, how to substitute electronic media for paper, how to expand television through cable systems, how to organize the storage and retrieval of information, and how to use computers in the educational system (Bell, 1980: 38–39). These changes—particularly the growing use of computers to process information—have already altered society in important ways and will continue to effect radical changes in the near future (see SEL 20.2).

SOCIOLOGY AND EVERYDAY LIFE 20.2
The Computer Home

For millions of people in today's industrialized world, "home" is little more than a place to sleep, eat a meal or two, and store personal possessions. Most our waking hours are spent somewhere else—on the job, in a classroom, out shopping, eating in restaurants, at public entertainments, or simply moving from place to place in some form of transportation.

Yet, for most of recorded history, home was the center of every aspect of life. Until the industrial revolution and the bureaucracy it spawned forced workers into factories and offices, most people worked where they lived. Whether you were a farmer, merchant, or craftsman, your job seldom took you more than a few hours' journey by foot away from your house. The home, even if only four walls and a roof, was designed to remain in use 24 hours a day. . . .

Surprising as it may seem, the home of the future may be more like the home of the past than it is like the home of the present. But whereas, in the past, life at home was often confining and oppressive, the home-centered life of the future may be exhilarating and mind-expanding, thanks to worldwide networks of electronic communications. . . .

Small computers connected to existing telephone and television systems will enable people to exchange written information, pictures, money (in the form of credit and debit statements—the electronic equivalent of today's paper checks and cash), as well as spoken messages and recorded sounds, over any distance. This development will allow many of today's office jobs to be performed at home. . . .

But the true home computer will do much more than help people conduct business. It can become the eyes, ears, voice, and brain of the house itself—to the point where it might be more accurate to call it a "computer home.". . .

The microprocessor will precipitate the next step in the evolution of the house by making it possible for more and more household devices and systems to monitor and exert automatic control over their own operations. Stoves can automatically turn off the heat under pans that begin to scorch; electronic timers can turn lights on or off following a pre-determined schedule; new security devices use motion or heat sensors to detect potential burglars *before* they break in and respond by sounding an alarm or notifying authorities. . . .

But each system still works in isolation. The next phase of house evolution will be the joining together of separate systems through a central processor or home computer, a step that might be compared to the development of the spinal cord and brain in higher animals. This house brain will be crude at first, a "slave mentality" that will depend entirely on humans to choose its goals. But it will be capable of coordinating the operation of many different systems to achieve a particular objective once it is chosen. For example, a house brain could coordinate heating, air-conditioning, humidity control, and energy flow to maintain a comfortable environment while using the least possible amount of fuel. . . .

The addition of telecomputing capabilities to radio, TV, phonograph, and other home entertainment devices will transform today's family room into a "media room." Of course, not all the telecommunications and electronic entertainment devices will be placed in the same room. But the home computer will tie all the separate systems together and provide the central focus or "electronic hearth" around which the family will gather for work, play, and fellowship.

The ultimate house may be a structure whose computer brain, equipped with sensors and

Here a woman "cooks by computer." Recipes are stored in a memory bank and displayed through a Videotex system on her television screen.

linked through telecommunication networks to computer data banks and the "brains" of other houses, has developed an awareness of its own existence and an intimate knowledge of its inhabitants.

Advances in computer technology are making it possible for computers to synthesize human speech sounds and reply with words and actions to spoken commands. This development will greatly add to our ability to "believe" in the computer as a conscious entity. Once your house can talk to you, you may never feel alone again. Like it or not, it may become impossible to convince yourself that no one's home.

Source: Excerpted from Roy Mason and Lane Jennings, "The Computer Home: Will Tomorrow's Housing Come Alive?" *The Futurist* 16 (February 1982): 35–39. (Published by the World Future Society, 4916 St. Elmo Avenue, Washington, D.C. 20014.) Used by permission.

PREDICTING THE FUTURE

In recent years, experts from a variety of fields have grown concerned with predicting the future and planning social change. Their efforts to forecast the future have met with both success and failure (Lipset, 1979; Henshel, 1982). The complexity of society makes it difficult to predict the distant future with any accuracy, and even the near future is often hard to anticipate. Sociologists are better at explaining social change at specific times and places than at predicting broad changes in society over long periods. Often they encounter difficulty in isolating variables, measuring them precisely, and testing the relationship between them over time. Because predictions about the future can have important ramifications for social policy, sociologists need to be cautious in forecasting the future (Lipset, 1979).

One way that social scientists have dealt with the problem of predicting the future is to use *social indicators*, statistical measures of the quality of life in a society (Bauer, 1966; Andrews and Withey, 1976). A report by the President's Commission for a National Agenda for the Eighties (1980b) recommends the development of a national social report that would help policy makers assess social conditions, would make national concerns more visible, and would allow for an evaluation of the results of public programs. One social indicator that might be included in this national social report would be survey responses to questions about satisfaction with various aspects of personal life and satisfaction with the condition of the nation as a whole (Campbell, Converse, and Rodgers, 1976). Other indicators might be various measures of physical and mental health—including life expectancy, infant mortality rates, rates of death by heart disease and cancer, and rates of admission to mental hospitals. Measures of housing quality, such as overcrowdedness and affordability, would also tell us about the quality of life in the society. A national social report could also include information about crime rates, leisure time, activities in the arts, educational quality, working conditions, and welfare benefits.

Increased attention to the quality of life requires a careful assessment of the pros and cons of technological progress. Improvements in well-being are but one part of any evaluation of the consequences of change, for those improvements often have costs such as resource depletion or environmental pollution. Today a growing number of professional forecasters, some of whom call themselves ''futurists,'' are concerned with understanding, predicting, and planning the future of society. Sociologists have played and will continue to play an important part in these efforts to comprehend and even alter the process of social change.

Summary

All societies change or at least contain the potential for change, but the speed and the scope of change vary considerably from society to society. Sociologists do not agree on a single theory of social change, but they do focus on certain sources of change.

Environmental factors can cause a change in the social structure, but usually they simply set broad limits for the development of society. Changes in the size and structure of a population also affect many aspects of a society, including its schools and families. Perhaps the source of change that has received most attention is technology, an aspect of material culture that develops in a cumulative way and that sets off a chain reaction of changes in nonmaterial culture. When nonmaterial culture changes more slowly than material culture, we call it cultural lag. Sometimes changes in ideas, values, and beliefs—which are components of nonmaterial culture—also cause social change. Both nonmaterial and material culture are diffused from one society to another, and this is an important source of change.

Evolutionary theories of social change include the early theories of Comte, Spencer, and Durkheim, and the neoevolutionary theories of Lenski and Parsons. These neoevolutionary theories treat change as a complex, multilinear process that is not necessarily inevitable. They focus on changes in technology and the processes by which societies become more specialized. Closely associated with evolutionary theory is modernization theory, an approach that emphasizes the social consequences of industrialization and the growth in complexity.

Cyclical theories such as Spengler's, Toynbee's, and Sorokin's are efforts to trace very broad trends in the rise and fall of societies. These theories do not pinpoint the cause of change, and they are generally out of favor with sociologists today.

Equilibrium theory treats society as a stable set of interlocking institutions, each of which has consequences for each other and for the whole society. Change is simply the process by which a society moves from one state of equilibrium to another. This kind of theory has been criticized for paying too little attention to change as basic to the social structure and for being conservative.

Conflict theory focuses on change as a basic aspect of all social systems. Marx's theory of class conflict and Dahrendorf's generalization of that theory to all authority relationships are two important conflict theories. Recent theories of revolution have stressed the relative autonomy of the state and the organization of agriculture in developing societies. World-system theory is a conflict theory that emphasizes the importance of the stratification of the world's states into a capitalist Western core and a Third World periphery.

The emergence of postindustrial society opens the way for increased control over the development of society, something that seems incompatible with certain theories of social change. In the future, social indicators will probably be used increasingly to understand, monitor, and plan social change. Sociologists will continue to play an important part in that process of change.

Important Terms

CHANGE AGENT **(475)**
CULTURAL LAG **(480)**
CYCLICAL THEORY **(479)**
DIFFERENTIATION **(478)**
DIFFUSION **(475)**
EQUILIBRIUM THEORY **(480)**
EVOLUTIONARY THEORY **(476)**
MODERNIZATION **(478)**
NEOEVOLUTIONARY THEORY **(477)**
REVOLUTION **(482)**
SOCIAL CHANGE **(469)**
SOCIAL INDICATOR **(486)**
WORLD-SYSTEM THEORY **(484)**

Suggested Readings

Richard P. Appelbaum. *Theories of Change.* Chicago: Markham, 1970. A brief treatment of the major types of social change theories discussed in this chapter.

Daniel Bell. *The Coming of Post-Industrial Society: A Venture in Social Forecasting.* New York: Basic Books, 1973. An important examination of social changes that are dramatically altering the society in which we live.

Angus Campbell, Philip E. Converse, and Willard L. Rodgers. *The Quality of American Life: Perceptions, Evaluations, and Satisfactions.* New York: Russell Sage Foundation, 1976. A detailed exploration of a variety of social indicators that can be combined into a national social report.

Daniel Chirot. *Social Change in the Twentieth Century.* New York: Harcourt Brace Jovanovich, 1977. A well-done textbook that treats all aspects of social change and presents world-system theory in a lucid way.

Seymour Martin Lipset, ed. *The Third Century: America as a Post-Industrial Society.* Stanford, Calif.: Hoover Institution Press, 1979. An important collection of essays on changes in religion, law, politics, gender roles, racial and ethnic relations, education, and the mass media.

Wilbert E. Moore. *Social Change,* 2nd ed. Englewood Cliffs, N. J.: Prentice-Hall, 1974. A brief introduction to the major concepts in the study of social change.

Alvin Toffler. *The Third Wave.* New York: Morrow, 1980. A popular, provocative examination of the future of society.

Important Terms

ACADEMIC FREEDOM (284) The opportunity to conduct the search for truth without external pressure to produce results that support particular interests.

ACCULTURATION (204) The process by which a group adopts the dominant culture.

ACHIEVED STATUS (149) A social position that a person acquires by choice, effort, or merit.

AFFECTIVE DEVELOPMENT (74) The learning of emotions and feelings.

AFFIRMATIVE ACTION (205) A policy that tries to correct abuses caused by past discrimination against minority groups by encouraging structural assimilation.

AGE COHORT (397) A group of people born in a specified period of time.

AGENTS OF SOCIALIZATION (76) The people, groups, and organizations that transmit culture.

AGRARIAN SOCIETY (370) A society whose primary mode of subsistence is farming that employs the plow to increase the fertility of the soil.

ALIENATION (381) A worker's sense of separation from the products that he or she makes.

ALIGNING ACTION (140) An effort to maintain or reestablish an impression that a person wishes to convey to an audience.

AMALGAMATION (204) The assimilation of a group into a society by intermarriage with other groups.

ANOMIE (103) The sense of normlessness and frustration that is a product of the way that society is organized; a condition in which culturally defined goals and the norms that regulate the means to achieve those goals are not in harmony.

ANTICIPATORY SOCIALIZATION (89) The effort to learn the roles associated with a status that a person expects to attain in the future.

ARTIFACT (52) An object that is part of material culture because it has been given meaning by people.

ASCRIBED STATUS (149) A social position assigned to a person by others at birth or at some later stage in the life cycle.

ASSIMILATION (204) The absorption of a minority group into the larger society.

AUTHORITY (159) The acknowledged right of those who occupy certain positions to exercise their will over others.

AUTOMATION (370) The mechanization of production.

BUREAUCRACY (159) A formal organization that emphasizes the rational and efficient pursuit of goals through a highly structured network of statuses and roles.

BUSING (290) The policy of transporting students from one neighborhood to a school in a different community in order to reduce the segregation of schools by race.

CAPITALISM (373) An economic system based on private ownership of the means of production and little government regulation of the market forces of supply and demand.

CAREER MOBILITY (183) A change in social position over the course of a person's lifetime.

CARRYING CAPACITY (410) The number of people who can be sustained by the ecosystem.

CASE METHOD (356) A technique of teaching in law schools that involves intensive analysis of decisions that have been written by judges.

CASTE (172) A position in a stratification system that is ascribed at birth on the basis of family position; people are expected to marry others of the same caste.

CENSORSHIP (450) The restriction of information.

CENSUS (396) A systematic measurement of the size, composition, and distribution of a population.

CENTRAL CITY (424) The core of a metropolitan area that is usually characterized by large size, high population density, and diversity.

CHANGE AGENT (475) A person committed to and informed about a particular innovation who tries to get others to adopt it.

CHARISMATIC AUTHORITY (324) Authority derived from a person's unique vision, inspiration, or sense of destiny.

CHILD ABUSE (253) Physical and emotional abuse, sexual abuse, neglect, or abandonment that parents or other caretakers inflict on children.

489

CHURCH (302) A religious organization with a relatively large number of members who worship regularly in formal rituals.

CITY (421) A large, densely populated, and heterogeneous community.

CIVIL RELIGION (311) A belief system that elevates aspects of the secular world to the status of the sacred and interprets national history in terms of a transcendant reality.

CLASS (172) A category of people who have a similar social standing or rank based on economic resources, political power, social honor, or life style.

CLASS MODEL (337) A model of the political system that treats the dominant class in the economic system as a ruling class that is capable of exercising control over all sectors of society.

COGNITIVE SKILLS (74) Intellectual abilities such as reasoning, thinking, remembering, and using language.

COHABITATION (263) A situation in which people who define themselves as a couple live together but do not marry.

COLLECTIVE BARGAINING (383) A peaceful form of conflict in which representatives of a union and representatives of management negotiate wages, hours, working conditions, and fringe benefits such as health insurance and retirement pensions.

COLLECTIVE BEHAVIOR (445) Spontaneous, unstructured, and temporary action by a large number of people who interact with each other or respond to a common stimulus.

COMMUNE (265) A household that includes at least three adults and can also include children; members pool their resources and divide household tasks among themselves.

COMMUNISM (328, 330) A classless society in which property is communally owned and the state begins to "wither away"; a form of totalitarianism that emphasizes public property and that has a single political party.

COMMUNITY (421) A relatively permanent group of people who interact to meet common goals and needs and who live in one location.

COMPENSATORY EDUCATION (290) A policy of creating intensive educational programs for disadvantaged students to bring them up to the level of other students.

COMPETITION (129) A form of interaction in which the parties seek the same limited goal and agree to abide by certain rules in their efforts to reach that goal.

COMPOSITIONAL PERSPECTIVE (434) The position that aspects of a population's composition such as income, age, ethnicity, and occupation influence life in the city.

CONCENTRIC-ZONE MODEL (429) A model that portrays the city as a series of circles within circles, with each circle or zone differing in the way land is used.

CONFLICT (131) A struggle over scarce resources in which one party seeks to eliminate, defeat, destroy, or neutralize the opposition in order to achieve a desired goal.

CONFLICT THEORY (15) The theoretical perspective that stresses conflict and competition among groups of people for scarce resources, such as wealth, power, and prestige.

CONSUMERISM (386) An organized moral, economic, and legal effort to improve the lot of people who buy and use goods and services.

CONTAGION (456) The spread of behavior and beliefs among crowd participants through interaction and imitation.

CONTROL GROUP (34) A group of subjects in an experiment who are not exposed to the independent variable in order to provide a base line to which any changes in the behavior or attitudes of the experimental group can be compared.

CONTROL THEORY (106) The theory that people who lack intimate attachments to parents, teachers, and peers and who also lack the aspirations and moral beliefs that link them to a law-abiding life are free to violate norms.

CONVERGENCE THEORY (374, 457) The idea that capitalist and socialist economic systems might gradually evolve toward a middle ground that includes certain common elements; also, the idea that crowds develop when people who have similar characteristics, attitudes, or needs before joining a crowd come together for collective action.

COOPERATION (129) A form of interaction in which people strive for a common goal, share a definition of the situation, and depend on each other.

CORPORATION (376) An organization that is chartered by the state and that has a legal existence apart from its directors, managers, stockholders, and lower-level employees.

CORRELATION (31) A relationship between two variables in which changes in the value of one variable are related to proportionate changes in the value of another variable.

COUNTERCULTURE (62) A set of norms and values that contradict the norms and values of the dominant culture.

COURT (358) A formal organization that resolves disputes and determines how a society's idea of justice will be implemented.

CRAZE (450) Action by people who share an unquestioned belief that something will be rewarding to them.

CREDENTIALISM (284) The requirement that a worker have a degree that is not actually necessary for the performance of a job.

CRIME (99) An act that violates a legal norm and is punishable by the state.

CRIME TARIFF (353) The effect of the criminal law in raising the prices of goods and services that are made illegal.

CROSS-SECTIONAL STUDY (26) A research project that gathers evidence on subjects at just one point in time.

CROWD (452) A relatively large and temporary gathering of people in one place who have a purpose and who are aware of each other.

CRUDE BIRTH RATE (400) The annual number of live births for every 1,000 people in a population.

CRUDE DEATH RATE (403) The annual number of deaths for every 1,000 people in a population.

CULT (303) A religious group that emphasizes a specific belief or practice and that is led by a charismatic individual.

CULTURAL HEGEMONY (64) The principle that the dominant group in any repressive system will impose its values, norms, attitudes, beliefs, and morality on all other groups in the society in order to maintain and enhance its advantageous position.

CULTURAL LAG (480) The condition that exists when two parts of a culture that were once in adjustment with each other change at different rates and become incompatible with each other.

CULTURAL RELATIVISM (61) The view that no culture is better than another, and that cultural diversity should be tolerated, understood, and appreciated, rather than ethnocentrically condemned.

CULTURAL TRANSMISSION THEORY (109) A theory that explains deviant behavior in terms of socialization to norms, values, motives, and skills that differ from those of the dominant culture.

CULTURAL UNIVERSAL (65) A general trait shared by all cultures.

CULTURE (49) A system of symbols that a group of people share to help them make sense of the world.

CULTURE SHOCK (59) The sense of anxiety, confusion, and disorientation that occurs when one comes into contact with a different culture.

CYCLICAL THEORY (479) The idea that societies rise and fall, grow and decline.

DEMOCRACY (330) The form of the state in which authority is vested in the people.

DEMOGRAPHIC TRANSITION (409) A model that describes changes over time in fertility, mortality, and population growth rates.

DEMOGRAPHY (395) The study of population.

DENOMINATION (303) A branch of a church that coexists on a more or less equal basis with other religious organizations.

DEPENDENCY RATIO (399) The number of economically dependent people divided by the number of economically productive people in a population.

DEPENDENT VARIABLE (25) A variable that is influenced or depends on changes in an independent variable.

DESEGREGATION (201) The elimination of a spatial barrier between groups.

DETERMINIST PERSPECTIVE (432) The position that life in the city is a direct outcome of the size, density, and diversity of the community.

DETERRENCE (362) The idea that punishment, by instilling fear, can prevent crime.

DEVIANCE (99) An act that violates a norm.

DIFFERENTIAL ASSOCIATION THEORY (109) The theory that all criminal behavior is learned through face-to-face interaction and is the product of an excess of definitions favorable to violation of the law over definitions unfavorable to violation of the law.

DIFFERENTIATION (478) The process by which a society becomes more specialized over time.

DIFFUSION (475) The spread of values, ideas, and technology from one society to another.

DISASTER (455) A situation of collective stress and social disruption that is caused by human or natural means.

DISCRIMINATION (201) The treatment of people in a systematically negative way because they are members of a socially disvalued group or category.

DIVISION OF LABOR (157) A set of interrelated, specialized tasks within a social structure.

DIVORCE (266) The formal termination of the legal contract of marriage.

DOUBLING TIME (408) The number of years that it will take a population to become twice its current size, given its current rate of growth.

DRAMATURGICAL APPROACH (18) An interactionist perspective that analyzes behavior in much the same way that one would analyze the presentation of a play to an audience.

DYSFUNCTION (14) A consequence of an institution that fails to serve the well-being of society.

ECONOMIC EXCHANGE (368) The process by which individuals and organizations give each other valuable goods and services in return for different goods and services.

ECONOMIC SOCIALIZATION (368) The process through which people learn to regard the economic system as legitimate and learn the values and behavior needed to fill positions in the division of labor.

ECONOMIC SYSTEM (367) The institution that produces and distributes goods and services.

ECOSYSTEM (66) The complex and self-sustaining system of all living and nonliving things in a particular area.

ECUMENISM (315) A movement to achieve harmony among various religious groups by emphasizing what they have in common rather than stressing their doctrinal differences in a competition for new members.

EDUCATION (273) The formal process by which people are systematically taught knowledge, skills, and values.

ELITE MODEL (337) A model of the political system that suggests that any institution is controlled by a small group of leaders.

EMBOURGEOISEMENT (190) The process by which manual and blue-collar workers develop a life style much like that of the middle class or bourgeoisie.

EMERGENT-NORM THEORY (458) The idea that people in a crowd come to share the same views and develop a group structure that reflects specific norms and values.

EMPIRICAL DATA (23) Types of evidence that result from careful observation and exact measurement.

"EMPTY NEST SYNDROME" (93) The sense of purposelessness that many parents feel in the absence of the children to whom they have devoted years of their lives.

ENDOGAMY (257) Marriage within certain defined groups and categories.

EQUILIBRIUM THEORY (480) The idea that at any given time a society is either in a state of balance or moving toward such an integrated condition.

ETHNIC GROUP (197) A "people" that is defined by a common cultural or national identity that sets it off from other groups.

ETHNOCENTRISM (61) The judgment of a culture as inferior, undeveloped, barbaric, backward, or immoral in comparison to the culture of the person making the judgment.

ETHNOMETHODOLOGY (138) An approach to the study of social interaction that seeks to understand and describe people's efforts to make sense of the world and seeks to discover the underlying rules and formal structures of routine daily life.

EVOLUTIONARY THEORY (476) The idea that social change is an orderly, gradual process that leads to greater complexity and the progressive improvement of societies.

EXCHANGE (128) A process in which people give and receive rewards in a mutually satisfying way.

EXOGAMY (257) Marriage outside a specific group or category.

EXPERIMENT (23) A controlled type of research in which human subjects are treated in various ways to determine the effects of that treatment on their behavior and attitudes.

EXPERIMENTAL GROUP (34) A group of subjects in an experiment who are exposed to the independent variable in order to see its effects on their behavior and attitudes.

EXPRESSIVE CULTURE (52) The ideas, beliefs, values, and customs that serve to express people's emotional needs and help them to interpret the world.

EXTENDED FAMILY (254) A family consisting of a husband and a wife, their children, the parents of one or both spouses, and possibly the brothers, sisters, nephews, and nieces of the spouses.

FAD (450) A new and relatively trivial activity that many people adopt quickly and enthusiastically.

FAMILISM (401) The value that encourages people to marry and bear children.

FAMILY (249) A socially defined set of relationships between at least two people who are related by birth, marriage, or adoption.

FAMILY PLANNING (415) A process of conscious decision making by married couples to have only as many children as they want to have.

FASCISM (329) A form of totalitarianism that has a one-party dictatorship headed by a charismatic leader and that emphasizes private property along with state control over the economy.

FASHION (451) A style of appearance or behavior.

FECUNDITY (400) The reproductive potential of women.

FERTILITY (400) The actual number of children that women have.

FORMAL ORGANIZATION (157) A large, complex secondary group that is deliberately created to achieve certain goals.

FUNCTION (12) A consequence or effect that an institution has on the rest of society.

FUNCTIONAL ILLITERACY (273) The inability to read and write well enough to be an effective (or functioning) member of society.

FUNCTIONALISM (12) The theoretical perspective that sees each structure as serving a certain function for society.

GENDER (221) The social, cultural, and psychological aspects of maleness or femaleness, or masculinity or femininity.

GENDER IDENTITY (221) The socially learned part of the self that results from a person's recognition that he or she is a man or a woman, or a boy or a girl.

GENDER ROLE (221) The kinds of behavior that are typically expected of the members of a particular sex.

GENERALIZED OTHER (87) The broader perspective of a group or a society that is learned in the development of the self.

GENOCIDE (206) The deliberate and systematic elimination of a racial or ethnic group.

GENTRIFICATION (436) The movement of middle-class and upper-class people into the city from the suburbs and the permanent settlement in the city of middle-class and upper-class people who in the past probably would have moved to the suburbs.

GOVERNMENT (323) The group of people who hold office in a political system at a given time.

GRADE INFLATION (280) An increase in the grades awarded by schools without an increase in actual academic achievement.

"GREEN REVOLUTION" (413) A change in agricultural technology that made it possible to increase greatly the yield of land by using new varieties of wheat and rice.

GROSS NATIONAL PRODUCT (GNP) (371) A monetary measure of the total value of goods and services produced in a given year.

GROUP (153) A set of relationships among people

who interact on a face-to-face basis over time; a group has a defined membership, a set of interrelated statuses and roles, common values and norms, and an identity.

HAWTHORNE EFFECT (35) The effect that participation in an experiment has on a dependent variable.

HIDDEN CURRICULUM (274) A set of values and norms that is subtly instilled through the educational process; it includes learning behavior that is conducive to the smooth functioning of the school and the society at large.

HOMOGAMY (257) The selection of spouses with similar social characteristics.

HORIZONTAL MOBILITY (182) Movement from one position in a stratification system to another position at the same level.

HORTICULTURAL SOCIETY (370) A society whose primary mode of subsistence is raising plants by farming that is based mainly on human labor.

HUMAN ECOLOGY (395) The study of the relationship of people to other living and nonliving things in the ecosystem.

HUNTING–GATHERING SOCIETY (369) A society that relies for food primarily on the hunting of animals and the gathering of food that grows in the natural environment.

HYPOTHESIS (25) A tentative statement about the relationship between variables.

IDEAL TYPE (154) A composite of a set of general characteristics showing the essence of a social phenomenon.

IMPRESSION MANAGEMENT (140) The process of trying to convey particular kinds of information to others to get them to respond in a desired way.

INCAPACITATION (362) The use of prison to prevent crime by keeping offenders off the street.

INCEST TABOO (257) The rule that people cannot marry or have sexual relations with family members or kinfolk to whom they are closely related.

INCOME (175) A type of property derived from personal labor or from the use of capital over a given period of time.

INDEPENDENT VARIABLE (25) A variable that influences or causes changes in a dependent variable.

INDETERMINATE SENTENCE (364) An inexact period of time in custody.

INDUSTRIAL SOCIETY (370) A society whose primary mode of subsistence is based on mechanical sources of energy and that uses science and advanced technology to produce goods and services.

INDUSTRIALIZATION (370) The process by which an economy based primarily on energy supplied by animals and humans changes to one based mainly on mechanical sources of energy such as the steam engine and electricity.

INFANT MORTALITY RATE (403) The annual number of deaths of children in the first year of life for every 1,000 live births in a population.

INFLATION (385) A continuing increase in the general level of prices for goods and services.

INFORMAL STRUCTURE (164) Patterns of interaction, friendships, personal behavior, "common knowledge," and informal authority, which differ from the practices specified in the rules and procedures of an organization.

INSTITUTION (164) A stable cluster of values, norms, statuses, and roles that enjoys wide support in a society.

INSTITUTIONAL RACISM (202) The social practices and policies that lead to the unequal treatment of a racial group.

INSTITUTIONAL SEXISM (229) A pattern of discrimination and a set of beliefs that are built into a society's institutions and policies, causing members of one sex to deny opportunities and rewards to members of the other sex.

INSTITUTIONALIZATION (164) The process by which institutions are created.

INTEGRATION (201) The actual social interaction of the members of different groups.

INTERACTIONISM (18) A theoretical perspective that focuses on the ways that individuals direct and choreograph their interactions with each other.

INTEREST GROUP (336) A group that attempts to influence decision making by elected officials and government bureaucrats in ways that are favorable to group members.

INTERGENERATIONAL MOBILITY (183) Movement in a stratification system from the level occupied by a person's parents.

INTERLOCKING DIRECTORATE (376) A condition in which the boards of directors of different corporations include many of the same individuals.

INTERNAL MIGRATION (406) Population movement from one area to another within the same country.

INTERNATIONAL MIGRATION (404) The movement of people from one country to another.

INTERVIEW (28) A face-to-face encounter in which trained researchers ask respondents a series of questions and record their answers.

IRON LAW OF OLIGARCHY (163) The tendency of an organization to become increasingly dominated by a small group of people.

LABELING PERSPECTIVE (110) The approach that focuses on the interaction between rule-breakers and those who label or stigmatize them as deviants.

LAISSEZ-FAIRE (373) A "hands-off" policy in which the state allows the market forces of supply and demand to operate in an unrestricted way.

LANGUAGE (57) A set of words and rules of grammar for the use of those words.

LATENT FUNCTION (14)   A consequence of an institution that is not intended or obvious.

LAWYER (355)   A trained specialist in legal rules and procedures.

LEGITIMACY (323)   The belief that the exercise of power by others is appropriate.

LIFE CYCLE (82)   The orderly sequence of events between birth and death.

LIFE EXPECTANCY (403)   The average number of years that a person of a particular age can expect to live.

LIFE SPAN (403)   The maximum number of years that people might live.

LOBBYING (336)   A tactic of pressuring lawmakers and agency officials in order to influence policy.

LONGITUDINAL STUDY (26)   A research project that follows a group of people over time.

LOOKING-GLASS SELF (87)   The sense of personal identity that is the image that reflects off the ''mirror'' of other people.

MAGIC (301)   A technique for manipulating and controlling matters that seem to be beyond human control and that often involve danger and uncertainty.

MANIFEST FUNCTION (14)   An obvious and intended consequence of an institution.

MASS (446)   A large and heterogeneous number of people who are not in the same physical location but who will all react to a common stimulus.

MASS HYSTERIA (446)   A response by physically dispersed individuals to a common perception that they face a great and unpreventable threat.

MASS MEDIA (80)   The instruments of large-scale communication—including television, radio, movies, magazines, and newspapers—which transmit information and symbolic material to a large, unorganized, and dispersed group of people.

MASTER STATUS (148)   The most important status in a person's life, the one that determines his or her social identity.

MATERIAL CULTURE (52)   The tangible and physical aspects of culture, including artifacts and technology.

MEGALOPOLIS (424)   A number of metropolitan areas that are connected by urban, semiurban, or suburban areas to form a more or less continuous urban community.

METROPOLIS (423)   A central city, its suburbs, and the surrounding towns and rural areas that are socially and economically linked together.

MIGRATION (404)   The movement of people from one area to another.

MINORITY GROUP (198)   A category of people that has common traits and is subordinate in the stratification system of a society.

MOB (455)   An emotional crowd that cooperates in striving for a common goal or in expressing a shared hostility with violence.

MODERN SOCIETY (167)   A society in which relationships are relatively impersonal, there is diversity of values and norms, and achieved statuses and secondary groups are important.

MODERNIZATION (478)   A change from a simple, preindustrial society to a complex, industrial one.

MONOGAMY (255)   The marriage of one husband and one wife.

MORAL ENTREPRENEUR (100)   People who oppose certain behavior and support laws to prohibit that behavior.

MORTALITY (403)   The number of deaths in a population.

MULTINATIONAL CORPORATION (379)   A firm based in one nation that buys, produces, and sells goods and services in other nations.

MULTIPLE-NUCLEI MODEL (431)   A model that shows cities as having different centers that affect land use and rents in surrounding neighborhoods.

MYTH (300)   A story that defines the relationship of believers to their ancestors, to nature, or to life after death.

NEOEVOLUTIONARY THEORY (477)   The idea that there is a general trend toward a more complex technology and a more elaborate division of labor; it does not assume that change is inevitable nor that change invariably proceeds along the same path.

NET GROWTH RATE (408)   The rate of natural increase plus the net migration rate.

NET MIGRATION RATE (404)   The difference between immigration and emigration, expressed as a net number of people per 1,000 in a population who enter or leave an area during one year.

NEW TOWN (439)   A planned and largely self-contained community that is often built on open land.

NORM (56)   A rule or expectation about appropriate behavior for a particular person in a specific situation.

NORM OF RECIPROCITY (128)   The expectation that people are obliged to help and not to harm those who have helped them.

NUCLEAR FAMILY (254)   A family unit composed of a married couple and their children.

OBSERVATION (23)   Watching social behavior in a systematic way.

OPEN CLASSROOM (278)   An approach that tries to minimize the formality and impersonality of the school bureaucracy by adapting seating patterns and the structure of the classroom to the educational and expressive needs of students rather than to the needs of the school's administrators and teachers.

OPERATIONAL DEFINITION (26)   The definition of abstract, general concepts in concrete, measurable terms.

PANIC (454)   Sudden flight by a crowd that is responding to a belief about an ambiguous and uncontrollable threat.

PARTICIPANT OBSERVATION (37)   A research

strategy that requires the scholar to become personally involved in a group in some capacity in order to observe the group's behavior.

PASTORAL SOCIETY (370)   A society whose primary mode of subsistence is the domestication of animals.

PEER GROUP (76)   People who are of the same age and roughly equal in authority.

PERSONAL SPACE (137)   The unoccupied area that people feel must be maintained around themselves in order to be safe and comfortable.

PLEA BARGAINING (359)   A process in which the prosecuting attorney, the defense attorney, the defendant, and the judge agree on the charge to which the defendant will plead guilty and the sentence that the defendant will receive.

PLURALISM (205)   A situation in which a variety of distinct racial and ethnic groups coexist side by side in the same society.

PLURALIST MODEL (337)   A model of the political system that portrays society as composed of multiple and competing groups.

POLICE (353)   A formal organization designed to preserve order and to provide public service.

POLITICAL PARTY (335)   A formal organization that mobilizes resources and voter support in order to win power.

POLITICAL SOCIALIZATION (330)   The process through which people learn political attitudes and behavior.

POLITICAL SYSTEM (323)   The institution that meets society's needs for internal order, protection from external enemies, resolution of group differences, and the definition and pursuit of societal goals.

POLYGAMY (255)   A form of marriage that involves multiple spouses.

POPULATION (28, 395)   The total group of people to which a researcher wishes to generalize from the data on a sample; the number of people living in an area at a given time.

POPULATION PYRAMID (397)   A diagram that shows the age and sex composition of a population.

POPULATION TRANSFER (206)   A policy that creates spatial separation among racial and ethnic groups; it includes expulsion, exclusion, and partition of a country.

POSTINDUSTRIAL SOCIETY (371)   A society in which a large proportion of all workers are employed in the tertiary or service sector, and a decreasing number of workers are employed in the primary sector.

POVERTY (184)   A condition in which people have too little money to afford the basic necessities of life.

POWER (178)   The ability to impose one's will on another, even if that person does not wish to comply.

PREJUDICE (199)   A belief that individuals can be evaluated by their membership in a group or a category.

PRESTIGE (176)   The respect, deference, and social honor that are given voluntarily to a person by others.

PRIMARY GROUP (153)   A relatively small group whose members interact on a regular and intimate basis.

PROFANE (297)   The everyday and routine, as distinguished from the sacred.

PROFIT (373)   The result of charging more for goods and services than they cost to produce.

PROPAGANDA (450)   The deliberate and calculated presentation of distorted, one-sided, and selective information to the public in order to change its opinion in a desired way.

PROPERTY (175)   The set of rights and obligations attached to the ownership of money, goods, and services.

PROTESTANT ETHIC (306)   A value system inherent in the religious beliefs of Calvinism that emphasizes the acquisition and reinvestment of wealth.

PUBLIC (449)   A large number of people who share a common sentiment on some issue.

PUBLIC OPINION (449)   An attitude or position on an issue that is held by the members of a public.

PULL FACTOR (408)   Something that induces people to move to another area.

PUNISHMENT (362)   A sanction administered by a legitimate authority.

PUSH FACTOR (408)   Something that induces people to move from a country or an area.

RACE (195)   An inherited set of physical traits that are thought to distinguish large categories of people from one another.

RACISM (199)   Prejudice in the form of a coherent set of beliefs (or ideology) that physical differences among groups determine differences in behavior among those groups.

RATE OF NATURAL INCREASE (408)   The difference between the crude birth rate and the crude death rate.

RATIONAL–LEGAL AUTHORITY (325)   Authority based on the formally defined rights and obligations of people who occupy the status of official.

REFERENCE GROUP (154)   A group or a category that people use to evaluate themselves and their behavior.

REHABILITATION (362)   The idea that punishment can change offenders so that they will give up their criminal activities.

RELATIVE DEPRIVATION (458)   The discrepancy between a group's expectations of what it is legitimately entitled to and the actual conditions that the group experiences or feels are possible within the existing social system.

RELIGION (297)   A stable and shared set of beliefs, symbols, and rituals that focus on the sacred.

RESEARCH DESIGN (26)   An orderly plan for collecting, analyzing, and interpreting data.

RESOCIALIZATION (90)   A process that involves unlearning old ways of doing things and the adoption of new identities, values, norms, and behavior.

RESOURCE-MOBILIZATION THEORY (463) The theory that regards social movements as purposive activity based on the organization and use of a body of supporters, financial resources, legal talent, access to the news media, and other resources.

RESPONSE RATE (29) The proportion of a sample of subjects who provide complete information to a researcher.

RETRIBUTION (362) The idea that people who have done wrong deserve to suffer.

RETROSPECTIVE INTERPRETATION (113) A process by which people respond to an act of rule-breaking by reassessing the individual as a whole person, searching for other behavior or characteristics that seem compatible with the rule-breaking.

REVOLUTION (482) A basic and rapid change in a society's political, economic, and stratification systems.

RIOT (455) People banded together in a relatively spontaneous, unplanned, and temporary way to act in an openly violent fashion against other people or their property.

RITUAL (301) A traditional and stylized practice that defines the relationship of believers to the sacred.

ROLE (148) The behavior expected of a person who occupies a particular status.

ROLE CONFLICT (151) An incompatibility between two or more roles that a person is expected to play.

ROLE ENGULFMENT (114) The tendency of a labeled rule-breaker to be engulfed or swallowed up in a deviant role.

ROLE PERFORMANCE (151) The actual behavior of a person who occupies a status.

ROLE SET (151) The various roles attached to a single status.

ROLE STRAIN (152) An incompatibility in the expectations of a single role, making it difficult to perform the role.

ROUTINIZATION OF CHARISMA (304) The process by which the leadership of a charismatic figure is institutionalized in an organization.

RUMOR (451) A piece of unverified but not necessarily incorrect information that is transmitted from person to person relatively rapidly.

SACRED (297) The ideal and the supernatural that are not observable and that stand apart from daily life.

SAMPLE (28) A representative group of people chosen from a larger population.

SANCTION (56) A reaction to the violation of a norm.

SAPIR–WHORF HYPOTHESIS (58) The idea that language influences the way that people see the world.

SCIENTIFIC METHOD (8) A way to gather evidence and test ideas by careful observation, exact measurement, accurate recording of findings, and thoughtful interpretation of results.

SECONDARY GROUP (154) A group that is usually larger and more complex than a primary group, and less personal and intimate.

SECT (303) A relatively small religious organization that recruits its members through conversion and that engages in relatively informal and emotional worship practices.

SECTOR MODEL (431) A model of a city that emphasizes the way the transportation paths affect land use and divide the city into sectors shaped like pieces of pie.

SECULARIZATION (319) The process by which other institutions become increasingly separated from religion.

SEGREGATION (201) The forced spatial separation of a group.

SELF (83) That sense of identity of oneself as separate from the rest of society, while still living in it.

SENTENCE DISPARITY (360) A difference in criminal penalties for offenders with similar criminal records who commit similar offenses.

SEX (221) The biological characteristic of being male or female.

SEX RATIO (400) The number of males in a population for every 100 females in that population.

SEXISM (229) The ideology that people of one sex are innately superior to people of the opposite sex.

SIGNIFICANT OTHER (87) A person whose reactions are important to an individual.

SLUM (435) An area with high population density and run-down housing that is occupied by the poor.

SOCIAL CHANGE (469) The process by which whole societies, institutions, patterns of interaction, work and leisure activities, roles, and norms are altered over time.

SOCIAL CONTROL (102) The process that brings about conformity to society's norms.

SOCIAL DISTANCE (200) An indicator of how much intimacy a person would be willing to allow the members of a different group.

SOCIAL INDICATOR (486) A statistical measure of the quality of life in a society.

SOCIAL INTERACTION (127) The response of individuals to one another.

SOCIAL MOBILITY (182) The movement of people from one position to another in the stratification system.

SOCIAL MOVEMENT (445) A set of attitudes and self-conscious actions by people who seek to change society's structure or ideology.

SOCIAL STRATIFICATION (171) The ranking of individuals and categories of people in terms of valued things, such as income or social honor.

SOCIAL STRUCTURE (147) Interaction among people that recurs in a regular and stable pattern over time; the form or shape of social relationships.

SOCIALISM (328) A society in which property is publicly owned and there is a ''dictatorship of the proletariat.''

SOCIALIZATION(74)   The process by which people learn the culture of a society and become full participants in that society.

SOCIETY(165)   A self-perpetuating social structure or set of institutions that is relatively self-sufficient, endures beyond the lifetimes of its members, and occupies a specific territory.

SOCIOBIOLOGY(51)   A discipline that tries to explain social behavior in biological terms.

SOCIOLOGICAL IMAGINATION(4)   The effort to relate individual behavior to larger social influences.

SOCIOLOGY(3)   The systematic study of relationships among people.

STANDARD CONSOLIDATED STATISTICAL AREA (SCSA)(424)   Two or more contiguous or adjoining Standard Metropolitan Statistical Areas that are integrated with each other socially and economically.

STANDARD METROPOLITAN STATISTICAL AREA (SMSA)(423)   An area that includes a city of at least 50,000 people and the adjacent counties with urban populations that are economically and socially integrated with the city.

STATE(323)   An organization that has a monopoly on the legitimate use of physical force within a defined territory.

STATISTICAL SIGNIFICANCE(32)   A term describing a relationship between variables that is unlikely to have been produced by chance.

STATUS(148)   A position within a social structure.

STATUS CONSISTENCY(178)   A condition in which a person's rankings in terms of property, prestige, and power are all about equal.

STATUS GROUP(176)   People who recognize each other as roughly equivalent in prestige.

STEREOTYPE(111)   A caricature or simplified picture that sometimes contains an element of truth but exaggerates the differences between those it depicts and the rest of the society.

STRAIN THEORY(103)   The theory that the organization or disorganization of society causes anomie, which leaves people confused about what norms should regulate their behavior.

STRUCTURAL ASSIMILATION(205)   The process by which people of different racial and ethnic groups participate in both the primary and secondary groups of the larger society.

SUBCULTURAL PERSPECTIVE(434)   The position that the size, density, and diversity of the city are conducive to the formation of primary group ties.

SUBURB(426)   A community outside the central city but within the metropolitan area.

SURVEY(23)   A study in which a representative group of people are asked to answer a prepared list of questions.

SYMBOL(18)   Something that stands for something else or has a meaning deeper than the surface aspect of the symbol.

SYMBOLIC INTERACTIONISM(18)   A theoretical perspective that examines the way that participants in social interaction choose and agree on the meaning of symbols.

TECHNIQUE OF NEUTRALIZATION(108)   A justification for committing a deviant act.

TECHNOLOGY(52)   The practices, tools, materials, skills, and methods of organization that people use to manipulate the environment for their own purposes.

TENURE(284)   A lifetime contract that is contingent on competent job performance.

THEISM(300)   A belief system that includes a god or gods who are more powerful than humans and who should be worshipped.

THEOLOGY(300)   An elaborate set of doctrines, teachings, and philosophical speculations about religious matters.

THEORETICAL PERSPECTIVE(11)   A general approach to the study of reality; a set of assumptions and interrelated concepts that provide a way of seeing the world.

THEORY(24)   A formal statement of the relationships among concepts.

TOTAL INSTITUTION(158)   An organization that relies on coercion to motivate its members, often has nearly full control over all important aspects of an individual's daily life, and frequently isolates the individual from contact with the outside world.

TOTALITARIANISM(328)   A centralized state that is relatively intolerant of opposition and that manipulates its citizens through its control of basic social institutions.

TOTEM(301)   An object worshipped by a community of believers.

TRACKING(286)   The placement of students in different educational programs according to their academic skills and their career interests.

TRADITIONAL AUTHORITY(324)   Authority that is based on customs and long-standing practices.

TRADITIONAL SOCIETY(167)   A society in which social relationships are relatively simple, people share values and norms, and ascribed statuses and primary groups are important.

TWO-CAREER FAMILY(262)   A family in which the husband and the wife both work at jobs that have a career path and that they expect to work at for many years.

URBAN ECOLOGY(429)   The study of the relationship of people to each other and to their environment in an urban setting.

URBAN HOMESTEADING(438)   A policy of giving abandoned buildings or selling them for small amounts to people who agree to pay overdue property taxes, repair the buildings with low-interest loans, and live in the buildings for a certain period.

URBAN PLANNING (438) The rational effort to design, build, and change a city.

URBAN RENEWAL (438) A type of urban planning that tries to improve the city by tearing down old buildings and constructing new ones.

URBANISM (431) A special way of life in the city.

URBANIZATION (421) The process by which societies become "citified" as people move from small communities to large cities.

VALUE (55) An abstract and shared idea about what is desirable, good, or correct.

VALUE-ADDED THEORY (459) A theory that collective behavior and social movements develop through a specific sequence of stages that are related to social conditions.

VARIABLE (25) A measurable characteristic or trait that differs from one subject (person or thing) to another, or over time for the same subject.

VERTICAL MOBILITY (182) Movement upward or downward in a stratification system.

VICTIMLESS CRIME (118) A violation of the law for which there is usually no victim who is willing to report the crime to the police.

VOLUNTARY ASSOCIATION (157) An organization whose members freely participate, often in their spare time.

VOUCHER (292) A form that parents can use to pay the tuition at any school that their children attend.

WEALTH (175) Income that has been accumulated or invested.

WHITE-COLLAR CRIME (116) A punishable violation of the law by otherwise respectable people of high social standing who engage in criminal acts in the course of their legitimate work.

"WHITE FLIGHT" (291) The migration of whites from the cities to the suburbs.

WORLD-SYSTEM THEORY (484) The theory that the "core" states of the capitalist West have developed economically and maintained their dominance by exploiting the "peripheral" states of the Third World.

ZERO POPULATION GROWTH (ZPG) (408) A rate of natural increase that is zero because the crude birth rate and the crude death rate are the same.

Bibliography

Aaker, David A., and George S. Day, eds. *Consumerism: Search for the Consumer Interest*, 4th ed. New York: Free Press, 1982.

ABC News–Harris Survey. "Leisure Time Activities." New York: Chicago Tribune Syndicate, January 1, 1979.

Aberle, D. F., et al. "The Functional Prerequisites of a Society," *Ethics* 60 (January 1950): 100–111.

Abrahamson, Mark. *Sociological Theory: An Introduction to Concepts, Issues, and Research*. Englewood Cliffs, N.J.: Prentice-Hall, 1981.

Acquaviva, S. S. *The Decline of the Sacred in Industrial Society*, trans. by Patricia Lipscomb. New York: Harper & Row, 1966, 1979.

Adam, Margaret. *Single Blessedness: Observations on the Single Status in Married Society*. New York: Basic Books, 1976.

Adams, Karen L., and Norma C. Ware. "Sexism and the English Language: The Linguistic Implications of Being a Woman," in Jo Freeman, ed., *Women: A Feminist Perspective*, 2nd ed. Palo Alto, Calif.: Mayfield, 1979, pp. 487–504.

Akers, Ronald L. *Deviant Behavior: A Social Learning Approach*, 2nd ed. Belmont, Calif.: Wadsworth, 1977.

Alba, Richard D. "Social Assimilation among American Catholic National-Origin Groups," *American Sociological Review* 41 (December 1976): 1030–1046.

————, and Gwen Moore. "Ethnicity in the American Elite," *American Sociological Review* 47 (June 1982): 373–383.

Albin, Rochelle Semmel. "Has Feminism Aided Mental Health?" *The New York Times*, June 16, 1981, pp. C1, C3.

Alex, Nicholas. *Black in Blue: A Study of the Negro Policeman*. New York: Appleton-Century-Crofts, 1969.

Alexander, Karl L., and Martha A. Cook. "Curricula and Coursework: A Surprise Ending to a Familiar Story," *American Sociological Review* 47 (October 1982): 626–640.

Alford, Robert R., and Roger Friedland. "Political Participation and Public Policy," in Alex Inkeles, James Coleman, and Neil Smelser, eds., *Annual Review of Sociology*, vol. 1. Palo Alto, Calif.: Annual Reviews, 1975, pp. 429–479.

Allen, Michael Patrick. "The Structure of Inter-Organizational Elite Cooptation: Interlocking Corporate Directorates," *American Sociological Review* 39 (June 1974): 393–406.

Allport, Gordon W. *The Nature of Prejudice*, abridged ed. Garden City, N.Y.: Doubleday, 1958.

————, and Leo Postman. *The Psychology of Rumors*. New York: Holt, Rinehart and Winston, 1947.

Alpert, Irvine, and Ann Markusen. "Think Tanks and Capitalist Policy," in G. William Domhoff, ed., *Power Structure Research*. Beverly Hills, Calif.: Sage Publications, 1980, pp. 173–197.

Amir, Yehuda. "Contact Hypothesis in Ethnic Relations," *Psychological Bulletin* (May 1969): 319–342.

Andelman, David A. "City Crime Wave Spreading to Suburbs," *The New York Times*, January 30, 1972, p. 49.

Andenaes, Johannes. *Punishment and Deterrence*. Ann Arbor, Mich.: University of Michigan Press, 1974.

Andrews, Frank M., and Stephen B. Withey. *Social Indicators of Well-Being: Americans' Perceptions of Life Quality*. New York: Plenum, 1976.

Antunes, George, and A. Lee Hunt. "The Impact of Certainty and Severity of Punishment on Levels of Crime in American States: An Extended Analysis," *Journal of Criminal Law and Criminology* 64 (December 1973): 486–493.

Ardrey, Robert. *The Territorial Imperative: A Personal Inquiry into the Animal Origins of Property and Nations*. New York: Atheneum, 1966.

Arensberg, Conrad M., and Arthur H. Niehoff. *Introducing Social Change: A Manual for Community Development*, 2nd ed. Hawthorne, N.Y.: Aldine, 1971.

Arenson, Karen W. "Are Administration Tax Cuts as Good as Money in the Bank?" *The New York Times*, July 11, 1982, p. E4.

Ariès, Philippe. *Centuries of Childhood: A Social History of Family Life*. New York: Alfred A. Knopf, 1962.

Armor, David J. "The Double Double Standard: A Reply," *Public Interest* 30 (Winter 1973): 119–131.

————. "White Flight and the Future of School Desegregation," in Walter G. Stephan and Joe R. Feagin, eds., *School Desegregation: Past, Present, and Future*. New York: Plenum, 1980, pp. 187–226.

Arons, Stephen, and Ethan Katsh. "A Television Cop in King Richard's Court," in John J. Bonsignore et al., eds., *Before the Law: An Introduction to the Legal Process*, 2nd. ed. Boston: Houghton Mifflin, 1979, pp. 152–158.

Aronson, Sidney H. "The Sociology of the Bicycle," in Marcello Truzzi, ed., *Sociology and Everyday Life*. Englewood Cliffs, N.J.: Prentice-Hall, 1968, pp. 293–303.

Asch, Solomon E. "Opinions and Social Pressure," *Scientific American* 193 (November 1955): 31–35.

Ash, Roberta. *Social Movements in America*. Chicago: Markham, 1972.

Ashcraft, Norman, and Albert E. Scheflen. *People Space*. Garden City, N.Y.: Doubleday, 1976.

Astin, Alexander W. *Four Critical Years*. San Francisco: Jossey-Bass, 1977.

——————. "The Measured Effects of Higher Education," *Annals of the American Academy of Political and Social Science* 404 (November 1972): 1–20.

Atchley, Robert C. "Retirement as a Social Institution," in Ralph H. Turner and James F. Short, Jr., eds., *Annual Review of Sociology*, vol. 8. Palo Alto, Calif.: Annual Reviews, 1982, pp. 263–287.

Austin, Charles. "Decline in Church Membership Nearly Stopped, Council Says," *The New York Times*, June 26, 1983, p. 18.

Babbie, Earl R. *The Practice of Social Research*, 3rd. ed. Belmont, Calif.: Wadsworth, 1983.

Babchuk, Nicholas, and Alan Booth. "Voluntary Association Membership: A Longitudinal Analysis," *American Sociological Review* 34 (February 1969): 31–45.

Bahr, Howard M. "Shifts in Denominational Demography of Middletown, 1924–1977," *Journal for the Scientific Study of Religion* 21 (June 1982): 99–114.

Baird, Leonard L., Mary Jo Clark, and Rodney T. Harnett. *The Graduates*. Princeton, N.J.: Educational Testing Service, 1973.

Baldwin, John, and Michael McConville. "Criminal Juries," in Norval Morris and Michael Tonry, eds., *Crime and Justice: An Annual Review of Research*, vol. 2. Chicago: University of Chicago Press, 1980, pp. 269–319.

Bales, Robert F. "Attitudes toward Drinking in the Irish Culture," in David J. Pittman and Charles R. Snyder, eds., *Society, Culture, and Drinking Patterns*. New York: Wiley, 1962, pp. 157–187.

——————. "The Equilibrium Problem in Small Groups," in Talcott Parsons, Robert F. Bales, and Edward A. Shils, eds., *Working Papers in the Theory of Action*. New York: Free Press, 1953, pp. 111–161.

——————. *Interaction Process Analysis: A Method for the Study of Small Groups*. Cambridge, Mass.: Addison-Wesley, 1951.

——————. *Personality and Interpersonal Behavior*. New York: Holt, Rinehart and Winston, 1970.

——————, and Philip E. Slater. "Role Differentiation in Small Decision-Making Groups," in Talcott Parsons and Robert F. Bales, ed., *Family, Socialization and Interaction Process*. New York: Free Press, 1955, pp. 259–306.

Bales, Robert F., and Fred L. Strodtbeck. "Phases in Group Problem Solving," *Journal of Abnormal and Social Psychology* 46 (1951): 485–495.

Bandura, Albert, Dorothea Ross, and Sheila A. Ross. "Transmission of Aggression through Imitation of Aggressive Models," *Journal of Abnormal and Social Psychology* 62 (1961): 575–582.

Bane, Mary Jo. *Here to Stay: American Families in the Twentieth Century*. New York: Basic Books, 1976.

——————. "Is the Welfare State Replacing the Family?" *Public Interest* 70 (Winter 1983): 91–101.

Banks, Olive. *The Sociology of Education*. New York: Schocken Books, 1968.

Banks, W. Curtis, et al. "Perceived Objectivity and the Effects of Evaluative Reinforcement upon Compliance and Self-Evaluation in Blacks," *Journal of Experimental Social Psychology* 13 (September 1977): 452–463.

Baran, Paul A. *The Political Economy of Growth*. New York: Monthly Review Press, 1957.

Bard, Morton. *Training Police as Specialists in Family Crisis Intervention*. Washington, D.C.: U.S. Government Printing Office, 1970.

Barkan, Steven E. "Strategic, Tactical and Organizational Dilemmas of the Protest Movement against Nuclear Power," *Social Problems* 27 (October 1979): 19–37.

Barnet, Richard, and Ronald Müller. *Global Reach: Power and the Multinational Corporations*. New York: Simon and Schuster, 1974.

Barnett, H. G. *Innovation: The Basis of Cultural Change*. New York: McGraw-Hill, 1953.

Barry, Herbert, III, Margaret K. Bacon, and Irvin L. Child. "A Cross-Cultural Survey of Some Sex Differences in Socialization," *Journal of Abnormal and Social Psychology* 55 (1957): 327–332.

Barthelme, Marion Knox. "A Woman's Life in the Priesthood," *The New York Times Magazine*, September 5, 1982, pp. 20–38.

Barton, Allen H. *Communities in Disaster: A Sociological Analysis of Collective Stress Situations*. Garden City, N.Y.: Doubleday, 1970.

Bassis, Michael. "The Campus as Frog Pond: A Reassessment," *American Journal of Sociology* 82 (May 1977): 1318–1326.

Bauer, Raymond A., ed. *Social Indicators*. Cambridge, Mass.: M.I.T. Press, 1966.

Baxter, Sandra, and Marjorie Lansing. *Women and Politics: The Invisible Majority*. Ann Arbor: University of Michigan Press, 1980.

Beaulac, Willard L. "The Latin American Church: Marxist Inroads," *National Review* 33 (April 17, 1981): 422–423.

Beck, E. M. "Labor Unionism and Racial Income Inequality: A Time-Series Analysis of the Post-World War II Period," *American Journal of Sociology* 85 (January 1980): 791–814.

Becker, Howard S. *Outsiders: Studies in the Sociology of Deviance*. New York: Free Press, 1973.

—————, Blanche Geer, and Everett C. Hughes. *Making the Grade: The Academic Side of College Life*. New York: Wiley, 1968.

Bedau, Hugo Adam, ed. *The Death Penalty in America*, 3rd ed. New York: Oxford University Press, 1982.

Beirne, Piers, and Richard Quinney, eds. *Marxism and Law*. New York: Wiley, 1982.

Bell, Alan P., and Martin S. Weinberg. *Homosexualities: A Study of Diversity among Men & Women*. New York: Simon and Schuster, 1978.

Bell, Carolyn Shaw. "Reaganomics: Time to Ask Some Questions," *The Boston Globe*, July 13, 1982, p. 44.

Bell, Daniel. *The Coming of the Post-Industrial Society: A Venture in Social Forecasting*. New York: Basic Books, 1973.

—————. *The Cultural Contradictions of Capitalism*. New York: Basic Books, 1978.

—————. *The End of Ideology: On the Exhaustion of Political Ideas in the Fifties*, rev. ed. New York: Free Press, 1962.

—————. "The 'Rediscovery' of Alienation," in Shlomo Avineri, ed., *Marx's Socialism*. New York: Lieber-Atherton, 1972, pp. 59–79.

—————. *The Winding Passage: Essays and Sociological Journeys, 1960–1980*. Cambridge, Mass.: Abt Books, 1980.

Bell, Donald H. "Up from Patriarchy: The Male Role in Historical Perspective," in Robert A. Lewis, ed., *Men in Difficult Times: Masculinity Today and Tomorrow*. Englewood Cliffs, N.J.: Prentice-Hall, 1981, pp. 306–323.

Bellah, Robert N. *The Broken Covenant: American Civil Religion in Time of Trial*. New York: Seabury Press, 1975.

—————. "Civil Religion in America," *Daedalus* 96 (Winter 1967): 1–21.

—————. "Religion and Legitimation in the American Republic," *Society* 15 (May–June 1978): 16–23.

—————, and Phillip E. Hammond. *Varieties of Civil Religion*. San Francisco: Harper & Row, 1980.

Ben-Horin, Daniel. "Television without Tears: An Outline of a Socialist Approach to Popular Television" *Socialist Revolution* 35 (September–October 1977): 7–35.

Benbow, Camilla, and Julian Stanley. "Sex Differences in Mathematical Ability: Fact or Artifact?" *Science* 210 (December 1980): 1262–1264.

Bensman, Joseph, and Bernard Rosenberg. *Mass, Class, and Bureaucracy: An Introduction to Sociology*. New York: Praeger, 1976.

Berelson, Bernard, and Gary A. Steiner. *Human Behavior: An Inventory of Scientific Findings*. New York: Harcourt Brace Jovanovich, 1967.

Berg, Ivar. *Education and Jobs: The Great Training Robbery*. New York: Praeger, 1970.

—————, Marcia Freedman, and Michael Freeman. *Managers and Work Reform: A Limited Engagement*. New York: Free Press, 1978.

Berg, Ivar, and Mayer N. Zald. "Business and Society," in Ralph H. Turner, James Coleman, and Renée C. Fox, eds., *Annual Review of Sociology*, vol. 4. Palo Alto, Calif.: Annual Reviews, 1978, pp. 115–143.

Berger, Bennett, Bruce M. Hackett, and R. Mervyn Millar. "Child-Rearing Practices in the Communal Family," in Hans Peter Dreitzel, ed., *Recent Sociology, No. 4: Family, Marriage, and the Struggle of the Sexes*. New York: Macmillan, 1972, pp. 271–300.

Berger, Peter L. *Facing up to Modernity: Excursions in Society, Politics, and Religion*. New York: Basic Books, 1977.

—————. *The Heretical Imperative: Contemporary Possibilities of Religious Affirmation*. Garden City, N.Y.: Anchor Press/Doubleday, 1979.

—————. *The Sacred Canopy: Elements of a Sociological Theory of Religion*. Garden City, N.Y.: Doubleday, 1967.

Berk, Bernard. "Face-Saving at the Singles Dance," *Social Problems* 24 (June 1977): 530–544.

Berk, Richard A. *Collective Behavior*. Dubuque, Iowa: William C. Brown, 1974a.

—————. "A Gaming Approach to Crowd Behavior," *American Sociological Review* 39 (June 1974b): 355–372.

—————, Harold Brackman, and Selma Lesser. *A Measure of Justice: An Empirical Study of Changes in the California Penal Code, 1955–1971*. New York: Academic Press, 1977.

Berk, Sarah Fenstermaker, and Donileen R. Loseke. "'Handling' Family Violence: Situational Determinants of Police Arrest in Domestic Disturbances," *Law and Society Review* 15 (1980–1981): 317–346.

Berkowitz, Leonard, and Nigel Walker. "Law and Moral Judgments," *Sociometry* 30 (December 1967): 410–422.

Berle, Adolph A., Jr., and Gardiner C. Means. *The Modern Corporation and Private Property*, rev. ed. New York: Harcourt Brace Jovanovich, 1932, 1968.

Bernard, Jessie. *The Future of Marriage*. New York: World, 1972.

Bibby, Reginald W. "Why Conservative Churches Are *Really* Growing: Kelley Revisited," *Journal for the Scientific Study of Religion* 17 (June 1978): 129–137.

Bird, Caroline. *The Case against College*. New York: McKay, 1975.

Black, Norman. "Group Decries TV Distortion of Women," *The Boston Globe*, November 23, 1982, p. 41.

Blankenship, Ralph, ed. *Colleagues in Organization: The Social Construction of Professional Work*. New York: Wiley, 1977.

Blau, Peter M. *Exchange and Power in Social Life*. New York: Wiley, 1964.

—————. *Inequality and Heterogeneity: A Primitive Theory of Social Structure*. New York: Free Press, 1977.

—————, and Otis Dudley Duncan. *The American Occupational Structure*. New York: Wiley, 1967.

Blau, Peter M., and Marshall W. Meyer. *Bureaucracy in Modern Society*, 2nd. ed. New York: Random House, 1971.

Blau, Peter M., and W. Richard Scott. *Formal Organiza-*

tions: A Comparative Approach. San Francisco: Chandler, 1962.

Blau, Zena Smith. *Black Children-White Children: Competence, Socialization, and Social Structure.* New York: Free Press, 1981.

Blauner, Robert. *Alienation and Freedom: The Factory Worker and His Industry.* Chicago: University of Chicago Press, 1964.

—————. "Internal Colonialism and Ghetto Revolt," *Social Problems* 16 (Spring 1969): 393–408.

—————. *Racial Oppression In America.* New York: Harper & Row, 1972.

Block, Fred. "The Fiscal Crisis of the Capitalist State," in Ralph H. Turner and James F. Short, Jr., eds., *Annual Review of Sociology,* vol. 7. Palo Alto, Calif.: Annual Reviews, 1981, pp. 1–27.

Blood, Robert O., Jr. *Love Match and Arranged Marriage: A Tokyo–Detroit Comparison.* New York: Free Press, 1967.

—————, and Donald M. Wolfe. *Husbands and Wives.* New York: Free Press, 1960.

Bluestone, Barry, and Bennett Harrison. *The Deindustrialization of America: Plant Closings, Community Abandonment and the Dismantling of Basic Industry.* New York: Basic Books, 1982.

Blumberg, Abraham S. *Criminal Justice: Issues & Ironies,* 2nd ed. New York: New Viewpoints, 1979.

Blumberg, Rae Lesser. *Stratification: Socioeconomic and Sexual Inequality.* Dubuque, Iowa: William C. Brown, 1978.

Blumer, Herbert. "Collective Behavior," in Joseph B. Gittler, ed., *Review of Sociology: Analysis of a Decade.* New York: Wiley, 1957, pp. 127–158.

—————. "Collective Behavior," in Alfred McClung Lee, ed., *Principles of Sociology,* 3rd. ed., New York: Barnes & Noble, 1969a, pp. 65–121.

—————. "Social Problems as Collective Behavior," *Social Problems* 18 (Winter 1971): 298–306.

—————. *Symbolic Interactionism: Perspective and Method.* Englewood Cliffs, N.J.: Prentice-Hall, 1969b.

Blumstein, Alfred, Jacqueline Cohen, and Daniel Nagin. *Deterrence and Incapacitation: Estimating the Effects of Criminal Sanctions on Crime Rates.* Washington, D.C.: National Academy of Sciences, 1978.

Bogardus, Emory S. *Social Distance.* Yellow Springs, Ohio: Antioch College Press, 1959.

Boggs, Carl. *Gramsci's Marxism.* London: Pluto Press, 1976.

Boggs, Sarah L. "Formal and Informal Crime Control: An Exploratory Study of Urban, Suburban, and Rural Orientations," *Sociological Quarterly* 12 (Summer 1971): 319–327.

Bonacich, Phillip, and John Light. "Laboratory Experimentation in Sociology," in Ralph H. Turner, James Coleman, and Renée C. Fox, eds., *Annual Review of Sociology,* vol. 4. Palo Alto, Calif.: Annual Reviews, 1978, pp. 145–170.

Boocock, Sarane Spence. "The Social Organization of the Classroom," in Ralph H. Turner, James Coleman,

and Renée C. Fox, eds., *Annual Review of Sociology,* vol. 4. Palo Alto, Calif.: Annual Reviews,, 1978, pp. 1–28.

Booth, Alan, and Lynn White. "Thinking about Divorce," *Journal of Marriage and the Family* 40 (August 1980): 605–616.

Borland, Dolores Cabic. "Three Ethnic Groups of Women: A Theoretical Position," *Journal of Marriage and the Family* 44 (February 1982): 117–129.

Bornschier, Volker, and Thanh-Huyen Ballmer-Cao. "Income Inequality: A Cross-National Study of the Relationships between MNC-Penetration, Dimensions of the Power Structure and Income Distribution," *American Sociological Review* 44 (June 1979): 487–506.

Bornschier, Volker, Christopher Chase-Dunn, and Richard Rubinson. "Cross-National Evidence of the Effects of Foreign Investment and Aid on Economic Growth and Inequality: A Survey of Findings and a Reanalysis," *American Journal of Sociology* 84 (November 1978): 651–683.

Bornschier, Volker, and Jean-Pierre Hoby. "Economic Policy and Multinational Corporations in Development: The Measurable Impacts in Cross-National Perspective," *Social Problems* 28 (April 1981): 363–377.

[*The Boston Globe.*] "Bangladesh to Sterilize 1.4 Million in 2 Years," *The Boston Globe,* December 3, 1982, p. 12.

—————. "Survey Raps 'Fantasy World' of TV Crime," *The Boston Globe,* January 10, 1983, p. 3.

Bowen, Howard R. *Investment in Learning.* San Francisco: Jossey-Bass, 1977.

Bowles, Samuel. "Unequal Education and the Reproduction of the Social Division of Labor," in Jerome Karabel and A. H. Halsey, eds., *Power and Ideology in Education.* New York: Oxford University Press, 1977, pp. 137–153.

—————, and Herbert Gintis. *Schooling in Capitalist America: Educational Reform and the Contradictions of Economic Life.* New York: Basic Books, 1976.

Bradbury, Katharine, Anthony Downs, and Kenneth A. Small. *Urban Decline and the Future of American Cities.* Washington, D.C.: Brookings Institution, 1982.

Braithwaite, John. "*The Myth of Social Class and Criminality* Reconsidered." *American Sociological Review* 46 (February 1981): 36–57.

Braverman, Harry. *Labor and Monopoly Capital: The Degradation of Work in the Twentieth Century.* New York: Monthly Review Press, 1974.

Briggs, Kenneth A. "Mainstream U.S. Evangelicals Surge in Protestant Influence," *The New York Times,* March 14, 1982, pp. 1, 50.

Brim, Orville G., Jr. "Adult Socialization," in John A. Clausen, ed., *Socialization and Society.* Boston: Little, Brown, 1968, pp. 182–226.

—————. "Socialization through the Life Cycle." in Orville G. Brim, Jr., and Stanton Wheeler, eds., *Socialization after Childhood: Two Essays.* New York: Wiley, 1966, pp. 25–33.

Brinton, Crane. *The Anatomy of Revolution,* rev. and expanded ed. New York: Vintage, 1938, 1965.

Britton, Gwyneth E. "Danger: State Adopted Texts May Be Hazardous to Our Future," *The Reading Teacher* 29 (October 1975): 52–58.

Brody, Jane E. "Male Hormones Tied to Aggressive Acts," *The New York Times*, March 7, 1981, p. 12.

————. "Noise Poses a Growing Threat, Affecting Hearing and Behavior," *The New York Times*, November 16, 1982a, pp. C1, C5.

————. "Unemployment: Consequences and Damages," *The New York Times*, November 3, 1982b, pp. C1, C12.

Bromley, David G., and Anson D. Shupe, Jr. "Financing the New Religions: A Resource Mobilization Approach," *Journal for the Scientific Study of Religion* 19 (September 1978): 227–239.

————. *"Moonies" in America: Cult, Church, and Crusade*. Beverly Hills, Calif.: Sage Publications, 1979.

Bronfenbrenner, Urie. "Soviet Methods of Character Education: Some Implications for Research," *American Psychologist* 17 (August 1962): 550–564.

————. *Two Worlds of Childhood: U.S. and U.S.S.R.* New York: Russell Sage Foundation, 1970.

Brookover, Wilbur B., and Edsel L. Erickson. *Sociology of Education*. Homewood, Ill.: Dorsey Press, 1975.

Brooks, Andree. "Child Support: A Growing Problem of Nonpayment," *The New York Times*, June 14, 1982, p. B10.

Brophy, Jere E., and Thomas L. Good. *Teacher–Student Relationships: Causes and Consequences*. New York: Holt Rinehart and Winston, 1974.

Broverman, Inge K., et al. "Sex Role Stereotypes: A Current Appraisal," *Journal of Social Issues* 28 (No. 2, 1972): 59–78.

Brown, Bruce W. *Images of Family Life in Magazine Advertising: 1920–1978*. New York: Praeger, 1981.

Brown, Dee. *Bury My Heart at Wounded Knee*. New York: Holt, Rinehart and Winston, 1970.

Brown, Lester R. *Food or Fuel: New Competition for the World's Cropland*, Worldwatch Paper No. 35. Washington, D.C.: Worldwatch Institute, 1980.

————. *Population Policies for a New Economic Era*, Worldwatch Paper No. 53. Washington, D.C.: Worldwatch Institute, 1983.

————. *The Twenty-Ninth Day: Accommodating Human Needs and Numbers to the Earth's Resources*. New York: Norton, 1978.

Brown, Michael, and Amy Goldin. *Collective Behavior: A Review and Reinterpretation of the Literature*. Pacific Palisades, Calif.: Goodyear, 1973.

Browning, Edgar K. "How Much More Equality Can We Afford?" *Public Interest* 43 (Spring 1976): 90–110.

————, and William R. Johnson. "Taxes, Transfers, and Income Inequality," in Gary M. Walton, ed., *Regulatory Change in an Atmosphere of Crisis: Current Implications of the Roosevelt Years*. New York: Academic Press, 1979, pp. 129–152.

Brownmiller, Susan. *Against Our Will: Men, Women and Rape*. New York: Simon and Schuster, 1975.

Bryan, James H. "Apprenticeships in Prostitution," *Social Problems* 12 (Winter 1965): 278–297.

————. "Occupational Ideologies and Individual Attitudes of Call Girls," *Social Problems* 13 (Spring 1966): 441–450.

Burgoon, Judee K., and Stephen B. Jones. "Toward a Theory of Personal Space Expectations and Their Violations," *Human Communication Research* 2 (Winter 1976): 131–146.

Burnham, Walter Dean. "Party Systems and the Political Process," in William Nisbet Chambers and Walter Dean Burnham, eds., *The American Party Systems: Stages of Political Development*, 2nd ed. New York: Oxford University Press, 1975, pp. 277–307.

Burstein, Paul. "The Sociology of Democratic Politics and Government," in Ralph H. Turner and James F. Short, Jr., eds., *Annual Review of Sociology*, vol. 7. Palo Alto, Calif.: Annual Reviews, 1981, pp. 291–319.

Busby, Linda J. "Sex Role Research on the Mass Media," *Journal of Communication* 25 (Autumn 1975): 107–131.

Butterfield, Fox. "2 Areas Show a Path to Jobs in Technology," *The New York Times*, August 8, 1982, pp. 1, 30.

Cameron, Paul. "Social Stereotypes: 3 Faces of Happiness," *Psychology Today* 8 (August 1974): 63–64.

Campbell, Angus, Philip E. Converse, and Willard L. Rodgers. *The Quality of American Life: Perceptions, Evaluations, and Satisfactions*. New York: Russell Sage Foundation, 1976.

Campbell, Angus, et al. *The American Voter: An Abridgement*. New York: Wiley, 1964.

Campbell, Donald T., and H. Laurence Ross. "The Connecticut Crackdown on Speeding: Time-Series Data in Quasi-Experimental Analysis," *Law and Society Review* 3 (August 1968): 33–53.

Campbell, Ernest Q. "Adolescent Socialization," in David A. Goslin, ed., *Handbook of Socialization Theory and Research*. Chicago: Rand McNally, 1969, pp. 821–859.

Caplovitz, David. *Making Ends Meet*. Beverly Hills, Calif.: Sage Publications, 1979.

————. *The Poor Pay More: Consumer Practices of Low-Income Families*. New York: Free Press, 1963.

Caplow, Theodore. "Christmas Gifts and Kin Networks," *American Sociological Review* 47 (June 1982a): 383–392.

————. "Religion in Middletown," *Public Interest* 68 (Summer 1982b): 78–87.

————. *Two against One: Coalitions in Triads*. Englewood Cliffs, N.J.: Prentice-Hall, 1969.

Carlin, Jerome. *Lawyers' Ethics: A Survey of the New York City Bar*. New York: Russell Sage Foundation, 1966.

Carmichael, Stokely, and Charles V. Hamilton. *Black Power: The Politics of Liberation in America*. New York: Random House, 1967.

Carnegie Council on Policy Studies in Higher Education.

3000 Futures: The Next Twenty Years in Higher Education. San Francisco: Jossey-Bass, 1980.

Carter, Hugh, and Paul C. Glick. *Marriage and Divorce: A Social and Economic Study.* Cambridge, Mass.: Harvard University Press, 1976.

Castillo, Angel. "Judges Flip the Family Album," *The New York Times*, May 3, 1981, p. E9.

Cater, Douglass, and Stephen Strickland. *TV Violence and the Child: The Evolution and Fate of the Surgeon General's Report.* New York: Russell Sage Foundation, 1975.

Chagnon, Napoleon. *Yąnomamö: The Fierce People*, 2nd ed. New York: Holt, Rinehart and Winston, 1968, 1977.

Chambliss, William J., ed. *Crime and the Legal Process.* New York: McGraw-Hill,1969.

—————, and Robert Seidman. *Law, Order, & Power*, 2nd ed. Reading, Mass.: Addison-Wesley, 1982.

Charon, Joel M. *Symbolic Interactionism: An Introduction, An Interpretation, An Integration.* Englewood Cliffs, N.J.: Prentice-Hall, 1979.

Cheek, Neil H., Jr., and William R. Burch, Jr. *The Social Organization of Leisure in Human Society.* New York: Harper & Row, 1976.

Chein, Isidor, et al. *The Road to H: Narcotics, Delinquency, and Social Policy.* New York: Basic Books, 1964.

Cherlin, Andrew, and Pamela Barnhouse Walters. "Trends in United States Men's and Women's Sex-Role Attitudes: 1972 and 1978," *American Sociological Review* 46 (August 1981): 453–460.

Chickering, Arthur W. *Education and Identity.* San Francisco: Jossey-Bass, 1969.

Chilton, Roland J. "Delinquency Area Research in Baltimore, Detroit, and Indianapolis," *American Sociological Review* 29 (February 1964): 71–83.

Chinoy, Eli. *Automobile Workers and the American Dream.* Boston: Beacon Press, 1955.

Chira, Susan. "Elite Colleges Dipping into the Adult Market," *The New York Times*, August 22, 1982, Section 12, pp. 1, 31.

Chiriboga, David A., and Loraine Cutler. "Stress Responses among Divorcing Men and Women," *Journal of Divorce* 1 (Winter 1977): 95–106.

Chirot, Daniel. *Social Change in a Peripheral Society: The Creation of a Balkan Colony.* New York: Academic Press, 1976.

—————. *Social Change in the Twentieth Century.* New York: Harcourt Brace Jovanovich, 1977.

—————, and Thomas D. Hall. "World-System Theory," in Ralph H. Turner and James F. Short, Jr., eds., *Annual Review of Sociology*, vol. 8. Palo Alto, Calif.: Annual Reviews, 1982, pp. 81–106.

Choldin, Harvey M. "Urban Density and Pathology," in Ralph H. Turner, James Coleman, and Renée C. Fox, eds., *Annual Review of Sociology*, vol. 4. Palo Alto, Calif.: Annual Reviews, 1978, pp. 91–113.

Christenson, James A. "Urbanism and Community Sentiment: Extending Wirth's Model," *Social Science Quarterly* 60 (December 1979): 387–400.

Citrin, Jack. "The Alienated Voter," *Taxing and Spending*, October 1978, pp. 1–7.

Clapham, W. B., Jr. *Human Ecosystems.* New York: Macmillan, 1981.

Clark, Burton R., and Martin Trow. "The Organizational Context," in Theodore M. Newcomb and Everett K. Wilson, eds., *College Peer Groups: Problems and Prospects for Research.* Hawthorne, N.Y.: Aldine, 1966, pp. 17–70.

Clark, Kenneth B. "The Role of Race," *The New York Times Magazine*, October 5, 1980, pp. 25–33.

Clark, Terry Nichols. "Community Power," in Alex Inkeles, James Coleman, and Neil Smelser, eds., *Annual Review of Sociology*, vol. 1. Palo Alto, Calif.: Annual Reviews, 1975, pp. 271–295.

Clarke, Stevens H. "Getting 'Em out of Circulation: Does Incarceration of Juvenile Offenders Reduce Crime?" *Journal of Criminal Law and Criminology* 65 (December 1974): 528–535.

Clausen, John. "Family Structure, Socialization, Personality," in Lois Wladis Hoffman and Martin L. Hoffman, eds., *Review of Child Development Research*, vol. 2. New York: Russell Sage Foundation, 1966, pp. 1–53.

Clayton, Richard R., and Harwin L. Voss. "Shacking up: Cohabitation in the 1970s," *Journal of Marriage and the Family* 39 (May 1977): 273–283.

Clinard, Marshall B. *The Black Market: A Study of White Collar Crime.* Montclair, N.J.: Patterson Smith, 1952, 1969.

—————. *Cities with Little Crime: The Case of Switzerland.* Cambridge, Engl.: Cambridge University Press, 1978.

—————. "Rural Criminal Offenders," *American Journal of Sociology* 50 (July 1944): 38–45.

Cloward, Richard A., and Lloyd E. Ohlin. *Delinquency and Opportunity: A Theory of Delinquent Gangs.* New York: Free Press, 1960.

Clymer, Adam. "Campaign Costs Soar as Median Spending for Senate Seat Hits $1.7 Million," *The New York Times*, April 3, 1983a, p. 20.

—————. "PAC Money's Roles in Congress Raises Suspicions," *The New York Times*, January 19, 1983b, p. A20.

—————. "Studies Find Future in Political Parties," *The New York Times*, April 20, 1981, p. B6.

Coale, A. J. "The Demographic Transition Reconsidered," Paper presented at the International Population Conference, Liège, Belgium, 1973.

—————, and N. W. Rives, Jr. "A Statistical Reconstruction of the Black Population of the United States, 1880–1970," *Population Index* 39 (January 1973): 3–36.

Coale, A. J., et al., eds. *Aspects of the Analysis of Family Structure.* Princeton, N.J.: Princeton University Press, 1965.

Cohen, Albert K. *Delinquent Boys: The Culture of the Gang.* New York: Free Press, 1955.

—————, and Harold M. Hodges. "Characteristics of the Lower-Blue-Collar Class," *Social Problems* 10 (Spring 1963): 303–334.

Cohen, Jacqueline. "The Incapacitative Effect of Imprisonment: A Critical Review of the Literature," in Alfred Blumstein, Jacqueline Cohen, and Daniel Nagin, eds., *Deterrence and Incapacitation: Estimating the Effects of Criminal Sanctions on Crime Rates*. Washington, D.C.: National Academy of Sciences, 1978, pp. 187–243.

Cohen, Julius, Reginald A. H. Robson, and Alan Bates. *Parental Authority: The Community and the Law*. New Brunswick, N.J.: Rutgers University Press, 1958.

Cohen, Muriel. "Coleman Cites Private Schooling," *The Boston Globe*, April 3, 1981, p. 3.

————. "College Board Scores Rise for First Time in 19 Years," *The Boston Globe*, September 22, 1982, pp. 1, 10.

Cohen, Sharon. "Paralyzed Man Upset by Rule on Marriage," *The Boston Globe*, January 27, 1982, p. 65.

Cohn, Alvin W., and Emilio C. Viano, eds. *Police Community Relations: Images, Roles, Realities*. Philadelphia: Lippincott, 1976.

Cohn, Norman. *The Pursuit of the Millenium*. New York: Oxford University Press, 1962.

Cole, Charles Lee. "Cohabitation in Social Context," in Roger W. Libby and Roberty N. Whitehurst, eds., *Marriage and Alternatives: Exploring Intimate Relationships*. Glenview, Ill.: Scott, Foresman, 1977, pp. 62–79.

Cole, Steward G., and Mildred Wiese Cole. *Minorities and the American Promise*. New York: Harper & Row, 1954.

Coleman, James S. *The Adolescent Society*. Garden City, N.Y.: Doubleday, 1961.

————. *Equality of Educational Opportunity*. Washington, D.C.: U.S. Government Printing Office, 1966.

————. "Public Schools, Private Schools, and the Public Interest," *Public Interest* 64 (Summer 1981): 19–30.

————, Thomas Hoffer, and Sally Kilgore. "Cognitive Outcomes in Public and Private Schools," *Sociology of Education* 55 (April–July 1982a): 65–76.

————. *High School Achievement: Public, Catholic, and Private Schools Compared*. New York: Basic Books, 1982b.

Coleman, Richard P., and Lee Rainwater. *Social Standing in America*. New York: Basic Books, 1978.

Collins, Glenn. "Stepparents: Erasing the 'Wicked' Image," *The New York Times*, June 21, 1982, p. A17.

Collins, Randall. *Conflict Sociology: Toward an Explanatory Science*. New York: Academic Press, 1974.

————. *The Credential Society: An Historical Sociology of Education and Stratification*. New York: Academic Press, 1979.

————. "Functional and Conflict Theories of Educational Stratification," *American Sociological Review* 36 (December 1971): 1002–1018.

Collins, Sharon M. "The Use of Social Research in the Courts," in Lawrence E. Lynn, Jr., ed., *Knowledge and Policy: The Uncertain Connection*. Washington, D.C.: National Academy of Sciences, 1978, pp. 147–182.

Condry, John, and Sandra Condry. "Sex Differences: A Study of the Eye of the Beholder," *Child Development* 47 (September 1976): 812–819.

Conklin, John E. *Criminology*. New York: Macmillan, 1981.

————. *"Illegal but Not Criminal": Business Crime in America*. Englewood Cliffs, N.J.: Prentice-Hall, 1977.

————. *The Impact of Crime*. New York: Macmillan, 1975.

————. *Robbery and the Criminal Justice System*. Philadelphia: Lippincott, 1972.

Conner, Walker. "Nation-Building or Nation-Destroying?" *World Politics* 24 (April 1972): 319–355.

Conrad, Peter, and Joseph W. Schneider. *Deviance and Medicalization: From Badness to Sickness*. St. Louis: Mosby, 1980.

Converse, Philip E. "Country Differences in Time Use," in Alexander Szalai, ed., *The Use of Time: Daily Activities of Urban and Suburban Populations in 12 Countries*. The Hague, The Netherlands: Mouton, 1972, pp. 145–177.

————, et al. *American Social Attitudes Data Sourcebook 1947-1978*. Cambridge, Mass.: Harvard University Press, 1980.

Cook, Karen S., and Richard M. Emerson. "Power, Equity and Commitment in Exchange Networks," *American Sociological Review* 43 (October 1978): 721–739.

Cook, Philip J. "Research in Criminal Deterrence: Laying the Groundwork for the Second Decade," in Norval Morris and Michael Tonry, eds., *Crime and Justice: An Annual Review of Research*, vol. 2. Chicago: University of Chicago Press, 1980, pp. 211–268.

Cooley, Charles Horton. *Human Nature and the Social Order*. New York: Scribner's, 1903.

————. *Social Organization*. New York: Schocken Books, 1909, 1963.

Coser, Lewis A. *The Functions of Social Conflict*. New York: Free Press, 1956.

Couch, Carl J. "Collective Behavior: An Examination of Some Stereotypes," *Social Problems* 15 (Winter 1968): 310–322.

Council on Environmental Quality and the Department of State. *The Global 2000 Report to the President: Entering the Twenty-First Century*, vol. 1. Washington, D.C.: U.S. Government Printing Office, 1981.

Cox, Allan. *The Cox Report on the American Corporation*. New York: Delacorte, 1982.

Cox, Harvey. *Turning East: Why Americans Look to the Orient for Spirituality—and What That Search Can Mean to the West*. New York: Simon and Schuster, 1977.

Coxon, Anthony P. M., and Charles L. Jones. *The Images of Occupational Prestige*. London: Macmillan, 1978.

Crain, Robert L. "School Integration and Occupational Achievement of Negroes," *American Journal of Sociology* 75 (January 1970): 593–606.

Crampton, Gertrude. *Tootle*, pictures by Tibor Gergely. New York: Golden Press, 1945.

Crano, William D., and Joel Aronoff. "A Cross-Cultural Study of Expressive and Instrumental Role Complementarity in the Family," *American Sociological Review* 43 (August 1978): 463–471.

Cressey, Donald R. *Other People's Money: A Study in the*

Social Psychology of Embezzlement. Belmont, Calif.: Wadsworth, 1953, 1971.

Crosby, John F. "A Critique of Divorce Statistics and Their Interpretation," *Family Relations* 29 (January 1980): 51–58.

Cullen, John B., and Shelley M. Novick. "The Davis–Moore Theory of Stratification: A Further Examination and Extension," *American Journal of Sociology* 84 (May 1970): 1424–1437.

Cummings, Scott, and Del Taebel. "The Economic Socialization of Children: A Neo-Marxist Analysis," *Social Problems* 26 (December 1978): 198–210.

Curtis, James. "Voluntary Association Joining: A Cross-National Comparative Note," *American Sociological Review* 36 (October 1971): 872–880.

Curtis, Richard F., and Elton F. Jackson. *Inequality in American Communities.* New York: Academic Press, 1977.

Curtiss, Susan. *Genie: A Psycholinguistic Study of a Modern-Day "Wild Child."* New York: Academic Press, 1977.

Dahl, Robert A. *Dilemmas of Pluralist Democracy: Autonomy vs. Control.* New Haven, Conn.: Yale University Press, 1982.

————. *Who Governs?* New Haven, Conn.: Yale University Press, 1961.

————, and Charles E. Lindblom. *Politics, Economics, and Welfare: Planning and Politico-Economic Systems Resolved into Basic Social Processes,* 2nd ed. Chicago: University of Chicago Press, 1976.

Dahrendorf, Ralf. *Class and Class Conflict in Industrial Society.* Stanford, Calif.: Stanford University Press, 1959.

Daley, Suzanne. "Panel Asks Stress on English Studies," *The New York Times,* May 6, 1983, pp. Al, D15.

Darwin, Charles. *On the Origin of Species by Means of Natural Selection, or the Preservation of Favoured Races in the Struggle for Life.* London: John Murray, 1859.

Davidson, James D., Gerhard Hofmann, and William R. Brown. "Measuring and Explaining High School Interracial Climates," *Social Problems* 26 (October 1978): 50–70.

Davies, James C. "Toward a Theory of Revolution," *American Sociological Review* 27 (February 1962): 5–19.

Davies, R. W., and Dennis J. B. Shaw, eds. *The Soviet Union.* London: George, Allen and Unwin, 1978.

Davis, John A. "Justification for No Obligation: Views of Black Males toward Crime and the Criminal Law," *Issues in Criminology* 9 (February 1974): 69–87.

Davis, Kingsley. *Human Society.* New York: Macmillan, 1949.

————, and Wilbert E. Moore. "Some Principles of Stratification," *American Sociological Review* 10 (April 1945): 242–249.

Dawson, Carl A., and Warner E. Gettys. *An Introduction to Sociology,* rev. ed. New York: Ronald Press, 1935.

Day, Robert A., and JoAnne V. Day. "A Review of the

Current State of Negotiated Order Theory: An Appreciation and a Critique," *Sociological Quarterly* 18 (Winter 1977): 126–142.

Deaux, Kay. *The Behavior of Women and Men.* Monterey, Calif.: Brooks/Cole, 1976.

DeLone, Richard H. *Small Futures: Future Inequality and the Limits of Liberal Reform.* New York: Harcourt Brace Jovanovich, 1979.

Demerath, Nicholas J., III. *Social Class in American Protestantism.* Chicago: Rand McNally, 1965.

————, and Phillip E. Hammond. *Religion in Social Context: Tradition and Transition.* New York: Random House, 1969.

Demerath, Nicholas J., III, and W. C. Roof. "Religion—Recent Strands in Research," in Alex Inkeles, James Coleman, and Neil Smelser, eds., *Annual Review of Sociology,* vol. 2. Palo Alto, Calif.: Annual Reviews, 1976, pp. 19–33.

Dempewolff, J. A. "Some Correlates of Feminism," *Psychological Reports* 34 (April 1974): 671–676.

Dentler, Robert A., Bernard Mackler, and Mary Ellen Warshauer, eds. *The Urban R's: Race Relations as the Problem in Urban Education.* New York: Praeger, 1967.

Denzin, Norman K. *Childhood Socialization.* San Francisco: Jossey-Bass, 1977.

de Tocqueville, Alexis. *Democracy in America.* New York: Vintage, 1831, 1945.

Dewey, Richard. "The Rural–Urban Continuum: Real but Relatively Unimportant," *American Journal of Sociology* 66 (July 1960): 60–66.

Diggory, James C., and Doreen Z. Rothman. "Values Destroyed by Death," *Journal of Abnormal and Social Psychology* 63 (1961): 205–210.

Dionne, E. J., Jr. "Why Everyone Else Seems to Vote," *The New York Times,* March 20, 1983, p. E4.

DiPrete, Thomas A. "Unemployment over the Life Cycle: Racial Differences and the Effect of Changing Economic Conditions," *American Journal of Sociology* 87 (September 1981): 286–307.

Domhoff, G. William. *The Bohemian Grove and Other Retreats: A Study in Ruling-Class Cohesiveness.* New York: Harper & Row, 1974.

————. *The Higher Circles: The Governing Class in America.* New York: Random House, 1971.

————, ed. *Power Structure Research.* Beverly Hills, Calif.: Sage Publications, 1980.

————. *The Powers That Be: Processes of Ruling-Class Domination in America.* New York: Random House, 1978a.

————. *Who Really Rules? New Haven and Community Power Reexamined.* New Brunswick, N.J.: Transaction Books, 1978b.

————. *Who Rules America?* Englewood Cliffs, N.J.: Prentice-Hall, 1967.

Douglas, J. W. B. *The Home and the School: A Study of Ability and Attainment in the Primary School.* London: MacGibbon and Kee, 1964.

Downs, Anthony. "The Impact of Housing Policies on

Family Life in the United States since World War II," *Daedalus* 106 (Spring 1977): 163–180.

Downton, James V., Jr. "An Evolutionary Theory of Spiritual Conversion and Commitment: The Case of Divine Light Mission," *Journal for the Scientific Study of Religion* 19 (December 1980): 381–396.

Dowse, Robert E., and John A. Hughes. *Political Science.* New York: Wiley, 1972.

Drew, David E. *Competency, Careers, and College: New Directions for Education and Work.* San Franscisco: Jossey-Bass, 1978.

Drew, Elizabeth. "A Reporter at Large: Legal Services," *The New Yorker,* March 1, 1982, pp. 97–113.

Duberman, Lucille. *The Reconstituted Family: A Study of Remarried Couples and Their Children.* Chicago: Nelson-Hall, 1975.

—————. *Social Inequality: Class and Caste in America.* Philadelphia: Lippincott, 1976.

Duffy, Mike. "The Medium's Message: Call It Distorted," *The Boston Globe,* December 13, 1982, p. 35.

Dullea, Georgia. "First Year at College Can Strain Family Tie," *The New York Times,* August 23, 1982, p. B5.

Dumazedier, Joffre. *Sociology of Leisure.* Amsterdam, The Netherlands: Elsevier, 1974.

Duncan, Otis Dudley, David L. Featherman, and Beverly Duncan. *Socioeconomic Background and Achievement.* New York: Seminar Press, 1972.

Durkheim, Emile. *The Division of Labor in Society,* trans. by George Simpson. New York: Free Press, 1893, 1933.

—————. *The Elementary Forms of Religious Life,* trans. by Joseph W. Swain. New York: Free Press, 1912, 1947.

—————. *The Rules of Sociological Method,* trans. by Sarah A. Solovay and John H. Mueller and ed. by George E. G. Catlin. New York: Free Press, 1895, 1938.

—————. *Suicide: A Study in Sociology,* trans. by John A. Spaulding and George Simpson. New York: Free Press, 1897, 1951.

Duverger, Maurice. *Political Parties: Their Organization and Activity in the Modern State,* rev. ed., trans. by Barbara and Robert North. New York: Wiley, 1959.

Easterlin, Richard A. *Birth and Fortune: The Impact of Numbers on Personal Welfare.* New York: Basic Books, 1980a.

—————, ed. *Population and Economic Change in Developing Countries.* Chicago: University of Chicago Press, 1980b.

Ebaugh, Helen Rose Fuchs, and C. Allen Haney. "Shifts in Abortion Attitudes: 1972–1978," *Journal of Marriage and the Family* 40 (August 1980): 491–499.

Eder, Richard. "Franglais Work Has the French in Tizzy Again," *The New York Times,* June 7, 1981, p. 19.

Edwards, Lyford P. *The Natural History of Revolutions.* Chicago: University of Chicago Press, 1927.

Ehrlich, Paul R., Anne H. Ehrlich, and John P. Holdren. *Ecoscience: Population, Resources, Environment.* San Francisco: Freeman, 1977.

Ehrlich, Thomas. "Legal Pollution," *The New York Times Magazine,* February 8, 1976, pp. 17–24.

Eisinger, Peter K. "Racial Differences in Protest Participation," *American Political Science Review* 68 (June 1974): 592–606.

Ekman, Paul. *The Face of Man: Expression of Universal Emotions in a New Guinea Village.* New York: Garland, 1980.

Elashoff, Janet D., and Richard E. Snow. *Pygmalion Reconsidered.* Worthington, Ohio: Charles A. Jones, 1971.

Elder, Glen H., Jr. "Age Differentiation and the Life Course," in Alex Inkeles, James Coleman, and Neil Smelser, eds., *Annual Review of Sociology,* vol. 1. Palo Alto, Calif.: Annual Reviews, 1975, pp. 165–190.

Elkind, David. "Erik Erikson's Eight Ages of Man," *The New York Time Magazine,* April 5, 1970, pp. 25–27, 84–92, 110–119.

—————. "Giant in the Nursery: Jean Piaget," *The New York Times Magazine,* May 26, 1968, p. 25–27, 50–62, 77–80.

Emerson, Richard M. "Social Exchange Theory," in Alex Inkeles, James Coleman, and Neil Smelser, eds., *Annual Review of Sociology,* vol. 2. Palo Alto, Calif.: Annual Reviews, 1976, pp. 335–362.

Emerson, Robert M. "Observational Field Work," in Ralph H. Turner and James F. Short, Jr., eds., *Annual Review of Sociology,* vol. 7. Palo Alto, Calif.: Annual Reviews, 1981, pp. 351–378.

Empey, LaMar T. *American Delinquency: Its Meaning and Construction,* rev. ed. Homewood, Ill.: Dorsey Press, 1982.

—————, and Steven G. Lubeck. *Explaining Delinquency: Construction, Test, and Reformulation of a Sociological Theory.* Lexington, Mass.: Heath, 1971.

Engels, Friedrich. *The Origin of the Family, Private Property, and the State,* ed. and with an intro. by Eleanor Burke Leacock. New York: International, 1884, 1972.

Epperson, Arlin, Peter A. Witt, and Gerald Hitzhusen. *Leisure Counseling: An Aspect of Leisure Education.* Springfield, Ill.: Charles C. Thomas, 1977.

Epstein, Cynthia Fuchs. *Women in Law.* New York: Basic Books, 1981.

Erickson, Maynard L., and Jack P. Gibbs. "On the Perceived Severity of Legal Penalties," *Journal of Criminal Law and Criminology* 70 (Spring 1979): 102–116.

Erikson, Erik H. *Childhood and Society.* New York: Norton, 1950.

Erikson, Kai T. *Everything in Its Path.* New York: Simon & Schuster, 1977.

—————. *Wayward Puritans: A Study in the Sociology of Deviance.* New York: Wiley, 1966.

Erlanger, Howard S., and Douglas A. Klegon. "Socialization Effects of Professional School: The Law School Experience and Student Orientations to Public Interest Concerns," *Law and Society Review* 13 (Fall 1978): 11–35.

Etzioni, Amitai, and Richard Remp. *Technological Short-*

cuts to Social Change. New York: Russell Sage Foundation, 1973.

Etzioni-Halevy, Eva. *Social Change: The Advent and Maturation of Modern Society.* London: Routledge & Kegan Paul, 1981.

Evan, William M., ed. *The Sociology of Law: A Social-Structural Perspective.* New York: Free Press, 1980.

Evans, Joel R. "An Inter-Industry Analysis of Consumerism," in Joel R. Evans, ed., *Consumerism in the United States: An Inter-Industry Analysis.* New York: Praeger, 1980a, pp. 391–439.

——————. "A New Approach to the Study of Consumerism," in Joel R. Evans, ed., *Consumerism in the United States: An Inter-Industry Analysis.* New York: Praeger, 1980b, pp. 1–10.

Evans, Peter B. "Recent Research on Multinational Corporations," in Ralph H. Turner and James F. Short, Jr., eds., *Annual Review of Sociology,* vol. 7. Palo Alto, Calif.: Annual Reviews, 1981, pp. 199–223.

——————, and Michael Timberlake. "Dependence, Inequality, and the Growth of the Tertiary: A Comparative Analysis of Less Developed Countries," *American Sociological Review* 45 (August 1980): 531–552.

Fatemi, Nasrollah S., Gail W. Williams, and Thibaut de Saint-Phalle. *Multinational Corporations,* 2nd ed. South Brunswick, N.J.: A. S. Barnes, 1976.

Feagin, Joe R., and Douglas Lee Eckberg. "Discrimination: Motivation, Action, Effects, and Context," in Alex Inkeles, Neil J. Smelser, and Ralph H. Turner, eds., *Annual Review of Sociology,* vol. 6. Palo Alto, Calif.: Annual Reviews, 1980, pp. 1–20.

Feagin, Joe R., and Clairece Booker Feagin. *Discrimination American Style: Institutional Racism and Sexism.* Englewood Cliffs, N.J.: Prentice-Hall, 1978.

Featherman, David L., and Robert M. Hauser. "Sexual Inequalities and Socioeconomic Achievement in the United States, 1962–1973," *American Sociological Review* 41 (June 1976): 462–483.

Feinberg, Susan. "The Classroom Is No Longer Prime Time," *Today's Education* 66 (September 1977): 74–75.

Feldman, Kenneth A., and Theodore M. Newcomb. *The Impact of College on Students.* San Francisco: Jossey-Bass, 1969.

Fellmeth, Robert C. "The Regulatory–Industrial Complex," in Bruce Wasserstein and Mark J. Green, eds., *With Justice for Some: An Indictment of the Law by Young Advocates.* Boston: Beacon Press, 1970, pp. 244–278.

Fergusson, Adam. *When Money Dies: The Nightmare of the Weimar Collapse.* London: William Kimber, 1975.

Ferrero, Gina Lombroso. *Criminal Man according to the Classification of Cesare Lombroso.* New York: Putnam, 1911.

Fiedler, William R., Ronald D. Cohen, and Stephanie Feeney. "An Attempt to Replicate the Teacher Expect-

ancy Effect," *Psychological Reports* 29 (December 1971): 1223–1228.

Fields, Cheryl M. "Why the Big Drop in S.A.T. Scores?" *Chronicle of Higher Education,* September 6, 1977, p. 1.

Firebaugh, Glenn. "Structural Determinants of Urbanization in Asia and Latin America, 1950–1970," *American Sociological Review* 44 (April 1979): 199–215.

Fischer, Claude S. "The Public and Private Worlds of City Life," *American Sociological Review* 46 (June 1981a): 306–316.

——————. *To Dwell among Friends: Personal Networks in Town and City.* Chicago: University of Chicago Press, 1981b.

——————. *The Urban Experience.* New York: Harcourt Brace Jovanovich, 1976.

Fiske, Edward B. "Academic Decline in High Schools Can Be Explained Theoretically," *The New York Times,* March 7, 1976, Section 4, p. 9.

——————. "School Study Said to Fail to Emphasize Main Point," *The New York Times,* April 26, 1981, p. 40.

Flacks, Richard, and Gerald Turkel. "Radical Sociology: The Emergence of Neo-Marxian Perspectives in U.S. Sociology," in Ralph H. Turner, James Coleman, and Renée C. Fox, eds., *Annual Review of Sociology,* vol. 4. Palo Alto, Calif.: Annual Reviews, 1978, pp. 193–238.

Flast, Richard. "Survey Finds That Most Children Are Happy at Home but Fear World," *The New York Times,* March 2, 1977, p. 12.

Fleming, Elyse S., and Ralph G. Anttonen. "Teacher Expectancy or My Fair Lady," *American Educational Research Journal* 8 (March 1971): 241–252.

Fleming, Macklin. "The Law's Delay: The Dragon Slain Friday Breathes Fire Again Monday," *Public Interest* 32 (Summer 1973): 13–33.

Fogelson, Robert M., and Robert B. Hill. "Who Riots? A Study of Participation in the 1967 Riots," in *Supplemental Studies for the National Advisory Commission on Civil Disorders.* Washington, D.C.: U.S. Government Printing Office, 1968, pp. 221–243.

Foley, Donald L. "The Sociology of Housing," in Alex Inkeles, Neil J. Smelser, and Ralph H. Turner, eds., *Annual Review of Sociology,* vol. 6. Palo Alto, Calif.: Annual Reviews, 1980, pp. 457–478.

Ford, W. Scott. "Interracial Public Housing in a Border City: Another Look at the Contact Hypothesis," *American Journal of Sociology* 78 (May 1973): 1426–1447.

Form, William. "Comparative Industrial Sociology and the Convergence Hypothesis," in Alex Inkeles, James Coleman, and Ralph H. Turner, eds., *Annual Review of Sociology,* vol. 5. Palo Alto, Calif.: Annual Reviews, 1979, pp. 1–25.

Foster, Jack D., Simon Dinitz, and Walter C. Reckless. "Perceptions of Stigma Following Public Intervention for Delinquent Behavior," *Social Problems* 20 (Fall 1972): 202–209.

Fox, Thomas, and S. M. Miller. "Occupational Stratification and Mobility," *Studies in Comparative International Development* 1 (No. 1, 1965): 1–9.

Fraiberg, Selma. "Should You Go Back to Work?" *Harper's Bazaar*, July 1978, pp. 100, 117.

Frank, André Gunder. *Capitalism and Underdevelopment in Latin America*. New York: Monthly Review Press, 1967.

Frankel, Marvin E. *Criminal Sentences: Law without Order*. New York: Hill and Wang, 1973.

Freedman, Jonathan L. *Crowding and Behavior*. New York: Viking, 1975.

Freedman, Samuel G. "Requests for Corporate Funds Rise as Federal Aid Declines," *The New York Times*, September 12, 1982, p. E6.

Freeman, Jo. "The Origins of the Women's Liberation Movement," *American Journal of Sociology* 78 (January 1973): 792–811.

—————. "Resource Mobilization and Strategy: A Model for Analyzing Social Movement Organization Actions," in Mayer N. Zald and John D. McCarthy, eds., *The Dynamics of Social Movements*. Cambridge, Mass.: Winthrop, 1979, pp. 167–189.

Freeman, Richard B. *The Overeducated American*. New York: Academic Press, 1976.

Freud, Sigmund. *Civilization and Its Discontents*, trans. by James Strachey. New York: Norton, 1930, 1962.

Fried, Marc. "Grieving for a Lost Home," in Leonard J. Duhl, ed., *The Urban Condition*. New York: Basic Books, 1963, pp. 151–171.

Friedan, Betty. *The Feminine Mystique*. New York: Norton, 1963.

—————. "Feminism's Next Step," *The New York Times Magazine*, July 5, 1981, pp. 13–15, 32–35.

—————. "Twenty Years after the Feminine Mystique," *The New York Times Magazine*, February 27, 1983, pp. 35–36, 42, 54–57.

Frieden, Bernard J., et al. *The Nation's Housing, 1975 to 1985*. Cambridge, Mass.: Joint Center for Urban Studies of M.I.T. and Harvard University, 1977.

Friedman, Lawrence M. *Law and Society: An Introduction*. Englewood Cliffs, N.J.: Prentice-Hall, 1977.

Friedrich, Carl J., and Zbigniew Brzezinski. *Totalitarian Dictatorship and Autocracy*, vol. 2. Cambridge, Mass.: Harvard University Press, 1965.

Fromm, Erich. *Escape from Freedom*. New York: Holt, Rinehart and Winston, 1941.

Frueh, Terry, and Paul E. McGhee. "Traditional Sex Role Development and Amount of Time Spent Watching Television," *Developmental Psychology* 11 (January 1975): 109.

Fuchs, Victor R. *Who Shall Live? Health, Economics and Social Choice*. New York: Basic Books, 1974.

Fukuyama, Yoshio. "The Major Dimensions of Church Membership," *Review of Religious Research* 2 (Spring 1961): 154–161.

Furstenberg, Frank F., Jr. "Public Reaction to Crime in the Streets," *American Scholar* 40 (Autumn 1971): 601–610.

Fyfe, James J. "Blind Justice: Police Shootings in Memphis," *Journal of Criminal Law and Criminology* 73 (Summer 1982): 707–722.

Gaiter, Dorothy J. "Barbara Bush Says Illiteracy Is an Epidemic," *The New York Times*, September 16, 1982, p. B6.

Gallup, George H. *The Gallup Poll: Public Opinion 1981*. Wilmington, Del.: Scholarly Resources, 1982, pp. 21–23.

Gallup Opinion Index. *How Americans View the Public Schools*, Report No. 151. Princeton, N.J.: American Institute of Public Opinion, February 1978.

—————. *Religion in America 1976*, Report No. 130. Princeton, N.J.: American Institute of Public Opinion, 1976.

—————. *Religion in America 1977–78*, Report No. 145. Princeton, N.J.: American Institute of Public Opinion, 1977.

—————. *Religion in America 1981*. Report No. 184. Princeton, N.J.: Gallup Organization and the Princeton Religion Research Center, January 1981.

Gamson, William A. *The Strategy of Social Protest*. Homewood, Ill.: Dorsey Press, 1975.

—————, Bruce Fireman, and Steven Rytina. *Encounters with Unjust Authority*. Homewood, Ill.: Dorsey Press, 1982.

Gans, Herbert J. *The Levittowners: Ways of Life and Politics in a New Suburban Community*. New York: Pantheon, 1967.

—————. *More Equality*. New York: Pantheon, 1973.

—————. *The Urban Villagers*, updated and expanded ed. New York: Free Press, 1962, 1982.

—————. "Urbanism and Suburbanism as a Way of Life," in Arnold M. Rose, ed., *Human Behavior and Social Processes: An Interactionist Perspective*. London: Routledge & Kegan Paul, 1962, pp. 625–648.

Garfinkel, Harold. "Conditions of Successful Degradation Ceremonies," *American Journal of Sociology* 61 (March 1956): 420–424.

—————. *Studies in Ethnomethodology*. Englewood Cliffs, N.J.: Prentice-Hall, 1967.

Gecas, Victor. "The Self-Concept," in Ralph H. Turner and James F. Short, Jr., eds., *Annual Review of Sociology*, vol. 8. Palo Alto, Calif.: Annual Reviews, 1982, pp. 1–33.

Geertz, Clifford. *The Interpretation of Cultures*. New York: Basic Books, 1973.

Geller, William, and Kevin J. Karales. "Shootings of and by Chicago Police: Uncommon Crises. Part I: Shootings by Chicago Police," *Journal of Criminal Law and Criminology* 72 (Winter 1981): 1813–1866.

Gellhorn, Walter. "Individual Freedom and Governmental Restraints," in Lawrence M. Friedman and Stewart Macaulay, eds., *Law and the Behavioral Sciences*, 2nd ed. Indianapolis: Bobbs-Merrill, 1977, pp. 705–714.

Gerstel, Naomi R. "The Feasibility of Commuter Marriage," in Peter J. Stein, Judith Richman, and Natalie

Harmon, eds., *The Family: Functions, Conflicts, and Symbols*. Reading, Mass.: Addison-Wesley, 1977, pp. 357–367.

Geschwender, James A. *Racial Stratification in America*. Dubuque, Iowa: William C. Brown, 1978.

Gibbs, Jack P. *Crime, Punishment, and Deterrence*. New York: Elsevier, 1975.

Giddens, Anthony. *Capitalism and Modern Social Theory: An Analysis of the Writings of Marx, Durkheim and Max Weber*. Cambridge, Engl.: Cambridge University Press, 1971.

————. *Central Problems in Social Theory: Action, Structure and Contradiction in Social Analysis*. Berkeley, Calif.: University of California Press, 1979.

————. *New Rules of Sociological Method: A Positive Critique of Interpretative Sociologies*. New York: Basic Books, 1976.

Giele, Janet Zollinger. *Women and the Future: Changing Sex Roles in Modern America*. New York: Free Press, 1978.

Gillespie, Dair L. "Who Has the Power? The Marital Struggle," *Journal of Marriage and the Family* 33 (August 1971): 445–458.

Gintis, Herbert. "Education, Technology, and the Characteristics of Worker Productivity," *American Economic Review* 61 (May 1971): 266–279.

Gist, Noel P., and Sylvia Fleis Fava. *Urban Society*, 6th ed. New York: Crowell, 1974.

Gitlin, Todd. "Prime-Time Ideology: The Hegemonic Process in Television Entertainment," *Social Problems* 26 (February 1979): 251–266.

Glaser, Daniel. *Crime in Our Changing Society*. New York: Holt, Rinehart and Winston, 1978.

————. "Criminality Theories and Behavioral Images," *American Journal of Sociology* 61 (March 1956): 433–444.

Glass, Robert. "If It's a Sexist Term, You Won't Find It in Roget's Latest Edition," *The Boston Globe*, April 23, 1982, p. 25.

Glazer, Nathan and Daniel P. Moynihan. *Beyond the Melting Pot: The Negroes, Puerto Ricans, Jews, Italians, and Irish of New York*, 2nd rev. ed. Cambridge, Mass.: M.I.T. Press, 1970.

Glenn, Norval D., and Sara McLanahan. "Children and Marital Happiness: A Further Specification of the Relationship," *Journal of Marriage and the Family* 44 (February 1982): 63–72.

Glenn, Norval D., and Charles N. Weaver. "The Contribution of Marital Happiness to Global Happiness," *Journal of Marriage and the Family* 43 (February 1981): 161–168.

Glick, Paul C., and Arthur J. Norton. "Marrying, Divorcing, and Living Together in the U.S. Today," *Population Bulletin* 32 (October 1977): 3–39.

Glick, Paul C., and Graham B. Spanier. "Married and Unmarried Cohabitation in the United States," *Journal of Marriage and the Family* 42 (February 1980): 19–30.

Glock, Charles Y., and Robert N. Bellah, eds. *The New Religious Consciousness*. Berkeley, Calif.: University of California Press, 1976.

Glock, Charles Y., and Rodney Stark. *Religion and Society in Tension*. Chicago: Rand McNally, 1965.

Glock, Charles Y., and Robert Wuthnow. "Departures from Conventional Religion: The Nominally Religious, the Nonreligious, and the Alternatively Religious," in Robert Wuthnow, ed., *The Religious Dimension: New Directions in Quantitative Research*. New York: Academic Press, 1979, pp. 47–68.

Goering, John M. "The Emergence of Ethnic Interests: A Case of Serendipity," *Social Forces* 49 (March 1971): 379–384.

Goffman, Erving. *Asylums: Essays on the Social Situation of Mental Patients and Other Inmates*. Garden City, N.Y.: Doubleday, 1961.

————. *Encounters*. Indianapolis: Bobbs-Merrill, 1966.

————. *Gender Advertisements*. New York: Harper & Row, 1976.

————. *The Presentation of Self in Everyday Life*. Garden City, N.Y.: Doubleday, 1959.

————. *Relations in Public*. New York: Harper & Row, 1971.

Goldberg, Philip. "Are Women Prejudiced against Women?" *Trans-Action* 5 (April 1968): 28–30.

Goldberg, Susan, and Michael Lewis. "Play Behavior in the Year-Old Infant: Early Sex Differences," in Judith M. Bardwick, ed., *Readings on the Psychology of Women*. New York: Harper & Row, 1972, pp. 30–34.

Goldman, Ari L. "Couple in Jersey Are Accused of Trying to Trade in Their Baby for Used Sports Car," *The New York Times*, September 5, 1980, p. B1.

————. "Scores Rise at School after Nearby Subway Is Quieted," *The New York Times*, April 26, 1982, p. B4.

Goldman, Marshall I. "The Soviet Economic Problem: A System That Has Outlived Its Time," *The New York Times*, November 14, 1982, p. F2.

Goldsen, Rose K. *The Show and Tell Machine: How Television Works and Works You Over*. New York: Dial Press, 1977.

Goldstone, Jack A. "The Comparative and Historical Study of Revolutions," in Ralph H. Turner and James F. Short, Jr., eds., *Annual Review of Sociology*, vol. 8. Palo Alto, Calif.: Annual Reviews, 1982, pp. 187–207.

————. "The Weakness of Organization: A New Look at Gamson's *The Strategy of Social Protest*," *American Journal of Sociology* 85 (March 1980): 1017–1042.

Goldthorpe, John H., et al. *The Affluent Worker in the Class Structure*. London: Cambridge University Press, 1969.

Goleman, Daniel. "The 7,000 Faces of Dr. Ekman," *Psychology Today* 15 (February 1981): 42–49.

Goode, William J. *The Family*, 2nd ed. Englewood Cliffs, N.J.: Prentice-Hall, 1982.

————. "The Theoretical Importance of Love," *American Sociological Review* 24 (February 1959): 38–47.

——————. *World Revolution and Family Patterns*. New York: Free Press, 1963.

Goodman, Norman, and Kenneth A. Feldman. "Expectations, Ideals, and Reality: Youth Enters College," in Sigmund E. Dragastin and Glen H. Elder, eds., *Adolescence in the Life Cycle: Psychological Change and Social Context*. New York: Wiley, 1975, pp. 147–169.

Gordon, Hans. "Robert Michels and the Study of Political Parties," *British Journal of Political Science* 1 (April 1971): 155–172.

Gordon, Milton M. *Assimilation in American Life: The Role of Race, Religion and National Origins*. New York: Oxford University Press, 1964.

Gortmaker, Steven L. "Poverty and Infant Mortality in the United States," *American Sociological Review* 44 (April 1979): 280–297.

Gough, Kathleen. "Nayar: Central Kerala," in David M. Schneider and Kathleen Gough, eds., *Matrilineal Kinship*. Berkeley, Calif.: University of California Press, 1961, pp. 298–384.

——————. "The Origin of the Family," *Journal of Marriage and the Family* 33 (November 1971): 260–270.

Gouldner, Alvin W. "The Norm of Reciprocity: A Preliminary Statement," *American Sociological Review* 25 (April 1960): 161–178.

Gove, Walter R., ed. *The Labelling of Deviance: Evaluating a Perspective*, 2nd ed. Beverly Hills, Calif.: Sage Publications, 1980.

——————, and Jeannette F. Tudor. "Adult Sex Roles and Mental Illness," *American Journal of Sociology* 78 (January 1973): 812–835.

Gracey, Harry L. "Learning the Student Role: Kindergarten as Academic Boot Camp," in Dennis Wrong and Harry L. Gracey, eds., *Readings in Introductory Sociology*. New York: Macmillan, 1967, pp. 288–299.

Granovetter, Mark. "The Strength of Weak Ties," *American Journal of Sociology* 78 (May 1973): 1360–1380.

Greeley, Andrew M. *The American Catholic: A Social Portrait*. New York: Basic Books, 1977.

——————. *The Denominational Society*. Glenview, Ill.: Scott, Foresman, 1972.

——————. *Ethnicity, Denomination, and Inequality*. Beverly Hills, Calif.: Sage Publications, 1976.

——————. *Ethnicity in the United States: A Preliminary Reconnaissance*. New York: Wiley, 1974.

——————. *Why Can't They Be Like Us: Facts and Fallacies about Ethnic Differences and Group Conflicts in America*. New York: Institute of Human Relations Press, 1969.

——————, William C. McCready, and Kathleen McCourt. *Catholic Schools in a Declining Church*. Kansas City: Sheed & Ward, 1976.

Green, Charles S., III, and Richard G. Salem, eds. *Liberal Learning and Careers*. San Francisco: Jossey-Bass, 1981.

Greenberg, David F. "The Incapacitative Effect of Imprisonment: Some Estimates" *Law and Society Review* 9 (Summer 1975): 541–580.

Greenberg, Ellen F., and W. Robert Nay. "The Intergenerational Transmission of Marital Instability Reconsidered," *Journal of Marriage and the Family* 44 (May 1982): 335–347.

Greenberg, Joel. "Study Finds Widowers Die More Quickly than Widows," *The New York Times*, July 31, 1981, pp. A1, A10.

Gregory, Michael S., Anita Silvers, and Diane Sutch, eds. *Sociology and Human Nature*. San Francisco: Jossey-Bass, 1978.

Griffin, Susan. "Rape: The All-American Crime," *Ramparts* 10 (September 1971), 26–35.

Gross, Harriet Engel. "Dual-Career Couples Who Live Apart: Two Types," *Journal of Marriage and the Family* 42 (August 1980): 567–576.

Gruenberg, Barry. "The Happy Worker: An Analysis of Educational and Occupational Differences in Determinants of Job Satisfaction," *American Journal of Sociology* 86 (September 1980): 247–271.

Gulino, Denis G. "Study Says More Women Staying Childless," *The Boston Globe*, February 8, 1981, p. 12.

Gullahorn, J. T. "Distance and Friendship as Factors in the Gross Interaction Matrix," *Sociometry* 15 (February–May 1952): 123–134.

Gurr, Ted Robert. *Why Men Rebel*. Princeton, N.J.: Princeton University Press, 1970.

Gusfield, Joseph R. *Symbolic Crusade: Status Politics and the American Temperance Movement*. Urbana, Ill.: University of Illinois Press, 1963.

Gustavus, Susan O., and James R. Henley, Jr. "Correlates of Voluntary Childlessness in a Select Population," in Ellen Peck and Judith Senderowitz, eds., *Pronatalism: The Myth of Mom & Apple Pie*. New York: Crowell, 1974, pp. 284–294.

Guterbock, Thomas M. "Social Class and Voting Choices in Middletown," *Social Forces* 58 (June 1980): 1044–1056.

Hacker, Helen. "Women as a Minority Group," *Social Forces* 30 (October 1951): 60–69.

Hadden, Jeffrey K., and Charles E. Swann. *Prime Time Preachers: The Rising Power of Televangelism*. Reading, Mass.: Addison-Wesley, 1981.

Hadley, Arthur T. *The Empty Polling Booth*. Englewood Cliffs, N.J.: Prentice-Hall, 1978.

Hagan, John. "Extra-Legal Attributes and Criminal Sentencing: An Assessment of a Sociological Viewpoint," *Law and Society Review* 8 (Spring 1974): 357–383.

——————. "The Legislation of Crime and Delinquency: A Review of Theory, Method, and Research," *Law and Society Review* 14 (Spring 1980): 603–628.

Hall, Edward T. *Beyond Culture*. Garden City, N.Y.: Doubleday, 1981.

——————. *The Hidden Dimension*. Garden City, N.Y.: Doubleday, 1966.

——————. *The Silent Language*. Garden City, N.Y.: Doubleday, 1959.

Hall, Jerome. *Theft, Law and Society*, 2nd ed. Indianapolis: Bobbs-Merrill, 1952.

Hall, Robert H. "The Concept of Bureaucracy: An Empirical Assessment," *American Journal of Sociology* 69 (July 1963): 32–40.

Hamilton, V. Lee, and Laurence Rotkin. "Interpreting the Eighth Amendment: Perceived Seriousness of Crime and Severity of Punishment," in Hugo Adam Bedau and Chester M. Pierce, eds., *Capital Punishment in the United States.* New York: AMS Press, 1976, pp. 502–524.

Handel, Warren. *Ethnomethodology: How People Make Sense.* Englewood Cliffs, N.J.: Prentice-Hall, 1982.

Handler, Joel F. *Social Movements and the Legal System: A Theory of Law Reform and Social Change.* New York: Academic Press, 1978.

Haney, Craig, Curtis Banks, and Philip Zimbardo. "Interpersonal Dynamics in a Simulated Prison," *International Journal of Criminology and Penology* 1 (February 1973): 69–97.

Hannan, Michael T., and Nancy Brandon Tuma. "Income and Independence Effects on Marital Dissolution: Results from the Seattle and Denver Income-Maintenance Experiments," *American Journal of Sociology* 84 (November 1978): 611–633.

Hare, A. Paul. *Handbook of Small Group Research,* 2nd ed. New York: Free Press, 1976.

Harlow, Harry, and Margaret K. Harlow. "Social Deprivation in Monkeys," *Scientific American* 207 (November 1962): 137–147.

Harper, Dean, and Frederick Emmert. "Work Behavior in a Service Industry," *Social Forces* 41 (December 1963): 216–225.

Harris, Anthony R., and Gary D. Hill. "The Social Psychology of Deviance: Toward a Reconciliation with Social Structure," in Ralph H. Turner and James F. Short, Jr., eds., *Annual Review of Sociology,* vol. 8. Palo Alto, Calif.: Annual Reviews, 1982, pp. 161–186.

Harris, Chauncy D., and Edward L. Ullman. "The Nature of Cities," *Annals of the American Academy of Political and Social Science* 242 (November 1945): 7–17.

Harris, Louis, and Associates, Inc. *A Study of Attitudes toward Racial and Religious Minorities and toward Women.* New York: National Conference of Christians and Jews, 1978.

Harris, Marvin. *Cannibals and Kings: The Origins of Cultures.* New York: Random House, 1977.

————. *Cows, Pigs, Wars, and Witches: The Riddles of Culture.* New York: Random House, 1974.

————. *Cultural Materialism: The Struggle for a Science of Culture.* New York: Random House, 1979.

Harrison, Bennett. *Education, Training, and the Urban Ghetto.* Baltimore, Md.: Johns Hopkins University Press, 1972.

Harrison, James. "Warning: The Male Sex Role May Be Dangerous to Your Brain," *Journal of Social Issues* 34 (No. 1, 1978): 65–86.

Hauser, Robert M., and David L. Featherman. *The Process of Stratification: Trends and Analysis.* New York: Academic Press, 1977.

Heath, Dwight B. "Drinking Patterns of the Bolivian Camba," in David J. Pittman and Charles R. Snyder, eds., *Society, Culture, and Drinking Patterns.* New York: Wiley, 1962, pp. 22–36.

Hechter, Michael. *Internal Colonialism.* Berkeley, Calif.: University of California Press, 1975.

Heilbroner, Robert L. *Business Civilization in Decline.* New York: Norton, 1976.

————. "Does Capitalism Have a Future?" *The New York Times Magazine,* August 15, 1982, pp. 20–22, 38, 44, 52–60.

Heilman, Samuel C. "The Sociology of American Jewry: The Last Ten Years," in Ralph H. Turner and James F. Short, Jr., eds., *Annual Review of Sociology,* vol. 8. Palo Alto, Calif.: Annual Reviews, 1982, pp. 135–160.

Helmreich, William B. "Stereotype Truth," *The New York Times,* October 15, 1981, p. A27.

Henley, Nancy. "The Politics of Touch," in Phil Brown, ed., *Radical Psychology.* New York: Harper & Row, 1973.

Henretta, John C., and Richard T. Campbell. "Net Worth as an Aspect of Status," *American Journal of Sociology* 83 (March 1978): 1204–1223.

Henry, Diane. "'Divorcing' Parent from Child," *The New York Times,* February 24, 1981, p. C11.

Henshel, Richard L. "Sociology and Social Forecasting," in Ralph H. Turner and James F. Short, Jr., eds., *Annual Review of Sociology,* vol. 8. Palo Alto, Calif.: Annual Reviews, 1982, pp. 57–79.

Henslin, James M., and Mae A. Biggs. "Dramaturgical Desexualization: The Sociology of the Vaginal Examination," in James M. Henslin, ed., *Studies in the Sociology of Sex.* New York: Appleton-Century-Crofts, 1971, pp. 243–272.

Herberg, Will. *Protestant, Catholic, Jew,* rev. ed. Garden City, N.Y.: Doubleday, 1960.

Herbers, John. "As U.S. Aid to Cities Withers, Private Money Gets Bigger Role," *The New York Times,* August 14, 1982a, p. A18.

————. "A Demographer in Demand, Unlikely as It Seems," *The New York Times,* December 24, 1982b, p. A12.

————. "Florida's Generation Conflicts Seen as Hint of Future," *The New York Times,* June 13, 1981a, pp. 1, 12.

————. "Measuring Poverty: Perplexing Task Insures a Debate," *The New York Times,* April 15, 1982c, p. A29.

————. "New Mass Transit Data Rekindle Urban Issue," *The New York Times,* March 31, 1983, pp. A1, B14.

————. "Private School Rolls Fell by a Third from '64 to '79," *The New York Times,* October 4, 1982d, p. A14.

————. "Report to Carter on Cities: Scholars 1—Politicians 0," *The New York Times,* January 12, 1981b, p. A17.

————. "Rural Growth: Issue of 1980's," *The New York Times*, March 9, 1981c, p. B10.

————. "Urban-Rural Data: Confusing Census," *The New York Times*, December 12, 1981d, p. 10.

Hess, Robert D., and Judith V. Torney. *The Development of Political Attitudes in Children*. Hawthorne, N.Y.: Aldine, 1967.

Heumann, Leonard F. "Housing Needs and Housing Solutions: Changes in Perspective from 1968–1978," in Gary A. Tobin, ed., *The Changing Structure of the City: What Happened to the Urban Crisis*. Beverly Hills, Calif.: Sage Publications, 1979, pp. 233–260.

Hewitt, John P., and Randall Stokes. "Disclaimers," *American Sociological Review* 40 (February 1975): 1–11.

Hill, Reuben, and Joan Aldous. "Socialization for Marriage and Parenthood," in David A. Goslin, ed., *Handbook of Socialization Theory and Research*. Chicago: Rand McNally, pp. 885–950.

Hill, Robert B. "The Illusion of Black Progress: A Statement of the Facts," in Charles Vert Willie, ed., *Caste & Class Controversy*. Bayside, N.Y.: General Hall, 1979, pp. 76–79.

Hindelang, Michael J. *Criminal Victimization in Eight American Cities: A Descriptive Analysis of Common Theft and Assault*. Cambridge, Mass.: Ballinger, 1976.

————, Michael R. Gottfredson, and James Garofalo. *Victims of Personal Crime: An Empirical Foundation for a Theory of Personal Victimization*. Cambridge, Mass.: Ballinger, 1978.

Hindelang, Michael J., Travis Hirschi, and Joseph G. Weis. "Correlates of Delinquency: The Illusion of Discrepancy between Self-Report and Official Measures," *American Sociological Review* 44 (December 1979): 995–1014.

Hinds, Michael de Courcy. "Rising Concern on Consumer Issues Is Found in Harris Poll," *The New York Times*, February 17, 1983, p. A18.

Hirschi, Travis. *Causes of Delinquency*. Berkeley, Calif.: University of California Press, 1969.

Hodge, Robert W., Paul M. Siegel, and Peter H. Rossi. "Occupational Prestige in the United States: 1925-1963," in Reinhard Bendix and Seymour Martin Lipset, eds., *Class, Status, and Power*, 2nd ed. New York: Free Press, 1966, pp. 322–334.

Hodge, Robert W., Donald J. Treiman, and Peter H. Rossi. "A Comparative Study of Occupational Prestige," in Reinhard Bendix and Seymour Martin Lipset, eds., *Class, Status, and Power*, 2nd ed. New York: Free Press, 1966, pp. 309–321.

Hodges, Harold M., Jr. *Social Stratification: Class in America*. Cambridge, Mass.: Schenkman, 1964.

Hoffer, Eric. *The True Believer*. New York: Harper & Row, 1951.

Hoffman, Lois Wladis. "Changes in Family Roles, Socialization, and Sex Differences," *American Psychologist* 32 (August 1977): 644–657.

————, and Ivan Nye. *Working Mothers*. San Francisco: Jossey-Bass, 1974.

Hofstadter, Richard. *Social Darwinism in American Thought*. Boston: Beacon Press, 1955.

Hollander, Paul. *Soviet and American Society: A Comparison*. New York: Oxford University Press, 1973.

Hollingshead, August B., and Frederick C. Redlich. *Social Class and Mental Illness: A Community Study*. New York: Wiley, 1958.

Holmstrom, Lynda Lytle. *The Two-Career Family*. Cambridge, Mass.: Schenkman, 1972.

————, and Ann Wolbert Burgess. *The Victim of Rape: Institutional Reactions*. New Brunswick, N.J.: Transaction Books, 1983.

Homans, George C. "Bringing Men Back in," *American Sociological Review* 29 (December 1964): 809–818.

————. *Social Behavior: Its Elementary Forms*, rev. ed. New York: Harcourt Brace Jovanovich, 1974.

Hope, Keith. "A Liberal Theory of Prestige," *American Journal of Sociology* 87 (March 1982a): 1011–1031.

————. "Vertical and Nonvertical Class Mobility in Three Countries." *American Sociological Review* 47 (February 1982b): 99–113.

Horner, Matina. "Fail: Bright Women," *Psychology Today* 3 (November 1969): 36–38, 62.

Horning, Donald N. M. "Blue-Collar Theft: Conceptions of Property, Attitudes toward Pilfering, and Work Group Norms in a Modern Industrial Plant," in Erwin O. Smigel and H. Laurence Ross, eds., *Crimes against Bureaucracy*. New York: Van Nostrand Reinhold, 1970, pp. 46–64.

Howard, Ebenezer. *Garden Cities of To-morrow*. London: Faber and Faber, 1902.

Hoyt, Homer. *The Structure and Growth of Residential Neighborhoods in American Cities*. Washington, D.C.: U.S. Government Printing Office, 1939.

————. "The Structure of American Cities in the Post-War Era," *American Journal of Sociology* 48 (January 1943): 475–492.

Huber, Bettina J. *Embarking upon a Career with an Undergraduate Sociology Major*. Washington, D.C.: American Sociological Association, 1982.

Huber, Joan, and Glenna Spitze. "Considering Divorce: An Expansion of Becker's Theory of Marital Instability," *American Journal of Sociology* 86 (July 1980): 75–89.

Hughes, Everett C., Howard S. Becker, and Blanche Geer. "Student Culture and Academic Effort," in Nevitt Sanford, ed., *The American College: A Psychological and Social Interpretation of the Higher Learning*. New York: Wiley, 1962, pp. 515–530.

Humphreys, Laud. *Out of the Closets: The Sociology of Homosexual Liberation*. Englewood Cliffs, N.J.: Prentice-Hall, 1972.

————. *Tearoom Trade: Impersonal Sex in Public Places*, enlarged ed. Hawthorne, N.Y.: Aldine, 1975.

Hunt, Chester L., and Lewis Walker. *Ethnic Diversity*. Homewood, Ill.: Dorsey Press, 1974.

Hunt, Janet G., and Larry L. Hunt. "The Dualities of Careers and Families: New Integrations or New Polarizations?'' *Social Problems* 29 (June 1982): 499–510.

Hunter, Floyd. *Community Power Structure.* Chapel Hill, N.C.: University of North Carolina Press, 1953.

——————. *Community Power Succession: Atlanta's Policy-Makers Revisited.* Chapel Hill, N.C.: University of North Carolina Press, 1980.

Hunter, Marjorie. ''More Women Having First Child in 30's,'' *The New York Times,* May 28, 1982, p. B6.

Hurn, Christopher J. *The Limits and Possibilities of Schooling: An Introduction to the Sociology of Education.* Boston: Allyn and Bacon, 1978.

Hyman, Herbert H., and Charles R. Wright. *Education's Lasting Influence on Values.* Chicago: University of Chicago Press, 1979.

——————, and John Shelton Reed. *The Enduring Effects of Education.* Chicago: University of Chicago Press, 1975.

Inkeles, Alex, and Peter H. Rossi. ''National Comparisons of Occupational Prestige,'' *American Journal of Sociology* 61 (January 1956): 329–339.

Irwin, John. *The Felon.* Englewood Cliffs, N.J.: Prentice-Hall, 1970.

Isaac, Larry, and William R. Kelly. ''Racial Insurgency, the State, and Welfare Expansion: Local and National Level Evidence from the Postwar United States,'' *American Journal of Sociology* 86 (May 1981): 1348–1386.

Jackson, Philip W. *Life in Classrooms.* New York: Holt, Rinehart and Winston, 1968.

Jacobs, David. ''Inequality and Police Strength: Conflict Theory and Coercive Control in Metropolitan Areas,'' *American Sociological Review* 44 (December 1979): 913–925.

Jacobs, Jane. *The Death and Life of Great American Cities.* New York: Vintage, 1961.

——————. *The Question of Separatism: Quebec and the Struggle for Sovereignty.* New York: Random House, 1980.

Janowitz, Morris. ''The Study of Mass Communication,'' in David L. Sills, ed., *International Encyclopedia of the Social Sciences,* vol. 3. New York: Macmillan & Free Press, 1968, pp. 41–55.

Jaspan, Norman. *Mind Your Own Business.* Englewood Cliffs, N.J.: Prentice-Hall, 1974.

Jellinek, E. M. *The Disease Concept of Alcoholism.* New Brunswick, N.J.: Hillhouse Press, 1960.

Jencks, Christopher, et al. *Inequality: A Reassessment of the Effect of Family and Schooling in America.* New York: Basic Books, 1972.

——————, et al. *Who Gets Ahead? The Determinants of Economic Success in America.* New York: Basic Books, 1979.

Jenkins, J. Craig, and Charles Perrow. ''Insurgency of the Powerless: Farm Worker Movements (1946–1972),'' *American Sociological Review* 42 (April 1977): 249–268.

Jennings, M. Kent, and Richard G. Niemi. *The Political*

Character of Adolescence: The Influence of Families and Schools. Princeton, N.J.: Princeton University Press, 1974.

Jensen, Arthur R. *Bias in Mental Testing.* New York: Free Press, 1980.

——————. ''How Much Can We Boost IQ and Scholastic Achievement?'' *Harvard Educational Review* 39 (Winter 1969): 1–123.

——————. *Straight Talk about Mental Tests.* New York: Free Press, 1981.

Johnson, Barclay D. ''Durkheim's One Cause of Suicide,'' *American Sociological Review* 30 (December 1965), 875–886.

Johnson, Stephen D., and Joseph B. Tamney. ''The Christian Right and the 1980 Presidential Election,'' *Journal for the Scientific Study of Religion* 21 (June 1982): 123–131.

Johnstone, Ronald L. *Religion and Society in Interaction: The Sociology of Religion.* Englewood Cliffs, N.J.: Prentice-Hall, 1975.

Joint Committee on New York Drug Law Evaluation. *The Nation's Toughest Drug Law: Evaluating the New York Experience.* Washington, D.C.: U.S. Government Printing Office, 1978.

Josephy, Alvin M., Jr. *Now That the Buffalo's Gone: A Study of Today's American Indians.* New York: Alfred A. Knopf, 1982.

Judah, J. Stillson. *Hare Krishna and the Counterculture.* New York: Wiley, 1974.

Judson, Horace Freeland. *Heroin Addiction in Britain: What Americans Can Learn from the English Experience.* New York: Harcourt Brace Jovanovich, 1974.

Kalmuss, Debra S., and Murray A. Straus. ''Wife's Marital Dependency and Wife Abuse,'' *Journal of Marriage and the Family* 44 (May 1982): 277–286.

Kalven, Harry, Jr., and Hans Zeisel. *The American Jury.* Boston: Little, Brown, 1966.

Kammeyer, Kenneth C. W. ''The Dynamics of Population,'' in Harold Orel, ed., *Irish History and Culture: Aspects of a People's Heritage.* Lawrence, Kan.: University Press of Kansas, 1976, pp. 189–223.

Kanter, Rosabeth Moss. *Men and Women of the Corporation.* New York: Basic Books, 1977.

Karabel, Jerome. ''Community Colleges and Social Stratification: Submerged Class Conflict in American Higher Education,'' in Jerome Karabel and A. H. Halsey, eds., *Power and Ideology in Education.* New York: Oxford University Press, 1977, pp. 232–254.

Kasarda, John D., and Morris Janowitz. ''Community Attachment in Mass Society,'' *American Sociological Review* 39 (June 1974): 328–339.

Kassebaum, Gene, David A. Ward, and Daniel M. Wilner. *Prison Treatment and Parole Survival: An Empirical Assessment.* New York: Wiley, 1971.

Katz, Daniel, et al. *Bureaucratic Encounters.* Ann Arbor, Mich.: Survey Research Center Institute for Social Research, 1975.

Katz, Elihu, and Paul Lazarsfeld. *Personal Influence*. New York: Free Press, 1955.

Katz, Joseph, et al. *No Time for Youth: Growth and Constraint in College Students*. San Francisco: Jossey-Bass, 1968.

Katzell, Raymond A. "Changing Attitudes toward Work," in Clark Kerr and Jerome M. Rosow, eds., *Work in America: The Decade Ahead*. New York: Van Nostrand Reinhold, 1979, pp. 35–57.

Kaysen, Carl. "The Corporation: How Much Power? What Scope?" in Reinhard Bendix and Seymour Martin Lipset, eds., *Class, Status, and Power*, 2nd. ed. New York: Free Press, 1966, pp. 231–239.

Kee, Wan Fook, and Ann Sarah Lee. "Singapore," *Studies in Family Planning* 4 (April 1973): 117–118.

Keller, George C. "Jobless: 35%? No." *The New York Times*, January 28, 1981, p. A23.

Kelling, George L., et al. *The Kansas City Preventive Patrol Experiment*. Washington, D.C.: Police Foundation, 1974.

Kellner, Douglas. "TV, Ideology, and Emancipatory Popular Culture," *Socialist Review* 45 (May-June 1979): 13–53.

Kellogg, Frederic R. "From Retribution to 'Desert': The Evolution of Criminal Punishment," *Criminology* 15 (August 1977): 179–192.

Kelsen, Hans. *The Communist Theory of Law*. New York: Praeger, 1955.

Kemper, Theodore D. "Marxist and Functionalist Theories in the Study of Stratification: Common Elements That Lead to a Test," *Social Forces* 54 (March 1976): 559–578.

Kennedy, Ruby Jo Reeves. "Single or Triple Melting Pot? Intermarriage in New Haven, 1870–1950," *American Journal of Sociology* 58 (July 1952): 56–59.

—————. "Single or Triple Melting Pot? Intermarriage Trends in New Haven, 1870–1940," *American Journal of Sociology* 49 (January 1944): 331–339.

Kephart, William M. *The Family, Society, and the Individual*, 5th ed. Boston: Houghton Mifflin, 1981.

Kessler, Ronald C., and Paul D. Cleary. "Social Class and Psychological Distress," *American Sociological Review* 45 (June 1980): 463–478.

Kessler, Ronald C., and James A. McRae, Jr. "The Effect of Wives' Employment on the Mental Health of Married Men and Women," *American Sociological Review* 47 (April 1982): 216–227.

—————. "Trends in the Relationship between Sex and Psychological Distress, 1957–1976," *American Sociological Review* 46 (August 1981): 443–452.

Kessler, Suzanne J., and Wendy McKenna. *Gender: An Ethnomethodological Approach*. New York: Wiley, 1978.

Killian, Lewis M. *The Impossible Revolution? Black Power and the American Dream*. New York: Random House, 1968.

Kindleberger, Charles P. *American Business Abroad*. New Haven, Conn.: Yale University Press, 1969.

King, Nick. "State Grapples with Lawyer Incompetence," *The Boston Globe*, March 9, 1982, pp. 1, 28.

King, Seth S. "Even Miracles Have Their Price, Green Revolutionaries Discover," *The New York Times*, January 11, 1981, p. E24.

—————. "How U.S. Puts Together Unemployment Statistics," *The New York Times*, January 10, 1982, p. 48.

Kinsey, Alfred C., Wardell B. Pomeroy, Clyde E. Martin. *Sexual Behavior in the Human Male*. Philadelphia: Saunders, 1948.

—————, and Paul H. Gebhard. *Sexual Behavior in the Human Female*. Philadelphia: Saunders, 1953.

Kitagawa, Evelyn, and Philip M. Hauser. "Education Differentials in Mortality by Cause of Death, United States, 1960," *Demography* 5 (No. 1, 1968): 318–353.

Kitsuse, John I. "Societal Reaction to Deviant Behavior: Problems of Theory and Method," in Howard S. Becker, ed., *The Other Side: Perspectives on Deviance*. New York: Free Press, 1964, pp. 87–102.

Kittrie, Nicholas N. *The Right to Be Different: Deviance and Enforced Therapy*. Baltimore, Md.: Johns Hopkins University Press, 1971.

Klapp, Orin. *Collective Search for Identity*. New York: Holt, Rinehart and Winston, 1969.

Klemesrud, Judy. "Two-Career Couples: Employers Listening," *The New York Times*, June 27, 1981a, p. 21.

—————. "Voice of Authority Still Male," *The New York Times*, February 2, 1981b, p. A16.

Klemke, Lloyd W. "Does Apprehension for Shoplifting Amplify or Terminate Shoplifting Activity?" *Law and Society Review* 12 (Spring 1978): 391–403.

Kluckhohn, Clyde. *Mirror for Man*. New York: McGraw-Hill, 1949.

—————, and Dorothea Leighton. *The Navaho*. Cambridge, Mass.: Harvard University Press, 1946.

Kluegel, James R., and Eliot R. Smith. "Beliefs about Stratification," in Ralph H. Turner and James F. Short, Jr., eds., *Annual Review of Sociology*, vol. 7. Palo Alto, Calif.: Annual Reviews, 1981, pp. 29–56.

The Knapp Commission Report on Police Corruption. New York: George Braziller, 1973.

Kneeland, Douglas E. "Urbanization of Rural U.S. Called Peril to Farmland," *The New York Times*, June 16, 1981, p. B8.

Knox, Richard A. "An Aging Society Ponders the Future," *The Boston Globe*, December 8, 1982, pp. 1, 24.

Kohl, Jürgen. "Trends and Problems in Postwar Public Expenditure Development in Western Europe and North America," in Peter Flora and Arnold J. Heidenheimer, eds., *The Development of Welfare States in Europe and America*. New Brunswick, N.J.: Transaction Books, 1981, pp. 307–344.

Kohlberg, Lawrence. "A Cognitive-Developmental Analysis of Children's Sex-Role Concepts and Attitudes," in Eleanor Maccoby, ed., *The Development of Sex Differences*. Stanford, Calif.: Stanford University Press, 1966, pp. 82–173.

—————. *The Philosophy of Moral Development: Moral Stages and the Idea of Justice*. San Francisco: Harper & Row, 1981.

Kohn, Melvin L. "Bureaucratic Man: A Portrait and an Interpretation," *American Sociological Review* 36 (June 1971): 461–474.

——————. *Class and Conformity: A Study in Values.* Homewood, Ill.: Dorsey Press, 1969.

——————. "Occupational Structure and Alienation," *American Journal of Sociology* 82 (July 1976): 111–130.

——————. "Social Class and Parent-Child Relationships: An Interpretation," *American Journal of Sociology* 68 (January 1963): 471–480.

Komarovsky, Mirra. *Blue-Collar Marriage.* New York: Vintage, 1967.

——————. "College Women and Careers," *The New York Times*, January 23, 1981, p. A23.

——————. *Dilemmas of Masculinity: A Study of College Youth.* New York: Norton, 1976.

Kourvetaris, George A., and Betty A. Dobratz. "Political Power and Conventional Political Participation," in Ralph H. Turner and James F. Short, Jr., eds., *Annual Review of Sociology*, vol. 8. Palo Alto, Calif.: Annual Reviews, 1982, pp. 289–317.

Kowinski, William Severini. "Suburbia: End of the Golden Age," *The New York Times Magazine*, March 16, 1980, pp. 16–19, 106–109.

Kozol, Jonathan. *Prisoners of Silence: Breaking the Bonds of Adult Illiteracy in the United States.* New York: Continuum, 1980.

Kreps, Juanita M., and Joseph J. Spengler. "The Leisure Component of Economic Growth," in Howard R. Bowen and Garth L. Mangum, eds., *Automation and Economic Progress.* Englewood Cliffs, N.J.: Prentice-Hall, 1966, pp. 128–134.

Kübler-Ross, Elisabeth. *On Death and Dying.* New York: Macmillan, 1969.

Kurdek, Lawrence A., and Albert E. Siesky. "Children's Perception of Their Parents' Divorce," *Journal of Divorce* 3 (Summer 1980): 339–378.

Kurtz, Howard. "President's Economic Program Evaluated," *The Boston Globe*, September 14, 1982, p. 3.

Ladd, Everett C. *Where Have All The Voters Gone? The Fracturing of America's Political Parties.* New York: Norton, 1978.

Lane, Robert, Jr. "Catholic Charismatic Renewal," in Charles Y. Glock and Robert N. Bellah, eds., *The New Religious Consciousness.* Berkeley, Calif.: University of California Press, 1976, pp. 162–179.

Langbein, John H. "Torture & Plea Bargaining," *Public Interest* 58 (Winter 1980): 43–61.

Lanternari, Vittorio. *The Religions of the Oppressed: A Study of Modern Messianic Cults*, trans. by Lisa Sergio. London: MacGibbon & Kee, 1963.

LaPiere, Richard T. "Attitudes vs. Actions," *Social Forces* 13 (December 1934): 230–237.

Lasch, Christopher. *Haven in a Heartless World: The Family Besieged.* New York: Basic Books, 1979.

Laslett, Peter, ed. *Household and Family in Past Time.* Cambridge, Engl.: Cambridge University Press, 1972.

——————. *The World We Have Lost*, 2nd ed. New York: Scribner's, 1973.

Latané, Bibb, and John M. Darley. *The Unresponsive Bystander: Why Doesn't He Help?* New York: Appleton-Century-Crofts, 1970.

Law and Society Review 13 (Winter 1979). Special issue on plea bargaining.

Law Enforcement Assistance Administration. *Criminal Victimization in the United States 1973.* Washington, D.C.: U.S. Government Printing Office, 1976.

LeBon, Gustave. *The Crowd: A Study of the Popular Mind*, 2nd ed. Dunwoody, Ga.: Norman S. Berg, 1896, 1968.

Lee, Everett S. "A Theory of Migration," *Demography* 3 (No. 1, 1966): 47–57.

Lee, Gary R., and Eugene Ellithorpe. "Intergenerational Exchange and Subjective Well-being among the Elderly," *Journal of Marriage and the Family* 44 (February 1982): 217–224.

Lemert, Edwin M. *Instead of Court: Diversion in Juvenile Justice.* Washington, D.C.: U.S. Government Printing Office, 1971.

——————. "Isolation and Closure Theory of Naive Check Forgery," *Journal of Criminal Law, Criminology, and Police Science* 44 (September–October 1953): 293–307.

——————. *Social Pathology.* New York: McGraw-Hill, 1951.

Lenski, Gerhard. *Power and Privilege: A Theory of Social Stratification.* New York: McGraw-Hill, 1966.

——————. *The Religious Factor*, rev. ed. Garden City, N.Y.: Doubleday, 1963.

——————, and Jean Lenski. *Human Societies: An Introduction to Macrosociology*, 4th ed. New York: McGraw-Hill, 1982.

Lerner, Barbara. "American Education: How Are We Doing?" *Public Interest* 69 (Fall 1982): 59–82.

Lerner, Gerda. *The Majority Finds Its Past: Women in History.* New York: Oxford University Press, 1979.

Lesy, Michael. *Wisconsin Death Trip.* New York: Pantheon, 1973.

Levenson, Hanna, et al. "Are Women Still Prejudiced against Women? A Replication and Extension of Goldberg's Study," *Journal of Psychology* 89 (1975): 67–71.

Lever, Janet. "Sex Differences in the Complexity of Children's Play and Games," *American Sociological Review* 43 (August 1978): 471–483.

——————. "Sex Differences in the Games Children Play," *Social Problems* 23 (April 1976): 478–487.

Levine, James P. "The Potential for Crime Overreporting in Criminal Victimization Surveys," *Criminology* 14 (November 1976): 307–330.

——————. "Reply to Singer," *Criminology* 16 (May 1978): 103–107.

Levine, Steven B. "The Rise of American Boarding Schools and the Development of a National Upper Class," *Social Problems* 28 (October 1980): 63–94.

Levinson, Daniel J. *The Seasons of a Man's Life.* New York: Ballantine, 1978.

Levitan, Sar A., and Richard S. Belous. *What's Happening to the American Family?* Baltimore, Md.: Johns Hopkins University Press, 1981.

Lewin, Julius. *Studies in African Law*. Philadelphia: University of Pennsylvania Press, 1947.

Lewis, Anthony, et al. "If Inequality Is Inevitable, What Can Be Done About It?" *The New York Times*, January 3, 1982, p. E5.

Lewis, C. S. "The Humanitarian Theory of Punishment," in Stanley E. Grupp, ed., *Theories of Punishment*. Bloomington, Ind.: Indiana University Press, 1971, pp. 301–308.

Lewis, Edwin C. *Developing Women's Potential*. Ames, Iowa: Iowa State University Press, 1968.

Lewis, Robert A. "Emotional Intimacy among Men," *Journal of Social Issues* 34 (No. 1, 1978): 108–121.

Lewis-Beck, Michael S. "Some Economic Effects of Revolution: Models, Measurement, and the Cuban Evidence," *American Journal of Sociology* 84 (March 1979): 1127–1149.

Libby, Robert W. "Creative Singlehood as a Sexual Life Style: Beyond Marriage as a Rite of Passage," in Bernard L. Murstein, ed., *Exploring Intimate Life Styles*. New York: Springer, 1978, pp. 164–195.

Liebert, Robert M., and Robert A. Baron. "Some Immediate Effects of Televised Violence on Children's Behavior," *Developmental Psychology* 6 (1972): 469–475.

Liebow, Elliot. *Tally's Corner: A Study of Negro Streetcorner Men*. Boston: Little, Brown, 1967.

Lindblom, Charles E. *Politics and Markets: The World's Political-Economic Systems*. New York: Basic Books, 1977.

Linden, Fabian. "Demographics: The Boom Next Time," *The New York Times*, May 2, 1982, p. F2.

Lindenfeld, Frank, and Joyce Rothschild-Whitt, eds. *Workplace Democracy and Social Change*. Boston: Porter Sargent, 1982.

Lindert, Peter H. "Child Costs and Economic Development," in Richard A. Easterlin, ed., *Population and Economic Change in Developing Countries*. Chicago: University of Chicago Press, 1980, pp. 5–79.

Lindsey, Robert. "The New Asian Immigrants," *The New York Times Magazine*, May 9, 1982, pp. 22–42.

Lipset, Seymour Martin. *The First New Nation*. New York: Basic Books, 1963a.

————. *Political Man: The Social Bases of Politics*. Garden City, N.Y.: Doubleday, 1959.

————. "Predicting the Future of Post-Industrial Society," in Seymour Martin Lipset, ed., *The Third Century: American as a Post-Industrial Society*. Stanford, Calif.: Hoover Institution Press, 1979, pp. 1–35.

————. "Social Mobility and Equal Opportunity," *Public Interest* 29 (Fall 1972): 90–108.

————. "The Sources of the 'Radical Right,'" in Daniel Bell, ed., *The Radical Right*. Garden City, N.Y.: Doubleday, 1963b, pp. 307–371.

————. "Three Decades of the Radical Right: Coughlinites, McCarthyites, and Birchers," in Daniel Bell, ed., *The Radical Right*. Garden City, N.Y.: Doubleday, 1963c, pp. 373–446.

————, and Reinhard Bendix. *Social Mobility in Industrial Society*. Berkeley, Calif.: University of California Press, 1959.

Lipset, Seymour Martin, et al. 'The Psychology of Voting: An Analysis of Political Behavior," in Gardner Lindzey, ed., *Handbook of Social Psychology*, vol. 2. Reading, Mass.: Addison-Wesley, 1954, pp. 1124–1175.

Lipset, Seymour Martin, Martin A. Trow, and James S. Coleman. *Union Democracy*. Garden City, N.Y.: Doubleday, 1962.

Lipsky, Michael. "Protest as a Political Resource," *American Political Science Review* 62 (December 1968): 1144–1158.

Lipton, Douglas, Robert Martinson, and Judith Wilks. *The Effectiveness of Correctional Treatment Evaluation Studies: A Survey of Treatment*. New York: Praeger, 1975.

Little, Roger W. "Buddy Relations and Combat Performance," in Oscar Grusky and George A. Miller, eds., *The Sociology of Organizations: Basic Studies*. New York: Free Press, 1970, pp. 361–375.

Lo, Clarence Y. H. "Countermovements and Conservative Movements in the Contemporary U.S.," in Ralph H. Turner and James F. Short, Jr., eds., *Annual Review of Sociology*, vol. 8. Palo Alto, Calif.: Annual Reviews, 1982, pp. 107–134.

Lofland, John, and Rodney Stark. "Becoming a World Saver: A Theory of Conversion to a Deviant Perspective," *American Sociological Review* 30 (December 1965): 865–875.

Lohr, Steve. "The Company That Stopped Detroit," *The New York Times*, March 21, 1982a, pp. F1, F26.

————. "Tokyo Air Crash: Why Japanese Do Not Sue," *The New York Times*, March 10, 1982b, pp. A1, D5.

Lopreato, Joseph. *Peasants No More*. San Francisco: Chandler, 1967.

Lorence, Jon, and Jeylan T. Mortimer. "Work Experience and Political Orientation: A Panel Study," *Social Forces* 58 (December 1979): 651–676.

Lowney, Jeremiah, Robert W. Winslow, and Virginia Winslow. *Deviant Reality: Alternative World Views*, 2nd ed. Boston: Allyn and Bacon, 1981.

Luckenbill, David F. "Criminal Homicide as a Situated Transaction," *Social Problems* 25 (December 1977): 176–186.

Luckey, Eleanor Braun, and Joyce Koym Bain. "Children: A Factor in Marital Satisfaction," *Journal of Marriage and the Family* 32 (February 1970): 43–44.

Lurie, Alison. *The Language of Clothes*. New York: Random House, 1981.

Lyman, Stanford M. *Chinese Americans*. New York: Random House, 1974.

Lyon, Larry, et al. "The National Longitudinal Surveys Data for Labor Market Entry: Evaluating the Small Effects of Racial Discrimination and the Large Effects of Sexual Discrimination," *Social Problems* 29 (June 1982): 524–539.

Maccoby, Eleanor E. "The Development of Moral Values and Behavior in Childhood," in John A. Clausen, ed., *Socialization and Society*. Boston: Little, Brown, 1968, pp. 227–269.

————, and Carol Nagy Jacklin. *The Psychology of Sex Differences*. Stanford, Calif.: Stanford University Press, 1974.

Mackenzie, Gavin. *The Aristocracy of Labor: The Position of Skilled Craftsmen in the American Class Structure*. London: Cambridge University Press, 1973.

Macklin, Eleanor D. "Nonmarital Heterosexual Cohabitation," *Marriage and Family Review* 1 (No. 2, 1978): 1–12.

Maeroff, Gene I. "Community Colleges Defy Recession," *The New York Times*, August 22, 1982a, Section 12, pp. 1, 31.

————. "More States Testing Teachers in Response to School Critics," *The New York Times*, February 1, 1982b, pp. A1, A11.

————. "U.S. Tackling Crisis in Science and Math," *The New York Times*, August 10, 1982c, pp. C1, C7.

Malinowski, Bronislaw. *Magic, Science and Religion*. New York: Free Press, 1954.

————. "Parenthood, the Basis of Social Structure," in Rose Laub Coser, ed., *The Family: Its Structure and Functions*. New York: St. Martin's Press, 1964 (orig. publ. 1930), pp. 3–19.

Malthus, Thomas Robert. *Essay on the Principle of Population*, ed. by Gertrude Himmelfarb. New York: Modern Library, 1798, 1960.

Mancusi, Peter. "Tuning in to TV's Effect on Studies," *The Boston Globe*, November 10, 1980, pp. 1, 12.

Mandle, Joan D. *Women & Social Change in America*. Princeton, N.J.: Princeton Book Company, 1979.

Marger, Martin N. *Elites and Masses: An Introduction to Political Sociology*. New York: Van Nostrand, 1981.

Mariani, John. "Television Evangelism: Milking the Flock," *Saturday Review*, February 3, 1979, pp. 22–25.

Marsh, Dave. "The Once and Forever King," *Rolling Stone*, May 28, 1981, pp. 46–49.

Marshall, Victor W. *Last Chances: A Sociology of Aging and Dying*. Monterey, Calif.: Brooks/Cole, 1980.

Martin, Michael J., and James Walters. "Familial Correlates of Selected Types of Child Abuse and Neglect," *Journal of Marriage and the Family* 44 (May 1982): 267–276.

Marx, Gary T. "Religion: Opiate or Inspiration of Civil Rights Militancy among Negroes?" *American Sociological Review* 32 (February 1967): 64–72.

————, and James L. Wood. "Strands of Theory and Research in Collective Behavior," in Alex Inkeles, James Coleman, and Neil Smelser, eds., *Annual Review of Sociology*, vol. 1. Palo Alto, Calif.: Annual Reviews, 1975, pp. 363–428.

Marx, Karl. "Contribution to the Critique of Hegel's Philosophy of Right," in Karl Marx and Friedrich Engels, *On Religion*. New York: Schocken, 1844, 1964, pp. 41–58.

————. *Economic and Philosophic Manuscripts of 1844*.

Moscow: Foreign Languages Publishing House, 1844, 1961.

————, and Friedrich Engels. *The Communist Manifesto*. Middlesex, Engl.: Penguin, 1848, 1967.

Maslow, Abraham M. *Toward a Psychology of Being*, 2nd ed. Princeton, N.J.: Van Nostrand Reinhold, 1968.

Masnick, George, and Mary Jo Bane. *The Nation's Families: 1960–1990*. Cambridge, Mass.: Joint Center for Urban Studies of M.I.T. and Harvard University, 1980.

Massey, Douglas S. "Dimensions of the New Immigration to the United States and the Prospects for Assimilation," in Ralph H. Turner and James F. Short, Jr., eds., *Annual Review of Sociology*, vol. 7. Palo Alto, Calif.: Annual Reviews, 1981, pp. 57–85.

Matthiessen, Peter. *In the Spirit of Crazy Horse*. New York: Viking, 1983.

Matza, David, and Gresham M. Sykes. "Juvenile Delinquency and Subterranean Values," *American Sociological Review* 26 (October 1961): 712–719.

Maurer, David W. *Whiz Mob: A Correlation of the Technical Argot of Pickpockets with Their Behavior Pattern*. New Haven, Conn.: College & University Press, 1964.

Mauss, Marcel. *The Gift*. New York: Free Press, 1925, 1954.

Mazur, Allan, et al. "Physiological Aspects of Communication via Mutual Gaze," *American Journal of Sociology* 86 (July 1980): 50–74.

McCandless, Boyd R. "Childhood Socialization," in David A. Goslin, ed., *Handbook of Socialization Theory and Research*. Chicago: Rand McNally, 1969, pp. 791–819.

McCarthy, John D., and Mayer N. Zald. "Resource Mobilization and Social Movements," *American Journal of Sociology* 82 (May 1977): 1212–1241.

————. *The Trend of Social Movements in America: Professionalization and Resource Mobilization*. Morristown, N.J.: General Learning Press, 1973.

McCone, J.A., ed. *Violence in the City: An End or a Beginning?* Los Angeles: California Governor's Commission on the Los Angeles Riots, 1965.

McEwen, C. A. "Continuities in the Study of Total and Nontotal Institutions," in Alex Inkeles, Neil J. Smelser, and Ralph H. Turner, eds., *Annual Review of Sociology*, vol. 6. Palo Alto, Calif.: Annual Reviews, 1980, pp. 143–185.

McGaw, Douglas B. "Commitment and Religious Community: A Comparison of a Charismatic and a Mainline Congregation," *Journal for the Scientific Study of Religion* 18 (June 1979): 146–163.

McGowan, William. "Iliterasee att Wurk," *The New York Times*, August 19, 1982, p. A27.

McGrath, Joseph E. "Small Group Research," *American Behavioral Scientist* 21 (May–June 1978): 651–671.

McKeown, Thomas, and R. G. Brown. "Medical Evidence Related to English Population Changes in the Eighteenth Century," *Population Studies* 9 (November 1955): 199–141.

McKeown, Thomas, and R. G. Record. "Reasons for the Decline of Mortality in England and Wales during the

19th Century," *Population Studies* 16 (November 1962): 94–122.

McLaughlin, Loretta. "China's Success in Controlling Population Raises Questions about Repressive Policies," *The Boston Globe*, March 14, 1982, p. 48.

McNamara, Eileen, and Hank Klibanoff. "Condo Evictions and Fire," *The Boston Globe*, March 31, 1981, pp. 17, 20.

McPartland, James M., and Edward L. McDill. "Control and Differentiation in the Structure of American Education," *Sociology of Education* 55 (April–June 1982): 77–88.

McRoberts, Hugh A., and Kevin Selbee. "Trends in Occupational Mobility in Canada and the United States: A Comparison," *American Sociological Review* 46 (August 1981): 406–421.

Mead, George Herbert. *Mind, Self, and Society*, ed. by Charles W. Morris. Chicago: University of Chicago Press, 1934.

Mead, Margaret. *Sex and Temperament in Three Primitive Societies*. New York: Morrow, 1935, 1963.

Meadows, Donella H., Dennis L. Meadows, Jørgen Randers, and William W. Behrens, III. *The Limits to Growth: A Report for the Club of Rome's Project on the Predicament of Mankind*, 2nd ed. New York: Universe Books, 1974.

Medalia, Nahum Z., and Otto N. Larsen. "Diffusion and Belief in a Collective Delusion: The Seattle Windshield Pitting Epidemic," *American Sociological Review* 23 (April 1958). 180–186.

Mehegan, David. "The Squeeze on the Dollar," *The Boston Globe Magazine*, May 17, 1981, pp. 12–13, 26–43.

Melman, Seymour. *Pentagon Capitalism: The Political Economy of War*. New York: McGraw-Hill, 1970.

Melton, J. Gordon. *Encyclopedia of American Religions*. Gaithersburg, Md.: Consortium Books, 1979.

Melville, Keith. *Marriage and Family Today*. New York: Random House, 1980.

Mercy, James A., and Lala Carr Steelman. "Familial Influence on the Intellectual Attainment of Children," *American Sociological Review* 47 (August 1982): 532–542.

Merton, Robert K. *Social Theory and Social Structure*, 1968 enlarged ed. New York: Free Press, 1968.

Meyer, John W., John Boli-Bennett, and Christopher Chase-Dunn. "Convergence and Divergence in Development," in Alex Inkeles, James Coleman, and Neil Smelser, eds., *Annual Review of Sociology*, vol. 1. Palo Alto, Calif.: Annual Reviews, 1975, pp. 223–246.

Meyers, Jerome K., and Lee L. Bean. *A Decade Later: A Follow-up of Social Class and Mental Illness*. New York: Wiley, 1968.

Michels, Robert. *Political Parties*, trans. by Eden and Cedar Paul. New York: Collier, 1915, 1962.

Miles, Betty. *Channeling Children: Sex Stereotyping in Prime-Time TV*. Princeton, N.J.: Women on Words and Images, 1975.

Milgram, Stanley. "The Experience of Living in Cities: A Psychological Analysis," *Science* 167 (March 13, 1970): 1461–1468.

————. *Obedience to Authority: An Experimental View*. New York: Harper & Row, 1973.

————, and Hans Toch. "Collective Behavior: Crowds and Social Movements," in Gardner Lindzey and Elliot Aronson, eds., *Handbook of Social Psychology*, 2nd. ed., Vol. 4. Boston: Addison-Wesley, 1969, pp. 507–610.

Miliband, Ralph. *Marxism and Politics*. New York: Oxford University Press, 1977.

————. *The State in Capitalist Society*. New York: Basic Books, 1969.

Miller, Abraham H., Louis H. Bolce, and Mark Halligan. "The J-Curve Theory and the Black Urban Riots: An Empirical Test of Progressive Relative Deprivation Theory," *American Political Science Review* 71 (September 1977): 964–982.

Miller, Joanne, and Howard H. Garrison. "Sex Roles: The Division of Labor at Home and in the Workplace," in Ralph H. Turner and James F. Short, Jr., eds., *Annual Review of Sociology*, vol. 8. Palo Alto, Calif.: Annual Reviews, 1982, pp. 237–262.

Miller, Walter B. "Lower Class Culture as a Generating Milieu of Gang Delinquency," *Journal of Social Issues* 14 (No. 3, 1958): 5–19.

Mills, C. Wright. *The Power Elite*. New York: Oxford University Press, 1956.

————. *The Sociological Imagination*. New York: Oxford University Press, 1959.

Mills, Theodore. *The Sociology of Small Groups*. Englewood Cliffs, N.J.: Prentice-Hall, 1967.

Mintz, Beth, and Michael Schwartz. "The Structure of Intercorporate Unity in American Business," *Social Problems* 29 (December 1981): 87–103.

Money, John. "The 'Givens' from a Different Point of View: Lessons from Intersexuality for a Theory of Gender Identity," in Evelyn K. Oremland and Jerome D. Oremland, eds., *The Sexual and Gender Development of Young Children: The Role of the Educator*. Cambridge, Mass.: Ballinger, 1979, pp. 27–33.

————. *Love and Love Sickness: The Science of Sex, Gender Difference, and Pair-Bonding*. Baltimore, Md.: Johns Hopkins University Press, 1980.

————, and Anke Ehrhardt. *Man and Woman, Boy and Girl*. Baltimore, Md.: Johns Hopkins University Press, 1972.

Money, John, and Patricia Tucker. *Sexual Signatures: On Being a Man or a Woman*. Boston: Little, Brown, 1975.

Montero, Darrel. "The Japanese Americans: Changing Patterns of Assimilation over Three Generations," *American Sociological Review* 46 (December 1981): 829–839.

Montgomery, Paul L. "Major Faiths in City Undertaking First United Effort against Cults," *The New York Times*, August 1, 1982, pp. 1, 33.

Moore, Barrington, Jr. *Injustice: The Social Bases of Obedience and Revolt*. White Plains, N.Y.: M. E. Sharpe, 1978.

Moore, Gwen. "The Structure of a National Elite Network," *American Sociological Review* 44 (October 1979): 673–692.

Moore, Wilbert E. "Occupational Socialization," in David A. Goslin, ed., *Handbook of Socialization Theory and Research*. Chicago: Rand McNally, 1969, pp. 861–883.

—————. *Social Change*, 2nd ed. Englewood Cliffs, N.J.: Prentice-Hall, 1974.

Morris, R. N. *Urban Sociology*. New York: Praeger, 1968.

Morse, Nancy, and Robert Weiss. "The Function and Meaning of Work and the Job," *American Sociological Review* 20 (April 1955): 191–198.

Mortimer, Jeylan T., and Roberta G. Simmons. "Adult Socialization," in Ralph H. Turner, James Coleman, and Renée C. Fox, eds., *Annual Review of Sociology*, vol. 4. Palo Alto, Calif.: Annual Reviews, 1978, pp. 421–454.

Morton, Henry W. "Soviet Cities: A Review Essay," *Comparative Urban Research* 5 (No. 1, 1977): 40–45.

Moskos, Clark C., Jr. "The American Combat Soldier in Vietnam," *Journal of Social Issues* 31 (No. 4, 1975): 25–37.

Moynihan, Daniel Patrick. *The Negro Family: The Case for National Action*. Washington, D.C.: U.S. Department of Labor, 1965.

Mueller, Charles W., and Hallowel Pope. "Marital Instability: A Study of Its Transmission between Generations," *Journal of Marriage and the Family* 39 (February 1977): 83–92.

Murdock, George P. *Culture and Society*. Pittsburgh, Pa.: University of Pittsburgh Press, 1965.

—————. *Ethnographic Atlas*. Pittsburgh, Pa.: University of Pittsburgh Press, 1967.

—————. *Social Structure*. New York: Macmillan, 1949.

Murstein, Bernard I. "Stimulus-Value-Role: A Theory of Marital Choice," *Journal of Marriage and the Family* 32 (August 1970): 465–481.

Muson, Howard. "Teenage Violence and the Telly," *Psychology Today* 11 (March 1978): 50–54.

Muth, Richard F. *Cities and Housing: The Spatial Pattern of Urban Residential Land Use*. Chicago: University of Chicago Press, 1969.

Myrdal, Gunnar. *An American Dilemma: The Negro Problem and Modern Democracy*. New York, Harper & Row, 1944, 1962.

Nader, Ralph. *Unsafe at Any Speed: The Designed-in Dangers of the American Automobile*. New York: Grossman, 1965.

Nam, Charles B. "Sociology and Demography: Perspectives on Population," *Social Forces* 61 (December 1982): 359–373.

National Advisory Commission on Civil Disorders. *Report*. New York: Bantam, 1968.

National Advisory Council on Economic Opportunity. *Twelfth Report: Critical Choices for the 80's*. Washington, D.C.: U.S. Government Printing Office, 1980.

The National Commission on the Causes and Prevention of Violence. *To Insure Justice, To Establish Domestic Tranquility*. Washington, D.C.: U.S. Government Printing Office, 1970.

National NOW Times. June–July 1982, p. 3.

Neubauer, David W. *Criminal Justice in Middle America*. Morristown, N.J.: General Learning Press, 1974.

Neugarten, Bernice L. "Adult Personality: A Developmental View," *Human Development* 9 (1966): 61–73.

—————. "Patterns of Aging: Past, Present, and Future," *Social Service Review* 47 (December 1973), 571–580.

[*The New York Times*.] "B.A. Degree Worth $329,000 in Earnings," *The New York Times*, March 14, 1983, p. A12.

—————. "Black Teen-Age Job Plight: Lack of Skill and Hope," *The New York Times*, April 19, 1983, p. A14.

—————. "Census Did Not Count 1.3 Million U.S. Blacks," *The New York Times*, April 5, 1982, p. A18.

—————. "Controls on Guns Supported in Poll," *The New York Times*, June 20, 1983, p. A16.

—————. "Data on Protestant Churches Show Losses May Be Ending," *The New York Times*, June 15, 1982, p. A8.

—————. "Disturbed Residents of Poisoned Suburb Are Deeply Divided," *The New York Times*, January 1, 1983, pp. 1, 5.

—————. "Infant Mortality Highest in Capital," *The New York Times*, December 13, 1981, p. 37.

—————. "Martial Arts Fever Sweeps China off Its Feet," *The New York Times*, September 12, 1982, p. 10.

—————. "Nine Killed in Zaire in Crush to Join Pope in Mass," *The New York Times*, May 5, 1980, pp. A1, A7.

—————. "Survey Finds 'Bleak' Outlook for Cities Losing Federal Aid," *The New York Times*, January 3, 1983, p. A15.

—————. "That Costly White-Collar Mob," *The New York Times*, January 2, 1977, Section 3, p. 15.

—————. "Women Are Increasing Lead in Enrollment on Campuses," *The New York Times*, March 21, 1983, p. A13.

Newcomb, Paul R. "Cohabitation in America: An Assessment of Consequences," *Journal of Marriage and the Family* 41 (August 1979): 597–603.

Newcomb, Theodore M. *Persistence and Change: Bennington and Its Students after 25 Years*. New York: Wiley, 1967.

—————. "Persistence and Regression of Changed Attitudes: Long-Range Studies," *Journal of Social Issues* 19 (No. 4, 1963): 3–14.

Newman, Oscar. *Defensible Space: Crime Prevention through Environmental Design*. New York: Macmillan, 1972.

Newman, Peter. "Malaria and Mortality," *Journal of the American Statistical Association* 72 (June 1977): 257–263.

Newport, Frank. "The Religious Switcher in the United States," *American Sociological Review* 44 (August 1979): 528–552.

Nie, Norman H., Sidney Verba, and John R. Petrocik. *The Changing American Voter*. Cambridge, Mass.: Harvard University Press, 1976.

Niebuhr, H. Richard. *The Social Sources of Denominationalism*. New York: Meridian, 1929, 1957.

Niemi, Richard G., and B. I. Sobieszek. "Political Socialization," in Alex Inkeles, James Coleman, and Neil Smelser, eds., *Annual Review of Sociology*, vol. 3. Palo Alto, Calif.: Annual Reviews, 1977, pp. 209–233.

Nimkoff, M. F., and Russell Middleton. "Types of Family and Types of Economy," *American Journal of Sociology* 66 (November 1960): 215–225.

Nisbet, Robert. *History of the Idea of Progress*. New York: Basic Books, 1979.

——————, and Robert G. Perrin. *The Social Bond*, 2nd ed. New York: Alfred A. Knopf, 1977.

Nolan, William, and David W. Swift. "The Community College," in David W. Swift, ed., *American Education: A Sociological View*. Boston: Houghton Mifflin, 1976, pp. 118–124.

Norman, Michael. "The New Extended Family: Divorce Reshapes the American Household," *The New York Times Magazine*, November 23, 1980, pp. 27–29, 44–54, 147, 162–173.

North, David S., and Marion F. Houstoun. *The Characteristics and Role of Illegal Aliens in the U.S. Labor Market: An Exploratory Study*. Washington, D.C.: Linton and Company, Inc., 1976.

Nortman, Dorothy. "Changing Contraceptive Patterns: A Global Perspective," *Population Bulletin* 32 (August 1977): 1–37.

Nossiter, Bernard D. "U.N. Gets a Report on African Slaves," *The New York Times*, August 26, 1981, p. A11.

Novak, Michael. *The Spirit of Democratic Capitalism*. New York: Simon and Schuster, 1982.

Oberschall, Anthony. "Theories of Social Conflict," in Ralph H. Turner, James Coleman, and Renée C. Fox, eds., *Annual Review of Sociology*, vol. 4. Palo Alto, Calif.: Annual Reviews, 1978, pp. 291–315.

O'Connor, James. *The Fiscal Crisis of the State*. New York: St. Martin's Press, 1973.

Ogburn, William F. *On Culture and Social Change: Selected Papers*, ed. and with an intro. by Otis Dudley Duncan. Chicago: University of Chicago Press, 1964.

——————. *Social Change*. New York: Viking, 1922, 1950.

O'Reilly, Jane. "The Death and Life of the E.R.A.," *The Boston Globe Magazine*, July 18, 1982, pp. 8, 18–23.

Oreskes, Michael. "Retraining of Workers Becomes a Priority," *The New York Times*, Section 12, October 17, 1982, p. 5.

Orum, Anthony M. *Introduction to Political Sociology: The Social Anatomy of the Body Politic*, 2nd ed. Englewood Cliffs, N. J.: Prentice-Hall, 1983.

Ostrow, Ronald J. "Same Cases, but Different Sentences in Study of U.S. Judges," *The Boston Globe*, March 17, 1982, p. 9.

Owens, David M., and Murray A. Straus. "The Social Structure of Violence in Childhood and Approval of Violence as an Adult," *Aggressive Behavior* 1 (1975): 193–211.

Packer, Herbert L. *The Limits of the Criminal Sanction*. Stanford, Calif.: Stanford University Press, 1968.

Paige, Jeffery M. *Agrarian Revolution: Social Movements and Export Agriculture in the Underdeveloped World*. New York: Free Press, 1975.

Palen, J. John. *The Urban World*. New York: McGraw-Hill, 1975.

Park, Robert E., Ernest W. Burgess, and Roderick D. McKenzie, eds. *The City*. Chicago: University of Chicago Press, 1925.

Parke, Ross D. "The Father of the Child," *The Sciences* 19 (April 1979): 12–15.

Parkinson, C. Northcote. *Parkinson's Law*. Boston: Houghton Mifflin, 1957.

Parsons, Talcott. *Essays on Sociological Theory*. New York: Free Press, 1954.

——————. *The Evolution of Societies*. Englewood Cliffs, N. J.: Prentice-Hall, 1977.

——————. *The Social System*. New York: Free Press, 1951.

——————. *Societies: Evolutionary and Comparative Perspectives*. Englewood Cliffs, N. J.: Prentice-Hall, 1966.

——————. *The System of Modern Societies*. Englewood Cliffs, N.J.: Prentice-Hall, 1971.

——————, and Robert F. Bales. *Family Socialization and Interaction Process*. New York: Free Press, 1955.

Patrick, Ted. *Let Our Children Go*. New York: Ballantine, 1976.

Pavalko, Ronald M., ed. *Sociology of Education: A Book of Readings*, 2nd ed. Itasca, Ill.: F. E. Peacock, 1976.

Payne, Charles. "On the Declining—and Increasing—Significance of Race," in Charles Vert Willie, ed., *Caste & Class Controversy*. Bayside, N. Y.: General Hall, 1979.

Pear, Robert. "Blacks Moving to Suburbs, but Significance Is Disputed," *The New York Times*, August 15, 1982a, p. 18.

——————. "Census Says 3 Plans Would Raise Many above Poverty Line," *The New York Times*, April 15, 1982b, pp. A1, A28.

——————. "Federal Study Finds Immigrants Are Not a Burden on Taxpayers," *The New York Times*, September 22, 1980, pp. A1, A15.

——————. "Population Drop Predicted in U. S.," *The New York Times*, November 9, 1982c, p. A19.

Pearce, Diana. "The Feminization of Poverty—Women, Work, and Welfare." Unpublished Manuscript, Department of Sociology, University of Illinois, Chicago Circle, 1978.

——————. "Gatekeepers and Homeseekers: Institutional Factors in Racial Steering," *Social Problems* 26 (February 1979): 325–342.

Peattie, Lisa, and Jose A. Aldrete-Haas. "'Marginal' Settlements in Developing Countries: Research, Advocacy of Policy, and Evolution of Programs," in Ralph H. Turner and James F. Short, Jr., eds., *Annual Review of Sociology,* vol. 7. Palo Alto, Calif.: Annual Reviews, 1981, pp. 157–175.

Pelto, Pertti J., and Ludger Müller-Wille. "Snowmobiles: Technological Revolution in the Arctic," in H. Russell Bernard and Pertti J. Pelto, eds., *Technology and Social Change.* New York: Macmillan, 1972, pp. 166–199.

Pendleton, Brian J., Margaret M. Poloma, and T. Neal Garland. "Scales for Investigation of the Dual Career Family," *Journal of Marriage and the Family* 42 (May 1980): 269–275.

Perrucci, Robert. *Circle of Madness: On Being Insane and Institutionalized in America.* Englewood Cliffs, N.J.: Prentice-Hall, 1974.

Persell, Caroline Hodges. *Education and Inequality: The Roots and Results of Stratification in America's Schools.* New York: Free Press, 1977.

Petersen, William. "International Migration," in Ralph H. Turner, James Coleman, and Renée C. Fox, eds., *Annual Review of Sociology,* vol. 4. Palo Alto, Calif.: Annual Reviews, 1978, pp. 533–575.

————. "The Social Roots of Hunger and Overpopulation," *Public Interest* 68 (Summer 1982): 37–52.

Pettee, George Sawyer. *The Process of Revolution.* New York: Harper & Row, 1938.

Pettigrew, Thomas F., and Robert L. Green. "School Desegregation in Large Cities: A Critique of the Coleman 'White Flight' Thesis," *Harvard Educational Review* 46 (February 1976): 1–53.

Piaget, Jean. *The Moral Judgment of the Child.* New York: Free Press, 1932, 1948.

————, and Bärbel Inhelder. *The Psychology of the Child.* New York: Basic Books, 1969.

Piliavin, Irving, and Scott Briar. "Police Encounters with Juveniles," *American Journal of Sociology* 70 (September 1964): 206–214.

Pincus, Fred L. "The False Promises of Community Colleges: Class Conflict and Vocational Education," *Harvard Educational Review* 50 (August 1980): 332–361.

Pines, Maya. "Recession Is Linked to Far-Reaching Psychological Harm," *The New York Times,* April 6, 1982, pp. C1, C2.

Piven, Frances Fox, and Richard A. Cloward. *The New Class War: Reagan's Attack on the Welfare State and Its Consequences.* New York: Pantheon, 1982.

————. *Poor People's Movements: Why They Succeed, How They Fail.* New York: Pantheon, 1977.

Platt, Anthony M. *The Child Savers: The Invention of Delinquency,* 2nd ed. Chicago: University of Chicago Press, 1977.

Pleck, Joseph H. "Men's Power with Women, Other Men, and Society: A Men's Movement's Analysis," in Elizabeth H. Pleck and Joseph H. Pleck, eds., *The Amer-*

ican Man. Englewood Cliffs, N.J.: Prentice-Hall, 1980, pp. 417–433.

————, and Robert Brannon, eds. "Male Roles and the Male Experience," *Journal of Social Issues* 34 (No. 1, 1978).

Polsby, Nelson W. *Community Power and Political Theory,* 2nd ed. New Haven, Conn.: Yale University Press, 1980.

Pomper, Gerald M. "The Decline of the Party in American Elections," *Political Science Quarterly* 92 (Spring 1977): 21–41.

————, ed. *Party Renewal in America: Theory and Practice.* New York: Praeger, 1980.

————, with Susan S. Lederman. *Elections in America: Control and Influence in Democratic Politics,* 2nd ed. New York: Longman, 1980.

Pool, Ithiel de Sola, ed. *The Social Impact of the Telephone.* Cambridge, Mass.: M.I.T. Press, 1977.

Pope, Hallowel, and Charles W. Mueller. "The Intergenerational Transmission of Marital Instability: Comparisons by Race and Sex," *Journal of Social Issues* 32 (No. 1, 1976): 49–66.

Population Reference Bureau. *Interchange* 7, January 1978.

Porter, Judith R., and Robert E. Washington. "Black Identity and Self-Esteem: A Review of Studies of Black Self-Concept, 1968–1978," in Alex Inkeles, James Coleman, and Ralph H. Turner, eds., *Annual Review of Sociology,* vol. 5. Palo Alto, Calif.: Annual Reviews, 1979, pp. 53–74.

Postman, Neil. *The Disappearance of Childhood.* New York: Delacorte, 1982.

The President's Commission for a National Agenda for the Eighties. *A National Agenda for the Eighties.* Washington, D.C.: U.S. Government Printing Office, 1980a.

————. *The Quality of American Life in the Eighties.* Washington, D.C.: U.S. Government Printing Office, 1980b.

The President's Commission on Law Enforcement and the Administration of Justice. *The Challenge of Crime in a Free Society.* Washington, D.C.: U.S. Government Printing Office, 1967.

Presser, Harriet B., and Linda S. Salsberg. "Public Assistance and Early Family Formation: Is There a Pro-Natalist Effect?" *Social Problems* 23 (December 1975): 226–241.

Preston, Marilynn. "A Disturbing Study of Kids and TV," *The Boston Globe,* June 7, 1981, pp. B1, B4.

Preston, Samuel H. "Causes and Consequences of Mortality Declines in Less Developed Countries during the Twentieth Century," in Richard A. Easterlin, eds., *Population and Economic Change in Developing Countries.* Chicago: University of Chicago Press, 1980, pp. 289–360.

————. "Mortality Trends," in Alex Inkeles, James Coleman, and Neil Smelser, eds., *Annual Review of Sociology,* vol. 3. Palo Alto, Calif.: Annual Reviews, 1977, pp. 163–178.

Prial, Frank J. "More Women Work at Traditional Male Jobs," *The New York Times*, November 11, 1982, pp. A1, C20.

Pynoos, Jon, Robert Schafer, and Chester W. Hartman. *Housing Urban America*, 2nd ed. Hawthorne, N. Y.: Aldine, 1980.

Quarantelli, E. L., and Russell R. Dynes. "Response to Social Crisis and Disaster," in Alex Inkeles, James Coleman, and Neil Smelser, eds., *Annual Review of Sociology*, vol 3. Palo Alto, Calif.: Annual Reviews, 1977, pp. 23–49.

Quinley, Harold E., and Charles Y. Glock. *Anti-Semitism in America*. New York: Free Press, 1979.

Quinn, Robert P., and Graham L. Staines. *The 1977 Quality of Employment Survey*. Ann Arbor, Mich.: Institute for Social Research, 1979.

Quinney, Richard. *Criminology: Analysis and Critique of Crime in America*, 2nd ed. Boston: Little, Brown, 1979.

Rabin, A. I. "The Sexes: Ideology and Reality in the Israeli Kibbutz," in Georgene H. Seward and Robert C. Williamson, eds., *Sex Roles in Changing Society*. New York: Random House, 1970, pp. 285–307.

Radelet, Louis A. *The Police and the Community*. Beverly Hills, Calif.: Glencoe Press, 1973.

Radzinowicz, Sir Leon, and Joan King. *The Growth of Crime: The International Experience*. New York: Basic Books, 1977.

Rainwater, Lee. "Fear and the House-as-Haven in the Lower Classes," in Robert Gutman, ed., *People and Buildings*. New York: Basic Books, 1972, pp. 299–313.

————, and William L. Yancey. *The Moynihan Report and the Politics of Controversy*. Cambridge, Mass.: M.I.T. Press, 1967.

Rapoport, Rhona, and Robert Rapoport. *Dual-Career Families Re-examined*. New York: Harper & Row, 1976.

Raskin, A. H. "The Air Strike Is Ominous for Labor," *The New York Times*, August 16, 1981, pp. F1, F24.

Razzell, E. "Population Change in Eighteenth Century England: A Reappraisal," in Michael Drake, ed., *Population in Industrialization*. London: Methuen, 1969, pp. 128–156.

Read, Piers Paul. *Alive: The Story of the Andes Survivors*. Philadelphia: Lippincott, 1974.

Redfield, Robert. *The Folk Culture of Yucatan*. Chicago: University of Chicago Press, 1941.

Reed, Judith. "Working with Abusive Parents," *Children Today* 4 (May 1975): 6–9.

Reimann, Bernard C. "Parkinson Revisited: A Component Analysis of the Use of Staff Specialists in Manufacturing Organizations," *Human Relations* 32 (July 1979): 625–641.

Reinhold, Robert. "An 'Overwhelming' Violence-TV Tie," *The New York Times*, May 6, 1982, p. C27.

Reiss, Albert J., Jr. *The Police and the Public*. New Haven, Conn.: Yale University Press, 1971.

————, and David J. Bordua. "Environment and Organization: A Perspective on the Police," in David J. Bordua, ed., *The Police: Six Sociological Essays*. New York: 1967, pp. 25–55.

Reiss, Ira L. "The Universality of the Family: A Conceptual Analysis," *Journal of Marriage and the Family* 27 (November 1965): 443–453.

Reiterman, Tim, with John Jacobs. *Raven: The Untold Story of the Rev. Jim Jones and His People*. New York: Dutton, 1982.

Renshon, Stanley Allen, ed. *Handbook of Political Socialization: Theory and Research*. New York: Free Press, 1977.

Rich, John Martin. *Challenge and Responsibility*. New York: Wiley, 1974.

Rich, Spencer. "Noncash Welfare Grants Miss Two-Fifths of Poor—U.S. Study," *The Boston Globe*, July 7, 1982, p. 6.

Richardson, Laurel Walum. *The Dynamics of Sex and Gender: A Sociological Perspective*, 2nd ed. Boston: Houghton Mifflin, 1981.

Riegel, Klaus F. *Foundations of Dialectical Psychology*. New York: Academic Press, 1979.

————. *Psychology of Development and History*. New York: Plenum, 1976.

Riesman, David, with Reuel Denney and Nathan Glazer. *The Lonely Crowd: A Study in the Changing American Character*. New Haven, Conn.: Yale University Press, 1950.

Riley, Matilda White, and Anne Foner. *Aging and Society*. New York: Russell Sage Foundation, 1968.

Rist, Ray C., ed. *Desegregated Schools: Appraisals of an American Experiment*. New York: Academic Press, 1979.

————. *The Invisible Children: School Integration in American Society*. Cambridge, Mass.: Harvard University Press, 1978.

Ritchey, P. Neal. "Explanations of Migration," in Alex Inkeles, James Coleman, and Neil Smelser, eds., *Annual Review of Sociology*, vol. 2. Palo Alto, Calif.: Annual Reviews, 1976, pp. 363–404.

Ritzer, George. *Working: Conflict and Change*, 2nd ed. Englewood Cliffs, N.J.: Prentice-Hall, 1977.

Robbins, Thomas, and Dick Anthony. "Deprogramming, Brainwashing and the Medicalization of Deviant Religious Groups," *Social Problems* 29 (February 1982): 283–297.

————. "The Sociology of Contemporary Religious Movements," in Alex Inkeles, James Coleman, and Ralph H. Turner, eds., *Annual Review of Sociology*, vol. 5. Palo Alto, Calif.: Annual Reviews, 1979, pp. 75–89.

Robbins, William. "Data on Jobs Show Variety of Ills in U.S.," *The New York Times*, January 11, 1982, pp. A1, D10.

Rochford, E. Burke, Jr. "Recruitment Strategies, Ideology, and Organization in the Hare Krishna Movement," *Social Problems* 29 (April 1982): 399–410.

Roethlisberger, Fritz J., and William J. Dickson. *Manage-*

ment and the Worker. Cambridge, Mass.: Harvard University Press, 1939, 1964.

Rogers, Everett M. *Diffusion of Innovation.* New York: Free Press, 1962.

Rojek, Dean G., and Maynard L. Erickson. "Reforming the Juvenile Justice System: The Diversion of Status Offenders," *Law and Society Review* 16 (1981–1982): 241–264.

Roof, Wade Clark, and Christopher Kirk Hadway. "Denominational Switching in the Seventies: Going Beyond Stark and Glock," *Journal for the Scientific Study of Religion* 18 (December 1979): 363–378.

Rose, Arnold M. *The Power Structure: Political Process in American Society.* New York: Oxford University Press, 1967.

Rosen, Bernard C., and Carol S. Aneshensel. "Sex Differences in the Educational–Occupational Expectation Process," *Social Forces* 57 (September 1978): 164–186.

Rosenbaum, James E. "The Structure of Opportunity in School," *Social Forces* 57 (September 1978): 236–256.

—————. "Track Misperceptions and Frustrated College Plans: An Analysis of the Effects of Tracks on Track Perceptions in the National Longitudinal Survey," *Sociology of Education* 53 (April 1980): 74–88.

Rosenberg, Morris, and Roberta G. Simmons. *Black and White Self-Esteem: The Urban School Child.* Washington, D.C.: American Sociological Association, 1971.

Rosenhan, D. L. "On Being Sane in Insane Places," *Science* 179 (January 19, 1973): 250–258.

Rosenthal, Robert, and Lenore Jacobson. *Pygmalion in the Classroom: Teacher Expectation and Pupils' Intellectual Development.* New York: Holt, Rinehart and Winston, 1968.

Rosett, Arthur, and Donald R. Cressey. *Justice by Consent: Plea Bargains in the American Courthouse.* Philadelphia: Lippincott, 1976.

Rosnow, Ralph L., and Gary Alan Fine. *Rumor and Gossip: The Social Psychology of Hearsay.* New York: Elsevier, 1976.

Rosnow, Ralph L., and Allan J. Kimmel. "Lives of a Rumor," *Psychology Today* 13 (June 1979): 88–92.

Rosow, Irving. *Socialization to Old Age.* Berkeley, Calif.: University of California Press, 1974.

Ross, Heather L., and Isabel V. Sawhill. *Time of Transition: The Growth of Families Headed by Women.* Washington, D.C.: Urban Institute, 1975.

Rossides, Daniel W. *The American Class System: An Introduction to Social Stratification.* Lanham, Md.: University Press of America, 1976.

Rothman, Robert. *Inequality and Stratification in the United States.* Englewood Cliffs, N.J.: Prentice-Hall, 1978.

Rothman, Sheila M. *Women's Proper Place.* New York: Basic Books, 1978.

Rothschild-Whitt, Joyce. "Private Ownership and Worker Control in Holland," *Working Papers* 8 (March–April 1981): 22–25.

Rothstein, Edward. "Scholars Sign on with Semiotics," *The New York Times,* October 18, 1981, p. E11.

Roy, Donald. " 'Banana Time': Job Satisfaction and Informal Interaction," *Human Organization* 18 (Winter 1959–1960), 158–168.

—————. "Efficiency and the 'Fix': Informal Intergroup Relations in a Piecework Machine Shop," *American Journal of Sociology* 60 (November 1954): 255–266.

—————. "Quota Restriction and Goldbricking in a Machine Shop," *American Journal of Sociology* 62 (March 1952): 427–442.

Roy, William G. "The Unfolding of the Interlocking Directorate Structure of the United States," *American Sociological Review* 48 (April 1983): 248–257.

Rubin, Jeffrey Z., Frank J. Provenzano, and Zella Luria. "The Eye of the Beholder: Parents' View on Sex of Newborns," *American Journal of Orthopsychiatry* 44 (July 1974): 512–518.

Rubin, Lillian Breslow. *Worlds of Pain: Life in the Working-Class Family.* New York: Basic Books, 1976.

Rudé, George. *The Crowd in History: A Study of Popular Disturbances in France and England, 1730–1848.* New York: Wiley, 1964.

Rushing, William A., and Suzanne T. Ortega. "Socioeconomic Status and Mental Disorder: New Evidence and a Sociometric Formulation," *American Journal of Sociology* 84 (March 1979): 1175–1200.

Russell, Candyce Smith. "Transition to Parenthood: Problems and Gratification," *Journal of Marriage and the Family* 36 (May 1974): 294–301.

Rutter, Michael. *Fifteen Thousand Hours: Secondary Schools and Their Effects on Children.* Cambridge, Mass.: Harvard University Press, 1979.

Rytina, Joan Huber, William H. Form, and John Pease. "Income and Stratification Ideology: Beliefs about the American Opportunity Structure," *American Journal of Sociology* 75 (January 1970): 703–716.

Sagan, Carl. *The Cosmic Connection: An Extraterrestrial Perspective.* Garden City, N.Y.: Anchor Press/Doubleday, 1973.

St. John, Nancy. *School Desegregation: Outcomes for Children.* New York: Wiley, 1975.

Salem, Richard G., and Charles S. Green, III. "An Experiment in the Teaching of Applied Sociology: Career Tracks, Internship Experience, and Ethical Practices." A paper presented at the Annual Meeting of the American Sociological Association, San Francisco, 1982.

Sawyer, Kathy. "Grade-Schoolers down 20% Since '70," *The Boston Globe,* May 18, 1981, p. 5.

Scanzoni, John. "A Social Systems Analysis of Dissolved and Existing Marriages," *Journal of Marriage and the Family* 30 (August 1968): 452–461.

Schachter, Stanley, and Harvey Burdick. "A Field Study on Rumor Transmission and Distortion," *Journal of Abnormal and Social Psychology* 50 (1955): 363–371.

Schafer, Stephen. *The Political Criminal: The Problem of Morality and Crime.* New York: Free Press, 1974.

Schafer, Walter E., Carol Olexa, and Kenneth Polk.

"Programmed for Social Class: Tracking in High School," *Trans-Action* 7 (October 1970): 39–46, 63.

Scheflen, Albert E., and Norman Ashcraft. *Human Territories*. Englewood Cliffs, N.J.: Prentice-Hall, 1976.

Schlegel, Alice, ed. *Sexual Stratification: A Cross-Cultural View*. New York: Columbia University Press, 1977.

Schlesinger, Y. "Sex Roles and Social Change in the Kibbutz," *Journal of Marriage and the Family* 39 (November 1977): 771–779.

Schmeck, Harold M., Jr. "Extending the Life Span May Be Just Impossible," *The New York Times*, May 3, 1981, p. E7.

Schmemann, Serge. "New Soviet Rituals Seek to Replace Church's," *The New York Times*, March 15, 1983, pp. A1, A9.

Schnore, Leo F. "Community: Theory and Research on Structure and Change," in Neil J. Smelser, ed., *Sociology: An Introduction*, 2nd ed. New York: Wiley, 1973, pp. 67–125.

Schultz, Duane P. *Panic Behavior: Discussion and Readings*. New York: Random House, 1964.

Schumann, Howard, and Stanley Presser. "Attitude Measurement and the Gun Control Paradox." *Public Opinion Quarterly* 41 (Winter 1977–1978): 427–430.

Schur, Edwin M. *Crimes without Victims: Deviant Behavior and Public Policy*. Englewood Cliffs, N.J.: Prentice-Hall, 1965.

——. *Interpreting Deviance: A Sociological Introduction*. New York: Harper & Row, 1979.

——. *Labeling Deviant Behavior: Its Sociological Implications*. New York: Harper & Row, 1971.

——. *Radical Nonintervention: Rethinking the Delinquency Problem*. Englewood Cliffs, N.J.: Prentice-Hall, 1973.

——, and Hugo Adam Bedau. *Victimless Crimes: Two Sides of a Controversy*. Englewood Cliffs, N.J.: Prentice-Hall, 1974.

Schwartz, Barry. "The Effect in Philadelphia of Pennsylvania's Increased Penalties for Rape," *Journal of Criminal Law, Criminology, and Police Science* 59 (December 1968): 509–515.

Schwartz, Michael, Naomi Rosenthal, and Laura Schwartz. "Leader-Member Conflict in Protest Organizations: The Case of the Southern Farmers' Alliance," *Social Problems* 29 (October 1981): 22–36.

Schwartz, Pepper, and Janet Lever. "Fear and Loathing at a College Mixer," *Urban Life* 4 (January 1976): 413–431.

Schwartz, Richard D. "Law in the Kibbutz: A Response to Professor Shapiro," *Law and Society Review* 10 (Spring 1976): 439–442.

——. "Social Factors in the Development of Legal Controls: A Case Study of Two Israeli Settlements," *Yale Law Journal* 63 (February 1954): 471–491.

Scott, Marvin B., and Stanford M. Lyman. "Accounts," *American Sociological Review* 33 (February 1968): 46–62.

Sears, David O. "Political Socialization," in Fred L. Greenstein and Nelson W. Polsby, ed., *Micropolitical*

Theory: Handbook of Political Science, vol. 2. Reading, Mass.: Addison-Wesley, 1975, pp. 93–153.

Sechrest, Lee, Susan O. White, and Elizabeth D. Brown, eds. *The Rehabilitation of Criminal Offenders: Problems and Prospects*. Washington, D.C.: National Academy of Sciences, 1979.

Seeman, Melvin. "Alienation Studies," in Alex Inkeles, James Coleman, and Neil Smelser, eds., *Annual Review of Sociology*, vol. 1. Palo Alto, Calif.: Annual Reviews, 1975, pp. 91–123.

Seidman, Robert B. "Witch Murder and *Mens Rea*: A Problem of Society under Radical Social Change," *Modern Law Review* 28 (January 1965): 46–61.

Sen, Amartya. *Poverty and Famines: An Essay on Entitlement and Deprivation*. Oxford, Engl.: Clarendon Press, 1981.

Serrin, William. "Labor's Concessions Stir Worried Debate over Shifts in Power," *The New York Times*, April 25, 1982a, pp. 1, 30.

——. "Worry Grows over Upheaval as Technology Reshapes Jobs," *The New York Times*, July 4, 1982b, pp. 1, 29.

Shapiro, Allan E. "Law in the Kibbutz: A Reappraisal," *Law and Society Review* 10 (Spring 1976): 415–438.

Sharp, Lauriston. "Steel Axes for Stone-Age Australians," *Human Organization* 11 (Summer 1952): 17–22.

Shaw, Clifford R., and Henry D. McKay. *Juvenile Delinquency and Urban Areas*, rev. ed. Chicago: University of Chicago Press, 1969.

Sheehy, Gail. *Passages: Predictable Crises of Adult Life*. New York: Dutton, 1976.

Shepard, Ron M. "Technology, Alienation, and Job Satisfaction," in Alex Inkeles, James Coleman, and Neil Smelser, eds., *Annual Review of Sociology*, vol. 3. Palo Alto, Calif.: Annual Reviews, 1977, pp. 1–21.

Sherif, Muzafer. "Experiments in Group Conflict," *Scientific American* 195 (November 1956): 54–59.

Sherman, Lawrence W., ed. *Police Corruption: A Sociological Perspective*. Garden City, N.Y.: Anchor Press/Doubleday, 1974.

Shibutani, Tomatsu. *Improvised News: A Sociological Study of Rumor*. Indianapolis: Bobbs-Merrill, 1966.

Shinnar, Shlomo, and Reuel Shinnar. "The Effects of the Criminal Justice System on the Control of Crime: A Quantitative Approach," *Law and Society Review* 9 (Summer 1975): 581–611.

Shlay, Anne B., and Peter H. Rossi. "Keeping up the Neighborhood: Estimating Net Effects of Zoning," *American Sociological Review* 46 (December 1981): 703–719.

Short, James F., Jr., and Fred L. Strodtbeck. *Group Process and Gang Delinquency*. Chicago: University of Chicago Press, 1965.

Shorter, Edward. *The Making of the Modern Family*. New York: Basic Books, 1977.

Shupe, Anson D., Jr., and David G. Bromley. *The New Vigilantes: Deprogrammers, Anti-Cultists, and the New Religions*. Beverly Hills, Calif.: Sage Publications, 1980.

Siegel, Barry. "Juries Want T.V. Justice," *The Boston Globe*, July 13, 1980, pp. A1, A4.

Siegel, Jacob S., and Jeffrey S. Passel. *Coverage of Hispanic Population of the United States in the 1970 Census*. Washington, D.C.: Current Population Reports, 1979.

Silberman, Charles E. *Criminal Violence, Criminal Justice*. New York: Random House, 1978.

————. *Crisis in the Classroom: The Remaking of American Education*. New York: Random House, 1970.

Sills, David L. *The Volunteers*. New York: Free Press, 1958.

Simmel, Georg. "The Metropolis and Mental Life," in *The Sociology of Georg Simmel*, trans., ed., and with an intro. by Kurt H. Wolff. New York: Free Press, 1905, 1950.

————. *The Sociology of Georg Simmel*, trans., ed., and with an intro. by Kurt H. Wolff. New York: Free Press, 1950.

Simmons, John, and William J. Mares. "Reforming Work," *The New York Times*, October 25, 1982, p. A19.

Simmons, Roberta G., et al. "Self-Esteem and Achievement of Black and White Adolescents," *Social Problems* 26 (October 1978): 86–96.

Simon, Julian L. *The Ultimate Resource*. Princeton, N.J.: Princeton University Press, 1981.

Simpson, George E., and J. Milton Yinger. *Racial and Cultural Minorities: An Analysis of Prejudice and Discrimination*, 4th ed. New York: Harper & Row, 1972.

Simpson, John H. "Sovereign Groups, Subsistence Activities, and the Presence of a High God in Primitive Societies," in Robert Wuthnow, ed., *The Religious Dimension: New Directions in Quantitative Research*. New York: Academic Press, 1979, pp. 299–310.

Singer, Simon I. "A Comment on Alleged Overreporting," *Criminology* 16 (May 1978): 99–103.

Singh, B. K. "Trends in Attitudes towards Premarital Sexual Relations," *Journal of Marriage and the Family* 40 (May 1980): 387–393.

Sjoberg, Gideon. *The Preindustrial City*. New York: Free Press, 1960.

Skocpol, Theda. *States & Social Revolutions: A Comparative Analysis of France, Russia, & China*. Cambridge, Engl.: Cambridge University Press, 1979.

Skolnick, Jerome H. *Justice without Trial: Law Enforcement in Democratic Society*, 2nd ed. New York: Wiley, 1975.

Slater, Philip. *The Pursuit of Loneliness: American Culture at the Breaking Point*. Boston: Beacon Press, 1970.

————. *The Pursuit of Loneliness: American Culture at the Breaking Point*, rev. ed. Boston: Beacon Press, 1976.

————. "Role Differentiation in Small Groups," in A. Paul Hare, Edgar J. Borgatta, and Robert F. Bales, eds., *Social Groups: Studies in Social Interaction*. New York: Alfred A. Knopf, 1955, pp. 498–515.

Smelser, Neil J. *Social Change in the Industrial Revolution*. New York: Free Press, 1959.

————. *The Sociology of Economic Life*, 2nd ed. Englewood Cliffs, N.J.: Prentice-Hall, 1976.

————. *Theory of Collective Behavior*. New York: Free Press, 1962.

Smidt, Corwin. "Civil Religious Orientations among Elementary School Children," *Sociological Analysis* 41 (Spring 1980): 25–40.

Smith, A. Wade. "Racial Tolerance as a Function of Group Position," *American Sociological Review* 46 (October 1981): 558–573.

Smith, Adam. *Inquiry into the Nature and Causes of the Wealth of Nations*. New York: Modern Library, 1776, 1937.

Snow, David A., and Cynthia L. Phillips. "The Lofland-Stark Conversion Model: A Critical Reassessment," *Social Problems* 27 (April 1980): 430–447.

Snow, David A., Louis A. Zurcher, Jr., and Sheldon Ekland-Olson. "Social Networks and Social Movements: A Microstructural Approach to Differential Recruitment," *American Sociological Review* 45 (October 1980): 787–801.

Snyder, David, and Charles Tilly. "Hardship and Collective Violence in France, 1830–1960," *American Sociological Review* 37 (October 1972): 520–532.

Sobel, Dava. "Work Habits in Childhood Found to Predict Adult Well-Being," *The New York Times*, November 10, 1981, pp. C1, C4.

Sokoloff, Natalie J. *Between Money and Love: The Dialectics of Women's Home and Market Work*. New York: Praeger, 1980.

Solmon, Lewis C., and Paul J. Taubman, eds. *Does College Matter? Some Evidence on the Impacts of Higher Education*. New York: Academic Press, 1973.

Sommer, Robert. *Personal Space: The Behavioral Basis of Design*. Englewood Cliffs, N.J.: Prentice-Hall, 1969.

Sorokin, Pitirim A. *Social and Cultural Dynamics*. Cincinnati, Ohio: American Book Company, 1937.

Spanier, Graham B., and Robert A. Lewis. "Marital Quality: A Review of the Seventies," *Journal of Marriage and the Family* 41 (November 1980): 825–839.

Spengler, Oswald. *The Decline of the West*. New York: Modern Library, 1918, 1965.

Spohn, Cassia, John Gruhl, and Susan Welch. "The Effect of Race on Sentencing: A Reexamination of an Unsettled Question," *Law and Society Review* 16 (1981–1982): 71–88.

Sprafkin, Joyce N. and Robert M. Liebert. "Sex Therapy and Children's Television Preferences," in Gaye Tuchman, Arlene Kaplan Daniels, and James Benét, eds., *Hearth and Home: Images of Women in the Mass Media*. New York: Oxford University Press, 1978, pp. 228–239.

Squires, Gregory D., Ruthanne DeWolfe, and Alan S. DeWolfe. "Urban Decline or Disinvestment: Uneven Development, Redlining and the Role of the Insurance Industry," *Social Problems* 27 (October 1979): 79–95.

Srole, Leo, et al. *Mental Health in the Metropolis: The Midtown Manhattan Study*, rev. and enlarged ed. New York: New York University Press, 1977.

Stack, Steven. "The Effect of Direct Government Involvement in the Economy on the Degree of Income Inequality: A Cross-National Study," *American Sociological Review* 43 (December 1978): 880–888.

Staines, Graham L., and Robert P. Quinn. "American Workers Evaluate the Quality of Their Jobs," *Monthly Labor Review* 102 (January 1979): 2–12.

Stampp, Kenneth M. *The Peculiar Institution: Slavery in the Ante-Bellum South.* New York: Alfred A. Knopf, 1956.

Stark, Rodney, and William Sims Bainbridge. "American-Born Sects: Initial Findings," *Journal for the Scientific Study of Religion* 20 (June 1981): 130–149.

————. "Networks of Faith: Interpersonal Bonds and Recruitment to Cults and Sects," *American Journal of Sociology* 85 (May 1980): 1376–1395.

————. "Of Churches, Sects, and Cults: Preliminary Concepts for a Theory of Religious Movements," *Journal for the Scientific Study of Religion* 18 (June 1979): 117–133.

————, and Daniel P. Doyle. "Cults of America: A Reconnaissance in Space and Time," *Sociological Analysis* 40 (Winter 1979): 347–359.

Stark, Rodney, and Charles Y. Glock. *American Piety: The Nature of Religious Commitment.* Berkeley, Calif.: University of California Press, 1968.

————. "Prejudice and the Churches," in Charles Y. Glock and Ellen Siegelman, eds., *Prejudice U.S.A.* New York: Praeger, 1969, pp. 70–95.

Stearns, Marion S. *Report on Preschool Programs: The Effectiveness of Preschool Programs on Disadvantaged Children and Their Families.* Washington, D.C.: U.S. Government Printing Office, 1971.

Stein, Peter J. *Single Life: Unmarried Adults in Social Context.* New York: St. Martin's Press, 1981.

Stein, Robert B., Lon Polk, and Barbara Bovee Polk. "Urban Communes," in Nona Glazer-Malbin, ed., *Old Family/New Family: Interpersonal Relationships.* New York: Van Nostrand Reinhold, 1975, pp. 171–188.

Sterba, James P. "Peking Announces Austerity Plan; Private Business to Be Encouraged," *The New York Times,* March 1, 1981, pp. 1, 9.

Sternglanz, Sarah H., and Lisa A. Serbin. "Sex Role Stereotyping in Children's Television Programs," *Developmental Psychology* 10 (September 1974): 710–715.

Sternlieb, George, and Robert W. Burchell. *Residential Abandonment: The Tenement Landlord Revisited.* New Brunswick, N.J.: Center for Urban Policy Research, Rutgers University, 1973.

Stewig, John Warren, and Mary Lynn Knipfel. "Sexism in Picture Books: What Progress?" *Elementary School Journal* 76 (December 1975): 151–155.

Stinchcombe, Arthur L. "Institutions of Privacy in the Determination of Police Administration," *American Journal of Sociology* 69 (September 1963): 150–160.

Stokes, Randall, and John P. Hewitt. "Aligning Actions," *American Sociological Review* 41 (October 1976): 838–849.

Straus, Murray A. "Wife Beating: How Common and Why?" *Victimology* 2 (Nos. 3–4, 1978): 443–458.

————, Richard J. Gelles, and Suzanne K. Steinmetz. *Behind Closed Doors: Violence in the American Family.* Garden City, N.Y.: Anchor Press/Doubleday, 1980.

Stryker, Sheldon. *Symbolic Interactionism: A Social Structural Version.* Menlo Park, Calif.: Benjamin/Cummings, 1980.

————, and Anne Statham Macke. "Status Inconsistency and Role Conflict," in Ralph H. Turner, James Coleman, and Renée C. Fox, eds., *Annual Review of Sociology,* vol. 4. Palo Alto, Calif.: Annual Reviews, 1978, pp. 57–90.

Sussman, Marvin B. "The Isolated Nuclear Family: Fact or Fiction," *Social Problems* 6 (Spring 1959): 333–340.

Sutherland, Edwin H. "The Diffusion of Sexual Psychopath Laws," *American Journal of Sociology* 56 (September 1950): 142–148.

————. *White Collar Crime.* New York: Holt, Rinehart and Winston, 1949, 1961.

————, and Donald R. Cressey. *Criminology,* 10th ed. Philadelphia: Lippincott, 1978.

Suttles, Gerald D. *The Social Construction of Communities.* Chicago: University of Chicago Press, 1972.

————. *The Social Order of the Slum: Ethnicity and Territory in the Inner City.* Chicago: University of Chicago Press, 1968.

Swank, Duane H. "Does Crime Really Pay? The State, Social Disorder, and the Expansion of Social Welfare in the Post-World War II United States." A paper delivered at the Annual Meeting of the American Political Science Association, New York, 1981.

Swanson, Guy E. *The Birth of the Gods: Origins of Primitive Beliefs.* Ann Arbor, Mich.: University of Michigan Press, 1960.

Swidler, Ann. "Love and Adulthood in American Culture," in Neil J. Smelser and Erik H. Erikson, eds., *Themes of Work and Love in Adulthood.* Cambridge, Mass.: Harvard University Press, 1980, pp. 120–147.

Sykes, Gresham M. *The Society of Captives.* New York: Atheneum, 1958.

————, and David Matza. "Techniques of Neutralization: A Theory of Delinquency," *American Sociological Review* 22 (December 1957): 664–670.

Szymanski, Albert. *The Capitalist State and the Politics of Class.* Cambridge, Mass.: Winthrop, 1978.

Szasz, Thomas. *The Manufacture of Madness: A Comparative Study of the Inquisition and the Mental Health Movement.* New York: Harper & Row, 1970.

Taeuber, Irene B. "Japan's Demographic Transition Reexamined," *Population Studies* 14 (July 1960): 28–39.

Talland, George A. "Task and Interaction Process: Some Characteristics of Therapeutic Group Discussion," *Journal of Abnormal and Social Psychology* 50 (1955): 105–109.

Talmon, Y. "Sex-Role Differentiation in an Equalitarian Society," in Thomas E. Lasswell, John H. Burma, and Sidney H. Aronson, eds., *Life in Society.* Glenview, Ill.: Scott, Foresman, 1965, pp. 144–155.

Tanke, Elizabeth Decker, and Tony J. Tanke. "Getting off a Slippery Slope: Social Science in the Judicial Process," *American Psychologist* 34 (December 1979): 1130–1138.

Tatel, David S. "Depriving Deprived Children," *The New York Times*, March 23, 1983, p. A27.

Tauskey, Curt. "Meaning of Work among Blue Collar Men," *Pacific Sociological Review* 12 (Spring 1969): 49–55.

Tawney, R. H. *Religion and the Rise of Capitalism*. New York: Harcourt, Brace, and World, 1926.

Taylor, Ian, Paul Walton, and Jock Young. *The New Criminology: For a Social Theory of Deviance*. London: Routledge & Kegan Paul, 1973.

Taylor, Stuart, Jr. "Young Lawyers: A Taste of Failure," *The New York Times*, October 21, 1982, p. B14.

Tedlock, Barbara. "Boundaries of Belief," *Parabola* 4 (No. 1, 1979): 70–77.

Teltsch, Kathleen. "Lower Profits and Economic Uncertainty Threaten Corporate Philanthropy," *The New York Times*, September 22, 1982, p. A20.

—————. "Survey Finds Young People Lack Work Skills," *The New York Times*, January 16, 1983, p. 21.

Terkel, Studs. *Working: People Talk about What They Do All Day and How They Feel about What They Do*. New York: Pantheon, 1974.

Thomas, Jo. "Study Finds Miami Riot Was Unlike Those of '60's," *The New York Times*, May 17, 1981, p. 28.

Thomas, Robert McG., Jr. "11 Killed and 8 Badly Hurt in Crush before Rock Concert," *The New York Times*, December 4, 1979, pp. A1, A13.

Thompson, Warren S., and David T. Lewis. *Population Problems*, 5th ed. New York: McGraw-Hill, 1965.

Thurow, Lester C. "Why Women Are Paid Less than Men," *The New York Times*, March 8, 1981, p. F2.

—————. *The Zero-Sum Society: Distribution and the Possibilities for Economic Change*. New York: Penguin, 1980.

Tietze, Christopher, and Deborah A. Dawson. "Induced Abortion: A Factbook," *Reports on Population Family Planning*, No. 14 (December 1977): 1–51.

Tiger, Lionel, and Joseph Shepher. *Women in the Kibbutz*. New York: Harcourt Brace Jovanovich, 1975.

Tilly, Charles. *From Mobilization to Revolution*. Reading, Mass.: Addison-Wesley, 1978.

—————. "Introduction," in Louise A. Tilly and Charles Tilly, eds., *Class Conflict and Collective Action*. Beverly Hills, Calif.: Sage Publications, 1981, pp. 13–25.

Titmuss, Richard. *The Gift Relationship: From Human Blood to Social Policy*. New York: Pantheon, 1971.

Tittle, Charles, R., Wayne K. Villemez, and Douglas A. Smith. "The Myth of Social Class and Criminality: An Empirical Assessment of the Empirical Evidence," *American Sociological Review* 43 (October 1978): 643–656.

Tobias, Sheila. *Overcoming Math Anxiety*. New York: Norton, 1978.

Toffler, Alvin. *Future Shock*. New York: Random House, 1970.

—————. *The Third Wave*. New York: Morrow, 1980.

Tolchin, Martin. "General Negative Feeling toward City Shown in Congressional Refusal of Aid," *The New York Times*, May 25, 1975, pp. 1, 38.

Tönnies, Ferdinand. *Community and Society*. East Lansing, Mich.: Michigan State University Press, 1887, 1957.

Toynbee, Arnold. *A Study of History*. New York: Oxford University Press, 1946.

Traugott, Mark. "Reconceiving Social Movements," *Social Problems* 26 (October 1978): 38–49.

Trebach, Arnold S. *The Heroin Solution*. New Haven, Conn.: Yale University Press, 1982.

Treiman, Donald J. *Occupational Prestige in Comparative Perspective*. New York: Academic Press, 1977.

—————, and Kermit Terrell. "Sex and the Process of Status Attainment: A Comparison of Working Women and Men," *American Sociological Review* 40 (April 1975): 174–200.

Troeltsch, Ernst. *The Social Teachings of the Christian Churches*. London: Allen and Unwin, 1931.

Tuchman, Gaye. "Women's Depiction by the Mass Media," *Signs* 4 (Spring 1979): 528–542.

—————, Arlene Kaplan Daniels, and James Benét, eds. *Hearth and Home: Images of Women in the Mass Media*. New York: Oxford University Press, 1978.

Tumin, Melvin M. "Some Principles of Stratification: A Critical Analysis," *American Sociological Review* 18 (August 1953): 387–394.

Turnbull, Colin M. *The Mountain People*. New York: Simon and Schuster, 1972.

Turner, Jonathan H. *The Structure of Sociological Theory*, 3rd ed. Homewood, Ill.: Dorsey Press, 1982.

Turner, Ralph H. "Collective Behavior," in Robert E. L. Faris, ed., *Handbook of Modern Sociology*. Chicago: Rand McNally, 1964, pp. 382–425.

—————, and Lewis M. Killian. *Collective Behavior*, 2nd ed. Englewood Cliffs, N.J.: Prentice-Hall, 1972.

Turner, Stanley. "The Ecology of Delinquency," in Thorsten Sellin and Marvin E. Wolfgang, eds., *Delinquency: Selected Studies*. New York: Wiley, 1969, pp. 27–60.

Turow, Scott. *One L*. Boston: Little, Brown, 1977.

Tyler, Ralph W. "The Federal Role in Education," *Public Interest* 34 (Winter 1974): 164–187.

Tylor, Edward. *Primitive Culture*. New York: Harper & Row, 1871, 1958.

Tyree, Andrea, Moshe Semyonov, and Robert W. Hodge. "Gaps and Glissandos: Inequality, Economic Development, and Social Mobility in 24 Countries," *American Sociological Review* 44 (June 1979): 410–424.

Udy, Stanley H., Jr. "'Bureaucracy' and 'Rationality' in Weber's Organizational Theory: An Empirical Study," *American Sociological Review* 24 (December 1959): 791–795.

United Nations. *Demographic Yearbook—1978*. New York: United Nations, 1979.

U.S. Bureau of the Census. *Historical Statistics of the United States: Colonial Times to 1970*. Washington, D.C.: U.S. Government Printing Office, 1975.

—————. *Money Income and Poverty Status of Families and Persons in the United States: 1981.* Washington, D.C.: U.S. Government Printing Office, July 1982.

—————. *Social Indicators III.* Washington, D.C.: U.S. Government Printing Office, 1980.

—————. *Statistical Abstract of the United States, 1981.* Washington, D.C.: U.S. Government Printing Office, 1981.

—————. *Statistical Abstract of the United States, 1982–83.* Washington, D.C.: U.S. Government Printing Office, 1982.

U.S. Department of Labor, Employment and Training Administration. *Dictionary of Occupational Titles,* 4th ed. Washington, D.C.: U.S. Employment Service, 1977.

U.S. National Center for Health Statistics. *Monthly Vital Statistics Report.* Washington, D.C.: U.S. Department of Health and Human Services, September 17, 1981.

U'Ren, Marjorie B. "The Image of Women in Textbooks," in Vivian Gornick and Barbara K. Moran, eds., *Women in Sexist Society: Studies in Power and Powerlessness.* New York: Basic Books, 1971, pp. 218–225.

Useem, Bert. "Solidarity Model, Breakdown Model, and the Boston Anti-Busing Movement," *American Sociological Review* 45 (June 1980): 357–369.

Useem, Michael. "Corporations and the Corporate Elite," in Alex Inkeles, Neil J. Smelser, and Ralph H. Turner, eds., *Annual Review of Sociology,* vol. 6. Palo Alto, Calif.: Annual Reviews, 1980a, pp. 41–77.

—————. "The Inner Group of the American Capitalist Class," *Social Problems* 25 (February 1978): 225–240.

—————. "The Social Organization of the American Business Elite and Participation of Corporation Directors in the Governance of American Institutions," *American Sociological Review* 44 (August 1979): 553–572.

—————. "Which Business Leaders Help Govern?" in G. William Domhoff, ed., *Power Structure Research.* Beverly Hills, Calif.: Sage Publications, 1980b, pp. 199–225.

Van de Walle, Etienne, and John Knodel. "Europe's Fertility Transition: New Evidence and Lessons for Today's Developing World," *Population Bulletin* 34 (February 1980): 3–43.

Van der Tak, Jan, Carl Haub, and Elaine Murphy. "Our Population Predicament: A New Look," *Population Bulletin* 34 (December 1979): 1–48.

Van Dyke, Jon M. *Jury Selection Procedures: Our Uncertain Commitment to Representative Panels.* Cambridge, Mass.: Ballinger, 1977.

Van Loon, Eric E. "The Law School Response: How to Make Students Sharp by Making Them Narrow," in Bruce Wasserstein and Mark J. Green, eds., *With Justice for Some: An Indictment of the Law by Young Advocates.* Boston: Beacon Press, 1970, pp. 334–352.

Van Maanen, John. "Rookie Cops and Rookie Managers," *Wharton Magazine* 1 (Fall 1976): 49–55.

Veblen, Thorsten. *The Theory of the Leisure Class: An Economic Study of Institutions.* New York: Modern Library, 1899, 1918.

Veevers, Jean E. "Voluntarily Childless Wives: An Exploratory Study," *Sociology and Social Research* 57 (April 1973): 356–365.

Verba, Sidney, and Norman H. Nie. *Participation in America: Political Democracy and Social Equality.* New York: Harper & Row, 1972.

Vidich, Arthur J. "Inflation and the Social Structure: The United States in an Epoch of Declining Abundance," *Social Problems* 27 (June 1980): 636–649.

Von Hirsch, Andrew. *Doing Justice: The Choice of Punishments.* New York: Hill and Wang, 1976.

Voss, Harwin L. "Ethnic Differentials in Delinquency in Honolulu," *Journal of Criminal Law, Criminology, and Police Science* 54 (September 1963): 322–327.

Wahlke, John C., Heinz Eulau, William Buchanan, and LeRoy C. Ferguson. *The Legislative System: Explorations in Legislative Behavior.* New York: Wiley, 1962.

Walker, Kathryn E. "Time Spent by Husbands in Household Work," *Family Economics Review* 4 (1970): 8–11.

Wallace, Anthony F. C. *Religion: An Anthropological View.* New York: Random House, 1966.

Wallerstein, Immanuel. *The Capitalist World-Economy: Essays.* Cambridge, Engl.: Cambridge University Press, 1979.

—————. *The Modern World-System: Capitalist Agriculture and the Origins of the European World-Economy in the Sixteenth Century.* New York: Academic Press, 1974.

—————. *The Modern World-System II: Mercantilism and the Consolidation of the European World-Economy, 1600–1750.* New York: Academic Press, 1980.

Wallerstein, Judith S., and Joan Berlin Kelly. *Surviving the Breakup: How Children and Parents Cope With Divorce.* New York: Basic Books, 1980.

Walsh, Edward J. "Resource Mobilization and Citizen Protest in Communities around Three Mile Island," *Social Problems* 29 (October 1981): 1–21.

Walter, Eugene Victor. *Terror and Resistance: A Study of Political Violence.* New York: Oxford University Press, 1969.

Walum, Laurel Richardson. "The Changing Door Ceremony," *Urban Life and Culture* 2 (January 1974): 505–515.

Warner, W. Lloyd. *The Family of God.* New Haven, Conn.: Yale University Press, 1961.

Weaver, Warren, Jr. "Republicans Spent 5 Times More Than Foes on '80," *The New York Times,* February 21, 1982, p. 24.

Webb, Eugene J., et al. *Nonreactive Measures in the Social Sciences,* 2nd ed. Boston: Houghton Mifflin, 1981.

Weber, Max. *From Max Weber: Essays in Sociology,* 2nd ed., trans. by Hans H. Gerth and C. Wright Mills. New York: Oxford University Press, 1918, 1949.

—————. *The Protestant Ethic and the Spirit of Capital-*

ism, trans. by Talcott Parsons. New York: Scribner's, 1904, 1958.

————. *The Sociology of Religion*, trans. by Ephraim Fischoff. Boston: Beacon Press, 1922, 1963.

————. *The Theory of Social and Economic Organization*, trans. by A.M. Henderson and Talcott Parsons. New York: Free Press, 1925, 1947.

Webster, William H. *Crime in the United States, 1981: Uniform Crime Reports*. Washington, D.C.: U.S. Government Printing Office, 1982.

Weeks, H. Ashley. "Income and Disease—The Pathology of Poverty," in Lawrence Corey, Michael F. Epstein, and Steve E. Saltman, eds., *Medicine in a Changing Society*, 2nd ed. New York: Mosby, 1977, pp. 53–65.

Wegner, Eldon L. "Graduate Education," in David W. Swift, ed., *American Education: A Sociological View*. Boston: Houghton Mifflin, 1976, pp. 215–224.

Weinberg, Martin S. "Sexual Modesty, Social Meanings, and the Nudist Camp," *Social Problems* 12 (Winter 1965): 311–318.

Weis, Kurt, and Sandra S. Borges. "Victimology and Rape: The Case of the Legitimate Victim," *Issues in Criminology* 8 (Fall 1973): 71–115.

Weiss, Robert S. *Going It Alone: The Family Life and Social Situation of the Single Parent*. New York: Basic Books, 1979.

————. *Marital Separation*. New York: Basic Books, 1975.

Weitz, Shirley. *Sex Roles: Biological, Psychological, and Social Foundations*. New York: Oxford University Press, 1977.

Weitzman, Lenore J., et al. "Sex-Role Socialization in Picture Books for Preschool Children," *American Journal of Sociology* 77 (May 1972): 1125–1150.

Wellin, Edward. "Water Boiling in a Peruvian Town," in Benjamin D. Paul, ed., *Health, Culture, and Community*. New York: Russell Sage Foundation, 1955, pp. 71–103.

Wells, B. W. P. "The Psycho-social Influence of Building Environment: Sociometric Findings in Large and Small Office Spaces," *Building Sciences* 1 (1965): 153–165.

Wells, Robert V. "Household Size and Composition in the British Colonies in America, 1675–1775," *Journal of Interdisciplinary History* 4 (Spring 1974): 543–570.

Welsh, William A. *Leaders and Elites*. New York: Holt, Rinehart and Winston, 1979.

Westoff, Charles F. "The Blending of Catholic Reproductive Behavior," in Robert Wuthnow, ed., *The Religious Dimension: New Directions in Quantitative Research*. New York: Academic Press, 1979, pp. 231–240.

————. "The Decline of Unplanned Births in the United States," *Science* 191 (January 1976): 38–41.

Weston, Peter J., and Martin T. Mednick. "Race, Social Class, and the Motive to Avoid Success in Women," *Journal of Cross-Cultural Psychology* 1 (September 1970): 283–291.

Whitt, J. Allen. "Can Capitalists Organize Themselves?" in G. William Domhoff, ed., *Power Structure Research*. Beverly Hills, Calif.: Sage Publications, 1980, pp. 97–113.

Whyte, William Foote. *Street Corner Society: The Social Structure of an Italian Slum*, 3rd ed. Chicago: University of Chicago Press, 1943, 1981.

Wiatrowski, Michael D., David B. Griswold, and Mary K. Roberts. "Social Control Theory and Delinquency," *American Sociological Review* 46 (October 1981): 525–541.

Wilford, John Noble. "9 Percent of Everyone Who Ever Lived Is Alive Now," *The New York Times*, October 6, 1981, pp. C1, C2.

Williams, Robin M., Jr. *American Society: A Sociological Interpretation*, 3rd ed. New York: Alfred A. Knopf, 1970.

Willie, Charles Vert. "The Inclining Significance of Race," in Charles Vert Willie, ed., *Caste & Class Controversy*. Bayside, N.Y.: General Hall, 1979, pp. 145–158.

Wilson, Bryan R. *Religion in Secular Society*. London: Watts, 1966.

Wilson, Edward O. *On Human Nature*. Cambridge, Mass.: Harvard University Press, 1978.

————. *Sociobiology: The New Synthesis*. Cambridge, Mass.: Harvard University Press, 1975.

Wilson, James Q. "The Police and Their Problems: A Theory," in Carl J. Friedrichs and Seymour Harris, eds., *Public Policy*, XII. Cambridge, Mass.: Harvard University Press, 1963, pp. 189–216.

————. *Thinking about Crime*. New York: Basic Books, 1975.

————. "'What Works?' Revisited: New Findings on Criminal Rehabilitation," *Public Interest* 61 (Fall 1980): 3–17.

Wilson, John. *Religion in American Society: The Effective Presence*. Englewood Cliffs, N.J.: Prentice-Hall, 1978.

————. "Sociology of Leisure," in Alex Inkeles, Neil J. Smelser and Ralph H. Turner, eds., *Annual Review of Sociology*, vol. 6. Palo Alto, Calif.: Annual Reviews, 1980, pp. 21–40.

Wilson, William Julius. *The Declining Significance of Race: Blacks and Changing American Institutions*. Chicago: University of Chicago Press, 1978.

————. "The Declining Significance of Race: Revisited but Not Revised," in Charles Vert Willie, ed., *Caste & Class Controversy*. Bayside, N.Y.: General Hall, 1979, pp. 159–175.

Winch, Robert F., and Rae Lesser Blumberg. "Societal Complexity and Familial Organization," in Robert F. Winch and Graham B. Spanier, eds., *Selected Studies in Marriage and the Family*, 3rd ed. New York: Holt, Rinehart and Winston, 1968, pp. 70–92.

Winn, Marie. "What Became of Childhood Innocence?" *The New York Times Magazine*, January 25, 1981, pp. 14–17, 44–68.

Wirth, Louis. "The Problems of Minority Groups," in Ralph Linton, ed., *The Science of Man in the World Crisis*.

New York: Columbia University Press, 1945, pp. 347–372.

——————. "Urbanism as a Way of Life," *American Journal of Sociology* 44 (July 1938): 3–24.

Wissler, Clark. *Man and Culture*. New York: Crowell, 1923.

Witkin, Herman A., et al. "Criminality In XYY and XXY Men," *Science* 193 (August 13, 1976): 547–555.

Wolf, Wendy C., and Neil D. Fligstein. "Sex and Authority in the Work Place: The Causes of Sexual Inequality," *American Sociological Review* 44 (April 1979): 235–252.

Wolfgang, Marvin E., Robert M. Figlio, and Thorsten Sellin. *Delinquency in a Birth Cohort*. Chicago: University of Chicago Press, 1972.

Wolfinger, Raymond E. *The Politics of Progress*. Englewood Cliffs, N.J.: Prentice-Hall, 1974.

——————, and Steven J. Rosenstone. *Who Votes?* New Haven, Conn.: Yale University Press, 1980.

Women on Words and Images. *Dick and Jane as Victims: Sex Stereotyping in Children's Readers*. Princeton, N.J.: Women on Words and Images, 1972.

Woodrum, Eric. "An Assessment of Japanese American Assimilation, Pluralism, and Subordination," *American Journal of Sociology* 87 (July 1981): 157–169.

Woodward, Kenneth L., et al. "Saving the Family," *Newsweek*, May 15, 1978, pp. 63–73.

Work in America: Report of a Special Task Force to the Secretary of Health, Education, and Welfare. Cambridge, Mass.: M.I.T. Press, 1973.

Wren, Christopher S. "China, to Relieve Unemployment, Gives Private Sector More Leeway," *The New York Times*, November 24, 1981, pp. A1, D17.

——————. "China's Birth Goals Meet Regional Resistance," *The New York Times*, May 15, 1982a, pp. 1, 7.

——————. "China's Minorities Find a Place in the Sun at Last," *The New York Times*, June 17, 1982b, p. A2.

——————. "Old Nemesis Haunts China on Birth Plan," *The New York Times*, August 1, 1982c, p. 9.

Wright, Erik Olin, et al. "The American Class Structure," *American Sociological Review* 47 (December 1982): 709–726.

Wrong, Dennis H. "The Oversocialized Conception of Man in Modern Sociology," *American Sociological Review* 26 (April 1961): 183–193.

——————. *Population and Society*, 4th ed. New York: Random House, 1977.

——————. *Power: Its Forms, Bases and Uses*. New York: Harper & Row, 1979.

Wuthnow, Robert. *Experimentation in American Religion: The New Mysticisms and Their Implications for the Churches*. Berkeley, Calif.: University of California Press, 1978.

——————. "The New Religions in Social Context," in Charles Y. Glock and Robert N. Bellah, eds., *The New Religious Consciousness*. Berkeley, Calif.: University of California Press, 1976, pp. 267–294.

——————, and Charles Y. Glock. "God in the Gut," *Psychology Today* 8 (November 1974): 131–136.

Yablonsky, Lewis. *The Violent Gang*. Baltimore, Md.: Penguin, 1966.

Yankelovich, Daniel. "Are You Taking Risks with Your Life?" *Parade Magazine*, May 24, 1981, pp. 4–6.

Yinger, J. Milton. *Countercultures: The Promise and the Peril of a World Turned Upside Down*. New York: Free Press, 1982.

——————. "Presidential Address: Countercultures and Social Change," *American Sociological Review* 42 (December 1977): 833–853.

——————. *The Scientific Study of Religion*. New York: Crowell-Collier and Macmillan, 1970.

Yoder, Jan D., and Robert C. Nichols. "A Life Perspective Comparison of Married and Divorced Persons," *Journal of Marriage and the Family* 42 (May 1980): 413–419.

Zahn, Gordon C. *The Military Chaplaincy: A Study of Role Tension in the Royal Air Force*. Toronto: University of Toronto Press, 1969.

Zald, Mayer N., and John D. McCarthy, eds. *The Dynamics of Social Movements: Resource Mobilization, Social Control, and Tactics*. Cambridge, Mass.: Winthrop, 1979.

Zaretsky, Eli. *Capitalism, The Family, and Personal Life*. New York: Harper & Row, 1976.

Zeisel, Hans, Harry Kalven, Jr., and Bernard Buchholz. *Delay in the Court: An Analysis of the Remedies for Delayed Justice*. Boston: Little, Brown, 1959.

Zeitlin, M. K., K. G. Lutterman, and J. W. Russell. "Death in Vietnam: Class, Poverty, and the Risks of War," *Politics and Society* 3 (Spring 1973): 313–328.

Zigler, Edward, and Jeanette Valentine, eds. *Project Head Start: A Legacy of the War on Poverty*. New York: Free Press, 1979.

Zimbardo, Philip G. "Pathology of Imprisonment," *Society* 9 (April 1972): 4–8.

——————. "The Prison Game." Hearings before Subcommittee #3 of the Committee on the Judiciary, House of Representatives, 92nd Congress, 1st Session, Part II, Serial No. 15, October 25, 1971. Reprinted in Norman Johnston and Leonard D. Savitz, eds., *Legal Process and Corrections*. New York: Wiley, 1982, pp. 195–198.

——————, et al. "A Pirandellian Prison: The Mind Is a Formidable Jailer," *The New York Times Magazine*, May 8, 1973, pp. 38–60.

Zimring, Franklin E., and Gordon J. Hawkins. *Deterrence: The Legal Threat in Crime Control*. Chicago: University of Chicago Press, 1973.

Zwerdling, Daniel. "The Food Monopolies," in Jerome H. Skolnick and Elliott Curie, eds., *Crisis in American Institutions*, 4th ed. Boston: Little, Brown, 1979, pp. 41–50.

Photo Credits

Name Index

Subject Index